Radical Jewish Politics

Radical Jewish Politics

A Global Perspective

EDITED BY
NATHANIEL DEUTSCH,
ALMA RACHEL HECKMAN, AND
TONY MICHELS

RUTGERS UNIVERSITY PRESS
NEW BRUNSWICK, CAMDEN, AND NEWARK, NEW JERSEY
LONDON AND OXFORD

Rutgers University Press is a department of Rutgers, The State University of New Jersey, one of the leading public research universities in the nation. By publishing worldwide, it furthers the University's mission of dedication to excellence in teaching, scholarship, research, and clinical care.

978-1-9788-4572-5 (cloth)
978-1-9788-4571-8 (paper)
978-1-9788-4573-2 (epub)

Cataloging-in-publication data is available from the Library of Congress.
LCCN 2025012636

A British Cataloging-in-Publication record for this book is available from the British Library.

∞ The paper used in this publication meets the requirements of the American National Standard for Information Sciences—Permanence of Paper for Printed Library Materials, ANSI Z39.48-1992.

rutgersuniversitypress.org

For Maya Karin Peterson (1980–2021), a dear friend and a brilliant colleague.

Contents

Radical Jewish Politics

Introduction

GLOBAL RADICAL JEWISH POLITICS

Nathaniel Deutsch, Alma Rachel Heckman, and Tony Michels

Radical Jewish politics have experienced a boom of interest in recent years. This is a significant departure from the late 1990s, when Ezra Mendelsohn noted with regret in the introduction to his *Essential Papers on Jews and the Left* that the book's subject matter held little attraction for other scholars as the twentieth century drew to a close. Most of the volume's articles, which all focused on Ashkenazi Jewish radicals in Europe, the United States, or the *Yishuv* (the term for Jewish settlement in Palestine before the establishment of Israel in 1948), had originally been published prior to the 1990s and their authors were "either 'veterans' . . . who were themselves involved with the old left in the interwar period, or members of the generation that arrived during the 1960s and 1970s."[1] Mendelsohn, one of the foremost historians of modern Jewish politics, hoped that his collection would help rekindle interest in Jews and socialism among future scholars. "Historians, like politicians, react to current events: we may have to wait for a new wave of left-wing activity in Europe, Israel, and America to produce a new interest in the history of Jewish socialism," Mendelsohn concluded. "For the meantime, may this volume testify both to the richness of the subject and to its central importance in modern Jewish history."[2]

When we first began writing this introduction several years ago, we originally followed this opening paragraph on Mendelsohn with an analysis of Bernie Sanders as an old-new symbol of the resurgent Left in the United States. At the time, Sanders seemed to represent the last link in a long tradition of radical Jewish politics. Sanders was a product of a New York Jewish milieu that had absorbed the influences of the old Jewish labor movement and oriented him toward social activism. Did Sanders represent the culmination of a certain kind of prewar, New York, democratic socialist Jewish heritage? It seemed so in 2016, during his first run for President.

Sanders's background signified a kind of authenticity and formed part of his appeal to many voters. His presidential bid helped to revive American leftist politics, and that revival included young Jews, who did not share a unitary outlook but were drawn to what seemed to be an exciting movement, at once old and new, rooted in the past yet headed into the future. It remains an open question today whether, after Sanders's second unsuccessful presidential campaign of 2020, democratic socialism is still on the rise. But in the intervening years, a particular strand of Jewish radicalism has surged.

Since the Hamas attack on Israelis of October 7, 2023, and the ensuing devastation in Gaza, Jewish anti-Zionist organizations have come to the fore, demanding a ceasefire and an end to the Israeli siege on Gaza; furthermore, some call for an end to Jewish national self-determination. Jewish students featured prominently in the Gaza solidarity encampments that sprang up across the country in the winter and spring of 2024, hosting anti-Zionist Shabbats and Passover seders among other activities. In addition to reinterpreting Jewish religious rituals and texts through the lens of their anti-Zionism, some of these activists have also explicitly identified with earlier Jewish radical movements.

For example, in February 2024, *The Forward* reported on a newly created organization calling itself the Bund, thus laying claim to the legacy of the first Russian Jewish workers' party, founded in 1897.[3] As the author of the article rightly noted, there were generational and ideological differences between the "old" Bund (which continues to exist in parts of the world) and the "new" Bund (which had no organizational roots in, or ties to, the original organization). The new Bund took inspiration from the older party's embrace of *doikayt* or "hereness," the view that Jews should be rooted wherever they live, and its original vehement opposition to Zionism, despite the fact that the Bund later accepted the establishment of the State of Israel in 1948.[4] Thus, many contemporary anti-Zionist Jews have positioned themselves as inheritors of an older Jewish radical tradition, not only in the United States but globally.[5] This is apparent in publications such a *Jewish Currents* and in the activities of the explicitly anti-Zionist organization Jewish Voice for Peace. While we leave the still-unfolding current political moment to be analyzed by future historians, its resonance with the themes undertaken in this volume is undeniable.

One of the main goals of this volume is to demonstrate that the phenomenon of Jewish radicalism represented for many by Bernie Sanders—an Ashkenazi Jew of Eastern European origin who volunteered on a kibbutz, marched for civil rights, and joined a socialist party—while worthy of the attention it has received in Mendelsohn's and others' work, only reveals part (albeit a large part) of a much broader relationship between Jews and radical politics around the globe. No single volume can address all the geographies and temporalities of radical Jewish politics. In this volume we have focused on those contexts with significant radical Jewish political history, especially those outside of the traditional European focus that has prevailed until very recently. Rather than focusing on radical Jewish politics in the Russian Empire, interwar Poland, or among Eastern European Jews in New York or Palestine—and later, Israel—as many fine works have already done, the essays in this volume instead engage with a much wider range of sites as well as illuminate largely unfamiliar aspects of radical Jewish politics in previously well-studied places, such as Mizrahi radicals in 1970s Israel, Jewish radicalism in Salonica between Ottoman and Greek rule, or the activities of Iraqi Jewish radical women. This volume also shines new light on aspects and impacts of Jewish radicalism that have typically fallen outside of the standard historiographical focus on communism, socialism, labor Zionism, and the Bund. These include varieties of anarchism and Revisionist Zionism, which itself is better known today for being politically conservative, but which absorbed important influences from—and was significantly shaped by—encounters with various forms of radicalism. In this volume, "radicalism" for the most part refers to Jewish engagement with leftist political formations. However, radical Jewish political movements have existed on a spectrum that at one extreme can include reactionary (right-wing) politics, such as Revisionist Zionism, and at the other end, anarchism. The "Unorthodox Radicalisms" addressed in Part IV bring together these extreme ends of the spectrum, including the previously ignored history of Sephardi participation in Revisionist Zionism. In short, the volume shows that the far right is also part of the far left's story.

For the first time, this volume centers the stories of Jewish radicals from across the Middle East and North Africa (the MENA), including Morocco, Algeria, Tunisia, Egypt, Israel, Iraq, and Iran, within a global narrative that also includes previously understudied aspects of radical Jewish politics in Eastern Europe—for example, labor Zionists in post–World War II Hungary—as well as Argentina, Brazil, South Africa, Salonica of the former Ottoman Empire and then Greece, and the Jewish Autonomous Oblast of Birobidzhan. When the picture is expanded in this way, new figures emerge to join the list of already well-known Jewish radicals of European and, especially, Eastern European origin. Alongside global icons such as Leon Trotsky, Rosa Luxemburg, Emma Goldman, and, of course, Bernie Sanders, we find figures like Léon René Sultan and Abraham Serfaty (Morocco), Shmuel Anvar and Harun Parviz Yesha'ya (Iran), Madeline Mir 'Ezer, and Sa'ida Mash'al (Iraq), and many others, who played significant roles in the history of radicalism in their respective countries, even if in many cases their contributions were later downplayed or suppressed, frequently by fellow radicals because of their Jewishness or by fellow Jews because of their radicalness. The lives of these individuals reveal the degree to which radical movements of different kinds exerted a profound attraction for Jews around the globe, even as the vast majority of Jews, wherever they were, eschewed political radicalism entirely, despite what right-wing critics frequently suggested to the contrary—a topic to which we will return below. While many different disciplines have valuable contributions to make regarding the study of radical Jewish politics, all of the contributors to this volume are historians who are well-positioned to examine the phenomenon of radical Jewish politics comparatively across the diverse array of contexts addressed here.

When we examine these geographies together, remarkable patterns and temporal convergences appear. Similar processes concerning Jewish political and social belonging within wider state and international entities unfolded around the world, albeit sometimes on different timetables and with different contextual options. For example, World War II was a kind of swan song for once thriving Eastern European Jewish political organizations like the Bund, which was utterly destroyed in Poland by the Holocaust. Overall, however, WWII represented a major watershed moment for Jewish participation in radical leftist politics around the world, even in places decimated by the Holocaust such as Eastern Europe under Soviet influence or control. For the Jews of the Middle East and North Africa, the period of the Second World War was one of political galvanization, of acceleration into radical politics as anti-fascist activism transformed into anti-colonial agitation. As Kamilia Rahmouni argues in chapter 3 of this volume, Jewish involvement in the Communist Party in Tunisia increased dramatically as a result of the Vichy regime's wartime persecution of local Jews and the Communist Party's anti-Nazi activism. Similarly, as Nathaniel Deutsch demonstrates in his essay on radical Jewish politics in Argentina (chapter 8), the rise of fascism helped to catalyze the rapid growth and popularity of ICUF (*Idisher Kultur Farband*), the Argentine branch of an international Yiddish-oriented communist organization that was founded in Paris in 1937, but which achieved its greatest influence in post–World War II Buenos Aires.

The Second World War is one watershed moment among many in the periodization and thematization of global radical Jewish politics. The modern history of political radicalism is often depicted as beginning with the French Revolution, a pivotal event that may also serve as a common starting point for the diverse radical political movements that would eventually attract Jews in places as disparate as Morocco and Lithuania, Baghdad and Buenos Aires. In 1791, the Jews of France were emancipated and became French citizens. The emancipation of French Jews often serves as the starting point for modern Jewish history because it heralds a new era in the global Jewish experience. No longer would Jews in France constitute a corporate entity to be governed collectively by the state while still subject in many respects to a communal Jewish authority. Instead, following emancipation, Jews would be treated as citizens within the French nation-state, as the Comte de Clermont-Tonnerre famously declared in 1789, "We must refuse everything to the Jews as a nation and accord everything to Jews as individuals." Neither the Jewish communities of Eastern Europe nor those in the Middle East and North Africa directly experienced this late-eighteenth-century moment of French Jewish emancipation, but questions of emancipation and political belonging would characterize much of their respective political histories in the nineteenth and twentieth centuries. It is therefore a common starting point for a periodization of radical Jewish political history around the globe, as much as it is a crucible for the forces that would shape Jewish modernity.

The centering of the MENA region within a global history of radical Jewish politics reveals the importance of colonialism, and, in the twentieth century, anti-colonialism, as key factors driving the political radicalization of Jews from a variety of backgrounds. The Napoleonic conquests not only ended centuries of ghettoization for Jews in cities like Venice and Frankfurt and helped spread emancipation across much of Europe, the French campaign in Syria and Egypt (1798–1801) also represented the first steps toward colonialism in the Middle East and

North Africa. In 1830, France dramatically accelerated this process by launching the invasion of Algeria. Several decades later, in 1860, Jews in France seeking to "regenerate" their co-religionists in the Muslim-ruled lands between Morocco and Iran and prepare them for the rights and responsibilities of citizenship in their home countries established the Alliance Israélite Universelle. For generations of Jews of the Middle East and North Africa, the French-based curriculum of the Alliance network of schools would serve as a gateway toward upward social mobility, and indirectly (and very unintentionally) for some alumni, political radicalization. In 1870, the French empire passed the Crémieux Decree, granting most Algerian Jews French citizenship. In the forty-year period between the initial French invasion of Algeria and the Crémieux Decree, Jews across much of Europe had been emancipated. One stark exception was the Russian Empire, where the world's largest Jewish population was concentrated in the Pale of Settlement—itself a colonized space, as we will argue below—where Jews would have to wait until the Revolution of 1917 to receive full rights.

During this era of dramatic changes, socialism, communism, and anarchism all blossomed, beginning in Europe and spreading across the globe. The emergence of these ideologies was coterminous with the rapid pace of European colonization over much of the Middle East, Africa, and Asia. By the early decades of the twentieth century, the *Maghrib* (the Arab West) had come under colonial rule, while the Ottoman Empire's extensive holdings in the *Mashriq* (Arab East) would become European Mandates following World War I, with Iran and Turkey escaping sustained overt European domination in the region. These developments would have profound political effects on the region's Jews, with most falling under either French or British authority, with pockets under Italian rule.[6] Prior to European colonialism, Jews and other religious minorities in the MENA had generally held inferior legal status to Muslims, though the *Tanzimat* reforms (1839–1876), implemented in response to emancipatory trends in Europe and the threat of nationalist independence movements within the empire, formally granted equality to all Ottoman subjects. By contrast, French and British authorities often privileged Jews over Muslims in their colonial holdings, positioning Jews, as Ethan B. Katz, Lisa Moses Leff, and Maud S. Mandel assert in their 2017 edited volume *Colonialism and the Jews*, "in the crosshairs" of imperial hierarchies and agendas.[7] As Katz, Leff, and Mandel put it: "Very often Jews were neither exactly masters nor victims of colonial exploitation. Instead, they often circulated between physical spaces of metropole and colony and enjoyed a status somewhere between equal citizens and oppressed subjects. Moreover, they could be both orientalist and Orientalized, and frequently knew the life of both the colonizer and the colonized."[8] This dynamic, plus differential Jewish philanthropic aid in the form of organizations like the Alliance Israélite Universelle, underscored the perceived connection between Jews and colonial powers.

The post–World War I period witnessed the emergence of mass anti-colonial movements in the MENA, including in areas that were nominally independent (Egypt, Iraq) but maintained a strong British military presence. Throughout the region, Arab nationalism came to take precedence over more universalist political approaches. At the same time, even communist parties in the region typically syncretized elements of Marxism with local forms of nationalism. As Alma Heckman has written: "Communism was often nationalist in colonial contexts. Although this would seem to contradict the central tenets of international Communism, and though each colonial context indeed differed, this was a common feature of what would eventually be called the Global South. Communist parties in the MENA and many other colonial contexts of the twentieth century were viable and popular alternatives to national liberation parties predicated on ethnocentric or religious identities."[9] Jews in the MENA who rejected European colonialism responded enthusiastically to such ideological maneuvers, as they viewed nationalist-inflected communist parties as the most capacious—and in some cases, the only—way to express national belonging in political contexts that often privileged an Arab-Muslim cultural identity. Consequently, Jews seeking to achieve full participation in the postcolonial futures of their respective home countries were often at the vanguard of socialist and communist movements in the MENA, helping to found organizations such as the Moroccan Communist Party and *Ila al-Amam* (Forward) in Morocco and the Egyptian Communist Party and *al-Haraka al-Misriyya lil-Tahrir al-Watani* (Egyptian Movement for National Liberation) in Egypt, and serving in leadership positions while also joining as rank-and-file members in disproportionate numbers across the region.

Colonialism is crucial to understanding the political radicalization of Jews in the Middle East and North Africa. It also provides a valuable new perspective on the trajectory of radical Jewish politics in other contexts. Thus, for example, in chapter 16, Arie Dubnov demonstrates that in the early 1940s, Revisionist Zionists in Palestine looked to the Easter Uprising of 1916 against British rule in Ireland for inspiration and engaged in a "Judaising of the language of anticolonial revolt," while "Jewish militants who joined the Irgun and later on the Lehi [Revisionist guerilla groups] . . . saw themselves as anonymous soldiers in a war of national liberation against a foreign and hostile colonial foreign rule." Surprisingly, perhaps, colonialism should also be seen as an important factor in the development of radical Jewish politics in the Pale of Settlement, where roughly 40 percent of the world's Jews lived in 1900. While nineteenth-century Russian imperial expansion into Siberia, Central Asia, and the Caucasus has frequently been described as a form of colonialism, the category is rarely applied to Russia's creation of the Pale of Settlement or to the special legal provisions that were imposed on its Jewish residents over the course of decades and which contributed to the leftward turn of younger Jews in particular.[10]

There are important contextual differences between Jewish life under colonial regimes in the MENA and that of Jews in imperial Russia. However, in both Russia and the MENA, Jews often served as go-betweens. In both cases, colonial policies regarding Jews segmented them from the wider Muslim-majority or Christian-majority populations in which they lived. In key ways, the Russian approach to Jews in the Pale greatly resembled those taken by other empires to the residents of their overseas colonies. In this regard, it is particularly telling that in the first decades of the nineteenth century, Jews were the only people in European Russia to be designated by the government as *inorodtsy*, a term typically translated as "aliens," and which was otherwise applied to colonized peoples in the empire's newly conquered territories in Asia and the Caucasus. As John Slocum has written,

> The term *inorodsty* first acquired a strict legal definition in 1822. . . . The *Ustav* [decree] placed in the category of *inorodtsy* various "eastern" peoples, mostly nomadic or semi-nomadic Siberian natives, whose way of life was based on herding, hunting, or fishing. Subsequent nineteenth-century expansion to the south and east brought new ethnic groups into the empire, and a decision had to be made in each case whether or not a given ethnic group should be assigned to the category of *inorodtsy*. In 1835, Russia's Jews were designated *inorodtsy*, despite the fact that Jews were a sedentary people and inhabited a European, rather than Asian milieu.[11]

The influence of Russian colonialism in the Pale of Settlement on the radicalization of its Jewish residents, and even whether the radical Jewish politics that emerged there at the end of the nineteenth century should be seen as antecedents to the anti-colonial movements that would soon erupt elsewhere around the globe, deserves its own study. For the present, it is enough to emphasize that by centering the MENA, the impact of colonialism on the origins of radical Jewish politics more broadly, including in the Russian Empire, comes into focus.

If colonialism serves as a perhaps unexpected bridge between Jewish political activism in the MENA and the Russian Empire, then Zionism reveals the distinctive pressures that Jewish radicals in the Middle East and North Africa faced. Whereas a broad swath of leftists in Eastern Europe, including members of the Bund, either condemned Zionism as reactionary for its nationalist orientation and supposedly bourgeois tendencies, the movement had a dramatically different significance in the MENA. There, Zionism was seen as an existential threat to local Arab political aspirations in Palestine, an affront to the broader Arab nationalist vision for the region, and an extension of European settler colonialism. For Jewish radicals in the MENA, the widespread suspicion that all Jews possessed Zionist sympathies would become a profound obstacle to their participation in local politics and, especially after the creation of the State of Israel, to even remaining within their home countries. As Joel Beinin, Rami Ginat, Orit Bashkin, Lior Sternfeld, and Alma Heckman have pointed out in their studies of Jewish radical politics in Egypt, Iraq, Iran, and Morocco respectively, Jewish radicals vociferously decried Zionism as a fracturing agent between Jews and their home countries, a foreign ideology that challenged the *doikayt* or "hereness," to borrow a term from the Eastern European context, of their Jewishness.[12] In other words, anti-Zionism was an expression of patriotism and belonging.

In Egypt, Jewish radical Marsil Shirizi went so far as to found the Jewish League to Combat Zionism (*al-Rabita al-Israiliyya lil-Mukafahat al-Sahyuniyya*) in 1946.[13]

As Shirizi wrote in 1947: "Zionism is now helping turn the Arab world, well known for its traditional friendship with Jews, into a fertile soil for anti-Jewish movements. . . . We regard Zionism as an anti-Jewish movement because it ultimately serves foreign interests that are, meanwhile, malevolent toward Jews. We declare that the sole direction Jews need to take rests with dedicated open engagement in the national life of the country in which they live."[14] Leftist Jews expressed similar sentiments across the Middle East and North Africa. As Abraham Serfaty of Morocco declared in 1969 in the pages of *Souffles-Anfas*, the Moroccan radical magazine of literature, art and politics, "Jews from the Arab world, prisoners of Zionism, will gain consciousness of their solidarity with the Arab revolution and will help to shatter the last historical attempt to lock Jews up in a ghetto—and what a ghetto . . . of global proportions!"[15] Beginning in the 1960s, Zionism and anti-Zionism would also help to shape the experiences of Jewish radicals in other regions, particularly in countries in the Global South, such as Argentina and South Africa, where some Jews on the Left were swept up in the post–Six Day War euphoria that engulfed Jews across the political spectrum, while others rejected Israel as a bastion of colonialism and allied themselves with the Palestinian cause as part of an emerging "Third World" political sensibility and as a mode of expressing patriotism within the Arab world specifically.

Like colonialism, the role of race has not been sufficiently incorporated into the existing historiography of radical Jewish politics. Yet, in a variety of ways, race theory, and the popular attitudes and state-sponsored policies developed around it, helped to shape the conditions for—and the subsequent course of—the political radicalization of Jews around the globe. Perhaps most fundamentally, from the nineteenth century on, Jewish difference was increasingly understood in racial terms, a development that inflected how Jews were represented and treated, and, in turn, how they became politically radicalized. In the MENA, race profoundly shaped European colonial regimes' differential treatment of local Jews, Muslims, settlers, and others (e.g., native Christians and Imazighen, i.e., Berbers).

Since the earliest years of the Muslim conquests across the Middle East and North Africa in the seventh century, Jews and others of the *ahl al-kitab* (People of the Book) were legally classified as *dhimmis*—protected minorities under Muslim rule. Dhimmi status included a number of restrictions and taxation in exchange for official protection and the ability to freely practice one's religion. However, it is important to note that dhimmi status was not uniformly enforced across place and time. Further, dhimmi status was not racialized; persecution of dhimmis, when it did happen, was religiously based. The beginning of colonial regimes in the MENA in the nineteenth century and the concomitant rise of national movements transformed the position of minorities in the region, including Jews. As Ethan Katz has written, "colonial administrators and ethnographers attempted—here as elsewhere—to differentiate among the native population. They established policies of divide and rule and authored reams of 'scientific' reports, struggling to establish clear categories such as 'white,' 'non-white,' 'European,' 'native,' 'Jew,' 'Muslim,' 'Arab,' and 'Berber.' In lands where Jews and Muslims had cohabited for centuries, the very articulation and hardening of such categories entailed the creation of sharper stereotypes and distinct policies regarding both groups."[16]

Over time, the result of these racialist policies was to alienate many Jews from their non-Jewish neighbors throughout the MENA. The WWII years represented a particularly acute spike in antisemitism in the region. North Africa under Vichy French rule saw the stripping of Algerian Jews' French citizenship and restrictions on Jewish employment, housing, and education across the French Maghrib. Libyan Jews under fascist Italian colonial rule faced increased antisemitism after the promulgation of the *leggi razziali* race laws in 1938, which escalated still further after Germany's takeover of Italy.[17] In Iraq, popular violence, including murder and looting, took place against Jews during what became known as the Farhud in early June 1941. The notorious Hajj Amin al-Husseini, once the British-appointed Grand Mufti of Jerusalem, met with Hitler after a sojourn in Iraq.[18] Across the region, the WWII years marked a crescendo of antisemitism, resulting in increased Jewish involvement in radical leftist politics to combat such divisive currents. While some Jews in the region came to identify with colonial regimes and embraced European culture, indeed even as a response to the traumas of the WWII period, others turned to radical politics as a means to overcome what they considered to be the false distinctions between Jews and non-Jews imposed by European powers and to advocate for a shared future in their home countries.

Some Jewish radicals in the MENA, most notably in Iraq, as Orit Bashkin reveals in chapter 5 of this volume, embraced the self-designation "Arab Jews" as a way of asserting solidarity as well as integration with their non-Jewish neighbors and rejecting any racial or ethnic difference between them in favor of a common cultural and national identity. Likewise, in Algeria, as Pierre-Jean Le Foll-Luciani argues in chapter 2, the persecution of local Jews by the antisemitic Vichy regime helped to radicalize some members of the Jewish community, leading them to reject France, identify explicitly as "natives," and, in some cases, join the anti-colonialist National Liberation Front (FLN) during the Algerian War of Independence.

While the segmented racialization of native populations by colonial regimes in the MENA has been well documented, most scholarship on the Russian Empire has either denied the salience of race or dismissed it as a Western European category with little significance for understanding the empire's group dynamics, a phenomenon that Eugene Avrutin has described as the "'absence' of race in Russian imperial historiography."[19] Yet Avrutin has identified a "gradual shift in documentation practices—from religion and social estate to ethnicity and race," at the end of the nineteenth century that included the growing racialization of the empire's Jews. Indeed, he argues, the Russian government responded to Jewish political radicalism by implementing a series of policies that inscribed Jewish difference in racial, rather than religious, terms: "Jews and Jewish radicalism 'threatened' to undermine and perhaps even destroy the social order . . . political conservativism intensified anti-Jewish fears and hostilities, marking the appearance of a modern, exclusionary imperial racism. . . . In St. Petersburg, Moscow, and Warsaw, police officials required Jewish merchants to display their forenames, patronymics, and surnames on all privately owned shops. . . . Like the French colonial administrators who inscribed *noir* to document ex-slaves in the Caribbean, Russian officials marked 'of Jewish origin' (*iz evreev*) on all official documentation for those Jews who converted to Russian Orthodoxy."[20]

Ironically, the Russian government's hardening of the line between Jews and non-Jews did not eliminate or even diminish the political radicalization of the empire's Jews; instead it almost certainly helped to drive more and more Jews into radical parties at the turn of the twentieth century. As Jewish difference was increasingly portrayed in racial or ethnic terms—Avrutin has argued that the two categories should be seen as coterminous in the late imperial Russian context—and, therefore, insurmountable by religious conversion or the liberal policies that had previously encouraged assimilation and integration, growing numbers of Russian Jews turned toward forms of radical politics that either promised a world in which Jewish difference would cease to exist entirely (i.e., communism) or that embraced Jewish difference *and* characterized it as harmonious with socialist ideals.

Among the latter movements, socialist Zionists argued that the confluence of capitalism, nationalism, and antisemitism imperiled Jews in Europe and elsewhere. The only way to solve the problems of discrimination, violence, and poverty, they argued, was through the creation of a Jewish homeland. Bundists, by contrast, believed that Jews could overcome capitalism and antisemitism in the countries where they lived by organizing Jewish workers into their own political party (and auxiliary institutions) in alliance with other, non-Jewish revolutionary parties. Their program called for Jewish national cultural autonomy in Russia rather than a homeland elsewhere. The Bundist principle of *doikayt* or "hereness," in Yiddish, dates back to interwar Lithuania, as Michael Casper discusses in chapter 12 of this volume. Even the Soviet Union, despite Bolshevik opposition to the Bund and socialist Zionism, sought a way to accommodate Jewish difference—at least in the near term—while furthering the global goal of socialist revolution. Bolsheviks did so, after 1917, by defining Jews as a national minority and establishing a Jewish commissariat, a Jewish section of the Bolshevik party, and an array of Yiddish-language educational, cultural, and juridical institutions. During the 1920s and 1930s, the Soviet government established Jewish colonies in Ukraine and Crimea, and the Jewish Autonomous Oblast of Birobidzhan. As Robert Weinberg writes in chapter 11, "The Birobidzhan experiment conformed to the [Soviet] dictum 'national in form, socialist in content.'" Thus, the Soviet Union implemented important aspects of the Bundist program and the Zionist principle of territoriality, albeit within an authoritarian state structure that made no room for independent political parties.

Beyond these imperial contexts, race also helped to shape the course of Jewish radicalism in other sites around the globe. In chapter 16, Arie Dubnov reveals that only the imposition of the *leggi razziali* or Italian racial laws, in 1938, ended the long-standing romance between Revisionist Zionists and Italy dating back to Vladimir Jabotinsky's student days in Rome. Among the direct consequences of the new racial laws was the forced departure of Isacco Sciaky, a Sephardi native of

Salonica who "was the *enfant terrible* of Italian Zionism, known for his fiery temperament and radical ideas," to Palestine in 1939, where he would join other Revisionists in challenging British colonial administration of the territory. And, as Dario Miccoli argues in chapter 7, intra-Jewish racism in the newly established State of Israel would contribute to the political radicalization of some of the country's Mizrahi Jewish population, leading to the creation of *Ha-panterim ha-shehorim* or "Black Panthers"—modeled on the African American organization—during the 1970s. Finally, while not directed at Jews, the oppressive racial laws of Apartheid-era South Africa would, from the 1940s on, serve as the chief impetus for the disproportionate involvement of Jews in radical politics in the country, as Milton Shain and Richard Mendelsohn demonstrate in chapter 10. Jewish leftists such as Joe Slovo, who became the general secretary of the South African Communist Party and a leader within the African National Congress (ANC), worked alongside African activists like Nelson Mandela, not to achieve Jewish political emancipation, as was done elsewhere, but to create a South Africa in which apartheid was a shameful relic of the past.

In his introduction to *Jews and Leftist Politics* (2017), an edited volume devoted exclusively to radical politics among Ashkenazi Jews in Europe, the United States, and Israel, Jack Jacobs has written: "The presence of Jews and individuals of Jewish descent in the leadership of leftist movements was, at one point in time, considerable, and was regularly disproportionate to the percentage of Jews in the general populations of the countries in which these Jews were active. Particularly in the first decades of the twentieth century, there were not only a remarkable number of Jews in the most prominent leadership positions of the leftist parties, but also a disproportionately high number of Jews in (somewhat) lower-ranking position within some of these parties, and in particular roles in party-related institutions."[21] By way of illustration, Jacobs notes that 23 percent of the Menshevik delegates to the 1907 congress of the Russian Social Democratic Workers Party were Jews and a still significant but smaller number were Bolsheviks. Eighteen of the twenty-nine commissars in the short-lived Hungarian Soviet Republic of 1919 were Jews. The German Social Democratic Party won the support of 42 percent of Jewish voters in 1924. Roughly 35 percent of the Communist Party of Poland were Jews as of 1930 and, Jacobs writes, "In 1949, it has been alleged, approximately half of those in the American Communist Party were Jews."[22] While similarly precise figures are not available for other sites around the globe, the essays in this volume make clear that Jews helped to found and lead numerous leftist parties in the MENA, as well as in areas with more recently settled Jewish immigrant communities, including in Latin America and South Africa, where they were often disproportionately represented in rank-and-file membership as well.

Like their counterparts from other backgrounds, Jews became radicalized for a wide variety of reasons, including a desire to eliminate social and economic inequality, improve working conditions for themselves and others, oppose colonialism, fight for national liberation, and, particularly for Jewish women who became radicalized, champion the rights of women. As Orit Bashkin writes regarding Iraq, "The Iraqi Communist Party also called for suffrage, expansion of women's education, and changes in the personal status laws, and strongly denounced honor killings," a platform that attracted Jewish (and other) women to the party, even as they were still subjected to sexism by their male comrades. Yet, in addition to these shared motivations, scholars, and in some cases Jewish radicals themselves, have long asked whether there was also something distinctive about Jewishness that helps to explain Jews' prominence in left-wing movements.

In his 2020 presidential campaign, Bernie Sanders indicated that the Jewish experience of persecution—rather than any religious or cultural traditions—had played a key role in his own political awakening. When asked at a town-hall, "How do you think your Jewish heritage impacts your vision of the world, your politics?" Sanders responded, "It impacts me very profoundly. You know, when I try to think about the views that I came to hold there are two factors. One, I grew up in a family that didn't have a lot of money. . . . And the second one is being Jewish." By way of explanation, Sanders remembered that upon learning about the Holocaust as a child, "tears would roll down my cheeks when I saw what happened to the Jewish people, six million were killed."[23] Elsewhere on the campaign trail, Sanders suggested that this history should lead Jews to embrace leftist politics, "If there's any group that should be trying to bring people together around a common and progressive agenda, it is the Jewish people."[24]

By contrast, other Jewish radicals have emphasized the decisive importance of Jewish religious traditions to explain the particular appeal of socialism for Jews. Abraham Menes, an alumnus of the prestigious Mirer and Grodno yeshivas in Eastern Europe, who later became a leader of the Bund, a Yiddish language journalist, and a historian of radical Jewish politics, offered one of the most succinct formulations of this approach in the late 1940s:

> Both Jewish socialism and Zionism gave expression to the age-old yearnings of the Jew for redemption. Although each was profoundly affected by the general social and national political tendencies of the surrounding world they remained essentially Jewish movements, bound up with Jewish life and with the cherished traditions of Jewish history. The Messianic-Utopian element in socialism appealed strongly to the Jewish intellectual and particularly to the working man. In the course of generations the Jews had come to constitute a "proletarian nation," a people without a land or government of its own. In the socialist propaganda for the new world, built upon the foundations of truth, peace and justice, the Jewish worker heard an echo of the old Biblical prophecies of eternal peace, of the "End of Days," when, along with the redemption of the entire world, the people of Israel, too, would be redeemed.[25]

Menes's explanation for the supposed affinity of Jews *as Jews* for radical politics contains key elements that have also appeared in many other sources, for example, Ernst Bloch, Ernest Renan, Russell Jacoby, and Michael Lowy. These elements include the claim that traditional Jewish texts, particularly the prophetic books of the Hebrew Bible, nurtured a predilection for utopianism, a redemptive approach to history, and a passion for social justice among Jews. In addition to these factors, Menes argued that the vicissitudes of history had resulted in a distinctively Jewish socioeconomic status or what he called a "'proletarian nation,' a people without a land or government of its own," that lent itself readily to socialism. Even a skeptic like Robert Wistrich, who wrote dismissively that "A great deal of speculative nonsense has been written about this subject, and about the alleged affinities between Judaism and Marxian socialism," nevertheless conceded that certain features of the Jewish experience were easily transposed into radical politics. Thus, he argued that for members of the "Russified and Polonized Jewish intelligentsia . . . Marxism had replaced Judaism (with its traditional isolation from the Gentile world) by a gospel of militant activism. *Das Kapital* became the Torah of this intelligentsia, over which they argued with a learning, skill in logical exposition and genius for abstract interpretation reminiscent of their rabbinical and Talmudic ancestors."[26] Wistrich added that the socialist shift in "loyalties from *nation* to *class*" was "easier for Jews than for non-Jews . . . at a time when there was no Jewish state or officially recognized 'Jewish' nationality."[27] Finally, he noted that antisemitism encouraged some Jews to embrace universalist versions of socialism and communism, while others responded to persecution by creating the "separatist Jewish socialism" of the Bund and Labor Zionism.[28]

Most famously, Isaac Deutscher, a former child Talmud prodigy turned Trotskyist, identified Jewish social marginality as the key factor producing what he called "the non-Jewish Jew," a figure who rejected Jewish peoplehood and all forms of nationalism in favor of "universal human emancipation." Deutscher posited a lineage of iconoclastic thinkers from Spinoza to Marx to Luxemburg and Trotsky, whom he considered "*a priori* exceptional" because they "dwelt on the borderlines of various civilizations, religions, and national cultures." "They lived on the margins or in the nooks and crannies of their respective nations. Each of them was in society and yet not in it, of it and yet not of it. It was this that enabled them to rise in thought above their societies, above their nations, above their times and generations, and to strike out mentally into wide new horizons and far into the future."[29] These "rootless" Jews, according to Deutscher, shared similar ways of thinking. They possessed an ingrained comparative perspective, rejected moral absolutes, and eschewed Jewish group belonging in favor of "the ultimate solidarity of man." Moreover, Deutscher made it clear that he viewed the "non-Jewish Jew" as a figure that was neither timeless nor uniquely Jewish. Indeed, the Palestinian scholar and critic Edward Said would later claim it for himself and for the growing number of "refugees, exiles, expatriates, and immigrants" possessing "the diasporic, wandering, unresolved, cosmopolitan consciousness of someone who is both inside and outside his or her community."[30] The figure of the "non-Jewish Jew," then, powerfully exemplified a certain Jewish experience of modernity that might fruitfully be applied to others or even be embraced by them.

Like most of the literature on radical Jewish politics, these proposed explanations have all focused on developments in Central and Eastern Europe or on immigrants from these regions who settled elsewhere. The notable exception to this tendency is Philip Mendes's survey, *Jews and the Left: The Rise and Fall of a Political Alliance* (2014), which argues that at least five factors encouraged Jews around the globe, including those in the Middle East and North Africa, to gravitate toward leftist movements.[31] These include high rates of Jewish poverty in places ranging from the Russian Empire to Iraq during the late nineteenth and early twentieth centuries, the impact of "ethnic oppression" or antisemitism, the influence of "Jewish cultural values" embedded in traditional texts and practices, leftist support for Jewish equality, and what he calls "other causes," including disproportionately high rates of urbanization and intellectualism, which cut across different geographical regions. According to Mendes, the distinctive ways that Jews were perceived and treated by others, as well as how they were differentially implicated in—and impacted by—much broader socioeconomic and cultural phenomena such as urbanization, influenced their radicalization at least as much as Jewish religious or cultural traditions. The essays in this volume reinforce the view that Jewishness, capaciously understood to include the different kinds of factors identified by Mendes, helped to shape the political radicalization of Jews around the globe. An important corollary is that Jewishness never existed—nor was it experienced—in a uniform way across the different regions in which Jews lived, even as certain shared phenomena cut across time and space. Put differently, the constellation of factors that constituted Jewishness in a particular place and time overlapped *and* differed from the factors that defined Jewishness elsewhere in the same period.

Prior to the nineteenth century, Jewishness in Europe, the Middle East, and North Africa comprised elements of what we now call religion, culture, and ethnicity. Wherever they lived, Jews traditionally identified as members of *am yisrael* or the "nation" or "people of Israel" and understood themselves—and were seen by others—as the physical descendants of biblical Israel. This genealogical self-conception was reinforced by Christian and Muslim legal prohibitions that barred members of their own communities from converting to Judaism. In addition to this shared collective identity, Jewish communities also possessed a common literary heritage in Hebrew and Aramaic that included the Tanakh (Hebrew Bible), the two Talmuds and other rabbinic sources, medieval and early modern legal texts such as Maimonides's Mishnah Torah and Joseph Karo's Shulhan Arukh, and different forms of the Kabbalah, including the Zohar and the Lurianic teachings of the sixteenth century, which quickly spread from Ottoman Palestine to Jews in Syria, Yemen, Morocco, Salonica, Germany, Poland, and all parts in between.

Just as important as this common heritage, however, were the distinctive customary practices (known as *minhag*) and liturgical traditions (or *nusach*) that were specific to Jewish communities around the globe. Eventually, in the early modern period, many of these differences coalesced around two major taxonomical categories that became known as "Sephardi" (Jews whose ancestors had lived in the

Iberian Peninsula or Sepharad prior to the Spanish and Portuguese expulsions) and "Ashkenazi" (Jews whose ancestors had lived in the Rhineland region or Ashkenaz during the medieval period). In practice, however, there remained countless, highly localized ways of being Jewish, including among those Jews living in Iran, Iraq, Italy, Yemen, Greece, Syria, parts of North Africa, and so on, whose ancestors were originally neither Sephardi nor Ashkenazi, even if in some cases they came to adopt such an identity over time, at least to a certain degree.

Traditionally, Jewishness was also defined in different places by elements of what would later be called "culture," once that concept became popular during the nineteenth century. This included a wide range of customary practices but also distinctive foods, musical traditions, dress, and languages, which in some cases, such as Ladino and Yiddish, sharply differentiated Jews from their non-Jewish neighbors, while in others, such as Judeo-Arabic or Judeo-Persian, served as a linguistic bridge while still maintaining elements of Jewish difference. Finally, Jewishness was also shaped by traditional Christian and Muslim religious attitudes toward Jews, the rise of racialized antisemitism, the civil and legal status conferred upon Jews by the states in which they resided—which, as we have seen, began to shift dramatically in many places during the nineteenth century—and, finally, by internal communal developments in the same period, such as the rise of the Haskalah (Jewish Enlightenment) and of Jewish religious denominations in Western Europe, beginning with the Reform movement, and of new educational institutions, including the modern yeshiva movement in Eastern Europe and the Alliance Israélite Universelle in the MENA. Rather than a single Jewish identity or experience, therefore, multiple versions of Jewishness coexisted historically, overlapping in some fundamental respects and differing dramatically in others.

Against this complex historical backdrop, it is not surprising that Jewishness, understood in the capacious sense we have been exploring, inflected the development of radical Jewish politics around the globe in a variety of ways. On one end of the spectrum, across North Africa and the Middle East, with some notable exceptions most Jews who became involved in radical politics did not seek to integrate their political activism with Jewish religious or cultural traditions; except for those who became Zionists, they did not participate in political movements that were predicated on the idea of Jewish nationality and therefore did not advocate for Jewish cultural or political autonomy within their own societies. At the same time, most Jewish radicals in the MENA did not claim that Jewishness would disappear once socialism was victorious, as did many leftists in Europe, going all the way back to Karl Marx in his essay *On the Jewish Question*. Instead, they tended to treat Jewishness as a private or domestic affair that was separate from the public sphere in which they were active politically, perhaps in part due to the influence of postrevolutionary French conceptions regarding the proper place of religion in society. Phrased differently, those Jews who embraced radical politics in the MENA did so as a means to become fully Moroccan, Iraqi, Algerian, and so on, even if in most cases they still maintained some form of private Jewish identity. As Alma Heckman has written regarding Jewish involvement in the Moroccan

Communist Party (PCM): "The Jewish members of the PCM . . . saw themselves as contributing to a truly emancipated Morocco, defined not by their Jewishness but by their Moroccanness first and foremost."[32]

Nevertheless, for many Jewish radicals in the region, the fact of their Jewishness played at least some role in their turn to politics in the first place and in their subsequent trajectories, even if they did not seek to integrate the radical and Jewish aspects of their identities. Indeed, regardless of their own self-conception, Jewish radicals in the MENA were typically treated by others as Jews, including by their non-Jewish political comrades and the states in which they lived. Whether in Morocco, Egypt, or Iraq, Jews were members of a minority group for whom radical politics represented a potential path to normalization and integration into a majority national identity, in an era when such national identities were being fiercely debated and defined. Indeed, Jewish radicals across the region were often in the vanguard of those arguing for the creation of national identities that would subsume traditional ethno-religious differences. In this regard, Jewish radicals had much in common with members of other minority groups, for example, Christian Arabs in Syria, Armenians in Iran, or Kurds in Iraq, who all played prominent roles in the emergence of radical political movements in their respective countries.

Within this broader context, Jewishness often played an important, even pivotal, role in the political awakening of many Jewish radicals in the Middle East and North Africa, but not because of anything particular or distinctive to Judaism. Rather, these radicals' Jewishness located them within a minoritized and sometimes discriminated against community whose future was in flux as colonialism gave way to nation-states across the region. This was particularly the case during the 1930s and 1940s, when rising antisemitism in both Europe and in the MENA, along with anti-Zionism, Arab nationalism, and anti-colonialism in the Middle East and North Africa, led to an increase in anti-Jewish sentiment and, in some cases, outbreaks of anti-Jewish violence, notoriously in Constantine, Algeria, in 1934, and during the *Farhud*, in which hundreds of Jews were either killed or injured, and their property looted, in Baghdad, Iraq, in 1941. These developments, in turn, provided Jewish radicals in the region with a powerful motivation to embrace a politics that downplayed Jewish difference and subsumed it within an emerging nationalist identity, whether Iraqi, Moroccan, or, more generally, Arab or Iranian. In this way, radical movements could serve as a means for minority groups, Jews among them, to become fully integrated.

While most Jewish radicals in the MENA embraced political activism primarily as a path to national acceptance or belonging, some turned to internationalism and affiliated with the Comintern or Third International (1919–1943), the Soviet-controlled initiative to spread Communism around the globe. As Rami Ginat demonstrates in chapter 4, among them were Joseph and Charlotte Rosenthal, members of an Ashkenazi Jewish family from Ottoman Palestine who moved to Alexandria, Egypt, by way of Beirut, at the end of the nineteenth century. Their story exemplifies the movement of Jewish radicals across borders, reflecting broader patterns of Jewish migration that played a key role in catalyzing the development of radical politics throughout the Middle East and North Africa. Indeed, the presence of multilingual Jewish migrants, refugees, and travelers in cosmopolitan cities like Alexandria, Cairo, and Casablanca transformed these sites into veritable hothouses of intellectual fermentation and radical political activism.

Joseph Rosenthal, who had first read Marx in Yiddish translation while living in Beirut, founded the Egyptian Socialist Party—later the Communist Party of Egypt—and established links with the Comintern in the early 1920s. Rosenthal's daughter, Charlotte, and her husband, Yehiel Kossoi, both became deeply involved with the Comintern after first being active in socialist Zionist organizations in Palestine. Charlotte, who spoke Arabic in addition to Italian, Yiddish, and several other languages, eventually moved to the Soviet Union, where she became a student in the Arab Section of the Communist University of the Toilers of the East, established in 1921 to train cadres to spread revolution in Asia, Africa, and the Middle East. The presence of an Ashkenazi Jew from Egypt by way of Palestine in the "Arab Section" of the Comintern was hardly unique, as Masha Kirasirova writes: " In the 1920s, the Arab Section was dominated by non-Arab minorities—including Armenians, Kurds, and Jews of Middle Eastern, Russian, Polish, and Ukrainian origins—a fact that reflected the composition of early communist parties in Palestine, Egypt, and Syria/Lebanon."[33] At the same time, internationalist and nationalist movements often overlapped in their membership, particularly in the urban centers of the MENA. One reason why leftist radical politics was so appealing to religious and ethnic minorities in the region was the universalism promoted by such groups at a time and in a place when many national liberation movements were predicated on Muslim or Arab identity.

Yet after the creation of the state of Israel in 1948, simply possessing a Jewish background, even if one was anti-Zionist, became a source of tension or worse for many Jewish radicals in the MENA. Government opponents seeking to delegitimate local socialist or communist parties found it useful to cast them as dominated by Jewish—and, therefore, they claimed, Zionist—members, as Orit Bashkin writes concerning the Iraqi Communist Party or ICP: "The Iraqi state used their Judaism to present them as Zionists in order to smear the ICP's image as a power disloyal to Arab interests, and concurrently, tried to strip them of their Iraqi citizenship and deport them to Israel. For example, in the 1949 encyclopedia of Iraqi Communists produced by the police, all the photos of arrested female Communists are of Jewish activists, although many members of varying religious affiliations were arrested in this period." In the face of such pressure, some Jewish radicals in the MENA even converted to Islam because it allowed them to remain in their respective countries at a time of heightened suspicion toward Jews, who were often accused of having Zionist sympathies or outright allegiance to Israel, despite their own protestations to the contrary. This phenomenon also went beyond radical circles. Famously, the Egyptian Jewish diva Layla Mourad (who was not a Communist), second only to the Egyptian national treasure Umm Kalthum in her fame, converted to Islam in part to maintain her career and remain in Egypt.[34] Across the region, pan-Arab and Arab nationalist politics emphasized solidarity with the

Palestinian Arab struggle against Jewish national ambitions in the territory. During the twentieth century, Jewishness and Zionist support were frequently and increasingly conflated by political parties and popular media across the MENA region. Hence, for Jews committed to a vision of Arab-Jewishness and patriotism in their home countries, disavowing Zionism in the most rigorous terms was critical.

Like their counterparts elsewhere in the Middle East, Jewish radicals in Iran were initially drawn to leftist politics because it offered the dual possibility of overcoming discrimination and of integrating into Iranian society, rather than out of a strong ideological commitment to socialism, as a radical named Habib recalled to Lior Sternfeld, "We [the Jews] were attracted to Tudeh [the Iranian Communist party] in order to become more Iranian," adding, "I knew nothing about Marx or Marxism when I joined Tudeh. I joined because this was the only place that they did not call me Johud [a derogatory name for Jews]. I learned Marxism in Qasr prison, shortly after I joined the party." Yet, in contrast to the rest of the Middle East and North Africa, Jewish radicals in Iran also sought ways of integrating their Jewishness with their politics. Instead of abandoning Jewish religious traditions, for example, members of the Jewish branch of the Communist Tudeh party, and later the Association of Jewish Iranian Intellectuals or *Jami'ah-i Rawshanfikran-i Kalimi-yi Iran*, created what Sternfeld describes in chapter 6 as "hybrid identities that were, in many ways, unique to Iran. They contained sentiments of nationalism and radical socialism, all mixed with Muslim and Jewish religiosity." Thus, many Jewish radicals in Iran viewed the Jewish, radical, and nationalist aspects of their identities as mutually reinforcing. In this regard, it is likely that they were influenced by other Iranian political movements that sought to integrate Shia Islam and socialism, beginning with the "Movement of God-Worshipping Socialists" founded by Muhammad Nakshab in the 1940s and continuing to the present day with the People's Mujahedin Organization or Mujahedin-e-Khalq.

Whereas Iran represented an outlier in the Middle East and North Africa, the cultivation of "hybrid identities," comprising strong Jewish and radical political elements, was common in Eastern Europe and among Eastern European Jewish immigrants and their descendants in the United States, Argentina, and elsewhere. Unlike in Iran, however, the Jews who embraced these hybrid identities did not do so in order to assimilate into a dominant national identity, be it Russian, Polish, or otherwise. On the contrary, by the beginning of the twentieth century, a majority of Jewish radicals from Eastern Europe either embraced secular Jewish nationalism in the form of left-wing Zionism or the Bund or, if they were anarchists or communists, they typically rejected nationalism altogether in favor of internationalism. Others, as Robert Weinberg demonstrates in chapter 11, even managed to square the circle, as it were, during the 1930s, by supporting the Soviet Union's creation of the Jewish Autonomous Region of Birobidzhan, where Yiddish language signs welcomed Jewish settlers from around the world to a self-described communist "Jewish homeland."

Already in the nineteenth century, Jewish thinkers from the northwest corner of the Russian Empire known as *Lita* in Yiddish sought to harmonize materialist views of the world with ideas drawn from a variety of traditional Jewish religious texts, including the profoundly recondite Kabbalah. The most influential figure in the creation of what the historian Eliyahu Stern has called "Jewish Materialism" was Aaron Shmuel Lieberman (1843–1880), later known as "the father of Jewish socialism" for the key role he played in translating and disseminating Karl Marx's works among Hebrew language readers in Eastern Europe. For Lieberman, who studied the Kabbalah with his grandfather as a youth before abandoning Orthodox religious practice, the teachings of prominent Kabbalists such as Isaac Luria and Moshe Chaim Luzzatto anticipated—and, he claimed, would one day be fulfilled by—socialism.

Paradoxically, perhaps, the many yeshivas or rabbinic academies established in Eastern Europe during the nineteenth century functioned as a crucial—if inadvertent—incubator for radical activism, much like the network of Alliance schools did in the MENA, despite the profound differences between these educational institutions. Yeshivas produced a native Jewish intelligentsia whose members were well-equipped from years of study to immerse themselves in radical literature.[35] Some yeshiva students attempted to reconcile Jewish tradition with their newfound revolutionary sympathies, while others rejected Judaism completely in favor of a radical orthodoxy. Among the latter were former yeshiva students who became Bolsheviks and later joined the *Yevsektsia*, the Jewish section of the Soviet Communist Party, which became notorious for its efforts to suppress Judaism following the Russian Revolution.

Like their non-Jewish counterparts, Jewish radicals in Eastern Europe frequently identified as atheists and almost all rejected rabbinic authority, often with great gusto. Nevertheless, many also realized the impossibility of neatly separating the religious and cultural aspects of Jewishness, especially for the Jewish masses whom they hoped to bring into the radical fold. Rather than jettison Judaism entirely, then, some Jewish radicals from Eastern Europe selectively embraced Jewish traditions, albeit in transformed ways, such as with socialist-themed Passover Seders that emphasized the holiday's message of liberation from bondage, instead of its miraculous aspects. Others re-read Jewish history through a radical lens.[36] For instance, Emma Goldman, born into an Orthodox Jewish family in Kovno (Kaunas), then part of the Russian Empire, constructed what Anna Torres describes in chapter 15 of this volume as a revisionist "genealogy of anarchism *within* Judaism, itself, citing Jesus of Nazareth, Hasidic mutual aid societies, and the radical Jewish thinker Moses Hess as links in a single chain." Hasidism, in particular, was reimagined by some Jewish radicals as a populist phenomenon. Thus, Goldman praised the "many anarchist elements among the Hasidim,"[37] while the Yiddish author and socialist Menashe Unger, who came from a prominent Hasidic family, described Hasidism as "a development of the Jewish popular masses" that "liberated the simple Jews, the humble people, from the hegemony, from the sovereignty of the powerful and the scholars."[38]

Perhaps most significantly, Jewish radicals in Eastern Europe and its diaspora created a distinctive culture of their own that was at once profoundly radical *and* Jewish. Tony Michels has argued that the cultural turn among Jewish radicals occurred in several stages. At first, during the 1890s, "Socialists did not think of themselves as building a new, Yiddish culture. . . . As far as most socialists were concerned, all they were doing was promoting enlightenment and spreading socialism in the Yiddish language."[39] Moreover, "Even as socialists built an all-Jewish, Yiddish-speaking movement, they professed an opposite goal: dissolution of the Jewish labor movement and, indeed, the entirety of Jewish culture, community, and identity."[40] By the turn of the twentieth century, however, a series of developments, including the emergence of the Bund and the Zionist movement, as well as the galvanizing effects of the Kishinev pogrom in 1903, helped to inspire a dramatic shift in attitude among many Jewish radicals on both sides of the Atlantic. Rather than merely promoting socialism in the Yiddish language, figures like Chaim Zhitlovsky and his childhood friend, S. An-sky, advocated for the creation of a secular Jewish culture or *yidishe kultur,* whose Jewishness would be as central as its socialism. In the following decades, a vibrant radical Jewish culture took shape in Eastern Europe, the Americas, South Africa, and other outposts, finding expression in an incredible range of leftist newspapers, books, and other publications, conferences, collective farms, theater groups, summer camps for "red diaper babies," schools, and cooperative buildings in the Bronx that were founded by Jewish socialists and communists—who then tried to keep their children from playing with one another due to ideological differences.

If Jewish radicals in Iran differed from their counterparts elsewhere in the MENA by seeking to combine Jewish religious traditions, socialist politics, and nationalism, then those in Hungary diverged from their counterparts in the rest of Eastern Europe by not participating in the radical Jewish culture that we have discussed above. Instead, the Jewish radicals who formed a majority of the "people's commissars" in the short-lived Hungarian Soviet Republic of 1919 and those who later constituted the "quartet" of top leaders—Mátyás Rákosi, Erno Gero, Mihály Farkas, and Jozsef Revai—in the Communist government established following World War II generally repudiated any attachment to Jewishness and, in the words of Peter Kenez in chapter 13 of this volume, "devoted their entire lives to the communist cause." In short, the hybrid identities that were common in Eastern Europe among Bundists, Zionists, anarchists, and even some Haredim were exceedingly rare in Hungary.[41]

Several factors help to explain the uniqueness of the Hungarian case. Whereas in Eastern Europe Jews were becoming increasingly proletarianized in the first decades of the twentieth century, a majority of Hungarian Jews were highly assimilated members of the bourgeoisie and formed a large percentage of the country's professional class, industrialists, financiers, and artists. While Yiddish provided Jews in most of Eastern Europe with a distinctly Jewish idiom in which to express themselves politically and culturally, Hungarian Jews overwhelmingly used Hungarian and Yiddish was only spoken by the country's Hasidic population, which was famous for being the most separatist and reactionary in Europe. Thus, Hungary was notable for having at once the most assimilated, the most politically radical, *and* the most reactionary Jewish population of any country in Eastern Europe.

Another place where a distinctive radical Jewish culture emerged was in the "Jewish metropolis" of Salonica. As Kostis Karpozilos and Paris Papamichos Chronakis describe in chapter 14, during the final years of Ottoman rule, Salonica experienced rapid industrialization and a large percentage of its Jews, including many young Jewish women, were proletarianized, working in some of the same industries—textiles, tobacco, printing—as their counterparts in Warsaw and Vilna. The extreme density and industrialization of the Jewish community, its famously vibrant Jewish life, the presence of a Jewish intelligentsia educated in the Alliance Israélite Universelle system, and its close ties with the other Jewish communities of the Balkans meant that the city was able to serve as the incubator for a political culture that was both profoundly Jewish and radical. As was the case with Yiddish in Eastern Europe, this was greatly facilitated by the widespread use of Ladino, which both united Jewish residents of the region and differentiated them linguistically from their non-Jewish neighbors.

In Salonica, a city whose Jewish character was so pronounced that it was popularly known as the "Jerusalem of the Balkans," the most important socialist leader of any background was Abraham Benaroya, an extraordinarily prolific political organizer, thinker, and author. Benaroya was raised in Bulgaria, where he joined a socialist organization while still in high school and published a book on the "Jewish Question" in Bulgarian. Benaroya briefly studied law before arriving in Salonica, where he would make his reputation soon after the Young Turk Revolution of 1908. During the brief window preceding the First Balkan War of 1912 and the transfer of Salonica to Greek rule, Benaroya catalyzed one of the most intense flowerings of radical Jewish politics in history. In short order, Benaroya and his comrades established a socialist club, a biweekly Ladino newspaper called *La Solidaridad Obradera* (later renamed *Avanti* and published as a daily until 1934), a socialist youth group, and the Socialist Workers' Federation of Salonica, a multiethnic affair that was nevertheless dominated by Ladino-speaking Jews and which the scholar Nikos Potamianos described as "the most significant socialist organization in the Ottoman Empire, and after 1912, in Greece."[42]

The goal of the Federation was to unite the city's different ethnic groups under a common class-based banner, while allowing each of them to retain their own cultural distinctiveness.[43] Whether this vision reflected the tradition of federative politics among socialists in the Balkans or the influence of Jewish Austro-Marxists such as Otto Bauer and Victor Adler, or whether it developed independently, is difficult to determine. Whatever its source(s), the Federation's ideology reflected the broad appeal of autonomism among Jewish socialists in the waning days of the Ottoman, Russian, and Austro-Hungarian empires alike. The Federation disseminated its political message to the city's working-class Jewish women and men via a wide range of educational and cultural activities in Ladino, including free classes, a lending library, a theater group that performed plays by Molière and Tolstoy in

Ladino translation, communal celebrations, and more. Looking back in 1968, Benaroya noted the uniqueness of the socialist movement in Salonica within the wider Sephardi world, as well as its close parallels with the Bund: "The labor movement in the city [Salonica] . . . was, as far as I know, the only socialist and syndicalist movement in the entire Sephardi Jewish diaspora. . . . This special movement had similarities and certain ideological connections, with the Bundist movement among Ashkenazi Jewry."[44]

In 1921, the future British prime minister Winston Churchill published an essay in the *Illustrated Sunday Herald*, in which he described Jews as the "mainspring of every subversive movement during the nineteenth century" and stressed that one could not "exaggerate the part played in the creation of Bolshevism and in the actual bringing about of the Russian Revolution by these international and for the most part atheistical Jews."[45] A decade and a half later, Joseph Goebbels, the Nazi propaganda minister, declared in a speech entitled "Communism with the Mask Off" that, "It was the Jew who discovered Marxism. It is the Jew who for decades past has endeavored to stir up world revolutions through the medium of Marxism. It is the Jew who is today at the head of Marxism in all the countries of the world."[46] More recently, right-wing conspiracy-mongers have accused George Soros, a Jewish financier and pro-democracy advocate originally from Hungary, of being "the motivating force behind revolutions aboard and even of trying to stage one in the United States."[47] All of these accusations reflect what Paul Hanebrink has called the "myth of Judeo-Bolshevism," an enduring phenomenon defined by Elissa Bemporad as "the belief that communism was a Jewish plot to destroy western civilization."[48]

If anything, the essays in this volume, exploring Jewish involvement in left-wing movements around the globe, might be said to provide further ammunition to those who would weaponize Jewish participation in radical politics for both antisemitic and anti-socialist ends. After all, while the classic Judeo-Bolshevik conspiracy theory focused on the Russian Revolution and subsequent developments in Europe, this book reveals that the participation of Jews in radical politics was far more geographically widespread and included Jews from many more backgrounds than the stereotypical Eastern European Jewish revolutionary. And yet, when collected together into a single volume, these accounts actually illuminate a profound and poignant truth that gives the lie to the fundamental claim underlying the myth of Judeo-Bolshevism. For rather than reflecting a "Jewish plot to destroy western civilization," Jews became involved in communism, socialism, and other left-wing movements in order to *belong*.

Beginning with the heated debates in the French National Assembly over whether Jews should receive citizenship in postrevolutionary France, the question of belonging was at the center of the Jewish experience during the nineteenth and much of the twentieth century. The "Jewish Question," as it became known, would emerge in societies across Europe and, eventually, with the spread of colonialism and then the rise of anti-colonialist and nationalist movements, in distinctive forms throughout the Middle East and North Africa as well. At its core, the "Jewish Question" asked whether there was something about Jewishness—be it racial, national, religious, or, in the case of Zionism, political—that prevented Jews from being fully integrated into their respective societies. Against this historical backdrop, radical politics, including its specifically Jewish forms, such as the Bund, Labor Zionism, and the Ladino socialism of Salonica, offered the possibility of overcoming the Jewish Question, whether by transcending Jewishness along with other ethnic and religious differences, transforming society so that Jewishness was no longer an obstacle to integration, or creating an entirely new society in which Jewishness would be the norm.

Given the potency of antisemitism, it is not surprising that this desire for belonging was not always reciprocated. Indeed, the Left had a mixed and sometimes shameful record when it came to the Jewish Question.[49] Especially during the nineteenth century, socialists of differing persuasions repeatedly expressed callous and even hostile opinions about Jews. In the 1860s, to give just one striking example among many, the Russian anarchist Mikhail Bakunin, maligned the Jews as "an exploiting sect, a bloodsucking people, a unique devouring parasite, tightly and intimately organized."[50] Yet, it would be a gross mistake to characterize the socialist movement overall as antisemitic. None of the major socialist parties advanced anti-Jewish programs. All of them favored equal rights for Jews. Despite Karl Marx's derogatory remarks about Jews and Judaism in his notorious 1844 essay *On the Jewish Question*, he unequivocally endorsed Jewish emancipation. Furthermore, by the turn of the twentieth century, many socialist leaders were vigorously denouncing antisemitism. The German Social Democrat August Bebel famously dismissed antisemitism as "the socialism of fools"—that is, a bogus form of anti-capitalism. Karl Kautsky, the most authoritative Marxist during the era of the Second International (1889–1914), repeatedly attacked antisemitism, as Jack Jacobs has documented. In an 1884 letter to Friedrich Engels, Kautsky wrote, "The anti-Semites are now our most dangerous opponent... because they pose as oppositional and democratic, [and] thus comply with the instincts of the workers."[51] Yet, if Marxists offered rigorous critiques of antisemitism, they rarely formulated an adequate understanding of the problem or its stubborn perniciousness. Most Marxists viewed antisemitism as a feudal holdover based in remnants of the old regime and the petty bourgeoisie, two declining social classes that were destined to disappear with the coming revolution.

Indeed, most Marxists argued that the solution to the Jewish Question was assimilation, describing it as both an inevitable and progressive process that would help to vanquish the antisemitic forces that aimed to exclude Jews from society. As a corollary, Marxists rejected political programs on the left that supported maintaining Jews as a discrete community, deeming them reactionary, separatist, and ultimately futile efforts to hold back inexorable socioeconomic processes. In light of these attitudes, Jewish radicals often faced a choice between staking a claim to belong as both radicals *and* Jews or rejecting their Jewishness in favor of a political identity that nevertheless contained the promise of a different kind of belonging. As Michael Stanislawski has written regarding Jewish Bolsheviks, "[they] viewed their Jewishness as an incidental artifact of their birth, with no meaning for them either religiously (as they were atheists) or nationally (as they regarded themselves as internationalists). Most famously, when Leon Trotsky was asked what his nationality was, he replied 'socialist.'"[52] During the 1930s, Trotsky began to revise his position on the Jewish Question, and one may speculate as to how far he would have gone during the 1940s had he not been murdered at the hands of a Soviet agent. Some of his followers did indeed undertake a reevaluation of the Jewish Question after the Holocaust in ways that showed new sympathy for Jewish national aspirations. Before World War II, however, most Marxists offered assimilationist solutions to the Jewish Question.

Above all, Jewish radicals, no matter what their orientation, worked to create political movements and, through them, new societies in which they could achieve the integration and normalcy that had otherwise eluded them. This was the case whether they hoped to build a communist Iraq where self-identified "Arab Jews" could live and work as equals alongside Shia and Sunni Arabs, Kurds, Assyrian Christians, Mandaeans, and others; a socialist Salonica, where the cultural and linguistic differences between Jews, Bulgarians, Greeks, and Turks would be respected; a Jewish Autonomous Oblast in the Soviet Union that would be Jewish—or, at least, Yiddish—in form but socialist in content; a socialist state in Israel where Jews could finally join the family of nations; or any of the other societies that Jewish radicals envisioned. In this regard, the stakes of radical politics for Jews were existential in a way that they were not for members of the majority population(s) among whom they lived. Yet for this very reason, the history of radical Jewish politics in all of its varieties is as much about failure as it is about hope.

NOTES

1. Ezra Mendelsohn, introduction to *Essential Papers on Jews and the Left*, ed. Ezra Mendelsohn (New York: New York University Press, 1997), 17.
2. Mendelsohn, introduction to *Essential Papers on Jews and the Left*, 17.
3. Andrew Silverstein, "In the Story of Two Jewish Bunds, a Stark Generational Divide over Israel," *The Forward*, February 21, 2024, https://forward.com/culture/584214/jewish-new-bund-zionism/.
4. On the relationship of the Bund to Zionism, see, for example, Jack Jacobs, "Bundist Anti-Zionism in Interwar Poland," in *Tel Aviver Jahrbuch für deutsche Geschichte*, vol. 33 (Tel Aviv: Institute for German History at Tel Aviv University, 2005), 239–259.
5. See, for example Ben Lorber, "Jewish Alternatives to Zionism: A Partial History," Jewish Voice for Peace, January 12, 2019, https://www.jewishvoiceforpeace.org/2019/01/12/a-partial-history-of-jewish-alternatives/.
6. See Jessica Marglin, *Across Legal Lines: Jews and Muslims in Modern Morocco* (New Haven: Yale University Press, 2016), as well as Ethan B. Katz, Lisa Moses Leff, and Maud S. Mandel, eds., *Colonialism and the Jews* (Bloomington: Indiana University Press, 2017).
7. Ethan Katz, Lisa Moses Leff, and Maud S. Mandel, "Engaging Colonial History and Jewish History," in *Colonialism and the Jews*, 1–25; 3.
8. Katz et al., "Engaging Colonial History," 11.
9. Alma Heckman, "Jewish Radicals of Morocco: Case Study for a New Historiography," *Jewish Social Studies*, 23, no. 3 (2018), 68.
10. A notable comparative study of Jews under French and Russian colonialism is Israel Bartal's chapter "Jews in the Crosshairs of Empire: A Franco-Russian Comparison" in *Colonialism and the Jews*, 116–126.

11. John Slocum, "Who, and When, Were the *Inorodtsy*? The Evolution of the Category of 'Aliens' in Imperial Russia," *The Russian Review* 57, no. 2 (April 1998), 174.

12. See Joel Beinin, *The Dispersion of Egyptian Jewry: Culture, Politics, and the Formation of a Modern Diaspora* (Cairo: The American University in Cairo Press, 2005); Rami Ginat, *A History of Egyptian Communism: Jews and Their Compatriots in Quest of Revolution* (Boulder and London: Lynne Rienner Publishers, 2011); Orit Bashkin, *New Babylonians: A History of Jews in Modern Iraq* (Stanford, CA: Stanford University Press, 2012); Lior Sternfeld, *Between Iran and Zion: Jewish Histories of Twentieth-Century Iran* (Stanford, CA: Stanford University Press, 2018); Alma Rachel Heckman, *The Sultan's Communists: Moroccan Jews and the Politics of Belonging* (Stanford, CA: Stanford University Press, 2021).

13. Moshe Behar and Zvi Ben-Dor Benite, eds., *Modern Middle Eastern Jewish Thought: Writings on Identity, Politics, & Culture, 1893–1958* (Brandeis: Brandeis University Press, 2013), 164–165.

14. Excerpt from Marsil Shirizi, *Awraq munadil Itali fii Misr* [Papers of an Italian fighter in Egypt] (al-Qahira, Egypt: Dar al-'Alam al-Thalith, 2002), 52–56, republished and translated into English as "Anti-Zionism for the Sake of Jews and the Sake of Egypt," in Moshe Behar and Zvi Ben-Dor Benite, eds, *Modern Middle Eastern Jewish Thought: Writings on Identity, Politics, & Culture, 1893–1958* (Brandeis: Brandeis University Press, 2013), 166–173; 168.

15. Abraham Serfaty, "Moroccan Jewry and Zionism (Excerpts)," translated form the French by Lia Brozgal and Olivia C. Harrison, first appeared in *Souffles* in 1969, republished in Olivia Harrison and Teresa Villa-Ignacio, eds, *Souffles-Anfas: A Critical Anthology from the Moroccan Journal of Culture and Politics* (Stanford, CA: Stanford University Press, 2015), 196–205; 196.

16. Ethan B. Katz, "An Imperial Entanglement: antisemitism, Islamophobia, and Colonialism," *American Historical Review* 124, no. 4 (October 2018), 1193.

17. For more on the Jews of North Africa during the Second World War, see Aomar Boum and Sarah Abrevaya Stein, eds., *The Holocaust and North Africa* (Stanford, CA: Stanford University Press, 2018).

18. See David Motadel, *Islam and Nazi Germany's War* (Cambridge, MA: Belknap Press, 2014); Jeffrey Herf, *Nazi Propaganda for the Arab World* (New Haven: Yale University Press, 2009); Israel Gershoni, ed., *Arab Responses to Fascism and Nazism: Attraction and Repulsion* (Austin: University of Texas Press, 2015).

19. Eugene Avrutin, "Racial Categories and the Politics of (Jewish) Difference in Late Imperial Russia," *Kritika: Explorations in Russian and Eurasian History* 8, no. 1 (Winter 2007), 14.

20. Avrutin, "Racial Categories," 33–34.

21. Jack Jacobs, *Jews and Leftist Politics: Judaism, Israel, antisemitism, and Gender* (New York: Cambridge University Press, 2017), 9.

22. Jacobs, *Jews and Leftist Politics*, 10.

23. "Sanders on Jewish Heritage: It Impacts Me Profoundly," CNN Politics (video), https://www.cnn.com/videos/politics/2020/02/07/jewish-heritage-bernie-sanders-new-hampshire-town-hall-sot-vpx.cnn/video/playlists/new-hampshire-2020-town-halls/

24. Elana Schor, "Sanders Defines a Jewish Identity His Way on the 2020 Trail," *AP News*, January 29, 2020, https://apnews.com/article/us-news-ap-top-news-caucuses-antisemitism-iowa-38d217df36e903a671089dfb4e669218.

25. Abraham Menes, "The Jewish Socialist Movement in Russia and Poland: From the 1870's to the Founding of the Bund in 1897," in *The Jewish People Past and Present*, vol. 2 (New York: Central Yiddish Culture Organization of New York, 1948), 355.

26. Robert Wistrich, *Revolutionary Jews from Marx to Trotsky* (London: George G. Harrap & Co., 1976), 18.

27. Wistrich, *Revolutionary Jews*, 19.

28. Wistrich, *Revolutionary Jews*, 13.

29. Isaac Deutscher, *The Non-Jewish Jew and Other Essays* (New York: Oxford University Press, 1968), 27.

30. Edward Said, *Freud and the Non-European* (London and New York: Verso, 2003), 53.

31. Philip Mendes, *Jews and the Left: The Rise and Fall of a Political Alliance* (London: Palgrave Macmillan, 2014).

32. Heckman, *The Sultan's Communists*, 105.

33. Masha Kirasirova, "The 'East' as a Category of Bolshevik and Comintern Ideology: The Arab Section of the Communist University of the Toilers of the East," *Kritika: Explorations in Russian and Eurasian History* 18, no. 1 (Winter 2017), 11.

34. Layla Mourad is the subject of a book by Hanan Hammad, *Unknown Past: Layla Murad, the Jewish-Muslim Star of Egypt* (Stanford, CA: Stanford University Press, 2022).

35. On this issue, see Leo Deutsch, "Der ershter yeshive bokhur in der rusisher revolutsion," *Di Tsufkunft* 20, no. 8 (1915): 713–718. Deutsch wrote that many Jewish revolutionaries in the Russian Empire were the "sort of Jewish young men who had spent their entire youths pouring over the *gemora* [Aramaic section of the Talmud] in a small shtetl somewhere and suddenly, at around nineteen or twenty years old or even later, they tore themselves from the *dalet amos* [four cubits] of the *bes hamedresh* [study house], left for a big city and with the same passion they now devoted themselves to *goyish* [gentile] knowledge. Just as the Jewish holy books had once occupied them, they devoured the works of Russian writers" (713).

36. This revisionist approach to Jewish history reached its fullest expression with Abraham Bick (1913–1990), a descendent of a prominent rabbinic family and committed socialist, who published numerous articles and books exploring the connections—both real and imagined—between Jews, Judaism, and socialism, including essays on the rabbinic backgrounds of prominent Marxist figures such as Rosa Luxemburg and the supposedly socialist leanings of important rabbinic figures like Moshe Sofer, widely considered to be the founder of Haredi Judaism.

37. Ruven Braynen, "Zeks froyen: di interesantste zeks froyen, vos ikh hob bagegent in meyn leben," *Der Tog*, September 22, 1935.

38. As quoted in Nathaniel Deutsch, *The Maiden of Ludmir: A Jewish Holy Woman and Her World* (Berkeley: The University of California Press, 2003), 39. Chaim Zhitlovsky, a committed socialist whose father was a Lubavitcher Hasid, wrote that "The holy word of the Baal Shem—socialism . . . has had the impact of the messiah's shofar." See Chaim Zhitlovsky, "Briv fun a yidishn sotsyalist," *Folks-shtime*, no. 1 (December 1906), 58–59, as quoted in Jonathan Frankel, *Prophecy and Politics: Socialism, Nationalism, and the Russian Jews, 1862–1917* (Cambridge, UK: Cambridge University Press), 285.

39. Tony Michels, *A Fire in Their Hearts: Yiddish Socialists in New York* (Cambridge, MA: Harvard University Press, 2009), 123.

40. Michels, *A Fire in Their Hearts*, 123.

41. On the hybridization of Haredi Judaism and socialism that produced Poale Agudas Yisroel as well as other phenomena, see Nathaniel Deutsch, "Kosher Socialism? A History of Haredi Judaism and the Left," in *New Trends in the Study of Haredi Culture and Society*, ed. David Myers and Nechumi Malovicki-Yaffe (West Lafayette, IN: Purdue University Press, 2024), 127–156.

42. Nikos Potamianos, "Internationalism and the Emergence of Communist Politics in Greece, 1912–1924," *Journal of Balkan and Near Eastern Studies* 21, no. 5 (2019), 2.

43. (Dumont 1994, 62). As cited in H. Sükrü Ilicak, "Jewish Socialism in Ottoman Salonica," *Southeast European and Black Sea Studies*2, no. 3 (September 2002), 115–146.

44. Abraham Benaroya, "Reshit ha-tenuah ha-sotsialistit ben Yehude Saloniki," *Zikhron Saloniki: gedulatah ve-hurbana shel Yerushalayim de-Balkan*, ed. David Recanati, vol. 1, (Tel Aviv: Ha-Vaad le-Hotsaat Sefer Kehilat Saloniki, 1971), 309.

45. Winston Churchill, "Bolshevism Versus Zionism: A Struggle for the Soul of the Jewish People," *Illustrated Daily Herald*, February 8, 1920.

46. Ellen Engelstad and Mímir Kristjánsson, "The Return of 'Judeo-Bolshevism,'" *Jacobin*, February 16, 2019, https://jacobin.com/2019/02/antisemitism-judaism-bolsheviks-socialists-conspiracy-theories.

47. Emily Tamkin, "Five Myths About George Soros," *Washington Post*, August 6, 2020, https://www.washingtonpost.com/outlook/five-myths/five-myths-about-george-soros/2020/08/06/ad195582-d1e9-11ea-8d32-1ebf4e9d8e0d_story.html.

48. Elissa Bemporad and Paul Hanebrink, "Jews and the Red Scare: The Mythology of Judeo-Bolshevism," *The Marginalia Review*, October 18, 2019, https://themarginaliareview.com/jews-and-the-red-scare-the-mythology-of-judeo-bolshevism/. See also Paul Hanebrink, *A Specter Haunting Europe: The Myth of Judeo-Bolshevism* (Cambridge, MA: Belknap Press, 2018).

49. For example, in "On the Jewish Question" (1843), Karl Marx wrote, "What is the secular foundation of Judaism? *Practical* needs, *egoism*. What is the secular cult of the Jew? *Huckstering.* What is his secular God? *Money.*" The Russian populist group Narodnaya Volya (People's Will), whose membership was disproportionately Jewish, even welcomed the outbreak of pogroms against Jews in 1881 as the first step toward the tsar's overthrow, before eventually repudiating the position.

50. As quoted in Robert Wistrich, *From Ambivalence to Betrayal: The Left, the Jews, and Israel*, (Lincoln and London: The University of Nebraska Press, 2012), 186.

51. Quoted in Jack Jacobs, "Marxism and antisemitism: Kautsky's Perspective," *International Review of Social History* 30, no. 3 (December 1985), 403.

52. Michael Stanislawski, "Why Did Russian Jews Support the Bolshevik Revolution?" *Tablet*, October 24, 2017, https://www.tabletmag.com/sections/news/articles/why-did-russian-jews-support-the-bolshevik-revolution.

PART I

The Middle East and North Africa

Until the publication of this book, the prevailing narrative of Jewish radical politics has largely focused on Eastern Europe and to some extent the United States, especially New York City. Centering radical Jewish histories from the Middle East and North Africa in a revised reading of comparative radical Jewish politics demonstrates several important thematic, temporal, and ideological connections across regions. Crucial among these connections is the history of colonialism and anti-colonial movements.

The history of radical Jewish politics in the Middle East and North Africa (the MENA) is characterized by anti-colonial activism. Even in those places not formally colonized, such as Iran, Jews militated against imperialist oppression in the form of the Western-backed Shah, as Lior Sternfeld shows in chapter 6. Extending from what are today the nation-states of Morocco in the west to Iran in the east as well as across the lands of the former Ottoman Empire, the Middle East and North Africa has been home to Jewish populations for millennia. In the second half of the twentieth century, nearly all of them left their homelands except for small pockets in Morocco and Turkey and a still significant number in Iran. However, this mass departure was not inevitable. While most Jews across the MENA were not involved in radical politics, those that were sought to carve out a place for Jewish citizens in the emerging nation-states of the region.

Nineteenth-century reformist movements and colonization, as well as the rise of nationalism and the political upheavals of the twentieth century, catalyzed radical politics among residents of the region, Jews included. A large portion of the region fell under some form of colonial rule before WWI; after the war and the dissolution of the Ottoman Empire, nearly the entire MENA region was colonized by European powers. As boundaries shifted, so did ideas of nationhood and citizenship and the place of minorities in states. For Jews, these formations included affinity with a colonial power, local forms of nationalism, and Zionism. Of the local forms of nationalism, those that were more universalist in their definition of the national appealed to Jews and were typically communist or socialist in leaning.

Organizing against fascism and antisemitism during the interwar period led to leftist nationalist politics for Jews following the Second World War. As chapters 1–3 by Heckman, Le Foll-Luciani, and Rahmouni all demonstrate, antisemitic legislation during the Vichy period in French North Africa particularly spurred Jewish politicization. While Egypt and Iraq had nominal independence from British colonial rule during the Second World War, Britain still maintained a strong military and political presence in each country. During the war, anti-British nationalist sentiment mixed with pro-German politics to produce the *Farhud* in Iraq (1941), two days of mass violence against Jews. In Egypt, pro-Axis sentiment also made limited inroads among Egyptian nationalists militating against the British presence. In each place, as chapters 4 and 5 by Rami Ginat and Orit Bashkin demonstrate, anti-fascist activism motivated Jews to join leftist movements alongside their co-nationals as well as Europeans.

In the wake of the near annihilation of European Jewry, Zionism became more popular among Jews around the world, including in the MENA region. Additionally, war had depleted the imperial powers of France and Britain. As during the First World War, soldiers from the colonies fighting in the Second World War hoped their participation would result in improved rights and recognition, yet they were once again disappointed. The conclusion of WWII strengthened the resolve of national liberation movements as well as intensified Jewish political discussions of the future. The establishment of the modern State of Israel in 1948 and the growing slippage of antisemitism and anti-Zionism pushed Jews of the MENA in two competing directions: stay and participate in anti-colonial nation-building efforts in their home countries or leave for Israel and participate in the construction of a Jewish state. For those Jews seeking to participate in national liberation efforts, leftist movements including communist parties provided the most convincing means of proving nationalist convictions, despite the apparent contradiction between communism and nationalism. Indeed, in much of the Global South, communist parties provided more universalist definitions of political belonging and citizenship in ways that were often appealing to religious and ethnic minorities. For most Jews of the MENA, rejection of Zionism was a critical component of patriotism, particularly from the 1950s onward. Meanwhile, the vast majority of Jews from the region (excluding Iran) migrated from their homelands during the 1950s and 1960s largely to Israel or former imperial metropoles. These Jews were anxious for their futures in countries increasingly defined by local nationalisms that often encouraged suspicion of Jews as Zionists or as being on the side of imperialists and therefore disloyal citizens. Once they arrived elsewhere, however, particularly in Israel, new political struggles were required, this time against discrimination as Mizrahi ("Eastern" or "Oriental" in Hebrew) Jews in a country whose social and political structures were dominated by Ashkenazim (Jews of Central and Eastern European origin), as Dario Miccoli demonstrates in chapter 7 regarding Mizrahi radical politics in Israel.

CHAPTER 1

Radicalism, Emancipation, and Nationalism

THE STORY OF MOROCCAN JEWISH COMMUNISTS

Alma Rachel Heckman

The radicalism of Moroccan Jews was perhaps not so radical after all. It was a radicalism fueled by the desire to belong to the Moroccan nation and to contribute to a more just version of that nation, a local iteration of a common mode of modern nationalist—and modern Jewish—politics. Radicalism itself can mean many things. Fundamentally, the word relates to the potential to root and uproot, an organic political metaphor to describe the relational aspirations of people and their networked places. Such relational aspirations are, of course, subject to change over time in precise contexts and are never stable (or "timeless") outside the imaginations of romantics. The radicalism of Moroccan Jews, which I will trace over the course of the twentieth century in the pages that follow, was like the radicalisms of other Jews in other contexts in that it was a distinctly modern phenomenon that developed in response to distinctly modern challenges—local, regional, and international.

Like Jewish radicalisms everywhere, the history of Jewish radicalism in Morocco is intimately connected to watershed moments of modern Jewish history. These include the emancipation of French Jews in 1790 and 1791, the growth of "race science" and antisemitism in nineteenth-century Europe and its spread through the vehicle of European colonization, the growing power of Romantic nationalism, two world wars, the establishment of the modern State of Israel, and the Cold War through to the modern neoliberal age. Unlike Jewish radicalisms in Europe and the Americas, Jewish radicalism in Morocco was born at the nexus of European (mostly French) colonial intervention with European (mostly French) Jewish assistance, rising Arab nationalisms and Moroccan nationalism in particular, and the growth of local Moroccan Zionism within a wider Zionist movement.

As such, Jewish involvement in radical politics in Morocco bears a close resemblance to Jewish involvement in radical politics elsewhere in the Middle East and

North Africa (MENA). Yet one of the major differences of the Moroccan case compared to other sites in the MENA is the "success" of Jewish radicalism in Morocco, not in retaining the Jewish population so much as in shaping the narrative of Jewish life in the country. As in most of the MENA region, most Moroccan Jews left their home country in the 1940s to 1970s. By most population projections, Moroccan Jewish life has been steadily declining since the massive outmigration of the 1950s and 1960s—from a 1945 height of approximately 250,000, to the current Jewish population in Morocco of around 2,000, according to somewhat fuzzy estimates. However, demographic increase or decline is less interesting than the endurance of a Jewish Moroccan national narrative. In this, the story of Moroccan Jewish radicalism is one of spectacular success—Moroccan Jewish radicals have become leading national heroes in their home country.

The following overview of Moroccan Jewish radical politics sheds light on several overlapping historiographical circles. These circles include Jewish studies, Middle Eastern and North African studies, and above all for the sake of the present volume, comparative study of Jews and radicalisms across traditional and regional and contextual boundaries. It argues that for Moroccan Jews, indeed as was the case for Jews in many other times and places, participation in radical politics was a means of constructing a place for Jews in an idealized pluralistic nation-state, if not quite assimilation. Radical political engagement also served as a method of fighting threats to Jewish belonging in the nation-state, including antisemitism, particularly as antisemitism became increasingly conflated with anti-Zionism over the course of the twentieth century. In Morocco as elsewhere, Jewish radicalism was, as others have previously argued, a particular "path of emancipation," simultaneously a form of nationalism and an assertion of local Jewish particularity.[1] Further, this chapter emphasizes that the history of Jews and colonialism is necessarily bound up with the history of Jewish radicalism.

The Alliance Israélite Universelle and Challenges of Belonging in the Early Colonial Period

Moroccan Jewish participation in radical politics was, perhaps counterintuitively (and quite unintentionally), the apotheosis of the work of the Alliance Israélite Universelle. The Alliance was the "path of emancipation" that set Jews on the path to radical politics.[2] The Alliance itself emerged from the humanist and universalist discourse of the Enlightenment, which found practical action in the French Revolution that began in 1789. The revolution produced, among other things, the emancipation of French Jews. This was a watershed moment for modern Jewish history—Jews were, for the first time, citizens, theoretically on equal legal and civic footing with their Christian compatriots. Religion was to be relegated to the domain of the private sphere, while the nation dominated the public sphere.[3] The Alliance was radical in its own right, transforming Jewish education and social hierarchies wherever it took root. It laid the critical educational and social groundwork for Jews in the MENA to embrace a republican political model of citizenship that in turn enabled some Jews to embrace radical national liberation politics. This was an unintended and undesired consequence of an organization whose political stance was to prepare Jews for citizenship in their home countries and functioned as handmaiden of the French colonial *mission civilisatrice* (civilizing mission), especially in French North Africa.

Adolphe Crémieux (1796–1880), a first-generation emancipated French Jew who rose to become the minister of justice among other prominent positions, was one of the founding figures of the Alliance. The Alliance was founded in Paris in 1860 with the goal of preparing Jews for the rights and obligations of citizenship in their home countries. The home countries in question extended from Morocco to Iran, and up through the Ottoman Balkans. In order to prepare the supposedly "backward" and benighted "Oriental" Jews for the rights and obligations of full emancipation, they first needed "regeneration." The preferred manner of "regeneration" was education. The Alliance ran what would become an extensive network of schools and training programs, with the first school established in the northern Moroccan city of Tetuan in 1862. The curriculum was largely in French, with some Hebrew and, over time, some local language instruction (the spoken languages used in local Jewish communities such as Ladino or Judeo-Arabic were denigrated as "jargon").[4] The teachers were initially from France, but as this model became unsustainable, the best and brightest students from Alliance schools were selected for rigorous training in Paris before being sent out to teach in the vast network of schools, rarely in their home countries.[5]

Despite French pretensions of "protecting" Moroccan Jews (a justification that often served as a pretext for colonial rule in the MENA region, whether directed toward Christian or Jewish minorities), Jews in Morocco had enjoyed a long history of relative stability in the country prior to European colonization. Jews and Christians, as *ahl al-kitab* (People of the Book), held *dhimmi* (protected) status pursuant to the dictates of the Pact of ʿUmar, which itself dates from the earliest years of Muslim expansion from the Arabian Peninsula. Jews were the only major religious minority indigenous to Morocco in the modern era, and thus they were the most prominent *dhimmi* population. Dhimmi status across the wider region meant different things in different contexts, and it was rigorously enforced in some places and barely at all in others. Overall, the Pact of ʿUmar outlined a series of restrictions for dhimmis, notably restrictions on building height (not to surpass mosques), requirements to remove shoes when passing a mosque, prohibitions on riding on horseback, payment of an annual poll tax (*jizya*), sartorial restrictions, and more in exchange for protection from the sultan and freedom to govern communal religious affairs with autonomy. Jews had historically served in prominent roles in the courts of Moroccan sultans (indeed, as with sultans elsewhere), and were influential in Morocco's international trade and diplomacy.[6] Meanwhile, Jews depended on the sultan for legal protections, as well as networks of allegiance to other Muslim officials. That being said, moments of violence and persecution did break out in Morocco and other MENA countries, including in the nineteenth century, which prompted figures such as Montefiore and Crémieux to intervene and made the protection of Jews an international "cause célèbre" of sorts.[7]

In practice, the Alliance, founded to improve Jews' lot in their home countries, often served instead as a wedge between Jews and Muslims.[8] This was particularly the case in French colonial North Africa, where Alliance education and Gallicization entrenched the popular perception of Jewish complicity with French colonization and disenfranchisement of the Arab Muslim majority. France began its official ingestion of the Maghrib beginning in 1830 when it launched the conquest of Algeria. Tunisia became a French protectorate in 1881, while Morocco was divided into two protectorates in 1912, a small Spanish zone in the north and a larger French zone in the rest of the country, including the major Moroccan imperial cities of Rabat, Fez, Meknes, and Marrakesh as well as the soon to be boomtown of Casablanca. The Mediterranean coastal city of Tangier was designated an international zone. By the time of the establishment of the French protectorate over Morocco, generations of Jewish students had passed through Alliance schools and had been taught French language, history, literature, and geography, all supposedly in the name of preparing them for citizenship in their home country.

Upon signing the protectorate treaty with the French in Fez in 1912, Sultan Abd al-Hafid abdicated, and the French propped up his brother, Yusef ben Hassan, in his stead.[9] Theoretically, the sultan still maintained autonomous power, albeit under the "guiding hand" of the French administrators. Jews had once depended on the sultan for "protection," a dynamic that had been challenged and diminished over the course of the nineteenth century and encroaching European power. With the protectorate treaty of 1912, following decades of Alliance education and other European Jewish influence, France became the self-appointed official "protector" of Jews in Morocco. Alliance teachers and administrators in Morocco taught accordingly, walking a difficult ideological tightrope that rhetorically maintained the sultan as a source of authority while vaunting France as a noble, protective, civilizing force in students' lives. Simultaneously, it inculcated an embrace of the nation-state model and the notion that Jews as citizens of a future Moroccan state (albeit dependent on France) would be important political and social actors.

Tensions in the Interwar Period

The French republicanism fostered by the Alliance in earlier decades reached full flower in the Jewish anti-fascist activism of the interwar period. This activism served as the starting point for Moroccan Jewish participation in radical politics, which began during the interwar period. Even before the start of the First World War, France had invested heavily in massive building and infrastructural projects, including railroads, mining operations, new ports, and industrial manufacturing projects, particularly around Casablanca. New employment opportunities lured vast numbers of Moroccans from rural areas as well as other cities to the burgeoning city, in addition to a flood of European workers (primarily French, Spanish,

Italian, and Portuguese) looking for cheap land and steady employment. This latter category expanded exponentially following the First World War, as did the Moroccan population in the city. Unequal pay and housing access between Moroccans and Europeans meant that sprawling shantytowns (*bidonvilles*) sprang up around the city.[10] Europeans were, as a rule, paid at least double what Moroccans took home. European and Moroccan workers overlapped, however, in canning and other food processing plants, as well as in factory and construction operations. Europeans included Moroccans in political organizing, and some organizations, including the Moroccan branch of the French Section of the Workers' International (SFIO—*Section française de l'internationale ouvrière*) and the nascent *Amicales* (labor associations), openly recruited Moroccans, calling for solidarity and equal pay.[11] While French protectorate authorities had outlawed such political miscegenation, it proved difficult to enforce.[12] By the mid-1930s, Moroccans outnumbered Europeans in a spate of mass strikes that swept the country, and growing numbers of Moroccans exchanged leftist political propaganda.

The French Communist Party (PCF—*Parti communiste français*) itself became involved in Moroccan domestic politics in the 1920s in response to the Rif War (1920–1927). The Rif War, named for the mountainous Rif region in the Spanish zone in northern Morocco where the conflict broke out, began with a charismatic Amazigh (Berber) Muslim legal scholar turned military leader, Abdelkrim al-Khattabi, who lead a series of successful military incursions against Spanish forces, humiliating the already rather sensitive formerly expansive empire and establishing a short-lived independent Riffian Republic. When Khattabi's forces pushed into the French zone, threatening the sultan's authority and French imperial interests, France began to draft troops into the conflict and eventually crushed it. The French Communist Party, itself established only in 1920 and signed onto the terms of Third International, had the opportunity to prove its anti-imperialist and anti-racist bona fides by inaugurating mass demonstrations against the conflict, sending telegrams of support to Abdelkrim al-Khattabi and his forces and encouraging French soldiers to defect or subvert and spread Communist propaganda among prospective Moroccan comrades.[13] The PCF would have a vexed relationship with Moroccan national liberation over the coming decades, but this initial push in the 1920s allowed the nascent Moroccan Communist Party (PCM—*Parti communiste marocain*) to recruit Moroccans more actively and to criticize French policies that discriminated against Moroccans more vociferously. The visibility of the PCM grew from there, eventually including a women's section, a youth league, literacy programs, soup kitchens, and more.[14]

The mainstream Moroccan nationalist movement also took off during the 1930s. Most historians agree that the so-called Berber Dahir sparked the mainstream Moroccan independence movement. A *dahir* is a decree signed into law by the sultan, which under the French protectorate became a legitimizing stamp for French imperial policy over which the sultan himself had little effective control. According to French racial-colonial "logic," Berbers (Imazighen in Tamazight, the Berber language), the indigenous inhabitants of North Africa before the Arab-Muslim conquests of the seventh and eighth centuries, were not "true" Muslims and were more "Latin" than "Arab." This "logic" justified French colonization in North Africa, built around the case that France was a "Latin" nation, North Africa had been Roman and therefore "Latin," and thus France was not invading a foreign territory but rather reclaiming a lost cousin.[15] Berbers, then, were not "true Muslims," but had been colonized by Arab Muslim invaders and converted from either Christianity or Judaism. The Berber Dahir of 1930 intended to put this discourse into legal practice, separating Berber customary law from Sharia (Islamic) law.[16] It backfired enormously, with major protests breaking out across the country starting in Morocco's traditional religious imperial center, Fez. Protests took the form of *Latif* prayers (invoked traditionally in times of extreme hardship, notably for rain) and began in mosques before spilling out into the street. The dahir did not, in the end, become law. Out of this popular protest arose Morocco's first major national liberation organization, the Moroccan Action Committee (CAM—*Comité d'Action Marocaine*), led by Moroccan elites who expounded a vision of Moroccanness predicated on Islam. These elites had the backing of French socialists (including Karl Marx's own grandson) and met with prominent political leaders in Paris and elsewhere. The CAM had, in the words of John Halstead, an "eclectic" mix of political influences and supporters. Although following the Second World War its descendant organization, the *Istiqlal* (Independence) Party, overtly rejected communism as antithetical to Morocco's Muslim values, the CAM was a bit more profligate in its alliances.[17]

Jews became involved in leftist radical politics not in response to the Berber Dahir, but rather in response to the growing menace of fascism and Nazism, both across the Mediterranean in Europe and at home in Morocco. Antisemitic, antirepublican politics had flourished in France during the Dreyfus Affair at the end of the nineteenth century, with violent ramifications in the Maghrib, most notably Algeria, where most Jews had received French citizenship via the 1870 Crémieux Decree, named for the Alliance founder Adolphe Crémieux. This legislation was not applied to the Tunisian or Moroccan protectorates, although some Jews (more in Tunisia than in Morocco) did achieve French naturalization. Since the Dreyfus Affair, antisemitic, anti-republican, militarist, monarchist, and increasingly fascist politics had been a fixture of French and French settler-colonial political life.[18] With the elevation of Adolf Hitler to German chancellor in January 1933 and the outbreak of local antisemitic incidents alongside news of antisemitism in the European Jewish world, Moroccan Jews began to take political action, much to the chagrin of protectorate administrators and Alliance officials.

Another important factor of Moroccan Jewish political life was Zionism. Zionism had emerged in Morocco toward the end of the nineteenth century, particularly in the Atlantic coastal city of Essaouira with its connections to the London-based Moroccan Jewish community. Zionism was not widely popular in Morocco until after the Second World War, and it must be understood within its particular Moroccan context. While Zionist magazines and societies were established in cities, and a certain messianic Zionism took root in the countryside, in the urban context Zionist publications did not call for Jews to leave Morocco and emigrate. Rather, Zionism was a mode of expression of solidarity for the troubles of Jews abroad, particularly in Europe, as well as of international Jewish cultural affinity. The Alliance decried Zionism until after WWII because it was squarely at odds with the organization's central mission: the Alliance called for Jews to become ideal citizens in their countries of residence, while political Zionism called for Jews to leave their countries of residence to build a national Jewish homeland in Palestine. That being said, some individual Alliance teachers expressed Zionist or communist political leanings, inculcating these possibilities in the hearts of their charges within the framework of French republicanism. Rhetoric and debates in the pages of a variety of Jewish journals recombined these ideas fluidly and challenged them, all while protectorate officials sought, unsuccessfully and desperately, to dampen any political fires among Moroccan society at large.[19]

The primary means for Jewish political action in interwar Morocco came through the Paris-based International League Against Antisemitism (LICA—*Ligue internationale contre l'antisémitisme*), initially founded by French Jew Bernard Lecache in 1927 as the "League Against Pogroms" before changing its name and broadening its scope. Following a wave of violence against Jews in Constantine, Algeria, in 1934 and other flares of violence in North Africa, Bernard Lecache embarked on a speaking tour across the Maghrib, including a long stint in Moroccan cities.[20] The LICA grew dramatically, including vast numbers of Moroccan Jews and a considerable number of Muslims as well—they were drawn to it in the name of universalist humanism and anti-fascism.[21] After 1936, a Moroccan branch of the French Popular Front party (which famously brought Léon Blum, France's first Jewish and first socialist prime minister, to elected office) gained steam as well. Membership of the LICA, the Popular Front, the SFIO, and the PCM all overlapped in the fight against anti-fascism, and it would be shared campaigns against racism, fascism, antisemitism, and workers' rights that would ultimately bring Jews into the membership of the Moroccan Communist Party, and through it, the struggle for Moroccan independence. On the eve of the Second World War, Moroccan Jewish politics included a wide array of ideological options, including French republicanism via the Alliance Israélite Universelle, communism, and Zionism.

World War II to 1948

When France fell to Nazi forces in the summer of 1940, the famous French republican slogan of *liberté, égalité, fraternité* (liberty, equality, brotherhood) became *travaille, famille, patrie* (work, family, fatherland) with the installation of the Nazi collaborationist Vichy regime.[22] Vichy rule betrayed the universalist, emancipationist promises of French republicanism and galvanized Jews into several national political directions, including anti-colonial communism as a Jewish mode of participating in Morocco's national liberation movement. Zionism, too, gained in popularity, which threatened the sense of belonging to Morocco that radical Jews increasingly sought to cultivate and demonstrate. The radical revelation, at least for some Moroccan Jews, was that France was not the protective power it had claimed to be, and that joining the national liberation struggle and appealing to the Moroccan sultan was the best hope for Jewish national belonging.[23]

Before France fell to Germany, streams of European Jewish refugees arrived in Morocco, looking for transit to the Americas. With the Vichy regime, many of these Jews became stuck, living either in cramped refugee camps or joining Moroccan Jewish households, while others were forcibly detained, and, for "political undesirables," put into labor camps. From late summer into early fall 1940 and onward, Vichy authorities passed a spate of antisemitic legislation, which differed regarding Moroccan Jews and European Jewish refugees. Legislation was unevenly and inconsistently enforced, and exemptions, while difficult to obtain, were possible. The Crémieux Decree was abrogated, stripping Algerian Jews of their French citizenship. A sizeable contingent of Algerian Jews resided in Morocco, including Léon René Sultan, born in Constantine, Algeria, but living in Casablanca and running a law practice since the late 1920s. In addition to his legal work, Sultan was an active member of the PCM. When it was abolished during WWII, Sultan continued subversive communist organizing, inflamed by his experience of having been forced to leave the legal profession due to Vichy quotas on Jews in a number of professions, as well as in schools.

Alliance schools and social institutions, meanwhile, became overburdened with European Jewish refugees and Moroccan Jewish students that had been ejected from French schools due to quotas. In some places, Moroccan Jews that had left the traditional *mellahs* or old Jewish quarters for the French-built *villes nouvelles* (new cities) were ordered to return. At the beginning of the Second World War in the fall of 1939, Alliance students had labored by lamplight sewing gloves and hats for French soldiers; one year later, many of their parents were out of work on account of their Jewishness. Indeed, Moroccan Jews had tried to volunteer to join the French army in 1939 as they had during WWI; in both wars, Jews were considered undesirable military candidates even before the start of the Vichy administration.

Jewish refugees deemed "undesirable" were placed in forced labor camps either to build the old colonial dream of a trans-Saharan railroad or working in mines to load the train cars that would travel on it. In a stroke of bitter irony, many of these refugees were cloaked in French foreign legion greatcoats, having been spurned by the nation for which they had been willing to die.[24] These Jewish "undesirables" joined others, including a large contingent of Spanish Civil War refugees and other anti-fascists that had made their way to Morocco. Moroccan Jews (with some exceptions based on foreign nationality) were spared the labor camps, but for all Jews in Morocco during the Vichy period, France had betrayed its republican promises.

Relief came with Operation Torch in the fall of 1942. From November 8–10, 1942, Allied forces launched Operation Torch, a military strategy to rout Axis powers by providing an additional Mediterranean front. Aerial raids and naval warfare echoed near the port of Casablanca as Vichy forces attempted to repel the Allies but conceded after a few days. The Americans became heroes to the majority

Moroccan Jewish community, and violence occasionally broke out among Jews, Muslims, and pro-Vichy Europeans when Jews celebrated Allied liberation in an overly jubilant manner. American popularity soared in Morocco, particularly with rumors that President Roosevelt had promised Sultan Sidi Muhammad Ben Yussuf help in ridding Morocco of the French yolk during the Casablanca Conference of January 1943.[25] In 1944, the Istiqlal Party emerged out of the now defunct CAM and proclaimed its intent to work for Moroccan independence. The Istiqlal required members to swear an oath over the Qur'an to join, and while several Jews did eventually join the organization, its ideological base was fundamentally informed by Islam.[26]

The PCM was a bit slower to embrace the cause for independence. The previously mentioned Léon René Sultan reestablished the Moroccan Communist Party in 1943, becoming its Secretary General. He joined the Free French forces but was wounded in Germany and ultimately succumbed to his injuries upon returning home to Casablanca. Sultan's death marked a change in the PCM's ideology and leadership. While under Sultan the party had embraced an "associationist" policy with France and not a complete break, with his death the party transformed into a full-fledged national leadership organization under Moroccan Muslim leadership.[27] The PCM issued its own manifesto for independence in 1946 and became the most popular political party for Jews seeking to participate in Morocco's national liberation struggle. The Second World War period was crucial for the politicization of Moroccan Jews more broadly, and specifically so for a number of Moroccan Jewish Communists who would play a prominent role in Morocco's national liberation struggle. This category included Edmond Amran El Maleh, Abraham Serfaty, and Simon Lévy, among others. These men would number among Morocco's most prominent Jewish radical nationalists.

Postwar to Independence

A critical number of Jews participated in national liberation movements from colonial rule across the MENA, including in Morocco. They were optimistic for the future of Morocco and the place of Jews within it. This participation coincided with significant global upheaval, including the beginning of the Cold War, the establishment of the modern State of Israel, anti-colonial movements, pan-Arab nationalisms, and Third Worldism. This context is critical for understanding Morocco's achievement of independence from French and Spanish colonialism in 1956 and the mass migrations of Moroccan Jews that accompanied it.

At the end of the Second World War, France was demonstrably weakened, the United States and the Soviet Union were hailed as victors and the world's two superpowers, and anti-colonial fervor heightened. As previously discussed, the Istiqlal Party, Morocco's most popular national liberation party, issued its manifesto for independence in 1944. The party's platform was a blend of Moroccan nationalism and Salafist Islam. Other parties arose as well but were less popular, including the Democratic Party for Independence (PDI—*Parti démocratique pour l'indépendence*) as well as the Moroccan Communist Party. At stake was the question of "Moroccan-ness"—who composed the nation, with what values, and with what traditions—as well as the future of Moroccan governance. Every viable political party upheld the sultan as the prospective leader of independent Morocco—no serious political party, including the PCM, called for the abolishment of the Alawite dynasty (the Alawite dynasty has held the throne in Morocco since the sixteenth century and claims descent from the Prophet Muhammad). The Moroccan sultan himself came out as an advocate for Moroccan independence at a famous speech in Tangier in 1947, transforming himself into the symbol of a Moroccan nation held captive. Protests, boycotts, demonstrations, and ultimately violence characterized Morocco from the late 1940s to the mid-1950s.

Most Jews were not involved in national liberation politics. Many Jews preferred, as Léon Sultan indeed had, to interpret the Vichy years as a kind of aberration from the values of the "true France," and to believe that the France of the postwar period would continue to protect Jewish interests. Further, anti-Arab propaganda had been circulating for decades pitting "Jews" and "Arabs" against one another as embodied categories replete with atavistic hatred. In the years leading to independence, Zionist propaganda issued dire warnings that if France left, Moroccan Jews would be at the mercy of the nebulously defined but inevitably hostile "Arabs."[28] While every major national liberation party appealed to Jews as full partners in the struggle for liberation, on the ground moments of violence belied such promises of partnership. This dynamic reached a crescendo in 1948.

The year 1948 was pivotal for Moroccan Jews in two major ways. First, it was the year of the establishment of the modern nation-state of Israel and the regional war that attended it. Second, a wave of violence broke out in the eastern cities of Oujda and Jerada on Morocco's border with Algeria that began with rumors of illegal Zionist migration. The events were connected and undermined a popular Moroccan Jewish sense of belonging as some newspapers and propaganda underscored the conflation of Jewishness and Zionism.[29] At the same time, the Moroccan sultan and prominent nationalist political actors both Muslim and Jewish vociferously and consistently distinguished between Zionists and Moroccan Jews and urged Moroccan Jews to reject Zionism and Moroccan Muslims to not conflate the two. Every major political actor decried violence against Moroccan Jews, and the PCM in particular issued reams of leaflets decrying imperialist machinations that sought to divorce Moroccan Jews from their "true" homeland.[30]

By the beginning of the 1950s, PCM membership was at its height, with cells in every major city and aspirations of reaching into the countryside. By 1949, Ali Yata, a Moroccan Muslim, had become the party's secretary general (a position he would hold onto until his death in 1997). Edmond Amran El Maleh, a Moroccan Jew born in the Atlantic coastal city of Safi, acted as the party's de facto secretary general when Yata was exiled by the French to Algeria and then to France in the late 1940s and early 1950s. As in the interwar period, Casablanca remained the center of radical leftist activism, including the Moroccan Communist Party. Members came from a variety of occupations and backgrounds, but the party was becoming increasingly "Moroccanized" and distanced from its European roots. However, the PCM had trouble convincing the broader Moroccan public of its national "authenticity," its legitimacy to represent the interests of the Moroccan people. Istiqlal members overtly refused to cooperate and collaborate with the PCM and accused it of being a European, atheistic, foreign import unsuited to Morocco. This would be a continual issue for the PCM—and for its Jewish members in particular, who also had to combat accusations of crypto-Zionism and loudly assert the primary Moroccan allegiance of Jews, even as Jews poured out of the country by illegal means, first to southern France and then onward to Israel.

Moroccan Jewish Communists, under the leadership of Edmond Amran El Maleh and prominent figures such as brother and sister pair Abraham and Evelyne Serfaty and Simon Lévy, issued numerous petitions and proclamations, sliding tracts under the doors of Jewish homes, synagogues, and other communal institutions urging Moroccan Jews to join the movement for independence and proclaim Morocco as their true home. Jewish PCM members organized protests and political action, and they struggled alongside their Muslim compatriots against the ills of imperialism, which, they asserted, was the original cause of any division among them. Yet, most of the Moroccan Jewish community saw these figures as liabilities to communal stability, as they had since the interwar period. Most Moroccan Jews were eager to continue to demonstrate loyalty to France or left for Israel out of Zionist political conviction, to follow other relatives, or pursuant to promises for improved employment and housing prospects in Israel. Between 1948 and Moroccan independence in 1956, approximately 92,000 Jews left the country for Israel out of a total population of approximately 250,000. Other waves would coincide with Israel's regional wars and anxieties over the stability of the postindependence Moroccan regime.

Despite this significant exodus, the moment of Moroccan independence itself was wreathed with optimism and proclamations of Muslim-Jewish unity to build a new Morocco under the leadership of the sultan-turned-king Muhammad V. The first independent government included Dr. Leon Benzaquen, a prominent Moroccan Jew and personal physician to the king, in a ministerial post. Despite the dire warnings of French and Zionist propaganda of imminent violence against Jews in an independent Morocco (a discourse that drew heavily on Orientalist understandings of Arabs and Muslims as inherently bloodthirsty and uncivilized), Moroccan Jews celebrated independence alongside Moroccan Muslims, with jubilations and prayers for the king intoned in the nation's synagogues. With the sponsorship of the palace, a group of Jews and Muslims founded the *al-Wifaq* (Accord) organization with the goal of fostering Muslim-Jewish Moroccan patriotism. One of Morocco's most famous musicians, the Jewish singer Sami el-Maghribi, performed at a large al-Wifaq gala attended by the king and crown prince Moulay Hassan.[31] Jewish emigration paused, and Jewish PCM members celebrated their role in achieving independence. The jubilation would prove short-lived, and the radical nationalist work of Moroccan Jewish Communists was just beginning.

From Independence to the "Years of Lead"

The initial postindependence period was one of exhilarating optimism. However, international events, particularly regional conflicts with Israel, menaced Jewish belonging. Mass exodus overlapped with a period of intense political repression, with emigration spikes following the Suez Crisis of 1956 (mere months after independence), the death of King Muhammad V and a state visit from Egyptian pan-Arabist president Gamal Abd al-Nasser that resulted in violence against Jews in 1961, a spate of bloodily suppressed uprisings in Casablanca in 1965, the 1967 Six Day War, two attempted coups against King Hassan II in 1971 and 1972, and the October War of 1973. As the Moroccan Jewish community diminished overall, the Moroccan Jewish radicals that remained figured among the most prominent Jewish voices, urging Jews to remain in their homeland as they had urged many times before, but their message fell on absent ears.[32]

While all political parties had hoped for a constitutional monarchy, the constitution itself was slow in coming. The PCM itself was dissolved by court order in 1960 pursuant to the false charges that the Communist Party was atheistic and sought to overturn the monarchy. A trial ensued, and prominent Jewish communists such as Raphael Benarosh and Joseph Levy represented the PCM in court. Ali Yata, the party's secretary general, and the PCM press cited the Qur'an and vociferously defended the party as wholly congruous with the values of the newly independent monarchy, but to no avail.[33] By this time, Ali Yata was married to Rosalie Rojel, the daughter of Spanish socialist immigrants to Morocco, and Simon Lévy would soon marry Rosalie's sister, Incarnation, meaning that the "first families" of the Moroccan Communist Party were connected by ties of blood and marriage, and, more importantly, represented a microcosm of the party's demographics and ideological influences: Muslim, Jewish, Moroccan, Algerian, French, and Spanish. Abraham Serfaty's first wife was also a radical Spanish woman, while his second would be a French woman who would be crucial in securing his release from prison in 1991, but that story is for the next section. During the 1960s, the PCM continued to operate clandestinely, distributing tracts and newspapers and calling for action, with individual members constantly in fear of arrest and imprisonment, if not worse. In 1962, the king finally ratified a new constitution and created a monarchist-apologist political party the year after, the Front for the Defense of Constitutional Institutions (FDIC—*Front pour la défense des institutions constitutionelles*). Istiqlal and the PCM, as well as other leftist groups such as Mehdi Ben Barka's socialist *Union nationale des forces populaires* (National Union of Popular Forces) that grew out of a split with Istiqlal, as well as a panoply of leftist student groups, all opposed the FDIC. Simon Lévy and Edmond Amran El Maleh, both educators in Casablanca, encouraged high schoolers to read Marx, agitate for equality, and denounce the failed promises of the regime.

Popular anger against the monarchy spilled over into protests in the streets and then riots in 1965, when the monarchy announced a policy to prevent youth over age seventeen from attending high school. Low literacy rates and inadequate access to education had been among the top complaints during the national liberation movement, and the new Moroccan state was supposed to prioritize these items but had not followed through, walking back a broad commitment to education. Further, poverty and joblessness continued well past independence, and the euphoric dreams of 1956 had become jaded. Organized student protests ballooned into mass uprising, which the regime put down with bloody, brutal force. Simon Lévy was kidnapped off the street during the fracas and tortured mercilessly for eight days before being dumped unceremoniously at his doorstep in the dead of night. Edmond Amran El Maleh fled Morocco to live in France in self-imposed exile until the early 2000s.

The party reemerged as the PLS—the *Parti de libération et du socialisme*—in 1968. Ali Yata remained secretary general, Simon Lévy remained prominent. Abraham Serfaty, however, left the PLS as he considered it insufficiently radical, founding the further-left party *Ila al-Amam* ("Forward" in Arabic) alongside the leftist poet Adellatif Laâbi and others from the literary *Souffles-Anfas* ("Breaths" in French and Arabic) circles he operated in. This move caused lasting ire between Lévy and Serfaty, though the two would ultimately be buried near one another in Casablanca's Ben M'sik Jewish cemetery, and each ultimately expressed admiration for the other in their last years. Over the same period that Morocco's leftist opposition gained strength and challenged the regime under the particularly unpopular King Hassan II, the vast majority of Moroccan Jews had already voted with their feet.

After two attempted coups d'état in 1971 and 1972, King Hassan II intensified his brutal crackdown on the opposition. The 1970s into the early 1990s are often characterized as the "Years of Lead" in Morocco, a grim period of history in which countless activists, protestors, and their families and friends were swept up into the regime's dragnet. Trials took place, but the outcome was clear in advance. Numerous political figures "disappeared," the most famous of whom was Mehdi Ben Barka, who was kidnapped in broad daylight and murdered in Paris in 1965. This pattern would continue in Morocco, especially around student protest movements and the independence claims of Western Sahara, which Abraham Serfaty and many others on the far left supported, which the Moroccan regime considered tantamount to treason. Abraham Serfaty was among many others who were captured and imprisoned in the early 1970s. Before he was arrested, Abraham's sister Evelyne, a radical Moroccan Jewish activist in her own right, was kidnapped off the streets of Rabat and tortured for information on her brother's whereabouts. Abraham's son Maurice was also imprisoned in retribution for his father's political activities.

The Moroccan monarch attempted to navigate between Cold War powers, Arab nationalism, and the need to crush the leftist opposition movement, with devastating consequences. Morocco sent a small force to fight in the 1973 October War to bolster regional credentials, but soon after, Morocco began to position itself as a peace broker between Israel and the wider Arab world. King Hassan II met with Israeli officials and Zionist immigration representatives clandestinely, but these meetings leaked to the popular press and he was called as a traitor to the

Arab and Palestinian cause. He became known as the chief "protector of the Jews" and encouraged Moroccan Jews living abroad to return home, at least for a short touristic jaunt if not to permanently resettle. All of this took place while Abraham Serfaty languished in solitary confinement following torture and a prison term that would fall just shy of that of Nelson Mandela.

Moroccan Jews were not uniform in their politics, but most, with the exception of Abraham Serfaty, supported Morocco's claim to Western Sahara. The issue of Western Sahara presented all Moroccans, including Jews, with the opportunity to demonstrate their patriotism. King Hassan II launched the 1975 Green March to claim Western Sahara, an irridentist movement to unify Morocco around its king, in order to shore up his regime's legitimacy and stability.[34] Moroccan Jews, at home and abroad, rushed to support King Hassan II's campaign; Simon Lévy was among the first to set foot in the contested territory. Ali Yata, leader of the dissolved PCM turned PLS, which was then reestablished in 1974 as the Party of Progress and Socialism (PPS—*Parti du progrès et du socialisme*), also leapt at the chance to demonstrate his party's patriotic bona fides and declared the PPS's endorsement of the Green March. For supporters of the march, Western Sahara was an integral part of Morocco and the fact that this territory was not yet internationally recognized as Moroccan was seen as a continued colonialist affront.

This historical event presents a good opportunity to reflect on competing Jewish radical histories in Morocco in the persons of Simon Lévy, Abraham Serfaty, and Edmond Amran El Maleh. While for Lévy the Green March represented the chance for Moroccan Jews to proclaim their loyalty to the Moroccan state in the face of international pressure, Abraham Serfaty rotted in prison for his support of the Western Saharan independence movement. Meanwhile, Edmond Amran El Maleh was writing in self-imposed exile in Paris, disgusted with the repressive regime of modern Morocco and the failures of the PCM and its subsequent iterations. Each man had his own relationship to his Jewishness as well—for Simon Lévy, Jewishness and Moroccanness were inextricable from one another, while Serfaty did not reflect on his Jewishness or that of his family until later in life, following a more universalist model of Moroccan citizenship. While it is unclear how El Maleh related to his Jewishness while he was active in the PCM leadership and organizing, he would later spend decades writing semi-autobiographical fiction that circled obsessively around his country's Jewish past and the predations of colonialism and Zionism in reducing the Jewish present.

During the 1980s and 1990s, Abraham Serfaty became one of Morocco's most famous political prisoners and in the process one of its most infamous Jews. He and other political prisoners corresponded from prison, and Serfaty ultimately became a cause célèbre for human rights organizations in Europe and beyond. The French Communist Party, Amnesty International, and a host of other Moroccan-specific organizations agitated for his release and that of his comrades, loudly decrying the vicious torture and solitary confinement employed by Hassan II's henchmen. Student groups remained particularly active, especially Moroccan students abroad in France who could militate with a reduced fear of reprisal. Simultaneously, King Hassan II positioned himself as a mediator for the intractable Israeli-Arab conflict, facilitating Egyptian President Anwar al-Sadat's treaty with Israeli Prime Minister Menachem Begin, as well as Sadat's historic trip to Israel and address in the Israeli Knesset. American diplomats and Zionist organizations praised Hassan II for his "enlightened" and "tolerant" policies, and his warm acknowledgment of his country's Jewish citizens and welcome for Moroccan Jews abroad. International Jewish groups never once spoke against the torture of countless leftists in Hassan II's prisons, and certainly never mentioned Abraham Serfaty by name, even as entire issues of the French Communist Party newspaper, *l'Humanité*, would be dedicated to his release and extradition to France in 1991. Moroccan Jewish radicals could be boons and liabilities to the state and the Moroccan Jewish community alike: figures like Simon Lévy were positive, albeit in earlier eras he was not always considered so; figures like Abraham Serfaty could only jeopardize the Moroccan Jewish community by association, and so its members sought to distance themselves from him as much as possible.

The dynamic of earlier eras, according to which Moroccan Jewish radicals had the distinct potential of destabilizing Jewish political security in the country, slowly eased when international pressure and a slew of contextual political events caused Hassan II to release many political prisoners, albeit in Serfaty's case the king stripped him of his Moroccan citizenship and booted him to France with the president of the Moroccan Jewish community as his chaperone. Upon King Hassan II's death in 1999 and the rise of the current King Muhammad VI to power, Serfaty and El Maleh returned to Morocco. Lévy ran for office successfully on a few occasions during the same interval and, in the middle of the 1990s, founded the Moroccan Jewish Heritage Center and Museum in the suburb of l'Oasis, adjacent to Casablanca. Each of these men lived to be hailed as national heroes and true emblems of Moroccan Jewish patriotism. After their deaths they still feature in newspapers and magazines and are the subject of state-sponsored documentaries; they each have foundations in progress or already in existence. They have achieved their political goal: belonging to the Moroccan nation.

Conclusion

In the end, Moroccan Jewish radical political figures became mainstays of the national political narrative and a major boon to contemporary Morocco. They each embodied profound Moroccan patriotism and critical idealism for Morocco. State officials attended the funeral of each man; yet Jews were relatively sparse in attendance. While these men were among the most prominent politically active Moroccan Jews, they did not represent the majority. Indeed, even as the state embraced them, most Moroccan Jews rejected them as the liabilities they had once been, first under French rule and then during the Years of Lead. In this, the Moroccan Jewish Communists described above are not terribly different from Jewish radicals in other contexts. Historically and in most lands, the majority of Jewish communities did not embrace political radicalism, preferring instead to carry on with their lives without incurring retribution. Those who were radically active presented liabilities to communal stability, particularly as non-Jewish communities might mistake the actions of a handful of Jews as reflective of the attitudes of the larger group. The Moroccan case study of radical Jewish politics contributes to a truly comparative understanding of the phenomenon of embracing such politics as a modern strategy of achieving emancipation and national belonging.

NOTES

1. I take this formulation from Pierre Birnbaum and Ira Katznelson, eds., *Paths of Emancipation: Jews, States, and Citizenship* (Princeton: Princeton University Press, 1995). *Paths of Emancipation* is mostly about Western Europe, although it includes contributions regarding the late Ottoman Empire and early Turkish Republic as well as regarding imperial Russia. However, many of the qualities of emancipation and modernity applicable in the predominantly nineteenth-century European context at hand in the volume extend to Jewish life in the colonial world. That being said, the colonial context is a critical difference, and one this volume (and this chapter) seeks to include in modern Jewish historiographical discussions.

2. See Aron Rodrigue, "From *Millet* to Minority: Turkish Jewry," in *Paths of Emancipation*, 238–261. In this chapter (the only one that touches on the Middle East and North African region in the volume), Rodrigue describes the growing influence of French among late Ottoman Jews alongside the *Tanzimat* reforms of the nineteenth century according to which the Ottoman Empire sought to centralize its government and eventually create an Ottoman shared citizenship model. Michelle Campos and Julia Phillips Cohen have both written excellent monographs that address the Jewish embrace of an Ottoman identity in the late imperial period. These books are Michelle U. Campos, *Ottoman Brothers: Muslims, Christians and Jews in Early 20th Century Palestine* (Stanford, CA: Stanford University Press, 2010) and Julia Phillips Cohen, *Becoming Ottomans: Sephardi Jews and Imperial Citizenship in the Modern Era* (Cambridge: Cambridge University Press, 2014). Regarding the Alliance's activities specifically in Morocco, see Michael M. Laskier, *The Alliance Israélite Universelle and the Jewish Communities of Morocco, 1862–1962* (Albany: State University of New York Press, 1983).

3. Salo Wittmayer Baron famously challenged the prevailing narrative of emancipation as a universal good for Jews and wrote against "lachrymose" historical narratives that characterized Jewish history as one unending slog of suffering until the emancipations of the nineteenth century. See Salo W. Baron, "Ghetto and Emancipation: Shall We Revise the Traditional View?" *Menorah Journal* 14, no. 6 (1928): 515–526. Historians of Jewish life in the MENA have also taken up this conceptualization to challenge the narratives of European emancipation (attended by colonialism) as "good for the Jews." See, for example, Ethan Katz, Lisa Moses Leff, and Maud S. Mandel, "Engaging Colonial History and Jewish History," in *Colonialism and the Jews*, ed. Ethan Katz, Lisa Moses Leff, and Maud S. Mandel (Bloomington: Indiana University Press, 2017): 1–25. As Katz, Leff, and Mandel put it, "As the essays in this volume show, the Imperial Turn has begun to transform our understanding of modern Jewish history in important ways. For too long, European Jewish historians remained wedded to a theory of Jewish modernization, first explicitly articulated by Salo Wittmayer Baron and later popularized by Hannah Arendt, that depicted the nation-state as the key political formation that shaped modernization for Jews everywhere" (4). Regarding emancipation in Morocco specifically, see Daniel Schroeter and Joseph Chetrit, "Emancipation and Its Discontents: Jews at the Formative Period of Rule in Colonial Morocco," in *Jewish Social Studies* 13, no. 1 (Autumn 2006): 170–206.

4. Aron Rodrigue, *Jews and Muslims: Images of Sephardi and Eastern Jewries in Modern Times* (Seattle: University of Washington Press, 2003). This volume contains excerpts of Alliance documents and analysis by Rodrigue. Regarding Jewish "jargons" in the MENA, see chapter 8, "The War of Languages" (pp. 125–134) in particular.

5. For a primer on the Alliance Israélite Universelle, see the work of Michael M. Laskier, Aron Rodrigue, and Frances Malino, among others.

6. For more on this topic, see Daniel Schroeter, *The Sultan's Jew: Morocco and the Sephardi World* (Stanford: Stanford University Press, 2002).

7. Jessica M. Marglin describes this dynamic thoroughly in her book *Across Legal Lines: Jews and Muslims in Modern Morocco* (New Haven: Yale University Press, 2016). Marglin emphasizes that "Montefiore's visit changed Moroccan Jews' perception of the potential of international appeals. Similarly, the Makhzan became increasingly aware of just how much pressure Jews could exert by appealing to international actors. Nonetheless, both Jews and the Makhzan continued to believe that the Moroccan state was the ultimate arbiter and guarantor of justice for its Jewish subjects" (131–132).

8. Indeed, non-Jews also attended Alliance schools but did not figure into the guiding institutional mission.

9. Abd al-Hafid himself had earlier overthrown a younger brother who had been sultan before him—Mulay Abd al-Aziz IV (r. 1894–1908).

10. For information on the history of Casablanca, see André Adam, *Histoire de Casablanca: des origins à 1914* (Aix-en-Provence: Éditions Ophrys, Publications des Annales de La Faculté de Lettres, 1968) and André Adam, *Casablanca: Essai sur la transformation de la société marocaine au contact de l'Occident. Tomes 1& 2* (Paris: Éditions du centre national de la recherche scientifique, 1972). Albert Ayache has a rich and thorough body of work regarding the history of leftist politics in Morocco with particular emphasis in Casablanca; in particular, see Albert Ayache, *Le Mouvement syndical au Maroc. Tome 1: 1919–1942* (Paris: Éditions l'Harmattan, 1982).

11. Ayache, *Le Mouvement syndical*, 95–96.

12. Theoretically, this policy was in place to preserve Moroccan "autonomy" under the terms of the protectorate.

13. See Ayache, *Le Mouvement syndical*, for more information on the Rif War and the PCF, as well as David Henry Slavin's doctoral dissertation of the same year, "Anticolonialism and the French Left: Opposition to the Rif War, 1925–1926" (PhD diss., University of Virginia, 1982).

14. For a much more thorough treatment of these themes (indeed, all of the themes in this chapter), see Alma Rachel Heckman, *The Sultan's Communists: Moroccan Jews and the Politics of Belonging* (Stanford: Stanford University Press, 2021). The archival material informing these conclusions comes from many boxes of material at the Centre des Archives diplomatiques de Nantes, which contains most of the French protectorate archives.

15. The Roman past of Libya likewise provided a pretext for Italian colonial rule in that country.

16. There are several excellent works on French colonial Berber attitudes, including Susan Gilson Miller, *A History of Modern Morocco* (Cambridge: Cambridge University Press, 2013); Jonathan Wyrtzen, *Making Morocco: Colonial Intervention and the Politics of Identity* (Ithaca: Cornell University Press, 2015); Edmund Burke III, "The Image of the Moroccan State in French Ethnological Literature: A New Look at the Origin of Lyautey's Berber Policy," in *Arabs and Berbers: From Tribe to Nation in North Africa*, ed. Ernest Gellner and Charles Micaud (Toronto: Lexington Books, 1972), 175–199; Gilles Lafuente, *La politiques berbère de la France et le nationalisme marocain* (Paris: Harmattan, 1999); Katherine Hoffman, "Berber Law by French Means: Customary Courts in the Moroccan Hinterlands, 1930–1956," *Comparative Studies in Society and History* 52, no. 4 (2010): 851–880; Patricia Lorcin, *Imperial Identities: Stereotyping, Prejudice, and Race in Colonial Algeria* (London: I. B. Tauris, 1995); and David Prochaska, *Making Algeria French: Colonialism in Bône, 1870–1920* (Cambridge: Cambridge University Press, 1990).

17. John P. Halstead, *Rebirth of a Nation: The Origins and Rise of Moroccan Nationalism, 1912–1944* (Cambridge: Harvard University Press, 1967), 265.

18. See Joshua Cole, *Lethal Provocation: The Constantine Murders and the Politics of French Algeria* (Ithaca: Cornell University Press, 2019), particularly chapter three, "The Crucible of Local Politics" (34–45).

19. Yaron Tsur, Mohammed Hatimi, Mohammed Kenbib, Jamaâ Baïda, Susan Gilson Miller, Emily Gottreich, Daniel Schroeter, and others have all addressed Moroccan Jewish Zionism.

20. See Cole, *Lethal Provocation*, for a thorough treatment of the Constantine riots of 1934.

21. For more information on LICA activities across the Maghrib, see Aomar Boum, "Partners Against antisemitism: Muslims and Jews Respond to Nazism in French North African Colonies, 1936–1940," *The Journal of North African Studies* 19, no. 4 (September 2014): 554–567.

22. Marrus and Paxton's work provides great detail on the Vichy regime in France but does not address North Africa (Michael R. Marrus and Robert O. Paxton, *Vichy France and the Jews* [New York: Basic Books, 1981]). For Vichy in the Maghrib, see Michel Abitbol's *Les Juifs d'Afrique du Nord sous Vichy* (Paris: G. P. Maisonneuve & Larose, 1983) and Aomar Boum and Sarah Abrevaya Stein's edited volume *The Holocaust in North Africa* (Stanford: Stanford University Press, 2019).

23. Jewish communal appeals to the sultan for protection preceded the colonial period. See Schroeter, *The Sultan's Jew*, and Marglin, *Across Legal Lines.*

24. See chapter 2, "Possibilities: World War II and Moroccan Jewish Belonging" in Heckman, *The Sultan's Communists.*

25. David Stenner, "Did *Amrika* Promise Morocco's Independence? The Nationalist Movement, the Sultan, and the Making of the 'Roosevelt Myth,'" *The Journal of North African Studies* 19, no. 4 (September 2014): 524–539.

26. See Wyrtzen, *Making Morocco.*

27. Danièle Joly, *The French Communist Party and the Algerian War* (London: Palgrave Macmillan, 1991); Heckman, *The Sultan's Communists.*

28. Joshua Cole provides an excellent discussion on this rhetoric, which indeed defines his book's argument. See Cole, *Lethal Provocation.*

29. See Mohammed Kenbib, *Juifs et Musulmans au Maroc: 1859–1948* (Rabat: Université Mohammed V, Faculté des Lettres et des Sciences Humaines, 1994).

30. See chapter 3, "Tactics: Jews and Moroccan Independence," in Heckman, *The Sultan's Communists.*

31. See Chris Silver's book for more information on North African Jewish popstars including Sami el-Maghribi: *Recording History: Jews, Muslims and Music Across North Africa* (Stanford: Stanford University Press, 2022).

32. Material in this section is a distillation of chapters 4, "Splinters: Disillusion and Jewish Political Life in the New Morocco" and 5, "Co-optation: The Moroccan Cold War, Israel, and Human Rights" in Heckman, *The Sultan's Communists.*

33. See Alma Rachel Heckman, "Sacred Values: Islam, Communism, and Moroccan Nationalism in the Long 1960s," in *Defending the Faith: Global Histories of Apologetics and Politics in the Twentieth Century*, ed. Hugh McLeod and Todd H. Weir (Oxford: Oxford University Press, 2020), 211–230.

34. As previously mentioned, Western Sahara had launched an independence movement, the Polisario Front, from its Spanish colonial overlords. Spanish colonization of Western Sahara predated the 1912 protectorates and was recognized in 1884 at the Berlin Conference. Spain retained Western Sahara after Moroccan independence from the French and Spanish protectorates in 1956; King Hassan II and General Francisco Franco had a tacit understanding that the issue would not be raised under after the latter's death. At the time of the Green March, General Franco was in ill health; King Hassan II seized the opportunity to shore up his popularity. Algeria supported the Polisario Front while neighboring Mauritania also sought control over the territory, making irridentist claims like Morocco.

CHAPTER 2

"Yes, We Are Native Algerian Jews . . ."

THE ANTI-COLONIALIST JEWS OF ALGERIA, CA. 1920–1970

Pierre-Jean Le Foll-Luciani
Translated from the French by Jane Teresa Kuntz

> *1940: Vichy and its decrees! Remember! Children thrown out of school, local businesses confiscated, so many of our brothers out of a job! . . . Not a single Algerian Jew should forget a single day of those wretched years. . . . For those of us who were only just coming of age during this time of humiliation, those years of our youth have left an indelible mark on our lives, and that is why we are* proud *of the insults hurled at us like a stigma:* Yes, we are native Algerian Jews . . . so what? *You will never get our hearts in exchange for citizenship documents that you use like the blade of a guillotine.*
>
> —Bulletin du Comité des Algériens israélites pour la négociation

This statement was published in 1957 by a group of Algerian Jews who had joined the National Liberation Front (FLN) during the war for independence (1954–1962). The young men who wrote it, their roots in the Maghreb going back centuries, were born in Algeria during the interwar years with the status of French citizen. Expelled from school, stripped of their citizenship, and relegated to the second-class status of *indigène* or a native colonial subject during the three Vichy years, they became communists after World War II. Refusing to be considered French, they claimed in 1957 the designation of *Algériens israélites*, Algerian Jews, and called upon the other Jews of Algeria to back the move toward decolonization.

At that time, the population of Algeria included some 8.5 million so-called Muslim colonial subjects compared to 1 million French citizens, 130,000 of whom were Jews. The Jewish presence in North Africa dates back to pre-Islamic antiquity, a period of Jewish immigration and of probable conversions of Berbers to

Judaism. In the modern era, this presence was bolstered in the Muslim Maghreb when the Jews were expelled from the Iberian Peninsula. When France launched its colonial campaign in 1830, the French authorities lumped together the local Jews and Muslims under the same derogatory heading of *indigènes* or natives. But they soon pursued differentiated policies in that regard,[1] the pinnacle of which was the Crémieux Decree: In 1870, the 35,000 "indigenous Jews of the *départements* of Algeria [were] declared French citizens,"[2] while the Muslims remained yoked to their legal status as subaltern indigenous subjects, as did the Jews of regions conquered by the French army after 1870.[3] An exception to the rule in the history of colonial imperialisms, this collective attribution of citizenship was accompanied by a so-called Gallicization policy. These two processes led to a widening socioeconomic, cultural, and political gap between Jews and Muslims.[4] But even though the status of "colonizer" was now attributed to Jews, a significant proportion of the French in Algeria sought to deny them this status: By the end of the nineteenth century, and during the interwar period in particular, leaders of anti-Jewish movements fought to have Jews divested of this citizenship.[5] After France's defeat by Nazi Germany, the Vichy regime fulfilled that wish in October 1940: The 110,000 Jews of Algeria, deprived of their citizenship, were returned to their earlier status of *indigènes* and subjected to a number of discriminatory practices. They would not fully recover their rights until October 1943, nearly a year after the Anglo-American landing in North Africa.[6] The Algerian war for independence began eleven years later, in November 1954, and came to an end between March 1962 (ceasefire) and July 1962 (proclamation of Algerian independence). The situation of Jews during this war seemed overall to conform with that of the other French citizens of Algeria, and by 1961–1962, most of them had left Algeria for France.

The handful of Jewish men and women, a few hundred in all, who had gotten involved in the anti-colonialist movement from the interwar period to the 1960s represented a tiny minority within the Jewish population, and more broadly, of the population of French citizens of Algeria. Starting in 2006, I proceeded to locate archives and living witnesses in order to gather biographical information about as many of these militants as I could. Ultimately, the archives and the memorial sources produced enough material for me to analyze in detail the trajectory of some fifty militants, a dozen of whom were women, born during the interwar period.[7] Compared to the radical engagements of Jews in other spatial-temporal contexts, what makes these biographical and political trajectories so unique lies in the radicalness of the identity movements they involved. In Algeria, these identity reconfigurations were even more intense than for the militant Jews of other colonized Muslim-majority countries. Unlike the overwhelming majority of the latter, subjected as they were to the legal status of colonized people, the Jews of Algeria effectively enjoyed the citizenship status of the colonizing country: Their anti-colonialist engagement was thus all the more at odds with their objective situation in the colonial society. Born French citizens, these militants were at first assigned socially (their entire lives) and then legally (under Vichy) to their Jewishness, and then they wished to be Algerians while often considering their Jewishness as a component of their Algerian-ness.

These marginal, radical lives might appear disconnected from the collective trajectory of the French citizens of Algeria, and perhaps even more from the trajectory of their Jewish "community" of origin. And yet, a study of the path they chose does indicate that although the story of their dissident trajectory cannot be reduced to their Jewishness, their life experience as Jews played a major role in the timeline of their involvement, and in how they acted upon and formulated their commitments.

"An Extremely Arab Surname, and an Extremely French Given Name"[8]: A Jewish Childhood in French Algeria (Interwar Period)

Until they began getting involved politically, the childhood of these fifty or so witnesses was fairly typical of other Algerian Jews of their generation. Despite their diversity, in the interwar years Jewish children grew up within the colonial world order, where Jewishness was a socially structuring fact that was meaningful in a number of ways.

First of all, being Jewish implied a connection to the indigenous society, despite their French citizenship generally dating back two or three generations. In most families, stories of ancient origins were undoubtedly sketchy, when they existed at all, though family names, whether Hebrew, Arab-Berber or Sephardic, may provide useful clues. But the children born in the interwar period grew up in proximity to a living sign of their Maghrebi roots: their grandparents. These were born for the most part in the 1870s and 1880s, when the Crémieux Decree had just been issued and compulsory schooling went into effect. Still, they remained essentially grounded in their society and culture of origin. Sometimes dressing "like the natives," they would have Arabic or Hebrew first names, spoke Arabic, Ladino, and/or Tamazight, and often knew no French at all. Many had almost no contact with the Europeans of Algeria, whereas they socialized on a daily basis with the Muslims of their social milieu. These Judeo-Muslim relations were not solely economic but were bound up in a variety of masculine and feminine forms of sociability, whether at the cafés of the Muslim quarters, at the hammam, at the market, or in the collective courtyards of their homes. When questioned about their relationship with their grandparents, some witnesses said they felt very close to them and were attracted to the indigenous culture that was tending to fade among the Jews of their own generation; others reported that they viewed their grandparents as quaint curiosities, and at times they disparaged this "Arabness," which they experienced as a sign of sociocultural inferiority.

For being Jewish also meant being a French citizen. The witnesses' parents' generation, born at the turn of the twentieth century, was the first to experience the tangible effects of this granting of citizenship on a broad scale. On the one hand, a sizable proportion of the fathers' generation were mobilized during World War I, totaling some 13,000 Algerian Jews. On the other, the vast majority of parents, although raised in the indigenous culture within their families, were now enrolled in French schools. The fathers—but also certain mothers—were thus able to access new jobs, often synonymous with upward socioeconomic mobility. Among these parents, as with the Jewish population of Algeria overall, merchants certainly accounted for a disproportionate share, and most sold to a Jewish and Muslim customer base. Still, a new middle tier arose within this generation: A number of parents practiced liberal professions, as accountants or midwives (with a Jewish and Muslim clientele), while others found mid-level jobs in state-run sectors such as transport, police, or public education. Regardless of their socioeconomic standing, the families valued academic achievement, and more generally, French culture and mainland France. Among the witnesses, close to 80 percent had earned a French *baccalauréat*, and a sizable proportion, some 60 percent, attended university in Algiers or in France.

For the witnesses' generation, being French seemed to be taken for granted, more so than for their parents. Even as children, they already had their sights set on French society, and did not experience any sort of culture shock when they started school. Even though its disappearance was not total, and depended on socioeconomic, sociocultural, and geographic factors, three major markers of the earlier generations' indigenous way of life tended to disappear between their parents' generation and their own: the Hebrew and Arab-Berber first names, the Arabic language, and the sociability between Jews and Muslims. For many parents, upward social mobility involved moving from small communities to larger cities, and out of Jewish or Judeo-Muslim quarters within cities into what were called the European quarters. Since so few Muslim children attended school, the young Jews who grew up in the European quarters of Algeria's cities—and even in some Judeo-Muslim quarters—had almost no social contact with Muslims of the same age. The only Muslim familiar to them was the housemaid, whose presence in even low-income Jewish households attests to the disruption of power relationships introduced by French colonization. The distancing from Muslims in some Jewish families sometimes involved demeaning language with regard to Muslims, or even racist speech, a trend further exacerbated among some families in Constantine by the anti-Jewish riots led by Muslims in August 1934.[9] Admittedly, these riots triggered a movement referred to as "Judeo-Muslim fraternity" throughout Algeria. Led by prominent Jewish community members, the militants of left-wing and "native" parties, as well as members of such associations as the International League Against Antisemitism (LICA), this movement supported the calls for equality in favor of Muslims and denounced all forms of racism.[10] But in most of the witnesses' families, as in the vast majority of Jewish—and more broadly, French—families, the issue of the fate of colonized Muslims was simply not raised.

However French and estranged from autochthonous society they might have been, the children did remain Jews nonetheless. No matter how observant their families were or were not, these children were overwhelmingly the product of communitarian endogamy. And unlike their grandparents, their parents tended to socialize almost exclusively among other Jews, and the witnesses' own childhood friends were almost always Jewish. And finally, nearly all of them experienced antisemitism from an early age, whether at school or in the street, at the hands of many Europeans. This antisemitism ran counter to their parents' massive investment in a practically unequivocal identification with France: Although they aspired to a more or less Jewish Frenchness, they and their parents remained perceived simply as Jews and nothing else in various representations and in daily social interactions.

"It's Entrenched at Gut Level, It's in Our Heads. It Was a Determining Factor in Our Lives"[11]: From the Vichy Laws to Zionist and Communist Commitments, 1940s

In 1940, the racial profiling of Jews sharpened markedly when the Vichy regime, the *État français*, took control of public institutions. In October, the Vichy authorities rescinded the Crémieux Decree and published the first Jewish status laws, the first set of discriminatory policies.

As children or adolescents between 1940 and 1943, the witnesses were experiencing these race-based laws at an age when they were only just learning how to relate to the world and to others. The early measures affected their parents, whom they saw humiliated and impacted economically: Businesses were placed into receivership and "Aryanized," public employees were dismissed and evicted from their lodgings, midwives were no longer allowed to practice, etc. This racial violence was all the more intensive in that the gap with Europeans was widening: Few parents experienced any solidarity from outside the Jewish community. Still, several witnesses assert that some Muslims who were close to their parents did sympathize with their situation. For their part, an overwhelming majority of the children experienced one measure in particular that many would later report as crucial to their path in life: They were expelled from school, a move that affected more than 20,000 Algerian Jews, starting in July 1941. Further, after the Allied landing in November 1942, the older boys who were drafted into military service were also subjected to anti-Jewish discrimination in the French army.

How did the young Jews react? Thanks to solidarity within the community, most of those expelled from school were reenrolled in private schools set up by Jewish institutions and the teachers that had been dismissed. Here, several witnesses assert that they immersed themselves in their schoolwork, "as a kind of revenge."[12] Several boys joined the Jewish community's Boy Scouts, the *Éclaireurs israélites*, which experienced a sharp increase in enrollments from 1940, since most youth organizations had been closed to Jews, creating a need for organizations where they would be sheltered from racism. In metropolitan France, where Jews were facing arrests and racial deportations carried out by German and French authorities, local Jewish scouts played an important role in the networks organized to rescue Jewish children and to channel young Jews into the political and armed resistance. In Algeria, a territory not occupied by the Germans, the Jewish Scouts did not represent an openly political space of resistance. The hundreds of young Jews who organized underground to neutralize the French political and military authorities the day of the Anglo-American landing on November 8, 1942, had no connection, for instance, to the Éclaireurs israélites. However, several witnesses acquired as scouts organizational skills that they would deploy a few months later in political youth movements: recruiting, organizing outdoor activities, and collective decision-making, as well as newspaper production, from writing and page layout to distribution. For the witnesses, the Vichy period and the months following the Allied landing of November 1942 and the end of the war together represented a time of revolt. This sense of indignation undoubtedly rallied most of the young victims of discrimination, though only a minority of them would then be spurred to organize and take action.

For a few of the witnesses, their political consciousness-raising began before the war. None of their parents were political activists, and certain fathers who feared that their Jewishness might jeopardize their safety advised their children "to be cautious"[13] when expressing their opinions. Still, most of the fathers did vote Left, as did most Jews of Algeria, who by the 1930s massively cast their votes in favor of the Radical-Socialists, the Socialists, and to a lesser extent, the Communists. Some parents attended street demonstrations with their children at the time of the *Front Populaire*, a rallying of left-leaning parties, whose electoral successes in Algeria in 1936 were owed in part to Jewish voters. Just like the hundreds of young Jews who joined the Socialist and Communist parties around 1936, some witnesses rallied to the Algerian Communist Party (PCA) prior to 1939. The Communists had been organizing in Algeria since 1920, first within local sections of the French Communist Party (PCF), then within the PCA, created in October 1936.[14] Until the early 1950s, the majority of communist militants came from Algeria's European and Jewish families. Still, the number of militants from Muslim families was growing steadily: In 1936, Muslims accounted for approximately 2,000 of the total 5,000 members of the PCA. The communists' political line underwent significant evolutions depending on strategies decided in Moscow and Paris. After a period of radical anti-colonialism featuring most notably the demand for Algerian independence, the PCA, as of 1936 and through World War II, put the anti-colonial struggle on the back burner in favor of the anti-fascist fight. During the Popular Front era, young Algerian Jews' involvement in the PCA was motivated mainly by anti-fascism and by social issues. The same went for the witnesses who joined the underground PCA during the Vichy regime, where they first became involved in illegal militancy.

In the final years of the war and into the postwar period, the police archives, along with the witnesses' recollections, give evidence of a state of ferment, an "excitement,"[15] among Jewish youth, a minority of whom were openly revolting. Unlike their parents, who seemed content with a return to the old order once the Vichy laws had been repealed, these young people sought a more radical change. Beyond mere politics as usual, this revolt had to do with embodied bitter realities: Pointing to racism and the barriers between faith communities, some spoke of feeling "stifled"[16] by an "unbearable" society.[17] The two avenues of political radicalization available to them at that time were communism and Zionism.

Communism attracted hundreds of young Jews after Vichy. While Jews were not especially over-represented within the PCA compared to Europeans, they most certainly were within youth organizations and communist student groups, a fact that testifies to an undeniable generational effect subsequent to Vichy. Zionism, on the other hand, proved less attractive. Very marginal during the interwar period in Algeria compared to Morocco and Tunisia, Zionist movements experienced a relative surge after World War II. They confined themselves mostly to informing Jews about Zionism and the situation in Palestine and were not particularly proactive when it came to organizing emigration. Still, it is striking to observe that around 20 percent of the witnesses had joined a Zionist movement before becoming communists. Though it may seem surprising at first, this passage from Zionism to communism actually makes sense. These young people were emerging from a period where their tendency to look toward France for a sense of identity and belonging had been dealt a serious blow. Both these movements promised an alternative to French citizenship and Frenchness. On the one hand, Zionism offered a way to politicize their Jewishness and to identify with a "Jewish nation." On the other, communism involved identification with a transnational dominated subject (the proletariat, the oppressed, etc.), but also with an Algerian homeland. Even though these involvements concerned only a minority of Jewish youth—the majority of whom had never experienced any form of political engagement—they still reveal the change brought about by Vichy.

"The Jewish Algerian Worker's Homeland Is Algeria"[18]: Communist "Algerians" in the Struggle for Independence, 1950–1962

Starting with their choice to join the PCA, the witnesses' trajectory followed the same arc as that of the Algerian communist movement more generally. As of 1946, anti-colonialism topped the PCA agenda, and the party aimed to become part of the Algerian anti-colonialist struggle. What made it so distinct from the other anti-colonialist parties on the scene was its desire to bring together militants of diverse origins. Around 1950, PCA membership topped out at some 20,000 adherents and the PCA obtained up to 20 percent of the vote on certain electoral ballots among the French citizens of Algeria. But a good number of French militants gradually strayed from the party as its anti-colonialist position started to harden: In 1954, on the eve of the war for independence, PCA membership had dropped to about 12,000 and the PCA recruited essentially among the colonized, who by then represented a narrow majority.

The PCA was thus a space of transgressive sociability with regard to the colonial world order. This aspect stirred the enthusiasm of the Jewish activists, for it was within the party that many of them first made friends with Europeans, and what's more, with Muslims. Their communist commitment did make them a minority within the Jewish population, thereby alienating them from some of their childhood friends, and sometimes from their own families when their affiliation created tension. Still, the militants did not experience their political engagement as a break with their community of origin, but rather as an opening up to other components of Algerian society. Most of the witnesses ended up marrying another

Jew, most often a communist. But some exogamous marriages were celebrated among communist militants, including between Jewish women and Muslim men. The PCA emphasized this aspect to defend its notion of an all-inclusive Algerian nation. In fact, the party prompted all its members to call themselves "Algerians," or even "Algerian patriots." Prior to 1954, patriotic discourses were mainly made by Muslim militants. But Jewish militants also asserted themselves as "Algerian patriots" at rallies and in articles or poems, whereas this affirmation was far less frequent among European militants.

Were these patriotic proclamations simply a matter of political strategy, or did they correspond to an affective reality? Questioned on this subject, several witnesses reported that they felt "Algerian." Others, less affirmative about their Algerian-ness, did say that, more importantly, they did not feel "French." To explain these feelings, some put forward the Vichy laws, which undermined "this already precarious [French] identity that [they] now could no longer completely believe in."[19] Others highlighted their "physical,"[20] "bodily"[21] attachment to the Algerian land, kindled by an awareness of their centuries-old heritage in the Maghreb. Of course, this sentimental attachment to the land was also widespread among the other French citizens of Algeria. But among the militants, it hinged on an undoing of their identification with France and an affective and political identification with the colonized Algerians: "Speaking for myself, I felt such solidarity with Algeria that in that sense, I felt Algerian."[22]

After the insurrection was touched off by the FLN in November 1954 and a genuine war for independence started taking shape over the following months, the participation of militant Jews in the fight for independence assumed several forms. Only a handful took direct part in the armed struggle inside the FLN or the PCA. A greater number lent logistic, material, legal or medical support to the FLN. But the majority worked directly within the underground networks of the PCA, which was banned in 1955, and whose hundreds of militants fell victim to repression. Their identification with Algeria was all the more visceral in that they experienced it in their bodies: Disguised and in hiding, suffering under torture, locked away in prison, their bodies participated in a shared destiny, struggling and suffering alongside all those who asserted themselves as Algerians. As a way of demonstrating their Algerian-ness, several witnesses adopted Arab pseudonyms when underground, laid claim to Algerian nationality in French courts of law, and learned Arabic from their fellow detainees in prisons and internment camps.

Jewish activists thus asserted themselves as Algerian first and foremost, and their communist training meant that they refrained from foregrounding their Jewishness. However, several militants leveraged the latter as a political weapon. Prior to the war for independence, communist cells in Jewish neighborhoods and PCA activists expressed themselves as Jews so as to more readily mobilize their fellow Jews for their anti-colonial agenda. At that time, they emphasized the analogy between antisemitism and anti-Arab racism, and between fascism and colonialism, and affirmed that the Muslims showed solidarity toward Jews under the Vichy regime. This agenda evolved during the war for independence: From 1956 onward, in underground print material, several Jewish activists within the FLN or PCA, sometimes grouped into specifically Jewish underground units, called into question the "Frenchification" of Algeria's Jews and emphasized the shared historic culture of Muslims and Jews, even declaring them a single people. Proclaiming the Algerian-ness of Algeria's Jews, they urged them to become one with colonized people in their struggle, so as to secure for themselves a future in independent Algeria. By the summer of 1956, this agenda had gained the support of the FLN, which helped spread the texts emanating from the Jewish activists.

Although the bulk of the Jewish population did not approve of this agenda or the various clandestine involvements, several militant Jews enjoyed support during the war from the Jews in their immediate circle, and even from the more institutionalized Jewish community: Nonpoliticized Jews were willing to hide militants and would come forward in court to attest to their good character, Jewish lawyers would defend them, one religious association vouched for one of them before the authorities, a rabbi regularly visited one of them in prison, and Jewish prison wardens would arrange for kosher meals and for Passover matzah for several of them.

"We Don't Belong Here": Facing State-Defined Algerian-ness in Independent Algeria, 1962–1970s

By the time Algeria was declared independent in July 1962, the majority of Jews, like the other French people of Algeria, had already left the country.[23] More than seven years of war, marked by violence against civilian populations perpetrated by the French army, the FLN, and the right-wing "ultras" favoring a French Algeria created a rift between populations that many believed could never be healed. Sharing with the mass of French citizens of Algeria a fear of Algerian nationalists and an apocalyptic vision of independent Algeria, Jews left in droves for France. A few thousand did choose Israel, a country that welcomed around 15,000 Algerian Jews between 1948 and 1963. Compared to the Jews of Tunisia and Morocco, only a minority of Algerian Jews opted for Zionism, which can be explained by their status as French citizens. A few weeks after independence, more than 100,000 French citizens of Algeria stayed behind. Among them were several thousand Jews, about whom we know very little. These French men and women from Jewish or European families who decided to live in independent Algeria were not all militants: only a few thousand had taken part in the anti-colonial struggle and considered themselves Algerian. These joined in the euphoria of festivities surrounding independence and envisioned their future in the country with enthusiasm: Despite their feeling abandoned at the departure of so many family members, childhood friends, neighbors and coworkers, independence was also their victory, and they wished to share in the building of a "socialist" Algeria.

However, by the early 1970s, between the coup d'état of June 1965 and the start of the new decade, the majority of Jewish militants, like the Europeans, had left Algeria. The witnesses cited several factors to explain this departure. A first set of factors accounts for not only their migration but also that of certain Muslim

Algerians: the authoritarian nature of the new regime, and the retrograde status of women. A second set explains more pointedly the migration of non-Muslims: the Arabization policy, the definition of Islam as the state religion, and the definition of what constitutes a "native national" in the nationality code[24] requiring that the person be Muslim. And finally, a third set of factors is specific to Jews: A minority among the witnesses observed anti-Jewish hostility, particularly during the 1967 Arab-Israeli conflict, the Six-Day War. Even if some of them had stood in solidarity with the Palestinians, they were adversely affected by the general tendency to conflate all Jews with Zionism and Israel.

Taken together, these factors contributed to a growing sense of illegitimacy among the witnesses regarding their presence in independent Algeria. But what affected them most was the state-mandated notion of Algerian-ness specified as exclusively Arab and Muslim. During the war for independence, several among them had already clashed with nationalist militants over this issue, especially in the prisons and camps. Still, the statements issued repeatedly by the FLN with respect to the status of Jews (and anti-colonialist Europeans) as true Algerians sounded reassuring. In early 1963, during parliamentary debates over the nationality code, several militant Jews spoke up, going on the offensive to publicly oppose the definition of "native national" as Muslim:

> While it is true that a foreigner should require a special favor to obtain the nationality of a country where he has lived only a short while, we feel entitled to believe, based on the fact that each one of us, having lived here over several generations, and sometimes, as is the case for the Jews, claiming no past other than in Algeria, that we have the right to be considered as autochthonous, native Algerians. . . . Thus, is it fair that this Jewish patriot, whose Algerian past dates back at least as far as any Algerian's, finds himself in a situation where, because the colonizer in 1870 declared him, *ex officio*, a Frenchman, he must now apply for naturalization? And the Algerian (of Muslim status) who *voluntarily* opted for French nationality, will be considered Algerian based on the sole fact of his status as Muslim?[25]

Outraged by the nationality code, a number of militants did not seek Algerian nationality: During the years 1963 through 1965, only 296 individuals were naturalized because of their participation in the struggle for independence, of whom seventy-three were Europeans of Algeria and twenty-one were Algerian Jews.

In light of their failed endeavor, it would be tempting to consider the course of action taken by this minority of anti-colonialist Jews as ultimately unrealistic and unachievable. The same might be said with regard to the trajectories of Moroccan and Tunisian Jews involved in their respective communist and nationalist movements. In June 1956, three months after Tunisia declared its independence, the Tunisian Jewish anti-colonialist intellectual Albert Memmi gave an account in one of his notebooks of a discussion with the Tunisian historian Paul Sebag, a Jew and a communist. Attempting to take stock of their respective trajectories, he wrote:

"1. I have to help the Tunisians because their cause is just [and then] 2. Leave, because their cause is not mine."[26] Still, we can decide not to endorse such a fatalistic view of history. On the one hand, because Maghrebi Jews who took part in the anti-colonial struggle did not consider themselves as outsiders to the cause: They felt it was theirs. On the other hand, because this marginalization and this failure were not a foregone conclusion: They resulted from power struggles within society and inside the institutions of both colonial and independent Algeria, whose victims were far more numerous than these few Jewish activists. Nor is it fair to assert that these militants acted in breach of their Jewishness or their Jewish community. "I think that we were the expression of our people's deep-seated reality,"[27] said one of them in 2008. He believed that his path and that of his fellow activists represented one of the possible conceivable and realizable choices for the Jews of his generation. To challenge the social confines of their family, to refuse the cautiousness instilled in them by their parents, to subvert the racial divisions of colonial society even in their own private lives, to disrupt the world order of French Algeria and risk their lives to bring it down—none of that implied a radical break with the Jews of Algeria or with the Jewish condition in colonial Algeria, said some of them. Quite the reverse: Several of them had stated that these acts formed an integral part of their family history and their experience as Jews, from which they more or less consciously drew their subversive resourcefulness.

NOTES

Epigraph: *Bulletin du Comité des Algériens israélites pour la négociation*, Fonds IVe Internationale, F delta 1733, ca. April 1957, La contemporaine, Nanterre, France.

1. Joshua Schreier, *Arabs of the Jewish Faith: The Civilizing Mission in Colonial Algeria* (New Brunswick, NJ: Rutgers University Press, 2010).

2. Decree signed at Tours on October 24, 1870, by Adolphe Crémieux, Léon Gambetta, Alexandre Glais-Bizoin, and Martin Fourichon, members of the French provisional Government after France's defeat against Prussia.

3. Sarah A. Stein, *Saharan Jews and the Fate of French Algeria* (Chicago: University of Chicago Press, 2014).

4. Lucette Valensi, *Juifs et musulmans en Algérie, VIIe-XXe siècle* (Paris: Tallandier/Projet Aladin, 2016).

5. Sophie Beth Roberts, *Jews, Citizenship, and Antisemitism in French Colonial Algeria, 1870–1943* (PhD diss., University of Toronto, 2011).

6. Michel Abitbol, *The Jews of North Africa During the Second World War* (Detroit: Wayne State University Press, 1989).

7. Pierre-Jean Le Foll-Luciani, *Les juifs algériens dans la lutte anticoloniale. Trajectoires dissidentes (1934–1965)* (Rennes: Presses Universitaires de Rennes, 2015).

8. Author interview with Paul Bouaziz, March 12, 2007.

9. Joshua Cole, *Lethal Provocation: The Constantine Murders and the Politics of French Algeria* (Ithaca, NY: Cornell University Press, 2019).

10. Pierre-Jean Le Foll-Luciani, "Les actions judéo-musulmanes pour une réforme de la citoyenneté en Algérie coloniale. Du Front populaire au *Manifeste du peuple algérien* (1936–1943)," in *La fabrique coloniale du citoyen. Algérie, Nouvelle-Calédonie*, ed. Éric Savarese and Éric De Mari (Paris: Karthala, 2019), 79–99.

11. Author interview with André Beckouche, March 29, 2007.

12. Author interview with Hubert Hannoun, April 11, 2007.

13. Author interview with Arlette Beckouche (née Bourgel), April 23, 2007.

14. Allison Drew, *We Are No Longer in France: Communists in Colonial Algeria* (Manchester, UK: Manchester University Press, 2014); Pierre-Jean Le Foll-Luciani, "The Communists in Algeria (1920–93)," in *Communist Parties in the Middle East: 100 Years of History*, ed. Laura Feliu and Ferran Izquierdo-Brichs (London: Routledge, 2019), 199–215.

15. Author interview with Emile Schecroun, June 23, 2011.

16. Author interviews with Jacques Azoulay, February 5, 2007, and Rolland Doukhan, May 24, 2007.

17. Author interviews with Claude Sixou, January 22, 2009, and Rubens Fitoussi, June 16, 2010.

18. William Sportisse, "Sionisme et antisémitisme," *Progrès* 2 (April–May 1953).

19. Interview by Liliane Verspeelt with Simone Aïach, February 24, 1995.

20. Author interview with Claude Sixou, February 12, 2007.

21. Author interview with Gabriel Timsit, December 20, 2006.

22. Author interview with Emile Schecroun, June 23, 2011.

23. Author interview with André Beckouche, March 29, 2007.

24. Law no. 63–96 of March 27, 1963, establishing the Algerian nationality code, *Journal officiel de la République algérienne* of April 2, 1963.

25. "Nationalité algérienne (document)," *Les Temps Modernes*, nos. 432–433 (July–August 1982): 294–299. The known signatories of this 1963 text are André Beckouche, Lucien Hanoun, Jean-Claude Melki, Francine Serfati, Claude Sixou (Algerian Jews), Jacqueline Guerroudj (metropolitan French Jew), and Colette Grégoire (French woman from Algeria).

26. Albert Memmi, *Tunisie, An I* (Paris: Éditions du CNRS, 2017).

27. Author interview with Jean Beckouche, December 10, 2008.

CHAPTER 3

Between Gallicism and Communism

JEWS AND POLITICS IN TUNISIA, 1881–1945

Kamilia Rahmouni

The creation in 1878 of a school of the Alliance Israélite Universelle[1] in Tunis and the establishment of the French Protectorate in Tunisia in 1881 deepened the exposure of the Jewish communities in the country to the influences of modern Europe. These influences brought about profound changes in the institutions, cultures, and religious practices of these communities, gradually leading many of their members to assimilation and identification with the French colonizers, namely through learning and speaking French, embracing the French lifestyle with its eating habits and clothing trends, and adopting French names.

The Second World War represented a shock to these communities. The defeat of France, the establishment of the Vichy regime with its anti-Jewish legislation (July 10, 1940, to August 20, 1944), and the occupation of Tunisia by the Germans (November 1942–May 1943) destroyed the image of an egalitarian France previously regarded as the emancipator and liberator of the Jews.[2] The upheavals engendered by the war had deep repercussions for the community's institutions, ideologies, and political affiliations. These repercussions were mainly reflected in the community members' political orientation and reorientation. Two main changes occurred following the end of the war: the decline of the old current of Gallicization, and the increased involvement in other types of political engagement, including Tunisian nationalism, communism, and Zionism.

In this chapter, I argue that the World War II years were of crucial importance for Tunisian Jews and global communism. The interwar period was characterized by the availability and fluidity of numerous political trends and ideologies, namely Gallicization, Zionism, and communism.[3] Borders and boundaries between these political trends were fluid and porous; this fluidity would harden in the crucible of the Vichy regime and the German occupation of Tunisia (from November 1942 through May 1943). The rampant repercussions of WWII profoundly transformed the Tunisian Jewish community. The disillusionment and disappointment with Vichy France due to its betrayal of long-preached values of democracy and equality led several Tunisian Jews to a search for new political models: communism, socialism, Zionism, and Tunisian nationalism. In this chapter, I will focus on the Jewish engagement in the Communist Party. For many Tunisian Jews, joining the Communist Party constituted a sociopolitical awakening that made them aware of the national problem; motivated them to fight for their country and for their fellow citizens regardless of their religion, gender or race; provided them with new forms of interactions with their Muslim compatriots; and deeply influenced their professional choices. Put pithily, for them communism was "the end of racism. We are neither Jews nor Muslims nor French. We are above all Bolsheviks. . . . We are all revolutionary militants. Religion, states and borders will disappear. Only the communist universe will remain where all the differences between men will be abolished. This is what we are fighting for" (my translation).[4]

The above quote is from a semi-autobiographical novel entitled *Gagou* (1980) written by Guy Sitbon, a Tunisian Jew who was an active member of the Communist Party. *Gagou*, along with other autobiographical and semi-autobiographical novels, namely Albert Memmi's *Pillar of Salt*,[5] will serve as historical references in my analysis of the impact of WWII on Tunisian Jews' self-identification and subsequent involvement in the communist movement. This analysis begins with an overview of the Gallicization current among Tunisian Jews (from the French occupation of Tunisia in 1881 until the beginning of WWII in 1939) then discusses the traumatic impact of WWII on Jewish social ideologies and political affiliations, concluding with an analysis of the main factors that attracted Tunisian Jews to the communist movement.

A Disillusioned Identity in the Face of Modernization: Gallicization

The French colonial presence in Tunisia had deep and divisive repercussions for Tunisian Jewish communities and the way they viewed themselves and defined their identity, an identity that had been already disillusioned by modernity. There were contradictory attitudes on the part of Tunisian rabbis toward modernity and the new technologies of the West. These attitudes can be categorized into three main groups. Members of the first group considered the West with its new technological powers and emancipated Jewries as a benevolent power that could assist and protect Tunisian Jews. Members of the second group viewed the West and the new cultural and religious changes it sought to bring as a danger to the Jewish identity and Judaism as a whole. Members of the third group were selective when it came to the changes wrought by modernity and remained thoroughly dedicated to traditional Judaism.[6] The contradictory attitudes of Tunisian rabbis were reflected in the Jewish community, whose members felt disillusioned by modernity and the various changes it brought; this disillusionment deepened with the establishment of the French protectorate in Tunisia.

When Tunisia became a French protectorate in 1881, a new era began for Tunisian Jews. The French revolutionary promise of *liberté, egalité, et fraternité* constituted a source of hope for many of them. A large number of Jews hoped to move away from what they saw as Muslim domination and segregation, an attitude that was reinforced—and many times imposed—by the French colonialist project and the Alliance Israélite Universelle's integrationist policy. Accordingly, "they were very receptive to the new French influences, even though they had a Christian European source."[7] Their quick reception of these French values facilitated their assimilation into French culture.[8] Many of the Tunisian Jews who were born under the protectorate quickly adopted French as their mother tongue instead of Judeo-Arabic, thus entering a long and ongoing process of Gallicization.[9]

Tunisian Jews were deeply influenced by European culture. The use of European instead of Hebrew or Arabic names, the adoption of European styles of dress, and the attempt to distance themselves from the majority Muslim population spread rapidly among educated Tunisian Jews.[10] Bourgeois families sent their children to Protestant and Catholic missionary schools, while the Alliance schools opened their doors to Jewish families of all social classes. The curriculum in the Alliance schools was based on the French educational system; it did, however, make a place for Jewish history and Hebrew language instruction. This led to a rapid increase in the number of educated Jewish children. Later on, these children had the opportunity to pursue higher education thanks to an improvement in the economic conditions of their families, and to be active participants in colonial economic and political life—an advantage that was denied to the majority of Tunisian Muslims.[11]

Tunisian Jews were quick to integrate into the colonial economy, even though many still performed traditional commercial activities like craftsmanship. Young university graduates increasingly engaged in other professions, mainly in industry, banks, stores, and insurance companies, and started working as lawyers, pharmacists, and doctors.[12] As a consequence, many Jews left the *hara* and moved to the newly established neighborhoods.[13] Acquiring French citizenship further improved their social and economic situations.

Many Jews were granted French citizenship, as shown in Table 2.1. Several other demands followed their naturalization. The extension of French jurisdiction to Tunisian Jews became one of the main demands of the modernist intelligentsia that was educated in French universities. Indeed, one can neither argue that all the Jewish communities in Tunisia went through the same Gallicization experience nor claim that there is a "one-size-fits-all" paradigm that can encompass all the processes of Tunisian Jews' self-identification during the colonial period. The existence of various and competing political movements had a deep and divergent influence on Tunisian Jews' identity formation and subsequent self-identification. This is especially clear in the autobiographic writings of the time, which illustrate the changing identities of Tunisian Jews during the colonial period (including Gallicism, Tunisian nationalism, socialism, communism, and Zionism).[14]

Impact of Colonialism on Tunisian Jews: The Rise of a Gallicized Identity

Many Tunisian Jews looked at the French colonial power as a source of great positive changes and started gradually detaching themselves from the surrounding Muslim society.[15] Haim Saadoun argues that the colonization of Tunisia by France gradually transformed Jewish-Muslim relations in the country.[16] This, he argues, was due to the Jews' assimilation to French culture, which increasingly detached them from the surrounding Tunisian Muslim society. Saadoun asserts that "The new colonial society gave Jews the freedom, within certain limitations, to choose how to live or identify themselves. . . . Consciously, then, but not necessarily by overt choice, the Jews tied their fate to that of French colonial rule, which eventually distanced them even more from the Muslim majority in Tunisia."[17]

Thus, many Jews advocated for a rapid acquisition of French nationality, which would allow them to benefit from the economic, financial, and legal advantages enjoyed by the French. These demands were mainly channeled through the *La Justice* newspaper, which was founded in Tunis in 1907 by Mardochée Smadja.[18] Smadja was very influenced by French culture and the ideals of the French Revolution. He believed that in order for Jews to achieve full emancipation, they needed to assimilate to French culture and ways of life. *La Justice* was named in homage to Georges Clémenceau and his campaign in favor of Alfred Dreyfus, and had as its subtitle "journal for the extension of France's rights and duties in Tunisia." It called on the French colonial authorities to grant Tunisian Jews French citizenship or at least to place them under the jurisdiction of French courts.[19]

According to Nataf,[20] *La Justice* newspaper (1907–1934) served as a unifying bond, during the interwar period, between a group of Jewish intellectuals from French universities who were strong advocates for French assimilation. They called for emancipation through naturalization and Gallicization through total integration of the Jewish community into French society and culture. These continuous calls were a driving force behind the adoption of the 1923 law allowing Jews to obtain French citizenship, which paved the way for the democratization of community institutions, especially judicial courts.[21] As a result, the political opponents of Gallicism attacked *La Justice* newspaper, considering it the platform of the "assimilation party."[22]

These strong calls for assimilation along with various French naturalization laws (July 29, 1887; February 28, 1899; October 3, 1910; August 15, 1914; November 8, 1921; December 20, 1923) resulted in the naturalization of many Tunisian Jews. Between 1911 and 1919, the majority of naturalized Tunisians were Jews, as Table 2.1 illustrates.

As is clear from the table, following both the 1910 and 1914 naturalization laws, the number of Tunisian Jews who were granted French citizenship increased considerably. However, with the growing demands of Muslims for equal rights through French naturalization, and with the increasing fear of the French authorities of the dual loyalty of the *Grana*[23] (especially after Italy showed its ardent ambitions to

TABLE 2.1.

NUMBER OF NATURALIZED FRENCH TUNISIANS (1891–1919)

1891–1898	23 Muslims
1899–1910	101 Muslims
1911–1919	55 Muslims and 106 Jews (number who naturalized as a result of the October 3, 1910, naturalization law)
1915–1919	22 Muslims and 107 Jews (number who naturalized as a result of the August 15, 1914, naturalization law)

Source: Charles Monchicourt, *La Tunisie Après La Guerre, Problèmes Politiques* (Paris: Comité de l'Afrique française, 1920–1921), 124.

take over the Tunisian territory), more Tunisian Muslims were granted French citizenship, particularly after the 1923 naturalization law. This does not mean, however, that the percentage of naturalized Muslims exceeded that of naturalized Jews. Following their colonial strategy of "divide and conquer," French authorities created and maintained divisions among the various religious factions of Tunisia by favoring some groups (Jews) over others (Muslims) especially when granting access to French citizenship along with all the advantages that came with it.

Under the provision of the 1923 naturalization law, after the age of twenty-one, and after proving that they could speak and write French fluently, Tunisians could apply for French citizenship if they met certain requirements.[24] From the beginnings of the protectorate, many Tunisian Jews had sent their children to French schools. Thus, by the enactment of the 1923 naturalization law, they had already met the conditions for obtaining French citizenship. In a population of 56,000, 5,549 Tunisian Jews were naturalized between 1921 and 1930.[25] This accounted for about 10 percent of the Jewish community. Although many Jewish demands for naturalization were rejected because they did not meet the criteria required by the French law, the percentage of Jews who were granted French nationality was much higher than the percentage of Muslims who were. Within the same period, in a population of more than two million, 1,016 Muslims were naturalized, accounting for about 0.05% of the Muslim population.[26] Indeed, one can account for this disparity in the number of naturalization cases by the French colonial policy of "divide and conquer."

This concept of internal colonialism and ethnic favoritism is not new in colonial discourses; most colonialist powers had used minorities to strengthen their influence over their colonies by endowing minority groups with certain privileges denied to the majority population. Thus, these measures do not necessarily represent an inclusive democratic advancement since they favor some groups over others. Some Jews, who constituted a minority in their community, felt that the Jewish minority could not achieve real and tangible progress unless this progress could be shared with Tunisian society as a whole.[27] Tapia asserts that "Thenceforth, a sole strategy was imposed: to accept the rights and advantages conferred by the dominant group (here, the colonial group), while refusing to sever ties with the majority population and working on raising their awareness of the injustices that affected, without distinction, all those who did not belong to the dominant group. This approach was mainly that of a few isolated individuals of bourgeois origin, distant from Judaism and its institutions, and sometimes openly rebelling against their families and social environment"(my translation).[28]

This quote outlines the path of several Tunisian Jews who chose to receive the privileges "offered" by the colonial power while at the same time remaining part of Tunisian society. Such a choice allowed them to "use" these privileges, including education in French schools and eloquence in the French language, to fight for universal justice for all Tunisians regardless of their religion. Tapia mentions that this approach was that of "some isolated individuals." However, the number of these individuals increased after WWII and the German occupation of Tunisia. The autobiographies published by Tunisian Jews are useful when discussing these changing identities and processes of self-identification among Tunisian Jews during the colonial period. All the discussed autobiographies were written in French, which reflects the francophone influence on Tunisian Jews.

Gagou is a semi-autobiographical novel written in French by Guy Sitbon[29] and published in 1980. It provides the reader with a detailed presentation of life in Tunisia between the two World Wars and offers an eloquent depiction of the author's personal story, life journey, and struggle with changing identities and competing loyalties. The itinerary followed by the young Gagou, the hero of the novel, perfectly illustrates the disillusionment of the third Jewish generation of the protectorate. As a young man, the protagonist desperately attempts to become integrated into French society and to be completely immersed in French culture. Gagou Benhassen is ashamed of his name and of his mother tongue (Arabic) because they reflect his non-French roots and they constantly remind him, and others around him, of his origin. At the French school, Gagou names himself Jojo to hide his "dubious" ethnic background: Arab, Jew, and colonized. With his friends and classmates, he makes valiant efforts to not speak Arabic and to properly speak French, the "language of the civilized."[30]

Such an attitude recalls that of Albert Memmi's similarly semi-autobiographical character, Alexander Mordekhai Benillouche.[31] The name of Memmi's protagonist reflects the warring identities within him. The name Alexander Mordekhai Benillouche has a triple dimension: Alexander represents the Western dimension, Mordekhai the Jewish heritage, and Benillouche the Berber origin. This triple identity creates in him a sense of self-fragmentation and a continuous tension between three contending sociocultural spaces: French, Jewish, and Tunisian. Consequently, Benillouche finds himself trapped in a continuous and deep colonizer/colonized dialectic, and experiences an increasing sense of self-rejection.

After numerous and arduous attempts to become a "true Frenchman," Gagou and Alexander come to a similar realization: Assimilation into French culture and values is not satisfying and, on many occasions, is not completely achievable. The two protagonists decide to explore other options and to turn to different political trends such as communism.[32] Gagou and Alexander's paths reflect the shift in self-understanding and self-identification that many Tunisian Jews witnessed throughout the French colonial presence and beyond. World War II and Nazism in particular greatly impacted Tunisian Jews.

WWII: An Introspective Turn in Self-Identification

The outbreak and repercussions of the Second World War had an immense impact on many Tunisian Jews, who had hoped and attempted to identify themselves with the French and to assimilate into the image of a cultured French metropolitan Jew. The rise of the Vichy regime in France (1940–1942) and the anti-Jewish legislation it promulgated[33] had a very negative impact on Tunisian Jewish communities.[34] The Nazi-inspired racial laws, applied in Tunisia from November 30, 1940, to June 10, 1943, destroyed the image of an egalitarian France, previously regarded as the emancipator of Tunisian Jews and the guarantor of their rights and liberties.[35] The defeat of France, the German occupation of Tunisia (November 1942–May 1943), the anti-Jewish measures enacted by the Germans and their French allies, and the unwillingness of the French to intervene to protect Tunisian Jews led many of those who previously wished to be Gallicized to reconsider their beliefs and lower their expectations.

In the meantime, the sympathetic attitude of Muslim officials to the Jewish cause led several Jews who had previously identified themselves with France to abandon their Gallicization and embrace Tunisian nationalism.[36] During that time, the Vichy regime in France enacted a series of anti-Jewish laws that were vigorously enforced in Algeria and Morocco. In Tunisia, however, the wartime rulers Ahmed Pasha Bey and, especially, his cousin Moncef Bey[37] were very sympathetic to the cause of Tunisian Jews. Satloff asserts that "a loophole in the Tunisian version of Vichy anti-Jewish laws gave the ruler the right to grant exemptions to native Tunisian Jews who had performed exceptional service to the state. Ahmed Bey took advantage of this oversight to exempt two leading Jewish personalities—Roger Nataf, an ophthalmologist, and Paul Ghez, the man who later served as head of the Jewish labor bureau during the German occupation."[38]

Moncef Bey became known as "the Protector of Jews"; he refused to sign anti-Jewish decrees and made efforts to ensure that these decrees were not put into effect. He also declared in front of numerous French officials that "Jews, just like Muslims, are my children," and just eight days after he became bey, he awarded about twenty Tunisian Jews the Nishan Iftikhar (Order of Glory), which constituted the highest distinction in the country.[39] He also appointed a prime minister, Mohamed Chenik, who had long-standing ties to the Tunisian Jewish community. Chenik helped many Tunisian Jews by regularly warning them of German plans, hiding them and intervening to prevent their deportation to work in labor camps.[40] This supportive treatment from the Muslim authorities collided with that of the French, who enacted anti-Jewish laws and were not quick to repeal them even after the defeat of the Germans.[41]

The discriminatory status that Vichy imposed on Tunisian Jews was only abrogated on August 8, 1943, two months after the liberation of Tunisia. The reluctance of the Giraud authorities in Algiers to put an end to the anti-Jewish legislation disappointed several Tunisian Jews who had earlier called for French assimilation.[42] This reluctance led many North African Jews to think that the racial laws had been not merely a pledge given by the Vichy regime to Germany; but rather the expression and concretization of a dormant anti-Jewish sentiment within the ruling circle in the Metropole and across the French Empire.[43]

During the six months of the German occupation, Tunisia was a battlefield between the belligerents. As such, its capital Tunis and several of its main interior cities were subjected to almost daily air bombardments. The war left the country in a very dire economic situation, with thousands of hectares of farmland devastated and numerous cities' infrastructure completely destroyed. Cities that had had large Jewish populations, such as Sfax, Sousse, Bizerte, and Beja, were deeply affected by the German occupation. This situation compelled a large number of Jews to move from the inland areas to Tunis; created a new social class of refugee; and led to the proletarianization and concomitant impoverishment of many members of the Jewish bourgeoisie, who lost their jobs and in many cases their properties.[44]

WWII along its devastating repercussions and upheavals had a scarring effect on the Tunisian Jewish community's institutions and ideologies as well as on the individual behaviors and convictions of Tunisian Jews. In the following sections, I identify the political and ideological changes that swept through the Tunisian Jewish community following the six-month German occupation of the country, namely the ebbing of the old sociocultural current of Gallicization and the rising tide of Jewish involvement in communism.

The Decline of Gallicization

WWII and the subsequent Italo-German occupation of Tunisia were a source of great disappointment to those who had linked progress, equality, and liberation with full integration into French society. The anti-Jewish laws instituted by the Vichy regime led the advocates of Gallicization to question their idealistic belief in France's *liberté*, *égalite*, and *fraternité*. Paul Ghez, one of the ardent supporters of French assimilationism, confessed in a conference: "We were sorely disappointed. We, who had always responded to the appeal of France, found ourselves alone, abandoned, rejected. More than the violence of the Germans, it is this sense of abandonment, the feeling of having been betrayed, which was the hardest to bear." Ghez added: "Of course we still love France, but our love is undoubtedly mingled with sadness and interrogation. . . . Have we been right in committing our co-religionists to follow us to this French homeland, if it has been able to reject us?" (my translation).[45]

In his semi-autobiography, Memmi (1953) reflected on how World War II, the Vichy regime, and the German occupation of Tunisia shaped his evolving sense of identity. He narrated that Vichy French soldiers targeted Tunisian Jewish communities, thus exposing the repression and hypocrisy of the colonial system. Alexander, the eponymous character, is subjected to a more systematic form of oppression and persecution in a Nazi labor camp in Tunisia. Close to half of the book's last part is dedicated to the description of his experiences in this camp. After the liberation of France, Benillouche decides to enlist in the Free French Forces of General de Gaulle but he is rejected because of his Jewish name.[46] He wonders, "If I rejected what I was becoming, would I be able to return to what I had been? . . . Perhaps, as I now straighten out this narrative, I can manage to see more clearly into my own darkness and to find a way out."[47] Memmi sees himself living in an internal darkness that reflects the colonial times, the oppressive decrees of Vichy, the Italo-German occupation of Tunisia, and its torturous labor camps.[48] Overall, Memmi's experience under the Vichy regime had a very deep impact on him; it made him feel "a sense of community" with "the Mohammedans" who were subject to the same derision and contempt[49] and made him question his belief in an egalitarian France and a West supposedly sympathetic to Jews, because, as he contends, "the West lies and is selfish."[50]

Hence, as Memmi's experience under the Vichy regime illustrates, the Gallicization trend started to gradually lose ground among the members of the Tunisian Jewish community. Before the war, French naturalization seemed to many young Tunisian Jews an ideal goal to be attained. According to Paul Sebag, 6,667 Tunisian Jews were naturalized French between 1924 and 1939. Between 1944 and 1955, while naturalization was facilitated in France, Sebag counted only 910 naturalizations.[51]

Disappointed by France, Tunisian Jews seemed to have looked elsewhere for better prospects of emancipation and better conditions of equal integration.[52] Some, comparing France's "betrayal" with the supporting attitude of the bey, believed that the development of Tunisian nationalism should now be considered.[53] For others, Zionism and religion came first in terms of belonging and self-identification.[54] Still others could identify themselves neither with nationalism, viewing it as mainly Islamist, nor with Zionism; they chose to adhere to leftist movements.

Leftist Movements: A Universalist Identity in a Fight for Freedom

The origin of the Communist Party in Tunisia goes back to the *Fedération Socialiste de Tunisie* (FST; Socialist Federation of Tunisia), which was established in 1908 under the initiative of Albert Cattan, a Tunisian doctor of Jewish origin.[55] In 1912, the FST was admitted to the *Section Française de l' Internationale Ouvrière* (SFIO).[56]

At the beginning of 1921, the FST experienced a split, which gave rise to two federations, one socialist and the other communist.[57]

Since the 1920s, Tunisian Jews had played an active role in the foundation of the Communist Front in Tunisia; Moise Zana, Joseph Uzan, Samuel Gozlan, and Maurice Abitbol were among the founders of the Fédération Communiste de Tunisie (CFT; Communist Federation of Tunisia) in 1921.[58] Victor Zana and Eugène Bessis[59] were among the three delegates that represented the Party in international communist meetings before the First World War. From WWII to Tunisia's independence in 1956, the party was led by the two Tunisian Jews Maurice Nizard[60] and Georges Adda[61] along with the two Muslims Ali Jrad and Mohamed Enafaa.[62] Many Tunisian Jews chose to document their communist activism in autobiographical form, as Guy Sitbon does in *Gagou*, where the protagonist decides to become a communist like his beloved uncle, Simon Temime.

Gagou becomes a communist because he aspires to melt into an inclusive universal ideology that embraces all religions and all nations of the world. He not only opens up to universal brotherhood, but also endeavors to achieve equality between the Tunisian and French peoples and to gain "bread, peace and liberty for everyone." He starts seeing Arabic "as a beautiful language" and Tunisian Muslims as his compatriots and comrades. Believing in the necessity of introducing them to communism, he forms a communist cell during his time in college, which many of his peers join. Religion is not a criterion of membership, only a belief in justice and equality for all. One of his Jewish friends, Vivi Bismuth, abandons Zionism, castigating the movement as "trivial," and joins Gagou in the "proletarian revolution."[63] Later, many Muslims join the cell, such as Mohammed Bechir and Hamadi Salah. Many Jews receive them with distrust; however, Gagou stands firm in his beliefs and asserts that "within the cell, there is no such a thing as religion or nationality, all the members are Bolsheviks."[64] In this context, one certainly could argue that Gagou's version of communism is heavily tinged with Tunisian nationalism. Gagou's strong attachment to Tunisia comes into tension with the idea of proletarian-communist revolution, which devalues national attachments in favor of class solidarity.

Gagou strongly believes in Tunisia as his homeland and wants to fight for its independence and bright, free future. In a conversation with his close Muslim friend Mohammed, Gagou seems very enthusiastic and optimistic about Tunisia's future. The whole conversation is worth citing, yet here I will cite only a small part that clearly reflects Gagou's ideological stance:

> MOHAMMED. Do you think that one day we will be independent? (Mohammed)
> GAGOU. Of course! If I did not believe in that, I would not have fought. We will be independent, and we will be socialist.
> MOHAMMED. When? Soon?
> GAGOU. I don't know. Two, three decades. Maybe less.
> MOHAMMED. And how about us?
> GAGOU. We would have fought for the future generations"(my translation).[65]

This conversation perfectly illustrates Gagou's enthusiastic belief in a unified Tunisia in which religion and race will not divide people. Similarly, in *Cristal*, Gilbert Naccache[66] describes his experience as a member of the Tunisian Left. Naccache was an active member of the group Perspectives Tunisiennes, also known as *Harakat al-'Amil al-Tounsi*, which was considered one of the main Tunisian opposition movements in the 1950s and 1960s.[67] He was persecuted and imprisoned because of his political activities within this group. In his autobiography,[68] Naccache states that "Some of my contemporaries have become Zionists and have disappeared from my horizon. Only communism was left for me, because I have never accepted the manifestations of racism of the French in Tunisia, the injustice that reigned . . . and the nationalist movement that often focused on Islam was hardly open to Jews."[69]

Michel-Ange Haïk,[70] who made his transition to communism through his early involvement in a railway workers' union and then a teachers' union, came to a similar observation, asserting that he "joined the Communist Party in 1945 when my friends had chosen Zionism. They sold their newspaper 'La Terre Retrouvée,' while we sold 'L'Avenir de la Tunisie.' I had Zionist friends, but it must be said that there was also an attraction to communism in the aftermath of the war, even if it sometimes took a fashionable effect. I followed a movement that I liked."[71]

As Haïk stated, several Tunisian Jews were attracted to Zionism, which first gained ground in Tunisia at the end of the nineteenth century.[72] It is important to note, however, that some Tunisian Jews who became part of the Zionist movement later decided to join the Communist Party. This was particularly the case with the leftist Zionist organization *Hashomer Hatzair* (The Young Guard; a secular Jewish youth movement founded in 1913 in Galicia, Austria-Hungary). The leaders of this organization were mostly interested in spreading their belief that the liberation of Jewish youth could only be accomplished by establishing a Jewish state in Palestine. The members of the Tunisian section, however, only became interested in anti-colonial and anti-imperialist action after the split that their movement experienced in the early 1930s. By 1934, members of Hashomer Hatzair with "progressive ideas" had joined the Tunisian Communist Party *en bloc*.[73]

The Communist Party was open to Tunisian women as well. Gladys Adda (1921–1995), wife of Georges Adda, was an active member of the Tunisian Communist Party and an ardent activist for independence and women's rights. In 1944, she was one of the co-founders of the Union of the Women of Tunisia (*Union des Femmes de Tunisie*, UFT), an organization associated with the local communist party. When trying to answer the question "Why the Communist Party?" Adda responded, "I hadn't read anything by Marx or Lenin yet, but I thought that the Communist Party was the only party that defended the weak, that fought against fascism, and that was important at that time."[74]

Similar thoughts were evoked by Béatrice Slama, who joined the Communist Party after earning her high school diploma from Lycée Armand-Fallières in Tunis in 1941.[75] Slama joined the party not only to stand against fascism, Nazism, and the German occupation of Tunisia but also to fight for women's rights and freedoms. After the war, Slama was one of the founders of a prominent feminist organization linked to the Communist Party known as the Union of Young Women in Tunisia (*Union des Jeunes Filles de Tunisie*). She led the organization from 1944 to 1948.[76] Describing her experience within the Communist Party and its impact on inter-religious relations in Tunisia (especially after the Allied victory in 1943 and the legalization of the Communist Party), Slama asserted that "invisible barriers between multiple groups were falling. . . . Slowly an organization was created in which Arabs, Jews, French, and Italians could be activists together."[77] To her, as to many of her co-religionists, the Communist Party represented a unique opportunity to be part of a larger national discourse, to develop a deep sense of national consciousness, to create a strong sense of unity with their Muslim compatriots, and to envision a clear path of career choices and professional outcomes.

For this segment of Tunisian Jewish intellectuals, communism was the tool that raised awareness of the national problem and motivated them to be active in the political battle for freedom and equality. Gagou states that "Communism is the end of racism. We are neither Jews nor Muslims nor French. We are above all Bolsheviks. . . . We are all revolutionary militants. Religion, states, and borders will disappear. Only the communist universe will remain where all the differences between men will be abolished. This is what we are fighting for."[78] The path followed by these Tunisian Jews clearly illustrates their willingness to transcend religious, cultural, and national boundaries and to identify themselves first as Tunisian and then as international citizens. The identity that these Tunisian Jews chose for themselves was an identity without stereotypes, social barriers, and religious divisions, an identity that was universal and shared by everyone.

Conclusion

After the establishment of the French protectorate in Tunisia, many Tunisian Jews embraced a new Gallicized identity and started identifying themselves as French. WWII, the defeat of France, and the subsequent Italo-German occupation of Tunisia left scars on those Tunisian Jews who previously identified themselves with the colonial powers. This created an introspective turn in the process of Tunisian Jews' identity formation, self-identification, and political orientation; it was a turn that signified a new relationship to the world based on a revaluation of the place of Jews in society and the acquisition of a new communal and universal sense of self. The rampant repercussions of WWII profoundly transformed the Tunisian Jewish community. The disillusionment and disappointment with Vichy France's betrayal of its long-preached values of democracy and equality led several Tunisian Jews, namely young French-educated Jews, to a search for new political models, including communism.

Communism represented an especially attractive option for Jewish youth in Tunisia. Its basic opposition to fascism and colonial racism attracted various young Tunisian Jews who refused to be included under the now-tainted umbrella of French assimilationism. For these young Jews who wanted to fight against the Vichy and

German anti-Jewish measures, to transcend colonial social hierarchies, and to abolish racial distinctions between indigenous peoples and Europeans, communism offered radical equality within an international framework.[79] It gave them the opportunity to identify themselves with international progressive forces, and provided them with an attractive "third space" in colonial cities, a space that was both European in orientation and inclusive in nature.[80]

Communism represented an oppositional current that rejected the premises of colonial assimilationism. It constituted a mediating ideology between local and global forces and a connecting force between the increasingly modern educated Jews of the 1930s and 1940s living in major colonial cities from Casablanca, Algiers, and Tunis, to Alexandria, Cairo, Beirut, and Baghdad and the worldwide struggle against racism and imperialism.[81] Additionally, the economic and social accomplishments of the Soviet Union presented for many young Tunisian Jews a viable model for resolving pressing problems at home and in Europe.[82]

It is often argued that North Africa and the Middle East have often been peripheralized in World War II scholarship and the study of global communism.[83] Through the examination and contextualized analysis of several Tunisian autobiographical and historical narratives, I attempt to reposition the narrative about North Africa and the Middle East by bringing it to the forefront of the broader landscape of regional politics, World War II, and global communism. This contextualized repositioning, I believe, will contribute to a richer understanding of the region, its politics, and its history.

NOTES

1. An international Jewish organization founded in 1860 in France to protect the rights of Jews around the world. It supports the principles of Jewish self-defense and self-sufficiency through education and professional development. It is known for establishing several French-language schools aimed at promoting French language and culture among Jews.

2. It is important to note here that being regarded as the protector and emancipator of Jews was an essential part of France's "divide and conquer" policy; French colonialist authorities endowed Jewish minority groups with certain privileges (such as easier access to French citizenship) that were denied to the majority Muslim population. It is also of equal importance to point out that not all Tunisian Jewish communities unconditionally embraced these "privileges"; there was a diversity of responses among these communities—some of them chose to embrace France while others chose not to be a part of France's Gallicizing colonialist project, namely the Jewish community of Djerba. These diverse responses might have been for different reasons than the French authorities imagined.

3. This echoes, in many ways, the experience of Moroccan Jews during the interwar period and following the Vichy period (1940–1942 in Morocco). For more information, see Alma Heckman, "Fissures and Fusions: Moroccan Jewish Communists Before, During, and After WWII," in *The Holocaust and North Africa*, ed. Aomar Boum and Sarah Stein (Stanford: Stanford University Press, 2019), 185–204.

4. Guy Sitbon, *Gagou* (Paris: Grasset, 1980), 83.

5. Albert Memmi, *La Statue de sel* (Paris: Gallimard, 1953).

6. See Zvi Zohar, "Sephardic Rabbinic Response to Modernity: Some Central Characteristics," in *Jews Among Muslims: Communities in the Pre-Colonial Middle East*, ed. Shlomo Deshen and Walter Zenner (New York: New York University Press, 1996), 64–80; Norman Stillman, *Sephardi Religious Responses to Modernity* (Australia: Harwood Academic Publishers, 1995).

7. Edith Haddad Shaked, "On the State of Being (Jewish) Between 'Orient' and 'Occident,'" in *Jewish Locations: Traversing Racialized Landscapes*, ed. Bat-Ami Bar On and Lisa Tessman (Lanham: Rowman & Littlefield, 2001), 185–199.

8. It is important to note that French laws aimed at emancipating Jews were not completely new to the Tunisian sociopolitical scene. The Tunisian bey had tried to implement the *Tanzimat* policies in Tunisia, such as the *Hatt-ı Hümayun of* 1856, which promised full legal equality for citizens of all religions, and the Nationality Law of 1869 aimed at creating a common Ottoman citizenship irrespective of religious or ethnic divisions. The existence of these reforms proves that the emancipatory values brought about by colonial French authorities did not represent a new start but rather the formalization of preexisting trends and policies.

9. During this period, Tunisian Jews also used situational code-switching and alternated between Judeo-Arabic and French. This was also dependent on social class; more educated and wealthier Jews were more likely to use French in their discourse.

10. Paul Sebag, *Histoire des Juifs de Tunisie* (Paris: L'Harmattan, 1992), 146–147.

11. Sebag, *Histoire des Juifs de Tunisie*, 260–261.

12. Sebag, *Histoire des Juifs de Tunisie*, 260.

13. It is important to note that many, if not most, remained very poor for a long time. The economic situation of Tunisian Jews was not homogeneous. There were clear class divisions among the Jewish communities of Tunisia, especially between the bourgeois community, which had access to better education and consequently better jobs, and poor communities that did not have equal educational and professional opportunities.

14. These changing identities mirrored the changes that were taking effect on the Tunisian sociopolitical scene at that time; the emerging main political trends (Gallicism, socialism, communism, nationalism, and Zionism) were themselves evolving and taking shape at the same time.

15. As with their reaction to modernity, Tunisian Jewish communities and their leaders were not unified in their attitude toward French claims of Jewish emancipation and liberation. The leaders of the community of Djerba in particular were skeptical of these claims and chose to distance their community members from the Gallicizing current and the influence of Alliance schools.

16. Haim Saadoun, "Tunisia," in *The Jews of the Middle East and North Africa in Modern Times*, ed. Reeva Simon, Michael Laskier, and Sara Reguer (New York: Columbia University Press, 2003), 49–64. For more information on Muslim-Jewish relations in Tunisia, please refer to Abdelkrim Allagui, *Al Aqaliyya al Yahoudiyya bi Tunis min Intisab al Himaya ila Sanat* (Tunis: Faculté des Sciences Humaines et Sociales de Tunis: 1992); Abdelkrim Allagui, *Juifs et musulmans en Tunisie. Des origines à nos jours* (Paris: Tallandier, 2016); Fayçal Cherif, "Jewish-Muslim Relations in Tunisia During World War II: Propaganda, Stereotypes, and Attitudes, 1939–1943," in *Jewish Culture and Society in North Africa*, ed. Emily Gottreich and Daniel Schroeter (Bloomington: Indiana University Press, 2011), 305–320; Sonia Fellous, *Juifs et musulmans en Tunisie: Fraternité et déchirements*, Actes du colloque Les relations judéo-musulmanes en Tunisie du Moyen Âge à nos jours: Regards croisés (Paris: Somogy, 2003).

17. Saadoun, "Tunisia," 447.

18. Mardochée Smadja was born in Tunis in 1864. His grandfather was chief rabbi of Tunisia from 1898 to 1900. He studied at an Alliance school in Tunis.

19. Habibi Kazdaghli, "La Justice (Tunis)," in *Encyclopedia of Jews in the Islamic World*, ed. Norman Stillman (Boston: Brill, 2010).

20. Claude Nataf, "Les mutations du judaïsme tunisien après la Second Guerre mondiale," *Archives Juives* 39, no. 3 (2006): 125–136.

21. Nataf, "Les mutations," 129.

22. Kazdaghli, "La Justice (Tunis)."

23. Jewish families who migrated from Tuscany (Livorno) in the seventeenth century to settle in Tunisia. They were called *Granas* in Arabic and *Gorneyim* (גורנים) in Hebrew.

24. The groups eligible for naturalization included

- –Graduates of various schools and colleges such as Sadiki College, Émile-Loubet Professional School, teacher training colleges, and holders of the Arab higher certificate;
- –veterans of the First World War or those with a dead son or three surviving sons who had served with the French army;
- –Individuals who had worked for ten years in the French public administration or in a French company;
- –Individuals with at least five children enrolled in French schools; and
- –Individuals deemed to have "rendered important services to the interest of France."

See Jacob Hurewitz, *The Middle East and North Africa in World Politics* (New Haven: Yale University Press, 1979), 270–271.

25. Daniel Goldstein, *Libération ou annexion. Aux chemins croisés de l'histoire tunisienne* (Tunis: Maison Tunisienne de l'Edition, 1978), 486.

26. Goldstein, *Libération ou annexion.*

27. Claude Tapia, "Ruptures et continuités culturelles, idéologiques chez les Juifs d'origine tunisienne en France," in *Juifs et musulmans de Tunisie. Fraternité et déchirements*, ed. Sonia Fellous (Paris: Somogy éditions d'art, 2003), 78.

28. Tapia, "Rupture et continuités."

29. Guy Sitbon, né Isaac Shetboun, is a journalist and writer who was born in Monastir, Tunisia, on January 9, 1934.

30. Sitbon, *Gagou*, 13.

31. Albert Camus wrote the preface to Memmi's *Statue de sel*, which was first published in 1953 and was awarded the Fénéon Prize in 1954.

32. Gagou's decision to adhere to communism is influenced by readings such as the Manifesto of the Communist Party, but mainly by his uncle, Simon Témime, who is the deputy secretary general of the Tunisian Communist Party.

33. Such as the Statute on Jews, a series of anti-Jewish laws enacted by the Vichy regime in France between 1940 and 1941. These laws affected metropolitan France as well as its overseas territories and were aimed at denaturalizing Jews and depriving them of the right to hold public office, designating them as a lower class, and depriving them of citizenship.

34. Nataf, "Les mutations," 126.

35. Nataf, "Les mutations," 125.

36. Nataf, "Les mutations," 130.

37. Bey of Tunis between June 19, 1942, and May 14, 1943.

38. Robert Satloff, *Among the Righteous* (New York: Public Affairs, 2006), 120.

39. Satloff, *Among the Righteous.*

40. Satloff, *Among the Righteous*, 121.

41. For instance, Albert Bessis, one of the Jewish community's notables, participated at the end of the war in the committee formed for the return of Moncef Bey, who was dethroned by the French colonial authorities. After Moncef Bey's death, Albert Bessis declared his allegiance to Lamine Bey, who made him one of his trusted consultants (Nataf, "Les mutations," 130). Other Tunisian Jews chose to take part in the Destour nationalist party by actively participating in its preliminary meetings, discussions, and important decisions (see Habib Kazdaghli, "L'engagement des juifs tunisiens dans l'anticolonialisme 1919–1956," in *Histoire communautaire, histoire plurielle: La communauté juive de Tunisie* [Tunis: Centre de publication universitaire, 1999], 217).

42. Nataf, "Les mutations," 126.

43. Nataf, "Les mutations."

44. Nataf, "Les mutations."

45. Paul Ghez, *Le Petit Matin* (June 15, 1947), quoted in Nataf, "Les mutations," 130.

46. What is interesting in this particular case is that Alexander actually volunteers and registers—he could have been exempted but wants to feel part of the Tunisian Jewish proletarian community, and he ends up leading religious services.

47. Albert Memmi, *Pillar of Salt*, trans. by Edouard Roditi (Lexington: Plunkett Lake Press, 2013), x.
48. Alexander also has the tragic experience of seeking protection from his former French mentor and being rejected.
49. Memmi, *Pillar of Salt*, x.
50. Memmi, *Pillar of Salt*, 335.
51. Sebag, *Histoire des Juifs de Tunisie*, 183.
52. This was the case for many Gallicized Tunisian Jews, but not for all of them; many were inclined to view the interwar period as a brief aberration in the story of the "true France" and still maintained an ardent Gallicism.
53. This chapter focuses on Jewish involvement in communism. For more information about Jewish involvement in Tunisian nationalism and Zionism, please see Nataf, "Les mutations"; Habib Kazdaghli, "L'engagement des juifs tunisiens"; Abdelwahab Meddeb and Benjamin Stora, *A History of Jewish-Muslim Relations* (Princeton: Princeton University Press, 2013).
54. Zionism was established as a political organization in 1897 under Theodor Herzl. However, not until the Balfour Declaration (1917), the San Remo Conference (1920), and the Allied Victory in North Africa (1943) did Zionism start to arouse widespread enthusiasm among North African Jews.
55. Albert Cattan was born in Tunis in March 1875. He came from a Jewish family of Algerian origin. He studied medicine in Lyon, where he was among the founders of a socialist student group (Kazdaghli, "L'engagement des juifs tunisiens," 224).
56. For more information on Tunisian Jews' involvement in socialism, see Élie Cohen-Hadria, *Du protectorat français à l'indépendance tunisienne : Souvenis d'un témoin socialiste* (Nice: Centre de la Méditerranée Moderne et Contemporaine, 1976).
57. Kazdaghli, "L'engagement des juifs tunisiens," 224.
58. Kazdaghli, "L'engagement des juifs tunisiens," 227.
59. Eugène Bessis (1871–1951) became a unionist in 1930; that same year he joined the Communist Party and in 1934 he became part of its underground leadership (Habibi Kazdaghli, "Bessis, Eugène," in *Encyclopedia of Jews in the Islamic World*).
60. Maurice Nizard was born in La Goulette on March 31, 1914. He studied law. He left for France in 1943 and returned to Tunisia in 1939 when he joined the underground leadership of the Tunisian Communist Party. In 1941, the Vichy government condemned Nizard to death, but he evaded arrest by going underground. After Tunisia achieved independence in 1956, Nizard earned a degree in Arabic. He left Tunisia in 1968. He earned a teaching degree in law in 1971 and became director of education at the Université Sorbonne Paris Nord (Habibi Kazdaghli, "Nizard, Maurice," in *Encyclopedia of Jews in the Islamic World*).
61. Georges Adda (b. 1916 in Tunis, d. 2008 in Tunis) was an activist and a former leader of the Tunisian Communist Party. Adda was a member of the Communist Party executive until 1957. After that, he remained a communist militant but without party responsibilities. He was married to Gladys Adda, who was also an active member of the Communist Party (Habibi Kazdaghli, "Adda, Georges," in *Encyclopedia of Jews in the Islamic World*).
62. Kazdaghli, "L'engagement des juifs tunisiens," 227.
63. Sitbon, *Gagou*, 81.
64. Sitbon, *Gagou*,.83
65. Sitbon, *Gagou*, 116.
66. Gilbert Naccache was a Tunisian writer of Jewish origin who was born January 15, 1939, in Tunis. He studied at the National Agronomic Institute in Paris. When he returned to Tunisia, he worked at the Ministry of Agriculture as an agricultural engineer from 1962 to 1968. He was active within the Tunisian Communist Party before being excluded in 1958, with the majority of the members of the communist cell of Paris, for "Trotskyist deviation" (Kazdaghli, "L'engagement des juifs tunisiens," 228).
67. The movement was founded in 1963 in Paris by an elite group of Marxist and nationalist intellectuals and students after the Communist Party of Tunisia was banned.

68. Naccache published *Cristal* in 1982, with Salammbô Editions. The book is entitled *Cristal* because he wrote it in prison on cigarette packaging of the Cristal brand.

69. Gilbert Naccache, *Cristal* (Tunis: Salammbô, 1982), 142. My translation.

70. Michel-Ange Haïk was born in Tunis in 1923. He studied at an Alliance school, then at Lycée Carnot from 1935 to 1942. He became a teacher at the same Alliance school where he studied. He came from a small bourgeois Tunisian Jewish family in the *Sidi Bahri* neighborhood. M. A. Haïk has been living in France since 1966 (Kazdaghli, "L'engagement des juifs tunisiens," 227).

71. Quoted in Kazdaghli, "L'engagement des juifs tunisiens," 229 (my translation).

72. Saadoun, "Tunisia," 451.

73. Kazdaghli, "L'engagement des juifs tunisiens," 228.

74. Quoted in Kazdaghli, "L'Engagement Des Juifs Tunisiens," 230. My translation.

75. Béatrice Slama, (née Saada) was born in Tunis in 1923 to a wealthy Livornese family from the southern Tunisian town of Gabès. Slama left Tunisia for Paris in 1965 and died in 2018 (Kazdaghli, "L'engagement des juifs tunisiens," 229).

76. Habibi Kazdaghli, "Slama, Béatrice," in *Encyclopedia of Jews in the Islamic World*).

77. Habibi Kazdaghli, "Slama, Béatrice," in *Encyclopedia of Jews in the Islamic World*).

78. Sitbon, *Gagou*, 83 (my translation).

79. Robert Watson, "Between Liberation(s) and Occupation(s): Reconsidering the Emergence of Maghrebi Jewish Communism, 1942–1945," *Journal of Modern Jewish Studies* 13, no. 3 (2014), 381.

80. Sebag, *Histoire des Juifs de Tunisie*, 245–246.

81. Orit Bashkin, *New Babylonians* (Palo Alto: Stanford University Press, 2012), 141–182; Joel Beinin, *Dispersion of Egyptian Jewry: Culture, Politics, and the Formation of a Modern Diaspora* (Berkeley: University of California Press, 1998), 142.

82. Watson, "Between Liberation(s) and Occupation(s)," 383.

83. Heckman, "Fissures and Fusions," 185.

CHAPTER 4

Communist Jews and Egypt's Struggle for National Liberation

Rami Ginat

The origins of the Jewish community in Egypt predated the Babylonian Exile. It continued to exist for many years, and a tiny group still lives there today. Egyptian Jews were a heterogenous ethnic and religious minority. The disintegration and dispersion of the deeply rooted Egyptian Jewish community began with the formation of the State of Israel and gathered momentum thereafter with the exacerbation of the Arab-Israeli conflict. The size, status, and position of the community were not static and fluctuated throughout history. The number of Jews in the 1940s was estimated at 75,000–80,000.[1] Following the Six-Day War, the number continued to decrease, and by late 1968 only 1,000 remained.[2]

Numerous studies have dealt with the Egyptian Jewish community of the first half of the twentieth century—the period under discussion—concentrating on issues related to the ethnically and culturally heterogeneous Jewish community, including its patterns and ways of life; its ethno-national identity; its internal diversity and its openness to local and external cultural influences, Egyptian, Middle Eastern, and European; its interrelations with and attitude to Zionism; and its position toward the Arab-Israeli conflict throughout its various historical phases. The existence or nonexistence of antisemitism in Egypt and the gradual dispersion of the Egyptian Jewish community around the globe have been additional focal points of such works.[3] Nonetheless, only few studies refer to the substantial role played by Egyptian Jews in the emergence and development of communism in Egypt.[4]

Ever since its formation in the early 1900s, Egyptian organized communism was characterized by the existence of splinter and rival groups as well as ephemeral unifications between various organizations. Jews featured prominently in the various communist groups, particularly in those of the 1930s and 1940s. Along with the Jewish communists, the members included Egyptian Muslims and Christians, Greeks, Armenians, Britons, Russians, and others. Egyptian society was characterized by being cosmopolitan and, like many Jews in Egypt, Jewish communists were sophisticated and moved in international circles. Many of them studied in foreign schools (such as the French lycées) and spoke several languages. Like many other young Jews worldwide they were attracted to communism as they perceived it as a secular and modern doctrine that would facilitate their integration within society irrespective of religious, ethnic, or socioeconomic origins. Furthermore, it offered a proper and thorough solution to their complex identity. The contribution of Jews to the development of Egyptian communism was not exceptional—Jews were also involved in the rise of communism in other Middle Eastern and North African countries. Moreover, Jews featured prominently in the international socialist movement during the periods of the First, Second, and Third Internationals (Karl Marx, Rosa Luxemburg, Edward Bernstein, Leon Trotsky, and many others). Our discussion of the participation of Jewish communists in Egypt's struggle for national liberation may add another dimension to a broader discussion on the motives of Jewish communists for such involvement in other parts of the Middle East.[5]

The heterogenous Jewish community in Egypt increased significantly following the British occupation (1882) as they perceived that country as "a land of opportunity" (not necessarily in materialist terms), adding another social layer to the existing homegrown Karaite and Mizrahi/Sephardi communities who had lived in Egypt for centuries. For instance, Ashkenazi Jews arrived from Eastern Europe as a result of the waves of antisemitic pogroms and persecutions they experienced following the assassination of Czar Alexander II in 1881. Some other Jews (Ashkenazi and Sephardi) who were expelled by the Ottomans from Palestine during World War I also settled in Egypt. The first waves of Jewish communists arrived in Egypt from Eastern Europe in the early twentieth century.

In my definition of the terms "Jewish" and "Egyptian," I avoid the essentializing notions of a history written from a national(ist) perspective. I therefore choose to employ the approach of transnational history, which "seeks to understand ideas, things, people, and practices which have crossed national boundaries"[6]—that is, to study the relationship that exists between the nation and those factors that go beyond it. I therefore consider anyone who was of Jewish origin as "Jewish," and anyone who lived in Egypt and regarded the country as his/her homeland as "Egyptian." The purpose of this chapter is to examine the role and contribution of Egyptian Jewish communists, who were active within a variety of communist organizations, to their country's struggle for liberation during the monarchy (1922–1952). As noted, these Jewish communists were part of a minority community and together with comrades from other minority groups they featured prominently in radical Egyptian communist movements.

In their search for identity, many of these Jews adopted the most extreme nationalist view prevalent at the time—an extreme form of the secular type of Egyptian territorial nationalism. In the immediate context in which they acted, they regarded themselves primarily as Egyptian nationalists, but in their long-term perception, their commitment to internationalism was unequivocal. In this regard, their actions may align with Marxist theories, which emphasize the role of class and social struggle in shaping political identity. These ideas can also be interpreted through Émile Durkheim's sociological framework, which—though non-Marxist—helps explain how collective identities contribute to social cohesion and integration, particularly in times of political transformation.[7] This framework connects to early modernization theory, particularly as articulated by Clifford Geertz, who emphasized the role of emerging collective identities in the formation of modern nation-states. Geertz's formulation suggests that the development of such identities would eventually lead to the creation of new states, ultimately supplanting premodern affiliations. In addition, the broader societal implications of minority group involvement in national liberation movements will be examined.[8] Building on these theoretical perspective, I argue that Egyptian Jewish communists—as a politically engaged minority—embody Richard Martin's claim that "minorities often play a role in the social change of the larger society. For instance, they may serve as an irritant that provokes social change, and they may provoke or may be provoked into clashes with the dominant culture, causing social dissatisfaction and unrest."[9] Seen in this light, their participation can be understood not only as a pursuit of identity or ideology, but also as a catalyst for structural transformation within Egyptian society during a period of nationalist upheaval.

The Emergence of Organized Communism

The Egyptian Left emerged in the early twentieth century and ever since then it was numerically small. However, its contribution to the political and mainly social development of Egypt was significant. The Egyptian Left encompassed a wide spectrum of ideological currents—social democrats, Fabianists, Marxists, Trotskyites, internationalist communists, Marxist nationalists, and others. The communist movements constituted a key component of the Egyptian Left in the first half of the twentieth century. Nevertheless, the Egyptian communists were divided over the issue of internationalism *versus* nationalism—that is, some were fully committed to the international communist movement and some wished to nationalize socialism and communism and to accommodate them to Egypt's special conditions and circumstances.

The intellectual forerunners of socialist thought in Egypt were both Egyptians and Arab immigrants from the Fertile Crescent who settled in Egypt at the outset of the twentieth century. Among them were Shibli Shumayyil (1850–1917) and Niqula al-Haddad (1878–1954). The former, who was a firm believer in science and socialism, envisaged a universal society built on harmony among nations inspired by science. Shumayyil laid the foundation for a new school of socialism that despite its lack of immediate success had long-term repercussions. Among his disciples were Salama Musa, Mustafa Hasanain al-Mansuri, and Niqula al-Haddad. The latter developed Shumayyil's ideas, presenting socialist theory in a logical and simple manner.[10] However, the foundations of Egyptian organized communism were laid shortly after the Bolshevik Revolution in Russia in 1917. Many of the founders were foreigners of European origin who were archetypal cosmopolitans, yet among them were also Egyptians.[11]

The most prominent of these was Joseph Rosenthal (1872–1966), the founding father of Egyptian organized communism. Rosenthal maintained strong transnational ties. His admiration for Marxist-Leninist doctrine made him enthusiastic to import, implant, develop, and execute such revolutionary ideas in his new homeland. He wanted to see Egypt go through a social revolution and subsequently be inextricably bound up with Soviet Russia, the homeland of communism.

Rosenthal's background prior to his arrival in Egypt is of great interest. He was born in 1872 in Safed, a city in Ottoman Palestine, to an Orthodox Jewish family. He received his primary education in a *shtiebel*—a traditional religious Jewish framework. He kept his traditional religious practices until his early teenage years. However, a sharp turn took place in Rosenthal's life when he discovered that his late father, David, had held a progressive worldview and was drawn toward Enlightenment ideas. In his late teenage years, Rosenthal moved from Palestine to Beirut to live with his older sister. It was there that he was exposed to socialist and Marxist ideas. In fact, he was an autodidact as far as his secular education was concerned.

The first Marxist literature—a summary of *The Communist Manifesto*, written in Yiddish, and an abbreviated version of Karl Marx's *Capital* (1887)—was given to him in Beirut by a Londoner, who claimed to have links to a Jewish worker organization. Rosenthal embarked on a long journey of research on social affairs. He also established links with British labor activists. His jewelry shop in Beirut gradually became a central place for political discussions on world affairs and modern ideas. It attracted the attention of Jewish students from Palestine, who studied at the American University of Beirut. Among his clients were also vicars, the son of the Beirut Mufti, Greeks, Jews, and others. The Ottoman authorities in Beirut, who noticed his activities, were not happy with the atheist and progressive content of the debates in his shop—Beirut was no longer a safe place for him. In 1897 he immigrated with his family to Egypt and settled in Alexandria, where he soon joined an ideological circle of anarchists and socialists, many of whom were Italians and a few of whom were Jews; some held radical revolutionary views, whereas others were social democrats. Unlike his peers, who called for change in their own homelands and showed no interest in Egypt, Rosenthal called for radical social change in Egypt.[12]

Rosenthal's earlier activities coincided with the emergence of modern Egyptian nationalism represented by two political parties. The first, the National Party (*al-Hizb al-Watani*) was founded by Mustafa Kamil (1874–1908), was depicted by Gershoni and Jankowski as "a passionate exponent of Egyptian territorial patriotism and a vehement opponent of the British occupation"; yet at the same time it preached solidarity with the Ottoman Empire, which Kamil believed would help to terminate the British occupation and subsequently lead to Egypt's liberation. Although the party was established in 1907 shortly before Mustafa Kamil's untimely death, his intellectual activities took place about a decade earlier in the form of publications in a variety of forums, mainly his journal *al-Liwa'*. Kamil's zeal for independence and anti-imperialist struggle impacted generations of Egyptian nationalists and culminated in the 1952 July Revolution. The second was the Party of the Nation (*Hizb al-Umma*), led by Ahmad Lutfi al-Sayyid, the iconic Egyptian liberal nationalist, who edited its newspaper *al-Jarida*, a forum where he expressed his opposition to political ties with the Ottoman Empire and advocated for Egyptian territorial nationalism—a territory of which Sudan was seen as an integral part.[13]

Kamil, the young and popular nationalist leader of the 1900s who led the anti-British struggle for liberation, appealed to Rosenthal and raised his hopes that the former might also be the ideal popular figure to advance a social platform. Rosenthal established contacts with Kamil and moved to Cairo to support his anti-British struggle. Yet, to Rosenthal's resentment, he soon realized that Kamil showed no interest in social change and concentrated his political zeal on Egypt's national liberation.[14]

Jewish Communists and the National Question: The Interwar Period

Egypt was formally part of the Ottoman Empire until 1914. Its formal status did not change even after the British occupation of 1882. In the wake of the outbreak of World War I in 1914, Egypt became a British protectorate, which lasted until 1922. After the end of the war in 1918, the Egyptian national movement, led by the *Wafd* Party, took pains to advance Egypt's route to independence. The British rejection of Egypt's national demands intensified the anti-British struggle for independence, culminating in the national revolt of March 1919—a popular uprising that took the British by surprise. Consequently, Britain arrived at the conclusion that the protectorate should be discontinued. Following the collapse of negotiations with the nationalist movement led by Sa'd Zaghlul, the British decided unilaterally to end their protectorate and to grant Egypt independence in February 1922. However, the nature of this independence did not meet the nationalists' demands—Britain continued to dominate Egypt's economy and defense and foreign policy. Under the new constitution of 1923 Egypt became a constitutional monarchy and in 1924 its first parliament was elected in free elections. The parliamentary game was nevertheless unfair since the king, who was granted supreme powers by the constitution, along with the British, the true master of Egypt, thwarted the activities of the government and the parliament whenever their interests clashed. Consequently, the period 1924–1939 witnessed growing social and political discontent, even after the conclusion of the Anglo-Egyptian treaty of 1936—a treaty designed to broaden Egypt's independence but still protect Britain's vast interests (and control) in Egypt.[15]

The first waves of organized communism in Egypt emerged in the late 1910s in two separate frameworks: the main one in Alexandria founded and led by Joseph Rosenthal and a smaller, less influential group in Cairo. The Cairo group was organized and led by A. Krauss, who belonged to a group of Jewish refugees of Russian and Eastern European origin who had fled to Egypt after the failed 1905 revolution in Russia. That group was short-lived, disbanded and reorganized twice for a short period of time before and after World War I. By the eve of the war, many of these Russians and Eastern Europeans activists had left Egypt, believing that advancing socialism there was unrealistic. A group of new recruits from among the Italian community joined Krauss, yet by the end of the war this small organization had dissolved. It was reestablished after the war with the participation of a group of exiled communist activists from Palestine, most of whom were Jews. Both the Alexandria and Cairo groups collaborated with a cluster of Egyptian socialist intellectuals—Muslims and Christians alike—including Salama Musa, 'Ali al-'Anani, and Muhammad 'Abdallah 'Anan. Together they founded the short-lived Egyptian Socialist Party (ESP) in August 1921.[16]

From its early days the ESP was split over the issue of the struggle for national liberation. The Alexandria section of internationalists (led by Husni al-'Urabi, the secretary general of the party, and Rosenthal) believed that Egypt's national struggle for independence should be dual, both political and social. The nationalists represented by the Cairo group of intellectuals (led by Salama Musa) believed that the party should concentrate on the struggle for national liberation and that social issues should be relegated to second place. Nevertheless, the party focused its main activity on social affairs, yet it also gave a full support to the Wafd and played an active role in the national movement for independence.

The Wafd (formed in 1918) was Egypt's most popular and influential political movement (it was abolished by the military regime in 1953). It led the 1919 anti-British uprising, which has been perceived by Egyptians as the 1919 Revolution. For several decades the Wafd spearheaded the anti-British struggle for national liberation. The young ESP, which could not compete with the mighty Wafd, had no choice but to declare its support for the latter in its struggle for independence. When the talks between the Egyptian delegation, headed by Prime Minister 'Adli Yakan, and the British government on the terms of ending the British protectorate opened in London in late 1921, the Wafd, headed by Sa'd Zaghlul, led stormy anti-British demonstrations attacking both the British and Yakan's delegations, portraying Yakan as a puppet manipulated by the British. The Wafd argued that Yakan had no mandate from the Egyptian people to conclude a deal with Britain. The demonstrations were followed by violent clashes between the Egyptian authorities and the demonstrators, culminating in Zaghlul's banishment to the Seychelles in December 1921. Both the ESP and *Confédération Générale du Travail* (CGT—the largest labor organization in Egypt at the time), which was founded and led by Rosenthal, were fully involved in the riots and expressed support for Zaghlul.[17] The ESP's support was welcomed by the Wafd. Makram 'Ubaid, a Wafd leader, was quoted as saying to Rosenthal, "we must do all we can to keep the fire of enthusiasm burning in the students, for Zaghlul must conduct the negotiations with Great Britain."[18]

The Egyptian Ministry of the Interior monitored the contacts between Wafd leaders and ESP leaders throughout 1921—a year that witnessed a marked escalation in the national struggle for liberation. For instance, it was reported that Mustafa al-Nahhas, a Wafd leader, visited Rosenthal on August 10, 1921. He showed

Rosenthal (in his capacity as president of the CGT) a paper that Zaghlul was going to publish before the elections.[19] A direct link existed between Zaghlul and Rosenthal, stated Muhammad Abu al-Ghar. He asserted that Zaghlul made it clear in his conversations with Rosenthal that his main interest was Egypt's struggle for liberation rather than social affairs. "The social aspects of the liberation were not clear enough to Zaghlul, but he appreciated Rosenthal and agreed with him," wrote Abu al-Ghar.[20] In light of the evidence, it can be said that an effective working relationship was maintained between the Wafd and the ESP at the time, when the Wafd needed the support of as many Egyptian opposition groups as possible.

Following its admission to the Comintern in December 1922, the ESP decided to change its name to the Egyptian Communist Party (ECP). The ECP was consequently compliant with the instructions and dictates of that institution. As noted, from its outset the ESP followed two parallel lines—the nationalist and the internationalist ones. The latter was dominated by Rosenthal and the Alexandria section (the cradle of organized Egyptian communism) and was in close touch with the Comintern as early as 1920. In fact, Rosenthal was the motive power behind the ESP's decision to join the Comintern. Consequently, he was held accountable by the nationalists for the dissolution of the ESP. Salama Musa, an eminent Egyptian (Christian) intellectual and founding member of the ESP, feared that the reorientation would have adverse implications for the Egyptian national movement. To quote Musa: "Our loyalty to Egypt must be stronger than our loyalty to socialism. Independence is our primary goal and socialism is secondary."[21] Musa attacked Rosenthal, whom he held responsible for the split within the ESP. He and his nationalist followers abandoned the ESP in the latter part of 1922.

To his resentment, Rosenthal was removed from the ECP by its central committee in December 1922 following an internal conspiracy concocted by his former allies within the ESP (Husni al-'Urabi in particular).[22] Nevertheless, even after his removal Rosenthal remained highly popular and admired by workers and left-wing circles. His political activities were severely interrupted in late 1924 by the Egyptian authorities. The government, led by the Wafd (January–November 1924) enjoyed broad popular support after winning the first free elections with an overwhelming majority of over 90 percent of the parliamentary seats. Once in power, the Wafd government was not enthusiastic about sharing the leadership of the national struggle with other political parties, let alone with the ECP. In its sociopolitical platform, the Wafd presented conservative views, and its leaders were anti-communist. As we have seen, in the years 1919–1923, while it was leading the anti-British struggle for independence and was therefore persecuted by the British, the Wafd did not hesitate to seek assistance from all political groups including the communists and the labor movement. The ECP's leaders obviously misinterpreted the Wafd's victory and were somehow inclined to believe that the new government would be more attentive to the workers' needs.[23]

Jewish communists were among the victims of the Wafd government's anti-communist campaign. On October 6, 1924, Avram Katz and Hillel Zandberg, senior members of the ECP, along with Husni al-'Urabi, the secretary general, were sentenced to three years in prison. Husni al-'Urabi was accused of playing a major role in linking the ECP with the Comintern, whereas Zandberg and Katz were held responsible for a series of workers' strikes that broke out in Alexandria in February and March 1924. However, they did not serve their prison terms, as they managed to escape to Moscow. Other Jewish communists, Samuel Zaslavsky and Grigorii Shoklender, were deported to the Soviet Union—the latter on November 11, 1924, and the former several months later. Joseph Rosenthal, who by then was not a member of the ECP, was also among those meant to be deported, but he was luckier as the authorities gave him a stark and foreboding choice: either drop politics or face deportation from Egypt. Rosenthal, who regarded Egypt as his homeland, chose the former.[24] Indeed, despite the fact that Rosenthal was forced to quit politics, many Egyptian nationalist figures still regarded him as the authentic representative of the Egyptian Left. While in opposition to Ahmad Ziwar's government (November 1924–June 1926), the Wafd (whose government had halted Rosenthal's political activities) took pains to rally all political opposition groups, in an effort to discredit the government's public support. At one point, the Egyptian press reported in amazement a surprise visit of Mustafa al-Nahhas to Joseph Rosenthal in Alexandria. Nahhas, who was soon to take over Zaghlul's position, maintained contacts with the Egyptian Left. The purpose of his meeting with Rosenthal was to ask the latter for his opinion on a manifest that the Wafd was going to publish. Unfortunately, there were no further references to the Nahhas-Rosenthal dialogue.[25]

There were other prominent Jewish figures with a left-wing orientation—although they were not communists—who supported the Wafd in its struggle for national liberation. Among them was Leon Castro, an affluent Jewish lawyer, who maintained close links with the Wafd. In wake of the 1919 national uprising, Castro set out on a publicity campaign in Europe to explain the nature of the events and to seek support for Egypt's struggle for liberation. He was the founder and editor of *La Liberté*, a pro-Wafd newspaper in French, a language used by educated circles within Egypt. *La Liberté*'s articles concentrated on issues related to state and society. Many dealt with the national question and the liberation of Egypt and others focused on social progressive ideas. The newspaper presented the Wafd leader as a moderate statesman working indefatigably to achieve his country's independence. It is noteworthy that in 1924, shortly after Sa'd Zaghlul formed the first Wafd government, he held talks in London with representatives of the British government on the future of Egypt; Castro was among his aides and acted as his translator during the negotiations.[26] In the late 1920s Castro founded *Les Essayistes*, a scientific-cultural society. It operated as an ideological umbrella consisting of liberals, democrats, and leftists that attracted many Jews, Italians, Greeks, and other foreigners as well as a small group of Egyptian intellectuals. The group's activities focused mainly on the struggle against fascism and antisemitism. One of its chief target audiences was the school network of the lycées, where there were many Jewish students. The importance and relevance of *Les Essayistes* to our discussion is that from this ideologically incohesive group emerged the Union of Peace

Supporters in 1934. It constituted the nucleus for the birth of a new generation of Egyptian communists—notably, *al-Fajr al-Jadid* (The New Dawn), which is discussed below.[27]

The late 1930s and early 1940s witnessed the appearance of several leftist groups that focused their activities on anti-fascism, anti-Nazism, and social affairs. Most of them supported the formation of a broad popular front to fight against fascism, in accordance with the doctrinaire line formulated by the Seventh Congress of the Comintern in 1935. The Comintern determined that it was the order of the day for all colonial and semi-colonial countries to form an anti-imperialist united front.[28] The communist organizations were called to lead the formation of such fronts. They should "engage the broad masses in a national liberation movement against growing imperialist exploitation."[29]

The Soviet Union and Egypt established diplomatic relations in August 1943. Until then the Soviet Union had refrained from maintaining diplomatic relations with ruling Arab elites, who were perceived as bourgeoisie with links to Western imperialism. Moreover, British imperialists controlled Egypt's foreign relations, and forging diplomatic relations with communist Russia was out of the question. However, in the period 1936–1939, there was a positive change in the Soviet attitude toward the Wafd, especially when the latter was in opposition. The Comintern advised the ECP to unite all anti-imperialist forces who were struggling for independence—including the "national bourgeoisie" and Wafd in particular. This fitted in with the Comintern's paradigm of a popular united front.[30]

The Comintern ideas were gradually disseminated to the Egyptian liberal educated classes, Muslims as well as non-Muslims, and a large number of people within the foreign communities, including many Jews, Italians, Greeks and Armenians, who were frustrated with the sociopolitical situation at the time. They were disappointed with the Wafd's failure to advance social reforms, in particular, with its inability to gain full independence for Egypt—for them, the 1936 treaty with Britain was a fiasco. They also perceived the alternative to the Wafd with mounting distress—particularly those doctrines suggested by the two strong extra-parliamentary movements the Muslim Brothers and Young Egypt (*Misr al-Fatat*), which were explicitly radical Islamic and radical nationalist, respectively. Their concern was amplified by the prevalent international circumstances, the rise of fascism and Nazism. They were looking for an alternative, and the communist formula of worldwide anti-fascist popular fronts as presented by the Seventh Congress of the Comintern appeared attractive to many of them.

The prevailing belief among many scholars is that the two movements *Misr al-Fatat* and (to a lesser extent) the Muslim Brothers, who attracted educated Egyptian youth, embraced fascist organizational practices and resembled European fascist organizations.[31] Israel Gershoni argues that the vast majority of Egyptian society totally rejected fascism and Nazism and draws a distinction between the Muslim Brothers and Misr al-Fatat, stressing that the latter was vocal and resembled a fascist movement in the period 1938–1939. It expressed admiration for Germany and Italy, seeing Nazism and fascism as role models to bring about the restoration of Egyptian society. The movement, Gershoni argues, took a virulent antisemitic line, asserting that the Jews took control of Egypt's economy and were stealing Arab Palestine. However, on the eve of World War II Misr al-Fatat aligned with the anti-fascist Egyptian consensus and its leader Ahmad Husain declared that Egypt should side with its British ally. As for the Muslim Brothers, Gershoni asserts that the movement took a passive and disinterested approach to the struggle between the liberal democracies and fascist and Nazi dictatorships. Nazism and fascism were also perceived as "Western," European, foreign, and furthermore "racist" and "imperialist."[32]

Indeed, these two right-wing groups tilted toward xenophobia and antisemitism and displayed sympathy for the anti-British fascist-Nazi alliance, yet they were not the Egyptian branch of that alliance. True, antisemitic expressions were voiced by these two movements, yet their bearers did so mainly because they confused Judaism with Zionism. Besides, those Jews who joined left-wing groups did not do so because they were anxious over the rise of Egyptian right-wing radicalism. In fact, this was not a significant factor in their decision to do so.[33]

Jewish Communists and the National Struggle for Liberation in the Post–World War II Years

The early 1940s witnessed the emergence of several communist organizations, the most important of which were the Egyptian Movement for National Liberation (EMNL; *al-Haraka al-Misriyya lil-tahrir al-Watani*), Iskra (*al-Sharara*—a spark, in Russian), The People's Liberation (*Munathamat tahrir al-Sha'b*), and The New Dawn (*al-Fajr al-Jadid*; FJ). The EMNL was established by Henri Curiel (1914–1978), an Egyptian Jew (Curiel's father Daniel was the second generation of the family in Egypt from Italy and his mother Zéphira was born in Istanbul), in 1943. Curiel's father was a well-to-do Jewish banker and big landowner. Henri Curiel received his basic and higher education at prestigious European institutions in Cairo, one of which was the Jesuit Primary School, which bestowed him with human values and a general worldview that led him at a later stage of his life to Marxism.[34] Like Rosenthal, Curiel was an influential Jewish communist leader who was caught between the nationalist and internationalist pincers.

Iskra was founded in 1942 by Hillel Schwartz (1923–2007), an Egyptian Jew of Eastern European origin (his father was born in Romania and his mother in Odessa). The People's Liberation was founded in 1940 by Marcel Israel, an Egyptian Jew holding Italian citizenship. Israel played a pivotal role in the emergence of the new Egyptian Left in the late 1930s and early 1940s. He was a founder of the short-lived Democratic Union (1938–1939), a Marxist-oriented organization that was the cradle of the EMNL, Iskra, and The People's Liberation.[35] The fourth group, FJ, was founded in the early 1940s by Ahmad Sadiq Sa'd, Yusuf Darwish, Raymond Duwayk, and Ahmad Rushdi Salih. The first three founders were Egyptian Jews.[36] Hillel Schwartz and Marcel Israel adhered to internationalism, albeit each with his own specific perspective on the issue. Sadiq Sa'd, Darwish, and Duwayk, on the other hand, were among the initiators of the new trend within the Egyptian Left—"Marxist nationalism," which was to become influential in the early 1960s following Nasser's shift to socialism.[37]

During World War II, the communists, who raised the banner of a broad antifascist front, condemned the British occupation. They formulated the slogan "against fascism . . . but not with the English" (*Didda al-Fashiyya . . . wa-lakinna laisa ma'a al-Ingiliz*).[38] Attempts by the Egyptian government to revise the 1936 treaty with Britain in the immediate post–World War II years were met by growing public discontent, particularly in February 1946 following the formation of a government led by the notorious politician Isma'il Sidqi. In the 1930s Sidqi headed an unpopular antidemocratic government that nearly ruined the foundations of Egypt's parliamentarism. His intention to reach a compromise agreement with the British in late 1946 was met by stern opposition. Mobilized by dissident political groups, the Egyptian masses took to the streets and held wild demonstrations.[39]

The first half of 1946 (February–July) witnessed a mounting wave of social and political discontent in Egypt both in the political arena and in civil society. The National Committee of Students and Workers (NCWS) emerged as a vocal and vital opposition to the government. This sociopolitical movement included members of the Wafdist Vanguard (*al-Tali'a al-Wafdiyya*), communist activists from the EMNL and Iskra, and students and workers, but no peasants. The NCWS, whose activities focused mainly on the cities, propagated a twofold struggle—the national and the social—and adopted the following goals: to eradicate all forms of colonialism; to eliminate its domestic allies who benefited from colonial rule (feudalists and capitalists); to unite all anticolonial forces within Egypt; and to establish contacts with international anti-imperialist movements.[40]

The NCWS achieved certain gains in its efforts to mobilize the anti-British struggle for national liberation. Many Egyptians took to the streets to take part in the demonstrations and strikes organized by the NCWS. Yet, like previous left-wing anti-establishment fronts, the NCWS too was an ephemeral experience. There were three main reasons for its disintegration: First, structurally it was unstable; second, it lacked a cohesive ideology; and third, its leadership was split and divided. Also, the anti-democratic measures taken by Isma'il Sidqi's government to stamp out all manifestations and activities of opposition proved temporarily efficient.[41] Although short-lived, the NCWS contributed a modified formula for collaboration between various leftist and nationalist political groups to the Egyptian political arena in the late 1940s. As we have seen, collaboration between left-wing frameworks and nationalist organizations, including the Wafd, did exist at earlier stages of the anti-British struggle in Egypt. However, unlike previous left-wing frameworks, the NCWS demonstrated that radical and progressive forces could play a leading role in the struggle for national liberation and take it out of the hands of the traditional nationalist parties, notably the Wafd.

At the time, the Wafd was ideologically divided between two main factions: the right-wing represented by the veteran and conservative generation, and the left-wing represented by the younger generation associated with the Wafdist Vanguard, a group that pursued a totally different sociopolitical agenda that in many ways may be perceived as closer to Marxist nationalism.[42] Indeed, at that stage, the three communist organizations—EMNL, Iskra, and FJ—had a noticeable impact on the development of the Wafdist Vanguard. That group became more influential in the post–World War II years, when Egyptian youth intensified their struggle for national liberation. The Wafdist Vanguard endeavored "to shift the Wafd's center toward the left acting as a pressure group within the Wafd . . . [it] provided the party with a revolutionary social and nationalist program, devoting considerable attention to the struggle for Egypt's national liberation. . . . The group expressed support for the USSR and other socialist powers and maintained that these powers could promote Egypt's interests internationally."[43]

Curiel, the EMNL leader, asserted that his movement was behind the formation of the NCWS and played a central role in the national unrest.[44] His assertion has been questioned by scholars.[45] Yet, it would be unfair to overlook the contribution of the EMNL to the radicalization of the Egyptian working class and to the bonds formed between the workers' struggle and that of the students in the broader struggle for national liberation. Also, the cooperation between Iskra and the EMNL, the two main communist organizations, during the anti-establishment social and political discontent of 1946, though not always efficient, was one of the factors leading to their historical decision to unite and form the Democratic Movement for National Liberation (DMNL) in 1947.

Jewish Communist, Zionism, and the Thorny Issue of Palestine

Since the formation of the Arab League in 1945, the Palestine question had occupied a central place in inter-Arab politics. It also became a central theme on Egypt's political agenda and political parties of all stripes displayed unquestionable support for the Arabs inhabiting Palestine in their escalating conflict with the Zionists over the future of that country in the post–World War II years. The communist movements led by Jews adopted a rigid anti-Zionist position. Indeed, opposition to Zionism was a central tenet of many Jewish communists. In this regard, they held a more radical view compared to mainstream Egyptian politics. They regarded the Zionist movement and its causes as a concrete threat that could irreversibly jeopardize the status and future of Egypt's heterogeneous Jewish community. The activity of the Zionist movement in Egypt was not a success story. True, Zionist activity had already commenced in the Nile Valley in the early twentieth century, yet it had made little headway. Until 1942–1943 it had a small social base. To quote Beinin, "most Egyptian Jews were relatively secure and comfortable during the 1930s, few saw the point of risking their position by ostentatious support for Zionism. Moreover, before 1948, the small minority of Jews who identified themselves as political Zionists rarely expressed this in the form of immigration to Palestine."[46]

It was Marcel Israel who in mid-1947 founded the Jewish Anti-Zionist League (*al-lajna al-Yahudiyya limukafahat al-Sahyuniyya*). Israel also formulated its doctrinal line. Its driving force, however, was Ezra Harari, a former Iskra member, in his capacity as the League's secretary. At that stage, EMNL, Iskra, and most of Marcel Israel's group joined forces and founded the Democratic Movement for National Liberation (DMNL)—by far the largest Egyptian communist organization. The League launched a publicity campaign in the Jewish community and identified its interests and goals with those of Egypt and its struggle for national liberation.[47]

The League was nevertheless disbanded in late 1947 by Nuqrashi Pasha, the then prime minister of Egypt. Nuqrashi ignored remonstrations made by Harari and members of the League, who regarded his steps as a pro-Zionist move.[48] It is noteworthy that the motives behind Nuqrashi's action remain obscure and debatable.[49] Moreover, shortly thereafter, communist Jews faced an uneasy dilemma following the decision of the Soviet Union to support the two-state solution in Palestine in November 1947, which was approved by the Zionists. This was a dramatic policy change given that until late 1947 the Soviets had supported a unitary binational state in Palestine—a policy that was in line with the Arab demand. All Egyptian communist organizations reluctantly endorsed the new Soviet policy toward Palestine. By doing so, they swam against the Arab nationalist current, a move that immediately had adverse effects on the communist movement in general and the Egyptian Jewish communists in particular.

With the outbreak of the 1948 Arab-Israeli War, the Egyptian authorities launched an anti-communist campaign, and by the end of 1948 most of the communist leaders and activists were in prison. The authorities unfoundedly established a link between Zionism and communism and questioned Jewish communists' loyalty to Egypt and the Arab nationalist cause. Soon after the 1948 war, most of the Jewish activists were expelled from Egypt, including the foremost leader Henri Curiel, who was forced to leave his homeland in 1950. He settled in France, where he remained in exile until his tragic death in 1978. In Paris he formed the Rome Group (*Majmu'at Ruma*), which included many exiled Egyptian Jewish communists. Majmu'at Ruma became the external branch of DMNL, assisting the latter in financial and ideological matters. The group also played an important role in advancing peace initiatives for settling the Arab-Israeli conflict in the 1950s.

In 1958 the main Egyptian communist organizations decided to unite by forming the United Egyptian Communist Party. One of the prerequisites for unity was the demand that DMNL cut its ties with Majmu'at Ruma—a condition that was fully implemented. Curiel's group was instructed by its Egyptian headquarters to disband. Curiel and his colleagues were displeased and disappointed by the DMNL's move. Nevertheless, they continued to support national liberation movements in other countries, such as the Algerian National Liberation Front (FLN) and also continued with their endeavors to help resolve the Arab-Israeli conflict.[50]

The Egyptian communist movements of the 1940s swam against the nationalist current on two key issues—Palestine and Sudan—and paid a heavy price for it. Their dissenting policy over Palestine, which endorsed the two-state solution, was later adopted by the political establishment in Egypt. The same applies to the communists' stand on the Sudan issue. In brief, the Sudan question, known as the doctrine of the unity of the Nile Valley (*wahdat wadi al-nil*), was a fundamental factor in forming Egypt's national identity under the monarchy. It was a consensual issue that united Egyptians of all political and nationalist stripes. They all viewed Sudan as an integral part of the Egyptian homeland, with one exception—the communists. Curiel's EMNL formulated a dissenting approach in the early 1940s. In contrast to the national consensus that demanded the unification of Egypt and Sudan under the Egyptian crown, the communists called for a common Sudanese-Egyptian struggle against British imperialism and for granting the Sudanese people their right to self-determination. In other words, they insisted that the Sudanese people alone should have the right to determine their future. Later, their stand was embraced and implemented by the ruling military elite (the Free Officers) that executed the July 1952 revolution.[51]

Ever since their emergence, organized communist groups had perceived themselves as the vanguard of the struggle against imperialism. They condemned the intention of the Egyptian government to negotiate with the British to modify the 1936 treaty in the post–World War II period.[52] Instead, they called for the termination of the 1936 treaty, a move they believed would enable the Egyptian government to negotiate with Britain as an equal and not from the inferior position stipulated by the treaty.[53] The concept of anti-British armed struggle, which the communist organizations of the 1940s worked tirelessly to promote, became a reality in late 1951.[54] The Anglo-Egyptian dispute intensified considerably under the Wafd government (1950–1952) and reached its pinnacle following the government's decision (in October 1951) to unilaterally abrogate the treaty of 1936. Domestically, this drastic move was to have far-reaching political repercussions as many Egyptians subsequently perceived the presence of British troops in the Suez Canal area as illegal. The severe deterioration in Anglo-Egyptian relations manifested itself in the outbreak of anti-British popular guerrilla warfare in the Suez Canal area with the participation of activists from various political groups—including communists, Muslim Brothers, and young nationalist students. Although in exile, Curiel, as noted, remained active in Egyptian communism and politics. He was pleased with the Egyptian government's decision to abrogate the 1936 treaty with Britain. He called on his Egyptian comrades to intensify the anti-British armed struggle and urged more communist volunteers to take an active part in it. Indeed, members of DMNL were active in the anti-British guerrilla warfare in the Suez Canal zone.[55]

The British forces responded harshly with excessive use of force and their military actions involved the occupation of the Suez Canal area. Anti-British rage and sentiment spread across Egypt. On January 26 the capital witnessed unprecedented anti-British riots, which the authorities failed to control. Mobs indiscriminately looted and burned businesses, entertainment establishments, banks, and anything they deemed Western or related to the British—these riots became known as the Cairo Fire. The following day the Wafd government was dismissed by King Farouk.[56]

Conclusion

Curiel's political senses were proven to be correct. The participation of DMNL's activists in the anti-British armed struggle and the contacts they made with members of the Free Officers movement, who "aided and abetted irregular units carrying out guerrilla activities,"[57] strengthened the trust and collaboration between the DMNL and the Free Officers movement that months later led the military coup of July 23, 1952. Through its military branch and printing unit, DMNL was directly embroiled in the preparation and implementation of the coup.

A great deal of the communists' intellectual and sociopolitical activities took place in theoretical forums through which they formulated, disseminated, and propagated a revolutionary platform. Many of their ideas slowly spread among Egyptian policymakers, who adopted and implemented them, though with some modifications and adjustments to accommodate the changing sociopolitical reality. For instance, the communist groups of the 1940s vehemently called upon the Egyptian government to embrace a policy of neutralism in the emerging Cold War and to develop and advance relations with the USSR. The Wafd government, dominated by Muhammad Salah al-Din, the foreign minister, who led the left-wing faction within the Wafd government (1950–1952), was the first to tighten relations with the Soviet Union and to pursue a neutralist policy in the inter-bloc dispute. Revolutionary Egypt led by Nasser followed suit.[58]

Jewish communists, along with their compatriots, had played a vital role in Egypt's anti-imperialist struggle before and after the July Revolution. Marcel Israel stated that he fought with the Egyptian nationalist movement against imperialism throughout his activity in Egypt. He did not feel foreign and was fully connected to Egypt and its people—he was proud to be Egyptian. However, the Egyptian political elite thought otherwise and expelled him and his Jewish comrades from their homeland. They had to watch reluctantly from their exile how Egypt's revolutionary regime successfully completed the prolonged anti-imperialist struggle that they were part of. During the early post-monarchical years, and despite the 1948 war and the formation of the State of Israel, a considerable number of Jews continued to live in Egypt (although not for long). However, only a few Jewish communists remained in that country at the time (such as the three founders of FJ, who converted to Islam for practical reasons). The vast majority were scattered across several continents. Several joined the local communist parties in their new countries (like Marcel Israel in Italy and a few activists in Israel); some, like Curiel's Rome Group, continued to be active in Paris, as noted earlier. Others like Hillel Schwartz (deported with his wife, who was also a communist, in 1953 after years in prison) abandoned their political activities and lost faith and interest in international communism.[59]

These communists Jews were altruistic idealists driven by universal, humanist revolutionary values that sought to challenge the established order. Though they formed a tiny minority, they understood the provisional nature of their leadership—devoting themselves to building frameworks for dissent and mentoring others who would continue their path. While their efforts were eventually curtailed by state repression and rival factions, they nonetheless contributed "unpretentiously and indirectly to many of the changes that Egypt underwent." [60]

Acknowledgments

I would like to thank the Israel Science Foundation (ISF) for their generous research grants (1001/12 and 4887), which helped me pursue this study. The chapter draws on my book *A History of Egyptian Communism: Jews and Their Compatriots in Quest of Revolution* (Boulder, CO: Lynne Rienner Publishers, 2011), and I would like to thank the publisher for allowing me to cite from the book.

NOTES

1. Based on data drawn from the American National Archives and presented by Selma Botman, *The Rise of Egyptian Communism, 1939–1970* (Syracuse: Syracuse University Press, 1988), 26–27.

2. Michael M. Laskier, *The Jews of Egypt, 1920–1970: In the Midst of Zionism, antisemitism, and the Middle East Conflict* (New York: New York University Press, 1992), 290.

3. See, for instance, pioneering and important studies by Laskier, *The Jews of Egypt* and "Egyptian Jewry Under the Nasser Regime, 1956–70," *Middle Eastern Studies* 31, no. 3 (July 1995): 573—619; Gudrun Krämer, *The Jews in Modern Egypt: 1914–1952* (London: I. B. Tauris, 1989); Joel Beinin, *The Dispersion of Egyptian Jewry: Culture, Politics, and the Formation of the Modern Diaspora* (Berkeley: University of California Press, 1998); Muhammad Abu al-Ghar, *Yahud Misr min al-Izdihar ila al-Shatat* (Cairo: Dar al-Hilal, 2004). On the Jews of Egypt in earlier periods, see, for instance, Jacob M. Landau, *Jews in Nineteenth-Century Egypt* (New York: New York University Press, 1969); Shimon Shamir, ed., *The Jews of Egypt: A Mediterranean Society in Modern Times* (Boulder: Westview Press, 1987); Shelomo Dov Goitein, *Jews and Arabs: Their Contacts Through the Ages* (New York: Schocken Books, 1964). On Jewish emigration to Egypt and the Egyptian Jewish community under Ottoman rule, see Stanford J. Shaw, *The Jews of the Ottoman Empire and the Turkish Republic* (New York: New York University Press, 1991), 33–35, 40, 55–56, 95, 101, 143, 158.

4. Beinin, *The Dispersion of Egyptian Jewry* and Abu al-Ghar, *Yahud Misr* discussed peripherally the subject of Jewish communists. See also a profound study on Jewish Egyptian communists in the period 1937–1964 by Irmgard Schrand, *Jews in Egypt: Communists and Citizens* (Hamburg: Lit, 2004).

5. See, for instance, Orit Bashkin, *New Babylonians: A History of Jews in Modern Iraq* (Stanford: Stanford University Press, 2012); Musa Budeiri, *The Palestine Communist Party, 1919–1948: Arab and Jew in the Struggle for Internationalism* (London: Ithaca Press, 1979); Alma R. Heckman, *The Sultan's Communists: Moroccan Jews and the Politics of Belonging* (Stanford: Stanford University Press, 2021).

6. Ann Curthoys and Marilyn Lake, eds., *Connected Worlds: History in Transnational Perspective* (Canberra: Australian National University Press, 2005), 5.

7. On Durkheim's theory, see, for instance, Leo Driedger, *The Ethnic Factor: Identity in Diversity* (Toronto: McGraw-Hill Ryerson, 1989), 17–22.

8. On Geertz's analysis, see Clifford Geertz, "The Integrative Revolution: Primordial Sentiments and Civil Politics in New States," in *The Interpretation of Cultures: Selected Essays* (New York: Basic Books, 1973), 255–310. A well-presented analysis of the approaches of Marx, Durkheim, and Geertz in the context of minorities in the Middle East may be found in Gabriel Ben-Dor, "Minorities in the Middle-East: Theory and Practice," in *Minorities and the State in the Arab World*, ed. Ofra Bengio and Gabriel Ben-Dor (Boulder: Lynne Rienner Publishers, 1999), 1–30.

9. Richard C. Martin, "From *Dhimmis* to Minorities: Shifting Constructions of the Non-Muslim Other from Early to Modern Islam," in *Nationalism and Minority Identities in Islamic Societies*, ed. Maya Shatzmiller (Montreal: McGill-Queen's University Press, 2005), 14.

10. Ginat, *A History of Egyptian Communism: Jews and Their Compatriots in Quest of Revolution* (Boulder: Lynne Reinner Publishers), 9–14.

11. To name a few: Joseph Rosenthal, Avigdor (Yehiel Kossoy), Sholom Polak, Charlotte Rosenthal (Jews); Sakellaris Yanakakis, Alexandra Pierride (Greeks); Husni al-'Urabi, Muhammad Sharif, M. Mahmud Ibrahim (Egyptians).

12. Ginat, *A History of Egyptian Communism*, 28–30.

13. Israel Gershoni and James Jankowski, *Egypt, Islam and the Arabs: The Search for Egyptian Nationhood, 1900–1930* (Oxford: Oxford University Press, 1987), 6–10. See also Rami Ginat, *Egypt and the Struggle for Power in Sudan: From World War II to Nasserism* (Cambridge, UK: Cambridge University Press, 2017), 36, 41.

14. Ginat, *A History of Egyptian Communism*, 30.

15. On various aspects of the history of monarchical Egypt, see, for instance, Arthur Goldschmidt, Amy J. Johnson, and Barak A. Salmoni, eds., *Re-Envisioning Egypt: 1919–1952* (Cairo: The American University in Cairo Press, 2005); Robert Tignor, *Egypt: A Short History* (Princeton: Princeton University Press, 2010), 228–255; P. J. Vatikiotis, *The History of Modern Egypt: From Muhammad Ali to Mubarak* (London: Weidenfeld & Nicolson, 1991), 249–374; Botman, *Egypt from Independence to Revolution, 1919–1952* (Syracuse: Syracuse University Press, 1991).

16. Ginat, *A History of Egyptian Communism*, 43–45.

17. Ginat, *A History of Egyptian Communism*, 59–60.

18. See the record of the conversation between Rosenthal, Makram 'Ubaid, and an undercover British agent, December 22, 1921, attached to letter 1077 (13592/4), Cairo, Foreign Office (FO) 371/7744, E 336/189/16, National Archives (NA), London.

19. Report on Joseph Rosenthal, September 28, 1921, FO 141/779, NA, 258.

20. Abu al-Ghar, *Yahud Misr*, 179.

21. Salama Musa, "al-Dawliyya al-Thalitha wa-al-Ishtirakiyya," *al-Ahram*, August 9, 1922.

22. See Ginat, *A History of Egyptian Communism*, 77–86.

23. For a detailed account of the plot concocted against Rosenthal from within his party, see Ginat, *A History of Egyptian Communism*, 73–89.

24. Ginat, *A History of Egyptian Communism*, 124–127.

25. Rif'at al-Sa'id, "Al-Tali'a al-Wafdiyya 'Indama Taltaqi al-Markisiyya bi-Shabab al-Wafd," *al-Yasar al-Jadid*, 6, 7 (Winter 2004): 148–158. On Rosenthal's relations with the Wafd leaders, see Muhammad al-Jindi's version in Marsil Shirizi, *Awraq Munadil Itali fi Misr* (Cairo: Dar al-'Alam al-Thalith, 2002), 223–224.

26. Abu al-Ghar, *Yahud Misr*, 63, 94; Beinin, *The Dispersion of Egyptian Jewry*, 34; Botman, *The Rise of Egyptian Communism*, 6; Rif'at al-Sa'id, *Ta'rikh al-Munazzamat al-Yasariyya al-Misriyya, 1940–1950* (Cairo: Dar al-Thaqafa al-Jadida, 1976), 104.

27. Ginat, *A History of Egyptian Communism*, 208–209.

28. On the Comintern's Seventh Congress and its implications for the ECP and the anti-imperialist struggle, see Ginat, *A History of Egyptian Communism*, 190–193. See also Shirizi, *Awraq Munadil Itali fi Misr*, 196–198.

29. Ginat, *A History of Egyptian Communism*, 190–191.

30. Ginat, *A History of Egyptian Communism*, 190–198. On the origins of Soviet-Egyptian relations, see Ginat, "British Concoction or Bilateral Decision? Revisiting the Genesis of Soviet-Egyptian Relations," *International Journal of Middle East Studies* 31, no. 1 (1999): 39–60.

31. See, for instance, P. J. Vatikiotis, *The History of Modern Egypt*, 319–333; Joel Beinin and Zachary Lockman, *Workers on the Nile: Nationalism, Communism, Islam, and the Egyptian Working Class* (Princeton: Princeton University Press, 1989), 286; Botman, *The Rise of Egyptian Communism*, 20; Donald M. Reid, *Cairo University and the Making of Modern Egypt* (Cambridge: Cambridge University Press 1990), 128–129; Elie Kedourie, *Politics in the Middle East* (Oxford: Oxford University Press, 1992), 186–188; Beinin, *The Dispersion of Egyptian Jewry*, 34, 64.

32. Israel Gershoni, *Dame and Devil—Egypt and Nazism, 1935–1950* (Tel-Aviv: Resling, 2012); book review by Rami Ginat, in *Haaretz Culture and Literature* (Hebrew), April 18, 2013. See also Israel Gershoni, *Light in the Shade: Egypt and Fascism, 1922–1937* (Tel Aviv: Am Oved, 1999); book review by Rami Ginat, in *Hamizrah Hehadash* 47 (2008): 360–366 (Hebrew).

33. On this subject, see Rami Ginat, "The Rise of Homemade Egyptian Communism: A Response to the Challenge Posed by Fascism and Nazism?," in *Arab Responses to Fascism and Nazism 1933–1945: Attraction and Repulsion*, ed. Israel Gershoni (Austin: University of Texas Press, 2014), 195–215.

34. Henri Curiel, *Pages autobiographiques: Une contribution à l'histoire de la naissance du Parti Communiste Égyptien de 1940 à 1950*, 1978, file 402, 23, Papers of the Egyptian Communists in Exile (ECE), International Institute of Social History (IISH), Amsterdam Cited in Ginat, *A History of Egyptian Communism*, 255.

35. On the Democratic Union, see Ginat, *A History of Egyptian Communism*, 219–222.

36. Rif'at al-Sai'd, *Ta'rikh al-Munazzamat*, 290–293.

37. On Nasser's shift to socialism and the role played by Marxist nationalists in shaping and implementing his brand of socialism, see Rami Ginat's detailed account, *Egypt's Incomplete Revolution: Lutfi al-Khuli and Nasser's Socialism in the 1960s* (London: Routledge, 1997).

38. al-Sa'id, *Ta'rikh al-Munazzamat*, 92–96.

39. 'Abd al-Raḥman al-Rafi'i, *Fi A'qab al-Thawrah al-Misriyyah—Thawrat 1919*, al-Juz' al-Thalith (Cairo: Dar al-Ma'arif, 1989), 190.

40. Quoted from Botman, *The Rise of Egyptian Communism*, 60. On the NCWS, see also Walter Z. Laqueur, *Communism and Nationalism in the Middle East* (London: Routledge & Kegan Paul, 1957), 54–55; Beinin and Lockman, *Workers on the Nile*, 335–344; Tareq Y. Ismael and Rifa'at El-Sa'id, *The Communist Movement in Egypt, 1920–1988* (New York: 1988), 57.

41. Botman, *The Rise of Egyptian Communism*, 61–67. On the rise and fall of the NCWS, see also Beinin and Lockman, *Workers on the Nile*, 340–344.

42. See also Shuhdi 'Atiyya -al-Shafi'i, *Tatawwur al-Haraka al-Wataniyya* (Cairo: al-Dar al-Misri lil-Kutub, 1956), 87–109.

43. Ginat, *A History of Egyptian Communism*, 217.

44. Henri Curiel, "L'histoire de la lutte du Mouvement Egyptien de Libération Nationale (MELN) et Mouvement Démocratique de Libération Nationale jusqu'à la declaration de la Loi Martiale, en mai 1948," September–October 1951, file 110, 5–10, ECE, IISH, Amsterdam.

45. Ra'uf Hamid 'Abbas, *Awraq Henri Curiel wa-al-haraka al-shuyu'iyya al-misriyya* (Cairo: Sina lil-Nashr, 1988), 60.

46. Beinin, *The Dispersion of Egyptian Jewry*, 121.

47. al-Sa'id, *Ta'rikh al-Munazzamat*, 192–193. See also Letter DS (E) 20/2/24, attached to Despatch 134 from Ronald Campbell, British Ambassador, Cairo, March 18, 1948, FO 371/69250, J 1890/1262/16, NA; Letter DS (E) 200/124 from R. M. Shields, British Security Services Representative (SSR), to British Embassy, Cairo, December 1, 1947, FO 141/1158, NA.

48. Al-Sa'id, *Ta'rikh al-Munazzamat*, 194.

49. al Sa'id, *Ta'rikh al Munazzamat*, 193–194; Abu al Ghar, *Yahud Misr*, 96–100.

50. On the Rome Group, see a detailed account in Beinin, *The Dispersion of Egyptian Jewry*, chapter 6.

51. See a detailed account in Ginat, *Egypt and the Struggle for Power in Sudan*.

52. Rushdi Salih, *al-Fajr al-Jadid*, no. 16, January 11, 1946, 3.

53. Ahmad Sa'id, *al-Fajr al-Jadid*, no. 27, March 27, 1946, 10.

54. Rif'at al-Sa'id, "al-Haraka al-Shyu'iyya al-Misriyya 'Abr Sib'in 'Aman," *Qadaya Fikriyya*, July 1996, 21–37.

55. See a report from Curiel to the DMNL, January 1952, file 327, ECE, IISH, Amsterdam.

56. On the guerrilla warfare and the Cairo Fire, see Rami Ginat and Odelya Alon, "En Route to Revolution: The Communists and the Free Officers—Honeymoon and Separation," *British Journal of Middle Eastern Studies* 43, no. 4 (October 2016), 594–597. For a broader discussion of the Cairo Fire, see Nancy Reynolds, *A City Consumed: Urban Commerce, the Cairo Fire, and the Politics of Decolonization in Egypt* (Stanford: Stanford University Press, 2012).

57. Joel Gordon, *Nasser's Blessed Movement: Egypt's Free Officers and the July Revolution* (Oxford: Oxford University Press, 1992), 46.

58. On Egypt's policy of neutralism and its relations with the Soviet Union in the first half of the 1950s, see Rami Ginat, *The Soviet Union and Egypt, 1945–1955* (London: Routledge, 1993), 107–204. On the DMNL and Free Officers' cooperation, see, for instance, Rif'al-Sa'id, *Munazzamat al-Yasar al-Misri, 1950–1957* (Cairo: Dar al-Thaqafa al-Jadida, 1983), 86–102; Yusuf al-Jindi, *Masirat Hayati* (Cairo: Dar al-'alam a-Thalith, 2006), 106–108; Henri Curiel, *Min Ajil Salam 'Adil fi al-Sharq al-Awsat* (Cairo: Dar al-Thaqafa al-Jadida, 1999), 23.

59. On the history of the Egyptian Jewish community following the formation of the State of Israel and the intensification of the Arab-Israeli conflict and its effect on that community, see detailed accounts in Laskier, *The Jews of Egypt*; Beinin, *The Dispersion of Egyptian Jewry.* The latter discusses at length issues related to Jewish communist émigrés. See also Ginat, *A History of Egyptian Communism*, 253–254, 376–377.

60. Ginat, *A History of Egyptian Communism*, 380.

CHAPTER 5

Subjugated Homeland, Unhappy People

IRAQI JEWISH COMMUNIST WOMEN, 1941–1966

Orit Bashkin

In 2016, an eighty-seven-year-old woman by the name of Su'ad Khayri joined a demonstration protesting Iraqi politics in front of the Iraqi Embassy in Stockholm. Su'ad enthusiastically chanted the slogan of the Iraqi Communist Party (the ICP), "A free homeland, a happy people" (*watan hurr, sha'ab sa'id*).[1] Su'ad Khayri is identified with the struggles of the ICP for social justice and equality and against incarceration of political prisoners of the 1950s; she organized communist cells, propagated communist publications, and led hunger strikes in Baghdadi jails. She is also a leading scholar of the ICP, having authored a number of significant books on the party's history.[2] Su'ad also, however, has another history, as a Jewish woman. She was born with the name Sa'ida Mash'al to a Jewish Baghdadi family in 1929. While Su'ad is remembered, the history of Sa'ida, and the history of how Sa'ida became Su'ad, are often forgotten. This chapter will shed light on these processes.

The Jewish community to which Sa'ida belonged thrived in the Iraqi nation-state. Its members were an essential part of the urban middle classes and received excellent education in a network of Western private schools. The community was one of the most Arabized Jewish communities in the Middle East because many Jews lived in mixed neighborhoods with Arab Muslims and Christians and many more studied Arab history and Arabic language and literature in private and public schools. Jewish intellectuals, writers, poets, and journalists participated in Arabic literary and cultural institutions and saw Iraq as their homeland; some even referred to themselves as Arab Jews.

These visions were challenged during the mid-1930s, as pro-fascist and pro-German forces gained influence in the public sphere. The massacre of over 170 Iraqi Jews in a series of urban riots after a failed pro-German military coup (April–May 1941), known as the *Farhud*, shattered their faith in Iraqi patriotism. However, between the years 1942 and 1948 Jews pursued integration into the cultural, economic, and political spheres of Iraq. Tragically, the Arab-Israeli conflict ended this pluralistic historical moment. From the creation of the State of Israel in May 1948 until the end of 1951, Jews were fired from positions at government ministries and a well-orchestrated right-wing campaign smeared them as treasonous Zionists. The State of Israel, for its part, negotiated secretly with Iraqi governments in order to bring Iraqi Jews to the new state. Though they were highly dismissive of the Iraqi Jews' Arab culture, Israeli officials both feared for the lives of Iraqi Jews and saw them as important potential settlers.

Responding to these changing conditions, young Jews joined the illegal Iraqi Communist Party during the 1940s. Established in 1929, the ICP gained influence after World War II. It attracted Jews who admired the Soviet Union as a power able to battle antisemitism and right-wing nationalism. Jews played an important role in the ICP as cell members, union leaders, translators, journalists, and party secretaries. Iraqi Jewish communism also represented an attempt to propagate a radical model of Arab-Jewish identity, as the party used the term "Arab Jew" in its publications. In 1946 Jewish communists established the League for Combating Zionism (*'Usbat mukafahat al-sahayuniyya*), which, although legal for only three months, organized successful demonstrations and rallies. However, as part of a brutal anti-communist campaign conducted by the Iraqi state in the years 1948–1949, many Jewish communists were arrested and jailed, and some were even stripped of their citizenship. These Jews did not foresee an end to this persecution, and thus emigrating became the only option.[3]

These communist Jews who left for Israel became part of a massive wave of Iraqi Jewish migration to Israel, which led to the displacement of the Iraqi Jewish community and its complete impoverishment. In the years 1949–1951 the majority of the Iraqi-Jewish community (over 124,000 individuals) arrived in Israel because of the difficult circumstances they lived through after the creation of the State of Israel. The immigrants were denationalized from their Iraqi identity and legislation passed in 1951 froze most of their assets in Iraq and left them penniless. These displaced Iraqi Jews now lived in horrendous poverty in shacks and tents. In the early 1950s radical Iraqi Jews turned to the Israeli Communist Party (*Maki*), the only legal non-Zionist organization in Israel, which served as an important political organization for the Palestinians who remained in Israel and for radical Jews.[4]

Reflecting on this radical context, this chapter tells the story of three female Jewish communists, who were active in the upper echelons of the ICP's organizations: Allen Darwish, Madeline Mir 'Ezer (or Ezra), and Sa'ida Mash'al/Su'ad Khayri. All were Jewish, all held positions in the party's organizations, all were married to party leaders, and all were sentenced to lengthy periods of jail time by Baghdadi courts as a result of their communist activities. I argue that family relations shaped their communist engagements and that the composition of their families is essential to our understanding of their life choices. Communist Jewish women joined the party because of their Jewish relatives, as Jewish men convinced their sisters, nieces, fiancés, and wives to join the ICP. Their tragic lives, moreover, were shaped in no small measure by what happened to the male members of their families. Their husbands, cousins, and brothers were killed, tortured, and jailed by the Iraqi state. In some cases, when threatened with torture and death, some of their relatives turned them in. Not all men followed this path; in fact many communist men protected female activists. And yet others did not withstand the pressure of state violence and oppression, and Iraqi Jewish women and their families paid a heavy price as a result.

This chapter also delves into why historians know so little about these women. Allen, Madeline, and Sa'ida, as well as other Jewish women communists, faced three overlapping circles of exclusion—as women, as communists, and as Jews. Historians in the fields of Middle Eastern and Jewish studies excluded them, until very recently, from the histories of Arab feminism and of the ICP.[5] Even gifted Iraqi Jewish novelists, who were once members of the ICP and *Maki*, preferred writing about lower-middle-class Muslim women or women who belonged to the urban poor (especially prostitutes and workers) rather than telling the stories of their female comrades. Moreover, some women themselves tended to minimize their Jewish identity in their own writings and in their confessions to the police.

In addition to historiographical marginalization among scholars and communists, the women's convictions led to the their marginalization and persecution in real time, as the Iraqi state tried to crush communism with all its power. The Iraqi state used their Judaism to present them as Zionists in order to smear the ICP's image as a power disloyal to Arab interests and, concurrently, tried to strip them of their Iraqi citizenship and deport them to Israel. For example, in the 1949 encyclopedia of Iraqi communists produced by the police, all the photos of arrested female communists are of Jewish activists, although many members of varying religious affiliations were arrested in this period.[6]

This chapter offers a modest remedy by recounting the tragic and heroic histories of these women. I do so by exploring the intertwined Jewish, Iraqi, and radical circles that made up their identities. Allen, Madeline, and Sa'ida turned to communism because they were Jewish; the support shown by Iraqi nationalist elites to Nazism and fascism during the years of World War II and the Holocaust traumatized them. The radical Left offered the three women a form of inclusion freed from the paternalism of nationalist Iraqi elites, whose members granted selected citizenship rights to minorities. In the vision of these national elites, Jews, including those who called themselves Arab Jews, could play a part in Iraq's culture as long as they did not critique the state's social policies toward silenced groups such as peasants and women. Communist Jews, however, refused to celebrate the cultural aspects of their Arab identity without a radical change in socioeconomic power relations. Their convictions gave birth to a radical Jewish subculture that challenged Iraqi Jewish upper- and middle-class values, strongly emphasized integration into the Iraqi state's bureaucratic and commercial networks, and accepted British involvement in Iraq's geostrategic affairs and its oil industry.

However, Allen, Madeline, and Sa'ida also turned to communism because they were Iraqi. They faced a society whose politics privileged Arab Sunni men, and they witnessed the struggles of Shiites, Kurds, Assyrians, and women (of all religious and ethnic communities) to attain equality and citizenship rights. While the state labeled all these groups as "minorities," radicals from these religious and ethnic communities wanted to distance themselves from sectarian and tribal agendas. The ICP also called for women's suffrage, expansion of women's education, and changes in the personal status laws, and strongly denounced honor killings. These positions greatly attracted Iraqi women. Working in the ICP, Allen, Madeline, and Sa'ida were introduced to different women and men within Iraqi society and fostered relations with students and fellow Iraqi radicals. Furthermore, when the state defined their Judaism as a marker of Zionism, and when the communists themselves feared that the religious identity of some of their most loyal Jewish comrades would lead to the party's representation as pro-Zionist, Madeline and Sa'ida converted to Islam, in part in order to avoid deportation to Israel and subsequent denationalization.

Allen, Madeline, and Sa'ida also played a role in global and Middle Eastern contexts. In the Middle East, as Rami Ginat, Alma Heckman, and Lior Sternfeld show in this volume, networks of Jewish communists saw the radical Left as key to liberation from colonial oppression and gender and social inequality. The Arabic books, newspapers, and pamphlets these women read and circulated referenced radical publications in French, English, and Russian, and the leadership of their parties worked under instructions from the Soviet Union. Reconstructing their histories captures the moment in which women in the Global South searched for venues for decolonization, modernization, and emancipation and found them in radicalism.

Most crucially, Allen, Madeline, and Sa'ida were women. Discrimination against them as women pushed them to the ICP, but it also allowed the Iraqi state, Arab nationalists, Zionists, and fellow Iraqi communists to use their gender against them. Despite their ideological commitments, these women were reminded frequently that their sexuality, family life, place of residence, identity, and citizenship were to be decided by men, who disregarded and brutally crushed the values they held most dear. And yet, Allen, Madeline, and Sa'ida fought back; this chapter reconstructs and pays tribute to their brave and deeply tragic battles.

Three Communist Leaders: The Rise of the Communist Family

Allen, Madeline, and Sa'ida became involved in the ICP during the late 1940s. These were crucial years for the party. From 1941 to 1945, the British ignored communist activities because of the ICP's anti-Nazi stance. Following the war, and similar to other communist parties across the globe, the ICP expanded its ranks. Under the direction of its Christian leader Yusuf Salman Yusuf, known as "Fahd," it organized cells, strikes, and demonstrations in the years 1946–1947. It played a pivotal role in the *Wathba*, a series of grassroots demonstrations against the state's pro-British politics and in favor of social justice, during January 1948. The state retaliated brutally and arrested many activists; the leaders of the party—Fahd, Zaki Basim, and Muhammad Husayn al-Shabibi—were executed in 1949.

Since 1942 Iraq's socioeconomic conditions had improved and more women entered public life and the labor market. Iraqi colleges and vocational schools opened their doors to women, who enrolled in large numbers, especially in the Baghdadi Teachers Training College. However, even under these conditions, women could not vote or be elected to the Iraqi Parliament and Senate, and tribal women were tried under a different legal system that greatly discriminated against them. As Noga Efrati has shown, the social democrats and especially the communists intertwined demands for women's suffrage with a general critique of Iraq's electoral and judicial systems and this platform attracted educated Iraqi women.[7]

In the mid-1940s, women joined the ICP as members of cells. The party's leader, Fahd, and major party's publications, put forward the idea that women were citizens with the same political, social, and economic rights as men. The party demanded that all women be given an education and allowed to participate in Iraq's political life; this element of the party ideology led conservative and religious elites to argue that the party's secular attitude toward women would bring about a moral and religious crisis, and the communists were thus denigrated in nationalist and religious circles as promiscuous and as disrespectful of the structure of the Iraqi family. Initially, the ICP created different cells for men and women, and women's cells were organized or led by men; later on, however, women began to lead their own cells.

ICP women participated in demonstrations, disseminated pamphlets, and were involved in campaigns to uproot illiteracy. In 1943 The Women's League Against Fascism was established. This left-leaning and communist organization continued to be active after the war, providing classes for illiterate women and men and holding informational meetings. In 1952, the League for Defense of Women's Rights articulated its demands for suffrage, a democratic political system, independence, and welfare rights. As violent protesters took to the streets, especially during the Wathba, women joined in, sometimes as separate groups and sometimes marching alongside men.[8] Despite this history of participation, women and Jewish Iraqis formed only a small part of the ICP's leadership.[9]

Jewish women had joined the party starting in 1941. Baghdadi Jewish women were educated and consequently exposed to communist activities in high schools and in colleges such as the Law College, the Medical College, and the Teachers Training College. Joining the ICP was no small feat: as Jewish women they faced pressure within their community to refrain from illegal political activity that might smear not only their reputation but also that of their community; they were therefore closely monitored by both their families and the state. During the late 1940s, the ICP's women's committees counted seven Jewish women, thirty-two Muslims, and one Christian in their ranks; the number of Jewish members as a whole declined sharply after the Jewish exodus in the years 1950–1951.[10] Male Jewish members in Baghdad and Basra worked in tandem with these women's organizations.[11]

Fahd recommended that men organize the female members of their families so that the former would not be accused of immoral conduct with women.[12] Thus the Jewish family became a key locus of recruitment; male and female Jewish communists urged their female relatives to join and recommended them as members to the ICP, and sisters and wives of members in turn entered the party's ranks. The careers of Madeline Mir Ezra, Allen Darwish, and Sa'ida Mash'al fit this pattern. Madeline was the sister of Sabih Mir Ezer (born 1928); both were born and grew up in Nasiriyya. They were initially Zionists, following the waves of antisemitism during the late 1930s and the Fahrud, but turned to communism and moved to Baghdad to disseminate the party's message more effectively. Allen Darwish, born in 1925 in Baghdad, was the wife of Ibrahim Naji Shumail (1912–1966), who joined the party in 1946. Her husband was a partner at a prospering Baghdadi drug store, as was her cousin Ya'qub Ephraim Shayyek (1912–1992); both were communists and major funders of the ICP. Allen's home became a communist safe house, as she and her husband often hosted, and hid, party members. Key party meetings, including ones with Fahd and Zaki Basim, took place at Allen's home.[13]

Sa'ida Mash'al was born in 'Amara. Her oldest sister Habiba was a communist. Sa'ida's family moved to Baghdad in 1941 so that she could complete her elementary and high school education. She was drawn to communism because of the gaps she saw in the neighborhoods of the city between the rich and the poor, because of the sectarian city that she found after the Farhud,[14] and especially because Habiba's fiancé, Hesqel Qujman, was a persuasive advocate for communism. Hesqel's brother Ya'qub and his sister Najia were also communists. Hesqel, who later married Habiba, brought Sa'ida, Habiba, and Najia to the party. World events were another factor that directed Sa'ida toward communism. Her family, whom she described as educated and cultured, had a radio, and during World War II she listened for news about the victories of the Red Army. After graduating from high school, Sa'ida studied medicine at first but then shifted to the Teachers Training College, where she studied math. There, she met Shlomo Sasson Dallal, a fellow Jew who had joined the ICP in 1946 and was one of the party's leading members. He convinced Sa'ida to leave college and become more active in the party as she had leadership potential. Specifically, she was needed for the organizing of women's cells and the spreading of the party's message, duties she thereupon assumed.[15]

Fahd and the ICP leadership, entrusted Madeline, Allen, and Sa'ida with positions of responsibility, though the tasks they performed were those typically assigned to women.[16] Madeline served as a member of the ICP central women's committee. Allen joined her in this committee and also organized women's cells. She became the most important courier when the party's leaders, Fahd, Zaki Basim, and Husayn Muhammad al-Shabibi were arrested and imprisoned in the Kut jail in 1947. The three led the ICP from jail; since Allen's husband, Ibrahim, was also among the communists serving long prison sentences in the jail, she used to visit him and was thus able to pass along letters from him, the party's three leaders, and other jailed Jewish communists to other ICP members.[17] Sa'ida reported on the women's cells she organized to her fiancé, Sasson Dallal, and to another party member, Rafiq Jalak. She participated in the ICP's major demonstrations, including the 1946 demonstrations of the League for Combating Zionism against the partition of Palestine and in the Wathba.[18]

The confession of Doris Sha'ul, Sa'ida's aunt, to the Iraqi police reveals how Sa'ida brought her political concerns into the family domain. Sha'ul lived in 'Amara, and as a teenager came to Baghdad. where she lived in the apartment of her sister Anisa and attended the Jewish middle school for girls in Batawin:

> I like the communist party. Sa'ida, my niece, used to tell me about communism. I participated in the recent demonstrations. I read about the execution of Fahd. I used to talk to Sa'ida at home because my sister did not allow me to go outside the house. She taught me and my nephew Fu'ad, who is now arrested. . . . When talking to me about communism, Sa'ida used to tell me that the class of workers and peasants do much for the country and therefore we should help them. . . . I did not read any books because I do not read well.[19]

This testimony provides a few important details about activities of Jewish women. It locates communist activity within the family: Two nieces and a cousin were gradually being exposed to communist ideology. Doris claims that she did not read well, although she attended a respectable school for girls in a middle-class Jewish neighborhood. Nonetheless, despite her claims of ignorance (which may have been tailored to the gendered expectations of her investigators), she still speaks about the political events that brought her to the ICP, and about her actions, such as going to demonstrations (over her family's objections). Sa'ida, was a mentor to her, as she was for many other women in her college and in her city, Baghdad.

Breaking Up the Family

The most difficult years for Iraqi Jewish communists were 1948–1949. Jewish involvement in the ICP helped deflect to some extent the ill will generated by the war in Palestine, because the ICP offered Jews a patriotic Iraqi framework in which they could act. Although the communists accepted the Partition of Palestine because of Soviet pressures, they objected to Zionism and argued that antisemitism would disappear once the class struggle was resolved. Jews who joined the ICP thus perceived themselves as loyal to Iraq's social interests, as committed to Arab anti-colonial concerns, and as promoting a framework that was concurrently Jewish, Iraqi, and Arab. The anti-communist campaign following the Wathba, however, led to the arrests of Jewish activists who received substantial jail sentences, and two secretaries, Sasson Dallal and Yehudah Sadiq, both Jews, were executed by the state. Communist Jewish families were broken apart in the most horrific ways in these years because communist Jews were pressured to provide information about their wives, sisters, husbands, and cousins to the police.

Allen was arrested in 1949. Having already been arrested the year before and given a probation sentence of eleven months that ended up lasting for five years, she faced a lengthy jail sentence. During her investigation, she showed great courage. Asked repeatedly whether she had delivered letters to Fahd, Zaki Basim, and Husayn al-Shabibi, she denied any connections to the three, pointing out she was accompanied by a guard when she visited her husband in jail. However, the investigation turned up ample evidence against her: She was found in an apartment where the newspapers of the party, such as *al-Rabita* and *al-Majalla*, were kept; when the Jewish activist and organizer Mir Yaʿqub Cohen was arrested, the police found letters addressed to her; Malik Sayif, a Christian and a key party member who chose to betray his friends in exchange for his life, provided her name to the police; and letters found with Yehuda Sadiq named her as a courier. For her part, she tried unsuccessfully to use her gender to distance herself from communism: She argued that the newspapers found in the apartment belonged to her husband, that she was not a member of the party, and that she merely visited her husband from time to time.[20]

The attempt to downplay the role of communist Jewish women as mere cooks and cleaners in order to conceal their real roles in the party was common to the confessions of Jewish men and women arrested at the time. After being arrested, Jewish communist Yaʿqub Mir Masri, for example, stated that his sister, ʿAmuma (b. 1923), did nothing more than cook for the party's members. ʿAmuma, however, who was born in Madali and moved with her brother Yaʿqub to Baghdad, wrote the protocols for women cells' meetings, was a member of the women's central committee, acted as a courier, and worked in the ICP's printing house.[21] When the police investigated her later, in 1949, she downplayed her role in the ICP. She acknowledged that she was a communist yet insisted that all she did was cook and clean for the male members staying in the apartment where she lived, saying "I did not organize anyone because I do not read and write well. I graduated from the third grade in elementary school."[22] Her only fault was that she was in an apartment with other communists.[23] This line of reasoning did not help her much—she was sentenced to twenty years in jail.

On February 19, 1949, Saʿida Mashʿal was arrested and jailed. It was difficult for her to defend herself, because her own brother Fu'ad and her fiancé Sasson Dallal provided incriminating information against her. The latter, who was arrested on February 20, 1948, was charged with disseminating communist propaganda in the army and was eventually executed for this crime. In his confession to the police, he reported that she was an organizer, that she delivered messages about what transpired in women's cells to him and other leaders, and that she was an important courier. He also gave the names of her sister, Habiba Qujman, and Habiba's sister-in-law, Najia Qujman. Sasson was criticized for these acts, yet from his full confession it is clear that he did not provide all the information that he had, that he saved other members, and that he died for his beliefs. It might have been the case that he knew that the family connections between Najia, Habiba, Fu'ad, and Saʿida had already been exposed. His testimony nonetheless helped the authorities eliminate the Mashʿal-Qujman communist network.[24]

The most devastating testimony came from Saʿida's brother, Fu'ad Sasson. Arrested at the age of fifteen, Fu'ad, who apparently had a problematic relationship with Saʿida, outlined the activities of the family network. First, he told investigators that he was nominated for the party by Hesqel Qujman. Then he revealed that his sister Saʿida felt he was lazy and not strongly committed to the party because he questioned the party's ideology. Finally, he spoke about how Sa'ida spent long hours outside of the home, claiming her sister Habiba had taught her how to be a seamstress, in order to cover up her activity, and that she became a zealot after she fell in love with a big man in the party (meaning Sasson Dallal). He said that he feared that Dallal would kill him. The party, he confessed, wanted to expel him, but Sai'da was afraid that as a disgruntled member of the party he would act against her. He ended his testimony with a plea to be forgiven for his crimes.[25] Another teenager, Sa'ida's aunt Doris Sha'ul, to whom I referred before, also identified her as a cell leader. Fearing for their lives, then, these petrified teenagers were forced to produce confessions against their own relative. Sa'ida was sent to jail for the next ten years.[26]

In her memoirs, Sa'ida notes that her incarceration and her decision to marry a Muslim man, ICP member Zaki Khayri, after she was released from jail destroyed her relationship with her Jewish family. Her mother spent the years 1949–1958 visiting her children and relatives in the jails. Harsher jailing conditions were imposed in Sa'ida's case, and consequently her mother was not allowed to see her daughter. Yet after Sa'ida was released, her mother did not approve of her marrying a Muslim and continuing her communist activities. To her mother, her daughter's decisions torn the family apart.[27]

The Lost Voices of Sa'ida and Madeline: Reconstructing Silenced Histories

Allen, Sa'ida, and Madeline were jailed for almost a decade in Baghdad's central women's prison, although they all received lengthier prison sentences. Their fate changed only with the 1958 revolution of 'Abd al-Karim Qasim, which ended the Iraqi monarchic regime and led to the release of communist political prisoners. On top of being in jail, in 1951 another problem for them arose, denationalization and deportation to Israel. Most Jews, including communists, migrated to Israel, and the communists who were left behind were terribly isolated; in a few cases the state deported Jewish communists to Israel, a state which claimed responsibility for world Jewry. Fearing denationalization, Madeline married a communist Muslim man and converted to Islam. Sa'ida followed a similar path. Because they were now Muslim women, the state could not claim that Israel was their homeland any longer.

During the 1950s, Iraqi jails became spaces of resistance. The communists, men and women alike, saw themselves as political prisoners, and therefore challenged the legality of their arrests and protested their jail conditions. The hunger strike was the most common tactic to protest government abuse. Sa'ida emerged as a jail leader. She taught illiterate women how to read in jail and played an important role in organizing strikes protesting the women's jailing conditions and demanding that they be recognized as political prisoners. She went on hunger strikes a few times, and she had to be fed by force. One protest was sparked by the fact that women prisoners had to wash the uniforms of the sick inmates in the hospital of Baghdad's central jail. Sa'ida pointed out that this was dangerous, and the women wrote a petition protesting this health hazard. In response, she was transferred from the Baghdad jail to the Basra jail, where she could no longer rely on the friendships and networks of support she had with the female prisoners at Baghdad's jail. She went on a hunger strike in Basra to demand that she be returned to Baghdad. She was hospitalized and eventually returned to the Baghdad jail, where she found that the prisoners there had gone on a hunger strike demanding her return. During her stay in jail, a parliamentary delegation from the British Labor Party offered three Jewish communist female prisoners, including Sa'ida, the opportunity to be released from jail if they moved to Israel. The women refused, saying that they would stay in Iraq even if it cost them their lives.

Sa'ida was released in 1958 with the revolution of 'Abd al-Karim Qasim and managed to complete her education, eventually earning a PhD. She married Iraqi communist Zaki Khayri in 1964 and was now known as Su'ad (the name she took as a convert) Khayri. The regime that replaced Qasim in 1963 was nationalist, pro-American, and hostile to communists and many were arrested and killed. Consequently, Su'ad was forced to move to Moscow in the years 1963–1967. She returned to Iraq in 1967, sill upholding her communist ideals; in 1979 she was arrested and tortured for forty-two days. Su'ad then left for exile in Sweden. After the American occupation of Iraq and the rise of the new regime, which she also criticized, she was able to return for short visits.[28]

In interviews she has given over the last decade, Su'ad is very open about her life; she still talks fondly about her love for Iraq and the Left. She candidly discusses her Jewish background but prefers to discuss her conversion as little as possible. Nonetheless, when pressed on the matter, she identifies Islam as part of the culture of Iraq and subsequently claims that her conversion symbolized her Iraqi patriotism. The argument that Islam was a civilization with which Jews and Christians could identify was already current in Arab national circles in the interwar years and Su'ad adopts it to support her conversion. Concurrently, however, she downplays the fact that nationalists in Iraq had come to identify Judaism with Zionism, and that even the communists feared the fact that she was both a communist and a Jew. Su'ad thus emphasizes that her conversion was a patriotic act that curtailed her denationalization and deportation to Israel, enabled her to live with the Iraqi man she loved, Zaki Khayri, and reflected her love for both her husband and her people.

Su'ad was not always this forthright, however. Her 1974 book *Min ta'rkih al-haraka al-thawriya al-mu'asara fi'l 'iraq* (From the History of the Contemporary Revolutionary Movement in Iraq) is a case in point. In it, she makes a systematic attempt, inspired by Soviet historiography, which silenced the Jewish role in the history of communism, not to discuss any Jewish aspect of her life (in contrast to her more recent interviews). When she discusses the 1941 pro-German coup, she makes no mention of the Farhud. When she narrates the demonstration by the League for Combating Zionism (whose members were mostly Jewish), she does not mention the name of the Jewish man killed by the police, who is often held up as the first martyr of the party—yet she does mention by name the people killed in the major Wathba demonstrations. In addition, when discussing World War II, she does not mention the Holocaust. This war, according to the book, was the war of the USSR against Hitlerism. Nor does she make much of female membership in the party, focusing more on the death of a young woman in the demonstrations of 1948. The only space she devotes to female and Jewish activists is her discussion of the hunger strikes and the prison protests of the 1950s, although she does not even mention her own name when she writes about the strikes in which she participated. The part of the book that deals with the years 1941–1949, however, has one hero—the party's leader, Fahd, whose writings are quoted at length.[29] In later publications, she discusses gendered and Jewish issues, speaking about her Jewish household, the Farhud, and the fear of being a Jew and a communist in Baghdad, but in 1974, her silences regarding gender and Judaism were self-imposed. The ICP in Baghdad needed to tell a particular tale about its past, a tale in which there was little room for the Jewish religion of its key members.

Madeline faced even greater difficulties. She too was part of the women's resistance movement in jail. She was able to evade the police for a while but was finally arrested in 1953 and sentenced to ten years in prison. Before her jailing, she became romantically involved with a key Kurdish member of the party, Baha' al-Din Nuri, who would later become the party's secretary. Unmarried, she gave birth to their child in jail; Baha al-Din was arrested shortly after her; the two would eventually marry. Things got worse for her: She lost her brother, Sabih, who was arrested in Baghdad in 1950 and subsequently jailed. In 1952, he joined the prisoners in a strike in the Kut jail. The responses of the jail's leadership were harsh, as they cut off food, medical treatment, and water for drinking and sanitary purposes from the inmates. His leadership in this strike was costly; he was murdered by the chief warden, who shot him in the head at close range.[30]

We have two testimonies about Madeline's life, one by her Muslim husband Baha al-Din Nuri and another by a Muslim man who desired her, the celebrated modernist Iraqi poet Badr Shaqir al-Sayyab. Both testimonies show the cruelty she endured in her relationships with communist men. In his memoir, Baha al-Din Nuri was selective in providing details about his wife (although it is unclear when he actually married her). In what must be one of the most unromantic paragraphs ever written by a communist husband, Nuri provides the following description of his wife:

> I was twenty-five years old when I got married—in the year 1952—to the communist young girl Madeline Mir, a Jew from Baghdad. She was a progressive, active struggler [*munadila*]. She went into hiding after the authorities wanted to arrest her. Her personal and political conduct was fine and her appearance was acceptable [*kana shakluha maqbulan*], despite her short height and the fact that she could not be considered a beautiful woman. Khaled Bakdash [the leader of the Syrian Communist Party] once scolded me about marrying a Jewish woman and I replied that I had married a fighter and a good communist. In

truth, I never feared marrying a Jewish woman and I would not prefer any Muslim or Christian woman over her.[31]

Marrying a Jew, then, made Baha al-Din Nuri a good communist, as he chose to ignore the sectarian codes of Iraqi and Arab society; his tale about the marriage is not so much about his wife but about his own political commitments. This point of view surfaces in his description of how he suffered because of Madeline. When hiding out in an apartment in a conservative neighborhood they used to run away from police raids by jumping from roof to roof. According to Nuri, the neighbors saw Madeline running on the rooftops, and since they did not know she was his wife, they thought she was a prostitute. One neighbor told him, "[A]ll the people around you know you and how good you are. . . . They are all happy with you. It is unfortunate, however, that in your home resides a corrupt, immoral woman, who is your sister or something similar."[32] The couple thus had to live in another hiding place. No consideration in the husband's narrative is given to Madeline's fears and the fact that she was living as an unmarried woman at the time in a conservative neighborhood with a man.

Nuri does argue that Jews were persecuted unjustly by the Iraqi state, that they were true communists and not Zionists, and that they played a prominent role in the party. He even writes favorably about friends of his, such as an entire family of Jewish communists whose members were jailed with him and were willing to support him despite the harsh conditions.[33] His accounts about his wife, however, are alarming, like a very strange section in which he admits putting his pistol close to his wife's body and shooting her by mistake, or instances where he described letting her lag behind as he and his friends escaped the police.[34] These descriptions give us a glimpse into Madeline's difficult life. She was isolated from her Jewish family, persecuted by the state and thus having to run from place to place, and finally was married to a man who was possibly abusive and clearly prioritized the party, and himself, over her best interests and needs.

An even more distressing depiction is found in the memoirs of the modernist poet Badr Shaqir al-Sayyab (1926–1964), who is considered one of the most important bards in the Arab world. A one-time member of the ICP, Sayyab serialized his autobiographical vignettes in the Baghdadi newspaper *Al-Hurriyya* (Freedom) for seventeen weeks in 1959. They were later published as a book entitled *I Used to Be a Communist* (*Kuntu shiyuʿiyyan*).[35] The literary critic Elliot Colla, who studied the text, calls Sayyab "a Cold War public intellectual, quite willing to throw himself into the ranks of the anti-communist liberal front then emerging across Western Europe."[36]

What Sayyab's biographers often ignore is that *I Used to Be a Communist* reeks of antisemitism and popularizes the myth of Judeo-Bolshevism. The communists are depicted as Zionists and Iraqi Jewish communists are referred to via ugly terms like "the Ezekiel[s]" (*hasaqila*) (because many Jews in Iraq were named Hesqel, meaning Ezekiel), and as traitors and disloyal to the Iraqi nation. Even Jewish party leaders who converted to Islam to avoid deportation to Israel are labeled as "the Muslim Jews" (*al-yahudi al-muslim*), hence questioning the authenticity of their conversion. Sayyab states that Jews were neither loyal Iraqis nor loyal communists, that the Iraqi Muslim communists were the servants of the Jews, that Jews who converted to Islam could not be trusted as Muslims, and that Jews pushed the Soviet Union to go to war against Hitler. In addition, Jews were responsible for horrible crimes, from those committed in the USSR by Soviet Jewish doctors (one of the few times where Sayyab actually believes the Soviets) to the killing of novelist Maxim Gorky. Sayyab produced this text in order to discredit the ICP, and yet his venomous prose takes a very particular gendered turn when he writes about Jewish communist women. If communist women are depicted as either promiscuous or naïve (and Sayyab takes great delight in recounting two stories about ICP members who impregnated women outside of wedlock), Jewish female communists are depicted as immoral to the core because of their Judaism.

Surprisingly, perhaps, Sayyab admits that he fell in love with Madeline Mir 'Ezer. Unlike her disdainful husband, he applauds her beauty as a young communist teenager. Throughout the text she is referred to as "Madeline the Jew" (*Madlin al-yahudiya*). According to Sayyab, when he first met her, she complimented him on his poetry. He wanted to know which specific poems she liked, referencing a number he had written, but she wanted to read only revolutionary poetry; she cared little about love. The two met three times, during which they discussed revolutionary and other matters; he composed a love poem in her honor. Sayyab then planned a fourth meeting. This was crucial; he was going to take Madeline to a hotel in the city and sleep with her. Unfortunately, the communists learned that police were about to arrest her, and the date was canceled. Her communist comrades further discussed her fate; they knew she was a loyal and progressive party member, and were worried that she might be deported to Israel: "She is indeed a beautiful girl and the government wants to denationalize her and send her to Israel. If a Muslim marries her, she becomes a Muslim and the government cannot denationalize her. But who should marry her? I signed my name as a candidate."[37]

According to Sayyab, the communists made a list of all possible candidates for marriage, writing down their personal details, such as whether they were married or single; if their mothers were still alive; their party rank; and their family situation, and then, "We waited a week, without any results. When we asked about the fate of our request they told us to give up the thought, because Madeline found a safe haven and managed to hide from the police."[38] He then found out that she was now with Baha al-Din Nuri, who would not give away such a "precious catch" (*sayid nafis*). "What could she do after he attacked her, trying to rape her? He is stronger. Should she scream? At the moment she screams, the police would come [to arrest her]."[39] Sayyab explains that Baha al-Din Nuri and Madeline could not marry because they could not bring a rabbi or a qadi (judge) to the hiding place and thus no one was there to conduct the ceremony. Sardonically he continues his narrative with the birth of her son: "She gave birth to a baby boy whom she named . . . what do you think she named him? Salam [peace]. Is there anything more beautiful than peace? He is the son of the party after all."[40] Sayyab does note that a fellow female prisoner praised Madeline's commitment to her communist convictions; he ends by saying that she sacrificed her youth for the sake of the party.[41]

I have given space to Sayyab's memories not only because they expose the intersection between antisemitism and misogyny, as articulated by one of the most famed poets of Iraq, but also in order to shed light on the impossible situation in which Madeline found herself. One way of reading this account is to assume that Sayyab is lying or at least telling half-truths; Sayyab was evidently using Madeline's biography in order to present these ICP members as licentious. This generous reading can assume that the story about the list of candidates for marriage to Madeline is made up by Sayyab. But Sayyab, so vehemently antisemitic throughout the text, does admit that he fell in love with a Jew and that Madeline was a victim of the ICP; this is the only place in his text, in other words, where the communists are presented not as having been deceived by Jews, but as deceiving an innocent Jewish girl. Sayyab also provides a somewhat embarrassing account of his own desires (how he planned to seduce Madeline). Some of the stories in his biographical text regarding specific ICP members can actually be corroborated from other sources. If this is the case and he was writing truthfully about her life, Madeline's life seems even bleaker. It turns out that she faced misogyny, persecution, and torture at the hands of male members of her own party as well. We cannot know exactly what happened to her, as her voice is silenced by these communist men.

The Promised Land

Sa'ida Mash'al's sisters, Clair and Habiba, migrated to Israel, where they lived during the mid-1950s. Having been released from jail, Allen Darwish joined them as well, where she was reunited with her husband Ibrahim. These women lived in an unfamiliar and hostile space. In the years 1950–1951, the state settled most displaced Iraqi Jews in transit camps (*Ma'abarot*), alongside migrants from Poland, Iran, Romania, Yemen, and other countries. Living in tents and wooden shacks, they suffered from poor sanitary conditions, meager food rations, and a lack of appropriate water resources, and had to struggle to ensure proper education for their children. Women had to deal with high unemployment rates; those who managed to work outside the home found positions in factories and in agricultural work but were the first to be fired when factories experienced financial difficulties, for example.[42]

In response to these conditions, Iraqi men and women joined the Israeli Communist Party, *Maki*. The party was a hub of protest and dissent, organizing strikes and demonstrations and sending petitions to the state about the horrible conditions under which immigrant Jews lived. In Iraq, Hesqel Qujman played an important role in convincing Sa'ida and Habiba to join the ICP. In Israel, Hesqel, Habiba, Hesqel's brother Ya'qub, and his sister, Najia, became members of *Maki*. The two brothers rose to the middle echelons of *Maki*, and though they organized important activities in the transit camps they could never regain the central position they enjoyed in the ICP. The women in the family were valuable to the party as Jewish women who could speak Arabic to the Palestinian female activists. Sai'ida Mash'al's mother arrived in Israel in 1967, but did not care for it and subsequently moved between Paris, London, and Israel, where her sons resided.

Sa'ida's youngest sister, Clair, joined *Maki* as well. In 1975, when the party commemorated the fortieth anniversary of the ICP, Clair Mash'al (now taking her husband's family name, Cohen) took the stage, together with *Maki*'s members Tawfiq Zayad and Ya'qub Saheyek (Allen's cousin and her husband's partner), as well as other Iraqi Jewish activists, to speak to an Israeli-Palestinian audience about the accomplishments of Iraqi communism. For Iraqi Jews, becoming Israeli communists meant further marginalization. While the party opened its gates to Iraqi Jews and was willing to expose racism against Jews from Muslim and Middle Eastern countries, the party's Jewish leadership was mostly Ashkenazi. In sharp contrast to the situation in the Iraqi Communist Party, no Iraqi Jew has ever risen to a position of top leadership in *Maki*. Worse yet, the state's Zionist socialist elites considered *Maki* a national pariah and state authorities harshly discriminated all communists in domains relating to employment, education, and housing. Pressure by the authorities on the Qujman family eventually pushed these communists out, to London.

Allen and Ibrahim stayed in Israel, where they reconstructed a small social circle comprised of Baghdadi and leftist Iraqi Jews who now joined *Maki*. Ibrahim started working again, now in Ramat Gan, and the couple attained some measure of normalcy after years spent in Iraqi jails. Tragically, Allen died of cancer at the age of forty-one in 1966, having suffered through her short life from medical complications caused by the poor nutrition and abuse she endured as a prisoner in Iraq. Her husband Ibrahim could not stand the pain. He put an end to his life in 1967. Ever the communist, he ordered that his body would be given to medical research and that his fortune would be donated to Beilinson Hospital.[43]

Conclusion

This chapter has highlighted the lives of three heroines of mine, three extremely interesting historical figures whose biographies teach us much about gender, communism, and the histories of Iraq and Israel. Their histories, as I noted at the beginning of this chapter, are completely excluded from Israeli, Iraqi, and communist historiography. Present scholarship within Middle Eastern studies, moreover, tends to focus on contemporary forms of Islamic feminism and struggles forged within diasporic communities. This trend, albeit highly important, should not cause us to forget the significance of the secular, Marxist, feminist, and nationalist activists of the 1940s and 1950s, who shaped the region's history. Cold War politics and the Arab-Israeli conflict forced women like Sa'ida, Madeline, and Allen to deal with new realities as women, as Jews, and as communists. They lived in a world dominated by various kinds of men: those who were their loyal partners, those who betrayed them, and those who represented the state, like the policemen who hunted them down and their interrogators. Sa'ida, Madeline, and Allen made some choices that today might seem peculiar, like converting to Islam in order to maintain their Iraqi secular identity or going on hunger strikes that seemed futile in face of harsh state oppression. But in their world, these choices made much sense. To understand these choices requires the reconstruction of a silenced historical context and the rediscovery of models for activism and Arab-Jewish solidarity also relevant in our own times.

NOTES

1. The demonstration can be viewed here: https://www.youtube.com/watch?v=uxzwo640QTk.

2. Su'ad Khayri, *Thawrat 14 Tammuz* (Beirut: Dar Ibn Khaldun, 1980); Su'ad Khayri, *Fahd wa-al-nahj al-markisi al-Linini fi qadayat al-thawra* (Beirut: Dar al-Farabi, 1974).

3. Orit Bashkin, *New Babylonians: A History of Jews in Modern Iraq* (Stanford: Stanford University Press, 2012), 141–182. It is difficult to say how many Jews were in the ICP. Some estimate that there were a few hundred in Baghdad, less than a hundred in Basra, and fewer in the north, from a party that numbered about three to four thousand members in 1948. Zionist accounts give much higher numbers, arguing that large segments of the Jewish youth and middle classes adopted very positive opinions regarding communism and the Soviet Union. See Bashkin, *New Babylonians*, 145–147.

4. Esther Meir-Glitzenstein, *Ben bagdad le-ramat gan: Yots'ey 'iraq be-yisra'el* (Jerusalem: Yad Ben-tzvi, 2008); Orit Bashkin, *Impossible Exodus: Iraqi Jews in Israel* (Stanford: Stanford University Press, 2017). On Iraqi women in Israel, see also Chelsie May, "'Girls of the Eastern Communities': The Intersectionality of Female Arab Jewish Immigrants, Israel-Palestine 1947–1960," *The Journal of Jewish Identities* 11, no. 2 (2018): 245–266.

5. Orit Bashkin, *The Other Iraq: Pluralism and Culture in Hashemite Iraq* (Stanford: Stanford University Press, 2009), 87–125; Bashkin, *New Babylonians*, 141–182. On the ICP, see Tareq Y. Ismael, *The Rise and Fall of the Communist Party of Iraq* (Cambridge: Cambridge University Press, 2009); Hanna Batatu, *The Old Social Classes and the Revolutionary Movements of Iraq* (Princeton: Princeton University Press, 1978), 404–712; Al-Hizb al-Shuyu'i al-'Iraqi, *Shuhada' al-hizb, shuhada' al-watan: Shuhadā' al-Ḥizb al-Shuyu'i al-'Iraqi* (Beirut: al-Ḥizb al-Shuyu'i al-'Iraqi ; Tawzi': Dār al-Kunuz al-Adabiyya, 2001); 'Aziz Sibahi, *'Uqud min ta'rikh al-Hizb al-Shuyu'i al-'Iraqi* (Damascus: al-Thaqafa al-Jadida, 2002). A few scholars have addressed Jewish and gendered radicalism in the ICP: Noga Efrati deals with radical women's movements in *Women in Iraq: Past Meets Present* (New York: Columbia University Press, 2012); Yosef Meir unpacks the histories of Jews in Zionist and communist circles in Iraq in *Be'ikar ba-mahteret, yehudim u-politika be-'iraq* (Tel Aviv: Nayarim, 1993); and Chelsie May studies notions of race in the communist party in "'Not a Figure in the Past': Zionist Imperial Whiteness, the Iraqi Communist Party, and Their Reverberating Histories of Race and Gender, 1941–1951," *Journal of Middle East Women's Studies* 16, no. 1 (2020): 41–61.

6. The photographed women include Daisy Hesqel, Habiba Sasson Mas'al, Simha bint Yaq'ub, and Najiyya bint Menahem Qujman. See Al-Shurta al-'amma, *Mawsu'a siriyya khassa bi'l Hizb al-Shuyu'i al-'Iraqi*, 3vols. (Baghdad: Matba'at mudiriyyat al-tahqiqat al-jina'iyya, 1949); henceforth MS 1–3.

7. Efrati, *Women in Iraq*.

8. Orit Bashkin, "Representations of Women in the Writings of the Intelligentsia in Hashemite Iraq, 1921–1958," *Journal of Middle East Women's Studies* 4, no. 1 (2007): 64–69.

9. On Jews and women in the party, see: Batatu, *The Old Social Classes*, 647–648; Bashkin, *New Babylonians*, 93–95, 155.

10. Meir, *Be'ikar ba-mahteret*, 103.

11. Bashkin, *New Babylonians*, 93–95; entry on Ezra Fu'ad Sasson Mash'al, MS 3:694–696; entry on Mir Ya'qub Cohen, MS 2:349.

12. Meir, *Be'ikar ba-mahteret*, 185.
13. Bashkin, *New Babylonians*, 94–95, 150–151.
14. On the Farhud and its influence on the Jewish community, see Haim Cohen, "The Anti-Jewish Farhud in Baghdad, 1941," *Middle Eastern Studies* 3, no. 1 (1966): 2–17; Elie Kedourie, "The Sack of Basra and the 'Farhud' in Baghdad," in *Arabic Political Memoirs and Other Studies* (London: Cass, 1974), 283–314; Bashkin, *New Babylonians*, 100–140.
15. Entry on Shlomo Sasson Dallal, MS 3:560–569. For interviews with Su'ad Khayri, see Ibrahim Khalil al-Alaaf "Su'ad Khayri . . . on her 83rd Birthday," February 25, 2020, http://m.ahewar.org/s.asp?aid=296663; Balkis Hamid Hasan, "Qira'a fi kitab hamm li'l katiba Su'ad Khayri," January 27, 2005, http://www.balkishassan.com/index.php?option=com_content&view=article&id=213:2009-11-15-20-06-09&catid=12:m7a6at&Itemid=18; Nizar 'Askar, "Su'ad Khayri," https://alkompis.se/special/اتسنيت-يف-شيعت-ةيقارع-ةيدوهي-يريخ-داعس/ and "Yahudiyya 'iraqiyya rafa'at liwa' al-nisawiyya (last accessed 6/18/2025); "Media Personality Muhammad 'Ammad with Writer Su'ad Khayri in Sweden," posted June 26, 2013, by Imad Muhammad, YouTube, https://www.youtube.com/watch?v=NR-boJLJqHo.
16. Bashkin, *New Babylonians*, 93–95; Meir, *Be'ikar ba-mahteret*, 100.
17. Confession of Malik Sayyif, November 10, 1948, MS 1:37–38, 66; Meir, *Be'ikar ba-mahteret*, 100.
18. Entry on Shelmoa Sasson Dallal, MS 3:560–569.
19. Confession of Doris Sha'ul, cited in Meir, Be-'ikar ba-mahteret, 276
20. Entry on Shelmoa Sasson Dallal, MS 3:560–569; confession of Mir Ya'qub Cohen, MS 1:122–124; Meir, *Be'ikar ba-mahteret*, 263–265.
21. "The ICP," M15 to FO (Foreign Office), March 1949, National Archives (NA), London, FO 371/75131; confession of Malik Sayyif, November 10, 1948, MS 1:37–38; Meir, *Be'ikar ba-mahteret*, 100.
22. Confession of 'Amuma Misri, cited in Meir, *Be'ikar ba-mahteret*, 271-272, see also, ibid, 74.
23. Meir, *Be'ikar ba-mahteret*, 271-272, 74.
24. Entry on Shelmoa Sasson Dallal, MS 3:560–569.
25. Entry on Ezra Fu'ad Sasson Mash'al, MS 3:694–696.
26. Confession of Doris Sha'ul, cited in Meir, Be-'ikar ba-mahteret, 276
27. Su'ad Khayri, "Al Hayat al-Jadida, Hayat al-Huriyya," February 17, 2012, http://www.ahewar.org/debat/show.art.asp?aid=295624.
28. Hasan, "Qira'a fi kitab"; 'Askar, "Su'ad Khayri," and "Yahudiyya 'iraqiyya rafa'at liwa'"; "Media Personality Muhammad 'Ammad with Writer Su'ad Khayri in Sweden."
29. Su'ad Khayri, *Min ta'rkih al-haraka al-thawriya al-mu'asara fi'l 'iraq*, Baghdad, publisher not identified, 1974.
30. Meir, *Be'ikar ba-mahteret*, 99, Khayri, *Min ta'rikh*, 212–213.
31. Baha' al-Din Nuri, *Mudhakkirat Baha' al-Din Nuri: Sikritir al-lajna al-markazīyya li'l Hizb al-Shuyu'i al-'Iraqi* (London: Dar al-Hikma, 2001), 149.
32. Nuri, *Mudhakkirat*, 153.
33. Nuri, *Mudhakkirat*, 215.
34. Nuri, *Mudhakkirat*, 150.
35. Badr Shakir al-Sayyab, *Kuntu shuyu'iyan* (Cologne, Germany: Matba'at al-Jamal, 2007).
36. Elliott Colla, "Badr Shākir al-Sayyāb, Cold War Poet," *Middle Eastern Literatures* 18, no. 3 (2015), 248.
37. al-Sayyab, *Kuntu shuyu'iyan*, 88.
38. al-Sayyab, *Kuntu shuyu'iyan*, 88.
39. al-Sayyab, *Kuntu shuyu'iyan*, 88–89.
40. al-Sayyab, *Kuntu shuyu'iyan*, 89.
41. al-Sayyab, *Kuntu shuyu'iyan*, 89.
42. Bashkin, *Impossible Exodus*.
43. Sasson Somekh, *Baghdad Etmol* (Tel Aviv: Ha-Kibbutz Ha-Me'uhad, 2004), 100.

CHAPTER 6

The Roots of Jewish Radicalism in Iran

Lior B. Sternfeld

In summer 1941, a political earthquake shook Iran. The British and Soviet armies invaded the country and overthrew Reza Shah, who had ruled the country since 1925. The decision to overthrow Reza Pahlavi followed his refusal to join the Allied countries and his insistence on maintaining Iran's neutrality. Subsequently, the Anglo-Soviet occupation started, dividing the country into two (three following the American entrance in the war) zones: British in the south, and Soviet in the north. Ironically, Reza Shah's abdication and the inception of military occupation in Iran gave way to political liberties that had been largely forgotten under the iron-fisted rule of Reza Pahlavi. The political sphere opened once again; new freedoms emerged, including the right of parties, such as the Tudeh Communist Party, to organize. The political sphere in Iran diversified significantly; a wide array of ideas emerged, ranging from fascist ideologies to communism. This chapter will analyze the ways in which the Tudeh Party laid the foundation for decades of Jewish radical politics, and how it survived many national and international upheavals. In fact, the brand of Jewish politics that was born in the Tudeh Party continued to be influential decades after the party was no longer significant in the national arena. Another finding of interest appears in the formula of Jewish radicalism in Iran that considered Jewishness to be a central component of radical identity.

By the early 1940s, the millennia-old Jewish community in Iran (around 100,000 individuals) had been undergoing profound transformations. Like all Iranians, they had turned from subjects to citizens in the aftermath of the Constitutional Revolution (1906–1911) and grappled with the nation-building projects of the late Qajar (1789–1925) and early Pahlavi eras (1925–1941). Simultaneously, Iranian Jews moved in significant numbers to the cities and urban centers, engaging with political Zionism as a possible redemption and socialism in its various forms in Iran. Eventually, their collective identity reflected this. Iranian Jewish identity in the period went along the lines of Iranian nationalism, socialism, or communism. Zionism also gained ground, albeit in a very particular interpretation that was unique to Iran. In this chapter I use archival materials as well as oral interviews with Iranian Jews who were active in these organizations and parties.[1]

Minorities and the *Hizb-i Tudeh*

The *Tudeh* Party ("The Masses" in Farsi) was one of the oldest political organizations with which Jews sympathized, and they actively supported it. The party was established in 1941, and as Iraj Eskandari, one of Tudeh's founding members and prominent leaders, wrote in his political memoir, the party was created essentially as an anti-fascist organization.[2] This was the main appeal of the party to Iranian Jews.[3]

The Tudeh Party adamantly opposed fascism and for years published articles and editorials denouncing the fascist inclinations of nationalist groups in Iranian society, openly criticizing the prevailing antisemitic climate in Iran,[4] which manifested itself through the appearance and massive operation of pro-Nazi political organizations, such as the Pan-Iranist Party.[5] The Tudeh Party's enduring defense of the Jewish community and its message of equality for all—regardless of ethnic, religious, or socioeconomic status—attracted many young Jews from Iran's middle and lower middle classes.[6] Iraj Farhoumand, a Jewish Tudeh activist, explained that active Jewish participation in the party was inarguably connected to troubling developments in Europe, Iran's geographic proximity to Russia, and the party's inclusiveness.[7] He references the vast Jewish participation in the 1940s and 1950s and even cites Jews who were members of the party's central committee.[8] In those decades many Jews became loyal communists for a multitude of reasons, and not merely because of a strong investment in communist ideology.

An interviewee for this research, Pinhas, was born in 1931 to an impoverished lower-class family in Hamadan, one of the oldest cities in Iran. He had eleven siblings and attended a Jewish school until sixth grade. Pinhas's recollection of his first encounter with the Tudeh Party is particularly revelatory:

> I left school because we were many children in the house and one income was not enough. I had to get out and earn some money. I had a cart from which I sold anything I could find and a regular spot on the street. Across from where I was standing there was a building with a sign, *Hizb-i Tudeh*, so one day after work I walked in. Inside there were many people—young and adults—and there was a tennis table. They invited me in, and I played for a while. After I finished they invited me to stay for a lecture. I started to go there on a regular basis; to play ping-pong and listen to lectures. They talked about equality and basic economy and taught us all the Marxist and leftist ideals. Until this day, almost seventy years later, I still play ping-pong and I still believe in all these ideals.[9]

The Tudeh "club" welcomed people from all walks of life to socialize and become activists in what became the mission of their generation. Part of the charm was the chance to meet some of the most influential intellectuals of Iran at that time. Not surprisingly, the Tudeh club's appeal also centered on its social and entertainment opportunities.

Another interviewee for this research, Habib, was born in Tehran in the early 1930s and as of 2019 was residing in North America. At age sixteen he joined Tudeh and remained an active member for more than three decades. His political activity landed him in Qasr, the Shah's prison, a half dozen times before he left Iran. Habib recalls, "I knew nothing about Marx or Marxism when I joined Tudeh. I joined because this was the only place that they did not call me *Johud* [a derogatory name for Jews]. I learned Marxism in Qasr prison, shortly after I joined the party." Habib's story is by no means unique. Many minorities joined the party to combat the social ostracism they experienced.[10] "We [the Jews] were attracted to Tudeh in order to become more Iranian, and the Armenians also had cultural ties to Russia [the Soviet Union] so they already recognized the political language," concluded Habib.[11]

The importance of minorities in leadership positions was especially apparent in the literary output of Tudeh's official newspapers: *Rahbar* (The Leader), *Mardum* (People), and *Razm* (The Fight).[12] *Rahbar*, for example, published antiracist editorials and op-eds, and it counted Jewish writers among its regular staff. Shmuel Anvar, a Jewish journalist and Tudeh activist, also established and edited a semiofficial weekly newspaper, *Nissan*. Officially, *Nissan* was an organ of the Cultural and Social Society of Iranian Jews (CSSIJ; *Jam'eyat-e Farhangi va ijtima'i-yi yahudiyan-i iran*). Prominent Jewish writers including Ibrahim Faiz-Jav and Muhandes Ibrahim Iran-Mehr contributed to both *Nissan* and *Rahbar*.[13] Nissan also consistently defended minorities' rights. During periods when *Rahbar* was banned, *Nissan* continued to present the views and opinions of the party's leadership. Indeed, *Nissan* enjoyed wide exposure and far-reaching distribution.[14]

The close association of *Nissan* with Soviet-supporting factions of the Tudeh Party is obvious from articles appearing in the newspaper, as well as from the language used. The ambiguous response of Tudeh and the Soviet Union to Israel and Zionism in the late 1940s and early 1950s was unmistakable—and was presented as a conversation between different streams of thought in the party and in the community. *Nissan* covered local and global Jewish political issues extensively and provided editorial interpretation of ongoing events. It presented Zionism as a "puppet of American imperialism" (*alatidast imperialism amrika*). During the Prague trials of 1953, Nissan's journalists asserted that the "leaders of today's State of Israel have sold themselves to American imperialists and have used Zionist organizations to further American interests in the People's Democracies [the Eastern Bloc]."[15] In this article Zionism is described as the "political and nationalist movement of Jewish bourgeoisies."[16] Moreover, *Nissan* also translated articles from daily newspapers and magazines of the Israeli press such as *Ha'aretz* and *Ha'olam Hazeh*; its editorial board presented what they considered to be fallacies on the part of Israel and the Zionist project. One article examined the rift between two factions of the kibbutz movement (overwhelmingly perceived in Israel to be leftist-socialist, to varying degrees).[17] The article claimed that the kibbutzim (plural for kibbutz) who opposed Prime Minister David Ben-Gurion's anti-Soviet policies were targeted and harassed by the "right-wing" MAPAI (*Mifleget Po'ale Eretz Yisra'el*; National Council of the Workers' Party of the Land of Israel) and its supporters. The article mentioned especially Kibbutz Yad-Hanna, acknowledged to be an ardent communist kibbutz, and the "left-wing" *Mapam* (*Mifleget ha-Po'alim ha-Me'uhedet*; United Workers' Party) as integral to the socialist movement.[18]

One could argue that *Nissan*'s interest in Israeli discourse regarding the Soviet Union bordered on obsession. For example, a 1953 article titled "Israeli Press and People Condemn Anti-Soviet Provocations of Ben-Gurion" addresses the deterioration of diplomatic relations between the Soviet Union and Israel (following the Doctors' Plot in Moscow and the Prague trials). The author of this article underscores the Israeli public's resentment toward Ben-Gurion's miscalculated steps—such as de facto joining the American bloc in the Cold War—and the widespread agreement among Israelis regarding the necessity of improved relations with the Soviets. The article quotes Dr. Shemuel Elyashiv, Israeli ambassador in Moscow during this time. At a *Mapai* meeting in Tel Aviv, Elyashiv is quoted as saying that "the anti-Soviet policy of Ben-Gurion's government will only hurt the existence of Israel, hence showing dissent from within the Israeli political establishment."[19] Understandably, the trials in Moscow and Prague made some Jews wary of developments among communist movements around the world. In an occasional segment titled "Dialogue with Readers," a reader identified as Mr. Roshan from Kashan praised the role of *Nissan* in "awakening the Jewish community," but he added that he did not understand why the trials would cause "the Soviet government [to] cut its relations with Israel." *Nissan* responded by saying that Zionist organizations were plotting with the United States against Soviet interests. Eventually (after Stalin's death) the Soviet government acknowledged its wrongdoing, reversed criminal charges against Jews who had been unjustly accused, and put an end to the Doctor's Plot charges.[20]

Jewish radicals in Iran had no easy way to deal with their attitude toward Israel in the early 1950s. First, Israel's ruling government was a self-proclaimed socialist system. An important pillar of Israel's emerging *Mapai* (labor Zionist) coalition was the leftist-Marxist *Mapam*, founded in 1930. Second, the Soviet Union had supported the 1947 United Nations Partition Plan. Indeed, one of the declaration signatories had been Meir Vilner of the Israeli Communist Party, and even the Tudeh Party, overall, supported the establishment of Israel and considered it a just solution to the conflict in Palestine (in this it also followed the line of the Soviet Union). In short, *Nissan* (and Jewish radicals) could not easily dismiss Israel as yet another reactionary force or puppet of Western empires since, to varying degrees, a coalition of socialists and communists, along with Soviet support, had played a pivotal role in the "state story" of Israel.

Nissan kept its readers informed about ongoing events in the Eastern Bloc and beyond. In a way, the newspaper helped to create the sense that a global Jewish leftist community existed. Its reports from Israel, the Soviet Union, and the Eastern

Bloc were enriched at times by reports regarding Jewish matters in the West. Nissan turned its readers' attention to political affairs in Hollywood, for example, and specifically to the treatment of Jewish actors and progressive "human-loving" Jews. One article from May 1953 criticized the witch hunt carried out by the U.S. House Un-American Activities Committee, as well as attempts to intimidate political dissidents in Hollywood.

The same article reported that Charlie Chaplin had been denied a reentry permit by the U.S. government in 1952 because he had allegedly expressed communist sympathies. The article concluded, "There exists another America too: the America of the lovers of humanity, of people with honor, the America of workers and the oppressed, the America of Charlie Chaplin and the Rosenbergs, human-loving Jews who have always been deemed alien by the writers of the Zionist organ, whether in the U.S. or in *'Alim-i Yahud* [The Jewish World, the title of another Jewish-Zionist publication in Iran at that time]."[21]

Not surprisingly, the U.S. espionage trial of Julius and Ethel Rosenberg piqued the interest of Iran's Jewish community. On June 19, 1953, the Rosenbergs, two American Jews, were executed for allegedly spying for the Soviet Union. Their trial raised concerns about persecution based on religious beliefs, and many followed the trial with mixed feelings. On July 29, 1953, the CSSIJ held a memorial ceremony for the Rosenbergs. Over five hundred individuals attended. Homage was paid to the Rosenbergs and their struggle for peace. One attendee by the name of Mr. Amini acknowledged the CSSIJ for providing accurate information about the Rosenbergs amid the deluge of disinformation. Another attendee, Ms. Giahizadeh, spoke on behalf of prominent intellectuals such as Jean-Paul Sartre. The memorial service concluded with prayer and the adoption of a resolution addressed to President Dwight D. Eisenhower that protested the inhumane and unjust decision to execute the Rosenbergs.[22]

Periodicals like *Nissan* changed the political conversation for Iranian Jews. Journalists repeatedly provided reasons for Jews to feel proud, which was especially important in such a highly turbulent political atmosphere, with rising tensions with Western superpowers and antisemitic sentiments in the political sphere, in relation to Israel and beyond. While Zionist organizations laid claim to publications like *'Alim-i Yahud* and *Israiil*, the leftists (Zionist and non-Zionist alike) had another spectrum of opinions to discuss and from which to draw. In fact, the reach of *Nissan* went far beyond Tehran, home to the majority of Iranian Jews. Its readership extended to the much smaller, distant communities of Hamedan and Abadan as well. Nissan's representative in Abadan reported that the paper received a warm welcome in that community. The representative asserted that although other newspapers carried similar messages (to that of *Bani-Adam*), they were lacking in journalistic integrity or authenticity and therefore did not resonate with the Jewish community. *Nissan* and *Bani-Adam* (the subject of the next section), so says the author, truly represented the class concerns of the people, enabling these publications to draw a wider audience.[23]

Bani-Adam: Socialist Alliance in Iran, Israel, and Beyond

Bani-Adam, which translates from Hebrew as "children of Adam," enjoyed a primarily though not exclusively Jewish readership.[24] Edited by Loqman Salih, *Bani-Adam* (like *Nissan*) was published by the CSSIJ. However, in regard to a plethora of social and political issues, the two periodicals took different approaches. Although remaining staunchly leftist, the views published by *Bani-Adam* were lenient toward and supportive of Israel—whereas *Nissan*'s position continued to be, on the whole, more confrontational. As previously suggested, *Nissan* questioned whether Israel was not merely an agent of European colonialism and American imperialism. In contrast, *Bani-Adam* struggled to present Israel as a complex and multilayered society.[25] *Bani-Adam*, for instance, celebrated Israel's independence day while still hoping to advise Israel on the correct political path globally: Join the "progressive" people (socialist and Soviet-leaning countries), engage in a peace process with its Arab neighbors, and grant equal rights and privileges to the Mizrahi Jews and the Palestinians.[26]

The last paragraph of that article presents a plea on behalf of *Bani-Adam*: "Once again we ask the Iranian state to establish political and commercial relationships with the state of Israel, and stop insisting on separation and termination of all relations with the nation of Israel. This path is against the real interest of the Iranian nation and should not be pursued."[27] It is worth remarking here that Tudeh—as well as other leftist circles—viewed Israel as a partner in the struggle against Western imperialism. The promulgation of this view was central to their political platform for years to come.

On April 25, 1952, the seventeenth Majlis term began in Tehran. *Bani-Adam* underscored the Jewish community's expectations by addressing the Majlis thus: "The issue of recognizing the newly founded Israeli republic is also a question [that Iran's] Jewish community expects the 17th Majlis to address." The editorial went on to contend that, after years of struggling against the British, Israel's best option would be to establish solidarity with its neighbors; *Bani-Adam*'s editorial board therefore urged the parliament to form deep diplomatic and commercial relations with Israel. Their demands to the seventeenth Majlis also included directing deputies to "quickly end the poisonous antisemitic [*zid-i yahudi*] and anti-racial propaganda." Moreover, they articulated objectives that would remain in radical Jewish circles up until the 1979 revolution; that is, a call to end discrimination by official state bodies against Jews (and other minorities) in education, the civil service, and the armed forces.[28]

Questions of nationalism and the resistance to colonialism took front and center in left-wing Jewish Iranian politics. During the struggle for nationalization of the Anglo-Iranian Oil Company (AIOC), the Tudeh Party, along with *Nissan* and *Bani-Adam*, voiced unwavering support for Prime Minister Mosaddeq, who championed the cause of oil nationalization. Tudeh also debated the implications of Great Britain's legal challenge to Iran's nationalization bill. Headlines such as the following took prominence: "Whatever the International Court of Justice in the Hague Decides, the Iranian People Will Not Waver from Their Path." The May 1952 *Bani-Adam* article from which this headline is excerpted reads, "The Iranian nation has time and again declared that it nationalized the oil industry based on the Iranian nation's right to sovereignty over its natural resources and no organ can stop a nation from exercising its right to sovereignty."[29] Bringing attention to the struggles in Abadan (the city where most oil refineries were), *Bani-Adam* included the perspective of Abadani Jews and revealed the multitude of hardships experienced in Abadan amid the oil crisis. One letter printed in *Bani-Adam* reports the closing of Jewish shops near Shat al-Arab: "Such are the sad and heartbreaking conditions of the miserable Jewish classes who spend their life in wails, sighs, and tears. Yes, this is an example of Jewish life in Abadan; a land that, until a year ago, was immersed in black gold that left on massive ships destined for every corner of the world. Even then, these miserable people did not receive anything but hardship and a burdensome life."[30] This letter illuminates the status of those Jews shunned from the political and cultural center of Iranian Jewry—exiled, in fact, to Iran's social periphery. However, the political reality brought their plight to public attention.[31]

Furthermore, if the goal was to create solidarity between Jews and their non-Jewish compatriots, another letter printed in *Bani-Adam* in June 1952 did just that by reporting the suffering of other Abadanis: "But the majority of our non-Jewish brothers endure even worse conditions. They are all mired in poverty and a sad life. There are those [non-Communist newspaper publishers and reporters] who speak nonsense. These lackeys of colonialism who fill their moneymaking newspapers with cheap, useless, and half-cooked words are ordered by their bosses to push people away from the truth, to sow division and enmity among them. They [publishers and editors] should send reporters to see the heartbreaking conditions of these miserable people and not distort the truth."[32] The letter also discussed the Majlis elections and the campaign of *Nissan* and *Bani-Adam* to get Shmuel Anvar, another Jewish Tudeh journalist, elected. Anvar's platform, which received prominent space in both newspapers, resonated with the clear agenda of the Jewish leftists: to improve relations between Jewish and non-Jewish Iranians in fighting racism, antisemitism, and fascism and to work in solidarity for the betterment of conditions for all Iranians.

Jewish Iranian political activists adopted yet another strategy at this time: using religious holidays to immerse the Jewish population in Iranian nationalism, perhaps to communicate a message to non-Jewish Iranians as well. At the heart of that message was the idea that Jewish traditions inherently educate the masses appropriately regarding their civic roles, guiding Jewish Iranian citizens to contribute responsibly to their beloved homeland. For example, in June 1952 *Bani-Adam* connected the celebration of Shavu'ot with messages of freedom and liberty. According to Jewish tradition, this holiday commemorates the giving of the holy Torah at Mount Sinai. Jews traditionally view it as the first codification of the Divine Law that the Jewish people (the Israelites) accepted as part of their sacred covenant with the one God. The article reads,

> The feast of Shavu'ot, which the Jewish community celebrated two days ago, aims to remember these laws and commemorate them. These laws were like a strong light eradicating the darkness that surrounded us 30 centuries ago, and they surely deserve commemoration. Those who assault Jews everyday with all sorts of insults and accusations—fascists and followers of the despicable racial theory who take to history to prove their nonsense—these people are afraid of considering historical truths. They are blind and ignore the truth that the Jewish masses, like non-Jewish people, support justice, freedom, and understanding among all peoples and will fight to reclaim these ideals.
>
> They obfuscate truth with a false smokescreen and seek to spread division and enmity among the poor who share the same interests. However, on the one hand, the awakening of people and, on the other, the collective struggle of Jewish progressivists to introduce their community to their fellow compatriots, will neutralize the claims of these division-seekers and will further embolden the friendship and intimacy between Jews and followers of other religions.
>
> We congratulate our brothers on the feast of Shavu'ot and invite our fellow Jews to collectively struggle for the guarantee of justice, fraternity, and freedom.[33]

Bani-Adam and *Nissan* created a genre of Jewish political journalism that sought to bring individuals caught in social and geographical peripheries closer to the center. A primary goal was to engage Iranian Jews politically, not just locally in community institutions but, more importantly, at the national level. Far ahead of the global trend, *Bani-Adam* advocated for women's rights, lent unequivocal support for oil nationalization, and called for action[34] in a variety of key political arenas, such as through wider participation in the Majlis elections.[35]

More than any other venues, *Nissan* and *Bani-Adam* welcomed Iranian Jews into the Tudeh circle while demonstrating the need for radical activism. These publications began by asking the question, how could the Tudeh party transform critical social issues at the local level while integrating Jews more fully into the larger national conversation? Their answer centered on identifying with political forces that sought to include religious and ethnic minorities, forces endeavoring to redefine the boundaries of Iranian national identity. The Tudeh Party, by virtue of being a party of minorities, encouraged its Jewish membership to openly support political and cultural advancement for Jews, to fight fascism globally, and to eschew distancing themselves from major events taking place in the Jewish world.

At this pivotal time, Iranian Jews were bearing witness to their brethren, the European Jews, slowly emerging from ruins of the Holocaust. They were also witnessing the establishment of the State of Israel and being encouraged by Tudeh and other Jewish associations affiliated with the Communist Party to recognize Israel as Iran's partner rather than enemy. *Nissan* and *Bani-Adam*, as well as the individuals supporting these papers, wanted to see a transformation of the Jewish community in Iran, a reform movement allowing Jews to fit more seamlessly into Iranian society—one that would guarantee them a place at the table in the Shah's plan for modernization. Following the political and social developments resulting from Mohammad Reza Shah's ascendance in 1941, this movement envisioned rural Jews increasingly moving into Iranian cities and therefore contributing more directly to the urbanization of their nation. After the coup against Prime Minister Mosaddeq in 1953 the Tudeh Party was outlawed and transformed itself in Iran into a mostly underground operation. The first generation of Jewish Tudehists joined the party to combat antisemitism and to be part of an extremely popular national political movement. The second generation of Jewish Tudehists joined the party out of the conviction that an all-Iranian struggle against tyranny was in par with their being part of the educated urban middle class.

The Tudeh's Second Jewish Generation

In the 1970s, along with increased assimilation, Jews were immensely active in student organizations and other opposition movements. Jews sympathized with their compatriots, setting aside their community's alleged inherent support of the monarchy. This mindset of assimilation (and perhaps the feeling that it had arrived at its ultimate stage) could have stemmed from instilling the liberal nationalist ideals those organizations expressed and promoted. Also, it seems as though these organizations, with their apparent religious and ethnic diversity, allowed Jews to envision a multicultural society in which they, as part of a minority group, would have a central role. The result was growing involvement in existing organizations, such as the student confederations and the Tudeh Party, and the establishment of new organizations. The generation of Jews that came of age during the Shah's White Revolution (after 1963) was already acquainted with socialist theories and politics and expressed its views loudly and clearly as the rest of Iranian society prepared for a revolution.[36]

The connections between leftist groups in Iran and abroad were very strong. Not only did Iranian students collaborate on operations in Iran and communicate activities to Western outlets, but many of them returned to Iran and became involved in the local chapters once they graduated from institutions in the West. For example, one of the interviewees for this project, Mihrdad, studied in Europe and was part of the European Confederation of Iranian Students. He returned to Iran from Europe at the time when the opposition inside Iran was becoming more active and more explicit:

> When I returned to Iran in 1975, I met an old friend who suggested setting up an organization for the younger generation, rather than the old attachment to synagogues. So we established an organization called Council of Advancement of Jewish Social and Cultural Activism and it became very successful. We held our first events in a hotel, not a community center, and it became an attraction for the newer generation. We had very interesting events and lectures, which were

> not religious or pro-Israel. It was more general on an informative basis. We had intellectuals coming from the politically active community. Our events were full. Soon, the room given to us was not enough. It was the place for the young up and coming Jews to meet each other. . . . It had become a big community. We were both Jews and part of the wider community.[37]

This group's worldview was holistic—that is, they wanted to engage in every aspect of Jewish Iranian social life. The newly established council provided cultural and educational activities to as many Jews as it could find and recruit. Among other operations, it ran a summer camp, which aimed to bring together Jews from all over Iran (and especially Tehran) regardless of socioeconomic status. Mihrdad states:

> We organized the camp for fourteen- to sixteen-year-olds. We mixed Jews from South Tehran, the *mahallah* (the traditional Jewish neighborhood/quarter), with Jews from North Tehran, and said there is a dress code: jeans and a T-shirt, and we provide the T-shirt, so there was no room for showing off. For three summers successively, in 76–78, there were 1,000 kids going to this camp, and all the parents wanted their kids to come to this camp to get to know the others, because the ties within the community became looser and looser and they thought that this is it. Our success was that about a third [of the campers] came from poor families of Tehran and we did not charge them anything, and [we] charged the others double.[38]

By organizing these camps, the group addressed issues that received wide attention in Iran at that time, such as economic inequality, and were able to present them in their community and to try to find a popular and working solution. Although disparity was a much greater concern in the general public, the fact that the group was able to treat this issue inside the community must have been seen as a message of success regarding their leftist ideals.

The ultimate goal of this council was to connect Jews to broader social movements in Iran and bring them closer to political action. In its deeds the council laid the foundation for a far-reaching organization later that decade, when the revolutionary events started to take place. During the protests of the 1970s, while the Tudeh Party's activity was outlawed, two Jewish activists, Harun Parviz Yeshayaee and ʿAziz Daneshrad, were jailed for antimonarchical activity. After serving their time, they turned to political activity within the Jewish community.[39] Loyal to their leftist tendencies and religious identity, they gathered a dozen like-minded comrades and established the most significant Jewish organization in late 1970s Iran: the Association of Jewish Iranian Intellectuals (AJII; *Jamiʿah-i Rawshanfikran-i Kalimi-yi Iran*). Habib, an interviewee for this project, was a close friend of Yeshayaee and Danseshrad from their days in the Tudeh. He was also one of AJII's founders: "We established our office in an apartment on Firdawsi Street. There were four of us, and we did not know where exactly we were heading."[40] They did not have a well-thought-out plan, but they wanted to politicize the community and connect Jewish values and ideas to the political program of the Tudeh Party. AJII's significance is threefold. First, it organized the Jews under a Jewish ethnic banner to engage in revolutionary activity. Second, in 1978 it challenged the old-guard leadership of the community, which mostly identified with the Shah's regime and had connections with Zionist organizations, and gained control of the Jewish establishment.[41] And third (only in July 1979, after the revolution), its weekly publication, *Tamuz*, named after the Hebrew month that corresponds to June/July (the month in which its publication started), quickly became a highly circulated magazine that aspired to be a bridge between the Jewish community and the Iranian people. As mentioned before, there were overlaps in some of the individuals' affiliations, and so the association actively welcomed people with different political and organizational affiliations and became the main venue for leftist Jewish activists.

In an article celebrating the third anniversary of AJII, a *Tamuz* editorial outlined the organization's contribution to Jewish involvement in the revolution:

> From the beginning of the year 1357 [1978] a group of the Iranian Jews has participated in the great movement against imperialism and dictatorship. From the very beginning we tried to collaborate with the revolutionaries, especially the Muslim clerics at different levels, and we have done this work ever since. And at last, in the month of Shahrivar 1357 [August 1978], a Jewish group joined the protest for the first time under an Iranian-Jewish banner, and this group, in the month of Azar 1357 [November 1978], met with the late Ayatollah Taliqani, and announced the[ir] common goals.[42]

This quote shows that AJII was a much more sophisticated incarnation of the previous attempt to be part of a national movement. In November 1978 these groups believed that the revolution was about to happen and that the Shah would soon be overthrown, but it can still be regarded as a bold policy to approach a revolutionary figure such as Taliqani for collaboration and give publicity to such support.

Indeed, AJII was formed to show Jewish discontent with the monarchical regime. The organization was established in March 1978, as revolutionary events were already unfolding. The group immediately began collaborating with other rebelling factions, including with Muslim Iranian activists (most notably Ayatollah Taliqani): "We formed this group in order to show the rest of the people in Iran that we Jews were not woven from a different fabric of society than other Iranians, but that we also supported [the new government's professed] goals for democracy and freedom," said Sa'id Banayan, one of the association's founding fathers.[43] AJII became the most vocal supporter of the revolution among the Jewish community. Hushang, an interviewee for this project and a prominent figure in AJII and the Jewish community during the revolution, stated, "AJII was the most important Jewish organization during the revolution. At the core of it were left-leaning intellectuals and students, and later many other Jews joined in."[44] Initially, the Jewish community did not welcome the new AJII leadership and tried to prevent them from gaining influence in the *Anjuman* (in Persian, the association, the short name for the Jewish Association), the traditional community organization. However, after the elections for the Anjuman's council in March 1978, the new AJII leadership succeeded in establishing a "revolutionary" committee to run Jewish affairs.[45] Some AJII members had served time in the Shah's prisons during previous turmoil, where they had become acquainted with other political dissidents who were later involved in the revolutionary movement. The most significant relationship was with Khomeini's close ally, the popular thinker and a chief ideologist of the revolution, Taliqani.[46]

AJII saw indifference, separatism, and corruption as the main obstacles to advancement within the Jewish community. In order to win the hearts and minds of Jews, the association invested in many activities that correlated with their ideals. It sponsored activities with Muslim activists during the revolution and established a lecture series hosted in local synagogues that featured presentations from secular Muslim advocates of the revolution and high-ranking clerics who were deeply involved in the revolution.[47] For example, Hidayatullah Matin-Daftari, one of the National Front's leaders and the son-in-law of the revered prime minister, Mohammad Mosaddeq, came to talk about how important it was for the Jews to contribute to the revolution and participate in building a new Iranian society.[48]

The official AJII bylaws reflect hybrid identities that were, in many ways, unique to Iran. They contained sentiments of nationalism and radical socialism, mixed with Muslim and Jewish religiosity. Some of the articles in the AJII bylaws expressed this approach with a call for political action and Iranian social solidarity. Article 3, for example, reads, "[We encourage] active participation in the social life of the Iranian people, and the creation of a Jewish society that will struggle shoulder to shoulder with our Iranian brothers for the ultimate victory of the revolution and the building of a free and progressive Iran." Article 4 presents the utopian vision of creating a new society, describing the organization's commitment to "efforts to preserve the fruits of the revolution of the Iranian people in regards of social and personal rights and including those of the Iranian Jews in the Islamic Republic of Iran." Article 5 distinguishes between Jews and Zionism, since during the revolution there were factions that intentionally conflated the two. The article declares the organization's commitment to waging "war against imperialism, and any form of colonialism, including Zionism, and revealing the relationship between Zionism and world imperialism," as well as waging "war against any sort of racial discrimination, racism, and antisemitism." Article 6 talks once again about the revolutionary utopia, encouraging the community to adapt "to the new reality in Iran, by enjoying all the opportunities to have better conditions to religious and cultural life and welfare of the Iranian Jews."[49] These bylaws' articles efficiently reflected the mindset of the leftist movements in Iran during the revolution. They envisioned a sort of model society in which universal values of solidarity would yield a just and open community, one in which the Jews would be equal citizens.

AJII clearly envisaged a utopian republic of endless opportunities, which would be made possible only by deposing the monarchy and establishing the Iranian republic. The vision of a republic that emphasized fraternity, solidarity—particularly with Palestinians—and freedom for minorities is representative of the cultural identity that AJII members aspired to create. This cultural identity was primarily Iranian but expanded to include the Arab Middle East and Third World countries. By positioning the organization as anti-imperialist and anti-colonialist, AJII became relevant not only to the Iranian context but even to the broader Middle East.

Sapir Charity Hospital, the Revolution, and Ayatollah Taliqani

AJII pulled members from a variety of political realms, state employees, merchants, industrialists, community activists, and Sapir Hospital staff. Some of the senior officials in the hospital were involved to some extent in AJII, sympathized with its causes, and assisted the revolutionaries for various reasons (such as believing in the democratic mission of the group, opposing the brutal handling of the demonstrators by the Shah's army, and backing the humanitarian cause of saving lives). These facilitators included Gad Naim, who was part of AJII leadership and a senior administrator in Sapir Hospital;[50] Dr. Manuchihr Aliyasi, who was also among the hospital's senior staff and an AJII sympathizer;[51] and Yeshayaee, who was among the founders of AJII and *Tamuz* and became the hospital director after the revolution.[52] The story of the hospital during the revolution helps us to see the involvement of Jewish revolutionaries and nonrevolutionaries who became part of the movement for reasons that exceed any political goals.

On September 8, 1978, mass demonstrations erupted in Tehran. The Shah sent the army to shoot live ammunition into the crowd of protesters (Where were they principally gathered? All over Tehran. I mention Zhalah below as it was one of the most horrific events of the day). This event became known as Black Friday and came to directly involve the hospital. "That Friday the head nurse, Ms. Farangis Hasidim, called me and told me that they are bringing many casualties to the hospital," recalled Dr. Jalali, one of the senior officials in Sapir Hospital at that time. "I drove to the hospital but the Zhalah [avenue] was blocked, so I went by foot and there was shooting. . . . Since I was friendly with the ambulance services people, almost 90 percent of the injured people came to Sapir hospital, where we treated all of them in our four surgery rooms." At this point Jalali referred to the growing involvement of Ayatollah Taliqani and his personal relationship with him, which proved to be essential later on: "Five months prior to the revolution [following Black Friday] I had a building next to my office, I dedicated it to 'Taliqani Support Group' [in Persian, *Guruh-i Imdad-i Taliqani*]. . . . After 'Black Friday' he called me and told me how he appreciated all the humanitarian work we did there. And yes, everybody knew about it."[53]

Guruh-i Imdad-i Taliqani became an important apparatus that helped first responders to treat the wounded protesters in the big cities, especially Tehran. According to the Iranian press, there were two first response groups reporting to Taliqani. They had a relatively large staff of volunteer physicians, nurses, ambulances, and other staff, and their contributions toward ensuring the continuity of the protests cannot be overrated.[54]

The acquaintance of Taliqani with Jewish leaders in Tehran extended beyond his friendship with Jalali. Upon Taliqani's release from prison, a group of prominent Jewish figures went to visit him and stayed in close contact with him until his death in 1979. Taliqani became one of the foremost advocates for minority rights in postrevolutionary Iran.[55] Although Jalali was politically affiliated with AJII, some of the doctors were not. The story of the hospital is mostly a humanitarian one.

On December 11, 1978, one of the largest demonstrations against the Shah took place in Tehran. Newspapers called it a "demonstration of millions," and it set a milestone in the struggle against the Shah's regime. Jewish participation set records as well; according to some sources, five thousand Jews participated in these protests.[56] Other estimates were much higher. Hushang, a longtime leftist activist in the Jewish community and AJII, helped organize the massive Jewish appearance that day: "According to press reports close to twelve thousand Jews participated in these protests that day," he says. "The Jewish religious leaders marched in the front row and the rest of the Jews followed them, showing great solidarity with our Iranian compatriots."[57] The religious leadership sided with the young radical group and in a sense "legitimized" them. "From the first days of the revolution we had considerable support from religious leaders. Hakham Yedidia Shofet, Hakham Uriel Davidi, Rabbi David Shofet, Hakham Yosef Hamadani Cohen, and others attended and supported. . . . Other key figures were Parviz Yeshayaee, 'Aziz Daneshrad, Ya'qub Barkhurdar, Hushang Melamed, Dr. Manuchihr Aliyasi, and Ms. Farangis Hasidim—all played a major role," Hushang said.[58] According to him, the activities of AJII helped to reduce tensions between the Muslim majority and the Jewish minority. However, not all of the religious leaders who joined that day did so wholeheartedly. "It was my assignment to convince Hakham Shofet to join us, to get him in the picture," said Mihrdad. "He was sympathetic to the cause but felt heavy hearted. He was reluctant to come and we told him that it was for the sake and safety of the community. We even found rabbinic writing and a halachic ruling that say that if the community requires you to do such and such you do it not because this is your belief but because the decision would be for the good of the community. So he said he would come out."[59] Shofet, then, participated despite early reservations, which makes him a unique case in this story. Loyalty to both the Shah and the community meant a great deal to him. He came out that day and afterward not because he looked to facilitate integration of the community into the broader society but rather to seek protection for the community in a rapidly changing reality.

Habib's memories of this demonstration help us to understand the profound impact it had on the participants: "We met by Darvazah-i dawlat Synagogue in south Tehran and joined the main demonstration from there. . . . Our signs and chants were: *Yahudi-musalman hambastigi-i mubarak* [Jewish-Muslims blessed solidarity]. It was so exciting, I could not stop crying." Hakham Shofet's recollections of this day express the same sentiment:

> In every place we live we must respect the majority's opinion and to approve and respect their leadership [not necessarily the elected or ruling leadership]. Because of this rule, in those days, with respect to these people, we joined them in marching for the *Tasu'a* [the ninth day of the holy month of Muharram; in Shi'a tradition it symbolizes the day before the battle of Karbala and the preparations of Hossein] in 19 Azar Mah 1357 [December 9, 1978]. Muhandis Daneshrad and other members of the Jewish Community [Anjuman] board were on my side.... It was constructive and inspiring. Many of the Muslims that led this great march and were responsible for it welcomed us warmly, among them were many Shi'i clerics.[60]

This memory is interesting, especially because of the fact that Shofet did not openly oppose the Shah. There are multiple accounts of him positively commenting on the Shah's period as unprecedented for Iranian Jews and expressing his fear of the unclear future. In an interview, one of the people who made Shofet join the march said that Shofet stated he would do it for the sake of the community, but he wanted the march organizer to know that every Saturday, when he offered prayers for the health of the Shah, he meant it.

Muslim protesters greeted the Jewish group by chanting, "Jewish brother, welcome, welcome" (*Baradar-i yahudi khush amadi, khush amadi*).[61] When they passed by Madrasah-i 'Alavi,[62] they chanted, "Khomeini's leadership is the basis of national unity" (*Rahbari-yi Khomeini asas-i vahdat-i milli*). "That day," Habib says, "we all had tears of happiness. We were all in support of democracy, and freedom, and the revolution."[63]

Despite the presentation of national unity in the demonstration, given past experiences, it was obvious that the protest was not about to end peacefully. Sapir Hospital's personnel were well prepared for the events of Tasu'a and 'Ashura. "That morning they called me from Madrasah-i 'Alavi and asked to keep all the staff and doctors for the day. I received 70 or 80 percent of the injured from all over the city. All of them went either to Sapir, Kurush-i Kabir as it was called back then, or the Imperial Medical Center, this situation lasted for seventy-two hours," recalled Jalali.[64]

Following these events, in late 1978 a delegation of the Jewish community went to Paris to meet the leader of the revolution, Ayatollah Khomeini. The tacit purpose of this trip was to ensure that Jews would not be regarded as enemies of the revolution but rather as its supporters. This meeting was the first of many between the Jewish leadership and Khomeini.[65] Shortly after, the hospital received its first recognition from Khomeini: "For this reason [the humanitarian help] Imam Khomeini, before his return to Iran, had sent a letter of gratitude to the director of the hospital, recognizing his help and support for the wounded revolutionaries," said Dr. Siamak Moreh-Sedegh, one of the hospital's leaders and the current Jewish deputy in the Majlis in an interview. He described the assistance given to the revolutionaries and confirmed, once again, the story of the Shah's army siege in 1978.[66] Receiving Khomeini's recognition was no small feat. In many ways it secured the future of the Jews under the leadership of the revolution.

Shortly after the 'Ashura events, the revolution took a dramatic turn when, on January 15, 1979, Mohammad Reza Pahlavi left Iran for good. "Shah Raft" (the Shah left), announced the newspapers the next day to the overjoyed crowds, and about two weeks later they announced that the Imam had arrived (*Imam amad*). All major minority groups came to the airport to welcome Ayatollah Khomeini back to Iran. The Jewish delegation coordinated their participation with another prominent leader of the revolutionary movement, Ayatollah Mohammad Bihishti. According to Mihrdad, "Bihishti knew Yeshayaee from the time they were in jail together and helped to bring the Jewish community on board of the welcome ceremony." This acquaintance facilitated bringing the Jewish representatives into the reception plans.[67]

After the installation of the new regime, the hospital encountered controversy. Jalali stated, "One night after the revolution they called me to tell that a group of people from the regime came and changed the name of the hospital to 'Khusraw Golisurkhi Hospital.' A member of the left, Golisurkhi had been executed by the Shah.[68] It took us a long time, together with Parviz Yesha'ya, to change it to 'Dr. Sapir Hospital.'"[69] Simin, Sapir's relative, explained how they petitioned the government to have the name changed to Dr. Sapir: "I collected evidence from people that got treatment in the hospital, collected newspaper stories, letters from clerics about the hospital during the revolution, and gave it to them in a big box. After a short discussion they pronounced him a Shahid, a martyr of the revolution, and ordered to have the name changed to Dr. Sapir Hospital."[70] This episode of the name change became significant as the Jewish community retained management of the hospital and the government acknowledged the role it had played during the revolution. Still today, at the entrance to the hospital, there is a sign welcoming patients, staff, and visitors. The sign reads, in Hebrew and Persian, "Love thy neighbor as yourself" (Hebrew: *Ve'ahavta le're'acha kamocha*; Persian: *Hamnow'at ra mesl-i khodet dust bedar*), and this essentially captures the philosophy of this hospital from the time it was established by Sapir and onward.[71]

The same events, wars, philosophies, and ideologies that shaped revolutionaries elsewhere in the world inspired the generation that came of age in the 1970s in Iran. It was the time when American students demonstrated against the war in Vietnam and Sartre and Michel Foucault incited European students and supported various goals of Third World identity groups. At the same time that many countries experienced their first moments of independence, the Iranian students' local project was to struggle against the American-backed monarchy in Iran and institute a functioning socialist republic instead. This kind of republic, would obviously be founded on the ideals of an egalitarian society, where religious or ethnic affiliations play no part. Thus the promise was to create a multiethnic, multireligious society.

The involvement of the Jews can be explained by the level of assimilation that they had reached by this crucial moment. Whereas members of their parents' generation in the late 1960s and early 1970s spent their own youths paving the way to leave the mahallah and traditional Jewish life in order to pursue education and careers in the private and public sectors, their children felt they had to fight not for their status as a marginal minority but rather for a better society for Iran. Jewish identity at that point served as another component and possible affiliation in the greater social tapestry of minorities in Iran.

Jewish participants in the student movements, both in Iran and abroad, belonged at that point to the nationalist bourgeoisie, whether they recognized it or not. Their assimilation efforts were fruitful, and Jewish culture and identity were just additional labels they carried and that perhaps rooted them deeper in the Iranian soil. It is within this context that we can begin to understand the establishment of AJII, initiatives such as the ones involving Sapir Hospital during the revolution, or the participation of Jews in Muslim revolutionary movements. These represent the entire spectrum of national belonging, from the decision of AJII's members to profess Iranian nationalism as Jews, to Sapir Hospital's efforts to form a partnership to provide humanitarian assistance (again, even when some of the collaborators evidently supported the Shah), to a desire to assimilate through the adoption of all the identifiers of Iranian and Islamic symbolism and rhetoric. We see, however, that no matter what venue of activism Jewish participants ended up pursuing, they articulated their responses around their interpretation of Judaism and Jewish values. For many of them, radical politics through participation in the Tudeh and AJII, or writing for *Bani-Adam*, *Nissan*, or *Tamuz*, were all means to follow the halachic order "Love thy neighbor as thyself."

NOTES

1. To protect the identities of interviewees and for methodological reasons, I have used pseudonyms exclusively throughout the discussions of my research.

2. Eskandari mentions that in the conference of 1331 (by the Persian calendar; in the Gregorian calendar the year was 1952) "the question of fighting against fascism was especially important. A few people opposed it, but the vast majority voted for it and that is how we decided to start an anti-fascist newspaper, and this led to Soviet intervention in our work." There is good reason to believe that the date of the conference, because of the content Eskandari mentions, actually took place ten years earlier, in 1321 (1942). Iraj Eskandari, Babak Amir Khusravi, and Faridun Azamur, *Khatirat-i Siyasi* (France, 1336 [1957]), 28.

3. Ervand Abrahamian, *Iran Between Two Revolutions* (Princeton, NJ: Princeton University Press, 1982); Mark J. Gasiorowski, "The 1953 *Coup D'Etat* in Iran," *International Journal of Middle East Studies* 19, no. 3 (1987): 261–286, https://doi.org/10.1017/S0020743800056737; Aviva Halamish, *Meir Yaari: A Collective Biography* (Tel-Aviv: Am Oved, 2009); Aviva Halamish, *Meir Yaari: The Rebbe from Merhavia—The State Years* (Tel-Aviv: Am Oved, 2013); Anita Shapira, "Ha-kibbutz ve-ha-medina," *'Iyunim bi-tkumat Yisrael* 20 (2010): 193–207.

4. Faryar Nikbakht, "Yahudiyan Dar Nihzatha Va Ahzab-i Siyasi," in *Terua*, ed. Homa Sarshar (Beverly Hills, CA: Center for Iranian Jewish Oral History; Philadelphia: Jewish Publication Society, 1996), 79–81.

5. Abrahamian, *Iran Between Two Revolutions*, 257–258; Gasiorowski, "The 1953 Coup D'Etat."

6. Nikbakht, "Yahudiyan Dar Nihzatha," 81.

7. Abrahamian also mentions border proximity as a factor in Soviet influence. The Soviets enthusiastically supported groups rebelling against Iran's central government. Abrahamian, *Iran Between Two Revolutions*, 386.

8. Iraj Farhoumand, "Iraniyan-i Yahudi va Hizb-i Tudah-i Iran," in *Yahudiyan-i Irani Dar Tarikh-i Mu'asir*, ed. Homa Sarshar (Beverly Hills, CA: Center for Iranian Jewish Oral History; Philadelphia: Jewish Publication Society, 2000), 119–124.

9. Interview with Pinhas, May 15, 2014.

10. As historian Ervand Abrahamian suggests, minorities' massive engagement and the party's even wider popularity among minorities gained the Tudeh Party a reputation for being the party of Armenians, Jews, and Caucasian émigrés. Abrahamian mentions this reputation because the party's opponents cited it to discredit the organization. Abrahamian, *Iran Between Two Revolutions*, 452.

11. Interview with Habib, June 24, 2013.

12. Abrahamian, *Iran Between Two Revolutions*, 201–202; Jaleh Pirnazar, "Yahudiyan-i Iran, Huvviyyat-i Milli va Ruznamahnigari," in *Yahudiyan-i Irani*, 25.

13. *Nissan* was not officially connected to the Tudeh Party. Its status as a semi-official newspaper stemmed from Anvar's proximity to the party's leadership and his ability to communicate their messages efficiently when *Mardum*, *Rahbar*, or *Razm* was censored.

14. Pirnazar, "Yahudiyan-i Iran," 25–26.

15. Arnold Krammer, *The Forgotten Friendship: Israel and the Soviet Bloc, 1947–53* (Urbana: University of Illinois Press, 1974), 134. Judd Teller reports that the Soviet security forces murdered 433 Jewish artists and intellectuals after 1948. See Judd L. Teller, *The Kremlin, the Jews, and the Middle East* (New York: T. Yoseloff, 1957); Jacob Ari Labendz, "Re-Negotiating Czechoslovakia. The State and the Jews in Communist Central Europe: The Czech Lands, 1945–1990" (PhD diss., Washington University, Saint Louis, 2014), 51–52, 65. The assault on Soviet Jewish artists began even before the events of fall 1948. In January of that year, Soviet security forces in Belarus murdered Solomon Mikhoels, who led both the Moscow State Jewish Theater and the Jewish Anti-Fascist Committee. The Soviet anti-Zionist campaign culminated in 1952 with the trial and execution of fifteen functionaries of the latter organization, along with ten others. See Joshua Rubenstein, Vladimir Pavlovich Naumov, eds., and Laura Esther Wolfson, trans, *Stalin's Secret Pogrom: The Postwar Inquisition of the Jewish Anti-Fascist Committee*, abridged ed. (New Haven, CT: Yale University Press, 2001). The Doctors' Plot was a series of government attacks on a group of predominantly Jewish Moscow doctors and officials between 1952 and 1953. These individuals were accused of plotting to assassinate Stalin and other senior officials between 1948 and 1953. Stalin's death in 1953 put an end to this persecution and the case was dropped. The Prague trials concerned the 1952 Slánský Affair that took place in Czechoslovakia. Like the Doctors' Plot, this was yet another "show trial," this time of fourteen Communist officials, eleven of whom were Jews. These individuals were accused of having Trotskyite leanings, supporting Yugoslavia's Josip Broz Tito, and engaging in Zionist conspiracy. The majority of the defendants were hanged in Prague, but three received life imprisonment. I want to thank Jacob Ari Labendz for assistance with this information.

16. "Tashkilat-i sayunist alatidast-i imperialism amrika," *Nissan*, 17 Ordibehesht 1332 [May 7, 1953], 1, 4.

17. For analysis on the place of the kibbutz in Israeli society and the role of the kibbutz movement in the defining ethos of Israel, see Anita Shapira, "Ha-kibbutz ve-ha-medina"; Halamish, *Meir Yaari: A Collective Biography*; Halamish, *Meir Yaari: The Rebbe from Merhavia*.

18. At one point in the article, the author refers to Mapam as the "right-wing" party. This is certainly a mistake, as Mapam was not only known as a socialist party in the Israeli political spectrum but was also solidly committed to Stalin. "Tiror afkar va taftish 'aqayid bi-vasilah dulat amrikayii benguriun dar isra'il idamah darad," *Nissan*, 17 Ordibehesht 1332 [May 7, 1953], 1, 3.

19. "Matbu'at va mardum isra'il tahrikat zid-i shuru-yi bingurin ra mahkum mi-kunand," *Nissan*, 17 Ordibehesht 1332 [May 7, 1953], 1.

20. "Guftigu ba khvanandigan," *Nissan*, 17 Ordibehesht 1332 [May 7, 1953], 3.

21. "Halivud digar jai hunarmandan nist," *Nissan*, 17 Ordibehesht 1332 [May 7, 1953], 1, 3.

22. "Majlis yadibud," *Nissan*, 22 Murdad 1332 [August 13, 1953], 1, 4.

23. "Istiqbal bi-nazir yahudiyan Abadan az ruznamih Nissan," *Nissan*, 17 Ordibehesht 1332 [May 7, 1953], 1, 3.

24. Pirnazar, "Yahudiyan-i Iran."

25. In an article on Jewish publications of this era, Amnon Netzer categorized some of the newspapers discussed in this chapter. Netzer asserted that *Nissan*, edited by Anvar, was directly connected to the Tudeh, whereas he describes *Bani-Adam* as merely "leftist; pro-Tudeh." Interestingly, the newspapers *Israiil* and *'Alim-i Yahud* are categorized as "social Zionist" and "general," respectively. However, Netzer added that Jewish Tudeh sympathizers wrote for both newspapers and that they even formed the majority of *Israiil*'s editorial board. This contribution by Netzer demonstrates, perhaps better than other statistics, the degree to which Jews embraced leftist political ideologies at the time. Amnon Netzer, "Ha-'Itonut Ha-Yehudit," in *Iran*, ed. Haim Saadoun (Jerusalem: Yad Ben-Zvi, 2005), 141–154.

26. "Jashn aghaz chiharmin sal-i istiqlal: Israil ra bimilat-i israil tabrik miguyim," *Bani-Adam*, 14 Ordibehesht 1331 [May 4, 1952], 1, 3. Interestingly, this issue also included excerpts from the Israeli Declaration of Independence.

27. The second part of the article is confusing chronologically. There are a few references to 1949 as the year of Israel's establishment as a state, instead of 1948. "Jashn aghaz chiharmin sal-i istiqlal," 1, 3.

28. "Israiil va jonbash'ha-i azadi talibanih khavar miyanih," *Bani-Adam*, 14 Ordibehesht 1331 [May 4, 1952], 3.

29. "Divan dadgastri binalmilili lahih har tasmimi itikhad konid dar rah vurush millat iran kuchaktarin bin tasiri nakhvuhad dhasht," *Bani-Adam*, 4 Khordad 1331 [May 25, 1952], 1, 3.

30. "Namunih-i az vaz'i zandigi yahudiyan Abadan," *Bani-Adam*, 11 Khordad 1331 [June 1, 1952], 1, 4.

31. In mid-1952 *Bani-Adam* sought to provide a forum for these forgotten voices by publicizing an appeal on behalf of Abadani Jews written by fourteen members of Iran's Jewish community leadership. This letter, sent to the governor of Abadan, asked for the creation of election booths so that Abadan's four thousand Jews could participate in the general elections, thus insisting on their right to elect their (one) representative. A copy of the letter was also sent to Prime Minister Mosaddeq, the governor of Tehran, and the Tehran Jewish Society, and it was reprinted in *Bani-Adam*. "Faraman-dati mukhtarim Abadan," *Bani-Adam*, 4 Khordad 1331 [May 25, 1952], 3.

32. "Barrasi birnamih intikhabati aqayi anvar," *Bani-Adam*, 11 Khordad 1331 [June 1, 1952], 1, 3.

33. "Shabu'ot, 'id tajlil adalat va azadi," *Bani-Adam*, 11 Khordad 1331 [June 1, 1952], 1, 3.

34. "Arzash-i zan dar ijtima,'" *Bani-Adam*, 9 Aban 1330 [November 1, 1951], 1, 3.

35. "Intikhabat," *Bani-Adam*, 9 Aban 1330 [November 1, 1951], 1–2.

36. The White Revolution is the name of a rapid modernization project announced by Mohammad Reza Shah in 1963. It aimed to transform Iran, the Iranian economy, and Iranian society. The shah detailed his plan in a book he published by the same name. The program included land reform, agrarian reform, infrastructure, health, education, and more.

37. Interview with Mihrdad, January 22, 2013.

38. Interview with Mihrdad.

39. David Menashri, "The Jews in Iran: Between the Shah and Khomeini," in *antisemitism in Times of Crisis*, ed. Sander L. Gilman and Steven T. Katz (New York: New York University Press, 1991), 360.

40. Interview with Habib, June 24, 2013.

41. Kuhin provides another account of the events, which is interesting in light of Kuhin's own affiliation with the old guard and his political position:

> By the spring of 1979, the legal term of the Jewish Association leadership was also coming to an end. The Jewish university students organizations, the youth and graduate societies, had submitted a unified list of candidates among which were the names of only two members of the present association. The rest of the association members, those who were known as the "National Fund Group," had produced their own list. After several meet-

> ings, seminars and other activities, finally the candidates of the former group won the majority, and the community was faced with a new association. In the new association, engineer Aziz Daneshrad, who had been a member of the association in the past, was elected as the chairman. The reason for the defeat of the "National Fund Group" in a few words was that these gentlemen preferred connections over qualifications when recruiting their colleagues; instead of selecting experts and knowledgeable people they were after people who would obediently follow the head of the Fund. Also, by concentrating all the financial affairs and by controlling all the funds, they intended to ensure the obedience of all active organizations for themselves. The organizations, on the other hand, and in particular the university students and the youth, would not acquiesce anyway, and demanded that the National Fund disperse each organization's respective expenses without conditions, according to their bylaws, without interfering with the leadership and the activities of the organizations.

For the extended quotations from this memoir, I used translations by Faryar Nikbakht with Aziz Kuhin's permission. Kuhin, *Yusif Kuhin*, 302. Yousef Kohin: *Guzarish va Khaṭirat-i Fa"aliyat' ha-yi Siyasi va Ijtima'i* (Los Angeles: International Printing, 1993).

42. Editorial, "Fa'aliyyat-i Sah Salah-i Jami'ah-i Rawshanfikran-i Kalimi-yi Iran," *Tamuz*, September 25, 1981.

43. I would like to thank Karmel Melamed for referring me to this interview and contributing his own knowledge to this research; see Karmel Melamed, "Escape, Exile, Rebirth: Iranian Jewish Diaspora Alive and Well in Los Angeles," *Jewish Journal*, September 4, 2008, http://jewishjournal.com/news/los_angeles/community/65726/escape-exile-rebirth-iranian-jewish-diaspora-alive-and-well-in-los-angeles/.

44. Interview with Hushang, May 15, 2011.

45. In any case, a few months later, in the summer of 1978, they failed to be reelected. See Amnon Netzer, *Yehude Iran Be-Yamenu* (Jerusalem: Shazar Library, Institute for Contemporary Jewry, Hebrew University of Jerusalem, 1981), 21. Amnon Netzer, *Yehude Iran be-yamenu* (Jerusalem: Hebrew University of Jerusalem Press, 1981).

46. Read more about Taliqani and his pivotal role in the revolution in Hamid Dabashi, *Theology of Discontent: The Ideological Foundation of the Islamic Revolution in Iran* (New York: New York University Press, 1993), 216–272.

47. Netzer, *Yehude Iran be-Yamenu*, 22; "Fa'aliyyat-i Sah Salah-i," 6.

48. Amnon Netzer, "Yehudei Iran, Yisrael, ve-Ha-Republiqah Ha-Islamit Shel Iran," *Gesher* 26 (Spring–Summer 1980), 48.

49. Netzer, "Yehudei Iran, Yisrael," 49.

50. Iranjewish.com, "Ma Yahudiyan Mizrakhi Hastim va Fiqh Ghani Darim," Summer 1388 [2009], http://www.iranjewish.com/Essay/Essay_36_mizrakhi.htm.

51. 7Dorim.com, "Doktor Manuchehr Aliyasi," accessed July 7, 2011, http://www.7dorim.com/tasavir/Namayandeh_Eliasi.asp.

52. Interview with Dr. Jalali, May 15, 2011.

53. Interview with Dr. Jalali. Kuhin remembered the day very similarly. Given that Kuhin was at odds with Jalali, I believe this validates the account. Kuhin, *Yusif Kuhin*, 312.

54. "I'zam-i Ekip-i Pizashki-yi Ayatollah Taliqani," *Kayhan International*, April 24, 1979.

55. Goel Cohen, *Az Kargaran Ta Kar-Afarini* (Geneva: Sina, 2011), 190–191.

56. Netzer, *Yehude Iran Be-Yamenu*, 22.

57. Interview with Hushang, May 15, 2011.

58. Interview with Hushang.

59. Interview with Mihrdad, January 22, 2013.

60. Goel Cohen, ed., *Bar Bal-i Khirad: Jami'ah-i Yahudiyan-i Iran va Haftad Sal Rahbari-Yi Mazhabi, Gam Bah Gam Ba Hakham Yedidiya Shofet Dar Kashan, Tehran, va Los Angeles* (Los Angeles: Educational Foundation of Hacham Yedidia Shofet, 2010) 390.

61. Cohen, *Bar Bal-i Khirad*, 390.

62. Madrasah-i 'Alavi was a girls' school in Tehran. It was known to be an opposition-supporting institution. Upon his return from exile, Khomeini first resided there.

63. Interview with Habib, June 24, 2013.
64. Interview with Dr. Jalali, May 15, 2011.
65. Netzer, *Yehude Iran Be-Yamenu*, 22.
66. IranJewish.com, "Nishani Az Vahdat-i Milli Dar Bimaristan-i Duktur Sapir," Esfand 1386 [February–March 2008]. http://www.iranjewish.com/Essay/Essay_34_farsi_bimarestan_sepir.htm.
67. Interview with Mihrdad, January 22, 2013.
68. Golisurkhi was identified with some of the guerilla movements. His trial was televised and had a tremendous impact on the young revolutionaries. His iconic image became one of the symbols of the revolution. Read more about him in Maziar Behrooz, *Rebels with a Cause: The Failure of the Left in Iran* (London: I. B. Tauris, 1999), 69–70.
69. Interview with Dr. Jalali, May 15, 2011.
70. Interview with Simin, March 27, 2011.
71. I am thankful to Rabbi Dr. Oren Steinitz for his advice and clarification on this important issue.

CHAPTER 7

Panthers and Leashes

A HISTORY OF MIZRAHI RADICALISM

Dario Miccoli

"We have to organize a protest," Herzl said, and he lay down next to me on the grass, at the foot of my favorite palm tree. "We have to, do you understand?" "Do me a favor, just shut up," I told him, holding my intertwined hands under my head and looking at the silver moon. "My head hurts just listening to you." "We cannot do without a protest," Herzl said, "Impossible."

—*Eli Amir,* Tarnegol kapparot *(Scapegoat)*

These lines open a chapter of a 1984 novel by the Baghdad-born Israeli Eli Amir.[1] While in a kibbutz, where the parents agreed to send them so that the two could leave the *ma'abarah* (transit camp) and hopefully integrate into the new country, the protagonist Nuri and his friend Herzl—originally from Iraq—experience the cultural disorientation that many of their peers also felt upon their arrival in Israel in the 1950s. Herzl even thinks of organizing a protest against the Ashkenazi veterans of the kibbutz and the discriminatory attitude they have toward the Middle Eastern and North African young immigrants: Protesting seems to him the only way to make his voice heard.

Even though the story of the protest of Nuri and Herzl is fictional and based on the imagination of the novel's author Eli Amir, it reflects in quite a realistic manner the experience of social, cultural, and political marginalization of North African and Middle Eastern Jews during the process of *'aliyah ve-qlitah* (immigration and absorption) in Israel during the 1950s and 1960s, as well as some of the tactics that they put in place to subvert the situation or at least rebel against it.[2] To make sense of the reality in which Nuri and Herzl's protest developed, this chapter reconstructs the history of *Mizrahi* (lit. "Eastern") radicalism and political activism, by which I mean a set of practices that aim at transforming the status of *Mizrahim*—the Israeli Jews of Middle Eastern and North African origin—in Israeli society, while striving for inclusion in it too.[3] Mizrahi radicalism is to be regarded as a shifting cultural and political framework in which different ideas and political movements can be found: from the street riots of Wadi Salib in 1959 and the leftist and anti-establishment stances of *Ha-panterim ha-shehorim* (The Black Panthers) of the early 1970s, to the Sephardi religious party *Shas* (acronym of *Shomrei Torah sfaradim*; Sephardi Guardians of the Torah) of the 1980s, to more recent social movements like *Ha-qeshet ha-demoqratit ha-mizrahit* (Mizrahi Democratic Rainbow). Being radical and Mizrahi, in other words, meant and still means many different things, depending on context and contingency. However, what binds together these movements is the desire—as it happens in all cases of (Jewish) radicalism—to fundamentally change society.[4] Mizrahi radicalism wishes to construct another kind of Israel in which the rifts between sectors of the population—firstly between Ashkenazim and Mizrahim, but sometimes also between Israelis and Palestinians—will disappear. It is a broad political landscape in which global notions of Jewishness and internationalism can be debated and intersect with local discussions on Israeliness and *mizrahiyut* ("Eastern-ness"). For this reason, the case of the Mizrahim may help us see Jewish radicalism as a malleable political tool that has influenced both leftist and rightist movements.

Before I start to delve into the history of Mizrahi radicalism, it is important to note that the Jews of the Middle East and North Africa underwent significant changes during the late Ottoman and post-Ottoman periods, and up to the mass migrations of the 1950s and 1960s. Many took part in their countries' nationalist revivals—for example the Jews of Iraq and their involvement in politics and culture.[5] On the other hand, Zionism only marginally concerned most of them.[6] When Israel was founded in 1948, about 800,000 Jews lived in the Middle East and in North Africa.[7] After the 1948 Arab-Israeli War that lead to the establishment of the modern State of Israel, as well as because of decolonization and the diffusion of more exclusionary forms of Arab nationalism, vast numbers of Jews left the region for Israel, European nations, the United States, and elsewhere.[8] Between 1948 and the late 1960s, Israel saw the arrival of hundreds of thousands of *'olim hadashim* (new immigrants). These new immigrants found themselves in a nation-state characterized by socialist Zionism, led by an elite of European (primarily Ashkenazi) origin. From a Zionist perspective, the migration of Jews from the Middle East and North Africa (MENA) constituted another step toward the realization of the *kibbutz galuyiot* (ingathering of exiles), where Diaspora Jews would fuse with one another in the *kor ha-hitukh* (melting pot), giving life to a rejuvenated and united Jewish people.[9]

But the *'aliyot* from the Middle East and North Africa region complicated the pristine ideological vision of Israeli history, highlighting the ideological limits of the Zionist establishment.[10] Despite the fact that, as *Ba-ma'arakhah* (In Battle)—a journal published by the Sephardi Community Council of Jerusalem—argued already in 1962, "it is hard to include the exiles from the Lands of Islam and the East in a common denominator" given the heterogeneity of these diasporas, at the beginning the Israeli state classified the *'olim* as *'edot ha-mizrah* (Eastern ethnicities/tribes), and later as Mizrahim.[11] The definition soon gained a derogatory, Orientalist meaning and implied that the Jews of the Middle East and North Africa—as opposed to those of Europe who were the majority of the Zionist pioneers—belonged to backward environments and were religiously conservative and detached from Zionism.[12] Some scholars now suggest that it is more appropriate to utilize the category *Arab Jew*, as it underlines the identity and history that these men and women shared with their Arab neighbors.[13] That said, currently Mizrahi has become a label that even Israelis of Middle Eastern and North African origin utilize to self-identify and that has lost much of its derogatoriness and in some cases has even been politically reclaimed. However, the cleavages between Mizrahim and Ashkenazim have not entirely vanished.[14] But then, what did the Mizrahim do to address these issues, and how did notions of "Israeliness" and Zionism affect them?

Tin Shacks and Dreams: The Beginnings of Mizrahi Radicalism, 1950s–1970s

To answer this question, one needs to go back to the space where everything began: the transit camp. This is where *Sallah Shabati*, one of the most famous Israeli movies on the Mizrahim, directed in 1964 by Efraim Kishon, is set. The movie tells the story of a Mizrahi immigrant and his family, from the first months spent in a faraway *ma'abarah* up to the tragicomic attempts to get a flat in a *shikun* (housing project), where "every room has a window . . . for the air!"—a modest dream that seems unrealizable due to the family's social disorientation and lack of economic resources. As the recent documentaries *Sallah, poh zeh Eretz Israel* (Sallah, This Is the Land of Israel) and *Ma'abarot* (Transit Camps) show, the story of Sallah Shabati in the eponymous film symbolizes that of many immigrants trapped in what proved to be inconsistent state policies, aimed at populating the periphery of Israel through the founding of new settlements, which never reached the results the state had hoped for in terms of economic and industrial development.[15] Upon leaving the ma'abarot, many settled nearby in *'ayarot pituah* (development towns) built in areas like northern Galilee and the Negev.[16] In the 1950s about 30 percent of the Iraqi immigrants and 60 percent of the Moroccans were living in peripheral localities that did not exist before 1948. On the other hand, many 'olim from Europe were able to leave the transit camps more rapidly to settle in central areas, like the Tel Aviv region, that were and remained the more developed ones in terms of job and educational opportunities. In other words, the hopes and expectations that the immigrants had before their migration clashed with a much harder reality: For many, Israel was not a land of rebirth and a place to build a better life, but—at least in the immediate aftermath—a place of alienation and socioeconomic downgrading.[17]

Therefore, the period extending from the mid-1950s to the early 1970s saw the emergence of a multifaceted Mizrahi social and political identity through protests, acts of resistance, and activism. This mirrored a preexisting context in which one finds Jews involved in the development of Arab communism and socialism, as well as in the anti-colonial struggle and Zionism—as other chapters in this volume explain in detail.[18] Mizrahi activism included a myriad of other things: from writing a novel like Shimon Ballas did with *Ha-ma'abarah* in 1964, to working for Arabic broadcasts on Israeli national radio.[19] Be it the strike of the dockers of Ashdod in 1964 or the Hatiqvah uprising of 1965, when Mizrahi youth reacted against the poverty of their neighborhood, these acts intended to highlight the needs and everyday problems of people for whom—as the novelist Ronit Matalon, born in Ganei Tiqvah in 1959 in an Egyptian Jewish family, said many years later—there were "neither gardens [*ganei*] nor hope [*tiqvah*]."[20] They came to construct a network of informal actions that consolidated a new feeling of *mizrahiyut*, destined to become a central component of the political discourse.[21]

The famous Wadi Salib revolt, which erupted in 1959 in the eponymous quarter of Haifa, was rooted in the feeling of being marginalized and given fewer, if any, opportunities to improve one's status. The revolt, long considered the earliest case of Mizrahi radicalism, broke out when a policeman shot a man who had vandalized a coffeeshop while drunk. As rumors had it that the man had died in hospital, crowds of mostly North African *'olim* gathered in the streets and attacked police cars and shops. Dozens of people were hurt and others arrested.[22] Even though Ben-Gurion's government blamed the revolt on the rightist party *Herut* and organizations close to it, Wadi Salib constituted a rather spontaneous act of protest and sanctioned the self-awareness of the Mizrahim as "an oppressed majority of the Israeli Jewish society."[23] It should be read as one of the first "sites of [Mizrahi] contestation in which bodies, symbols, identities, and discourses [were] used to pursue . . . changes in institutionalized power relations."[24] While the media and political establishment discussed the protesters' demands, they neglected the ethnic and racialized elements of their discontent.[25] This does not mean that the political parties—especially opposition ones like the leftist *Mapam* and *Maki* and the rightist *Herut*—were ignoring the migrants from the Arab world. However, if it is true that even the *Histadrut*, the Israeli general trade union, and *Mapai* opened their ranks to the newcomers, it occurred only as long as they accepted "the Zionist parameters of the state, its ideology, and its ruling bodies."[26] This principle, which in many ways was the raison d'être of Zionist institutions and parties in general, had a profound impact on the evolution of Mizrahi radicalism and the ways in which its demands were to be framed if they wanted to be included in the national agenda.

From this perspective, the emergence of *Ha-panterim ha-shehorim* in 1971 represents the outcome of a preexisting history of radical activism, moving from the transit camp to the city. Initially a rather unorganized group of youths of Moroccan origin from the Jerusalem neighborhood of Musrara, *Ha-panterim ha-shehorim* became popular thanks to effective slogans shouted in demonstrations that eventually attracted thousands of people: "We want our share of the cake—and if not, there won't be a cake."[27] As a member of the movement recalled, everything started as "a huge explosion of popular discontent" of common people "mobilized against the conditions in which they were living, their housing, wages, education."[28] *Ha-panterim ha-shehorim* protested in very effective and original ways against the cleavages between Mizrahim and Ashkenazim, for example taking milk bottles from the doorsteps of houses in the middle-class Jerusalem neighborhood of Rehavia and redistributing them to poor Mizrahi families. Blending the model of the American Black Panthers and civil rights' movement with notions of Sephardi pride, *Ha-panterim ha-shehorim* were also among the first Israelis to meet with the PLO leader Yasser Arafat and assert the existence of a link between the pursuit of Israeli social equality and peace with the Palestinians.[29] "There will be no equality and no chance for the Mizrahim"—Reuven Abergel, one of the founders of *Ha-panterim ha-shehorim*, argued—"as long as there's occupation and a national struggle, and on the other hand, the national struggle will not be over so long as the Mizrahim are at the bottom of the ladder."[30]

Even though the labor prime minister Golda Meir dismissed the protesters as *lo' nehmadim* (not nice [people]) and the Mizrahim as Jews that until the *'aliyah* had lived "in caves . . . many did not know what a bed sheet or pajamas were," this did not stop *Ha-panterim ha-shehorim* from running for the elections of the *Histadrut* and for the parliamentary elections of 1973, but without gaining any seats.[31] One of the leaders of *Ha-panterim ha-shehorim*, Charlie Biton, was then elected to the Knesset in 1977 on the list of the communist party *Hadash*. In the 1980s, other members were to join new Sephardi political formations, several of which I will later talk about, like *Tami* (acronym for *Tnu'at masoret Israel*; Movement for the Tradition of Israel) and *Shas*. All this, together with the popular perception of *Ha-panterim ha-shehorim* as a noisy, semi-delinquent youth gang close to anti-Zionist organizations like *Matzpen*—and lastly the focus on security and defense more than social issues that followed the 1973 Yom Kippur War—led to the decline and breakup of the group in the late 1970s.[32] Nonetheless, the young men from Musrara were able to draw public attention to important social issues, showing to what extent poverty and inequality in Israel also had an ethnic dimension that could no longer be ignored.

From Radicalism to Populism?: The Mizrahim After 1977

Dissatisfied with *Ha-'Avodah*, the labor coalition founded in 1968 from the merging of *Mapai* with smaller left-wing parties, some Mizrahim started to see in *Likud*, a nationalist rightist movement established in 1973 by Menachem Begin and Ariel Sharon, a possibility for modifying the status quo. 1977 was the year of the *mahapakh* (upheaval), in which a right-wing party came to power for the first time since 1948, largely thanks to the vote of the Mizrahim. This change was brought about "not [by] a bitter and repressed population, but . . . a group that demanded a genuinely equal partnership and rejected the option of self-segregation and alienation, as well as the revolutionary methods of the Black Panthers."[33] Begin's *Likud* presented itself as "an inclusive populist movement that mobilized mass support," but—as opposed to *Ha-panterim ha-shehorim*—it offered an institutional response to the anger felt against the Israeli Left.[34]

However, as time went by, the political recipe of *Likud* proved to be not as successful as hoped. The early 1980s saw the formation of parties—like *Tami* and

Shas—that took upon themselves the task of representing the Mizrahim through an approach that combined a reappraisal of ethnicity with Sephardi Jewish religiosity and populism.[35] "Haredim of Eastern origin are preparing a list for the Knesset, inspired by Rabbi Ovadiah Yosef," the daily *Ma'ariv* wrote in February 1984.[36] For the party's former spokesman Itzik Suderi, *Shas* "was born from a scream . . . against the system in which the Ashkenazim were the rulers and the Sephardim were the black slaves."[37] Defining *Shas* is not easy, as in the course of time it evolved from a more traditional ultra-Orthodox party to a radical populist one with a Sephardi religious core.[38] Since 1984, it has co-opted a great number of Mizrahi voters thanks to an integrative message based upon a redefinition of Israeli Jewishness in a Sephardi ultra-Orthodox, yet not anti-Zionist, direction. The party envisions Israel as a Jewish state that needs to recuperate its religious tradition, and the Mizrahim as a group of *shqufim* (invisibles) despised by the establishment who need to fight *le-hahzir 'atarah le-yoshnah* (to restore the crown [of the Torah] to its ancient glory).[39] This redefinition would have practical effects too, first and foremost the improvement of the socioeconomic status of the Mizrahim.[40] Could *Shas* constitute another facet of Mizrahi radicalism and—as Sa'adiah Marciano, one of *Ha-panterim ha-shehorim*'s founders, said—be "the continuation of *Ha-panterim ha-shehorim*" as well as a response to the limited success of the solutions proposed by *Likud*?[41]

Shas can be inscribed in a larger scenario that, in the 1980s and even more so in the 1990s and early 2000s, has been characterized by a sort of populist radicalism, especially for the Right.[42] At the same time, those years witnessed the emergence of new leftist movements fighting against inequality. One of these is *Ha-qeshet ha-demoqratit ha-mizrahit* (Mizrahi Democratic Rainbow), founded in 1997 by second- and third-generation Mizrahim as an "apolitical, non-parliamentary social movement . . . with the aim of bringing a radical change into Israeli society as a whole and to its institutions. The organization is mizrahi . . . in its goals, universal in its beliefs."[43] In the early 2000s, *Ha-qeshet* was able to negotiate between the ethnic identity of its members and generalist demands of social justice and economic improvement—for example the successful land and housing campaign, which aimed to reduce disparities among Israeli citizens in land allocation and housing. But as opposed to earlier cases of Mizrahi leftist radicalism, like *Ha-panterim ha-shehorim*, in order to do so it embraced a Zionist national discourse that rarely included non-Jewish citizens of the state.[44]

An attempt to promote a more universal, and less particularistic, approach to the Mizrahi cause could be seen in the 1990s with the emergence of Mizrahi feminism. Viky Shiran is one example—one of the founders of the group *Ahoti* (My Sister), who fought against the effects of globalization on lower-class Israeli women, and for whom being a feminist began by acknowledging that Mizrahi women are discriminated against "on the basis of [their] gender, ethnicity, and often also socioeconomic status."[45] Mizrahi feminism is one of the spaces where an intersectional approach—which sees the marginal status of the Mizrahim in conjunction with that of the Palestinians and with the Arab-Israeli conflict—is apparent. According to members of *Ahoti*, Mizrahi women should fight for the improvement of their status and find an alternative path to their social and cultural emancipation, in tune with their history and identity.

Mizrahi social and political platforms have begun to engage this discourse in recent years, framing the demands of the groups that they represent in ways that overcome a clear-cut opposition between Left and Right. One can mention the short-lived *Tor ha-zahav* (The Golden Age), founded in 2016 by young Mizrahim of different political backgrounds: Some of its members come from the youth movements of *Shas* and *Likud*, others from center-leftist parties, while still others do not have a previous political affiliation. The members of *Tor ha-zahav* are convinced that "'social justice' . . . is not just the keyword of some people from Rothschild [Boulevard, i.e. from central Tel Aviv] . . . Judaism should unite and not divide us . . . Zionism is not only the *kibbutzim* and the *Palmah* but also Netivot and Beit She'an."[46] Here, whereas the *kibbutzim* and the *Palmah* (acronym for *Plugot mahatz*: "Smite troops," an elite unit of the pre-1948 Jewish defense forces that conducted underground attacks in British Palestine) symbolize the Ashkenazi elite and the Israeli establishment, the two towns of Netivot and Beit She'an—situated respectively in the south and north of the country—stand as metaphor for poorer Mizrahi Israelis.

By calling for a kind of Zionism other than that of the *kibbutzim* and a Jewish religiosity that is respectful of tradition without becoming ultra-Orthodox, *Tor ha-zahav* proposes an alternative to the "melting pot": "The melting pot is dead. I went to its funeral. Or better to say, the party. Since then, we can take a deep breath and are slowly freed from the petrifying image of the *sabra*: the new Jew, the Western *hiloni* [non-religious, secular], that forcedly ruled over here for many years."[47] A middle ground approach, rooted in Middle Eastern and North African Jewish history and that the anthropologist Harvey Goldberg resumed in the image of "a male attending synagogue on *Shabbat* morning and going to a soccer match in the afternoon,"[48] would constitute the solution for downplaying the rifts between Ashkenazim and Mizrahim, *datim* (religious) and *hilonim*, periphery and center. On the other hand, as opposed to the Mizrahi political movements of the 1970s, *Tor ha-zahav* refrained from expressing definitive opinions on the occupied Palestinian territories or on relations with the Palestinians—these are treated as secondary aspects that do not impact on the daily life of many Israelis—and preferred to focus on social and economic issues.[49]

Mizrahit meshutefet (Mizrahi-Palestinian Partnership), a joint Mizrahi-Palestinian coalition founded in 2016, opted for a more radical path: "We invite all the oppressed groups in Israeli society to join hands and walk together: Palestinians, Mizrahim, Ethiopians, Russian-speakers, the people who are living in conditions of poverty, everyone that is pushed to the periphery and the social margins."[50] While based upon the work of the Arab Joint List, *Mizrahit meshutefet* evokes the Moroccan-born Rabbi Meir Buzaglo, so as not to "forget the Jewish affinity to this country and the fact that love and longing for Zion have always been a central part of Jewish identity" and to "permit Jewish religious language to shake off the burden of Zionist secular thought and undermine the concept of exclusive rigid national sovereignty."[51] Even though, for the time being, they did not enter the Israeli electoral competition, these movements testify to the existence of a Mizrahi sociopolitical sphere, which includes groups like the successful literary collective *'Ars Po'etiqah*—founded in Tel Aviv in 2013 by the poetess Adi Keissar, in an attempt to show the possibility of combining high culture and the literary dimension with the popular world of the *'arsim* (pl. of *'ars*, lit. "pimp," a term used to indicate Mizrahi men lacking education)—and a number of blogs, social network pages, and magazines.[52]

(Un)leashed Panthers

In March 2016, the weekly magazine *Yediot 'Aharonot* published a portrait of the *Likud* parliamentarian and then Minister of Culture Miri Regev (who is of Moroccan ancestry) firmly holding the leashes of three black panthers. The title read: "A culture war? This is the Mizrahi War of Independence!"[53]

Explicitly evoking *Ha-panterim ha-shehorim*, Regev presented herself as one of the faces of a new Mizrahi political culture, far from the elite and close to those peripheral zones where many Mizrahim still live: "I am Miryam Sibonyi Regev from Qiriyat Gat, I have never read Chekov . . . I used to listen to Jo Amar and Spanish songs and I do not feel less cultivated than the consumers of Western culture."[54] Apparently, Regev wished to counter some of the stereotypes about the Mizrahim and transform them into aspects of an identity of which she feels proud. However, her line of thought—which echoes that of contemporary populist and anti-establishment groups like the Italian Five Star Movement or Donald Trump's Republican Party—goes in the direction of a populist radicalism of sorts that in the end strengthens those same stereotypes and negates the possibility of being, for example, both a reader of Chekov and a fan of Jo Amar. This is what the poetess Adi Keissar writes in one of her best-known poems, *Ani ha-mizrahit* (I am the Easterner), where she describes a more multidimensional Mizrahi woman than that of Regev: "I am the Easterner/we forget about/who can recite/all the songs/of Zohar Argov/and reads Albert Camus/and Bulgakov."[55]

It is clear that Mizrahi radicalism has been able to fit into different groups, both on the left and right side of the sociopolitical spectrum, depending on context and contingency. In recent years, the mass-protests of *Ha-panterim ha-shehorim* and the street riots of Wadi Salib were substituted with the poetry events of *'Ars Po'etiqah*.[56] But next to this, a more ambivalent yet politically appealing form of radicalism emerged: first with *Shas* and more recently with exponents of *Likud* like Regev. Seen from Israel and the perspective of the Mizrahim, radicalism is to be viewed as a malleable political framework whose ultimate goal is to achieve substantial political, cultural, and economic changes within (Israeli Jewish) society. This malleability may help us acknowledging how Jewish radicalism more generally has never been a homogeneous ideology but a set of "ideologies rooted in, stimulated by, applied to or perceived through, the particular sets of conditions and traditions of . . . societies and cultures."[57]

As regards the Mizrahim, it is worth noting that the transnational influences that could be traced at the beginning—from the legacy of Arab communism present in intellectuals like Shimon Ballas,[58] who after the migration to Israel continued to write in Arabic and collaborated with the Arabic newspaper of the Israeli Communist Party *Al-Jadid*, directed by the Palestinian intellectual Emile Habibi, up to the approach to the Palestinian issue of *Ha-panterim ha-shehorim*—have been abandoned in favor of an Israeli-centered scenario, dominated by a particularistic and at times populist identity. This confirms that the state's Jewish character, together with the preservation of one's ethnocultural background, are of utmost importance for most of them. They are—as the short-lived experience of *Ha-panterim ha-shehorim* on the one hand, and the success of *Shas* on the other, testify—a *conditio sine qua non* that one has to agree upon.[59] Such a trend seems to have increased even more in post–October 7, 2023, Israel, where political and cultural dialogue between Israelis and Palestinians has become extremely difficult against the background of Hamas's terrorist attacks, the war in Gaza, and an almost generalized shift of the Israeli public toward more nationalist positions. That said, if Mizrahi radicalism proper is less visible than in the 1970s, its foundational goals—from social justice to the end of ethnic discrimination—remain very relevant today for all the political movements and actors that emerged in the last decades. The panthers have been leashed, but their roaring can still be heard.

NOTES

1. Eli Amir, *Tarnegol kapparot* [Scapegoat] (Tel Aviv: Am Oved, 1984), 69.

2. Nancy Berg, "Sephardi Writing: From the Margins to the Mainstream," in *The Boom in Contemporary Hebrew Literature*, ed. Alan Mintz (Hanover: Brandeis University Press, 1997), 114–142; Adia Mendelson-Maoz, *Multiculturalism in Israel: Literary Perspectives* (West Lafayette: Purdue University Press, 2014), 76–84; Yochai Oppenheimer, *Mi-rehov Ben-Gurion le-shari'a 'al-Rashid* [From Ben-Gurion Street to Shari'a al-Rashid] (Jerusalem: Ben-Tzvi Institute, 2014). See also Orit Bashkin, *Impossible Exodus: Iraqi Jews in Israel* (Stanford: Stanford University Press, 2017); Bryan K. Roby, *The Mizrahi Era of Rebellion: Israel's Forgotten Civil Rights Struggle, 1948–1966* (Syracuse: Syracuse University Press, 2015); Yehudah Shenhav, *The Arab Jews: A Postcolonial Reading of Nationalism, Religion, and Ethnicity* (Stanford: Stanford University Press, 2006); Ella Shohat, "The Invention of the Mizrahim," *Journal of Palestine Studies* 29, no. 1 (Autumn 1999): 5–20.

3. Uri Ram, "Hebrew Culture in Israel: Between Europe, the Middle East, and America," in *Handbook of Israel: Major Debates*, vol. 1, ed. Eliezer Ben-Rafael, Julius H. Schoeps, Yitzhak Sternberg, and Olaf Glöckner (Oldenburg, Germany: De Gruyter, 2016), 68.

4. Sebastian Kunze and Frank Jacob, "Introduction: Thoughts on Jewish Radicalism as a Phenomenon of Global Modernity," in *Jewish Radicalisms: Historical Perspectives on a Phenomenon of Global Modernity*, ed. Frank Jacob and Sebastian Kunze (Berlin: De Gruyter, 2020), 23–74.

5. Orit Bashkin, *New Babylonians: A History of Jews in Modern Iraq* (Stanford: Stanford University Press, 2012), 141–182.

6. Michael Laskier, "The Evolution of Zionist Activity in the Jewish Communities of Morocco, Tunisia and Algeria: 1897–1947," *Studies in Zionism* 4, no. 2 (1983): 205–236; Rachel Simon, "Zionism," in *The Jews of the Middle East and North Africa in Modern Times*, ed. Reeva

Simon, Michael Laskier, and Sara Reguer (New York: Columbia University Press, 2003), 165–179.

7. As an introduction to this population, I refer to Simon, Laskier, and Reguer, eds., *The Jews of the Middle East and North Africa*.

8. Colin Shindler, *A History of Modern Israel*, 2nd ed. (Cambridge: Cambridge University Press, 2013), 38–65. On the early years of the Israeli state, see Laurence Silberstein, ed., *New Perspectives on Israeli History: The Early Years of the State* (New York: New York University, 1991).

9. See reference works like Walter Laqueur, *A History of Zionism* (London: I. B. Tauris, 2003) and Gideon Shimoni, *The Zionist Ideology* (Hanover: Brandeis University Press, 1995).

10. Sammy Smooha, "The Mass Immigrations to Israel: A Comparison of the Failure of the Mizrahi Immigrants of the 1950s with the Success of the Russian Immigrants of the 1990s," *The Journal of Israeli History* 27, no. 1 (2008): 1–27. More generally, see Dvora Hacohen, *Immigrants in Turmoil: Mass Immigration to Israel and Its Repercussions in the 1950s and After* (Syracuse: Syracuse University Press), 2003; Aziza Khazoom, *Shifting Ethnic Boundaries and Inequality in Israel: Or, How the Polish Peddler Became a German Intellectual* (Stanford: Stanford University Press, 2008); Doris Bensimon-Donath, *Immigrants d'Afrique du Nord en Israël* (Paris: Anthropos, 1970).

11. Eitan Yehezqeli, "'Al qlitatam shel yotzei-'artzot ha-'Islam" [On the absorption of the exiles from the Lands of Islam], *Ba-ma'arakhah*, July 3, 1962, 6.

12. Shohat, "Invention of the Mizrahim"; Ella Shohat, "Sephardim in Israel: Zionism from the Standpoint of Its Jewish Victims," *Social Text* , no. 19/20 (1988): 1–35.

13. Shenhav, *The Arab Jews*. See also Moshe Behar, "What's in a Name? Socio-Terminological Formations and the Case for Arabized Jews," *Social Identities* 15, no. 6 (2009): 747–771; Jonathan Gribetz, "'To the Arab Hebrew!': On Possibilities and Impossibilities," *International Journal of Middle East Studies* 46, no. 3 (August 2014): 589–592; Emily Gottreich, "Historicizing the Concept of Arab Jew in the Maghrib," *Jewish Quarterly Review* 98, no. 4 (2008): 433–451; Lital Levy, "Mihu yehudi-'aravi? 'Iyun meshaveh be-toldot ha-she'elah, 1880–2010" [Who is an Arab Jew? A comparative historical analysis of the question, 1880–2010], *Te'oriah u-viqoret*, no. 38–39 (2011): 101–135.

14. Yitzhaq Haberfeld and Yinnon Cohen, "Ha-mehagrim ha-yehudim le-'Israel: Shinuim be-ramot haskalah, ba-sekher u-va-hishtalvut kalkaliyim ba-shanim 1948–2008" [Jewish immigrants to Israel: Changes in educational status, income and economic integration in the years 1948–2008], *Megamot* 3, no. 4 (2012): 504–534.

15. David Deri, *Salah, poh zeh Eretz Israel* [*Salah, This Is the Land of Israel*], a four-part documentary broadcast at the beginning of 2018 on the Israeli TV channel Reshet 13: http://reshet.tv/vod/sallah/, and Dinah Zvi-Riklis,\; *Ma'abarot* [*Transit Camps*], broadcast in February/March 2019 on the public TV channel Kan: https://www.kan.org.il/page.aspx?landingpageid=1107#/. For a less critical approach, see Avi Picard, "Unsung Heroes: North African Immigrants in Development Tows," *Segula*, April 2019, 52–65.

16. Oren Yiftachel and Eretz Tzfadia, "Between Periphery and 'Third Space': Identity of Mizrahim in Israel's Development Towns," in *Israelis in Conflict: Hegemonies, Identities and Challenges*, ed. Adriana Kemp, Uri Ram, David Newman, and Oren Yiftachel (Eastbourne: Sussex Academic Press, 2004), 203–235; Oren Yiftachel, "'Ethnocracy' and Its Discontents: Minorities, Protests and the Israeli Polity," *Critical Inquiry* 26, no. 4 (2000): 725–756.

17. Sami Shalom Chetrit, *Intra-Jewish Conflict in Israel: White Jews, Black Jews* (London: Routledge, 2010), 54; Aziza Khazoom, "Did the Israeli State Engineer Segregation? On the Placement of Jewish Immigrants in Development Towns in the 1950s," *Social Forces* 84, no. 1 (2005): 115–134; Yaron Tsur, "Carnival Fears: Moroccan Immigrants and the Ethnic Problem in the Young State of Israel," *Journal of Israeli History* 18, no. 1 (1999): 73–103.

18. On Jews implicated in North African and Middle Eastern communist and anti-colonial movements, see Robert Watson, "Between Liberation(s) and Occupation(s): Reconsidering the Emergence of Maghrebi Jewish Communism, 1942–1945," *Journal of Modern Jewish Studies* 13, no. 3 (2014): 381–398; Pierre-Jean Le Foll-Luciani, *Les juifs algériens dans la lutte anticolo-*

niale. Trajectoires dissidentes (1934–1965) (Rennes, France: Presses universitaires de Rennes, 2016); Rami Ginat, *A History of Egyptian Communism: Jews and Their Compatriots in Quest of Revolution* (Boulder: Lynne Rienner Publishers, 2011); Joel Beinin, *The Dispersion of Egyptian Jewry: Culture, Politics and the Formation of a Modern Diaspora* (Berkeley: University of California Press, 1998), 143–178; Bashkin, *New Babylonians*, 141–182; Lior B. Sternfeld, *Between Iran and Zion: Jewish Histories of Twentieth-Century Iran* (Stanford: Stanford University Press, 2019), 40–62; Alma R. Heckman, "Fissures and Fusions: Moroccan Jewish Communists and World War II," in *The Holocaust and North Africa*, ed. Aomar Boum and Sarah A. Stein (Stanford: Stanford University Press, 2019), 185–204.

19. Bashkin, *Impossible Exodus*, 201.

20. Ronit Matalon, "'Al-ha-ke'ev ba-sifrut" [Of pain in literature], lecture given at the Hebrew University of Jerusalem, February 6, 2011, available at: https://www.youtube.com/watch?v=-N61T4ZjnHM. The quote plays with the name of Matalon's birthplace Ganei Tikvah (lit. "Gardens of hope").

21. Donatella Della Porta and Mario Diani, *Social Movements: An Introduction* (Malden: Blackwell, 2006), esp. 20–29; Roby, *The Mizrahi Era of Rebellion.*

22. Ehud Sprinzak, *Brother Against Brother: Violence and Extremism in Israeli Politics from Altalena to the Rabin Assassination* (New York: The Free Press, 1999), 129–131.

23. Roby, *The Mizrahi Era of Rebellion*, 152.

24. Verta Taylor and Nella Van Dyke, "'Get Up, Stand Up': Tactical Repertoires of Social Movements," in *The Blackwell Companion to Social Movements*, ed. David A. Snow, Sarah A. Soule, and Hanspeter Kriesi (Oxford: Blackwell, 2004), 268.

25. Sammy Smooha, *Israel: Pluralism and Conflict* (Berkeley: University of California Press, 1978), 211.

26. Bashkin, *Impossible Exodus*, 149.

27. Deborah Bernstein, "Conflict and Protest in Israeli Society: The Case of the Black Panthers of Israel," *Youth & Society* 16, no. 129 (1984), 138. See also the catalogue of the exhibition by the Jerusalem School of Photography of Musrara, *Ha-panterim ha-shehorim* [The Black Panthers] (Jerusalem: Beit ha-sefer le-tzilum Musrara, 1997), and Asaf Elia-Shalev, *Israel's Black Panthers: The Radicals Who Punctured a Nation's Founding Myth* (Berkeley: University of California Press, 2024).

28. Shalom Cohen and Kokhavi Shemesh, "The Origin and Development of the Israeli Black Panther Movement," *MERIP Reports*, no. 49 (1976), 19.

29. Oz Frankel, "The Black Panthers of Israel and the Politics of the Radical Analogy," in *Black Power Beyond Borders: The Global Dimensions of the Black Power Movement*, ed. Nico Slate (London: Palgrave, 2012), 81–106; Ktzia Alon, "Sihah 'im David Me'iri" [A conversation with David Me'iri], *Ha-kivun mizrah*, 6 (2003–2002): 39–43. Ha-panterim ha-shehorim were in contact with European radical leftist groups too, like the Italian *Lotta Continua*, as recalled by the Italian journalist Gad Lerner in *Scintille* (Milan: Feltrinelli, 2009), 153.

30. Jaclynn Ashli, "When Israel's Black Panthers Found Common Cause with Palestinians," *The Electronic Intifada*, March 7, 2019, https://electronicintifada.net/content/when-israels-black-panthers-found-common-cause-palestinians/26821.

31. André Fontaine, "'Le test' étant la signature de la paix: 'Il serait ridicule de demander aux Arabes la reconnaissance de la légitimité de l'État d'Israël,' nous déclare Mme Golda Méïr," *Le Monde*, October 15, 1971. See also As'ad Ghanem, *Ethnic Politics in Israel: The Margins and the Ashkenazi Centre* (London: Routledge, 2010), 69–71; Alex Lubin, *Geographies of Liberation: The Making of an Afro-Arab Political Imaginary* (Chapel Hill: University of North Carolina Press, 2014), 140–141.

32. Tali Lev and Yehuda Shenhav, "Kinnuno shel ha-'oyev mi-bifnim: Ha-panterim ha-shehorim ke-musa' shel paniqah musarit" [The social construction of the enemy from within: Israeli Black Panthers as a target of moral panic], *Sotziologiyah Israelit* 12, no. 1 (2010): 135–158.

33. Uri Cohen and Nissim Leon, "The Mahapach and Yitzhak Samir's Quiet Revolution: Mizrahim and the Herut Movement," *Israel Studies Review* 29, no. 1 (2014), 36–37.

34. Amir Goldstein, "Partial Establishment: Menachem Begin, Gahal and the Black Panthers," *Journal of Modern Jewish Studies* 17, no. 2 (2018): 236–251; Uri Cohen and Nissim Leon, "Merkaz tnu'at Herut ve-ha-mizrahim, 1965–1977: Mi-shutafut 'adnutit la-shutafut taharutit" [Herut's central committee and the Mizrahim, 1965–1977: From patronizing partnership to competitive partnership], *The Israel Democracy Institute*, Policy Paper no. 88, 2011; Yonathan Shapiro, *The Road to Power: Herut Party in Israel* (Albany: State University of New York Press, 1991).

35. *Tami* was founded in 1981 by Rabbi Aharon Abuhatzira. The birth of *Shas* in 1984 led to its rapid decline and merging into *Likud*.

36. "Haredim mi-'edot ha-mizrah meqimim reshimah la-Knesset" [Ultra-Orthodox of eastern origin found a list for the Knesset], *Ma'ariv*, February 6, 1984, 2. Ovadiah Yosef—who was born in Baghdad in 1920 and died in Jerusalem in 2013—was a rabbi and religious scholar and, until his death, the undisputed spiritual leader of *Shas*. He served as Sephardi chief rabbi of Israel from 1973 to 1983. Although considered a controversial figure in Israeli society, Rabbi Yosef was universally praised for his knowledge of Jewish law and is considered to have been one of the most important halachic authorities of the twentieth century.

37. Itzik Suderi, cited by Nancy J. Davis and Robert V. Robinson, *Claiming Society for God: Religious Movements and Social Welfare* (Bloomington: Indiana University Press, 2012), 64.

38. David Lehmann and Batia Siebzehner, *Remaking Israeli Judaism: The Challenge of Shas* (Oxford: Oxford University Press, 2006), 160–168.

39. Yaakov Yadgar, "Shas as a Struggle to Create a New Field: A Bourdieuan Perspective of an Israeli Phenomenon," *Sociology of Religion* 64, no. 2 (2003): 223–246; Shlomo Deshen, "Shorashim historyim ve-hoveh 'israeli ba-datiyut shel-yehudei-ha-mizrah" [Historical roots and Israeli present in the religiosity of the Eastern Jews], in *Shas: Hebetim tarbutyim ve-re'ayioniyim* [Shas: Cultural and ideological perspectives], ed. Aviezer Ravitzki (Tel Aviv: Am Oved, 2006), 15–40.

40. Yoav Peled, "Roar of the Lion: Shas and the Challenge to Israeli Identity," *Israel Studies Bulletin* 16, no. 2 (2001), 11.

41. I am quoting Marciano from the 2003 documentary by Elie Hamo and Sami Shalom-Chetrit, *Ha-panterim ha-shehorim medabrim* [The Black Panthers speak]. Others, like Shalom-Chetrit himself, are more skeptical of the reading of *Shas* as a radical movement; see Sami Shalom-Chetrit, "Milkud 17: Beyin harediyut le-mizrahiyut" [Trap 17: Between Haredism and Mizrahi identity], in *Shas: 'Etgar ha-israeliyut* [Shas: The challenge of Israeliness], ed. Yoav Peled (Tel Aviv: Yediot Aharonot, 2001), esp. 39–42.

42. Dani Filc and Udi Lebel, "The Post-Oslo Israeli Populist Radical Right in Comparative Perspective: Leadership, Voter Characteristics and Political Discourse," *Mediterranean Politics* 10, no. 1 (2005): 85–97.

43. From the manifesto of *Ha-qeshet ha-demoqratit ha-mizrahit* cited by Ofir Abu, "Citizenship, Identity, and Ethnic Mobilization in Israel: The Mizrahi Democratic Rainbow Between Universalism and Particularism," in *The Contradictions of Israeli Citizenship: Land, Religion and State*, ed. Guy Ben-Porat and Bryan Turner (London: Routledge, 2011), 111.

44. Gershon Shafir and Yoav Peled, *Being Israeli: The Dynamics of Multiple Citizenship* (Cambridge: Cambridge University Press, 2002), 87–95.

45. Viky Shiran, "Lifneah 'et-ha-koah, livro' 'olam hadash" [Deciphering the strength, building a new world], *Panim* 2 (2002), accessed May 27, 2024, at http://www.itu.org.il/?CategoryID=521&ArticleID=1415&Page=1, . See also Henriette Dahan-Kalev, "Tensions in Israeli Feminism: The Mizrahi Ashkenazi Rift," *Women's Studies International Forum* 24, no. 6 (2001): 669–684; Dahan-Kalev "Mizrahi Feminism in Israel," The Shalvi/Hyman Encyclopedia of Jewish Women, *Jewish Women's Archive*, last updated June 23, 2021, https://jwa.org/encyclopedia/article/mizrahi-feminism-in-israel; Smadar Lavie, "Mizrahi Feminism and the Question of Palestine," *Journal of Middle East Women's Studies* 7, no. 2 (2011): 56–88.

46. From the homepage of *Tor ha-zahav*'s website, accessed (May 27, 2020) at https://www.tor-hazahav.org.

47. Ofir Touboul, "Ha-masortiyut tahlif 'et-kor-ha-hitukh" [Traditionalism will change the melting pot], *Maqor rishon*, January 28, 2018, https://www.makorrishon.co.il/opinion/11809/.

The term *sabra* (lit. "prickly pear cactus") indicates the quintessential native Israeli, stubborn and straightforward on the outside but soft on the inside. This cultural archetype was constructed already before 1948 to describe the traits of the first Jewish immigrants to Palestine, represented as farmers and soldiers that had left the Eastern European Jewish villages (*shtetls*) to construct a Jewish state in the land of their forefathers. See Oz Almog, *The Sabra: The Creation of the New Jew* (Berkeley: University of California Press, 2000).

48. Harvey Goldberg, "The Ethnographic Challenge of *Masorti* Religiosity Among Israeli Jews," *Ethnologie française* 4, no. 43 (2013), 584.

49. See the interview of *Tor ha-zahav*'s activist Carmen Elmakyies-Amos: David Rosenberg, "Social Justice: Israel's Newest Political Party—for Sephardim," *Arutzsheva 7*, February 17, 2016, http://www.israelnationalnews.com/News/News.aspx/208207.

50. "Open Call: An Eastern Joint Initiative—'Mizrahi-Palestinian Partnership,'" https://mizrahipalestinianpartnership.wordpress.com.

51. "Open Call." The 2015 Joint List resulted from the alliance between four Arab-dominated parties: *Hadash*, the *United Arab List*, *Balad*, and *Ta'al*.

52. On *'Ars Po'etiqah*, see Dario Miccoli, *La letteratura israeliana mizrahi* (Florence: Giuntina, 2016), 83–96; Esther Schely-Newman, "Poetics of Identity: Mizrahi Poets Between Here and There, Then and Now," *Quest—Issues in Contemporary Jewish History* 16 (December 2019): 111–132.

53. Raz Shechnik, Yehuda Nuriel and Raviv Golan, "Milhemet tarbut? Zo milhemet ha-'atzma'ut ha-mizrahit!" [Culture war? This is the Mizrahi War of Independence!], *Sheva' leilot—Yediot 'Aharonot*, March 10, 2016, available at: https://www.yediot.co.il/articles/0,7340,L-4776622,00.html#google_vignette.

54. Na'ama Lansky, "'Atem lo' taktivu li mah nahon u-mah lo' nahon" [You are not going to tell me what is right and wrong], *Israel Ha-yom*, September 11, 2015, http://www.israelhayom.co.il/article/313067. Jo Amar (1930–2009) was a renowned Israeli singer of Moroccan Jewish origin and one of the founding fathers of Mizrahi music. On Miri Regev, see Omri Ben Yehuda, "Miri (Sibonyi) Regev: Masah 'al-ha-politiqah shel-ha-guf" [Miri (Sibonyi) Regev: An essay on body politics], in *Off Foto: Ha-tzad ha-ahori shel-ha-tzilum ha-'israeli* [Off photo: The other side of Israeli photography], ed. Ktzia Alon (Tel Aviv: Gama, 2017), 165–190.

55. Adi Keissar, *Shahor 'al-gabey shahor* [Black on black] (Tel Aviv: Hotza'at Tangir, 2014), 66. Zohar Argov was another famous Mizrahi singer of the 1970s and early 1980s, born into a Yemenite Jewish family.

56. Giulia Daniele, "Political and Social Protests from the Margins: The Role of Mizrahi Jews in Israeli Grassroots Activism," *Etnografica* 23, no. 1 (2019): 201–220.

57. Jaff Schatz, "The Riddle of Jewish Radicalism," *Nordisk Judaistik* 11, no. 1–2 (1990), 5.

58. See Re'uven Snir, "'Till Spring Comes': Arabic and Hebrew Literary Debates Among Iraqi-Jews in Israel (1950–2000)," *Shofar* 24, no. 2 (2006): 92–123.

59. Here I follow Nissim Mizrachi, "Sociology in the Garden: Beyond the Liberal Grammar of Contemporary Sociology," *Israel Studies Review* 31, no. 1 (2016): 36–65.

PART II

The Americas, South Africa, and Asia

Radical Jewish politics traveled around the globe with the great waves of Jewish immigration from across Europe during the nineteenth and early twentieth centuries. Immigration transformed the United States into the home of the largest Jewish population in the Western Hemisphere, but it was far from the only site in the Americas where Jews settled in significant numbers or where they became extensively involved in radical politics. In chapters 8 and 9, Nathaniel Deutsch and Michael Rom explore the rich history of radical Jewish politics in the two Latin American countries with the largest Jewish communities, Argentina and Brazil. While Jewish radicals like Fabio Grobart, who helped to found the Communist Party of Cuba during the 1920s and later played an important role in the 1959 revolution, were active throughout the Americas, it was in Argentina and Brazil that Jewish radicals had the biggest and most sustained impact over the course of the twentieth century, both through their participation in a wide range of socialist and communist parties alongside non-Jewish comrades from different backgrounds, and through their involvement in political and cultural organizations that were both radical *and* Jewish.

At the same time that Jewish immigrants were settling throughout the length and breadth of the Americas, another stream arrived in South Africa, whose Jewish community would eventually become the largest on the entire continent following the mid-twentieth-century mass emigration of North African Jews to Israel, France, and elsewhere. Unlike in the Americas, where Jews arrived from practically every part of Europe and, in much smaller numbers, from the Middle East and North Africa, roughly 90 percent of the South African Jewish population hailed from a single country—Lithuania—which was a veritable cradle of radical Jewish politics. In chapter 10, Milton Shain and Richard Mendelsohn demonstrate how Lithuanian Jewish immigrants, as well as those from Latvia and elsewhere in Eastern Europe, played important roles in the establishment and leadership of radical political organizations in South Africa during the first half of the twentieth century, and how, during its second half, Jewish radicals such as the

Lithuanian-born Joe Slovo, who became the general secretary of the South African Communist Party and a member of the Executive Committee of the African National Congress, helped to wage the struggle against apartheid.

Finally, in the 1930s Jewish radicals from around the world converged in the newly established Jewish autonomous region of Birobidzhan, located in far-eastern Russia on the border with China. Promoted as an alternative to the Zionist vision of a Jewish national home, Birobidzhan was intended, as Robert Weinberg writes in chapter 11, to be the truest form of Jewish emancipation from bourgeois oppression and particularist (Zionist) nationalist tendencies. Soviet leadership reconciled the apparent contradiction of hosting a Jewish national home within its borders by arguing that Birobidzhan represented an incremental step toward the full integration of Jews into the Soviet Union and the culmination of years of efforts to "normalize" the Jewish population. Idealists traveled from around the world to a remote, swampy, underdeveloped region where Jewish life and culture were supposed to bloom. Unfortunately, as Weinberg explains, Stalin all but ensured the failure of the Birobidzhan dream, and by the 1950s it was clear Birobidzhan would not become the hub of Jewish radical renewal.

CHAPTER 8

A Century of Radical Jewish Politics in Argentina

Nathaniel Deutsch

The growth of radical politics among Jews in Argentina coincided with the dramatic increase in Jewish immigration to the country during the final years of the nineteenth century and first few decades of the twentieth. By 1914, more than 100,000 Jews had settled in the agricultural colonies—most famously, Moisés Ville—established by Baron Maurice de Hirsh's Jewish Colonization Association, provincial cities like Córdoba and Rosario, and particularly in the teeming immigrant neighborhoods of Buenos Aires.[1] During the 1930s, the number of Jews grew to more than 200,000, constituting 2 percent of the overall population of Argentina, though their percentage was much higher in working-class *porteño* neighborhoods such as Villa Crespo, Flores, Barracas, and Once, whose heavily Jewish character drew numerous comparisons to the Lower East Side of New York City. A large majority of these Jews hailed from the Russian and Austro-Hungarian empires, part of a wave that brought well over two million immigrants to Argentina in the same period, most from Spain and Italy. Smaller but significant numbers of Jews also arrived from the Ottoman Empire, Morocco, independent Poland, and, in the 1930s, Nazi Germany. By that point, Argentina had become home to the largest Jewish population in Latin America by far, with an extraordinary range of Jewish cultural, educational, and, as we will see shortly, political organizations. While Jews in other Latin America countries, from Uruguay and Brazil to Mexico and Cuba, also participated in radical politics, nowhere was their engagement as extensive, as varied, and as long-lasting as in Argentina, where the size and diversity of the Jewish community, combined with the country's distinctive political culture, created an environment in which a robust tradition of Jewish radicalism could thrive across multiple generations.

The first Jew to play a prominent role in radical politics in Argentina was Augusto Kühn, a member of a circle of German immigrants known as *el Club Vorwärts*, who, like their counterparts in the United States, engaged in some of the earliest socialist activism in the country. Among other contributions, Kühn organized the first May Day workers' celebration in Argentina in 1890, co-founded the socialist newspaper *La Vanguardia* in 1894, and collaborated with the Argentine socialist pioneer Juan B. Justo on the first translation of Karl Marx's *Kapital* into Spanish in 1898.[2] The 1890s also witnessed the first wave of Jewish immigrants from the Russian Empire, among them individuals who quickly became integrated, both politically and personally, into the nascent socialist scene in Argentina. This early group of Jewish radicals included a number of women, most notably the three Chertkoff sisters, Fenia, Mariana, and Adela, natives of Odessa who went on to found the *Centro Socialista Feminino* in 1902 and worked to spread socialism in Argentina by focusing on education and the family.[3] All three sisters married prominent male socialists, both Jewish and non-Jewish: Fenia and Mariana wed Nicolás Repetto and Juan B. Justo, respectively, native-born Argentines who helped found the Socialist Party of Argentina in 1896, while Adela married Adolfo Dickmann, an Eastern European Jewish immigrant author, socialist politician, and brother of Enrique Dickmann, a longtime leader of the Socialist Party and, during the 1950s, the *Partido Socialista de la Revolución Nacional*, the left wing of the Peronist movement.

Despite the early involvement of these figures, Jose Moya, in a study of Jewish anarchists in Argentina, argued that "Temporally, the most salient feature of Jewish radicalism in Argentina is its belated appearance one or two decades later than in London or New York," a phenomenon that he attributes to the relative lag in Jewish immigrants to the country (for example, by 1890 only 5,160 Jews had arrived in Argentina from the Russian Empire, compared to a quarter of million to the United States).[4] As the number of Jewish immigrants to Argentina dramatically increased in the first few decades of the twentieth century, however, so did the number of Jewish radicals. In an epoch in which anarchism was popular around the globe, newly arrived Russian Jews collaborated with Italian and Catalan immigrants and native born Argentines to transform Buenos Aires into "probably the second most important center of anarchist activism, after Barcelona."[5] In addition to coming from parts of the world where anarchism was already popular, Moya argues that Russian Jewish and Catalan immigrants were also overrepresented among the skilled workers and artisans who tended to be the mainstay of the anarchist movement. The parallel development of anarchism and Jewish-dominated prostitution rings in the country, known colloquially as the "white slave trade," led Moya to conjecture that anarchism—rather than orthodox Marxism—was a draw for Jews involved in the booming sex trade in Argentina, since "anarchist rhetoric elevated, instead of disdaining or dismissing, as socialists normally did, the 'dregs of society.'"[6]

Along with their socialist rivals, anarchists in Argentina were also the driving force behind the organization of workers at the beginning of the twentieth century, producing a vibrant labor movement in which Jews played important roles as organizers, union leaders, and, in some industries (for example, garment and furniture manufacturing), rank-and-file members.[7] During this tumultuous period, Jewish immigrants were among the radicals who participated in a series of demonstrations, strikes, and assassinations—most notably of Buenos Aires's antisemitic chief of police Ramon Falcón by the young Russian Jewish immigrant and anarchist Simon Radowitzky in 1909—even as Jews still remained a small minority within the overall population of radicals in Argentina.[8] Nicknamed *rusos* in Spanish due to their country of origin, Russian Jews were associated with radicalism in the popular imagination due to revolutionary political developments in the Russian Empire. This association, amplified by contemporary antisemitic propaganda—homegrown, though much of it was imported from France—played a role in the violent attacks against members of the Jewish community in 1909–1910, and most notoriously a decade later during the infamous *la Semana Trágica* or Tragic Week of 1919.

On the one hand, the labor strikes and clashes between workers, activists—among them Jews—and police in Buenos Aires during the la Semana Trágica should be seen as part of the global conflict between radical and reactionary forces that was fought on many fronts during this period. In this regard, it is significant that the name itself was inspired by an earlier outbreak of strikes and street battles in 1909 between anarchists, labor unionists, socialists, and military forces in Barcelona, Spain, also called la Semana Trágica. Seen from this perspective, Jews in Buenos Aires were caught up in a broader reactionary backlash or, as Victor Mirelman has written, "Jews were attacked as part of the general reaction against foreign agitators in the workers' movement."[9] Yet, as Mirelman and others have also documented, Jewish residents of Once, Villa Crespo, and elsewhere in the city were brutally targeted by right-wing vigilantes, whether or not they were actually engaged in radical politics (some were children or elderly, for example). Moreover, antisemitism played a role in fanning the flames in these neighborhoods, with some attackers yelling "Death to the Jews," among other slogans, and raping Jewish women. For these reasons—and because la Semana Trágica coincided temporally with the violent attacks against Jewish communities during the Russian Civil War—some have described the events in Buenos Aires as "the first pogrom in Argentina."[10]

Along with numerous individuals, local Jewish institutions were also targeted for assault during la Semana Trágica, including the offices of the Argentine branches of the socialist Zionist organization Poale Zion (*Partido Socialista Sionista* in Spanish) and the Bund (or *Avangard* as it was called in Argentina during these years). First founded in the Russian Empire at the turn of the century, both organizations were established in Argentina by Russian Jewish immigrants following the 1905 Revolution, when many Jewish radicals left the country to escape persecution.[11] Bundists and socialist Zionists quickly became part of the vibrant radical political scene in Argentina, forming ties with local activists belonging to non-Jewish organizations and sometimes fighting among themselves, leading to the creation of different factions. Early on both groups also published their own newspapers (*Der Avangard* and *Broyt un ehre*, respectively), thereby helping to establish a vibrant radical Jewish print culture that would continue to thrive for decades to come in Argentina.[12]

Among the victims of la Semana Trágica was Avangard's young leader, Pedro "Pinnie" Wald, who was arrested along with his fiancée Rosa Weinstein and tortured for supposedly heading a "Soviet Argentino," a charge that the Argentine Jewish socialist, journalist, and human rights activist Herman Schiller would later dismiss as "so crude it seemed tragicomic."[13] In response to the attacks, members of Avangard invoked antisemitic violence in their native Russia to condemn both the government and right-wing vigilantes: "The police and the army not only permitted the criminal pogrom against the Jews, but with their weapons they helped to perpetrate the savage actions of la Guardia Blanca [The White Guard]. The Avangard organization sees in this the dark policy of the radical government, which resembles the now extinct pogromist policy of the former tsarist government in Russia, and declares that with great energy and determination it will pursue its socialist militancy for the achievement of a better life in Argentina."[14] For decades to come, la Semana Trágica would serve as a foundational moment to be invoked by later generations of Argentine Jews during times of crisis and rupture.[15]

The establishment of the Soviet Union and the Third International, or Comintern, led to the creation of communist organizations in countries around the world, including Argentina, where the Communist Party of Argentina split off from the Socialist Party. In the early 1920s, Eastern European Jewish immigrants in Argentina founded a Jewish section known in Spanish as *la Sección Judía del Partido Comunista* and in Yiddish as *Idishe Sektie des Komunistishes* Partei) or, as it was popularly known, *la Idsektie*. Although other "language sections" were established to address the specific needs of different immigrant communities (Italians, Yugoslavs, etc.), Daniel Kersffeld has argued that "Jews formed the most defined and differentiated ethnic sector of the Communist Party of Argentina," and that membership functioned as "a privileged frame of reference and, therefore, as a kind of extension of their European homeland in their new country of adoption."[16]

The Jewish section soon founded a society to encourage immigration to the Jewish Autonomous Region of Birobidzhan in the Soviet Union; launched the Yiddish newspaper *Der Royter Shtern* (The Red Star) that was widely distributed in Buenos Aires, the Argentine interior, as well as in Uruguay and Brazil; and established a network of cultural and educational institutions, including *arbeter klubn* (workers' clubs) and libraries. As Ariel Svarch has noted, the Jewish section was also "the only language section that consolidated its own network of associated schools, the *arbeter shuln* (workers' schools)," beginning with a first school in Villa Crespo in 1922.[17] These competed with their "principal enemy . . . the leftist Poale Zion that . . . had their own workers' schools, the *Ber Borojov Shuln*," named in honor of the Marxist-Zionist leader Ber Borochov.[18] The efforts of the Jewish section were so successful that, by the end of the 1920s, Jews constituted 14 percent of Communist Party membership in the greater Buenos Aires region, while *Der Royter Shtern* was the communist newspaper with the greatest circulation in Argentina after the official Spanish language party organ *La Internacional*.[19]

During the 1930s, like their counterparts elsewhere, Jewish radicals in Argentina rallied to fight growing antisemitism and fascism at home and abroad. As they did in many countries, Jews from Argentina volunteered on behalf of the Spanish Republic in numbers much higher than their percentage of the country's overall population.[20] Most Argentine Jews who volunteered in the International Brigades were communists and a significant number were women, including those who were already members of the Communist Party and others who were first radicalized by the Spanish Civil War. Among the former was Fanny Edelman, a daughter of Russian Jewish immigrants who joined the Communist Party of Argentina in 1934, worked with the International Red Aid (founded by the Comintern in 1922), and mobilized to Spain in 1937, along with her husband, Bernardo. After returning to Argentina in 1938, Edelman played a prominent role in radical politics, advocating especially on behalf of women's rights around the globe, and was eulogized as "the heart of the Communist Party of Argentina," when she passed away at 100.[21] Although Edelman and her Jewish comrades were committed communists, Raanan Rein has argued that Jewishness also shaped their attitudes toward the conflict in Spain, both because of their concern for the fate of European Jews under fascist regimes and because "a rebel victory would strengthen the Nacionalistas in Argentina."[22]

In this climate of global crisis, Jewish radicals from around the world met in Paris in 1937 to establish the *Yiddisher Kultur Farband* (Jewish Culture Association), whose communist-oriented leaders included the prominent Argentine Jewish activist, journalist, and translator Pinie Katz, longtime editor of the most popular Buenos Aires Yiddish daily *Di Presse*. The organization's mission was to save Jews and their cultural heritage in the face of impending destruction while disseminating radical politics via Yiddish cultural and educational institutions. While this message resonated in multiple countries, it was in Argentina where the local branch, known popularly as ICUF, achieved its greatest influence after being founded in 1941.[23] Although ICUF typically followed the lead of the pro-Soviet Communist Party of Argentina when it came to politics, it nevertheless remained profoundly committed to the Yiddish language and what it termed "progressive" Jewish culture throughout the 1940s and beyond.[24]

To this end, ICUF established an extensive network of schools, clubs, credit cooperatives, publications, and "houses of culture," as well as a Yiddish theater and the Zumerland summer camp.[25] Nerina Visacovsky has written that these institutions enabled participants to embrace "hybrid" identities that were at once "Argentine, Jewish, and leftist."[26] Numerous women played crucial roles in ICUF-affiliated institutions, serving as educators, writers (most notably, the prolific author Mimi Pinzón), and leaders, including of a Women's Organization founded in 1947 by Leike Kogan.[27] At the same time, the organization's emphasis on Yiddish meant that Argentine Jews with roots in Syria, Morocco, Turkey, and elsewhere in the Middle East and Mediterranean—around 10 percent of the overall Jewish population—were excluded from meaningful participation in many ICUF activities, let alone its leadership. This marginalization of non-Yiddish-speaking Jews "was hardly a chance occurrence," Israel Lotersztain has argued, "since ICUF press organs made quite manifest their disdain for those populations."[28]

In 1944, ICUF was permitted to run in elections for AMIA (*Asociación Mutual Israelita Argentina*), the umbrella organization of Jewish institutions in the country, and quickly achieved impressive results; in 1947, the organization was admitted to DAIA (*Delegación de Asociaciones Israelitas Argentinas*), which officially represented the various sectors of the Jewish community to the Argentine government.[29] Yet the creation of the State of Israel in 1948 soon led to tensions between ICUF and the Zionist-dominated leadership of the Jewish establishment, which even enlisted the historically anti-Zionist Bund in its efforts to isolate the organization.[30] ICUF had initially echoed the Soviet Union's support for Israel as a blow to British imperialism, a position that was shared by the Community Party of Argentina, whose chief ideologue on the Middle East, Orestes Ghioldi, not only pointedly criticized the Arab League as a tool of the British but also praised the creation of Israel as "a just historic reparation for a people ferociously persecuted for the sake of barbaric racial prejudices."[31] When Soviet policy soon shifted decisively against Israel, however, ICUF followed suit. This about-face, as well as the Soviet Union's growing persecution of Jews—which the ICUF leadership denied—eventually provoked DAIA to expel the organization from its network in 1952 and AMIA to withhold funding for its schools. Despite what members described as a *herem* (Hebrew; excommunication), ICUF maintained significant support within the Argentine Jewish community and continued to operate its institutions independently.

Like the Communist Party of Argentina, ICUF endured a hostile climate under the first Peronist government, which shuttered its newspaper *Tribuna* and the Jewish Folk Theater in 1953.[32] Many have characterized the relationship between Juan Perón and the country's Jewish community as overwhelmingly negative due to a number of factors, including Perón's infamous protection of Nazi war criminals following World War II, Argentina's abstention from the 1947 United Nations vote that partitioned Palestine, and perhaps most fundamentally, the populist nationalism of Peronism, which contributed to mistrust among the country's Jews. More recently, however, Raanan Rein has demonstrated that Perón made significant overtures to the Jewish community, even alienating some of his antisemitic right-wing supporters in the process, while at the same time, "There were not a few Jews who supported the first instantiation of Peronism. It is certain that the establishment of the community, in its majority, had reservations regarding the Peronist government and the Justicialist movement, but various Jewish leaders in the labor movement, for example, did not only identify with the nascent movement but also played an important role in the mobilization of support for Peronism."[33] Among the most important was Ángel Perelman, the co-founder and, in 1943, first secretary general of *la Unión Obrera Metalúrgica* (Metallurgical Workers Union). Along with his brother, Adolfo, Perelman belonged to a Trotskyist circle led by Jorge Abelardo Ramos, whose mother hailed from a family of Jewish socialists. In 1953, Ramos was among the founders of el Partido Socialista de la Revolución Nacional, the left wing of the Peronist movement, whose leader was Enrique Dickmann, then in the twilight of his long career as one of Argentina's most prominent socialists.[34]

By the end of the 1950s, the widespread use of Yiddish by Jewish radicals in Argentina was declining, part of a broader shift away from Yiddish and toward Spanish and Hebrew among Argentina's Jews, a phenomenon documented in detail by Alejandro Dujovne in his study of the country's vibrant Jewish publishing industry.[35] Even ICUF, which had long promoted Yiddish as the cornerstone of its mission to create a progressive Jewish culture in Argentina, stopped teaching the language in its network of schools starting in 1956.[36] These linguistic changes reflected the widespread assimilation of younger Jews, in particular, as well as the growing strength of Zionism within both the Ashkenazi and Sephardi sectors of the community, encouraged by leaders who increasingly viewed the movement as a means for strengthening Jewish identity among the young.[37]

These leaders included members of the Sephardi Elnecavé family, whose patriarch, David, was a native of Istanbul, where he founded the first Zionist newspaper in Ladino, *El Djudio*, in 1909, before pressure from the government prompted him to move to Bulgaria, where he continued to publish *El Djudio* throughout the 1920s. After immigrating to Argentina, Elnecavé founded the Zionist newspaper *La Luz* in 1931 and worked as a correspondent for the Jewish Telegraphic Agency, ultimately becoming one of the most influential Jewish journalists in Latin America.[38] In 1948, his son Nissim, who had lived on a kibbutz for a time in the 1930s, co-founded *Nueva Sion*, a newspaper affiliated with the socialist Zionist youth movement *Hashomer Hatzair*.[39] Among the members of its first editorial board was Jacobo Timmerman, then a young journalist and later a prominent publisher whose criticism of the military dictatorship in the 1970s led to his arrest, torture, and subsequent exile from Argentina, events that he recounted in his 1981 memoir *Prisoner Without a Name, Cell Without a Number.*

The 1960s began with an outburst of shocking antisemitic incidents in Argentina following the Eichmann Affair, the first in a series of domestic and international developments that would strengthen support for Zionism and also help to inspire a broader shift to the Left among different segments of the Jewish community, a process that would continue into the early 1970s. Along with many other Argentines, growing numbers of Jews began to question the long-standing identification of the country with Europe and instead stressed connections with the rest of Latin America, a region that was then experiencing a wave of radicalism, spurred by developments in Cuba.[40] At the same time, Argentine radicals, foremost among them Ernesto "Ché" Guevara, were helping to spread revolution throughout Latin America.[41] In Argentina itself, younger Jews in particular became involved in a wide range of radical political organizations, with varying degrees of Jewish orientation. Many, at least initially, turned to Zionism, with Hashomer Hatzair, in particular, achieving widespread popularity among both Ashkenazi and Sephardi youth. Belying a widely held stereotype of their community as apolitical, the latter established their own affiliated organizations *Tejezakna* and *Baderej*, which were active in neighborhoods such as Barracas, Flores, and Villa Crespo that had large Sephardi and Syrian Jewish populations, and whose members sought to maintain some degree of independence from what they viewed as the Ashkenazi-dominated orientation of the broader socialist Zionist movement.[42]

Rather than being in conflict with a progressive desire to reimagine Argentina politically, Beatrice Gurwitz has argued that for young Argentine Jews who embraced socialist Zionism in this period, the two impulses were often mutually reinforcing: "At the height of revolutionary restiveness in the late 1960s and early 1970s Jewish youth activists first, and later members of the older generation, reinvented the Jewish tradition and Zionism in radical terms and supported the Jewish community as supportive of 'national liberation' in Argentina. . . . Paradoxically, this particular reimagining of the proper relationship between Jews and Israel was also an outgrowth of the sympathy Jewish activists had for the revolutionary ferment in Argentina."[43] Nevertheless, the Six-Day War in 1967 would profoundly transform the political landscape for socialist Zionists, as in its wake radicals around the globe, including members of the *nueva izquerdia* or the New Left in Argentina, roundly condemned Israel as an agent of Western imperialism and racism.[44]

In response, some Jewish radicals in Argentina who had previously identified as Zionist abandoned the movement entirely and became harsh critics, others doubled down on their support of Israel, while still others attempted to create what Gurwitz has described as a "new Third-World Zionism: Zionism was a national liberation movement and Zionist youth groups were the revolutionary vanguard responsible for aliyah [i.e., immigration to Israel]."[45] In the late 1960s and early 1970s, such "Third World Zionists" focused much of their critique on the local Jewish establishment, while attempting to navigate their ongoing support of Zionism, on the one hand, and their desire to belong to the broader Argentine Left, on the other.[46] The apogee of these efforts was Amós, a group formed in 1969 by self-identified "revolutionary socialist Zionists," who nevertheless remained committed to Third World movements around the globe and to "national liberation" in Argentina.[47] Membership in the latter was made more difficult by the emergence of what Jessica Stites Mor has argued was a particularly powerful tradition of "South-South solidarity" between Argentine radicals and the Palestinian cause, as well as by attacks on Israel and its Jewish supporters by leftist organizations in Argentina that sometimes recycled classical antisemitic tropes and imagery, even as they formally denounced antisemitism itself.[48]

The debate over Israel also engulfed ICUF, which had "blamed the [Six-Day] war on 'Zionist-imperialist aggression,'" leading some members to leave and form a new progressive Zionist organization, *Fraie Schtime* (New Voice).[49] Meanwhile, ICUF idealogues, most prominently the journalist Ruben Sinay, criticized their longtime opponents in Hashomer Hatzair for being "reactionary," while defending the Soviet Union's policy in the Middle East and rejecting claims that it was engaging in antisemitism. Yet Emmanuel Kahan has demonstrated that activists within ICUF also sought to balance their "condemnation of the bellicose and annexationist Israeli policy" with what they viewed as the frequent double standard of Israel's leftist critics. As the organization's monthly *Tiempo* put it in 1968: "Many left-wing sectors engage in an ideological distortion when they identify Israel with imperialism and the Arab countries with progress and anti-imperialism; both sides have progressive and reactionary sectors . . . the global left has failed to criticize the warmongering chauvinism of progressive Arab sectors . . . they have failed to support the Arab and Jewish left wings so as to foster understanding; in short they have failed to truly adopt a peacemaking spirit."[50]

Other Jewish radicals in Argentina, including many who were influenced by the revolutionary climate in the country's universities, vehemently rejected Zionism from the beginning. As early as 1961, the Argentine Jewish academic León Perez observed of universities in cities like Buenos Aires, Córdoba, and La Plata, "Zionism is considered reactionary and Israel as a pillar of Yankee imperialism in the Middle East, that is opposed to Nasser's neutral foreign policy."[51] Instead, such Jewish youth joined the Communist Party and/or one or more of the new revolutionary organizations that were founded in the 1960s by activists frustrated with what they perceived to be the party's accommodationist approach.[52] In some cases, these Jewish activists hailed from families with long traditions of radical politics, dating back to the first few decades of the twentieth century. Among them was Lucila Edelman, one of the leaders of *el Partido Comunista Revolucionario*, which split from the Communist Party in 1967 and attracted strong support among university students in particular. Regarding her mother, Edelman observed, "She left me an important legacy for which I am grateful, although I must admit it has often been hard to be the daughter of the famous Fanny Edelman!"[53]

During the 1960s, Jewish activists also continued to play an important role in Argentina's Trotskyist left, which was also divided into several competing factions. In 1964, Jorge Altamira (aka José Saúl Wermus), who was born into a working-class Jewish family in Buenos Aires, founded the *Política Obrera*, a Trotskyist group whose leadership included numerous Jews, among them Altamira's brother Julio Magri (aka Natalio Ismael Wermus), Roberto Gramar (aka Marcelo Nowersztern), Norberto Malaj (aka Norberto Flexer), and Rafael Santos (aka Gustavo Eibuszyc).[54] While it was common for radicals from all backgrounds to adopt *noms de guerre*—most famously Lenin, Stalin, Trotsky, and many others, including in Argentina—it is possible that a desire to distance themselves publicly from their Jewish roots influenced at least some of these activists.[55] Nevertheless, their Jewishness remained well-known in leftist circles and a joke even circulated that "the only reason why the Central Committee of Política Obrera doesn't hold their meetings in Yiddish is because they have a Sephardi member."[56] Moreover, as Maximiliano Jozami has noted, "The background of many of PO's founding members seems to have been used in a derogatory way" by some of their Trotskyist competitors, who accused them of being closet Zionists.[57] In fact, some Jewish members of Política Obrera had been Zionists before joining the group but, following the Six Day War, they took an especially hard stance against Israel, even for the Argentine Left, with Altamira publishing an essay in which he called for the "liquidation of Israel's imperialist State form . . . that is the direct agent of the exploitation of the Jewish masses and the racial and social discrimination existing in that country."[58]

Whereas Jorge Altamira would remain within Política Obrera (renamed *Partido Obrero* in 1983) for more than half a century, many other Jewish radicals migrated from group to group as local and global conditions—and their own political sensibilities—shifted over the course of the 1960s and into the next decade.[59] A striking case was Marcos Otasinsky, who first joined *la Federación Juvenil Comunista*, the youth branch of the Communist Party, in 1960, at a time when its secretary general was Jorge Bergstein, another native son of La Plata. Of his own Jewish background, Bergstein later recalled, "The story of my father is of a Polish Jewish immigrant who was never able to leave poverty. . . . He was religious but only performed the most fundamental ceremonies [and] went to synagogue three times a year, in contrast to my mother who honored the ceremony of lighting the candles every Friday night and the norms of Shabbat."[60] In the mid-1960s, Osatinsky and his Jewish wife and comrade, Sara Solarz, joined the *Ejército de Liberación Nacional*, a revolutionary group established in support of Ché Guevara's guerilla campaign in Bolivia. Following Guevara's death, Osatinsky helped to found *las Fuerzas Armadas Revolucionarias* (FAR), an organization whose leadership included a number of other Jews, before ultimately becoming a leader of the *Montoneros*, a leftist militant Peronist faction that united with the FAR in the early 1970s.[61] After participating in a series of guerilla attacks against targets around the country, Osatinsky was killed by government forces in Cordoba in 1975.

By that point, the country was on the verge of the 1976 coup-d'état that would install a military dictatorship that remained in power until it was weakened by the country's defeat in the Falklands War in 1982 and was finally succeeded by the democratically elected government of President Raúl Alfonsin in 1983. In a self-styled "Dirty War," the junta arrested, tortured, and killed thousands of radicals (or those suspected of engaging in subversive activities); many other radicals went underground or into exile to escape the regime. In some cases, the fate of "disappeared" individuals or of their children who were kidnapped and placed for adoption—frequently with military families—has never been learned. In this environment of fear and persecution, the vast majority of institutions, including those within the Jewish community, avoided confronting or openly criticizing the junta.

Among the most notable exceptions, Jewish or otherwise, was *Nueva Presencia*, a weekly newspaper founded in 1977—initially as a Spanish language insert in the country's last Yiddish daily *Di Presse*—by Herman Schiller, a longtime socialist activist and Jewish journalist.[62] Under his editorial direction, *Nueva Presencia* regularly condemned the junta's human rights violations—a typical headline from October 17, 1980, declared "For Human Rights, Against Violence"—and lent support to the newly created *las Madres de la Plaza de Mayo*, a grass roots organization consisting of mothers of the disappeared. Despite the constant threat of arrest and the bombing of its presses on two occasions, *Nueva Presencia* continued to publish throughout the years of the dictatorship, and in 1983, Schiller co-founded *el*

Movimiento Judío por los Derechos Humanos (the Jewish Movement for Human Rights) with Rabbi Marshall Meyer.[63]

Following the fall of the regime, the impact of the Dirty War on Argentina's Jews has been hotly debated. Different figures for the number of Jewish *desaparacidos* or disappeared have been offered over the years, with *la Comisión Nacional para la Desaparición de Personas* (CONADEP) listing 937 Jewish cases out of 8,961 overall—that is, 10.46 percent of the total during a period in which Jews constituted roughly 1 percent of the overall population of Argentina.[64] This discrepancy begs the question of whether Jews were arrested by the regime at least in part because they were Jewish and, if so, whether this reflected an antisemitic campaign directed specifically at the country's Jewish community by the military junta. There is ample evidence, including from the detention centers, that many members of the regime were antisemitic and that, once arrested, Jewish prisoners were frequently treated with a "special brutality" incorporating antisemitic elements, some explicitly connected to the Nazis (for example, "Heil Hitlers," swastikas, etc.).[65] As Alberto Goldberg, who was detained soon after the military coup, later testified: "They tied up my extremities and there I became aware of my being a Jew, because they started to make jokes in relation to my circumcision and to say: What are the Jews doing in the country; that we dirtied what we stepped on and all the current antisemitic phraseology. The fact of being Jewish was not decisive in being disappeared or imprisoned but it aggravated the punishment . . . they tossed a bucket of water on me and started to shock me with an electric cattle prod . . . focusing especially on my penis."[66]

While some observers have invoked the Holocaust in relation to the regime's treatment of Jews, Daniel Goldman and Hernán Dobry have written, "We do not know for certain whether there existed in the country any type of 'official' persecution of the Jewish community during the military dictatorship. . . . In fact, being Jewish or belonging to a family with a Jewish member was neither the sole nor sufficient reason to become a victim of the repressive forces."[67] Citing a lack of documentary evidence for a governmental campaign against the country's Jews, Goldman and Dobry have instead pointed to certain demographic factors to explain what appears to be the overrepresentation of Jews among the disappeared.[68] Specifically, a high percentage of Jews belonged to "those groups that were the central object of the repression, in particular in university sectors (in medical careers, journalism, law, psychology, economics and exact sciences), cultural fields, and business."[69] As Graciela Fernández Meijide, the secretary of CONADEP, explained, "Jewish people . . . were not kidnapped because they were Jews, but because of their political, student, and union activism, because they were swept up in the indiscriminate action [of the regime]."[70] A little more than half a century after la Semana Trágica, therefore, Argentina's Jewish radicals once again found themselves in the crosshairs of the country's right-wing elements, victims of a broader campaign of state-sponsored terror. Like their predecessors in 1919, they became targets due to their politics and were subjected to antisemitic treatment because of their Jewishness.

NOTES

1. For these figures, see Ricardo Feierstein, *Historia de los Judíos Argentinos* (Buenos Aires: Galerna, 2006), 117. See also Ira Rosenwaike, "Jewish Population of Argentina: Census and Estimates, 1887–1947," *Jewish Social Studies* 22 (1960), 203–204.

2. Alfredo Bauer, *La Asociación Vorwärts y la lucha democrática en la Argentina* (Buenos Aires: Biblioteca Nacional, 2008), 27. On Augusto Kühn's own writings, see 26. See also Augusto Kühn, "Páginas de la historia revolucionaria argentina. Espigando," *Correspondencia Sudamericana* 2 (1926), 3-15. Despite forming less than 0.5 percent of the overall population of the country according to the national census of 1895, German immigrants played an outsize role in the early history of socialism in Argentina. For this figure, see Lucas Poy and Daniel Gaido, "Under German Eyes: Germán Avé-Lallemant and the Origins of Marxism in Argentina," *Science & Society* 75, no. 4 (2011), 482.

3. On the Chertkoff sisters, see Sandra McGee Deutsch, *Crossing Borders, Claiming a Nation: A History of Argentine Jewish Women, 1880–1955* (Durham: Duke University Press), 154–157.

4. Jose Moya, "The Positive Side of Stereotypes: Jewish Anarchists in Early Twentieth-Century Buenos Aires," *Jewish History* 18 (2004), 21.

5. Moya, "The Positive Side," 20.

6. Moya, "The Positive Side," 22.

7. For a detailed study of Jewish involvement in the furniture industry in particular, see Walter Ludovico Koppman, "Radiografía sobre la presencia obrera judía en la industria de la madera y del mueble de la ciudad de Buenos Aires, 1894–1921," *A Contra corriente: Una revista de estudios latinoamericanos* 17, no. 3 (Spring 2020): 143–172.

8. Sandra McGee Deutsch, "The Argentine Right and the Jews, 1919–1933," *Journal of Latin American Studies* 18, no. 1 (May 1986), 117, writes, "Although leftists of other ethnic backgrounds vastly outnumbered Jewish union members, socialists, anarchists, and, later, communists, the Russian origins of most Jews led other Argentines to suspect them of radical sympathies." On the description of Falcón as "infamous as a reactionary and anti-Semite," see Raanan Rein, "A Trans-National Struggle with National and Ethnic Goals: Jewish-Argentines and Solidarity with the Republicans During the Spanish Civil War," *Journal of Iberian and Latin American Research* 20, no. 2 (2014), 178.

9. Victor Mirelman, "The Semana Trágica of 1919 and the Jews in Argentina," *Jewish Social Studies* 37, no. 1 (1975), 64.

10. Juan Carulla, *Al filo del medio siglo* (Paraná: Ediciones Llanura, 1951), 156, as quoted in Mirelman, "The Semana Trágica," 63. For a more recent assessment of the events as a pogrom, see Eduardo Anguita and Daniel Cecchini, "La sangrienta historia del pogrom judío que quedó oculto dentro de la Semina Trágica," *Infobae*, January 14, 2019, https://www.infobae.com/historia-argentina/2019/01/14/la-sangrienta-historia-del-pogromo-judio-que-quedo-oculto-dentro-de-la-semana-tragica/.

11. For a history of the Bund in Argentina, see Israel Laubstein, *Bund: Historia del movimiento obrero judío* (Buenos Aires: Acervo Cultural, 1997).

12. On these organizations and their publications, see Edgardo Bilsky, Gabriel Trajtenberg, Ana Epelbaum de Weinstein, *El movimiento obrero judío en la Argentina* (Buenos Aires: AMIA, 1987).- It is worth noting that Richard Walter, "The Socialist Press in Turn-of-the Century Argentina," *The Americas* 37, no.1 (1980), does not mention any of these Jewish socialist publications.

13. For his own account of the events, see Pedro Wald, *Koshmar* (Buenos Aires, 1929). See also Herman Schiller, "El primer pogrom," *Página 12*, January 3, 1999, 16–17.

14. Schiller, "El primer pogrom," 16–17; see also Marcelo Dimentstein, "En busca de un pogrom perdido: Memoria en torno de la Semana Trágica de 1919 (1919–1999)," in *Marginados y consagrados: Nuevos estudios sobre la vida judía en la Argentina*, ed. Emmanuel Kahan, Laura Schenquer, Damián Setton, and Alejandro Dujovne (Buenos Aires: Ediciones Lumière, 2011), 125. Both Schiller and Dimentstein note that, at the time, some members of the Jewish community who had ties to the government rejected the description of the events as a pogrom.

15. Dimentstein, "En busca de un pogrom perdido," 135–141.

16. Daniel Kersffeld, "'*Judeocomunismo*': Aproximaciones y derivaciones de una identidad política en conflicto," in *Marginados y consagrados*, 164. In *Rusos y rojos: Judios comunistas en los tiempos de la Comintern* (Buenos Aires: Capital Intelectual, 2012), 113, Kersffeld notes that even though they rejected the competing Jewish nationalisms of the Bund and socialist Zionism, tensions arose over accusations within the Communist Party of Argentina that members of the Jewish section possessed "autonomist intentions."

17. Ariel Svarch, "Comunistas judíos o judíos comunistas? El activismo y la lucha de la rama judía del PC en un contexto de crisis identitaria (1920–1950)," *X Jornadas Interescuelas/Departamentos de Historia. Escuela de Historia de la Facultad de Humanidades y Artes, Universidad Nacional del Rosario. Departamento de Historia de la Facultad de Ciencias de la Educación, Universidad Nacional del Litoral, Rosario*, 2005, 6.

18. Svarch, "Comunistas judíos o judíos comunistas?" 7.

19. Kersffeld, "'*Judeocomunism*,'" 145; for the figures, see Emmanuel Kahan, "Los 'judíos progresistas' en Argentina: Posicionamientos, debates y tensiones frente a la Guerra de los Seis Días," in *Memoria y violencia en el siglo XX: Horizontes de un proyecto de investigación*, ed. Emmanuel Nicolás Kahan, Santiago Cueto Rua, and Laura Graciela Rodríguez (La Plata: Universidad Nacional De La Plata, 2018), 41.

20. Rein, "A Trans-National Struggle," 173: "The proportion of Jews among the volunteers [on behalf of the Republicans in the Spanish Civil War] from each particular country was in most cases far greater than their representation in the general population of that country, including Argentina." He estimates that at least 10 percent of the between 500 and 600 Argentines who volunteered for the Republican cause were Jewish, as compared to their 1.6 percent of the overall Argentine population (176). Jewish volunteers hailed from Buenos Aires, but also from Moisés Ville, Tucumán, and elsewhere. The Jewish presence among women who volunteered appears to have been especially pronounced.

21. Alejandro Rebossio, "Fanny Edelman, el corazón del Partido Comunista argentine," *El Pais*, November 2, 2011. https://elpais.com/diario/2011/11/03/necrologicas/1320274801_850215.html. . Edelman was the honorary president of the Communist Party of Argentina when she passed away.

22. Rein, "A Trans-National Struggle," 176. Seeking to continue the fight against fascism, many of the Jewish communist women involved in the Spanish Civil War, among them Fanny Edelman, would later join, and in some cases help to lead, the Junta de la Victoria after it was founded "to definitively annihilate fascism, establish peace, defend the rights of the woman and solve the problems of children's health and education." For this quote, which appears in Junta de la Victoria, *Estatutos* (Buenos Aires, n.d.), 3, see Sandra McGee Deutsch, "Changing the Landscape: The Study of Argentine Jewish Women and New Historical Vistas," *Jewish History* 18 (2004), 65.

23. For an illuminating and detailed history of ICUF, see Nerina Visacovsky, *Argentinos, judíos y camaradas: Tras la utopia socialista* (Buenos Aires: Editorial Biblos, 2017).

24. Israel Lotersztain, "The Abandonment of Yiddish by the Jewish-Argentine Communist ICUF," in *Splendor, Decline, and Rediscovery of Yiddish in Latin America*, ed. Alan Astro and Malena Chinski (Leiden, Netherlands: E. J. Brill, 2018), 71, writes that ICUF functioned as "the Jewish wing of the very orthodox and pro-Soviet Argentine Communist Party." By contrast, Kahan, "Los 'judíos progresistas' en Argentina," 43, writes, "in this organization [ICUF] the relation with the Communist Party was neither obvious nor explicit. In theory, ICUF was not more than a network of secular Jewish institutions."

25. Lotersztain, "The Abandonment of Yiddish," 72. See Svarch, "Comunistas judíos o judíos comunistas?" 10, for a list of ICUF branches around the country (e.g., Cordoba, Rosario, La Plata) as well as institutions within the Buenos Aires region.

26. Nerina Visacovsky, "Los judíos textiles de Villa Lynch y el I. L. Peretz. Síntesis de institución judía, club de barrio y centro cultural," 13. Jornadas Historia Política del Gran Buenos Aires en el siglo XX. El Centro de Estudios de Historia Política (Escuela de Política y Gobierno. Universidad Nacional de General San Martín). Buenos Aires, June 22–23, 2006. https://historiapolitica.com/datos/biblioteca/jornadas/Visacovsky.pdf.

27. Nerina Visacovsky, "Leike Kogan," The Shalman/Hyman Encyclopedia of Jewish Women, *Jewish Women's Archive*, last updated June 23, 2021, https://jwa.org/encyclopedia/article/kogan-leike. On Mimi Pinzón (aka Adela Weinstein-Shliapochnik), author of the important Yiddish novel *Hoyf on fenster*, among many other works, see Joanna Meadvin, "At *Heym* in the *Hoyf*: Mimi Pinzón's Argentine Yiddish World," *Prooftexts* 36, no. 1–2 (2017): 167–189.

28. Lotersztain, "The Abandonment of Yiddish," 73.

29. Svarch, "Comunistas judíos o judíos comunistas?" 12: "ICUF began running for AMIA elections in 1944 and completed the steps in order to enter DAIA in 1947. By the end of the decade, progressivism had already obtained a third of the votes in the AMIA elections and had become transformed into the largest minority." Lawrence Bell, "Bitter Conquest: Zionists Against Progressive Jews and the Making of Post-War Jewish Politics in Argentina," *Jewish History* 17, no. 3 (2003), 289, writes, "In 1946, an alliance of Bundists, Communists, and non-aligned Zionists succeeded in defeating a combined Zionist slate for control of the AMIA."

30. On the rise of Zionist leadership within AMIA and other Ashkenazi-dominated institutions in Argentina, see Silvia Schenkolewski-Kroll, "'La conquista de la comunidades': El movimiento sionista y la comunidad ashkenazi de Buenos Aires (1935–1949)," *Judaica Latinoamericana, Estudios Histórico-Sociales* 11 (1993): 191–201. For the most detailed account of how center and right-wing Zionists maintained power in Argentina's Jewish establishment organizations during the 1950s, largely at the expense of ICUF, see Lawrence Bell, "Bitter Conquest."

31. Orestes Ghioldi, *La Guerra en Palestina. El Estado de Israel defiende su independencia* (Buenos Aires: Anteo, 1948), 8–9, as cited in Mercedes Saborido, "'Es justo que los Judíos tengan sus u estado proprio en Palestina? Mil veces justo': El Partido Comunista de la Argentina y la creación del estado de Israel," *Historia Contemporánea* 46 (2013), 241. On communist support for the creation of the State of Israel, see also "Con motivo a la proclamación de un estado judío en Palestina," *Orientación*, no. 44, May 19, 1948. For their part, many Jewish socialists in the country, Enrique Dickmann most prominently among them, also strongly voiced support for the new state. See Raanan Rein, *Argentina, Israel y los judíos. Encuentros y desencuentros, mitos y realidades* (Buenos Aires: Ediciones Lumière, 2001), 101–102.

32. Bell, "Bitter Conquest," 299. Lotersztain, "The Abandonment of Yiddish," 72, notes that in the 1954 AMIA elections, ICUF candidates garnered 38 percent of the votes in the same year that Communist Party candidates for the Argentine national legislature received barely 1 percent. Regarding the attitude of the Perón government, he writes, "at times [it] cracked down on Argentine communists in general and, arguably, the ICUF in particular" (71).

33. Raanan Rein, "Un pacto de olvido: Peronismo y las divisiones en la colectividad," in *Pensar lo judío en la Argentina del siglo XXI*, ed. Alejandro Dujovne, Daniel Goldman, and Dario Sztainszrajber (Buenos Aires: Capital Intelectual, 2011), 182.

34. Like others in the Socialist Party of Argentina, Enrique Dickmann initially criticized Perón during the 1940s. After throwing his support to Perón in the early 1950s, Dickmann and his son, Emilio, were both expelled from the Socialist Party, which viewed Peronism as competing for the same constituencies in the country. On the tension between Perón and the Socialist Party, see Marcela Garcia Sebastiani, "The Other Side of Peronist Argentina: Radicals and Socialists in the Political Opposition to Perón (1946–1955)," *Journal of Latin American Studies* 35, no. 2 (May 2003): 311–339.

35. Alejandro Dujovne, "'Un acto de afirmación judía'. La edición en castellano entre 1938 y 1974: Sionismo, cultura y religion," in *Una historia del libro judío: La cultura judía argentina a través de sus editores, libreros, traductores, imprentas y bibliotecas* (Buenos Aires: Siglo XXI Editores, 2019).

36. Lotersztain, "The Abandonment of Yiddish," 72. Israel Lotersztain, "Los intelectuales judíos y la Guerra Fria: El caso del ICUF," in *Pensar lo judío*, 212, argues that members of ICUF styled themselves as *progresistas* (progressives) as a "mere euphemism so as to not utilize the more difficult, controversial, and dangerous definition in those years of 'communist' or 'fellow traveler.'"

37. See Adriana Brodsky, "Working for the Homeland: Zionism and the Creation of an 'Argentine' Sephardi Community," *Sephardi, Jewish, Argentine: Community and National Identity, 1880–1960* (Bloomington: Indiana University Press, 2016); "Electing 'Miss Sefaradí,' and 'Queen Esther': Sephardim, Zionism, and Ethnic and National Identities in Argentina, 1933–1971," in *The New Jewish Argentina: Facets of Jewish Experiences in the Southern Cone*, ed. Adriana Brodsky and Raanan Rein (Leiden: E. J. Brill, 2012).

38. See "David Elnecavé, Dean of Jewish Journalists in Latin America, Dead," *JTA*, June 3, 1963. http://pdfs.jta.org/1963/1963-06-03_104.pdf.

39. On the role played by Nissim Elnecavé, see Abrasha Rotemberg, "Testigo viviente de un siglo, el único sobreviviente de los fundadores de *Nueva Sión*, 70 años atrás," February 27, 2018, https://web.archive.org/web/20180302164153/http://www.nuevasion.com.ar/articulo.php?id=6532.

40. On this wider phenomenon, see Diana Sorensen, *A Turbulent Decade Remembered: Scenes from the Latin American Sixties, Cultural Memory in the Present* (Stanford: Stanford University Press, 2007).

41. On the New Left in Argentina, see Martin Mangiantini, "La 'Nueva Izquierda' en la Argentina. Claves y discusiones alrededor del concepto," *Astrolabio* 21 (2018): 27–52.

42. For the history of leftist Zionist Sephardi youth groups in Argentina during the 1960s, see Adriana Brodsky, "Argentine Sephardi Youth: Between Aliyah and Activism, 1960–1970," *Journal of Jewish Identities* 8, no. 2 (2015): 113–135.

43. Beatrice Gurwitz, *Argentine Jews in the Age of Revolt: Between the New World and the Third World* (Leiden: E. J. Brill, 2016), 3.

44. See Mercedes Saborido, "El Partido Comunista Argentino y la Guerra de los Seis Días," *Izquierdas*, 12 (2012), 57: "The general support for the Arab cause among progressives around the world became evident as the conflict unfolded. The Six-Day War has remained in the [leftist] collective imagination as the first unjust war initiated by Israel, in which that country passed from being victim to victimizer." By contrast, DAIA celebrated the Israeli victory. See Emmanuel Kahan, "Progressive Jews in Argentina and the Arab-Israeli Conflict: Stances on the Six-Day War (1967)," *Latin American Perspectives* 46, no. 3(2019), 46.

45. Beatrice Gurwitz, "Zionism, Third Worldism, and Argentine Youth at the Crossroads," *Journal of Jewish Identities* 8, no. 2 (July 2015), 21. Emmanuel Kahan, *Memories That Lie a Little: Jewish Experiences During the Argentine Dictatorship* (Leiden: E. J. Brill, 2019), 31, discusses the case of Marcos Blank, a former Zionist who condemned the movement in a letter to the leftist Zionist publication *Nueva Sión*. See Marcos Blank, "Carta de un antisionista," *Nueva Sión*, September 9, 1974, 5. Blank's letter prompted a defense by David Ben-Ami, "Respuesta de un sionista," *Neuva Sión*, September 9, 1974, 6. For an in depth discussion of these sources and their wider historical context, see also Emmanuel Kahan, "Jewish Youth in Times of Political Radicalization: Argentina 1960/1970," *Dubnow Institute Yearbook* 18, 2019, 417–433.

46. Gurwitz, "Zionism, Third Worldism," 27, argues that Third World Zionism came to an end with the rise of the military junta: "Finally, when the military assumed power in 1976 and launched a brutal campaign against leftist 'subversives,' very broadly defined, the remaining voices of Third-World Zionism were entirely silenced. . . . By 1975, however, the moment of youth rebellion had effectively ended. Both the fervent Zionism and Third-World leftism that had underpinned the youth rebellion had waned."

47. On Amós, see Adrián Krupnik, "Cuando camino al kibbutz vieron pasar al Che. Radicalización política y juventud judía: Argentina 1966–1976," in *Marginados y consagrados*, 319–326.

48. Jessica Stites Mor, "The Question of Palestine in the Argentine Political Imaginary: Anti-Imperialist Thought from Cold War to Neoliberal Order," *Journal of Iberian and Latin American Research* 20, no. 2 (2014): 183–197. On the use of classic antisemitic tropes and imagery by Argentine leftists in their critiques of Israel during the 1960s and early 1970s, even as they repudiated antisemitism and sought to distinguish it from anti-Zionism, see Maximiliano Jozami, "Argentine Left Parties and the 1967 Six-Day War Through the Prism of Global Networks and South-South Connections," *Jahrbuch für Geschichte Lateinamerikas—Anuario de Historia de América Latina* 56 (2019), 34–35.

49. See Gurwitz, *Argentine Jews in the Age of Revolt*, 106; Leonardo Senkman, "Repercussions of the Six-Day War in the Leftist Jewish Argentine Camp: The Rise of *Fraie Schtime*," in *The Six-Day War and World Jewry*, ed. Eli Lederhendler (Bethesda: The University of Maryland Press, 2000).

50. "Por la paz en el Medio Oriente," *Tiempo*, no. 1, July 30, 1968, as cited in Kahan, "Progressive Jews in Argentina," 50.

51. León Perez, "Situación del universitario judío en la Argentina," paper presented at Primera Conferencia de Investigadores y Estudiosos Judeo-Argentinos en el Campo de las Ciencias Sociales y la Historia, October 11–15, 1961, Centro Mark Turkow, box 22A, 7, as cited in Beatrice Gurwitz, "Generation and Innovation in the Rise of an Argentine-Jewish Community, 1960–1967," in *The New Jewish Argentina*, 242.

52. Beatrice Gurwitz, "Generation and Innovation," 235ff.

53. Nancy Caro Hollander, *Uprooted Minds: Surviving the Politics of Terror in the Americas* (New York: Taylor & Francis, 2014), 149. Lucila Edelman went on to a distinguished career as a psychiatrist and psychoanalyst specializing in the effects of trauma experienced under repressive political conditions, including the military dictatorship in Argentina.

54. Jozami, "Argentine Left Parties and the 1967 Six-Day War," 22–23. Regarding the Jewish background of the group's members, Roberto Gramar later observed to Jozam in an interview, "it was not a mere question of origin, we had a Jewish education, went to Jewish schools and some belonged to the Zionist left" (23, n. 22).

55. See, for example, the non-Jewish Argentine Trotskyist leader Nahuel Moreno (aka Hugo Bressano).

56. Interview with Efraim Davidi, in Jozami, "Argentine Left Parties and the 1967 Six-Day War," 23, n. 22. Claudio Waisbrod, a Jewish leader of Política Obrera in Córdoba, remembered that members "used to make ironic calls for the 'Christianization of PO,'" because the organization had so many Jews.

57. Jozami, "Argentine Left Parties and the 1967 Six-Day War," 23.

58. Jorge Altamira, "Aprender de la derrota sufrida por la Revolución Árabe," *Política Obrera* 17, June 28, 1967, as cited in Jozami, "Argentine Left Parties and the 1967 Six-Day War," 34.

59. Like many of his fellow radicals in Argentina who were not killed or "disappeared" by the regime, Jorge Altamira went into exile during the country's military dictatorship, in his case to neighboring Brazil, where he remained from 1978 to 1982. After returning to Argentina, Altamira reestablished the organization he had founded two decades earlier, now renamed the Partido Obrero, and subsequently ran as the party's candidate in multiple elections—1989, 1995, 1999, 2003, and 2011—for the presidency of Argentina. Although Altamira was unsuccessful in these campaigns, he was now arguably the country's most prominent radical *éminence grise*. Jozami, "Argentine Left Parties and the 1967 Six-Day War," 20, observes that Partido Obrero had "become the most important current of the Argentine left at the beginning of the 21st century."

60. Jorge Bergstein, *Vida pasión y testimonio* (Buenos Aires, Editorial Tesis 11, 2003), 23–24.

61. On Marcos Osatinsky, see Mora González and Emmanuel Kahan, "Identidad, política y etnicidad. La trayectoria militante de Marcos Osatinsky, fundador de las Fuerzas Armadas Revolucionarias (Argentina)," *Rubrica Contemporanea* 10, no. 19 (2021): 145–166. The authors provide a long list of Jews in las Fuerzas Armadas Revolucionarias, including the well-known writer Juan Gelman (158, n. 36). Osatinsky's sons, Mario and José, who were also involved in militant activities, were subsequently killed by the government; his wife, Sara Solarz, was arrested and imprisoned. Gonzalez and Kahan argue that Jewishness was not a central issue in Osatinsky's political engagements or his self-presentation (161–165). Nevertheless, he was "rejudaized," following the military dictatorship, first by members of the Jewish establishment who sought to include Osatinsky and others like him as Jewish victims of an antisemitic regime (for example, in the book *Homenaje a los Desaparacidos de la Comunidad Judía de Córdoba*), a process that also involved "a depoliticization of his militant trajectory" (164).

62. On the founding of *Nueva Presencia* and its role during the dictatorship, see "La prensa judía y los desaparecidos," in Daniel Goldman and Hernán Dobry, *Ser Judío en los años setenta:*

Testimonios del horror y la resistencia durante la última dictadura (Buenos Aires: Siglo Veintiuno Editores, 2014), 181–205; Kahan, "*Nueva Presencia* and Resistance to the Military Dictatorship," *Memories That Lie a Little*, 204–233.

63. See "El movimiento judío por los derechos humanos," in *Ser Judío en los años setenta*, 207–238.

64. Goldman and Dobry, *Ser Judío en los años setenta*, 35.

65. See, for example, the essay by the Argentine lawyer and judge Daniel Rafecas, "La especial brutalidad antisemita del terrorismo de estado durante la última dictadura militar en la Argentina," *Nuestra Memoria* 29 (Buenos Aires: La Fundación Memoria del Holocausto, December, 2007), 195–208. By contrast, Emmanuel Kahan, "Discursos y reprentaciones en conflicto sobre la actuación de la comunidad judía durante la última dictadura military: Análisis de los Informes sobre 'los detenidos-desaparacidos de origen judío,' 1984–2007," in *Marginados y consagrados*, 375, demurs from the commonly held view regarding any "special treatment of the Jews in the clandestine detention centers . . . beyond certain tortures specifically for the 'disappeared of Jewish origin,' they did not have any especially cruel treatment in respect to the other disappeared. That is to say, the cruel treatment in the clandestine detention centers was extended to all of their residents." Kahan asks, "What would be the difference between the accusation of 'shitty Jew,' 'shitty whore,' or 'shitty guerilla' . . . during a torture session? Or where would lie the distinction between making a detainee of Jewish origin shout 'Heil Hitler'! and the systematic violation of women and the robbery/appropriation of the children of those detainees who were pregnant?" (376, n. 61).

66. Goldman and Dobry, *Ser Judío en los años setenta*, 44–45.

67. Goldman and Dobry, *Ser Judío en los años setenta*, 35. For a critical approach to what he calls "the identification of the Holocaust and the experience of Jews under the military dictatorship" (324), see Emmanuel Kahan, "Esto no es un Holocausto. El testimonio de Jacobo Timerman y la represión a los judíos durante la última dictadura militar," in *Represión estatal y violencia paraestatal en la historia reciente argentina. Nuevos abordajes a 40 años del golpe de Estado*, Gabriela Águila, Santiago Garaño, and Pablo Scatizza, coordinators (Facultad de Humanidades y Ciencias de la Educación, Universidad Nacional de la Plata, 2016).

68. Kahan, "Discursos y reprentaciones en conflicto," in *Marginados y consagrados*, has written that "the use of the notion of 'overrepresentation' presents various methodological problems" (376).

69. Goldman and Dobry, *Ser Judío en los años setenta*, 36–37. CONADEP statistics reveal that a high percentage of Jews belonged to the four most common professions or occupations whose members were arrested by the regime, although the order was different for the Jewish and non-Jewish disappeared (for example, "workers" ranked highest for non-Jews and "students" ranked second, while "students" ranked highest for Jews and "workers" was fourth, and so on). They also note that the proportion of Jewish men and women who were disappeared is practically identical to those of non-Jews (38). Although most of the Jewish disappeared were Ashkenazi, reflecting their much greater percentage of the overall Jewish population, some were Sephardi or Syrian. On this subject, see Silvina Schammah Gesser and Susana Brauner, "Aesthetics, Politics and the Complexities of Arab Jewish Identities in Authoritarian Argentina," in *Contemporary Sephardic and Mizrahi Literature*, ed. Dario Miccoli (New York: Routledge, 2019); Susana Brauner, "De la Torá a la Patria Socialista: Jóvenes judíos de origen sirio en los 60'y 70'," *Nueva Sion*, March 16, 2021, http://www.nuevasion.com.ar/archivos/30485.

70. As cited in Goldman and Dobry, *Ser Judío en los años setenta*, 37.

CHAPTER 9

Jewish Radicals in Twentieth-Century Brazil

Michael Rom

Like other sites of twentieth-century Jewish mass migration, Brazil became home to a significant number of Jewish radicals. These radicals were active within Jewish leftist institutions, which included cultural centers, schools, newspapers, women's organizations, and summer camps, and which competed with Zionists for political hegemony within the Brazilian Jewish community. But they could also be found throughout the broader Brazilian Left, in the Brazilian Communist Party, clandestine Marxist organizations that fought against the Brazilian military regime (1964–1985), and in the new political parties that emerged following the return of democratic rule in 1985, like the Green Party and Workers' Party. Several factors shaped the distinctness of the Jewish radical experience in Brazil, including the relative lateness of Jewish mass immigration, the particularities of Brazilian politics, and the decisive impact of the Cold War.

Although Brazil was home to the first Jewish community in the Western Hemisphere, during the seventeenth-century Dutch occupation of the Brazilian northeast, the modern Jewish community is of much more recent origin.[1] Unlike Jewish mass migration elsewhere in the Americas, which primarily occurred from 1880 to 1920, the majority of Brazilian Jewish immigrants arrived during the interwar period, when Brazil was the fourth most popular destination for Jewish immigration.[2] While fewer than twelve thousand European and Middle Eastern Jews immigrated to Brazil between 1880 and 1920, largely from Alsace-Lorraine, northern Morocco, and southwestern Ukraine, more than fifty thousand arrived during the subsequent two decades, predominantly from southern Poland and northern Bessarabia.[3] By 1949, the Brazilian Jewish community had grown to over one hundred thousand people.[4]

The primary destination for Jewish immigrants who arrived in Brazil during the 1920s was Rio de Janeiro, Brazil's largest city and the national capital until 1960. These immigrants mainly settled in Praça Onze (Eleventh Square), an immigrant neighborhood to the immediate west of the central train station that was also home to Italian and Portuguese immigrants, migrants from northeastern Brazil, and a large community of Afro-Brazilians.[5] In 1928, Jewish communists established the Morris Winchevsky Workers' Center on Visconde de Itaúna Street in Praça Onze, which became home to the Arbeter Shul (Workers' School), attended by forty-eight students, and the Yiddish newspaper *Der Onheyb* (The Beginning), whose first issue came out in 1929.[6] Another important leftist institution was the *Arbeter Kikh* (Worker's Kitchen), a nonprofit restaurant that catered to Jewish immigrants. "We raised money to cover expenses," remembered a Bessarabian Jewish immigrant named Rifka Gutnik, "so that those people could eat at least one decent meal a day, because the majority lived on bread and bananas."[7]

While Jewish leftist immigrants predominantly focused their energies on Jewish institutions, their children gravitated to the Brazilian Communist Party (PCB), established in 1922. Leôncio Basbaum was born in Recife in 1907 to Jewish immigrants from Bessarabia. In 1926 he joined the PCB while a medical student in Rio de Janeiro, and the following year he created the *Juventude Comunista* (Communist Youth), becoming its first secretary general.[8] Maurício Grabois was born in São Paulo in 1912 to Jewish immigrants from Ukraine, and grew up in Salvador, in the State of Bahia. He joined the PCB in 1932 while studying at the Realengomilitary academy in Rio de Janeiro.[9] Jacob Gorender was born in Salvador in 1923 to Jewish immigrants from Ukraine. In 1942, while studying at the law school, he joined a PCB student cell.[10] Grabois and Gorender both became important PCB leaders, although they would eventually break with the party.

The Jewish communist with arguably the greatest influence on the PCB, however, probably never set foot in Brazil. Abraham Heifetz was a Bundist from Riga, who joined the Bolsheviks in 1919.[11] Under the alias August Guralsky, he arrived in Buenos Aires in 1930 as the Latin American representative of the Communist International.[12] Heifetz set to work on the political education of Luís Carlos Prestes, a captain in the Brazilian army who had led a column of rebellious officers on a 24,000-kilometer march throughout the Brazilian interior in protest against the oligarchical rule of the First Republic (1889–1930) beginning in 1924 before going into exile in 1927.[13] Prestes related that Heifetz "helped me to understand the significance of the Russian Revolution." He was equally enthusiastic about Prestes, calling him "the most important convert [to Marxism] I have ever made in all my career as a revolutionary."[14] In May 1931 Prestes issued a manifesto publicly declaring himself a communist, and that October he sailed to the USSR along with his mother and three sisters.[15]

The previous October, Getúlio Vargas came to power in a military coup, ending the First Republic and beginning a presidency that would last for fifteen years.[16] The Vargas regime centralized the Brazilian state and empowered a new generation of urban elites, but it failed to create a truly national, mass-based political party.[17] Into the breach stepped the two mass movements then making rapid headway throughout Europe and the Americas, communism and fascism. A conservative intellectual named Plínio Salgado founded a fascist political party called the Brazilian Integralist Action (AIB) in 1932, and by 1934 it had 180,000 members, making it the largest Brazilian party at the time.[18] Through its newspapers, the AIB denounced liberalism, capitalism, and communism, all of which it associated with Jews.[19] In order to mobilize opposition to the AIB and Vargas, the clandestine PCB established the National Liberating Alliance (ANL) in 1935, a popular front organization that united communists, socialists, leftist officers, and liberal democrats, and which named Prestes as its honorary leader.[20]

In May 1935, Prestes secretly returned to Brazil, along with Olga Gutmann Benario, a German Jewish communist who was posing as his wife.[21] Other Comintern agents slipped into Brazil around the same time, including another German Jew named Elisa Saborovsky and her husband Arthur Ewert, and the Argentines Rodolfo and Carmen Ghioldi.[22] Together with the PCB secretary general Antônio Maciel Bomfim, they coordinated the activities of the ANL, which at its height numbered between seventy thousand and one hundred thousand members.[23] In July 1935, Prestes issued a manifesto calling for the creation of a revolutionary government led by the ANL, prompting Vargas to ban the organization.[24] Driven underground, the ANL plotted to seize power through a popular uprising. While Prestes had initially planned the uprising for early December, communist officers in Natal revolted in their barracks on November 23, seizing control of the northeastern state of Rio Grande do Norte. The next day, communist officers in Recife joined the uprising, but they encountered significant resistance and were unable to extend the revolt beyond their barracks. On November 27, communist officers in Rio de Janeiro took control of their barracks at Praia Vermelha, but the federal government quickly suppressed the revolt, retaking Natal that same day and successfully quelling the uprising.[25]

As the army put down the uprising, Brazilian police targeted foreign-born political activists, most of whom had no direct connection to the revolt. Acting on a tip from an informer, police raided the Arbeter Kikh, arresting twenty-four men and six women, all of whom were Jewish immigrants, on the charge of belonging to a "revolutionary Jewish organization."[26] Many of those arrested were deported to Europe.[27] While Jews were not the only foreigners detained in the wake of the failed revolt, their arrests and subsequent deportations received significant attention in the Rio de Janeiro press, furthering the popular association between Jews and communist subversion.[28] Many newspapers assumed that all the arrested foreigners were Jewish, such as *O Globo*, which called Arthur Ewert a "son of Israel and agent of Moscow."[29] The Vargas regime, however, evidently knew the difference. While it allowed Ewert to remain in Brazil, albeit under inhuman prison conditions, the government deported Benario and Saborovsky to Nazi Germany, where both ultimately perished in concentration camps.[30]

Following the arrests of its leadership, the PCB virtually ceased to exist as a political force for the next decade, but Judeo-Bolshevism remained a potent tool for diplomats who wished to limit Jewish immigration to Brazil, especially in Poland, where the government attempted to use economic boycotts to promote mass Jewish emigration. The Brazilian ambassador to Poland, José Francisco de Barros Pimentel, appealed in September 1936 for more restrictive immigration policies against Jews, whom he called "the principal promoters and greatest propagandists of communism in all the continents."[31] His colleague José Latour, the Brazilian commercial attaché to Poland and a leading AIB member, echoed this call, sending an unsolicited forty-page report on the dangers of Jewish immigration to the Brazilian foreign ministry in November 1936.[32] These diplomats' campaign had its desired effect. Having already banned Soviet immigration to Brazil, the foreign ministry issued a circular in June 1937 that instructed Brazilian consuls to refuse visas to all Jewish applicants.[33]

As Brazil prepared for its 1938 presidential election, in which Getúlio Vargas was unable to run again having already completed two terms in office, the specter of Judeo-Bolshevism became a useful weapon for those who wished to prolong Vargas's rule and overthrow Brazil's nominal democracy. Seeking to implement a dictatorship, the army chief of staff General Pedro Aurélio de Góes Monteiro found a pretext in a forged plan for a communist uprising, which a member of his staff named Olímpio Mourão Filho had written. Falsely attributing the forgery to the Hungarian communist leader Béla Kun, Mourão Filho wrote Kun's name as Cohen to emphasize his Jewish origins. The war minister Eurico Gaspar Dutra read out selections from the "Cohen Plan" on the government radio program *Hora do Brasil* (Brazil Hour) on September 30, 1937, and the next day Congress approved a ninety-day state of siege.[34] On November 10, soldiers barred the entrance to Congress, and Vargas instituted the *Estado Novo* (New State) dictatorship, through which he would rule Brazil for the next eight years.[35]

Even though Vargas's new dictatorship took its inspiration from authoritarian regimes in Italy and Portugal, he approved the construction of U.S. air bases in northeastern Brazil, and after the United States entered World War II following the Japanese attack on Pearl Harbor, Brazil broke off relations with the Axis powers.[36] In August 1942, Brazil joined the war effort on the side of the Allies, making it the only Latin American nation to send troops to Europe.[37] Forty-two out of the twenty-five thousand soldiers in the Brazilian Expeditionary Force (FEB) were Jewish, many of whom were communists, such as Jacob Gorender, Salomão Malina, and Carlos Scliar.[38] Brazil's entry into the war prompted a resurgence of nationalism, leading to the widespread adoption of the myth of racial democracy, which claimed that Brazil was a land free of racism, symbolized by the integrated FEB, in sharp contrast to the segregated U.S. Army.[39] Its entry into the war also doomed the Estado Novo, as it quickly became apparent that Vargas could not maintain his authoritarian dictatorship if Brazil wished to play a role in the postwar international order.[40]

Seeing the writing on the wall, in February 1945 Vargas announced that democratic elections would take place that year, and in May he scheduled them for December. New political parties began to form, including the leftist Brazilian Labor Party (PTB), centrist Social Democratic Party (PSD), and rightist National Democratic Union (UDN), while formerly illegal parties such as the PCB started organizing openly; the PCB officially registered as a party in September.[41] With the support of the PTB, the Brazilian Socialist Party (PSB) candidate Eurico

Gaspar Dutra won the presidential election with 55 percent of the vote.[42] The PCB managed to obtain a respectable 9 percent of the vote in the congressional elections, gaining fourteen seats in the Federal Chamber of Deputies and one in the Senate.[43] Maurício Grabois won election as a federal deputy for the Federal District (Metropolitan Rio de Janeiro), and became the leader of the PCB's congressional caucus.[44] Other Jewish communists, such as the physicist Mário Schenberg and the educator Elisa Kauffmann Abramovich, were elected to the São Paulo state legislative assembly and São Paulo city council, respectively.[45] By 1946, the PCB had an estimated membership of 180,000 people, making it the largest communist party in the Western Hemisphere, although it would once again be declared illegal the following year.[46]

Brazilian Jews took advantage of the newly instituted political liberties to establish a wide range of political, educational, and cultural organizations, many of which were associated with Zionist, communist, and Bundist movements. In November 1945, the two largest Zionist organizations in Brazil, the socialist Poale Zion and liberal General Zionists, created the United Zionist Organization of Brazil.[47] Jewish communists in São Paulo founded the Brazilian Jewish Cultural Institute (ICIB), with the goal of building a "People's House" (known in Portuguese as *Casa do Povo*) that would include a Yiddish theater, library, and elementary school, while Jewish female communists in Rio de Janeiro created the Brazilian Jewish Women's Association (AFIB), which established branches throughout Brazil.[48] Brazilian Bundists were also active in the postwar years, establishing libraries in Rio de Janeiro and São Paulo and holding national conventions in 1948 and 1950.[49] Zionists, communists, and Bundists also worked together to create the Jewish state federations of São Paulo and Rio de Janeiro.[50]

Jewish activists in postwar Brazil were able to cooperate thanks to the USSR's unexpected support for the establishment of the State of Israel, which reversed its decades-long opposition to Zionism in an attempt to weaken British imperialism and acquire a new ally.[51] Once it became apparent that Israel would not become a Soviet satellite, however, the Soviet Union began to reconsider its policy toward the Jewish state.[52] Afraid that Soviet Jews' support for Israel would render them disloyal to the USSR, the Soviet Union moved to repress Soviet Jewish political and cultural life. After dissolving the Jewish Antifascist Committee, the only legal Jewish entity in the country, the Soviet regime proceeded to shut down all Yiddish newspapers, theaters, and publishing houses in the USSR, arrested prominent Soviet Yiddish writers, and instituted an antisemitic press campaign against "rootless cosmopolitans."[53]

Soviet antisemitism, which Zionists denounced and communists denied, irrevocably impacted Brazilian Jewish intracommunal relations. Polish Jewish Holocaust survivors who arrived in Brazil after 1945 played leading roles in Cold War campaigns to dislodge Jewish communists from the executive committees of the São Paulo and Rio de Janeiro Jewish federations, using venues such as Warsaw Ghetto Uprising commemorations and the pages of the Brazilian Yiddish press. In São Paulo, Konrad Charmatz, the local correspondent of the Poale Zion–

affiliated *Idishe Prese* (Jewish Press), called for the expulsion of communists from the São Paulo Jewish Federation executive, achieved in March 1950 when an all-Zionist electoral slate defeated a mixed slate of Zionists and communists.[54] The *Idishe Prese* editor David Markus played a similar role following his arrival in Rio de Janeiro in 1951, appealing for the expulsion of communist institutions from the Rio de Janeiro Jewish Federation.[55] While moderate communal leaders resisted these efforts, after the Prague show trial of November 1952, and the Moscow Doctors' Plot of January 1953, both of which contained overt antisemitic elements and which the Brazilian Yiddish communist newspaper *Unzer Shtime* (Our Voice) supported, the Rio de Janeiro Jewish Federation expelled its communist affiliates in May 1953.[56]

After Soviet premier Nikita Khrushchev denounced the Stalinist personality cult in a speech during the twentieth Communist Party Congress in February 1956, revealing, among other Stalinist crimes, that the Doctors' Plot had been fabricated on Stalin's orders, and the New York Yiddish newspaper *Forverts* (Forward) reported the murders of prominent Soviet Yiddish writers, Brazilian Jewish communist organizations were forced to reckon with these charges.[57] By mid-1957, the Casa do Povo, the flagship São Paulo Jewish communist institution that was only inaugurated four years earlier, found itself divided between critics of the Soviet Union and unrepentant Soviet loyalists. Although the former had a small majority on the Casa do Povo executive, a tightly fought election in November 1958 resulted in the victory of the latter, returning control of the institution to Soviet loyalists.[58] This schism, however, and the concurrent mass exodus of Jews from the PCB in the wake of the Khrushchev revelations, decisively weakened the communists as a force within Brazilian Jewish politics.[59]

The early 1960s were a time of mass mobilization within Brazilian civil society, led by students, workers, and peasant groups. New communist parties emerged to challenge the hegemony of the PCB within the Brazilian Left. In 1961, young activists from the PSB in Rio de Janeiro, members of the PTB youth wing in Minas Gerais, and representatives of the International Socialist League (LSI) in São Paulo established the Revolutionary Marxist Organization—Worker Politics (POLOP), whose chief theoretician was an Austrian Jewish Marxist named Erich Czaczkes Sachs.[60] The following year, a group of PCB dissidents including Maurício Grabois, who rejected the Soviet approach of "peaceful coexistence" with the capitalist West and sided with China in the Sino-Soviet split, broke with the party and created the Communist Party of Brazil (PCdoB).[61]

Following the military coup of 1964, many high school and university student activists broke with the PCB and POLOP over these organizations' opposition to armed struggle as a means of overthrowing the military dictatorship. Inspired by the Cuban Revolution and Che Guevara's "foco theory," which claimed that a small group of activists could lead a successful guerrilla war against a military regime, these activists created new organizations, including the National Liberating Alliance (ALN) and the 8th October Revolutionary Movement (MR-8), which broke away from the PCB, and the Revolutionary Popular Vanguard (VPR), which split from POLOP.[62] Jewish armed struggle activists included Alfredo Syrkis, who participated in the VPR's kidnapping of the West German and Swiss ambassadors, and Iara Iavelberg, an MR-8 activist whom police killed in Salvador in 1971.[63] While most Jewish armed struggle activists were of Eastern European descent, a few, like the ALN militant Maurice Politi and the VPR activist Maryse Farhi, were of Egyptian origin.[64]

While all the armed struggle organizations aspired to create *focos*, bases from which to launch a guerrilla war against the military regime, the only organization to actually do so was the PCdoB. Beginning in 1967, the PCdoB established a guerrilla base in the Amazonian region of Araguaia, whose leaders included Maurício Grabois.[65] The Brazilian army discovered this base in 1972, and in December 1973 it executed the guerrilla leadership, including Grabois and his son André, whose bodies were never found.[66] Brazilian state violence also targeted urban activists, such as the ALN activists Ana Rosa Kucinski Silva, a chemistry professor at the University of São Paulo, and her husband Wilson Silva, who disappeared on their way to celebrate their fourth wedding anniversary in April 1974.[67] The couple were never seen again, in spite of the tireless efforts of her father, Yiddish writer Meir Kucinski, to obtain information as to their whereabouts. The truth only came out in 1992, when a former police agent revealed that they had been taken to the House of Death (*Casa da Morte*) detention center in Rio de Janeiro and most likely murdered.[68]

Their deaths occurred during the regime of Ernesto Geisel, the fourth consecutive general to serve as president since the 1964 military coup, who pursued a policy of "decompression," in which the military regime attempted to use the electoral system to perpetuate its rule. The military had dissolved all political parties in 1965 and established two new parties, the pro-government National Renewal Alliance (ARENA) and the opposition Brazilian Democracy Movement (MDB), to provide a fig leaf of democracy for what was in reality a dictatorship.[69] In the congressional elections of November 1974, however, the MDB scored a decisive victory, winning 59 percent of the vote for the Senate and 48 percent of the vote for the Federal Chamber of Deputies, and marking a decisive failure for Geisel's decompression strategy.[70] Blaming the loss on the PCB, which it claimed had infiltrated the MDB, the dictatorship initiated a crackdown on the PCB in São Paulo in January 1975. This repression had an antisemitic element, focused on the alleged existence of a "Jewish sector" of the party, which police claimed was secretly financing party activity and was instrumental to the election of the MDB state deputy, a Jewish politician named Alberto Goldman, and resulting in the arrests of educators associated with the leftist Sholem Aleichem elementary school.[71]

The most notorious instance of antisemitic state violence targeting Jewish PCB activists, however, was the death of a Jewish journalist and PCB sympathizer named Vladimir Herzog in police custody in October 1975. Asked to appear for questioning, Herzog willingly presented himself to DOI-CODI (secret police) headquarters, where he was taken to an interrogation room, tied to a chair, and subjected to beatings and electric shocks that resulted in his death. Although police agents attempted to frame his death as a suicide, going as far as to photograph his corpse hanging from a noose in a prison cell, news of the murder, and the callous way in which it was falsified, caused mass indignation within São Paulo civil society. Thirty thousand university students went on strike for a week, forty-two bishops signed a statement condemning military state violence, and eight thousand people attended an ecumenical service for Herzog in the main cathedral of São Paulo.[72] This memorial service was a flashpoint for repressed anti-dictatorship sentiment and marked a major turning point in the opposition to the military regime.[73]

Following the end of the military dictatorship and the reinstitution of political democracy in 1985, Jewish activists played leading roles in new political parties associated with environmental and labor movements. Newly returned political exiles, such as the former VPR activists Alfredo Syrkis and Carlos Minc Baumfeld, were among the founders of the Brazilian Green Party (PV). Baumfeld won election as a Rio de Janeiro state deputy in 1986 and Syrkis became the top vote recipient as Rio de Janeiro city councilor in 1988.[74] Other Jewish environmentalists chose to work with more established political parties, such as Fábio Feldmann, who won election to the National Constituent Assembly in 1986 and wrote the chapter addressing environmental protection in Brazil's post-dictatorship 1988 National Constitution.[75] The Workers' Party (PT), a democratic socialist party founded in 1980, also became home to Jewish activists, such as Clara Levin Ant, who won election to the São Paulo state legislative assembly as a PT deputy in 1986 and became the leader of the PT state congressional caucus.[76]

During the presidencies of Fernando Henrique Cardoso of the Brazilian Social Democratic Party (1995–2002) and Luiz Inácio Lula da Silva of the PT (2003–2010), Brazilian Jews were at the forefront of struggles on behalf of memory politics and post-dictatorship transitional justice. The Iavelberg family launched a multiyear legal battle to prove that Iara Iavelberg had been killed by police rather than by suicide, as the military version claimed, enabling her family to move her corpse from the suicide wing of the São Paulo Jewish cemetery to a grave next to her parents.[77] Novels and films by the author Moacyr Scliar and filmmaker Cao Hamburger grappled with the loss of children and parents during the dictatorship.[78] Finally, returned exile Maurice Politi spearheaded efforts to transform sites of state violence, such as the former secret police headquarters in São Paulo, into memorials of resistance.[79]

These efforts notwithstanding, the incomplete reckoning of Brazilian civil society with the human rights abuses of the military dictatorship enabled the election of the far-right congressman and notorious dictatorship apologist Jair Bolsonaro to the presidency in 2018.[80] The Bolsonaro presidency sharply polarized the Brazilian Jewish community between his supporters, who highlighted his Christian Zionism and enthusiastic advocacy for the State of Israel, and his opponents, who condemned his sympathy for far-right political movements such as the Alternative for Germany (AfD) and brandished Jewish victims of dictatorship violence, including Herzog, Iavelberg, and Kucinski Silva, as symbols of opposition to his regime.[81] Bolsonaro's election also prompted the creation of new Brazilian Jewish civil society organizations, such as Jews for Democracy and the Jewish Observatory of Human Rights in Brazil, whose members differ in their approaches to Judaism and Zionism but are united in their defense of Brazilian democracy as it faces its gravest threat in thirty years.[82]

Over the past one hundred years, Jewish activists have consistently found themselves at the forefront of radical Brazilian political movements, from the Brazilian Communist Party during the Vargas era and postwar democracy, to clandestine armed struggle organizations during the military dictatorship, to new environmental, labor, and transitional justice movements following the return of Brazilian democracy in 1985. These ongoing political evolutions are indicative of the political engagement of Brazilian Jews, their rootedness in their Brazilian environment, and the diversity of the Jewish political experience in Brazil. As Brazilians continue to face daunting challenges in building a more democratic and equal society and in recovering from the legacies of military rule, the next century will undoubtedly feature even more transformations within radical Jewish politics in Brazil.

NOTES

1. Bruno Feitler, "Jews and New Christians in Dutch Brazil, 1630–1654," in *Atlantic Diasporas: Jews, Conversos, and Crypto-Jews in the Age of Mercantilism, 1500–1800*, ed. Richard Kagan and Philip Morgan (Baltimore, MD: Johns Hopkins University Press, 2009), 123–151; Jonathan Israel and Stuart Schwartz, *The Expansion of Tolerance: Religion in Dutch Brazil (1624–1654)* (Amsterdam: Amsterdam University Press, 2007).

2. On Jewish mass migrations to the Americas, see Gur Alroey, "Aliyah to America? A Comparative Look at Jewish Mass Migration, 1882–1914," *Modern Judaism* 28, no. 2 (2008): 109–133; Hasia Diner, *Roads Taken: The Great Jewish Migrations to the New World and the Peddlers Who Forged the Way* (New Haven: Yale University Press, 2015); Rebecca Kobrin, *Jewish Bialystok and Its Diaspora* (Bloomington: Indiana University Press, 2010).

3. Jeffrey Lesser, *Welcoming the Undesirables: Brazil and the Jewish Question* (Berkeley: University of California Press, 1995), 183; Jacob Lestschinsky, "Jewish Migrations," in *The Jews: Their History, Culture, and Religion*, vol. 3, ed. Louis Finkelstein (New York: Harper, 1960), 1554; Mark Wischnitzer, *To Dwell in Safety: The Story of Jewish Immigration Since 1800* (Philadelphia: The Jewish Publication Society, 1948), 293.

4. I. Schwartzbart to S. Federbush, June 13, 1949, box H65, folder 2, MS-361, World Jewish Congress Records, American Jewish Archives, Cincinnati, Ohio.

5. Bruno Carvalho, *Porous City: A Cultural History of Rio de Janeiro* (Liverpool: Liverpool University Press, 2013), 106–107; Fania Fridman, *Paisagem estrangeira: Memórias de um bairro judeu no Rio de Janeiro* (Rio de Janeiro: Casa da Palavra, 2007), 39–51; Samuel Malamud, *Recordando a Praça Onze* (Rio de Janeiro: Livraria Kosmos Editora, 1988), 17–25.

6. Avraham Milgram, "O 'milieu' judeu-comunista do Rio de Janeiro nos anos 30," in *Judaica Latinoamerica: Estudios Histórico-Sociales*, vol. 4 (Jerusalem: Magnes University Press, 2001), 213–234.

7. Quoted in Eva Alterman Blay, "Inquisição, inquisicões: Aspectos da participação dos judeus na vida sócio-política brasileira nos anos 30," *Tempo Social* 1 (1989): 105–130.

8. Helena Faria, "Basbaum, Leôncio," *Dicionário histórico-biográfico Brasileiro*, http://www.fgv.br/cpdoc/acervo/dicionarios/verbete-biografico/basbaum-leoncio.

9. Victória Grabois, interview with the author, February 15, 2016, Rio de Janeiro.

10. Emiliano José da Silva Filho, "A Revolução de Jacob Gorender," *Carta Capital*, July 3, 2013, https://www.cartacapital.com.br/cultura/a-revolucao-de-jacob-gorender-6327.

11. Manuel Caballero, *Latin America and the Comintern, 1919–1943* (Cambridge: Cambridge University Press, 1986), 158; Branko Lazitch, *Biographical Dictionary of the Comintern* (Stanford: Hoover Press, 1986), 159.

12. Stanley Hilton, *Brazil and the Soviet Challenge, 1917–1947* (Austin: University of Texas Press, 1991), 8.

13. Jacob Blanc, "The *Bandeirantes* of Freedom: The Prestes Column and the Myth of Brazil's Interior," *Hispanic American Historical Review* 101, no. 1 (2021): 101–132.

14. Quoted in Hilton, *Brazil and the Soviet Challenge*, 23.

15. Luís Carlos Prestes, "Carta aberta," in Abguar Bastos, *Prestes e a revolução social* (Rio de Janeiro: Calvino, 1946), 252–66.

16. On the Vargas regime, see Boris Fausto, *A Concise History of Brazil*, trans. Arthur Brakel (Cambridge: Cambridge University Press, 1999), 182–216; Robert Levine, *Father of the Poor?: Vargas and His Era* (Cambridge: Cambridge University Press, 1998), 18–49; Thomas Skidmore, *Politics in Brazil, 1930–1964: An Experiment in Democracy*, 40th anniversary ed. (Oxford: Oxford University Press, 2007), 3–47.

17. Leslie Bethell, "Politics in Brazil Under Vargas," in *The Cambridge History of Latin America, Volume IX: Brazil Since 1930*, ed. Leslie Bethell (Cambridge: Cambridge University Press, 2008), 19.

18. Sandra McGee Deutsch, *Las Derechas: The Extreme Right in Argentina, Brazil, and Chile, 1890–1939* (Stanford: Stanford University Press, 1999), 248–307; Robert Levine, *The Vargas Regime: The Critical Years, 1934–1938* (New York: Columbia University Press, 1970), 83.

19. Fausto, *A Concise History of Brazil*, 209.

20. Bethell, "Politics in Brazil Under Vargas," 38.

21. Fernando Morais, *Olga*, trans. Ellen Watson (New York: Grove Weidenfeld, 1990), 45–54.

22. Hilton, *Brazil and the Soviet Challenge*, 54–55.

23. Levine, *The Vargas Regime*, 79.

24. Luís Carlos Prestes, "Manifesto of the National Liberating Alliance," in *The Brazil Reader: History, Culture, Politics*, 2nd ed., revised and updated, ed. James N. Green, Victoria Langland, Lilia Moritz Schwarcz (Durham: Duke University Press, 2019), 340–343.

25. On the uprising, see Hilton, *Brazil and the Soviet Challenge*, 53–72; Levine, *The Vargas Regime*, 100–124; Marly de Almeida Gomes Viana, *Revolucionários de 35: Sonho e realidade* (São Paulo: Companhia das Letras, 1992).

26. Blay, "Inquisição, inquisicões"; Fridman, *Paisagem estrangeira*, 68–70; Milgram, "O 'milieu' judeu-comunista," 230–233.

27. Abraham Josef Schneider, *Histórias da BIBSA: Crônicas de um judeu progressista* (Rio de Janeiro: Associação Scholem Aleichem de Cultura e Recreação, 2000), 24–26.

28. "Numerosas prisões de israelitas," *A Noite* (Rio de Janeiro), November 27, 1935, 1; "Presos varios elementos extremistas de uma organização estrangeira," *Correio da Manhã* (Rio de Janeiro), November 27, 1935, 3; "Queriam transformar o Brasil em Nova Russia!" *Diário Carioca* (Rio de Janeiro), November 27, 1935, 7.

29. "Filho de Israel e agente de Moscou," *O Globo* (Rio de Janeiro), January 6, 1936, 1.

30. Morais, *Olga*, 178–242.

31. J. F. de Barros Pimentel to José Carlos de Macedo Soares, September 30, 1936, lata 622, maço 9650, Itamaraty Historical Archive, Rio de Janeiro (hereafter cited as AHI).

32. Jorge Latour to José Carlos de Macedo Soares, November 8, 1936, lata 622, maço 9650, AHI.

33. Circular no. 1127, June 7, 1937, lata 1292, maços 29653 to 29655, AHI.

34. Bethell, "Politics in Brazil Under Vargas," 49–51; Fausto, *A Concise History of Brazil*, 215–216; Hilton, *Brazil and the Soviet Challenge*, 129–142; Levine, *The Vargas Regime*, 145–151; Skidmore, *Politics in Brazil*, 27–30.

35. Getúlio Vargas, "Vargas and the Estado Novo," in *The Brazil Reader*, 349–352.

36. Bethell, "Politics in Brazil Under Vargas," 67.

37. Fausto, *A Concise History of Brazil*, 228–29; Levine, *Father of the Poor*, 69–70.

38. Israel Blajberg, *Soldados que vieram de longe: Os 42 heróis brasileiros judeus da 2ª guerra mundial* (Resende, Rio de Janeiro: Academia de História Militar Terrestre do Brasil, 2008).

39. David Nasser, "Últimas horas no Brasil!" *O Cruzeiro* (Rio de Janeiro), April 29, 1944, 61–66, 70.

40. Leslie Bethell, "Brazil," in *Latin America Between the Second World War and the Cold War, 1944–1948*, ed. Leslie Bethell and Ian Roxborough (Cambridge: Cambridge University Press, 1992), 43–44.

41. Fausto, *A Concise History of Brazil*, 231; Skidmore, *Politics in Brazil*, 55–60.

42. Bethell, "Brazil," 55–56.

43. Skidmore, *Politics in Brazil*, 64.

44. Alzira Alves de Abreu, "Grabois, Maurício," *Dicionário histórico-biográfico Brasileiro*, http://www.fgv.br/cpdoc/acervo/dicionarios/verbete-biografico/grabois-mauricio.

45. Dina Lida Kinoshita, *Mário Schenberg: O cientista e o político* (Brasília: Fundação Astrojildo Pereira, 2014); Fausto Salvadori Filho, "Ela não teve medo da vida," *Revista Apartes* (São Paulo), March–April 2014, 18–23.

46. Bethell, "Brazil," 61. By comparison, the Communist Party of the United States had 50,000 members in 1946. See Joseph R. Starobin, *American Communism in Crisis, 1943–1957* (Berkeley: University of California Press, 1972), 113.

47. Nachman Falbel, *Judeus no Brasil: Estudos e notas* (São Paulo: Humanitas, 2008), 417–420; Samuel Malamud, "Zionism in Brazil," *Encyclopedia of Zionism and Israel*, vol. 1 (New York: Herzl Press, 1971), 157–158.

48. "Manifest," CDAP 0029-Fanny Kon, Der Yidish Brazilyaner Kultur Institut Ekzekutiv Komitet, Center for Memory of the Jewish Museum of São Paulo, São Paulo (hereafter cited as CDM); Monique Sochaczewski Goldfeld, *Senhoras progressistas e uma terra de crianças: A história da criação da Associação Feminina Israelita Brasileira (1947) e da colônia de férias Kinderland (1952)* (Rio de Janeiro: O Autor, 2007).

49. YIVO Archives, New York, Bund Collection, RG 1400 ME-18, Box 23, Folder 87; YIVO, Bund Collection, RG 1400 ME-18, Box 36, Folder 152; YIVO, Bund Collection, RG 1400 ME-18, Box 37, Folder 160.

50. "Ata no. 1," December 26, 1946, *Atas das reuniões do executivo*, Federação das Sociedades Israelitas Brasileiras do Estado de São Paulo (hereafter cited as FISESP); Monica Grin, "Diáspora minimalista: A crise do judaísmo moderno no contexto brasileiro," in *Identidades judaicas no Brasil contemporâneo*, ed. Bila Sorj (Rio de Janeiro: Centro Edelstein de Pesquisas Sociais, 2008), 97.

51. Jonathan Frankel, "The Soviet Regime and Anti-Zionism: An Analysis," in *Jewish Culture and Identity in the Soviet Union*, ed. Yaacov Ro'i and Avi Beker (New York: New York University Press, 1990), 316–318; Arnold Krammer, *The Forgotten Friendship: Israel and the Soviet Bloc, 1947–53* (Urbana: University of Illinois Press, 1974).

52. Peter Brod, "Soviet-Israel Relations 1948–56: From Courtship to Crisis," in *The Left Against Zionism: Communism, Israel and the Middle East*, ed. Robert Wistrich (London: Vallentine, Mitchell & Co., 1979), 59; Yuri Slezkine, *The Jewish Century* (Princeton: Princeton University Press, 2004), 296–297.

53. Frankel, "The Soviet Regime and Anti-Zionism," 318–319; Zvi Gitelman, *A Century of Ambivalence: The Jews of Russia and the Soviet Union, 1881 to the Present* (Bloomington: Indiana University Press, 2001), 149–151.

54. Konrad Charmatz, "Ve-lo yavo bakahal," *Idishe Prese* (Rio de Janeiro), December 16, 1949, 5; "Ata da reunião de posse do executivo da Federação das Sociedades Israelitas Brasileiras do Estado de São Paulo," March 23, 1950, *Atas das reuniões do executivo*, FISESP.

55. On David Markus, see Michael Rom, "David Markus: From the Holocaust to the Cold War," *Jewish Quarterly Review* 111, no. 4 (2021): 521–524.

56. "Finfte kolumnikes farmishpet in Prag," *Unzer Shtime* (São Paulo), November 28, 1952, 1; "Moskver 'pravda' vegn der farshverung fun di doktoyrim-teroristn," *Unzer Shtime*, January 23, 1953, 1; "Dray yevsekishe institutsiyes zaynen oysgeshlosn gevorn fun der federatsiye," *Idishe Prese*, May 26, 1953, 2.

57. Gennady Estraikh, *Yiddish in the Cold War* (London: Legenda, 2008), 18–23; Harrison Salisbury, "Khrushchev Talk on Stalin Bares Details of Rule Based on Terror," *The New York Times*, June 5, 1956, 1.

58. "Vencedora a Chapa No. 2," *Unzer Shtime*, November 22, 1958, 12; "Shturmishe farzamlung in 'folks-hoyz,'" *Der Nayer Moment* (São Paulo), November 25, 1958, 2; "Dos 'folks-hoyz' blaybt vayter a nest fun soyne yisroel," *Idishe Prese*, December 7, 1958, 1.

59. Godel Kon, "Percurso do biso Godel," CDAP 0103-Godel Kon, CDM, 99–100.

60. Marcelo Badaró Mattos, "Em busca da revolução socialista: A trajetória da POLOP (1961–1967)," in *História do marxismo no Brasil*, vol. 5, ed. Marcelo Ridenti and Daniel Aarão Reis Filho (Campinas, São Paulo: Editora da Unicamp, 2002), 185–212; Joelma Alves de Oliveira, "POLOP: As origens, a coesão, e a cisão de uma organização marxista (1961–1967)" (master's thesis, Universidade Estadual Paulista-Araraquara, 2007); *POLOP: Uma trajetória de luta pela organização independente da classe operária no Brasil* (Salvador: Centro de Estudos Victor Meyer, 2009).

61. Abreu, "Grabois, Maurício."

62. Higor Codarin, *O MR-8 na luta armada* (São Paulo: Alameda, 2019); Jean Rodrigues Sales, "A Ação Libertadora Nacional, a revolução cubana e a luta armada no Brasil," *Tempo* 14, no. 27 (2009): 199–217; Carla Luciana Silva, *A revolução da VPR, a Vanguarda Popular Revolucionária* (Uberlândia, Minas Gerais: Navegando Publicações, 2021).

63. Alfredo Syrkis, *Os carbonários: Memórias da guerrilha perdida* (São Paulo: Global, 1980); Judith Lieblich Patarra, *Iara: Reportagem biográfica* (Rio de Janeiro: Editora Rosa dos Tempos, 1992).

64. Maurice Politi, *Resistência atrás das grades* (Rio de Janeiro: Garamond, 2014); Maryse Farhi, interview with the author, March 27, 2015, São Paulo.

65. Pedro Corrêa Cabral, *Xambioá: Guerrilha no Araguaia* (Rio de Janeiro: Record, 1993); Romualdo Campos Filho, *Guerrilha do Araguaia: A esquerda em armas* (São Paulo: Anita Garibaldi, 2012); Hugo Studart, *Borboletas e lobisomens: Vidas, sonhos e mortes dos guerrilheiros do Araguaia* (Rio de Janeiro: Francisco Alves, 2018).

66. Comissão Nacional de Verdade, *Relatório*, vol. 1 (Brasília: CNV, 2014), 710.

67. "Ana Rosa Kucinski Silva," *Comissão da Verdade do Estado de São Paulo Rubens Paiva*, http://comissaodaverdade.al.sp.gov.br/mortos-desaparecidos/ana-rosa-kucinski-silva.

68. Expedito Filho, "A lei da barbárie," *Veja* (São Paulo), November 18, 1992, 22–32.

69. Thomas Skidmore, *The Politics of Military Rule in Brazil, 1964–1985* (New York: Oxford University Press, 1988), 48.

70. Maria Helena Moreira Alves, *State and Opposition in Military Brazil* (Austin: University of Texas Press, 1985), 143–144.

71. Marvine Howe, "Political Police Report in Brazil Links Jews to Communist Party," *New York Times*, March 6, 1975, 16; Skidmore, *Politics of Military Rule in Brazil*, 175; Genny Serber, interview with the author, February 12, 2015, São Paulo.

72. Hamilton Almeida Filho, *Sangue-quente: A morte do jornalista Vladimir Herzog* (São Paulo: Alfa-Omega, 1978); Audálio Dantas, *As duas guerras de Vlado Herzog: Da perseguição nazista na Europa à morte sob tortura no Brasil* (Rio de Janeiro: Civilização Brasileira, 2012).

73. Alves, *State and Opposition in Military Brazil*, 156–158.

74. Kathryn Hochstetler and Margaret Keck, *Greening Brazil: Environmental Activism in State and Society* (Durham: Duke University Press, 2007), 89–94; Mara Caballero, "O fenômeno verde," *Jornal do Brasil* (Rio de Janeiro), November 24, 1988, 6.

75. Artur Ribeiro Neto, "Feldman, o 'verde' no Congresso, quer transparência do poder," *Folha de S. Paulo* (São Paulo), January 4, 1987, 4; Marco Antônio Coelho Filho, "Único verde no Congresso não quer partido ecológico," *Jornal do Brasil*, December 26, 1986, 2.

76. Clara Levin Ant, interview with Alexandre Fortes and Marieta de Moraes Ferreira, CPDOC/Fundação Getúlio Vargas, March 14, 2006, Rio de Janeiro.

77. "Suicídio de mulher de Lamarca é improvável, diz laudo," *Folha da S. Paulo*, June 27, 2005, A9.

78. Moacyr Scliar, *Mãe judia, 1964* (São Paulo: Companhia das Letras, 2004); Cao Hamburger, *O ano em que meus pais saíram de férias* (2006).

79. Maurice Politi, interview with Luciana Lombardo and Lucas Pedretti, Ciclo Memória, Movimentos Sociais e Direitos Humanos, April 5, 2019, Rio de Janeiro.

80. Michael Rom, "Understanding Bolsonaro's Brazil," *Luso-Brazilian Review* 58, no. 1 (2021): E1–E8.

81. "Dois empresários paulistas contam por que estimulam Bolsonaro," *Piauí* (Rio de Janeiro), February 19, 2018, https://piaui.folha.uol.com.br/dois-empresarios-paulistas-contam-por-que-estimulam-bolsonaro/; Thais Bilenky, "Judeus progressistas repudiam acenos de Jair Bolsonaro a Israel," *Folha de S. Paulo*, October 3, 2018, https://www1.folha.uol.com.br/poder/2018/10/judeus-progressistas-repudiam-acenos-de-jair-bolsonaro-a-israel.shtml; Rafael Kruchin and Sebastião Nascimento, "'Pro-Israel' Meets Neo-Nazi: Brazil's Bolsonaro Unveils His New Best Friends on the German Far Right," *Haaretz* (Tel Aviv), August 9, 2021, https://www.haaretz.com/world-news/2021-08-09/ty-article-opinion/.premium/pro-israel-meets-neo-nazi-brazils-bolsonaro-unveils-his-german-far-right-allies/0000017f-f48b-d487-abff-f7ff4d260000.

82. Michel Ehrlich, "Judeus contra Bolsonaro: Análise de três abaixo-assinados pela democracia e pela afirmação de uma judaicidade plural e democrática," *Cadernos do Tempo Presente* 12, no. 1 (2021): 24–48.

CHAPTER 10

Jewish Radicals

THE SOUTH AFRICAN EXPERIENCE

Milton Shain and Richard Mendelsohn

Radical Activism

Eight years after the victory of the National Party in the all-white South African general election of 1948 and the subsequent unfolding of its Apartheid policies, the Afrikaner-led government arrested and accused 156 activists of treason. The great majority were Black but twenty-three were white, and of these a disproportionate fourteen were Jewish, four of whom were women. The protracted trial ended in 1961 with the acquittal of all the accused. A year earlier, in the wake of the infamous Sharpeville massacre of 69 peaceful demonstrators and of the subsequent banning of the African National Congress, the preeminent liberation movement, resistance to Apartheid had turned from nonviolent means to armed struggle: "history left us with no option but to engage in armed actions as a necessary part of the political struggle," Joe Slovo, a Lithuanian-born Jewish radical, later recalled.[1] This new strategy was seriously disrupted in July 1963 when state security operatives carried out a successful raid on Liliesleaf Farm in Rivonia on the outskirts of Johannesburg. The farm had been purchased by Arthur Goldreich as the headquarters for the underground South African Communist Party and as a safe house for political fugitives. Among the seventeen accused, all five of the whites were Jewish.[2]

While Jews were indeed disproportionately represented in radical ranks, these activists were a tiny minority of a small Jewish population in the country that in itself constituted less than 5 percent of the country's white minority. They were part of a second wave of Jewish radicalism in South Africa. The first had arrived in the late nineteenth and early twentieth centuries from Eastern Europe. These immigrant radicals were a fraction of the predominantly Lithuanian Jewish influx attracted by the discovery of gold on the Witwatersrand in 1886. The newcomers supplemented and reinvigorated an existing Anglo-German Jewish community first established in the mid-nineteenth century. The Eastern Europeans had imbibed the subversive socialist ideals percolating through the Tsarist empire, ideas that would in 1897 forge the General Union of Jewish Workers in Lithuania, Poland, and Russia. A branch of this organization, better known as the Bund, was established in Cape Town in 1900. Small groups of Jewish immigrants organized unions and cooperatives among Jewish tailors, cabinetmakers, bakers, and cigarette makers at the turn of the century. However, these specifically Jewish initiatives were rapidly absorbed into existing unions as Jewish workers built solidarity across color and ethnic lines.[3] But individual Jews would continue to play a leading role in labor struggles for decades to come. For these activists, universalist ideals trumped Jewish particularism, including Zionism, to which a majority of South African Jews subscribed.

Among the reasons for the rapid disappearance of specifically Jewish unions was the absence of a substantial Jewish proletariat of the sort found in New York at this time, or in Leeds and Manchester. The South African economy already displayed the character and contours of a racialized capitalism where race and class divisions increasingly coincided. As whites in an expanding capitalist economy, Jewish immigrants were well positioned to enter a bourgeoning commercial sector, and most did. Yet some continued to challenge the social, economic, and racial order. A number found their home in the Yiddish-speaking branch of the International Socialist League, the forerunner of the Communist Party of South Africa, which was founded in 1921.[4]

In the interwar years Jewish radicals engaged directly with the emergent trade union movement that accelerated with South Africa's secondary industrialization. Emil Solomon (Solly) Sachs (1899–1976) and Rachel (Ray) Alexander (1913–2004), both immigrants from Eastern Europe, became iconic figures in the worker's struggle in South Africa. Sachs grew up in a poor family in Kamaai, a shtetl in Lithuania, where he excelled as a student at *cheder*. He left for South Africa in 1914 to join his father in Johannesburg. Here the family experienced considerable hardship. Ray Alexander grew up in Varaklani, a small town in Latvia, where her father, a socialist, taught Russian, German, and mathematics and also ran a *cheder*. Ray was exposed at an early age to socialist ideas and was a precocious recruit to the Latvian communist underground. Afraid that her daughter would be arrested for her political activities, her mother sent her to South Africa at the age of fifteen to join her brother and sister in Cape Town. Five days after landing she joined the Communist Party of South Africa.

Sach's route to socialism and the Communist Party of South Africa was via a harsh slum area in Johannesburg where he lived during his childhood and had firsthand experience of the poverty of its multiracial inhabitants—and through working as a *kaffireatnik*, an exploited shop assistant in a mining concession store.[5] After interrupted spells as a student at the University of the Witwatersrand and a trip to the Soviet Union, Sachs became general secretary of the Garment Workers' Union, where he devoted himself to the interests of its predominantly white Afrikaner women membership, much to the chagrin of Afrikaner nationalists, who were competing for the loyalty of the same constituency. Alexander was similarly deeply involved in union activity. She became general secretary of the militant Food and Canning Workers' Union in the Western Cape, a nonracial union serving workers in the fruit canning and fishing industries.[6]

Inevitably both Sachs and Alexander, were targets of the "McCarthyism" that followed the National Party's victory in 1948. Sachs was banned under the Suppression of Communism Amendment Act in 1952, which meant that his daily life was severely restricted. As a result, he went into exile in Britain the following year. Alexander was repeatedly banned, was forcibly prevented from taking her place as the elected "Native Representative" in parliament,[7] and eventually went into exile with her husband in 1965.

While Sachs and Alexander grew up in intensely Jewish milieus and had childhood experiences of antisemitism, both moved away from ethnic particularism. From an early age Alexander saw socialist internationalism rather than Zionism as the answer to antisemitism. When as a schoolgirl she was asked by local Zionists to defend the Balfour Declaration in a public debate, she refused the invitation. "Not all Jews could go to Palestine," she explained in her autobiography, "and what would happen to the Palestinians?"[8] Sachs was equally indifferent to matters Jewish, looking to socialism as a universal panacea.

From 1948 Jews were conspicuous among the handful of whites who actively supported the freedom struggle of the Black majority against the Apartheid state.[9] The lawyer Sam Kahn, a communist who had been a member of Young Israel in his youth, was a Native Representative in Parliament till the proscription of the Communist Party at the start of the fifties. Jewish radicals took part in the Defiance Campaign of 1952, a nonviolent challenge to Apartheid regulations, and were members of the clandestine South African Communist Party[10] and of the (white) Congress of Democrats. The latter was allied to the African National Congress and the other progressive groupings that convened the Congress of the People in 1955 at Kliptown, Soweto, where the Freedom Charter—the foundational document of the liberation struggle—was adopted. Lionel "Rusty" Bernstein played a key role in drafting this historic statement of African National Congress policy.[11]

In the wake of increasing state repression after the Sharpeville massacre, many activists went into exile, where they continued the anti-Apartheid struggle. Particularly prominent were Ruth First (1925–1982) and her husband Joe Slovo (1926–1995). First was born in Johannesburg and was the daughter of founding members of the Communist Party of South Africa. Her father, an immigrant from Latvia, was a successful furniture manufacturer. Ruth attended the University of the Witwatersrand in Johannesburg, where she combined academic success with political engagement. Subsequently she married Joe Slovo, a fellow communist activist, and became a journalist, working for *The Guardian*, a Johannesburg-based radical newspaper, where she earned a reputation for her investigative journalism, exposing the abuses of Apartheid society. Concurrently, she was involved in political activism and with her husband was one of the Treason Trialists in the late 1950s. In 1963 she was arrested under the draconian 90-Day Law and spent 117 days in solitary confinement. She went into exile the following year, where she forged a successful academic career. First was killed in Maputo, the capital of Mozambique, in 1982 by a letter bomb sent by agents of the Apartheid state.[12]

Ruth First's husband Joe Slovo arrived in South Africa from Lithuania in 1936 at the age of ten. He was a member of *Habonim*, a Zionist socialist youth movement, in *der heym*, but joined the more radical and Marxist *Hashomer Hatzair* in Johannesburg before becoming a member of the Communist Party at the age of sixteen. The adolescent Slovo was influenced by the socialist rhetoric—often confused and contradictory—that permeated the inner-city dwellings in Johannesburg where his impecunious family lodged. "My leaning towards left socialist politics was also formed partly by the bizarre and paradoxical embrace of socialism shared by many of the immigrants who filled the boarding houses in which we lived," writes Slovo in his autobiography. "I say 'bizarre' because they tended to combine a passionate devotion to the Soviet Union with Zionism and the vicious racism towards the majority of the South African population." Like many other young South African Jews, Joe Slovo joined the army during the Second World War and went "Up North." On their return to South Africa and demobilization, some of these young volunteers, inspired by the fight against fascism, joined the Springbok Legion, a short-lived multiracial anti-racist veterans' association. Slovo qualified as a lawyer at the University of the Witwatersrand and combined his legal practice with underground politics. He fled South Africa in 1963 and rose to prominence as a leader of *Umkhonto we Sizwe*, the armed wing of the African National Congress, and as the secretary general of the South African Communist Party in exile, where he remained an ideological hardliner unlike his intellectually less rigid wife. He returned from exile in 1990 shortly after the historic unbanning of the South African Communist Party and African National Congress and the release of Nelson Mandela from prison. He soon became a principal negotiator for the African National Congress in its tussle with the National Party and entered the first democratic government led by Mandela as the minister of housing.[13]

Almost all the South African Jewish radicals were "non-Jewish Jews" in Isaac Deutscher's classic formulation.[14] With their Marxist allegiances, they were committed to a universalism that left little space for ethnic particularism. As Pauline Podbrey, an activist of the forties who went into exile in the fifties, reminisced, "it now seems as if everybody was Jewish. But there was no sense of Jewishness amongst them. Nobody ever discussed their Jewishness or brought it forward as an issue, and it was quite irrelevant to the politics of the day. I suspect that quite a few of us were not too anxious to be identified as Jewish, although nobody made a conscious effort to deny it. But it just wasn't allowed to impinge on Party work. It would have been seen as a concession to nationalism."[15]

Roads to Radicalism

Scholars agree that Jews were overrepresented in the ranks of radical opposition to Apartheid. But they differ about the reasons for this. Immanuel Suttner, editor of a compendious collection of interviews with South African Jewish activists, argues that "Jewishness frequently acted as a subtle catalyst" in determining the activists' political choices. Though often deracinated, their "awareness of the historical dehumanisation of the Jews was the experiential ground in which blossomed the conviction that no one else should be dehumanised." Moreover, their dissent and iconoclasm were, in Suttner's estimation, quintessentially Jewish. The activists "are all idol smashers, people who refuse to bow before the consensus. The aspect of Jewish tradition they link up to is the tradition of non-conformism, rebuke and solidarity with the underdog; a tradition which manifested in biblical stories which established the dissenter . . . as the hero."[16]

Glenn Frankel, one-time South African correspondent of the *Washington Post* and author of a compelling narrative about the Rivonia Trial and its Jewish defendants, also identifies Jewishness as an important factor informing Jewish radicalism. "It was no surprise that many of the activists were openly hostile to Judaism and Jewish causes," he writes. "What none of them saw was that their alienation from Judaism and their radicalism were consistent with one wing of Jewish tradition—that even as rejectionists they were firmly within the larger family of their contentious and self-contradictory faith."[17]

Gideon Shimoni, author of a major scholarly text on Jewish political behavior in Apartheid South Africa, dismisses what he labels the "Judaic values" theory, the view that Jewish radicalism is rooted in Judaism's "this-worldliness and the attendant messianic belief in ultimate social perfectibility; emphasis on *tzedakah* (social charity) and mutual responsibility for the welfare of others that translates into social justice; and respect for learning, which promotes rationality in human affairs."[18] He contends that this is not borne out by the South African evidence, manifest in a rich autobiographical literature of South African Jewish radicals. Instead Shimoni pursues a sociological explanation, stressing the ethos within particular families as a possible key to explaining Jewish overrepresentation in activist politics. The immigrant home, where there were communist sympathies or affiliations, was, he argues, a major factor. But Shimoni also observes that many radicals cut their political teeth in the Zionist movement, which "provided a stimulus for political awareness and sometimes a training ground for radical activism."[19] A prime example that illustrates his case is Baruch Hirson, who in his autobiography acknowledged the critical role his involvement in *Hashomer Hatzair*, the radical Jewish movement, played in his—and others'—political education and turn to radicalism. "The number of people who left Hashomer Hatza'ir to join the political left," he writes, "indicates that Hashomer Hatza'ir was a crucible of political development."[20] Unlike the hardline communist Joe Slovo, Hirson chose a Trotskyist path. As part of the African Resistance Movement, he was imprisoned from 1964 to 1973 for sabotage.

James Campbell, an American scholar, discounts religious and cultural legacies and instead underlines the impact of migration and the consequent disruption and alienation. Immigration was a profoundly disruptive experience, he argues, and South Africa's celebrated Jewish radicalism may be less a product of community "tradition," handed down from generation to generation, than a function of historically specific processes of dislocation and conflict. Drawing once again on the rich genre of South African Jewish autobiography, including the memoirs of Hyman Basner, Baruch Hirson, Pauline Podbrey, and Joe Slovo, Campbell highlights common experiences of marginality and dislocation. Radical politics, he writes, "and the Communist Party in particular, represented more than just a new political affiliation. It offered community, human contact, a warmth and solidarity otherwise absent from their daily lives."[21] Pauline Podbrey, for example, endured an unhappy childhood in the 1930s in a struggling immigrant home with a remote and silent father. The Communist Party filled the void. While initially a committed Stalinist, she finally lost faith while in exile from South Africa and after the crushing of the Hungarian uprising in 1956.[22]

The divergences between Suttner, Frankel, Shimoni, and Campbell point to the difficulties in arriving at an overarching explanation for Jewish radicalism in South Africa. Each add a dimension to a complex problem. What is clear is that religious values in themselves play little part. If there is one axiomatic lesson to be drawn from the historical experience in South Africa, it is that on the continuum of political activism it was the less religious and the less Jewishly identified who were more likely to bravely challenge the racial order. What is less clear is that historical and cultural legacies can be easily dismissed. The relatively recent and direct experience of discrimination in Eastern Europe almost certainly played a part in the choices made by those who turned to radicalism in South Africa. Nor can we discount the Marxian prism—so powerful in the Eastern Europe from which they or their parents came—in making clear sense of the egregious inequalities and racial oppression of the society they inhabited.

Beyond the generation directly connected with the Jewish immigrant experience, the tradition of Jewish extra-parliamentary opposition continued through the 1980s, the dying decade of Apartheid. This was manifest in national organizations such as the United Democratic Front and the Mass Democratic Movement, and in small groups such as the End Conscription Campaign and Jews for Justice. Similarly, Jews played key roles in the nonracial trade unions. By then the Jewish establishment had moderated its earlier distancing from Jewish radicalism, which had been a source of intense discomfort. Driven by an acute sense of vulnerability, informed by the virulent Afrikaner antisemitism of the 1930s and 1940s, and the coming to power of the National Party in 1948, Jewish communal leaders were fearful of the potential consequences of the conflation of Jewishness and radicalism.[23] A new and more confident generation of leaders in the 1980s had fewer qualms about condemning the Apartheid system, and during the democratic transition of the 1990s embraced the returning Jewish radical exiles. At the funeral of Joe Slovo in 1996, the Glaswegian Cyril Harris, Chief Rabbi of South Africa, eulogized the late communist leader, saying "Shalom, dear brother, shalom." The tradition of South African Jewish radicalism had been recovered and inserted into the mainstream of South African Jewish historical memory. What was formerly disquieting or even taboo was now valorized and often proudly publicized. Jewish radicalism, once deeply embarrassing to the community and requiring explaining away, has been given pride of place in the search for a usable past in post-Apartheid South Africa.

NOTES

1. Richard Mendelsohn and Milton Shain, *The Jews in South Africa: An Illustrated History* (Johannesburg: Jonathan Ball Publishers, 2008), 148.

2. Strikingly, Jews were prominently involved in the defense of the accused in both the Treason and Rivonia Trials. Throughout their careers these Jewish lawyers bravely challenged the Apartheid system from within, using such space as the law allowed. Ironically, the state case against Mandela in the Rivonia Trial was also led by a Jew, a respected member of the Jewish establishment. See Glenn Frankel, *Rivonia's Children: Three Families and the Cost of Conscience in White South Africa* (Johannesburg: Jonathan Ball Publishers, 1999).

3. Evangelos Mantzaris, "Jewish Trade Unions in Cape Town 1903–1907: A Socio-Historical Study," in Mantzaris, *Labour Struggles in South Africa: The Forgotten Pages, 1903–1921*, (Windhoek: Collective Resources Publications, 1995).

4. Evangelos Mantzaris, "Radical Community: The Yiddish-Speaking Branch of the International Socialist League, 1918–1920," in *Class, Community and Conflict: South African Perspectives*, ed. Belinda Bozzoli (Johannesburg: Ravan Press, 1987).

5. Joseph Sherman, "Serving the Natives: Whiteness as the Price of Hospitality in South African Yiddish Literature," *Journal of Southern African Studies* 26, no. 3 (September 2000): 505–521.

6. For Solly Sachs and Ray Alexander, see Leslie Witz, "Servant of the Workers: Solly Sachs and the Garment Workers' Union, 1928–1952" (unpublished master's thesis, University of the Witwatersrand, 1984); Bernard Sachs, *South African Personalities and Places* (Johannesburg: Kayor Publishers, 1959); Emil Solomon (Solly) Sachs, *Rebels Daughters* (Manchester: Macgibbon & Kee, 1957); Ray Alexander Simons, *All My Life and All My Strength*, ed. Raymond Suttner (Johannesburg: STE Publishers, 2004); Immanuel Suttner, ed., *Cutting Through the Mountain: Interviews with South African Jewish Activists* (Johannesburg: Viking, 1997).

7. The vagaries of the South African constitution allowed for a handful of Whites to serve as "native representatives" in the all-White parliament. Some communists seized the opportunity to speak for the oppressed.

8. Simons, *All My Life*, 40.

9. It should be noted that Jews in South Africa were also conspicuous in mainstream liberal opposition to Apartheid. Most famously, Helen Suzman was the sole representative of the Progressive Party in the all-White parliament from 1961 to 1974.

10. The Communist Party of South Africa was renamed the South African Communist Party following its banning.

11. See Rusty Bernstein, *Memory Against Forgetting: Memoirs from a Life in South African Politics, 1934–1964* (London: Viking, 1999).

12. For Ruth First, see Milton Shain and Miriam Pimstone, "Ruth First, 1925–1982," The Shalvi/Hyman Encyclopedia of Jewish Women, *Jewish Women's Archive*, https://jwa.org/encyclopedia/article/first-ruth; Shula Marks, "Ruth First: A Tribute," *Journal of Southern African Studies* 10, no. 1 (October 1983): 123–128; Don Pinnock, *Voices of Liberation, vol. 2: Ruth First* (Pretoria: HSRC Press,1997); Gillian Slovo, *Every Secret Thing: My Family, My Country* (London: Abacus, 1997).

13. For Joe Slovo, see *Slovo: The Unfinished Autobiography* (Randburg: Ravan Press, 1995), 22.

14. See Isaac Deutscher, *The Non-Jewish Jew and Other Essays* (London: Merlin Press, 1981).

15. Pauline Podbrey interviewed in Suttner, *Cutting Through the Mountain*, 52. See also Pauline Podbrey, White Girl in Search of the Party (Pietermaritzburg: Hadeda Books, 1993).

16. See the afterword in Suttner, *Cutting Through the Mountain*, 597–627.

17. Glenn Frankel, *Rivonia's Children: Three Families and the Cost of Conscience in White South Africa* (Johannesburg: Jonathan Ball Publishers, 1999).

18. Gideon Shimoni, *Community and Conscience: The Jews in Apartheid South Africa* (Hanover: University Press of New England for Brandeis University Press, 2003), 75.

19. Shimoni, *Community and Conscience*, 90

20. Baruch Hirson, *Revolutions in My Life* (Johannesburg: University of the Witwatersrand Press, 1995), 125.

21. James Campbell, "Beyond the Pale: Jewish Immigration and the South African Left," in Milton Shain and Richard Mendelsohn, *Memories, Realities and Dreams: Aspects of the South African Jewish Experience* (Johannesburg: Jonathan Ball Publishers, 2002), 158.

22. Campbell, "Beyond the Pale."

23. For antisemitism in the 1930s and 1940s, see Milton Shain, *A Perfect Storm: Antisemitism in South Africa, 1930–1948* (Johannesburg: Jonathan Ball Publishers, 2015). For an overview of Jewish political behavior in the Apartheid era, see Gideon Shimoni, *Community and Conscience.*

CHAPTER 11

Radical Jewish Politics in the Key of Land, Language, and Labor

THE BIROBIDZHAN PROJECT

Robert Weinberg

Examination of Birobidzhan, a region located on the Soviet-Chinese border some 5,000 miles east of Moscow that was established as the national homeland of Soviet Jews, reveals the curious nature of the Kremlin's policy toward its Jewish population (as well as other ethnic and national minorities), which promoted national consolidation at the same time it proclaimed its commitment to international proletarian unity. The seeming paradox of fostering nationalism in a country devoted to internationalism based on class not nation was an integral element of the Soviet Union's approach to the national question. How did the mixing of socialism and nationalism shape radical Jewish politics in the Soviet Union during the first several decades of communist rule? What did such a politics look like in the Soviet Union, the world's first acknowledged communist society that constrained, if not forbade, political activism, even by organizations devoted to the building of communism? Jewish radicalism in the Soviet context meant transforming Soviet Jewry into a group of people who rejected Judaism and embraced the building of a secular society committed to socialist principles as determined by the Kremlin. Soviet policy toward Jews was inconsistent and unpredictable, with dire, and at times lethal, consequences for many Jews whose work as intellectuals and political activists included efforts to create a socialist Jewish culture and society.

Proponents of Birobidzhan emphasized that unlike political Zionism, which they believed represented the interests of the Jewish bourgeoisie, the Soviet Zion promoted the well-being of working-class Jews whose emancipation from all forms of exploitation and oppression could occur only within the Soviet Union. In socialist Birobidzhan Jews would not be prey to an avaricious bourgeoisie, an assertion that Soviet authorities consistently emphasized when rebutting the criticism of those who dismissed the establishment of a Jewish national homeland anywhere but in Eretz Israel. Even Labor Zionists who embraced Marxism, rejected the Jewish past, and advocated the regeneration of Jewish society through productive labor did not escape the wrath of Birobidzhan's defenders, who condemned all other forms of Jewish nationalism.

The Birobidzhan project illuminates key features of left-wing Jewish politics in the first half of the twentieth century, particularly the interplay of nationalism and socialism. Many observers viewed the Kremlin's policy toward Jews as a genuine effort to imbue progressive Jewish politics with elements of the particular (nationalism) and universal (socialism) and give voice to a radical, secular Jewish culture and identity outside Eretz Israel. The Soviet Union would supposedly serve as the proverbial "light unto the nations" and lead the struggle for a world free of exploitation, oppression, and strife. This could happen only in the world's first socialist society.

The reality of ruling a multinational empire with well over one hundred national and ethno-religious groups left the Soviet leadership no choice but to acknowledge the diversity of the Soviet Union's populace. Marxist theory stressed that socialism would emerge from the contradictions of capitalism, whose overthrow would render the remnants of capitalism, such as national distinctions, obsolete. National identities would crumble over time as a socialist society fused all cultures in a common socialist Soviet culture; socialism would doom to extinction all religious and national sentiments, loyalties, and attachments. Until that time, however, the Kremlin acknowledged that the promotion of national identity in terms dictated by the Communist Party would be an integral part of nationality policy. To be sure, national identity in the Soviet Union meant stripping nationalism of any positive reference to religion and other expressions of so-called bourgeois values and culture. Still, Soviet nationality policy promoted national identification among ethnic and national minorities as a way to promote culture built on socialist principles.[1]

As Ezra Mendelsohn noted in *On Modern Jewish Politics*, if Jews were to comprise a modern nation, they had "to possess national rights, which could mean anything from full-fledged statehood to some sort of national autonomy in the lands of their dispersion."[2] Ideally, people claiming to be a nation required a national language and culture that flourished in a politically sovereign nation-state. But if Jews were willing to forgo a sovereign territory of their own, then they could still enjoy national rights within a larger political entity. The latter formulation characterized the situation of Jews in the Soviet Union, particularly during the first three decades of communist rule. Birobidzhan, whose official name was the Jewish Autonomous Region, embodied the application of this theory to reality. Nevertheless, it must be acknowledged that the regime, not the Jews themselves, initiated the decision to territorialize Soviet Jewry.

Land and language formed two pillars of Soviet nationality policy. As Soviet nationality policy took shape, government and party officials gave thought to providing Jews with a territory that would become the cultural and national homeland of Soviet Jewry and address the poverty and antisemitism experienced by the vast majority of Jews. Joseph Stalin, an architect of the Kremlin's nationality policy, noted that a full-fledged nation in the multiethnic, multinational Soviet Union historically needed to inhabit its own territory and speak its own language. As he wrote, "among Jews there is no large and stable stratum connected with the land, which would naturally rivet the nation together."[3] In the case of Jews, who lacked a territorial homeland, Soviet authorities decided to "normalize" the situation by designating a national territory for them and promoting Yiddish as the lingua franca of Soviet Jews. Stalin and other leaders in the Communist Party, including Vladimir Lenin, shared the view that the disappearance of capitalism and the building of socialism would facilitate the integration of Jews into Soviet society as well as weaken popular antisemitism. As religion disappeared under socialism, the secularization of Soviet Jewish society would proceed apace and weaken obstacles to Jewish acculturation and integration.

Labor constituted the third pillar of Soviet nationality policy. Along with territorialization and national consolidation, the Kremlin set out to transform the socioeconomic profile of shtetl Jewry through productivization via agricultural work or employment at the factory bench. Critical to the success of settling Jews in their own territory was the productivization of Jewish labor. In other words, the ideologically suspect nature of traditional Jewish economic life, such as petty trade and shopkeeping, led to the decision by the authorities to resolve the so-called Jewish Question by refashioning the occupational profile of the Jews and transforming them into farmers.

The grinding poverty of most Jews living in the Soviet Union, along with the resurgence of popular antisemitism and pogroms in the three years following the Bolshevik seizure of power in 1917, concerned the Kremlin. The fledgling regime combated anti-Jewish violence and enacted legislation outlawing antisemitism of any kind, the first such effort by a European state. The overwhelming majority of Soviet Jews lived in small towns and cities located in the western part of the country, and eked out pitiful livings from petty commerce, retail sales, small-scale handicraft production, and unskilled labor. The collapse of the economy due to the combined impact of world war, revolution, civil war, and anti-Jewish violence between 1914 and 1920 hit Jewish society particularly hard. Government and party authorities engaged in efforts to spread the values of the revolution to Jewish society, adopting policies they hoped would transform the petty bourgeois and religious world of shopkeepers, traders, and handicraft workers. The architects of Jewish nationality policy hoped the socioeconomic transformation of Jewish society would both undercut popular antisemitism and create the basis of socialist Jewish society and culture within the borders of the Soviet Union.

This experiment in social engineering had roots in tsarist policy, which in the nineteenth century encouraged Jews to be agricultural colonists in southern

Ukraine as a way to foster Jewish integration and acculturation, as well as reduce antisemitism; this was rooted in the belief that Jews economically exploited peasants. Inspired by the thinking of European intellectuals and rulers who had advocated altering the socioeconomic profile of Jews since the latter part of the eighteenth century, Tsar Alexander I in 1804 encouraged Jews to farm by offering them land to till. These efforts never achieved their desired ends for a host of reasons, but by 1914, on the eve of World War I, more than fifty thousand Russian Jews (or 3 percent of the total Jewish population in the Russian Empire) had taken advantage of offers to settle on the land. The family of Leon Trotsky was among them.[4]

This notion of rendering Jews less likely to exploit the majority of Russians by making them more like the peasantry and thereby promoting their integration into Russian society informed the thinking of those Soviet officials, many of whom were themselves Jewish, tasked with developing a coherent state policy toward Soviet Jews in the 1920s. Hence, the regime devoted funds and other resources to helping Jews seeking to escape poverty and to start life anew by allotting land for colonization in various regions of the Soviet Union. Several Soviet and American organizations publicized, mobilized, and organized the movement of Jews to the land during the second half of the 1920s and the 1930s. In addition, foreign aid in the form of equipment and money courtesy of the American-based Agro-Joint, an offshoot of the American Jewish Joint Distribution Committee, became part of the effort.[5] By 1930 some 47,000 Jewish families, or approximately 231,000 persons, were engaged in agricultural activities.[6]

In sum, just like other full-fledged nations living in the Soviet Union, Soviet Jews were entitled to exercise cultural autonomy in the language of the Jewish street, namely Yiddish.[7] In addition, they were granted a territory in which they could endeavor to create a socialist Jewish society and culture that hewed closely to the ideological dictates of the Kremlin. In other words, between the late 1920s and the late 1940s, Jewish radicalism in the country of Lenin and Stalin entailed the building of a secular, Yiddish-speaking Jewish society and culture committed to the building of socialism by transforming the occupational profile of Soviet Jews, preferably in a territory earmarked for Jewish settlement. The Birobidzhan experiment conformed to the dictum "national in form, socialist in content."

Beginning in 1924, officials began searching for a territory that could serve as a base for Jewish agricultural settlement and the nucleus of a national homeland. In 1928 the Kremlin designated the Biro-Bidzhanskii District, a territory the size of Belgium and located along the Amur River near Khabarovsk, as the official territorial homeland of Soviet Jews.[8] Many prominent Jewish government and party officials voiced their opposition to creating a region more than 5,000 miles from the center of Jewish residence in the Soviet Union. But in the end Stalin endorsed the settlement of Jews in what would become known as Birobidzhan and, after 1934, the Jewish Autonomous Region. One advantage of Birobidzhan, in the eyes of the Kremlin, was the absence of a sizable indigenous population that would protest the allocation of land to Jewish interlopers. Another was its location along the Sino-Soviet border in a relatively underpopulated region rich with untapped economic resources and possessing geostrategic significance to counter Japanese expansionism.

In accordance with Soviet nationality policy, the proponents of the Birobidzhan project believed that the region would facilitate the development of a secular culture rooted in socialist principles and expressed in Yiddish, while at the same time ensuring the national and cultural consolidation of Soviet Jewry. Mikhail Kalinin, president of the Soviet Union, declared in 1926 that the creation of a Jewish national homeland would help to preserve Jewish culture and ensure the future of the Jewish people in the Soviet Union. He expressed hope that Birobidzhan would facilitate the transformation of Soviet Jewry into "an economically stable, agriculturally compact group."[9]

The regime publicized the benefits and promise of Birobidzhan, which excited those Soviet Jews committed to the socialist experiment. Semen Dimanshtein, the party official in charge of Jewish affairs, noted that populating Birobidzhan with Jews would "strengthen the tempo of the productivization of the Jewish poor."[10] Another advocate of Jewish agricultural resettlement claimed that it would lead to the "physical rebirth and renewal" of Soviet Jewry. One of the first Jews to move to the region proclaimed, "I thank you, comrades, for sending me here. Here I am getting settled and will stop living life like a 'Jew,' that is as a *luftmentsh*." Finally, one Jewish settler announced on behalf of himself and others soon after his arrival at a rice planation in 1928, "We came here to become peasants!"[11]

To be sure, farming was not the only physically taxing occupation that could appeal to Jews. Already before 1917 Jews labored in workshops and factories and nonmanufacturing jobs that required physical stamina, which belied the belief that Jews engaged in only nonphysical labor. According to the 1897 census, some 36 percent of Jews in the Russian Empire engaged in the manufacturing sector, and many others labored as unskilled manual workers.[12] But in a country where the overwhelming majority of people were peasants tilling the land, it is not surprising that advocates of the productivization of Jews focused on agriculture. Moreover, the Kremlin's decision to encourage land resettlement of Jews occurred before the Soviet Union embarked on its policy of rapid industrialization in the late 1920s. Proponents of Birobidzhan, therefore, continued to tout the benefits of Jewish farming, despite the fact that state policies prompted millions of peasants to flee their villages for towns and cities during the course of the 1930s.

Jewish settlement in Birobidzhan began in earnest in mid-1928, and by the end of the 1930s, some 18,000 Jews had migrated to a region that was home to nearly 110,000 people, Jew and non-Jew alike.[13] The designation of Birobidzhan as a region reserved for the settlement of only Jews was honored more in the breach than in reality. Several factors accounted for the failure of Birobidzhan to attract larger numbers of Soviet Jews as the national homeland of Soviet Jews. First, Jews from the western borderlands of the Soviet Union hesitated to uproot themselves and their families to make the daunting trip of some 5,000 miles to settle in an unfamiliar region far from established Jewish life and culture. Most preferred to leave their hometowns for urban centers such as Moscow, Minsk, Odessa, Kiev, and Leningrad, where work and educational opportunities abounded. Second, those Jews who did move to Birobidzhan found living and working conditions that were far from satisfactory, prompting many of them to return home or move to more established towns and cities in the Soviet Far East. It is not difficult to imagine that the rigorous and challenging life as a "peasant" did not appeal to many Jews, and the plan to populate Birobidzhan with large numbers of Jews was stillborn.[14] Finally, many Jews who embraced the Kremlin's policy to establish a national territory for Soviet Jewry were nevertheless reluctant to move to a region where an infrastructure for Jewish culture and society did not exist. But rejection of Birobidzhan as a viable experiment to create a socialist Jewish society and culture does not mean the project failed for lack of trying.

Government officials and Jewish intellectuals made a concerted effort to publicize Birobidzhan and attract money and Jewish settlers in the region's first decade. The regime issued public appeals to buy lottery tickets as a fundraising tactic and to recruit potential migrants, and in the United States and Canada organizations devoted to the settlement of Birobidzhan collected money.[15]

The Soviet state devoted resources and creative energy to developing policies that would embody the national sentiments of Soviet Jewry in Yiddish. The Kremlin sanctioned efforts to establish academic and educational institutions in Birobidzhan that would oversee intellectual endeavors of Jewish culture in Yiddish. The regime funded the establishment of a variety of Yiddish cultural institutions, including a newspaper, a library with a sizable Judaica collection, literary journals, schools, and a teachers' college during the course of the 1930s. Street signs, railway station signs, and postage stamps and postmarks appeared in both Yiddish and Russian, as both languages had official status. Finally, the Birobidzhan State Yiddish Theater, established in 1934, staged a repertoire of plays that portrayed Birobidzhan as the embodiment of Soviet Jewish statehood, notwithstanding the claim of Zionists outside the country.[16]

Yiddish schools reinforced this emphasis on socialist construction. As of 1937, sixteen schools existed, with close to two thousand students, where all subjects, including the natural sciences and math, were taught in Yiddish. Indeed, a Yiddish version of a school text on the geography and economic resources of Birobidzhan appeared even before a Russian language one. These schools omitted traditional Jewish instruction in religion and Hebrew, emphasizing instead ideological messages that instilled feelings of Soviet patriotism and loyalty to Stalin and his policies. Courses on Jewish literature included stories by Sholem Aleichem and Mendele Mokher Seforim because of their focus on impoverished Jews and the redemptive possibility of Birobidzhan. In turn, courses on Jewish history stressed class struggle and the exploitation of the Jewish poor by communal institutions controlled by rabbis and wealthy Jews.[17]

Not surprisingly, literary efforts focused on the transformation of Soviet Jews into "productive citizens" who labored in the collective and state farms and factories that began to dot the landscape of Birobidzhan. The Kremlin praised stories that highlighted how Birobidzhan was "laying the foundation of a new, multifaceted Jewish culture."[18] Well-known Yiddish writers and Jewish intellectuals visited the region and affirmed the official line that the Birobidzhan project represented the national and cultural aspirations of Soviet Jewry. In 1932, for example, the eminent Yiddish writer David Bergelson visited the region and participated in a literary club that served as a gathering place and source of inspiration for local writers. Bergelson lent his literary skills and reputation to efforts to promote Birobidzhan and wrote stories, pamphlets, and essays touting the achievements of the Soviet Jewish homeland in order to attract the support of Soviet Jewry and Jews abroad. Bergelson's visit to Birobidzhan inspired him to write the novel *Birobidzhaner*, which lauded Birobidzhan as the nucleus of a new Jewish way of life that rejected religious traditions and glorified Soviet power in the construction of socialism.[19]

This rejection of the past was a firm aspect of Soviet Jewish writing about Birobidzhan as can be seen in this 1935 poem by Peretz Markish. Like Bergelson and other Jewish writers who understood what the Kremlin expected of them, Markish, another luminary of Yiddish literature, publicly expressed support for Birobidzhan. "A People Is Coming to You, Taiga, To Become Young" glorifies the efforts of Soviet Jews to overcome the hold that traditional Jewish culture had on the older generation of Jews and underscores the struggle for the hearts and minds of Jewish youth in the building of a socialist Jewish homeland:

> The houses are going up
> On the first little streets, on the sprouting alleyways,
> And a struggle with ancient times for every stride.
> But when the call goes out
> To build and to make a republic,
> The Name is proudly proclaimed—Biro-bidzhan.[20]

The bloody purges launched by Stalin and the secret police between 1936 and 1938 targeted the region's Jewish leadership. This marked the beginning of the end of the Birobidzhan project, which fell victim to the shifting policy of the Kremlin. The campaign to uncover "enemies of the people" because of their purported support of Leon Trotsky or embrace of "bourgeois nationalism" signaled the end of the Kremlin's efforts to devote significant resources and attention to Birobidzhan. The change in policy reflected the Kremlin's unwarranted fear that Jewish activists were not working on behalf of the socialist dream.[21] The regime imprisoned and executed prominent advocates of Birobidzhan and shut down organizations dedicated to the recruitment of Jewish settlers to Birobidzhan. The state closed virtually all Yiddish schools in Birobidzhan as well as elsewhere in the Soviet Union. In this regard, the Jews of Birobidzhan were not signaled out for special treatment, since the government also clamped down on cultural and educational institutions of national minorities both in and out of their respective territorial enclaves. By the late 1930s Stalin's emphasis on Russian patriotism had come to the fore, and policies designed to facilitate the cultural expression of various national and ethnoreligious minorities fell to the wayside. Officials closed the division of the region's college that trained teachers for Jewish schools. On the eve of the German invasion of the Soviet Union in 1941 only two Jewish schools—a high school and an elementary school—still operated. But the status of Birobidzhan as the national territory of Soviet Jews remained, and the *Birobidzhaner shtern* (Birobidzhan Star) newspaper continued to appear on a daily basis.

By the outbreak of World War II, many observers concluded that the experiment to settle Jews in Birobidzhan was an abject failure. For example, Markish privately expressed doubts that the region would fulfill its promise. Markish's wife noted, for example, that her husband returned from his 1934 trip to Birobidzhan "disheartened and disillusioned."[22] In 1952, when he defended himself against charges of "Jewish nationalism" and "anti-Soviet activity," Markish admitted that as early as 1934 he "didn't think a smart Jew would go live in Birobidzhan when he already had everything [in Moscow]." As he confessed to his interrogators, during a conversation with Ben-Zion Goldberg, a prominent Jewish-American journalist, Markish had asked, "What stupid Jew would give up Moscow for Birobidzhan?"[23]

Married to Marusi (Marie) Rabinovich, a daughter of Sholem Aleichem, Goldberg was one of many American Jews who visited the region in the 1930s and effusively praised the project. He remained an enthusiastic advocate of Birobidzhan until the end of the 1940s, proclaiming the region a center of a vibrant Jewish culture, in spite of his knowledge that Jewish life and culture in Birobidzhan (not to mention the Soviet Union in general) were under attack. Goldberg, like many other left-leaning American Jews, remained committed to the Soviet Union for reasons of politics and ideology.[24]

The fact that Jews accounted for just 16 percent of the region's population in 1939 is stark evidence of the government's inability to build a genuinely Jewish region in the Soviet Far East. Birobidzhan never became a center of Soviet Jewry embodying the aspirations of a secular Yiddishist culture. By the late 1930s, notwithstanding the lip service paid by officials and literary figures, the Kremlin intended to efface Jewish identity. Assimilation into the emerging Soviet way of life—the development of *Homo sovieticus*—became the overriding goal of the Communist Party. The Kremlin, while not dismantling the structures dedicated to national consolidation, made clear that it desired to fuse national cultures into a common socialist culture, with Russian language and culture as the glue.

Ironically, as Soviet Jewry achieved a semblance of national and cultural consolidation, little was left of the specifically Jewish content of culture in the territory. Soviet policy had stripped the region of all manifestations of traditional Jewish culture, which was heavily rooted in Judaism. In the words of Ezra Mendelsohn, "Soviet communism and Jewish nationalism were unable to co-exist."[25] By the end of the 1930s the socialist content became more important than the national (and religious) structures in which Jewish culture was expressed. The universalism of the Soviet experiment trumped the particularism of ethnic identity.

The catastrophe of World War II and the Holocaust breathed life again into Birobidzhan, reviving efforts to realize the goals of cultural and social transformation. The end of hostilities brought the return of Jewish migration to Birobidzhan as many Jews sought to start life over again after the tragedy of the war. Official efforts to resuscitate Jewish settlement began in early 1946, when the government announced a plan to stimulate the development of Birobidzhan. As in the 1930s the Kremlin wanted to populate and develop the Soviet Far East for economic and political reasons. The plan focused on building factories and apartments, and offered free train tickets, loans, and other incentives to those who chose to resettle in Birobidzhan.[26] But the regime also wanted to help those Jews displaced by the war.

Between 1946 and 1948, nearly ten thousand Jews, along with thousands of gentiles, from all parts of the Soviet Union, migrated to Birobidzhan. Perhaps as many as thirty thousand Jews lived in the region at the end of 1948, again raising the hopes of Birobidzhan's advocates that the region might be elevated to the status of autonomous republic. Mikhail Kalinin, still president of the Soviet Union, reasserted his continued support of Birobidzhan when he announced in 1948 that he considered the region "a Jewish national state" that would "regenerate" Soviet Jewry through "creative toil."[27]

In mid-1947 Der Nister, one of the Soviet Union's preeminent Yiddish writers, made the arduous journey on board a train with one thousand Holocaust survivors. In his notebook Der Nister characterized the train as a "modern Noah's ark" and Birobidzhan as a territory that would restore "wholeness" to Jews living in the Diaspora.[28] Not only did tens of thousands of Soviet Jews find themselves displaced by the devastation wrought by the Germans, many returning to their homes after the war frequently faced hostile welcomes from their former Ukrainian, Russian, and Belarusian neighbors. Personal loss and a desire to escape the war-ravaged conditions of the western Soviet Union motivated many Jewish settlers. A Jewish woman from Moldova described why she wanted to move to Birobidzhan after the war: "I am a seamstress who lost all my relatives in the war. Only two nephews remain and they plan to move to Birobidzhan after demobilization."[29] That the region was officially reserved for Jewish settlement undoubtedly added to the lure of the place. As one couple from Vinnytsia reported, they had come to Birobidzhan to "help build Jewish Soviet statehood," while two other settlers proclaimed at a reception celebrating their arrival that they "had come home. Long live our native home."[30] It would be difficult to find a statement that more blatantly asserted that Birobidzhan, and not Eretz Israel, was the homeland of Soviet Jews.

The drive to populate Birobidzhan with Jews occurred as the Kremlin briefly relaxed its grip on Soviet society and permitted a resurgence of Jewish cultural life, which even included the opening of a synagogue. Communist Party chief Aleksandr Bakhmutskii spearheaded a campaign to revive the use of Yiddish in the region, instructing party organizations to "pay more attention to party propaganda in Yiddish" and to deliver "more speeches in Yiddish."[31] The party believed that its work accorded with the use of Yiddish, still an official language of the region. Bakhmutskii also ordered the increased circulation of the *Birobidzhaner shtern*, stressing that more efforts be taken to expand the number of subscribers to the paper.[32] Officials also opened a Yiddish publishing house for books, periodicals, and textbooks, and once again Yiddish became an obligatory subject in schools, including those where Russian was the language of instruction. The local government allocated funds to supply Birobidzhan with teachers who could teach history and literature as well as physics and mathematics in Yiddish, a phenomenon that occurred nowhere else in the Soviet Union.

A group of energetic and enthusiastic novelists, dramatists, and poets revived literary ventures and published several issues of a new literary and cultural journal entitled *Birobidzhan almanakh*, appearing between 1946 and 1948. In 1946 the city renamed a major thoroughfare in the city of Birobidzhan in honor of Sholem Aleichem on the thirtieth anniversary of the writer's death. The Yiddish theater expanded its repertoire and even performed plays about the war. As one actor noted at a party conference in 1947, Birobidzhan "exists so that the Jewish people could create in its native language a culture socialist in content."[33] Lectures, discussions, concerts, and other events lauding the renowned Yiddish writer took place throughout the region. In addition, one wing of the regional museum, which had opened in 1945, focused on Jewish history and culture since antiquity. An article in a local newspaper noted that the museum was "a museum about the Jews . . . that should reflect the culture and way of life of the Jewish laboring masses in the Soviet Union."[34] At the behest of Bakhmutskii, the director of the museum was negotiating the transfer to Birobidzhan of the remnants of the Judaica collection from Odessa as well as materials from museums in Leningrad and Moscow. Clearly, then, locals shared the optimism of the original settlers of Birobidzhan.

This campaign of national awakening, however, faced the same challenges as it did in the 1930s: Jewish artists and writers were still confined by the ideological constraints imposed by the Kremlin. Despite the relaxation of the party's grip on society, people had to tread carefully, ever fearful of transgressing the bounds of the politically acceptable. Once again Jewish authors found themselves writing odes to the efforts of the original settlers to clear Birobidzhan's forests, drain swamps, and build factories. Rules for a public competition "Soviet-Jewish song to mark the thirtieth anniversary" of the Bolshevik seizure of power held that the music and lyrics of the winning song "must reflect 1) the basic socioeconomic changes that have taken place in the life of the Jewish people during the years of Soviet power; 2) the active participation of Jewish toilers in socialist construction and defense of the homeland; 3) the construction of Soviet Jewish statehood; and 4) the boundless loyalty of Jewish toilers to the Bolshevik Party and the Great

Stalin." Possible themes included: "Comrade Stalin—Great Leader and Friend of the People" and "Jews as Stakhanovites[35] in Industry, Transport, and Agriculture."[36] In other words, these works lacked any specific Jewish or Yiddish content except for the fact that many were written in Yiddish by Jews describing life in Birobidzhan.

Officials also encouraged the production of paintings and drawings that depicted the flourishing of Jewish culture in Birobidzhan. In the best socialist realist fashion, some of these works were entitled *The Brigadier in the Field*, *Meeting of Brigadiers*, and *Portrait of a Young Tractor Driver*. Like the literary output from and about Birobidzhan, paintings lacked any specific reference to Jewish life except for the fact that they depicted Jews who were building socialism in Birobidzhan.

The dwindling number of students attending the two remaining all-Yiddish schools was another indicator of the weakness of the cultural awakening. The Jewish high school saw its number of students plummet from 497 in 1938–1939 to 11 during the 1946–1947 school year. Clearly, the vast majority of Jewish youths in Birobidzhan, many of whom spoke Yiddish at home but Russian elsewhere, realized that receiving an all-Yiddish education made little sense when all forms of higher education and employment were conducted in Russian.

This cultural awakening was short-lived. In early 1948 Stalin moved to extinguish expressions of Jewish culture and life throughout the Soviet Union, the result of a growing suspicion of the political loyalty of prominent Jewish intellectuals, writers, and cultural figures. These policies began before the establishment of Israel, building upon a campaign that had started during World War II to reduce the involvement of Jews in the arts as well as to ignore the German campaign to annihilate Jews. But the heating up of the Cold War and the celebration of Israeli independence by Soviet Jewry appeared to confirm Stalin's fears that Soviet Jews were unpatriotic and two-faced, guilty of, at best, dual political allegiance. His minions launched ruthless attacks on Jews who were demonized as "bourgeois nationalists," "Zionists," and "rootless cosmopolitans," which unleashed the combined force of popular and state-initiated antisemitism. Known as the "Black Years," the anti-Jewish attacks led to the execution of a dozen or so of the Soviet Union's preeminent Jewish literary figures in 1952, culminating in 1953 with the infamous Doctors' Plot, when the regime accused Jewish doctors of plotting to kill leading party officials. The death of Stalin in March 1953 put an end to this Jewish bloodletting, but Soviet Jews continued to live in fear as antisemitism reverberated on both the popular and official levels.[37]

Materials from the meetings of Communist Party officials in Birobidzhan demonstrate that policies occurred in lockstep with those emanating from Moscow.[38] The Kremlin-orchestrated murder of Solomon Mikhoels in early 1948 set in motion steps to persecute the Jewish intellectual, cultural, and political elite in Birobidzhan. Trouble began after a fact-finding commission reported to the Central

Committee in February 1948 that Birobidzhan was rife with ideological, political, and economic errors, abuses, and corruption and complained about the supposed domination of public life by Jews.[39]

Soon after the commission's visit and report, accusations began to fly at party meetings regarding the political mistakes of Birobidzhan's leadership. In general, the accusations attacked activities that had been sanctioned by the Kremlin only a few years earlier. Some allegations were contradictory in nature, such as the one claiming that writers, journalists, and artists were not "free of the vestiges of nationalism," which at the same time asserted that they "have been incapable of implementing the nationality policy of the Party." Another condemned the efforts to "artificially plant" Yiddish in education, though Yiddish as a language of instruction had been promoted by the central leadership.[40] Some critics noted the obligatory study of Yiddish in all schools by Jews and gentiles alike was misguided. Still other critics attacked Jewish writers for exhibiting "Jewish bourgeois nationalism" by failing to distinguish between the motivations of Soviet and non-Soviet Jews who had settled in Birobidzhan: Foreign Jews allegedly viewed the region as a "place of refuge," whereas Soviet Jews moved to Birobidzhan as part of their "socialist duty." Clearly these critics overlooked the statements of migrants who asserted that they moved to Birobidzhan after the war precisely because they saw the region as a haven. Moreover, the Jewish intelligentsia in Birobidzhan, accusers declaimed, wrongly emphasized the efforts to establish the region as the center of Soviet Jewish life since Jews lived throughout the Soviet Union. These attacks on efforts to make Birobidzhan a center of Jewish life acquired tragic consequences when local officials decided to destroy some thirty thousand volumes in Yiddish, Russian, and Hebrew of the Judaica collection in the regional library.[41] In short, efforts to promote the use of Yiddish and the spread of Jewish identity came into the crosshairs of a concerted government campaign to destroy Soviet Jewish culture.

By the late 1940s Stalin had adopted policies to insulate Soviet society from the capitalist West. Party activists issued vociferous denunciations of Jewish settlers who purportedly had ties with family and friends abroad. They complained that the arrival of letters, newspapers and literature from abroad, as well as goodwill parcels of clothing, money, and canned foods was stirring up nationalist sentiments among Jews. In addition, personal contacts with "nationalist elements" elsewhere in the Soviet Union undermined the stability of socialism. Clearly, then, these developments marked a shift in the Kremlin's policies toward Birobidzhan and threatened the region's status as the cultural and political center of Soviet Jewry. In a complete reversal of twenty years of policy toward Jews, the party condemned any statement that referred to Birobidzhan, rather than the whole Soviet Union, as the "homeland for Jews." Over the next several years, many Jewish writers, artists, and actors in Birobidzhan fell victim to the "struggle against rootless cosmopolitanism, Jewish bourgeois nationalism, and . . . the depravity of bourgeois culture."[42] The personnel of leading political, cultural, and intellectual institutions changed frequently.[43] All told, some forty Jewish writers, artists, and political leaders living in Birobidzhan received long prison sentences.[44]

The fate of Bakhmutskii, head of the Birobidzhan Communist Party, is particularly revealing of the Kremlin's complete reversal of policy and, as in the 1930s, reflects the unpredictable nature of the regime's policy toward Jews. In mid-1949 a report issued by the regional party organization condemned Bakhmutskii for having too many ties with Americans. Such connections "facilitated the dissemination of pro-American and bourgeois nationalist sentiments among some sectors of the population." The fear of contamination stemmed from the concern that American Jews of different social and political sympathies provided material support for Birobidzhan. The report also took Bakhmutskii to task for asserting that Birobidzhan was being built "only with the hands of Jews," a deliberate slap in the face of the "Great Russian people" who also contributed to socialist construction in the region. Finally, by accepting material assistance from American groups, Bakhmutskii "belittled the dignity of Soviet citizens."[45]

Ordinary citizens also fell victim to the probing eyes of the secret police. The hyper-patriotism that was so much a part of the Cold War mentality involved condemnation of contacts between inhabitants of Birobidzhan and relatives and organizations abroad. In a Uruguayan journal dedicated to news about Birobidzhan, the caption to a photo of a house in Birobidzhan states: "You see our house? It was sent to us as a gift" from Americans. One Birobidzhan resident had written to his relatives in the United States that his daughter had no shoes. The letter made its way into the American press and Bakhmutskii's detractors used it to illustrate the damage caused by contacts with the West. In yet another case, the authorities believed that American relatives who were innocently asking what they should send to their kin in Birobidzhan were working for U.S. intelligence.[46]

Not surprisingly, the party relieved Bakhmutskii of his post, the first step in the process of stripping him of his party membership for sowing the seeds of Jewish separatism. In the eyes of the party, Jews comprised a minority of the population in Birobidzhan, and Bakhmutskii's focus on strengthening the specifically Jewish character of the region was misguided and detrimental to the needs of non-Jews living there. His failure to weed out "bourgeois nationalists" from the party and government indicated his affinity with the capitalist West.

But Bakhmutskii did not go without a struggle. He admitted that he had tried to promote Yiddish and Jewish culture in Birobidzhan, as well as maintained ties with American Jewish organizations and individuals. But he refused to recant because he felt that he had legitimately followed party directives. At the meeting where he was stripped of his party card he interrupted his accusers, pointing out that, when he undertook the very actions for which he was now condemned, the party had sanctioned them. Bakhmutskii noted the irony of the fact that although he grew up in a Russified Jewish family and did not speak Yiddish, he now found himself under attack for promoting the Yiddish language. In a confrontational display of bravery, Bakhmutskii declared, "I didn't realize that something I once said could become inappropriate at a later date."[47] Even though the Kremlin had authorized all his activities and policies before 1948, Bakhmutskii fell victim to the changing political and ideological circumstances of the Cold War. Consequently, he and many others found themselves targets of a witch hunt. As one party member stressed in his attack on Bakhmutskii:

> Who gave the region's leadership the right to enter into such friendly relations with America? Did they bother to ask us, the rank-and-file Communists of the region, whether we agreed? Who gave them the right to accept charity and, thereby, expose our shortcomings to America? As if we cannot cope with our shortcomings without America, as if we lack the means to do so!"[48]

It was not until January 1951 that the state charged him with treason. He was sentenced to death by firing squad the following February, but his sentence was commuted to twenty-five years in prison. Bakhmutskii was released in 1956 and his party card was returned to him. He died in 1961 at the age of 50.

The fate of Birobidzhan demonstrates that Soviet communism vanquished Jewish nationalism. The combined impact of official state policy through gradual secularization along with the destruction wrought by the Holocaust led to dilution of all expressions of meaningful Jewish culture. Soviet Jews ended up acculturating, integrating, and even assimilating, notwithstanding the official stance of the Kremlin to promote and sustain Jewish national identity. Given the constraints placed on the content of Jewish national and cultural identity, along with the state's concerted embrace of openly antisemitic policies by the late 1940s, it is no wonder that Birobidzhan did not succeed. And yet the regime did not dismantle Birobidzhan, presumably because its continued existence served the propaganda needs of the Kremlin, which wanted to maintain the fiction that Jewish society and culture flourished in the Soviet Union.

Still, the excitement and enthusiasm that many Jewish activists inside and outside the Soviet Union displayed toward Birobidzhan underscores the appeal of the idea of a socialist Jewish homeland outside the Land of Israel. Ezra Mendelsohn noted that the "Jewish left consisted of all specifically Jewish organizations that believed the solution to the Jewish Question must include a thoroughgoing restructuring of Jews . . . society and the establishment of a new social order based on justice and the absence of exploitation."[49] To be sure, a diverse group of organizations fit the bill, ranging from socialist, Marxist, and communist to autonomist, territorialist, and Yiddishist. As we have seen, the Kremlin bestowed the seal of approval on a particular form of left-wing Jewish politics that constrained the open expression of Jewish identity. And yet Moscow saw fit not to extinguish all signs of Soviet-styled Jewish nationalism after the anti-Jewish purges of the late 1940s and early 1950s. Some seventy-five years after Stalin's death in 1953, the Jewish Autonomous Region continues to exist, with both Yiddish and Russian enjoying the status of official languages. To be sure, the dream of the region's early activists and advocates that Birobidzhan would become the center of Soviet Jewish life and culture are relics of a period when the promise of building socialism in the Soviet Union was not considered some kind of warped joke. The withering of pro-Soviet sentiments among many left-wing American radicals occurred at the same time the Kremlin made it clear that the Jewish Autonomous Region would be Jewish and autonomous in name only. The experiment to establish a socialist Jewish homeland entered a vegetative state, a victim of the Kremlin's campaign to kill efforts to fulfill the dream of building a promised land at the confluence of two rivers, the Bira and Bidzhan, in a remote part of the Soviet Far East. Birobidzhan was a far cry from the land of milk and honey envisioned along the banks of the Jordan River. By the mid-1950s it was abundantly clear to observers that the Birobidzhan project was not a viable alternative to a Jewish state located in the historic homeland of the Jewish people.

NOTES

1. Two of the best accounts of Soviet nationality policy in the 1920s and 1930s are Terry Martin, *The Affirmative Action Empire: Nations and Nationalism in the Soviet Union, 1923–1939* (Ithaca: Cornell University Press, 2001) and Yuri Slezkine, *Arctic Mirrors: Russia and the Small Peoples of the North* (Ithaca: Cornell University Press, 1996).

2. Ezra Mendelsohn, *On Modern Jewish Politics* (New York: Oxford University Press, 1993), 17.

3. Joseph Stalin defined a nation as "a historically evolved, stable community of people, formed on the basis of a common language, territory, economic life, and psychological make-up manifested in a common culture." Joseph Stalin, *Marxism and the National Question* (Moscow: Foreign Languages Publishing House, 1950), 16 and 64.

4. Robert Weinberg, *Stalin's Forgotten Zion: Birobidzhan and the Making of a Soviet Jewish Homeland* (Berkeley: University of California Press, 1998), 18.

5. On the Agro-Joint, see Jonathan Dekel-Chen, *Farming the Red Land: Jewish Agricultural Colonization and Local Soviet Power, 1924–1941*(New Haven: Yale University Press, 2005), *passim*.

6. Weinberg, *Stalin's Forgotten Zion*, 21.

7. The best discussion on efforts to bring the revolution to Soviet Jews remains Zvi Gitelman, *Jewish Nationality and Soviet Politics: The Jewish Sections of the CPSU, 1917–1930* (Princeton: Princeton University Press, 1972).

8. See Weinberg, *Stalin's Forgotten Zion*; Allan Laine Kagedan, *Soviet Zion: The Quest for a Russian Jewish Homeland* (New York: St. Martin's Press, 1994); Antje Kuchenbecker, *Zionismus ohne Zion: Birobidzhan: Idee und Geschichte eines jüdischen Staates in Sowjet-Fernost* (Berlin: Metropol, 2000).

9. Quoted in Gitelman, *Jewish Nationality and Soviet Politics*, 416–417.

10. *Tribuna evreiskoi sovetskoi obshchestvennosti* [Tribune of the Soviet Jewish Community], October 1, 1928, 1.

11. Koreans who had settled the region in the late nineteenth and early twentieth centuries were responsible for rice cultivation. For these quotations, see, respectively, A. Fabrikant, "Agrikulturnye cherty evreiskogo zemledeliia v SSSR," *Evreiskii krest'ianin*, no. 1 (1925), 24; *Tribuna evreiskoi sovetskoi obshchestvennosti*, September 1, 1928, 21; and State Archive of the Jewish Autonomous Region (SAJAR), fond 3, opis 1, delo 13, 4–5.

12. Gitelman, *Jewish Nationality and Soviet Politics*, 19.

13. The following discussion of the history of Birobidzhan is based on Weinberg, *Stalin's Forgotten Zion*.

14. The settlement of Birobidzhan coincided with the decision of the Kremlin to launch an all-out industrialization drive in tandem with the collectivization of agriculture. These twin policies contributed to the failure of agricultural settlement, especially because Jews interested in farming were skeptical of the collective farm system.

15. On the efforts of North American Jews and non-Jews to promote Birobidzhan, see Henry Srebrnik, *Jerusalem on the Amur: Birobidzhan and the Canadian Jewish Communist Movement,*

1924–1951 (Montreal: McGill-Queen's University Press, 2008) and *Dreams of Nationhood: American Jewish Communists and the Soviet Birobidzhan Project, 1924–1951* (Boston: Academic Studies Press, 2010).

16. Ber Boris Kotlerman, *In Search of Milk and Honey: The Theater of "Soviet Jewish Statehood" (1934–1949)* (Bloomington: Slavica Publishers, 2009).

17. Weinberg, *Stalin's Forgotten Zion*, 64. Finally, schools in which classes were conducted in Russian required students to learn Yiddish, complementing the system of educational institutions where Yiddish was the language of instruction.

18. Sh. Klitenik, "Evreiskii teatr na Da'nem Vostoke," *Tribuna evreiskoi sovetskoi obshchestvennosti*, August 1, 1937, 10–12. When the Yiddish literary journal *Forpost* (Outpost) appeared in 1936, critics hailed it as an important Soviet-Jewish journal, which "should be the central organ of not only local Birobidzhan forces, but of all creative forces of Soviet Jewish society interested in the construction of the Jewish Autonomous Region." A. Kashin, "*Forpost*, zhurnal Evreiskoi avtonomnoi oblasti," *Tribuna evreiskoi sovetskoi obshchestvennosti*, January 1, 1937, 12–13.

19. Joshua Rubenstein and Vladimir Naumov, eds., *Stalin's Secret Pogrom: The Postwar Inquisition of the Jewish Anti-Fascist Committee* (New Haven: Yale University Press, 2001), 144–150.

20. Rubenstein and Naumov, *Stalin's Secret Pogrom*, 123.

21. Other local minorities also suffered at the hands of the security forces, particularly the 4,500 Koreans who were deported in sealed freight trains to Central Asia in 1937.

22. Rubenstein and Naumov, *Stalin's Secret Pogrom*, 123.

23. Rubenstein and Naumov, *Stalin's Secret Pogrom*, 134.

24. Rubenstein and Naumov, *Stalin's Secret Pogrom*, 26–27.

25. Mendelsohn, *On Modern Jewish Politics*, 39.

26. Material on Birobidzhan after 1945 is based on Robert Weinberg, "Birobidzhan After the Second World War," *Jews in Eastern Europe* 3, no. 49 (Winter 2002): 31–46. See also Gennadii Kostyrchenko, *V plenu u krasnogo faraona* [Out of the red shadows] (Moscow, 1994).

27. Weinberg, *Stalin's Forgotten Zion*, 72.

28. Ber Kotlerman, *Broken Heart/Broken Wholeness: The Post-Holocaust Plea for Jewish Reconstruction of the Soviet Yiddish Writer Der Nister* (Brighton: Academic Studies Press, 2017), *passim*.

29. *Birobidzhanskaia zvezda* [Birobidzhan Star] May 25, 1946. I accessed the old newspaper articles at the *Российская государственная библиотека* (Russian State Library).

30. *Birobidzhanskaia zvezda*, July 1 and 4, 1947.

31. Russian State Archive of Socio-Political History (hereafter RGASPI), fond 17, opis' 46, delo 2666, 186–189.

32. *Birobidzhaner shtern* restarted publication in 1944 after a hiatus of three years.

33. RGASPI, fond 17, opis' 47, delo 2680, 144.

34. *Birobidzhanskaia zvezda*, July 19, 1946.

35. Stakhanovites were workers who emulated the efforts of Aleksei Stakhanov, a miner who, in 1935, was said to have mined a record amount of coal during one shift, about seven times his daily quota.

36. *Birobidzhanskaia zvezda*, May 17, 1947.

37. For discussions of Soviet policy toward Jews during the final years of Stalin's life, see Jonathan Brent, *Stalin's Last Crime: The Plot Against the Jewish Doctors, 1948–1953* (New York: HarperCollins, 2003); Yehoshua Gilboa, *The Black Years of Soviet Jewry, 1939–1953* (Boston: Little, Brown and Company, 1971); Gennadii Kostyrchenko, *Tainaia politika Stalina: Vlast' i antisemitizm* (Moscow: Mezhdunarodnye otnosheniia, 2001); Shimon Redlich, *War, Holocaust and Stalinism: A Documentary Study of the Jewish Anti-Fascist Committee in the USSR* (Reading: Harwood Academic Publishers, 1995).; Rubenstein and Naumov, *Stalin's Secret Pogrom*.

38. The following discussion is taken from Robert Weinberg, "Birobidzhan After the Second World War."

39. RGASPI, fond 17, opis' 118, delo 39, 105–110.

40. RGASPI, fond, 17, opis' 48, delo 2741, 10–11.
41. Weinberg, *Stalin's Forgotten Zion*, 84.
42. RGASPI, fond 17, opis' 49, delo 3000, 17–18.
43. Kostyrchenko, *V plenu u krasnogo faraona*, 175–178.
44. Gilboa, *The Black Years of Soviet Jewry*, 194.
45. The material on Bakhmutskii is culled from several documents that are similar in content. RGASPI, fond 17, opis' 117, delo 597, 44–54; fond 17, opis' 118, delo 428, 39–86; fond 17, opis' 118, delo 494, 154, and 156; and fond 17, opis' 49, delo 2999, *passim*.
46. RGASPI, fond 17, opis' 49, delo, 2999, 38–39, 137, and 130; fond 17, opis 118, delo 428, 50.
47. RGASPI, fond 17, opis' 49, delo 2999, *passim*; fond 17, opis' 118, delo 494, 152–158.
48. RGASPI, fond 17, opis' 118, delo 494, 156.
49. Mendelsohn, *On Modern Jewish Politics*, 28.

PART III

Eastern Europe and the Balkans

Eastern Europe is famous for its history of Jewish radicals. Previous volumes on the subject of Jews and radicalism have accordingly devoted considerable space to the region, particularly to the Russian Empire, where Jews played pivotal roles in establishing and leading a wide spectrum of radical parties. Between the 1820s and the Bolshevik Revolution of 1917, a long-term process of political radicalization took place among Jews living in the Russian Empire, a swathe of land that at that time included much of Eastern Europe beyond contemporary Russia's borders. This roughly one-hundred-year period witnessed the rise of revolutionary groups and parties that sought to overthrow the tsarist regime and to emancipate the proletariat and/or the peasantry, depending on the case. Individual Jews joined such organizations as the agrarian populist People's Will and the Marxist Russian Social Democratic Workers Party in small but steadily increasing numbers. In addition, Jews formed their own parties that combined socialism with Jewish nationalism. The first such party was the Bund, founded in 1897 through an alliance of Social Democratic groups located in Vilna and other cities in the northwest provinces of the Russian Empire. In subsequent years, the Bund developed a program that combined revolutionary Marxism with a kind of Jewish nationalism based on language and culture, rather than territory and political sovereignty. Other Jewish political parties emerged during the 1905 Revolution and its immediate aftermath. The Marxist Zionist Poale Zion advocated for a Jewish homeland in Palestine; the Zionist Socialist Workers Party argued for a territory wherever feasible; and the Jewish Socialist Workers Party proposed a territorialist solution, as well, but placed greater emphasis on Jewish communal autonomy in Russia. Through these Jewish political parties and general Russian parties, a significant portion of Eastern European Jews became radicalized by 1917.

Against this general backdrop, we focus on three places that played key roles in the history of radical Jewish politics in Eastern Europe: Lithuania, the cradle of the Jewish labor Bund and incubator for the concept of *doikayt* or "hereness"; Hungary, where Jews dominated the leadership of the Communist Party to an extraordinary degree that was unmatched anywhere else in Europe; and the Balkans, where Sephardi Jews, including activists from Bulgaria and Macedonia, created a dynamic socialist movement in the city of Salonica and later helped to found both the Socialist and Communist Parties of Greece. The distinctive character and trajectories of radical Jewish politics in each of these sites reveals the importance of local and regional conditions, even as striking parallels may also be seen, particularly between the Yiddish radical culture of the Bund in Lithuania and the Ladino radical culture of the Socialist Workers' Federation of Salonica. Indeed, their shared embrace of local Jewish culture *and* socialist politics—despite the differences between Ladino and Yiddish, and between Sephardi and Ashkenazi traditions—only highlights the contrast with Hungary, where Jewish communists typically sought to distance themselves from any expression of Jewish particularity, even as they were frequently dismissed as foreigners by their opponents.

In chapter 12, Michael Casper reveals how particular socioeconomic conditions in the northwestern region of the Pale of Settlement (the heartland of the old Lithuanian kingdom) very much shaped the early Jewish workers movement that gave rise to the Bund. This region was home to a large, deeply rooted, densely populated, and highly cohesive Yiddish-speaking Jewish community. Reinforcing Jewish group distinctiveness was the region's economic underdevelopment. While large, mechanized factories arose in the major cities such as Moscow, St. Petersburg, and Warsaw, the Lithuanian provinces lacked heavy industries. Furthermore, factory owners were reluctant to hire Jewish workers because they were perceived to be troublesome, more inclined to protest compared to their gentile counterparts, and refused to work on Saturdays, or so it was believed. Finally, gentiles actively resisted the hiring of Jews, whom they viewed as unwelcome competition. Consequently, Jews in the Lithuanian provinces found themselves largely excluded from modern factories and confined to small workshops. While this combination of factors weakened the economic position of Jews, they nonetheless fostered a strong sense of ethno-class solidarity that contributed to the emergence of the Bund. Moreover, Casper demonstrates that Lithuania was not only a critical node in the development of Bundism. During the interwar period, it was also the place where *doikayt* or "hereness"—the concept that Jews should strive to achieve national-cultural rights in the diaspora, as opposed to the Zionist concept of "thereness"—was first formulated. Not by Bundists, as has often been assumed because of the Bund's post–World War II embrace of the concept, but by what Casper describes as the "expressly Lithuanian regionalist party, the Folkists."

The October Revolution in Russia led to the establishment of communist parties across Europe and abroad. In many countries Jews joined these parties in disproportionate numbers, but nowhere did this phenomenon occur as dramatically as in Hungary. At least three quarters of the "people's commissars" of the short-lived Hungarian Soviet Republic of 1919 were of Jewish parentage, Peter Kenez writes in chapter 13. The entire top leadership of the post–World War II Hungarian Communist government was also Jewish. Hungary represented an extreme case for a variety of socioeconomic reasons but it nonetheless reflected a broader pattern found in other Eastern European "people's republics." Antisemites exploited the high concentration of Jews in the early Soviet leadership and communist parties elsewhere to bolster their allegations of Jewish subversion and world domination. The persistent canard of a "Judeo-Bolshevik" conspiracy presented a cruel irony. Many Jews joined revolutionary organizations and, after 1917, communist parties in countries like Hungary with the intention of transcending Jewish peoplehood and all forms of nationality. Once asked whether he considered himself a Jew or a Russian, Trotsky famously retorted, "I am neither a Russian nor a Jew, but an internationalist." For those Jews who embraced it, communism presented an "exit strategy," to quote the sociologist Zygmunt Bauman. Yet, in practice, communism served to reinforce a kind of Jewish particularity and heightened suspicions of Jews in the minds of many non-Jews. Even within communist countries themselves, Jews were often treated as a foreign element that was worthy of suspicion or worse. Indeed, Kenez writes, "In 1953, following Stalin's death, the Hungarian communist leaders were summoned to Moscow and were told that they 'should have more Hungarians in the leadership,' implying that Jews were not Hungarians. This was precisely what the Hungarians themselves thought." Some Jews in Hungary, as elsewhere, responded to this hostile climate by embracing Zionism. Between 1945 and 1948, Zionism was tolerated by the Hungarian Communist government, whose attitude was "ambivalent and contradictory," and the movement, which had never been that popular, enjoyed its greatest success in the country during this period. And yet, Kenez writes, "After 1948 Zionists were mercilessly repressed and their leaders jailed."

During both the late Ottoman era and, later, under Greek rule, Sephardi Jews in the city of Salonica—today's Thessaloniki—created a distinctive radical Jewish culture in Ladino that, as their leader Abraham Benaroya noted, had important parallels to the Yiddish language activism of the Bund in Eastern Europe. As Kostis Karpozilos and Paris Papamichos Chronakis note in chapter 14, Sephardi Jewish activists in Salonica (including those like Benaroya who were from Bulgaria or elsewhere in the Balkans) initially took advantage of the window of political opportunity produced by the Young Turk Revolution of 1908, which was launched from the city, by creating the Socialist Workers' Federation, described by the historian Paul Dumont as the most important socialist movement in the Ottoman Empire. The federation organized thousands of workers into unions; held massive May Day rallies, published a newspaper in Ladino, ran a library, theater group, and social club; and was recognized by the Second International as the official representative of the workers of Salonica. After 1912, when the city came under Greek rule during the First Balkan War, the federation was the biggest socialist organization in Greece, until its members helped to found the Socialist Labor Party (SEKE) in 1918, which, in turn, became the Communist Party of Greece (KKE) in 1924. This transformation was accompanied by the Bolshevik leadership's expulsion of Benaroya and several other prominent Jewish socialists from Salonica because of their social democratic orientation.

CHAPTER 12

Lithuania and the Making of the Jewish Working Class

Michael Casper

This chapter has a clumsy title, but it is one that meets its purpose. Sixty years after E. P. Thompson opened his magisterial study of the rise of class consciousness in England with this apologia, no historian need any longer defend the use of "making" or "class" to describe the emergence of an organized movement of workers. The title of this chapter is clumsy because it begins with a small place that played an outsized role in the formation of radical Jewish politics in Eastern Europe and, by extension, both revolutionary politics in Russia and the labor movement around the world. While the boundaries of Lithuania shifted over the centuries, the place maintained a surprisingly stable meaning for the Jews who lived there, and Jews' deep ties to the area fostered several political movements that privileged the role of Lithuania.

The historiography of Eastern European Jewish politics has, quite reasonably, focused on Russia and Poland, whose size, power, and centuries-long cultural hegemony over most of the region determined, to a great extent, the contours of local Jewish life. And yet this approach fails to acknowledge the unique place in Jewish history of Lithuania, situated between—and, more often than not, within—Russia and Poland. It was this intermediary position in the multiethnic borderlands of Russia and Poland that made Lithuanian Jewry unique both compared to other Eastern European Jews and as a constituency in Russia. One of the most notable features of Lithuanian Jewish life was peaceful cohabitation with non-Jewish neighbors, especially Poles, Belarusians, and Lithuanians, resulting in a low level of interethnic violence relative to other areas of western Russia in the late nineteenth and early twentieth centuries.[1] By the nineteenth century, Lithuanian Jews had already distinguished themselves from other Eastern European Jewish groups in many significant ways, including through their separate regional communal organization and a tradition of opposition to ecstatic Hasidism that favored rationalist Talmudic analysis. At the same time, outside factors, such as the piecemeal industrialization of Lithuania within the Russian Empire, put unique pressures on

Lithuanian Jews and contributed to a perspective on political economy that was particular to their region.

The Lithuanian Jewish regional identity was encapsulated in the figure of the "Litvak," the Lithuanian Jew who, in the Jewish imaginary, was studious and self-serious. But by the turn of the twentieth century, Jewish political activists advanced a form of radical Jewish political regionalism that put the area of Lithuania at the center of Jewish identity—sometimes in contrast with modes of Jewish integration in other parts of Europe and other times in opposition to territorial Zionism. Lithuanian-ness played a large, if underappreciated, role in the most influential and radical Jewish movement to emerge from Europe: the Jewish labor movement and its later socialist political organization, the Bund. The Lithuanian Jewish labor movement was militant, highly organized, Marxist in orientation, and left its mark on the Jewish labor movement across Eastern Europe and also globally, due to large-scale Jewish emigration at the peak of the movement's popularity around the turn of the century. Moshe Mishinski noted the "regional uniqueness of the historical context of the movement" in an important treatment of Lithuanian Jewish politics: "Organizationally and ideologically Lithuania was the birthplace of the [Jewish labor] movement. It also retained the hegemony in pre-Bund and Bund formation period and to some extent even later. And the unique stamp that Lithuania imposed upon the Jewish labor movement was not obliterated even in the post-war Bund of Poland."[2] Perhaps most significantly, the mass workers' struggle in Russia developed a strong Lithuanian strain. As Georgi Plekhanov, a leading Russian revolutionary, famously noted as early as 1896, Lithuanian Jewish workers who "don't even have the lowly rights of the Christian 'citizens' of Russia, have, in struggle with their exploiters, demonstrated so much determination and such good sense in understanding the social-political tasks of the contemporary labor movement that, in a certain sense, we can consider them the vanguard of the labor army in Russia."[3]

In addition to Mishinski, a number of scholars have noted Lithuania's special place in the radicalization of Russian Jewry, and this chapter is first and foremost a historiographic synthesis, building on the work of Jonathan Frankel, Eli Lederhendler, Ezra Mendelsohn, Yoav Peled, Gershon Shafir, and Joshua Zimmerman, among others. E. P. Thompson argued that the working class came into being as a result of a convergence of social, economic, and religious factors in the era of industrialization. Here, the focus is on the critical period between manumission of the serfs and founding of the Bund, or what one Bundist called the "erev Bund"—the "eve" of the Bund, or proto-Bund—when the social, economic, and political pressures of the Lithuanian context were most clearly manifest.[4]

A Double Periphery

In Jewish history and memory, Lithuania refers not to the area defined by the borders of the contemporary nation-state in the European Union but to a much larger territory that roughly corresponds with that of the medieval Grand Duchy of Lithuania. In 1323, Lithuanian Grand Duke Gediminas invited Jews to settle the city of Vilna (today Vilnius); sixty-five years later, Grand Duke Vytautas the Great signed a charter that granted local Jews sweeping privileges and protections, including freedom of religion, travel, trade, and standing before the law equal to Christians. Historian Simon Dubnow wrote, "Under the laws enacted by Vitovt [Vytautas] the Jews of Lithuania formed a class of free citizens, standing under the immediate protection of the Grand Duke and his local administration. They lived in independent communities, enjoying autonomy in their internal affairs as far as religion and property are concerned. . . . Accordingly the position of the Jews was more favorable in Lithuania than in Poland."[5] After the union of the Grand Duchy with Poland, in 1569, which formed the Polish-Lithuanian Commonwealth, Lithuania, and Lithuanian Jews, retained unique social features that only deepened with the centuries, such as a distinct Yiddish dialect and a religious tradition opposed to Hasidism that championed the systematic study of the Talmud. While Poland and Lithuania were politically united, the respective Jewish communities were distinct enough to warrant the formation, in 1590, of a breakaway governing body in Lithuania to handle the region's Jewish communal affairs, such as taxation, and which functioned for over 150 years. During this time, Jews were by and large concentrated in cities and market towns, where they worked in handicrafts; held leases to fish, log, and distill liquor; and managed the estates of Polish noblemen.

The Partitions of Poland (1792–1795) put most Lithuanian Jews in the Russian Empire's westernmost provinces, and Jews were restricted, with a few exceptions, from settling outside of this area, known as the Pale of Settlement. Over the course of the next century, the Jewish population of the culturally Polish towns and cities of this region swelled. After the emancipation of the serfs, in 1861, large numbers of dispossessed peasants moved to cities to seek work in the factories that defined the emergent capitalist economy. For centuries, Lithuanian Jews had worked as artisans and economic middlemen, and so their labor was in greatest demand at relatively high-skilled, labor-intensive workshops that were smaller than the mechanized factories whose owners preferred to hire non-Jews. Although the factory and shop owners were often Jewish themselves, Jewish workers were increasingly replaced by non-Jews, who were viewed at the time as less likely to organize for higher wages and more willing to work on the Sabbath (while all shops remained closed on Sundays). The resulting exclusion of Jewish workers from the industrialized economy in western Russia has been studied with great care by Yoav Peled and Gershon Shafir, who identify the process as critical to what they call Jews' "non- or 'abnormal' proletarianization" outside of the factory system.[6]

Within the Russian Empire, the so-called Northwest Provinces, whose area roughly coincides with historical Lithuania, presented a situation that was particularly dire for Jewish workers. The same intermediary place that had enriched Lithuania's culture became a hindrance to its economic development. According to Tomas Balkelis, "The Lithuanian provinces remained essentially an economic backwater of the Russian empire, a sort of 'double periphery,' as described by some writers. . . . As a result, [the] Lithuanian provinces largely missed out [on] the large-scale industrialization that took place in cities such as Riga, Warsaw, Bialystok, Lodz, Saint Petersburg, and Moscow, but barely in Vilna or Kovno," where the government invested in border-related military rather than industry.[7] Yet in the very place in western Russia where industrialization was lowest, and the population as a whole, including Jews, was relatively poor, Jewish concentration in handicrafts and manual labor was highest. These Jewish workers, who formerly worked for themselves or were supported by guild-like organizations, now competed with each other for the limited jobs at workshops. Excluded from factories, and yet concentrated in handicrafts, around 90 percent of Lithuanian Jews plied their trade in workshops where working conditions, pay, job security, safety regulation, and working conditions were typically worse than in the factories. The resulting "greater economic 'overcrowdedness' and the privation among Jews in this region also had their effect on the tempo of proletarization and its forms."[8] It also resulted in Lithuanian Jews' disproportionate alienation from their traditional craft. As a result of this, Mishinski observed, "The increase of the socio-economic weight of the workers category in the life of the Jewish community in Lithuania aided significantly in the crystallization of an independent class movement."[9]

A Working Class *Haskalah*

Despite the difficult conditions in which they labored in Lithuania, as artisans Jewish workers had some characteristics that aided them in the class struggle. While workers in other parts of Russia struggled to organize, Lithuanian Jews formed groups called *kasy* in Russian, or *kases* in Yiddish, which operated in the underground, much like unions, to collect money for strike funds. But in addition to organizing, *kases* supported libraries, reading groups, and other cultural activities. It was easier to spread knowledge and organize in smaller workshops than in large factories, and *kases* made connections between towns and cities across Lithuania, providing critical structure for the future labor movement.

One apparent influence on the formation of these distinctive *kases* was the existence of a network of *khevres*, or guild-like societies of Jewish artisans that had organized Jewish professional life for centuries.[10] While Ezra Mendelsohn cautioned against drawing a direct line between *khevres* and *kases*, citing the well-known hostility of the latter to the former, he nonetheless attributed the success of the *kases* to the local "organizational tradition."[11] The resulting artisan character of the Lithuanian-Jewish labor movement made it structurally "more a part of Central and Western Europe than the Russian Empire," and thus in line with the class-formation process in England outlined by E. P. Thompson.[12] In this model, the relatively more literate and less physically exploited artisans had the ability and energy to discuss ideas and collaboratively write and disseminate pamphlets, inspiring Mendelsohn's astute observation that the Jewish labor movement constituted a "working class 'Haskalah.'"[13] Here Mendelsohn used the Yiddish and Hebrew term for the earlier movement known as the "Jewish Enlightenment," which applied Enlightenment ideals to the question of Jewish social and political emancipations. In other words, the intellectual component of the class struggle can be seen as an extension of the Jewish fight for emancipation in the economic sphere.

Another striking similarity between the formation of the working classes in England and in Lithuania is the religious underpinnings of these phenomena. In the case of England, according to Thompson, "Methodism provided not only the forms of the class meeting, the methodical collection of penny subscriptions and the 'ticket,' so frequently borrowed by radical and trade union organisations, but also an experience of efficient centralised organisation."[14] Here, too, it would be a mistake to draw a direct line between religious organization and labor organization.[15] And yet the distinctive religious tradition of Lithuanian Jews may have contained within it a democratizing impulse that fed labor organization. While much of Russian Jewry came under the sway of Hasidism, a pietistic movement centered around charismatic holy men and, later, institutionalized dynasties of their descendants and pupils, Lithuanian Jews came to be known as the *misnagdim*, or "opponents" of Hasidism. The *misnagdim* emphasized textual study and interpretation, rather than ecstatic experience, and produced innovative institutions to support and spread various forms of rationalistic study of the Talmud and its main expositors. The most important of these new nineteenth-century institutions were the *kollel*, which supported full-time study for newly married men, and the yeshiva, a seminary that trained advanced students for the rabbinate.

The young men who attended yeshiva, and endured privation and loneliness while studying away from home, were ideal candidates for radicalization.[16] During the day, they were steeped in the particularly Lithuanian Jewish intellectual approaches to Talmud taught in the yeshivas, including *musar*, a method of analysis that emphasized ethics, and *lomdus*, a form of thorough analytical interpretation. While the primary goal of the yeshiva was to prepare young men for rabbinical ordination, they were famous hotbeds of intellectual and political activity including Zionism, socialism, and the revival of literary Hebrew, as young men shared newspapers, books, and ideas; applied yeshiva-style analysis to their secondary topics of interest; and made contacts from towns and cities throughout Lithuania. Not all Jewish labor leaders had a background in yeshiva study. But as the movement popularized and came to favor Yiddish over Russian, "ex-yeshiva students who had a better command of Yiddish than Russian, moved into key positions in the revolutionary hierarchy. Without them, the growing output of revolutionary material, papers and brochures, in Yiddish would not have been possible."[17] Indeed, revolutionary Julius Martov singled out the Lithuanian activists for their rationalism.[18] Lithuanian Jewish labor organizing was not inspired by Lithuanian Judaism per se but, as with Methodism in England, by an organized reaction within it.

Out of the Lithuanian Jewish labor movement emerged one of the most important modern Jewish political organizations: the General Jewish Labor Union in Lithuania, Poland and Russia, known more commonly as the Bund (the union). The Bund was founded in 1897 in Vilna, where Jews made up about half of the total population and "constituted the local working class."[19] Of the thirteen delegates at the founding of the Bund, in the attic of Yankev Rozental at Lukiškės Square, remembered one of the organizers, "ten of them were more or less active in Vilna in earlier years and had been sent from Vilna to other cities, where they founded and led the Jewish socialist organizations."[20] Of these, several had been core members of an underground circle of orthodox Marxist labor activists known as the Vilna Group, whose "Vilna Program" advocated (in Russian) for workers to agitate forcefully for their workplace demands. While some members of the Vilna Group prioritized organizing across ethnic lines, and went on to found the Russian Social Democratic Labor Party, the Bund sought to orient the large numbers of Yiddish-speaking Jewish workers toward class struggle and succeeded in becoming a driving force in Jewish politics until World War II.

Despite its sweeping goals, and ultimate geographic spread, the Bund was recognized in its heyday, and later by scholars, as very much a product of its Lithuanian social, economic, and intellectual context. The struggle for the eight-hour workday in Russia began in Jewish workshops in small towns in Lithuania, while Vilna's position as a culturally Polish intellectual center in Russia put it at the confluence of the Polish and Russian socialist trends that converged in Bundist ideology. Bundism spread throughout Russia and Poland in the early twentieth century, but "its leadership remained chiefly of 'Lithuanian' stock, and the primacy of Vilna, the movement's birthplace and the Jewish cultural capital of the region, was never challenged."[21] Jonathan Frankel argued that access to the Lithuanian dialect of Yiddish helped spread social democracy among Litvaks more than Polish or Ukrainian Jews, where labor activism nonetheless did take hold, especially in cosmopolitan centers such as Odessa.[22] The Bund's on-the-ground militancy was forged in the experience of strike and workday actions in Lithuania, its social organization and systematic programs based on existing standards, and its reliance on the dissemination of Marxist literature in Yiddish due to Vilna's status as a center of intellectual life and Jewish publishing. According to one observer, the "pioneers of the Bund were classic Litvaks," or Lithuanian Jews.[23] Reflecting the deeply rooted, historic "regional perception" of local Jews, in 1901 the Bund added Lithuania to the territorial definition in its name, although no such political entity existed on the map at that time.[24]

Doikayt and the Memory of Lithuanian Jewish Regionalism

While the Bund went on to forge important political alliances, publish dozens of newspapers, and become a major political party in interwar Poland, its general position of regionalism has been one of its most lasting legacies. Following World War II, the Bund's attachment to Lithuania, and to working in situ more broadly, has been encapsulated by Bundists and scholars alike under the aegis of the term *doikayt*, or "hereness" in Yiddish. Ezra Mendelsohn defined the term as supporting the "belief that the struggle for Jewish equality and national rights must be fought and won in the Russian empire and in the other centers of East European Jewish life."[25] But the term has been most often evoked to describe the Bund's specific investment in European politics as opposed to territorial Zionism and plans for Jewish life in Palestine, even being described as "a key Bundist idea before the Second World War" and "the Bund's central ideology."[26]

The pre–World War II Bund did prioritize working in the diaspora, and leading Bundist thinkers such as Vladimir Medem and Henryk Ehrlich deployed the terms *do* and *dort*—"here" and "there" in Yiddish—to differentiate the *Gegenwartsarbeit* (German for "work in the present") position of the Bund from the Palestinism of some strands of Zionism. But despite the strong postwar association of the Bund with *doikayt*, there is little evidence that *doikayt* circulated as a meaningful Bundist term before World War II. Some Polish Bundists did refer to *doikayt* after the war, perhaps as a result of the more direct political competition between Bundists and Zionists in late 1930s Poland, or having taken up the term from others who used it in the postwar period, or as a result of a combination of both.[27]

But *doikayt* does appear to have emerged from Lithuania. The term took on a special significance there, where the Zionist camp came into direct conflict with an expressly Lithuanian regionalist party, the Folkists. Folkism was pioneered by historian Simon Dubnow in 1906, in response to Russian Zionists' adoption of a *Gegenwartsarbeit* program at the at the Helsingfors Conference. The following year, in a Folkist manifesto, Dubnow outlined his plan for a general Jewish party that sought autonomous rights in Russia and other more liberal states in the future. While Dubnow was not against Zionism per se, his vision was for a party to represent all Jews, especially what he understood to be the vast majority who lived outside of Palestine. In Dubnow's other writings, he also championed a broader philosophy of Jewish diasporism that argued that Jews in Europe should be treated in the same manner as other peoples more commonly considered indigenous there.

In addition to this rights regime and the call to recognize the historic Jewish place in Europe, Lithuanian Folkism, in contrast to the iteration of the *Folkspartey* that formed in interwar Poland, drew on strains of Jewish Lithuanian regionalism that were circulating in the early twentieth century. Partly inspired by the emergent nationalist movement for speakers of Lithuanian, and partly by a romantic movement that sought to revive the medieval, multiethnic Grand Duchy of Lithuania, some Lithuanian Jewish political activists in the 1910s advanced the idea that Jews are indigenous to Lithuania. One such figure, Uriah Katzenelenbogen, was, at various times in his life, a Bundist, a member of the duchy revivalist circles, and a supporter of Lithuanian nationalism. In the 1910s and early 1920s, he and like-minded Jews published a journal called *Lite* ("Lithuania" in Yiddish) that aired these views for Jewish readers.[28]

Katzenelenbogen was among the Lithuanian Jews who put their energy into a Folkist party in the interwar republic of Lithuania, which ironically had a relatively weak Bundist movement compared to neighboring Poland and Latvia. In Lithuania, Folkists became the main adversaries of the very popular Zionist movement. Until 1926, Lithuania had in place a system of national cultural autonomy for certain minorities, including Jews, which prompted public debates over the nature of autonomous institutions such as the school system. Zionist political activists and Folkists alike supported the system of autonomy but sparred over issues such as the language of instruction (Yiddish versus Hebrew). In a period of renewed government support for autonomy, in 1926, leading Folkist Yudl Mark and Zionist politician Jacob Robinson exchanged essays in the Lithuanian Yiddish press over how the nature of Jewish autonomy in Lithuania raised important questions about the very nature of the Jews as a group. It was in this context that Mark introduced the term *doikayt* to distinguish the Folkists' permanent and principled investment in institutions of autonomy (and the diaspora more broadly) from the Zionists' temporary and practical enthusiasm for such projects. The meaning of *doikayt* became a central concern of this exchange. Many pre- and postwar Lithuanian Jewish texts that used the term *doikayt* associated it closely with the *Folkspartey*, rather than the Bund.[29]

The Folkists lacked a robust economic program—the movement positioned itself as a moderate Jewish alternative to socialism and Zionism—but they held a radical conception of Jewish place. Folkism and Bundism were working through similar problems and shared some intellectual influences. They were also led by one family: Simon Dubnow, of the *Folkspartey*, was the father-in-law of Henryk Ehrlich, the leading Polish Bundist. Significantly, the regionalisms of both the early Bund and of the Folkists who used the term *doikayt* were rooted in an attachment to the geography and historical particularity of Lithuania. It is no wonder that Ezra Mendelsohn remarked, "In Lithuania . . . the children of the Haskalah became the founders of modern Jewish politics."[30]

Conclusion

Lithuanian Jewish radical politics transformed Eastern Europe. But "the constant migration from the overcrowded and economically underdeveloped Lithuania" to the United States, South Africa, and elsewhere around the world was perhaps the Lithuanian Jewish labor movement's greatest legacy.[31] The global Jewish labor movement, as Tony Michels has shown, was not monodirectional, but existed for decades as a transatlantic exchange of ideas and strategies.[32] Nonetheless, the Lithuanian Jewish experience was common ground for Jewish activists as geographically diverse as Baruch Vladeck (born near Minsk in 1886), who helped shape public housing in New York City, to Joe Slovo (born in northern Lithuania in 1926), who was at the forefront of the fight against apartheid in South Africa. These Lithuanian Jews steeped in the labor tradition not only saw their surroundings through the lens of one corner of northeastern Europe but sought to shape the world in that image.

And yet, it was not preordained that Lithuanian Jewish workers would coalesce into a class-based movement, although it may seem that way today. Rather, Lithuanian Jews followed their own dangerous and radical path to a Jewish working class, a path whose contours, as some scholars have observed, were similar to that taken by the working class in England—for example, in the replacement of skilled men by women and agricultural workers, or the use of Russian scabs to replace Jewish workers, recalling Irish strikebreakers in England.[33] But it was also a path that cut through the particular historical terrain of Lithuanian Jewry, rooted in the locals' material realities. To paraphrase E. P. Thompson's memorable expression to describe the agency of English labor activists, the Lithuanian Jewish working class was present at its own making.

NOTES

1. Darius Staliūnas, "Dusetos, Easter 1905: The Story of One Pogrom," *Journal of Baltic Studies* 43, no. 4 (December 2012), 495.
2. Moshe Mishinski, "Regional Factors in the Formation of the Jewish Labor Movement in Czarist Russia," in *YIVO Annual of Jewish Social Science* XIV, ed. Shlomo Bickel et al. (New York: YIVO Institute for Jewish Research, 1969), 28–29.
3. As quoted, for example, in *Di geshikhte fun Bund I*, ed. G. Aronson, S. H. Dubnov-Erlich, Y. Sh. Hertz, E. Novogrudski, H. S. Kazdan, and Emanuel Scherer (New York: Unzer Tsait, 1960), 91–92. Plekhanov referred to Jews in "western Russia" where "factory industry was weakly developed" (i.e., Lithuania).
4. Matvei, "Der bibliograf fun 'Bund': Mordkhe Yevzerov ('Volodie')," in *Historisher zamlbukh: materyaln un dokumentn tsushtayer tsu der geshikhte fun algemeynem yidishn arbeterbund* (Warsaw: Ringen, 1948), 25.
5. Simon Dubnow, *History of the Jews in Russia and Poland*, vol. 1, trans. Israel Friedlaender (Philadelphia: Jewish Publication Society, 1916), 59–60.
6. Yoav Peled and Gershon Shafir, "From Caste to Exclusion: The Dynamics of Modernization in the Russian Pale of Settlement," *Studies in Contemporary Jewry*, vol. 3 (Jerusalem: Hebrew University of Jerusalem, 1987), 98 and 105.
7. Tomas Balkelis, *The Making of Modern Lithuania* (New York: Routledge, 2009), 2. The phrase "double periphery" was originally applied to the Soviet Union's Kaliningrad Oblast, bordering Lithuania on the Baltic Sea.
8. Mishinski, "Regional Factors," 39.
9. Mishinski, "Regional Factors," 39.
10. Ezra Mendelsohn, "The Russian Jewish Labor Movement, and Others," *YIVO Annual* XIV, 92.
11. Mendelsohn, "Russian Jewish Labor Movement," 93.
12. Mendelsohn, "Russian Jewish Labor Movement," 93. See also Eli Lederhendler, "Classless: On the Social Status of Jews in Russia and Eastern Europe in the Late Nineteenth Century," *Comparative Studies in Society and History* 50, no. 2 (April 2008), 518.
13. Ezra Mendelsohn, *Class Struggle in the Pale: The Formative Years of the Jewish Workers' Movement in Tsarist Russia* (Cambridge: Cambridge University Press, 1970), 37.
14. E. P. Thompson, *The Making of the English Working Class* (New York: Vintage, 1966), 43–44.
15. Eli Lederhendler makes such an argument about Hasidism and socialist organizing, but the movements have different geographic origins. See Lederhendler, "Classless," 525–530.
16. Eliyahu Stern, *Jewish Materialism: The Intellectual Revolution of the 1870s* (New Haven: Yale University Press, 2018), 132–134.
17. Jonathan Frankel, *Prophecy and Politics: Socialism, Nationalism, and the Russian Jews, 1862–1917* (Cambridge: Cambridge University Press, 1981), 173.
18. Mishinski, "Regional Factors," 44.
19. Inna Shtakser, *The Making of Jewish Revolutionaries in the Pale of Settlement: Community and Identity During the Russian Revolution and Its Immediate Aftermath, 1905–07* (New York: Palgrave, 2014), 25.
20. Arkadi Kremer, "Di grindung fun Bund," in *Arkadi: zamlbukh tsum ondenk fun Arkadi Kremer* (New York: Unzer Tsait, 1942), 361.
21. Mendelsohn, *Class Struggle*, xi.

22. Frankel, *Prophecy and Politics*, 203.

23. Joshua Zimmerman, *Poles, Jews, and the Politics of Nationality: The Bund and the Socialist Party in Late Tsarist Russia, 1892–1914* (Madison: University of Wisconsin Press, 2004), 41.

24. Zimmerman, *Poles, Jews, and the Politics of Nationality*, 123.

25. Ezra Mendelsohn, *The Jews of East Central Europe between the World Wars* (Bloomington: Indiana University Press, 1987), 44.

26. Roni Gechtman, "Nationalising the Bund? Zionist Historiography and the Jewish Labor Movement," *East European Jewish Affairs* 43, no. 3 (2013), 261 n. 41; Joshua Karlip, *The Tragedy of a Generation: The Rise and Fall of Jewish Nationalism in Eastern Europe* (Cambridge: Harvard University Press, 2013), 230.

27. For a detailed discussion of *doikayt*, see Michael Casper, "'Principled Diasporism': Folkists, Zionists, and the Meaning of *Doikayt*," *Simon Dubnow Institute Yearbook* 17 (2018): 57–85.

28. See Michael Casper, "Strangers and Sojourners: The Politics of Jewish Belonging in Lithuania, 1914–1940" (PhD diss., University of California, Los Angeles, 2019), chapter 1.

29. Casper, "'Principled Diasporism,'" 14–20.

30. Mendelsohn, *The Jews of East Central Europe*, 22.

31. Frankel, *Prophecy and Politics*, 173.

32. Tony Michels, *A Fire in Their Hearts: Yiddish Socialists in New York* (Cambridge: Harvard University Press, 2009).

33. Peled and Shafir, "From Caste to Exclusion," 106; Mendelsohn, *Class Struggle*, 101.

CHAPTER 13

Communists and Zionists in Hungary, 1945–1953

Peter Kenez

Hungarian Jewry was unique in many respects, including in its relationship to radical politics. In the century before the Holocaust, unlike in any other country, Jews came close to dominating the economy and the intellectual professions. They were also represented disproportionately in the leadership ranks of the country's socialist and communist movements. Moreover, nowhere was the gap wider between acculturated Jews, who were in the majority, and the significant Haredi or ultra-Orthodox minority, who were more separatist and religiously zealous when it came to issues such as anti-Zionism and the education of girls than in any other country. Finally, while much of Hungarian Jewry possessed a Western European, liberal sensibility, it existed in an Eastern European political environment that was conservative and autocratic.

Although Jews had lived in the Hungarian kingdom since its establishment in the Middle Ages, their number was small. Only after the liberation of the country from Ottoman occupation at the end of the seventeenth century did a sizeable community develop. After the devastation of 150 years of Ottoman rule the Habsburg court and the Hungarian nobility welcomed immigrants, among them Jews. Unlike in the Russian Empire, where the vast majority of Jews came to reside within its borders as a result of the three Partitions of Poland—that is, through processes of imperial expansion and colonialism—most Jews arrived in Hungary during this period voluntarily. Once there, they were encouraged by the state to help grow the economy and did not face the same kinds of draconian restrictions that marked the much larger Jewish population in the Pale of Settlement, as the territory to which most Jews were restricted in the Russian Empire came to be known.

In the nineteenth century, the Hungarian nobility sought to encourage the industrialization of the country, but it was not a task that its members were either able or willing to take on themselves. Hungarian-speaking nobles controlled political life and ruled over and exploited a multinational peasantry. Within this environment, Jews soon came to make up the middle class. The country offered numerous economic opportunities and Jews were ready to take advantage of them. In 1867, with the establishment of the Austro-Hungarian monarchy, Jews were emancipated—that is, special laws that had previously applied only to them were abolished. In the following decades, most Jews enthusiastically identified with the Hungarian nationalist cause, and typically defined themselves as Jewish Hungarians rather than Hungarian Jews.

This golden age for Hungarian Jewry, however, did not outlast the Austro-Hungarian Empire. The First World War was disastrous for Hungary. The country lost 72 percent of its territory and 64 percent of its population. In the short-lived communist regime or Hungarian Soviet Republic of 1919 that followed the peace, at least three-quarters of the "people's commissars" were Jewish, including its leader Béla Kun. Although most Hungarian Jews were neither socialists nor communists, it is not surprising that they dominated the communist leadership since it was largely made up of the intelligentsia, and the intelligentsia in Hungary was overwhelmingly Jewish. Some Jewish communist leaders came from Orthodox families and their rejection of their parents' faith pushed them into extreme solutions. Others rebelled against their bourgeois backgrounds, such as the famous Marxist philosopher Georg Lukács, the son of a newly ennobled Jewish industrialist, who rejected his father's wealth and status. A dramatic rise in antisemitism following the war also convinced many Jews that their integration into Hungarian society was less complete and more contested than they had previously believed. Against this backdrop, Marxist internationalism appeared to offer Hungarian Jewish radicals from a variety of backgrounds a path to normalization and national belonging.

The long-standing alliance between the ruling classes and Jewry that had propelled the latter into positions of prominence in numerous sectors of Hungarian society thus ended ignominiously. The interwar Hungarian regime, headed by Governor Admiral Horthy, was fervently nationalist, deeply conservative, and explicitly antisemitic. Nationalist propagandists equated Judaism and Bolshevism and narrowly defined the Hungarian nation to exclude Jews. Hungary was the first European country in the 1920s to introduce an explicitly antisemitic law—the *numerus clausus*—that limited the percentage of Jewish students at universities to the percentage of Jews in the population. Within a short period, the number of Jewish university students declined from 30 to only 5 percent.

Hungary also became an early ally of Nazi Germany because Hungarian nationalists expected that a victorious Germany would redraw the borders established at Versailles. In the late 1930s and in the beginning stages of the Second World War, the government passed ever stronger antisemitic laws designed to limit Jewish economic and cultural influence. Although the first years of the conflict were difficult for Hungary's Jews, their lives were not in danger. In spite of Hitler's repeated urging, Admiral Horthy had refused to consent to the deportation of the Jews to death camps. At the beginning of March 1944, around eight hundred thousand Jews were still living within Hungary's borders. Yet after the Germans occupied allied Hungary on March 19, 1944, deportations to Auschwitz almost immediately commenced. In a remarkably short time, with enthusiastic help from many Hungarians, the Nazis managed to murder two-thirds of the Jews who had lived in the country at the time of the outbreak of war.

The Eastern European nations that were liberated by the Red Army shared similar fates. Between 1945 and 1948 these countries moved from limited pluralist regimes to one-party dictatorships. Hungary differed from its sister states only in that the entire top leadership was Jewish. The so-called "quartet" of Mátyás Rákosi, Ernö Gerö, Mihály Farkas, and József Révai had spent the war years in the Soviet Union and therefore were well known to Stalin. Rákosi, Gerö, and Révai came from middle-class families and were regarded as intellectuals, while Farkas came from the bottom of society. All of them devoted their entire lives to the communist cause. Rákosi, the head of the Party, and therefore the leader of the country, was a particularly hated man in Hungary. He aimed to be the best student of comrade Stalin, and probably succeeded. Although Jews were represented disproportionately in all socialist and, in particular, communist leadership cadres, nowhere was the dominance of Jews as overwhelming and visible as in Hungary. It is impossible to exaggerate the significance of this fact. From the point of view of most Hungarians, the country was ruled by one group of foreigners (i.e., Russians), and administered by another group of foreigners (i.e., Jews).

In 1953, following Stalin's death, Hungarian communist leaders were summoned to Moscow and told that they should have more Hungarians in the leadership, implying that Jews were not Hungarians. This was precisely what a majority of Hungarians themselves thought. Indeed, Soviet leaders chose Imre Nagy to be Hungary's premier because he was not Jewish. Nevertheless, until after the Revolution of 1956, Jews continued to dominate the country's communist leadership and the fact that it was Hungary among all the countries of Eastern Europe that first rebelled against Soviet rule had much to do with native antisemitism.

In Hungary, as elsewhere in Eastern Europe, the remnants of the once large and economically thriving Jewish community found it extremely difficult to reestablish their way of life and adjust to the new Soviet-dominated country. In light of the enthusiastic collaboration of many Hungarians in the mass murder of their Jewish compatriots, many Jews, especially younger ones, came to the conclusion that they could have no place in communist Hungary. It was evident to any observer that the wartime suffering of Jews had not diminished popular antisemitism. When war criminals were brought to justice it seemed to many, if not most, Hungarians that this represented a Jewish vendetta rather than well-deserved punishment; Hungarians who were themselves responsible for Jewish suffering were unwilling to accept responsibility.

The fact that the communist leaders of the Soviet-installed regime in Hungary were disproportionally Jewish did not make the lives of the survivors easier. Jewish communist leaders well understood that helping other Jews who had returned to Hungary from concentration camps in the hopes of reclaiming their property was politically harmful. They could see that to identify the Communist Party with Jewish interests and concerns would make their unpopularity even greater. Jewish communist leaders therefore made every attempt to distance themselves and their regime from their own ethnic background and did not hesitate to encourage latent antisemitism by calling for a struggle against "black marketeers," which many Hungarians understood as a struggle against Jews.

The communists, given their hostility to free markets, naturally blamed the dire economic postwar situation on speculators. On this volatile issue their anticapitalist demagogy easily slipped into antisemitism, at times with tragic consequences. In 1946 a series of pogroms took place in Hungary. Communist agitation against small businesses and "speculators" contributed to the atmosphere in which such pogroms were possible. The party decided to use the dreadful economic situation and misery of the postwar period, including an extraordinarily high rate of inflation, widespread starvation, and the destruction of urban areas, to sharpen the class struggle, which in reality meant making small traders scapegoats for the country's genuine problems. In this struggle, the communists explicitly approved of—indeed, advocated for—mass spontaneous demonstrations, and even spontaneous murders.

The party had organized a struggle against "speculators" by promising to hang those who traded in the black market. The leaders knew or certainly should have known that many of these traders were Jewish, and even if they were not, in the eyes of the common folk they were. The government published posters in which the "enemy," the capitalist, the speculator, often had stereotypically Semitic features. The communists did not create antisemitism during this period, but consciously or unconsciously they contributed to its metastasis in Hungary.[1] In the industrial town of Miskolc the struggle against "speculators" turned into a pogrom against Jews. In the little town of Kunmadaras even the blood libel was resurrected. In Hungary, unlike in postwar Poland, the pogroms had only a handful of victims. Nevertheless, the negative attitude of a large segment of the Hungarian population toward their Jewish compatriots was unmistakable.

The new government, of course, rescinded antisemitic legislation that was the inheritance of the Horthy regime, and it officially condemned antisemitism. However, the Jews had reason to be concerned. The attitude of the regime to the Jews could already be seen from the very beginning. In the very first issue of *Szabad Nép* (Free People), the communist newspaper, on March 25, 1945 (i.e., even before all the concentration camps were liberated), József Darvas, a leader of the Peasant Party and a crypto-communist politician, published an important article.[2] Entitled "An Honest Word on the Jewish Question," its chief point was that the Jews should not expect special consideration because they had suffered during the war.[3] Darvas's argument, soon repeated many times by other politicians, was that other Hungarians had also suffered and by implication there was nothing special about the fate of the Jews. In this respect, Hungarian politicians were no different than the Soviet leadership, which also refused to discuss what had happened to the Jews in the very near past. Jews returning from camps should not necessarily be able to reclaim their lost and confiscated property. Those Jews who were not willing to live in a democratic country and work, as all other decent workers did, should be expelled together with all other saboteurs and reactionaries, Darvas wrote. One might say that at that historical moment such a statement had a rather unpleasant connotation, to put it mildly.

At a time of competition among parties for public support, the leaders of the major political parties well understood that paying much attention to Jewish suffering was not a way to build political capital. Among the parties the most complicated relations were between the Communist Party and the Jews. On the one hand, the top leaders, as nowhere else in the world, were almost exclusively Jewish. The Stalinist leadership had chosen these men because they had spent a large part of their careers in the Soviet Union and, consequently, Stalin was likely to know them personally. Jews played major roles in the security services because they had no Nazi background and were considered to be trustworthy. They also served in significant numbers in the propaganda apparatus, including the communist editorial offices, inasmuch as they were more likely to be intellectuals and therefore appropriate for the task. They were also more likely to know foreign languages than the native communists who had worked in the Hungarian underground.

Although most Jews in Hungary did not support the Communist Party, a larger percentage of them did than the population as a whole. According to contemporary estimates, in 1945 a quarter of Hungarian Jews voted for the communists at a time when the party received only 17 percent of the vote nationally.[4] Undoubtedly Jewish influence in Hungary was greatly overrated in the public mind. However unfair, for many Hungarians, Judaism and communism were almost identical. This identification at least in part may have reflected the survival of a major Nazi propaganda trope.

None of the Jewish communist leaders ever demonstrated genuine sympathy for Jewish causes. It was essential for them to avoid Jewish identification and consequently they were less hesitant to attract support from "little Nazis" who had provided the backbone of the short-lived *Nyilas* rule.[5] After all, in the 1930s the extreme right-wing party had attracted large working-class support. The ironic consequence was that the Communist Party, which attracted the most Jewish supporters and whose leaders were largely Jewish, was at the same time also the most antisemitic. The Communist Party had the largest percentage of people who had played minor roles in the short-lived Hungarian Nazi regime. In a speech at a university, Rákosi made it explicit: Those who had been responsible for terror should be severely punished, but those little people who had been misled must be forgiven. Rákosi argued that people who had been misled by fascist propagandists ought not be excluded from the work of national reconstruction.[6]

In this climate, it is not surprising that for the first time in Hungary's history, Zionists managed to build a significant movement and attract a sizeable following. Nevertheless, even though Zionists achieved their greatest success in Hungary in the postwar period, the desire to leave the country for Palestine among the country's Jews was not comparable to what was happening in the rest of Eastern

Europe. After the war, the remnants of once thriving Polish and Romanian Jewish communities for all practical purposes disappeared as most survivors left for Palestine or elsewhere. By contrast, a higher percentage of Hungary's Jews remained and today the country has the largest Jewish community in Eastern Europe. The explanation for this phenomenon should not be sought in differences between the policies of various communist regimes. It was the consequence of the simple fact that, despite their dreadful wartime experiences and the ongoing animosity of many of their compatriots, most Hungarian Jews continued to regard themselves as above all Hungarians—even though a majority of their countrymen viewed them as aliens. In short, due to their high degree of acculturation, a majority of Jews who had survived still believed that they could create a new life in the country of their birth. Therefore, although Zionists were able to attract a following, especially among the young, a majority of Hungarian Jews never accepted the promise of normalcy offered by Zionism.

Relations between communists and Zionists in postwar Hungary were initially complicated and ultimately highly contentious. These relations should be divided into two discrete periods, 1945–1948 and 1948–1953. At first, Zionist organizations could function legally and the attitude of the party leadership toward the movement was ambivalent and contradictory. After 1948, however, Zionists were mercilessly repressed and their leaders jailed. The postwar pogroms in Hungary had convinced Zionists that the reconstruction of the old way of life for Jews would not be possible.[7] Especially among the young, there was a sense that antisemitism was everywhere. Many of them became interested in the possibility of moving to a future Jewish state. This was the lesson that they had learned from the Holocaust and its aftermath in the country.

The Hungarian Zionist Organization, which in the interwar period hardly existed, had 37,000 members in 1948.[8] Remarkably, 12,000 of these were also members of the Communist Party, and perhaps an even larger number were members of the Socialist Party. Jews gravitated toward left-wing parties at least partly because they took it for granted that these would be the least likely to be antisemitic. Many Jews also regarded the Marxist promise of a more just society as harmonious with Jewish religious teachings. Even before the conclusion of the war in April 1945, the Hungarian socialist Zionists petitioned the leadership of the Socialist Party to be accepted as an independent organization under its umbrella. In their letter, the Zionists offered their most sincere cooperation but asked to be consulted on Jewish matters. The letter also pointed out that the socialist movement was very active in Palestine and that it was recognized as a member of the Second International.[9] However, the major goal of the Zionists (i.e., leaving the country legally), would prove to be impossible. At first, emigration was difficult because of British policies in Palestine and later because of the attitude of the Hungarian state.

Nevertheless, in the immediate postwar years, the Zionist movement flourished in Hungary. Zionist arguments against the assimilationists made sense in the prevailing environment. Zionist activists for the first time were able to acquire important roles in the leadership of the country's major Jewish organizations. In the provincial cities, the Zionists also managed to capture important leadership positions in local Jewish institutions. Zionists could point out that they had played a disproportionate role in the very small anti-Nazi movement. The fact that many Jewish leaders had been compromised by their efforts during the German occupation of the country to find a modus vivendi with the Nazis made the Zionists' task easier. The Zionists also won over some of Hungary's most influential rabbis, among them Fabian Hershkovits, who had been appointed head rabbi of the country's most important synagogue, on Dohány Street.[10] Hershkovits also served as the vice president of the Zionist organization and his sermons were delivered in a Zionist key. He was among the Jewish leaders who had behaved courageously during the Holocaust and consequently enjoyed prestige after liberation. When József Darvas published his aforementioned article blaming Jews who had returned from the camps for being too demanding, Hershkovits answered him.[11] The rabbi gave Darvas credit for bringing up the Jewish Question explicitly. From his point of view, mentioning that there was a Jewish Question was a positive step, for it implied that Jews were not simply Hungarians who had a different religion.[12]

The Zionist movement was further helped by the American Jewish Joint Distribution Committee or the Joint, which provided a generous amount of badly needed financial support in immediate postwar Hungary, alleviating starvation among the country's Jews. In addition, Zionist leaders acquired important positions in the Joint's leadership and helped to advance Zionist causes. In relation to the Joint the communist leaders were put in a difficult situation. On the one hand, they were well aware of the significance of the material support that the Jewish agency gave to the country. On the other hand, they regarded the Joint as a fundamentally hostile organization.[13] For some time, they hesitated to close down the organization's operations in Hungary, since the party directly benefitted from it financially. The organization again and again bribed the authorities to allow some Jews to leave the country. Its director, Israel Jacobson, an American Jew, represented the Joint in Hungary.[14] In December 1949, he was arrested, mistreated in prison, and forced to confess that the task of the organization was to spy in Hungary. After two weeks in jail, he was allowed to leave the country. In the spring of 1950, the Joint's activities in Hungary came to an end.[15]

From the outset, Communist Party took a hostile attitude to the Zionist movement. When for the first time Zionists demonstrated in the streets of Budapest in June 1945, singing in Hebrew, *Szabad Nép* published a short article about the demonstration, entitled "Bad Politics." According to the newspaper, people passing by in the street were reminded of Hitler Youth marches. In the opinion of the journalist, the demonstrators harmed both the cause of democracy and the interests of Hungarian Jews by underlining their separateness.[16] The prominent communist politician, playwright, and intellectual Gyula Háy went even further. In a bitterly hostile review of an insignificant play, *Timosa*, he equated Zionism and fascism. The play evidently attempted to demonstrate the distinctiveness of the country's Jews.[17] For Háy, the Zionist street demonstrations and speeches of Rabbi Hershkovits were fascist actions.

In the same period, Erik Molnár, a communist intellectual and politician, wrote an extensive article on the Jewish Question in a sociological journal. In his view, there were two possible solutions: The reactionary solution was Zionism; the Zionists were reactionaries even if they regarded themselves as socialists. The progressive solution was the complete integration of Jews into the nation. The victory of democracy would solve the Jewish Question.[18] After the pogrom in Kunmadaras, the Jewish Question had become so important to the party leadership that two months later, in the same sociological journal, Márton Horváth, a member of the Politburo, responded to Molnár's article. Horváth, unlike Molnár, came from a Jewish family.[19] Also, unlike Molnár, Horváth conceded that assimilation up to this point had been a failure. He argued that Hungarians should show understanding to the members of the Jewish petit bourgeoisie who assumed that assimilation had failed and therefore turned to Zionism. The task, he continued, was to explain to these people that the attempt to assimilate was not a mistake. The common task going forward, he argued, was to build a democratic society in which Jews could live as Hungarians. This slightly modified view of Zionism came to be the official communist position in 1949, in the window before the creation of a government fully controlled by communists.

The attitude of the Communist Party to Zionism was contradictory. On the one hand, the party opposed Zionism as an ideology with greater or lesser degrees of venom. On the other hand, at least in the earliest years, it silently tolerated Zionist activities. That toleration went so far that Budapest for a short time came to be an Eastern European center of Zionist activities. Zionists from Romania and Czechoslovakia came to Hungary and local Zionists provided them with places to stay and organized transports to Vienna from where they proceeded illegally to Palestine.[20] Perhaps thirty to fifty thousand foreign Jews passed through Hungary in this fashion. At the same time, the Zionist movement in Hungary was thoroughly penetrated by Jewish communist agents. The communist-dominated political police were well informed about Zionist activities. One can only speculate as to why, in spite of their often-expressed hostility to Zionism, the Jewish leaders of the Communist Party closed their eyes to what was happening. One reason might have been that Zionists paid for this tolerance by providing the party with much needed foreign currency. But perhaps the most significant reason was not monetary.

In view of what had happened to Hungary's Jews in the very recent past, including the small-scale pogroms that had received wide publicity, communist leaders did not want to embark on what would be perceived as an anti-Jewish campaign. Since the Soviet leadership was also aware of what was happening in the country and raised no objections, it might be that the approach of local communists served the Soviet goal of embarrassing the British, who, at this point, were restricting Jewish settlement in Palestine for their own reasons. Conceivably, the communist leaders also did not want to alienate international Jewry, for they believed, as so many had before and since, that Jews had considerable power in international life and Jewish influence might make a difference in the unfolding peace negotiations.

Indeed, representatives of Hungarian Jewry did request that the diplomats of the 1946 Paris Peace Conference should provide for a just peace for Hungary and help Hungarians with their dire economic situation.[21] After the 1946 pogroms were reported in the international media, Zionist leaders in Hungary repaid the tolerance showed by the Communist Party by supporting various communist causes and expressing sympathy for Soviet policies.

Soviet leaders supported the establishment of the modern state of Israel for their own reasons. They understood that the establishment of a Jewish state would alienate the Arab world from Britain and the United States and enable the Soviet Union to find allies in the Middle East. From this it followed that the Hungarian communists, who by 1948 were in effective control of the government, also supported Jews in Palestine. The government allowed Czechoslovak armaments to flow through the country to Jewish fighters, and the Zionists were allowed to collect financial support.[22] Yet even as the Hungarian communists and therefore the Hungarian government supported the establishment of the Jewish state, following the Soviet example they objected to the efforts of local Zionists to persuade the country's Jews to move to the Jewish state. While supporting the Jews in Palestine, therefore, Hungarian communists were nevertheless determined to destroy the Zionist movement in Hungary.

The year 1948 was a turning point in Soviet policy toward Jews. The enthusiastic reception that Soviet Jews gave to the first Israeli ambassador, Golda Meir, when she visited the country may have aroused fear that Jews had dual loyalty—and that could not be tolerated. The shifting Soviet attitude toward Jews, in general, had consequences for their treatment of Zionism in the Soviet sphere of influence. Soviet, and therefore Czechoslovak, support in giving munitions to the Jews in Palestine abruptly stopped. It may have been that after the establishment of Israel, it became increasingly clear that the state would follow a basically Western-oriented foreign policy. Moreover, since the British were out of Palestine, there was no longer any way to embarrass them by highlighting their "imperialist" behavior in the territory.

In Hungary, the attitude of the communist leadership changed immediately. In practical terms it led to the repression of the Zionist movement and jailing of numerous Zionist activists. Zionist organizations were also closed down. The campaign against Zionism, whose explicit goal had been to persuade Jews to leave the country for Israel, took place at a time when Hungary was introducing ever stricter regulations against free movement out of the country. This was done for political reasons: People needed to learn to behave since they no longer had the opportunity simply to go away. After all, a totalitarian regime cannot exist as long as its citizens have the choice of leaving. The country's borders came to be closed for all intents and purposes until the revolution of 1956. According to Béla Dénes, a leader of the Zionist movement, he had two conversations with Rákosi, who told him explicitly that the Zionist movement could exist in Hungary only as long as there was a coalition government. Yet once a "dictatorship of the proletariat" was established—in other words, once the communists achieved total power—the

Zionist movement would cease to exist and its leaders would be imprisoned.[23] The violent suppression of the Zionist movement in Romania that took place a short time before the Hungarian communists seized complete power was also a warning signal to Zionists in the country.

The Zionists naively believed that if their movement had a more left-wing orientation it would have a better chance of survival. As a consequence, the most communist-inclined individuals assumed positions of leadership within the Hungarian Zionist organization in the course of 1948. That, however, made no difference. Indeed, it was precisely those leaders who in March 1949 were compelled "voluntarily" to dissolve the Hungarian Zionist Union.[24] Some illegal emigration to Israel continued for a short while. According to George Garai's figures, in 1949 and 1950 something like nine thousand Hungarian Jews reached the Jewish state.[25] After the closing of the Austria-Hungary border most of the emigrants went through Czechoslovakia. Very soon, however, the Czechoslovak attitude changed. The border guards arrested those who had attempted to escape and sent them back to Hungary, where they were jailed.

In April and May of 1949, all of the prominent Hungarian Zionist leaders were arrested and Zionism became a criminal offense.[26] Its principles came to be regarded as treasonous. The accusations against the leaders included currency speculation, helping people to cross the border illegally, and spying for Israel. Between 1948 and 1949, Israel became an imperialist state in communist parlance. Béla Dénes was accused of regularly supplying the Israeli Embassy with spy reports. What kind of information would have been useful for the Israeli state was never made clear.

The chief Hungarian political purge trial that took place in 1949 was that of László Rajk, one of the few non-Jewish top communists and, at one time, minister of the interior. In that capacity, Rajk was responsible for repressing the opposition. The main theme of the trial was that Rajk had collaborated with the Yugoslav leader Tito, who was supposedly an agent of Western imperialism. By contrast, Zionism was only a minor theme at the trial. However, the second and third significant defendants were Tibor Szőnyi and András Szalai, both of whom had been at one point in their careers left-wing Zionists and communists. Under pressure, Szőnyi "confessed" that the Zionist movement had closely cooperated with the American Secret Service. Together with Rajk, Szőnyi, and Szalai were sentenced to death and subsequently executed.

However hostile the communist regime was to Zionism, diplomatic relations with Israel were not broken. Negotiations even continued concerning the possibility of allowing some Jews to leave. The communists' primary interest in these dealings was financial. In exchange for allowing 3,100 Jews to emigrate, Hungary received $30,000 per person. In addition, the Joint made a million-dollar contribution to the reequipment of the Jewish hospital, after which it was quickly nationalized by the regime.[27] Jewish emigrants could take with them valuables not exceeding 5,000 forints, which was more or less equivalent to leaving empty-handed. In the course of 1949, at a time when the Zionist Organization in Hungary had already dissolved itself, long negotiations nevertheless took place between Israeli diplomats and representatives of the Hungarian government. The final result was that Hungary allowed approximately three thousand individuals to leave. These were people who were older than fifty years old, had relatives in Israel, and in some cases had been leaders of the Zionist movement.[28] Even after signing the agreement, the Hungarian government made the departure of Jews so difficult that the last transport only left the country as late as 1951.

After 1949, Zionism, which never had deep roots in Hungary, had for all practical purposes disappeared from the country. The Alliance of Hungarian Zionists dissolved itself; the leaders were either allowed to emigrate or were in prison. Jewish cultural life became impoverished; Jewish schools and hospitals were closed down. Jews were particularly hard hit by the country's economic transformation and the nationalization of its institutions. Antisemitism, of course, did not disappear, but it was not government policy. Jews who were not admitted to universities, despite their good grades, were refused admission not because they were Jewish, but because they came from bourgeois families. Among those individuals who were deported from Budapest to distant and poor villages, allegedly to make room for more workers, were a disproportionate number of Jews. Indeed, according to estimates, fully a third of those deported from the capital were Jewish despite being approximately 2 percent of the overall population.[29] They became victims, however, not because of their religion, but because, from the regime's point of view, they represented the discredited and destroyed exploiting classes. Lajos Stöckler, the head of the organization of Hungarian Jewry, promised the regime that the organization would make it clear that the internal deportations had not taken place as part of an antisemitic program. His statement was sent on to Rákosi himself.[30] Yet Stöckler's attempt to cooperate did not save him—during the subsequent Eastern Europe–wide antisemitic campaign, he was arrested and mistreated so badly that his mind never recovered.

The last year of Stalin's life was the apogee of this antisemitic and anti-Zionist campaign. It was a time when even the Jewish wives of the president of the republic, Mikhail Kalinin, and of the foreign minister, Vyacheslav Molotov, were incarcerated in Soviet prison camps. Stalin's paranoid preoccupation with Jews concluded in the so-called Doctor's Plot, in which Jewish doctors were accused of attempting to murder high-ranking functionaries, including Stalin himself. They were saved only by Stalin's timely death.

For the rest of the Soviet bloc, especially in Romania and Czechoslovakia, the consequences of Stalin's death included the purging of high-ranking communist leaders. In Czechoslovakia, the prime victim was the Jewish Rudolf Slánský, the general secretary of the party, who was tried and executed. In Romania, the most important victim was Ana Pauker, at the conclusion of the Second World War the most powerful politician in the country. She was an obvious candidate for the purge since she was a Jew (her Orthodox father was a *shohet* or ritual slaughterer) and had a brother who lived in Israel. It is remarkable that in Hungary, where the proportion of leaders of Jewish background was by far the highest, the purge was relatively small-scale. The most prominent victim was Gábor Péter, the head of the political police, the man who had been primarily responsible for carrying out the party's terror campaign against its perceived opponents, initiated by Rákosi himself. Péter was accused of Zionist sympathies. Ironically, in his own preparation for the Rajk trial he had leveled the charge of Zionism against some of the Jewish accused.

The Communist paper *Szabad Nép* published a major editorial on January 15, 1953, concerning the Doctors' Plot, which emphasized the Jewish dimension of the conspiracy and held the Joint responsible, among other organizations. The editorial stressed that the Joint played a far greater role in Hungary than it did in the Soviet Union and pointed out that every shade of Zionism needed to be unmasked.[31] After 1953, the Zionist movement completely ceased to exist in Hungary. In 1956, following the defeat of the revolution the country's borders were temporarily opened and people emigrated, among them, according to estimates, approximately 20,000 Jews. Very few of these refugees chose Israel as their destination, yet another sign that Zionism never became a major force among Hungarian Jews.

The distinctive history of Hungary's Jews and, in particular, the vexed relationship between Zionists and communists in the postwar era raise interesting questions regarding Jewish social radicalism. Nowhere in the world did Jews play a greater role in the socialist and communist movements than in Hungary; nowhere were Jews more responsible for the suppression of a minor Zionist movement than in Hungary. The explanation for both of these phenomena must be found in the extraordinary success of Hungarian Jews during the late nineteenth and early twentieth centuries in the country's economic and cultural spheres. This success encouraged most Jews to identify with the Hungarian nationalist cause and think of themselves as good Hungarians. But this very success was also a source of rising antisemitism among the country's non-Jewish majority. While Jews may have thought of themselves as good Hungarians, most of their compatriots continued to think of them as aliens. Ultimately, their efforts at integration failed and that failure drove some Jews to Zionism and many more to forms of Marxist internationalism that promised to liberate humanity from the corrosive forces of nationalism.

NOTES

1. Peter Kenez, *Hungary from the Nazis to the Soviets: The Establishment of the Communist Regime in Hungary, 1944–1948* (New York: Cambridge University Pres, 2006), 159–160.
2. The Peasant Party was a left-wing organization that claimed to represent the interests of the poor in the countryside.
3. József Darvas, "Őszinte szót a zsidókérdésben," *Szabad Nép*, March 25, 1945.
4. Kenez, *Hungary from the Nazis to the Soviets*, 156.
5. The *Nyilaskereszt* Party or Arrow Cross Party was an extreme right-wing, antisemitic organization that existed in the 1930s and came to power on October 15, 1944. It was the closest Hungarian equivalent to the Nazi Party.
6. *Szabad Nép*, July 7, 1945, 3.
7. Kenez, *Hungary from the Nazis to the Soviets*, 159–161.
8. László Svéd, "A magyar zsidóság és a hatalom 1945–1955. Dokumentumok," *Múltunk*, vol. 2–3 (1993), 250.
9. Svéd, "A magyar zsidóság," 283

10. George Garai, *The Policy Towards the Jews, Zionism and Israel of the Hungarian Communist Party, 1945–1953* (PhD diss., London School of Economics, 1979), 49.
11. Darvas, "Őszinte szót a zsidókérdésben."
12. Strochlitz Institute for Holocaust Research, guide 2, Hungary, Hershkovits.
13. Zeitlinger, writing to Communist Party Central Committee, July 31, 1947, Ministry of Social Service, 274.
14. Gábor Kiszely, *AVH. Egy Terrorszervezet Tortenete* (Budapest, Korona, 2000), 291.
15. Kiszely, *AVH*, 276.
16. *Szabad Nép*, June 22, 1945, 3.
17. Gyula Háy, *Szabad Nép*, July 5, 1945, 5.
18. *Társadalmi Szemle*, no. 5 (1946): 326–334.
19. Márton Horváth, *Társadalmi Szemle*, no. 7 (1946): 495–501.
20. I base my account of Zionist activities in Budapest in 1945–1946 on Garai, *The Policy Towards the Jews*, 109–118, who interviewed many of the survivors in Israel and in the United States.
21. Svéd, "A magyar zsidóság," 249.
22. Garai, *The Policy Towards the Jews*, 122.
23. Béla Dénes, *Ávós világ Magyarországon* (Budapest: Kairos, 1999), 7.
24. Garai, *The Policy Towards the Jews*, 142.
25. Garai, *The Policy Towards the Jews*, 143.
26. Dénes, *Ávós világ Magyarországon*, 11.
27. Garai, *The Policy Towards the Jews*, 177. Garai interviewed Israeli diplomats.
28. *Levéltári közlemények* [Archival information] no.2 (2004), 155–232.
29. Garai, *The Policy Towards the Jews*, 193.
30. Magyar nemzeti levéltár [Hungarian National Archive] 276/65/367.
31. *Szabad Nép*, January 15, 1953.

CHAPTER 14

Jewish Radicalism Between Ottoman Socialism and Greek Communism, 1908–1936

Kostis Karpozilos and Paris Papamichos Chronakis

The history of Jewish radicalism in the southern tip of the Balkans is the history of Ottoman and Greek socialism. It is the history of a Jewish city, a multiethnic empire, and a nationalizing Christian state, too. It emerges at the turn of the century in the port city of Salonica (present-day Thessaloniki), the Sephardi metropolis and the "Babel of the Mediterranean," one of the most Jewish as well as most diverse cities in Europe.[1] This history includes the collapse of Ottoman rule and the territorial expansion of the Greek state in the region, and is bookended by the emancipatory moment of the Young Turk Revolution in 1908 and the tragic ending of Greek Jewry in the Holocaust. It unfolds during a period of wars, shifting borders, unprecedented population movements, global revolutionary upheavals, and violent processes of state building that transformed the world in which Jewish socialists operated time and again. Above all, it is an open history of multiple connections that questions the boundaries of Jewishness and Greekness. For that reason, it is a history of silences, too.

In the field of Jewish studies, the intersection of Jewishness and socialism has primarily been explored through the case of the Bund and, more broadly, the social history of Central and Eastern European Jewries. Although there has been recent interest in decentralizing and globalizing the narrative of Jewish socialism, it has not yet extended to a discussion of the social and political tensions and dynamics in the Balkans, particularly in the Ottoman and post-Ottoman regions.[2] Within national historiographies, too, the slow growth of Greek social and labor history, along with its theoretical reductionism and methodological ethnocentrism, left little space for the organic inclusion of minorities and for challenging the primacy of class over ethnicity and other markers of labor identities. Moreover, the broader antifascist narrative dominating left public discourse in the postwar period prioritized the memory (and later, study) of World War II, wrapping the prewar decades in a shroud of oblivion.[3] Recently, the surge of historiographic interest in Sephardic Jewry has dramatically expanded the scope of Jewish studies, but it has also produced silences of its own. Early "community" histories frequently produced homogenizing accounts of singular Jewish experiences, universalizing middle-class trajectories often in isolation from the surrounding environment.[4] Later approaches, although more expansive and integrative, usually concerned the mobile, "cosmopolitan" elites, and while they insisted on the plurality and porousness of Sephardic Jewish identities, they often left class considerations aside.[5] The broader, international retreat from a class-based social history since the 1990s has meant that early and important works have not been renewed or revised.[6] Consequently, our knowledge of Jewish radicalism in the Ottoman Empire and beyond is still highly uneven. It is largely the product of an early phase in labor history and the history of socialist thought, focused on institutions rather than social actors and on ideological debates rather than the circulation of ideas. Hence, it centers on the main socialist organization in the early twentieth century southern Balkans—the Socialist Workers' Federation of Salonica—and its founder and leader, the Bulgarian Jew Abraham Benaroya. It concentrates on the Federation's first, Ottoman phase, often constructing a two-part narrative of (Ottoman) rise and (Greek) fall, usually ending with the organization's dissolution in 1918. Finally, written mostly by historians working in the fields of Ottoman history and the history of socialism and communism, it downplays the organization's Jewishness, treating it as a demographic given rather than a critical aspect to be unpacked.[7]

Working through a rich but uneven literature, this chapter grapples with some of these imbalances by highlighting the multiplicity of scales within which Jewish radicals around the Federation and the Greek communist movement operated and the concomitant shifting of their horizons of action over time. Their popular appeal, ideological quests, and political choices were determined by their involvement in Jewish communal affairs and intra-Jewish disputes; collaboration with non-Jewish socialist circles across the Ottoman Empire and later Greece; regular contacts with the Balkans, especially Bulgaria; and, eventually, participation in the cross-European world of socialism and communism. This multiscalar approach also suggests a different periodization, which the chapter's organization reflects. Starting with the Ottoman phase of the Federation (1908–1912), we then highlight the importance of the "post-Ottoman" 1910s, emphasizing the pivotal role Jewish socialists from the nation's margins played in renewing Greek socialism during a fluid period beginning with the Balkan Wars of 1912–1913, traversing World War I, and concluding with the establishment of the Greek Socialist Workers' Party (SEKE) in 1918 and then its descendant, the Communist Party of Greece, in 1924. This focus on Greek Jewish socialist beginnings rather than Ottoman Jewish endings also drives our sustained attention to the oft-neglected interwar period, with which the chapter concludes. The tripartite periodization is also an interpretative proposition regarding the changing relationship between Jewishness and socialist and communist politics. In the late Ottoman period, we argue, an open, hegemonic Jewishness was the driving force behind the formation of the multiethnic Federation. In turn, during the 1910s, Jewish *self*-minoritization became the prerequisite for Greek socialism to emerge. Finally, in the interwar years, party Bolshevization and ideological Stalinization dictated the complete effacement of Jewish particularity, even if Salonican Jews still comprised a considerable and very militant part of the party's supporters. In short, Jews were actively involved in the making of both Ottoman and Greek socialism. Yet, as in other communist parties across and beyond Europe and the Americas, their Jewishness was uniquely present and absent as the protagonists of this story struggled with the role of their own cultural identities within movements that called for the unification of all those who suffered, regardless of origins and backgrounds.

Socialist Ottomanists

The rapid integration of the Ottoman Empire into the globalizing capitalist economy of the late nineteenth century, along with the parallel but slower introduction of large-scale manufacturing in textile production and tobacco processing, created the first nuclei of industrial labor in Istanbul, Western Anatolia, and chiefly, Ottoman Macedonia. At the same time, radical ideas ranging from socialism to anarchism reached the empire, circulating among the bustling port cities of the Eastern Mediterranean or influencing the various nationalist movements emerging in its European parts.[8] Beginning in the 1890s, labor unrest increased, with strikes first hitting the major tobacco center of Kavala in eastern Ottoman Macedonia in 1879 and shortly after the region's capital, Salonica, peaking in the years 1904–1906. During these decades, the tobacco industry turned into a laboratory of labor radicalism, and tobacco workers developed a distinct protest culture that challenged existing power relations in the workplace.[9] Jews were part of the multiethnic labor force in Kavala and formed the overwhelming majority of Salonica's workforce, especially in the tobacco processing sector, which included both genders. As such, they actively participated in shaping a nascent labor activism that was fundamentally cross-ethnic yet, in the case of Salonica, also predominantly Jewish. Tobacco workers were the most militant group—they were later praised as the first to develop a "class consciousness"—and Jews were an integral part of it.[10]

The lack of systematic research into late Ottoman labor, coupled with the historiographical tendency to treat the Young Turk Revolution of 1908 as a watershed (following a narrative first crafted by the leaders of the Federation), makes it difficult to trace any continuities of persons, practices, and ideas in Jewish radicalism before and after 1908. Yet, undoubtedly, the restoration of the 1876 Ottoman Constitution signaled a new era for Ottoman Jewish radicalism. Salonica, the birthplace of the revolution and the seat of its leaders in the Committee of Union and Progress (CUP), became "a city of liberty," a place to experience the revolution and a laboratory for testing new and transformative ideas.[11] As such, the city attracted militants and agitators from abroad, especially among Bulgarian socialists.

At the turn of the century, Bulgaria was the undisputed center of Balkan socialism. Moreover, Bulgarian irredentism and the quest for expansion among the largely Slav-speaking, struggling peasants of Ottoman Macedonia fused nationalist and socialist aspirations, rendering Ottoman Macedonia a critical ground for Bulgarian radical activism. In Salonica specifically, the teachers at the Bulgarian high school, mostly educated in Central Europe and the Russian Empire, were ardent nationalists but also communicators of anarchist and socialist ideas.[12] Building on this fertile ground, several socialists arrived from Bulgaria right after the Revolution of 1908. Aiming beyond the small Bulgarian community, they sought to integrate the Ottoman Empire into the broader world of the global socialist movement by establishing Salonica as the center of Ottoman socialism.[13]

Among them was a young Jew from Vidin, Abraham Benaroya. Charting the intellectual influences shaping Benaroya's thought and actions as he moved from Bulgaria to Salonica makes evident the multiple universes Jewish socialists inhabited at the time and the diversity of spatial scales Jewish socialism operated in—from Salonica's Jewish community to the Balkan hinterland and beyond. To begin with, Benaroya, born in 1887, received a modern European-style education at his hometown's school of the Alliance Israélite Universelle, the French Jewish organization steeped in the ideas of French republicanism that strove to emancipate the Jews of the East through reform by introducing them to Western schooling.[14] Benaroya then joined the ranks of the Bulgarian Workers' Socialist Democratic Party. He first sided with the hardline Marxist "Narrows," espousing their doctrine of class struggle, revolutionary socialism, and ideological purity, but soon switched to the more moderate faction of the "anarcho-liberals" and their advocacy for broader social coalitions. During this time, he also published, in Bulgarian, a booklet on social democracy and the Jewish question—an early sign of his engagement with the burning issue of the Jewish condition in the era of nationalism and of his awareness of Austrian Marxist thinking on the matter.[15] In fact, his decision to move to Salonica right after the revolution of 1908 was dictated by this double problematic: to organize the working classes and to work for a socialist society spacious enough to accommodate (Jewish) difference.

As a Bulgarian Jew in Salonica, Benaroya might have been a newcomer, but he was certainly not an outsider. Bulgaria exerted a multilayered ideological influence on Salonica's Jewish community, and contacts among Bulgarian Christians, Bulgarian Jews, and the Jews of Salonica were close. Thus, while Benaroya was bringing "Bulgarian" socialism to Jewish Salonica, the visit of the Maccabi Zionist gymnastics club from Plovdiv in the months following 1908 similarly spurred the birth of Zionist sports associations in the city.[16] Salonica's Jewry was already in a state of ideological fermentation, and communal developments further accentuate this. Upon his arrival, the "anarcho-liberal" Benaroya encountered the moderate, humanistic socialism of Jean Jaurès (a prominent French socialist politician) through contacts with its handful of followers among the Jewish freemasons, liberal bourgeois, and the small circle of French-educated intellectuals led by Joseph Nehama, the head of the local Alliance schools. Little is known about the influence of this group, but its formation indicates the increasing attention the fate of the community's laboring strata was already attracting.[17] In the early months of the revolution, a strike wave brought Salonica to a standstill. Jewish workers were at the forefront of this unprecedented labor agitation, and Jewish industrial firms and commercial establishments were particularly hard hit. Labor unrest was becoming a particularly Jewish problem, threatening not only established social hierarchies but also communal cohesion and Jewish economic dominance in the multiethnic market.[18] Consequently, Jewish middle-class social reformers like Nehama, and particularly those around the newly founded association of the *Cercle des Intimes*, sought to regulate labor protests and guide blue- and white-collar workers into respectable politics through the establishment of self-help societies comprising both employers and employees. The most important of these was the Benevolent Society of Tobacco Workers, which tellingly had a Jewish tobacco merchant at its helm.[19] Jewish labor was becoming a vexing question, turning into a new area of social and political intervention.

To gain knowledge of local conditions and better prepare himself for the challenges of labor activism, Benaroya sought employment in the two most radicalized trades of the day, first as a printer and then as a tobacco worker. This practice was common among labor organizers across ethnic groups, with the socialist Muslim journalist Rasim Hasmet following a similar course. Initially, Benaroya operated solely within Jewish circles, doing preparatory work through the establishment of the appropriately broad Circle of Social Studies.[20] At the same time, the newly arrived Bulgarian socialists were busy promoting trade unionism among Salonica's tobacco workers and typographers. Soon enough, the two groups combined forces, and in May 1909, the Socialist Workers' Federation was born. Its offices were appropriately located above an Albanian restaurant on Salonica's main street, a neutral space where multiethnic Salonica met and a perfect fit for an organization open to all.[21]

In 1931, Benaroya proudly declared that "the Federation was founded by Jews but with the ultimate aim of uniting in a natural and unforced manner all of Turkey's [i.e., the Ottoman Empire's] socialist forces."[22] Indeed, Jews dominated the founding group of the Federation. Some, like Benaroya and Abraham Hasson, a poorly educated tailor and native of Strumitsa, were "outsiders," a testament to the regional allure of Salonica and its Jewish community. In contrast, others, like Alberto Arditti, were socially ascending locals who had received a modern education in Salonica's Alliance school. Moreover, Hasson, although influenced by Plekhanov, remained firmly on the Left, opposing any diluting collaboration with liberal bourgeois forces like the Freemasons. Others, however, like Joseph Hazan, who succeeded Benaroya as the Federation's second secretary general, were much more moderate, being closer to the cooperative movement. Such ideological quests were also multiscalar. While Hasson's intellectual explorations connected the Federation to the Bulgarian Narrows, Arditti, Hazan, and David Recanati linked it to the liberal humanist intellectual circles of the community. Alberto Dassa, too, was probably connected to local Jewish social reformers, having founded the Labor League, a forerunner of the Federation.[23] Overall then, the social backgrounds of the Federation's leaders reflected the highly stratified yet open and diverse world of Jewish Salonica. This nascent Jewish radical microcosm was born out of the ideological diversity of Balkan socialism as well as the slow but visible intellectual fermentation within Salonica's Jewish community.

Jews also constituted nearly the entirety of the Federation's members. Nearly all of the fourteen labor unions the organization united were either Jewish or Jewish-dominated, spearheaded by the formidable unions of tobacco warehouse workers. Jewish visibility was not merely a reflection of the local workforce's ethnic distribution but also of the Federation's success in addressing Jewish workers' fears and aspirations both as workers and as Jews.[24] Although our knowledge of the Federation's place in the Jewish community remains almost as skeletal as Benaroya himself first remarked it was back in 1931, it can be safely argued that the organization capitalized on a growing sense of neglect and cultural distancing felt by Jewish workers toward the reformist middle classes and modernizing communal elite.[25] Practical labor religiosity was at odds with the increasing secularism of the middle classes, and the workers' continuing use of Ladino was widening the gap with the Alliance-schooled and French-speaking middle and upper classes. This cultural divide was breaking the community apart, making culture a class marker as much as it turned class into a cultural signifier. By permitting Sabbath prayers in its venue and publishing its newspaper in Ladino, the Federation addressed Jewish workers' resentment and fear of being left behind, helping to revalorize historic Jewish cultural practices and rendering the Federation a force of Jewish cultural nationalism. Moreover, accidents like the one in 1907, when a roof collapsed, killing seven poor Jews, might have revealed elite apathy to the plight of laborers, shaking the communal consensus built on bourgeois benevolence, paternalist care for the needy, and the promise of provision through philanthropic action and communal welfare, thus pushing workers toward protest and self-organization. In this context, the Federation's critique of limited representation and its advocacy for universal male suffrage in communal elections addressed a critical issue for the disenfranchised lower Jewish strata.[26] Thus, although the Federation distanced itself from the various "national societies" mushrooming in Salonica at the time and consciously downplayed communal bonds in favor of class solidarity, it nonetheless offered an alternative space for the uncensored expression of vernacular Jewishness as well as a powerful means for autonomous involvement in communal politics—a successful function it shared with its arch-enemies, the Zionists.[27]

Yet, the Jewishness of the Federation was firmly inscribed within a supra-communal framework that informed both its structure and ideology. Unlike other "national" socialist organizations, such as the Istanbul-based Greek groups and the Armenian revolutionary parties Dashnak and Henchak, the Federation aimed to attract workers from all the empire's ethnoreligious communities. Put differently, it was not an Ottoman replica of the Bund—a separate socialist organization for Jewish workers only—but an alternative model for doing Jewish radical politics. This digression was likely because, contrary to czarist Russia, institutionalized and violent antisemitism in the Ottoman Empire (and, to a lesser extent, Bulgaria) was nonexistent. Combatting antisemitism was not a critical concern for Ottoman Jewish workers, especially in cities like Salonica, where Jewish demographic predominance and economic prowess generated a rare sense of safety and hence self-confidence.[28] For that reason, the Federation did not also subsume or efface ethnic particularities under a purportedly common class similarity, as the Narrow Bulgarian socialists and their followers in Salonica did. Instead, the Federation accommodated difference, reflecting the institutional structure of the empire within which it operated and keeping in accordance with the Austro-Marxist approach to multiethnicity.[29] It was organized according to the federative principle, with a separate section for each of Salonica's four main ethnic groups: Jews, Orthodox Greeks, Bulgarians, and Muslims. Similarly, its newspaper was initially published in four different languages. As a result, the Federation was probably the first labor organization in the empire to transcend ethnoreligious boundaries both in theory and in practice.[30]

Building on this supra-ethnic framework, its ultimate objective was to establish a single Ottoman socialist party.[31] Starting at the local level, the Federation attempted to form multiethnic trade unions and promote joint strike actions, especially among the key, most militant industries: tobacco and textile manufacturing. The organization was also the first to surpass local bounds, with unions from the great tobacco centers of Ottoman Macedonia (namely, Xanthi, Drama, and Kavala) joining it in the summer of 1911, granting it an unprecedented regional and multiethnic character. During these same years, the Federation also developed contacts with other socialist groups across the empire—from the Greek socialist center of Istanbul and the Zionist Poale Zion in Palestine to the two main Armenian revolutionary organizations, Dashnak and Henchak—in an attempt to build a multiethnic, empire-wide socialist network. This network was also trans-Balkan thanks to amicable relations with the Serbian socialist party.[32] All these efforts eventually culminated in the first conference of socialist organizations from the European parts of the Ottoman Empire in Salonica in 1911. There, not only did Serb, Orthodox Greek, Ottoman Turkish, and Jewish delegates participate jointly, but the local "particularity" of multiethnicity was statutorily acknowledged as the basis for any social and socialist activity in the Ottoman Empire.[33]

Yet, the project ultimately failed. Not only was a unified Ottoman socialist party never created due to ideological divisions, but the Federation quickly lost most of its multiethnic credentials and remained firmly Jewish. Its leadership, where Muslim and Orthodox Greek presence was anemic from the start, was further homogenized when the small but active founding group of Salonica's Narrow Bulgarian socialists around Vasil Glavinov left in November 1909. They disagreed radically with the Federation's overall consensual strategy—its insistence on the federative principle, its critical support for the Young Turk constitutional regime, and its occasional collaboration with liberal bourgeois elements like Salonica's Freemasons. These policies were viewed as incompatible with a truly principled socialist party, to the point that a vengeful Glavinov even saw the Federation as merely a branch of the ruling CUP.[34] The Narrows did not have much of a following, yet the Federation's membership remained similarly monoethnic, especially after the autumn of 1909, albeit for different reasons. Despite the Federation's handful of Muslim and Greek supporters, Muslim workers' involvement was low, while Orthodox Greeks, suspicious of Bulgarian irredentism and Jewish leadership, remained firmly under the control of their national societies and never joined en masse. Union participation was also exclusively Jewish, even if relations between the Jewish tobacco workers' union and Muslim and Greek Orthodox mutual aid societies were generally cordial.[35]

Yet, this "Jewishness" of the Federation was fundamentally Ottomanist, a hyphenation that ultimately shaped the organization's relationship with workers and socialists from other ethnoreligious groups, as well as with the regime itself. Operating in a period of heightened nationalism in the empire and irredentist aspirations across the Christian Balkans, established in a city that was a hotbed of nationalist activity, and functioning in a region plagued by violent nationalist conflict, the Federation remained a staunch supporter of the empire's integrity. Unlike other socialists, its Jewish leadership was never involved in any turn-of-the-century nationalist movements, remaining strongly opposed even to Zionism.[36] In this sense, its stance was uncharacteristically Jewish, mirroring the overall Jewish support for the Ottoman imperial project, which had long guaranteed safety and prosperity for Ottoman Jews, especially in the context of mounting European antisemitism and Christian Balkan exclusive nationalism. The Ottomanism of the Federation was another manifestation of Salonican Jewry's pro-Ottomanist stance.[37]

In the case of the Federation, however, Ottomanism did not inform any specific (and competing) understandings of Jewishness but was instead integrated into class politics in multiple ways.[38] The Federation fought hard for the empire's integration until the bitter end and even beyond. While it distanced itself from the most manifest (and violent) forms of popular Ottomanist patriotism by avoiding involvement in the anti-Greek and anti-Austrian boycotts of 1909 and 1908, respectively, which had swept the empire's port cities and radicalized the port workers and other laboring strata where Jews were overrepresented, the Federation participated energetically in the massive demonstrations against the Italian invasion of Tripoli in 1911. The following year, it opposed the Balkan Wars of 1912–1913 and the partition of the Ottoman Balkans among the victorious Christian Balkan states, even advocating for the internationalization of Salonica.[39] Adopting the evolutionary logic of international socialism, the Federation's main objective was not revolution but the progressive development of the empire. In this line of thought, nationalism and the formation of nation-states were not necessary stages to struggle for, as other Balkan socialists pledged, but aberrations and practical obstacles to workers' organization.[40] Consequently, the Federation followed a policy of legality: It abided by the constitution, acted within its confines, and actively supported the Young Turk regime. When Benaroya joined the revolutionary troops marching from Salonica to quell the counter-revolutionaries in Istanbul in March 1909, he was probably not only thinking tactically, aiming to legitimize the newly founded organization and win the sympathy of the regime (as he somewhat apologetically explained to his Greek audience in his memoirs from 1931), but also acting in accordance with the Federation's key understanding of the Young Turks as a step forward from Hamidian autocracy.[41] After all, early on, the Young Turks were both popular and on good terms with the nascent labor movement. Workers in Salonica chanted pro-revolutionary songs during the strike wave of September 1908, viewing the new regime as protective of their interests against foreign (and local) employers. Similarly, tobacco balers in Kavala forged cordial relationships with the local CUP branch; European socialists welcomed the regime change; the Young Turks were positively positioned toward socialism and its Ottoman supporters; and, finally, the Bulgarian socialist MP Dimitar Vlahov acted as an intermediary between the CUP and the Federation once he joined it in 1909.[42] This stance, however, created tensions with more nationally minded socialist groups in the empire. The small group of Greek socialists in Istanbul, headed by Nikolaos Giannios and Stefanos Papadopoulos, and even more fiercely, Glavinov's Narrow Bulgarian socialists in Salonica, reacted against the Federation's stance on the national question. Glavinov, in particular, viewed the Young Turks as a reactionary bourgeois regime and considered the empire's dissolution a prerequisite for establishing a Balkan Federation.[43]

The view of the Federation as a pro-Ottomanist organization persisted after the end of Ottoman rule in the Balkans, quickly morphing into that of an antinationalist force of regime subversion, as will be seen. The sight of young Jewish men and women workers on strike, wearing red caps and armbands—a color denoting their presumed allegiance to Ottomanism as much as to socialism—terrified the Greek authorities and public opinion in the spring of 1914. It conjured memories of a detested Ottoman past as much as it foreshadowed images of an unwelcome socialist future.[44] However, after the honeymoon of the early revolutionary months, relations between the Federation and the reigning CUP soured, and the organization quickly became a target of repressive policies. Frightened by the strike wave of late 1908 and eager to placate foreign investors and maintain social peace, the new regime reversed course. In August 1909, it passed a new antistrike law, and in 1910, it began attacking the nascent labor and socialist movements. In the spring of 1912, Finance Minister Cavid Bey delivered an anti-socialist jeremiad in the railway of Salonica, and extensive persecution followed after the elections of April 1912, which the CUP won and against which the Federation had allied with other oppositional forces.[45] Benaroya himself, along with four of his socialist friends, had already been arrested twice in June 1911, imprisoned without trial, and then exiled to Serbia. He was arrested again in early 1912, placed under surveillance in Istanbul, and subsequently exiled to Greece.[46] The Federation's opposition to the anti-minority policies of the CUP—its support for the Albanian revolts of 1910 and 1912 and for Cretan autonomy—also played a role in provoking the Young Turkish reaction. Alongside the regime's opposition to socialism, this intolerance to ethnoreligious autonomy foreshadowed the merging of anti-socialist and anti-minority discourses and a pattern of state persecution that would only intensify in interwar Greece.[47]

The Ottomanist socialism of the Federation was more than a set of ideas; the organization strove to translate it into a lived reality by attempting to educate workers and reshape their everyday lives. Alongside the bourgeois versions of modernity that were restructuring public life and the urban landscape of the late Ottoman port cities—ranging from Western-type school buildings to offices, associational venues, and leisure spaces—the Federation sought to introduce another modernity, one informed by socialist principles of respectability and intellectual advancement, fit for the empire's workers.[48] As elsewhere, to be a socialist was to enter a distinct world, living as one from cradle to grave. The Federation was instrumental in introducing this counterculture to the empire, inserting—and thus remolding—time-honored Jewish plebeian identities into a modern cultural frame.[49]

The organization's newspaper, initially titled *Giornal de Lavorador* (Workman's Paper), then *Solidaridad Ovradera* (Workers' Solidarity) and, finally, *Avanti* (Forward), first appeared in four languages (Ladino, Greek, Ottoman Turkish, and Bulgarian), and then in two (Ladino and Bulgarian). As its titles suggest, it aspired to create an imagined socialist community connecting Salonica's socialists with the Ottoman, international, and Ashkenazi Jewish socialist movements. There was a Greek-language *Workman's Paper* in Istanbul (*Ephemeris tou Ergatou*) and a Yiddish one in New York (*Di Arbeter Tsaytung*), later renamed *Forverts*, or *Avanti* in Ladino.[50] The newspaper informed and educated, while its loud group readings generated a new culture of workers' sociability centered around solidarity and raised political consciousness. Evening classes, a lending library, and the socialist bookshop "Ferrer," named after the executed Spanish anarchist, also contributed to this effort. The youth organization expanded the Federation's outreach to a new and politically important age group, giving an intergenerational spin to the notion of living a socialist life. Dance evenings and a drama club restructured workers' leisure time, while meetings at venues with names like Café El Amaneser ("The Dawn" in Ladino) created a new socialist workers' public space, distinct from both the historic Ottoman coffeehouse and the modern bourgeois café.[51] The Federation introduced a new culture of conviviality, which was also visibly Jewish. It sought to radically reorganize working-class time and space, creating a new socialist topography of Salonica. Meanwhile, the 1909 workers' fair in the city's main leisure garden at Behcinar, and above all, the impressive demonstrations and massive May Day celebrations in 1909 and again in 1911, made workers visible as a distinct group in the urban landscape.[52] The size, sounds, and colors of their parades allowed them to stake a claim to Salonica's modern bourgeois spaces, from which they were typically excluded. Fashioning the new socialist individual also meant fashioning a new Jew and a new Salonican as well.

This new individual was nevertheless highly gendered. While the Federation strove to expand the workers' field of social action and political engagement, raising their self-consciousness and confidence, it did so by indirectly excluding women. Women, especially Jewish women, constituted the bulk of the workforce in Salonica's tobacco processing industry, a core Federation constituency. They were also militant, actively and massively participating in many of the strikes erupting after 1908, culminating with the great tobacco strike of 1914, when young Jewish female workers violently clashed with Muslim strikebreakers and the Greek police. Women (and children) could also be seen participating in the 1911 May Day celebration, a contradictory sign of both the importance of family in working-class political culture and of women's integration as individuals into the socialist movement. Moreover, the organization's newspaper and other publications occasionally touched on feminism and the plight of women workers in fictional and other pieces, while the Federation-linked tobacco workers' trade union established a female vocational section. Finally, the noticeable involvement of women workers in the regional tobacco movement of Ottoman Macedonia ensured that their demands were included in the program of the Ottoman Socialist Party in 1910.[53]

Yet, there were clear symbolic and institutional boundaries that grew tighter as unionization proceeded and the Federation's presence consolidated. The gendered division of labor in the tobacco processing sector—where male balers monopolized the most lucrative skilled jobs, confining women to the lower-paid unskilled tasks—often framed protest culture, strike demands, and unionization.[54] While women could comprise up to 80 percent of the strikers (as was the case in the processing plant of the Régie Ottoman Tobacco Company), making it impossible to wage a strike without first securing their active participation, all strike representatives were men. Moreover, although their involvement was vital, it was strictly controlled. When their embarrassingly unruly behavior challenged the established cross-class gender hierarchies, threatened (male) workers' credibility, and questioned their claims to (manly) respectability, women were swiftly withdrawn from the streets and made invisible anew, as the tobacco strike of 1914 vividly demonstrated. Similarly, maintaining "male" jobs, resisting employers' attempts to replace male with cheaper female workers, accepting wage cuts for women, and demanding union control over recruitment (an indirect means to exclude women), were core strike claims throughout the late Ottoman and immediate post-Ottoman periods. Women were also regularly not admitted to the unions, which, as was the case in Kavala and Drama (regional outposts of the Federation), only welcomed skilled (male) workers. Even in Salonica, where they were accepted, women were never represented in union management.[55] The unionization that the Federation so systematically pursued, by taking over and radicalizing the established guilds and mixed self-help societies in order to emancipate the laboring strata from their employers and thus disrupt class hierarchies, proved a reverse process gender-wise. It latently consolidated gender hierarchies, implicitly crafting the unionized working subject as a man in the (Jewish) socialist imaginary. This double trend, initiated in the late Ottoman period, continued unabated in the years following Salonica's annexation to Greece in 1912, a continuity among the many changes that the change of rule initiated.[56]

"Jewish" Federation and the Making of "Greek" Socialism

The Balkan Wars of 1912–1913 signaled a new and final phase in the history of the Federation, marked by both continuities and ruptures. When the conflict erupted in October 1912, Benaroya and his organization remained loyal to the empire. Adhering to their Ottomanist and socialist internationalist credentials, they condemned the war and the irredentism of the Christian Balkan states, pleading instead for complete cultural autonomy for the empire's nationalities and the formation of a Balkan Federation.[57] Once again, their approach to the vexing question of sovereignty stood at odds with that of other, more nationally minded Ottoman and Balkan socialist groups, particularly Greek and Bulgarian. Yet, while their stance demonstrated the fragmentation of Ottoman and Balkan socialist politics that the war had accentuated, it also evidenced how much the Federation shared the same viewpoint with other Salonican Jews of diverse ideological orientations.[58] Similar to Zionists and assimilationists, Jewish socialists were fearful of Christian Balkan states steeped in religious antisemitism and built on exclusive and minority-intolerant nationalism. They also dreaded the swift economic downfall of (Jewish) Salonica, which annexation would inevitably bring. Their reaction was therefore identical to that of Zionist and communal groups pleading for some sort of political autonomy and the preservation of the city's Ottoman status. As these groups pushed for Salonica's internationalization, the Federation similarly first proposed Ottoman governance in the context of a Balkan Federation and then, in May 1913, the autonomy of Ottoman Macedonia.[59] Socialism was yet another language available to articulate the interests of Salonican Jewry.

By the end of 1913, however, after the Second Balkan War and the signing of the Treaty of Bucharest in August 1913, the Federation swiftly accepted the irreversibility of the new postwar order and the triumph of nationalism in the region. The new space for socialist politics would be national, not imperial—namely Greece, a country that had near miraculously managed to double its territory by integrating most parts of former Ottoman Macedonia. Compared to Salonica, Greece was a socialist backwater, with a minuscule industrial working class and a handful of mildly socialist intellectuals with their largely introspective small groups of followers, all still mostly radicals molded in the cast of popular, progressive nationalism, which was itself widespread among the country's laboring strata. As Benaroya experienced firsthand when he arrived in Athens in 1912, Greek irredentism strongly colored their socialist views, and all supported the Greek war effort. To his amazement, the image of Jesus—not Marx—adorned the offices of the Socialist Center and the recently founded Athens Labor Center.[60]

This was the world the Federation would engage with and drastically change. Despite the destruction of multiethnic socialist ties brought by the wars (mainly the departure of Salonica's Bulgarian socialists and the massive flight of Muslim workers from the region's tobacco centers), the organization clung to its "Ottoman" open policy, pursued cross-ethnic collaboration, and actively sought to build links with Greek socialist organizations. Instead of resisting Hellenization, it aspired to fully transform itself into a Greek organization.[61] One of its Jewish MPs, Alberto Couriel, even believed that the Federation should rid itself entirely of its Jewish character and work to establish a Greek socialist party.[62] The "Greek" chapter of the Federation's story thus points to yet another path to nationhood and national integration for the Jews of Greece's "New Lands."

After 1912, the Federation became the most important force in Greek socialist politics but also its most disruptive. To the irredentism of Greek socialists like Platon Drakoulis and Nikolaos Giannios, it juxtaposed its internationalism. While the former supported Greece's entry into World War I on the side of the Anglo-French Entente and against the Ottoman Empire—in hopes of Greek territorial expansion and the national integration of the "unredeemed" Ottoman Greeks—the Federation pleaded for neutrality. Eventually, it established links with the Zimmerwald socialists, who rallied around a staunch anti-war agenda.[63]

Support of or opposition to the war divided Greek socialists as much as it did Greek society at large, creating a fault line that pitted the "alien" newcomers from the New Lands against the established leaders from "Old Greece."[64] Similarly, while the latter were attracted to the modernizing vision of the ruling Liberal Party and considered its leader Eleftherios Venizelos their preferred interlocutor, the Federation took the opposite course. In the first general elections of June 1915, it sided with the anti-war Royalists, practicing the same policy of strategic pragmatism and demonstrating the same aptitude for independent action that had led it to ally with national parties and the ideologically distant Ottoman Liberals against the CUP in the Ottoman elections of early 1912. In 1915, the Federation managed to elect two MPs, the Jewish Alberto Couriel and the Christian Aristotelis Sideris, continuing a tradition of involvement in parliamentary politics initiated by its first Ottoman MP, Dimitar Vlahov, back in 1909. This was yet another radical change it brought to Greek socialist political practices. Before 1912, Greek socialists refrained from any autonomous involvement in electoral and parliamentary procedures. Reversing this trend, the Federation introduced a new aptitude for open negotiation and an appreciation for the importance of parliamentary politics by negotiating with both major Greek parties for the inclusion of socialist candidates in their tickets. In 1915, socialism made its first national appearance in Greek electoral debate.[65]

To top it all, the concerted effort of the Federation to expand beyond its Jewish and Salonican core led to the disruption of the established hierarchies within the small, Athens-based socialist circles. Since the early days of the Greek occupation of Salonica in late autumn of 1912, the organization's dynamism appealed to young Greek soldiers like Yiannis Pikros. In the following years, it attracted several more Greeks from the laboring and intellectual ranks of both Old and New Greece, including Sideris, the candidate Panagis Dimitratos, and Yiannis Petsopoulos, the editor of *Rizospastis* (The Radical), the future official newspaper of the Greek Communist Party. This new generation of outsiders challenged the primacy of the old guard of Giannios and Drakoulis, renewing Greek socialist politics.[66] In essence, the Jewish socialism of Salonica created an alternative network of young radicals who were impressed by the Federation's mass following and its internationalist principles. In the case of socialism, what was considered the periphery—the New Lands—defined the evolution of the movement on a national scale. In a rapidly shifting political and social landscape defined by the redrawing of borders, population movements, the crisis of the Socialist International, and the impact of the Russian Revolution, the idea of a single, and not locally defined, Greek socialist party acquired new dynamism.

The Socialist Workers' Party of Greece was founded in November 1918 in Piraeus. The proceedings reveal the instrumental role of the Federation, and particularly Benaroya, in transitioning Greek socialism from "pre-history" to "history," as he phrased it in his memoirs.[67] Yet, Benaroya went on to credit not his Jewish comrades for this achievement (as he had done with the founding of the Federation) but the group of "(Greek) Macedonian socialists."[68] This act of self-effacement—or, preferably, of identity playing—points to the new place of Jewishness in the world of (Greek) socialism.

Early on, in 1913, the Federation abolished its federal structure.[69] Later, during the founding congress of the Greek socialist party, Benaroya opted not to stand for election to the party's executive committee, which was now fully Greek. He also advocated for the headquarters of the Workers Confederation to be based in Athens, even though Salonica was the nation's de facto labor and socialist capital. This was a response to accusations raised by moderate socialists, such as Nikolaos Giannios—who had attacked the Jews of Salonica, not censoring his antisemitic attitude—as being responsible for the limited progress of socialism in Greece.[70] Giannios appeared at the conference dressed in his military uniform, making a bold statement of how he envisioned the balance of power within the new party: as a party of Greeks. His small group left the conference following a dispute with Benaroya that essentially questioned the immediate inclusion of the Federation's mass following into the party ranks. Despite his victory, Benaroya was extremely cautious in provoking further reactions and thus insisted on measures that ensured the Hellenization of the new party.

Once the party was established, the Federation was dissolved and became the party's Salonican branch. Benaroya's self-effacing stance certainly echoed his earlier Ottomanist conviction of the importance of crossing ethnic boundaries while securing ethnic particularity. In this regard, the program of SEKE, with its attention to minority rights and cultural autonomy, offered enough space for the expression of Jewishness and a smoother path to Hellenization, especially when compared with the increasingly forceful assimilationist policies of the Greek state.[71] Yet, Jewish retreat was noticeable. In the late Ottoman period, Jewish socialists were at the forefront of organizing a multiethnic labor movement. Confidently moving beyond communal boundaries, much like their bourgeois peers, they displayed a hegemonic Jewishness strong and open enough to support a new culture of (socialist) conviviality.[72] The prominence of Jewish socialists was the flipside of socialist multiethnicity and vice versa, the two seamlessly interwoven. However, by the late 1910s, hegemonic Jewishness had given way to self-minoritization.

Jewish socialists remained a visible presence in the Greek socialist movement, but they did so from a consciously secondary position that they themselves had helped craft. In short, they now displayed not a majority but a minority mentality. Benaroya, forever a pragmatist, had realized that socialism in a nation-state could not but be "Greek," with Jews now firmly occupying the place of difference.

Yet, although the "Jewish" Federation was instrumental in establishing "Greek" socialism, for state authorities and the Greek public alike, its militancy cast socialism as unequivocally Jewish and Jews as comprehensively socialists. In March 1914, the organization masterminded a tobacco strike of unprecedented size and intensity. Being regional rather than local, the strike brought together thirty thousand Greek and Jewish workers, both men and women, from all the major tobacco centers of Greek Macedonia, including Salonica and Kavala.[73] Their demands were economic, but their significance was political. Less than two years into a still fragile Greek rule, workers from the newly annexed territories were determined to shape the terms of their integration, crafting new political subjectivities along the way.

Even though the strikers adopted the language of nationalism, claiming to act as good Greeks, the authorities read the strike's geographic spread, violent clashes between female Jewish workers and Muslim strikebreakers, and, above all, the prominent role of the "Jewish" Federation as a subversive act threatening the legitimacy of Greek rule in the region.[74] Rather than serving workers' rights, its motives were perceived as political. Once the strike was over, Benaroya and his fellow Jewish socialist Yionas were internally exiled to the Aegean island of Naxos, initiating a long line of ideological persecution in Greece. The first political prisoners were Jews. Meanwhile, another Jewish socialist leader, Arditti, was termed an "anarcho-socialist-Judeo-Bulgar," a mouthful of a label that accurately summed up the alleged foreignness of both socialism and Greece's Jews.[75] The interchangeability of these derogatory categories in the national imaginary would come to determine how both socialism and the Jews were viewed in the interwar period. While "Greek" socialism was condemned as unpatriotic and rootless internationalism (and later as a local manifestation of Judeo-Bolshevism), Greek antisemitism in turn primarily fed on the image of the socialist and pro-Bulgarian Jew embodied by the "Benaroyas of various hues."[76] Thus, Benaroya, the Bulgarian socialist Jew from Vidin who willfully stepped aside for Greek socialism to emerge, came to live a second life as an all-encompassing metaphor of inassimilable (and dangerous) ethnic and ideological alterity.

Jewish Communism, 1924–1936

In late 1923, the Socialist Workers' Party of Greece renamed itself the Communist Party of Greece, adhering to the principles of the Communist International.[77] This development marked a decisive break from the tradition of polycentric socialism, highlighted by the expulsion of the party's founding fathers. Abraham Benaroya was one of them. His disagreement with the idea of a centralized and revolutionary party under the auspices of the Communist International was perceived as a sign of reformism by a younger generation of revolutionaries who had limited respect for the old socialist traditions. It was a time of upheaval and renewal. National borders were redrawn, and hundreds of thousands of refugees arrived following the end of the Greco-Turkish War in 1922 and the subsequent compulsory exchange of populations between the two countries in 1923. Right from the outset, the Communist Party appeared as the party of those on the nation's fringes. It disputed state-sponsored nationalism, and its protagonists were individuals and groups deemed unreliable Greeks: young refugees drawn to radical politics, professional revolutionaries who had fled Istanbul and studied in Red Moscow before arriving in Greece, war veterans accused of the defeat of the Greek army, ethnic Macedonians, and Jews in Macedonia and Thrace.[78] Therefore, aside from advocating social revolution, the Communist Party was also a party of outsiders to the national political family. This explains the response of the Greek state: Communism was conceived as an external and existential threat to the nation and a dangerous force that hindered the Hellenization of the newly annexed regions of Northern Greece, including the "new Greeks," the resettled refugees.

The Macedonian Question encompassed the issue. The Communist International and its Balkan sectors argued for an independent Macedonia resulting from an uprising that would liberate the oppressed working classes and minorities from nationalism and imperialism.[79] In this context, the Communist Party portrayed Greek Macedonia, and specifically Salonica, as a case study in Greek state repression. The destitute refugees from Turkey, the ethnically diverse working-class, and the Macedonian, Jewish, and Muslim minorities of the region were seen as interconnected links in a chain of class exploitation and nationalistic oppression. Within this framework, the "Jews" or "Israelites" of Salonica appeared in party resolutions alongside ethnic Macedonians, Muslims, and Vlachs as victims of Greek "colonizing" policies.[80] They were exploited simultaneously both as *Jews* and *proletarians*.[81] Housing and social conditions in the poor, ghetto-like neighborhoods at the outskirts of Salonica—where more than forty thousand destitute Jews had been relocated following the devastating fire that ravaged the inner-wall city in 1917—incidents of discrimination in the army, the implementation of mandatory Sunday rest that would leave Jewish workers out of work for two consecutive days, and the segregation of Jewish voters in minority polling stations were all presented as proof of an official or state antisemitism that followed the general pattern of enforced Hellenization of the city and Greek Macedonia as a whole.[82]

At the same time though, the party promoted its own policy of class assimilation. The transition to the Bolshevik model of a disciplined party signaled the demise of autonomy and the incorporation of Jewish radicalism in a new emerging paradigm that followed the general pattern of communist politics. According to the party's structure, members, regardless of their origins and linguistic diversity, belonged to the same party cells. Meanwhile, the Ladino publications *Avanti* and *El Joveno* (The Young Man) were now published under the auspices of the

Salonica party organization. The young rising stars of the movement did not engage with the questions that had puzzled Abraham Benaroya's generation. Jacques Ventura (born in Salonica in 1899) played a pivotal role in forming the Federation of the Communist Youth of Greece (OKNE) in 1922, which advocated for transforming the Socialist Workers' Party (SEKE) into a communist one. OKNE's headquarters were initially situated in Salonica, where its founding conference took place, and three of the five members of its first central committee were from the Jewish community.[83] As with SEKE and GSEE, Jewish radicalism was once again central to the formation of "Greek" socialism and communism. Yet, party activities soon moved to Athens, following the by now familiar path of party Hellenization. A polyglot and journalist, Ventura was elected to parliament as the communist MP for Salonica in 1926. He consistently defended the party's positions on the prospect of an independent Macedonia and the right of the Jewish minority to cultural autonomy against the policies of the Greek state. Still, these positions did not originate from an original inquiry on the Jewish Question but were mainly reflections of the broader communist position on the importance of minorities with regard to the Macedonian Question.[84]

Therefore, we are confronted with a paradox. Jewish communism in interwar Salonica was a visible social and political movement. Electoral results indicate a persistent following among the city's working class, especially tobacco workers, and in poor Jewish neighborhoods. In 1932, the communist ballot garnered 21 percent of the vote in the separate Jewish polling stations, leading to the election of Michel (or Michalis, in Greek) Cazes to parliament, while a communist-backed "Popular Block" gathered 16 percent in the communal elections of 1934.[85] The appeal of communism was based on its ability to address the victims of the existing order as the protagonists in the fight for a bright new world. The consistent references to the "antisemitic" practices of the Greek state and the oppression of the Jewish working class went hand-in-hand with an atmosphere of social and political empowerment that would lead to a state of cultural autonomy and social justice, in the footsteps of the autonomous Jewish Oblast of Soviet Birobidzhan.[86] Concurrently, however, the communist identity required a radical subordination of working-class diversity to the ideal of a unified, disciplined, and monophonic party that essentially promoted the amalgamation of its pluralistic elements. If, following the Balkan Wars and particularly during the foundation of SEKE, Benaroya and his comrades opted for a voluntary Hellenization of the Federation, the transition to the communist era signified a novel setting of an ever diminishing supplementary and complementary role within a movement striving for uniformity along Bolshevik lines. This was by no means a Greek exception or something that applied only to Jews. It applied to the overall transformation of the Communist Parties, which marginalized—or more precisely, aimed to subordinate—linguistic and ethnic plurality in favor of the Leninist party of a new type.

In this context, Jewish communists were active in promoting party campaigns and activities within their communities. "Mass work" involved electoral campaigns with leaflets produced in Ladino, meetings where speakers addressed community members or participated as representatives of the "Jewish working class" in the party's central election rallies, the publicizing of photos of Jewish candidates with short biographical notes, contributing to financial campaigns, and, obviously, mobilizing voters. In essence, Jewish communist activity relied on a translation, both literal and metaphorical, of the party's line, not just for a class but for an entire community that the Greek state perceived as outsiders to the national family. The backbone for this activity was provided by the party's Jewish cultural clubs, which originally appeared in 1927 and were reorganized in 1932, following the party's final step toward Stalinization.[87] We do not know much about their activities due to the lack of a full run of *Avanti*, even though references to them pop up in the testimonies of Holocaust survivors. Cultural clubs under the auspices of Communist Parties were a common practice and often operated as distinct, but not autonomous, spaces for immigrant and diasporic workers.[88] The Jewish cultural clubs (or *Koultourelles*) of Salonica promoted a red agenda by catering to the idea of working-class education and leisure through theater, excursions and picnics, talks on contemporary and past affairs, and the creation of working-class football clubs.

These activities were intertwined with the construction of a militant working class and revolutionary identity that presented the communist world as the only alternative to the harsh realities of capitalist exploitation. There was very little room for nuance. The dichotomous class analysis of the Communist International, especially during its Third Period, was applied to all spheres of social and cultural reproduction. In the rhetoric and praxis of Jewish communist activists, class enemies were seen as equally active both outside and inside the community. Communal leadership was attacked in the Greek-language communist press as representatives of capitalist exploitation and agents of the Greek state. Zionism, which attracted the interest of the working class, was elevated to the status of an archenemy, promoting unrealizable ideas of a "Jewish pseudo-nationalism" that divided the common interests of the laboring classes. By challenging the concept of common Jewish interests—the foundational stone of elite communal politics—and denouncing the "disgrace of emigration" to an illusory motherland as serving British imperialism, the communists presented their activities as an integral part of the global class war that had entered a novel phase since 1917.[89] These were not merely rhetorical exercises; they were translated into practice.

Interwar Salonica was a space of violent and multilayered confrontations. The rapid demographic changes brought about by the arrival of roughly one hundred thousand Greek refugees and the departure of native Muslims, the devastating fire of 1917, the nationalizing policies of the Greek authorities, and the protracted social and political crisis transformed the city into a virtual and actual battleground with different but interconnected fronts, from left radicalism to refugee disciplining and Jewish assimilation.[90] In this context, communist politics focused on the urban landscape. The pressing housing issue became synonymous with the social question, as it was a vivid spatial marker of widening class cleavages. Local initiatives by fire-stricken Jews and resettled refugees demanded—through petitions and protests to the communal and state authorities, respectively—improved conditions, the erection of new houses, and access to public services. The communist press repeatedly reported on the plight of the Jewish working-class families displaced by the 1917 fire, comparing their situation to that of the devastated refugees.[91] Obviously, the situation on the ground was much more complicated. Tension between the old Jewish inhabitants of the city and the "Greek" newcomers was fueled by antagonism over the disposition of houses and public buildings. A 1924 manifesto in Ladino by the Congress of the Federation of the Residents of all the Popular Neighborhoods, a communist-led initiative, included a demand for the evacuation of buildings occupied by the refugees.[92] Even so, organizing along neighborhood lines helped the communists make their presence visible in the city by hosting public meetings and acting as representatives of the socially segregated inhabitants, often in direct competition with the Zionists, who equally sought to win over the lower strata through similar neighborhood initiatives.[93]

These activities were linked to the rising militancy of the labor movement. The interwar financial crisis of the early 1930s had a profound effect on the numerous and well-organized tobacco workers, who were considered to represent the avant-garde of the working class given their militant tradition that dated back to the Ottoman years. It goes beyond the scope of this chapter to reconstruct the complex world of the tobacco industry and the equally complicated world of labor unions that represented diverse ideological, ethnic, and skill-based trends.[94] The overall picture, however, indicates the centrality of violence across the field. Strikes escalated to bloody incidents, such as the assassination of a Jewish worker in 1926; workers were beaten by thugs; and communists, socialists, left oppositionists, and mainstream labor activists frequently clashed in meetings at the Labor Center of Salonica.[95] In this process, the communists developed semi-militarized groups. Even though their activities were not extensively publicized for obvious reasons, it is not difficult to discern the presence of young working-class Jews in their ranks. They likely played leading roles in clashes and skirmishes with Zionists in the Jewish quarters of the city, creating an additional front of confrontations regarding spatial and political dominance.[96] Their activities acquired novel significance in the late 1920s. The implementation of state legislation against communism and the rising activities of antisemitic groups led the Communist Party to conclude that Salonica was becoming the forefront of a fascist takeover. The pogrom and arson of the Jewish working-class quarter of Campbell in the summer of 1931, organized by the antisemitic and anti-communist "National Union of Greece," seemed to confirm this analysis.[97] The Campbell pogrom was not the climax of antisemitism. On the contrary, it paved the way for new rounds of attacks and distributions of inflammatory pamphlets. The communist response came in the form of an anti-fascist organization, including a Jewish component, that made its intentions clear: to beat the fascists off the streets.[98]

Finally, Jewish communist activities were targeted by the anti-communist practices of the Greek state. The targeting of Jewish radicalism that began in the years following the Balkan Wars acquired an additional layer with the consolidation of the Judeo-Bolshevism theory, which informed the shaping of Greek anti-communism. Aristeidis Andronikos, former consulate of Greece in Saint Petersburg, wrote one of the first books on the question of communism in 1925. Andronikos had witnessed the events of 1917 and had translated *The Protocols of the Elders of Zion* into Greek.[99] His book was devoted to the issue of Judeo-Bolshevism, and he went to extensive lengths to prove that most Bolsheviks were Jews and made similar remarks about the evolution of Greek communism in Salonica. The election in 1926 of two communist Jews, Jacques Ventura and David Soulam, to the Greek parliament raised concerns regarding the disloyalty of the Jewish population as a whole. The debates on the Macedonian Question, which led to the first measures to combat communism, involved remarks about disloyal tendencies within the community. This prompted apologetic efforts by conservative Jewish members of the parliament, who argued that these tendencies were a consequence of the Greek state's indifference to the suffering of the Jewish masses.[100] Within the community, Zionists and conservatives of all stripes attacked the communists, claiming that their activities posed a threat to the interests of the Jewish population by contributing to discrimination and the rise of antisemitism.[101] Salonica became the epicenter of anti-communism. *Avanti* was targeted, its offices were frequently raided, and its editors, along with leading figures of Jewish communist activities, were imprisoned and exiled. The conservative press of the city systematically questioned their Greekness.[102] *Maκedonia*, the newspaper that had incited the Campbell pogrom with its inflammatory rhetoric, responded to the election of Michalis Cazes to the parliament in 1932 by stating, "A Jew is and always will be a Jew."[103]

Cazes himself would have possibly argued that he was, above all else, a communist. Born in 1905, Cazes was a printer and a dedicated party member who rose to prominence by siding with the new Stalinist leadership during the years of internal disputes. In 1934, he was arrested, tortured, and exiled. After his release, he traveled illegally to Moscow to study at an international communist school.[104] The rise of Nazism, the persecution of Jews, and the harsh targeting of his comrades in Salonica, along with the conviction that the Jewish working class was being targeted both economically and culturally, were not lost on him. However, these concerns appeared in a theoretical and practical horizon defined by the codified Marxism-Leninism of his era. The same can be said for his own persecution and, more broadly, the harsh treatment of Jewish communism in Salonica. Antisemitism added yet another layer to the Greek state's strategic policy to eradicate communist influence, which it viewed as a threat to the established order and a promoter of Salonica's secession from the national body. Jewish communists were primarily communists. This shaped their identity according to the principles of the Stalinist party of the 1930s while also defining their harsh treatment by the Greek state.

The final episode in the battle between communism and anti-communism in Salonica occurred in May 1936. A tobacco workers' strike escalated into a popular uprising. The capital of Greek Macedonia fell into the hands of strike committees and order was suspended, echoing parallel events in civil-war Spain. The protagonists were the city's poor and marginalized: workers, refugees, and Jews. The authorities responded with escalating violence. The bloody suppression of the strike, which led to dozens of deaths, involved police raids across the city and attacks on any form of union or communist activity.[105] By August, the events in Salonica had led to the implementation of a dictatorship that blended aspects of fascism, authoritarianism, and anti-communism. It was the end of an era. The Communist Party was outlawed, its activists imprisoned, and soon their world evaporated under the pressures of illegality and police infiltration of their ranks. If the 1914 strike had marked the dynamic entrance of Jewish socialism and working-class politics into the national arena, the 1936 one signaled the defeat of the movement. Jewish communists were arrested and exiled alongside their comrades. In 1941, political prisoners were handed over to the occupying German and Italian forces. Jacques Ventura, David Soulam, and Michalis Cazes, the three communist members of parliament in the interwar years, did not survive the war. Ventura perished in a concentration camp, while Soulam and Cazes were executed in the prisons of Salonica in retaliation for attacks by the communist-led national resistance movement. Even in death, their fate was determined by their communist, not Jewish, identity.

Conclusion: Left Aside

The Holocaust and the near total extermination of Salonica's Jewish community marked the terminus of the lengthy tradition of Jewish radicalism in Greece. Few sympathizers and party members escaped the deportations, joining the communist-led national resistance movement and fleeing to the mountains.[106] However, their survival led to new hardships. Following the country's liberation in 1944 and for the next five years, the Greek Communist Party was involved in a chaotic civil war. The state responded by outlawing its activities, while those associated with the resistance movement were accused of being communists or fellow travelers and systematically persecuted. The small number of Jews with links to the resistance faced confinement and imprisonment. Discrimination against them was based solely on their alleged or actual political leanings, with the specter of Judeo-Bolshevism being replaced by the all-encompassing accusation of a "Slav-inspired" mutiny. Despite these challenges, their background offered an alternative. Young male Jews detained in Makronisos—a prison island aimed at rehabilitating dangerous citizens—were offered the choice of emigrating to the young State of Israel in exchange for their Greek citizenship.[107] Abraham Benaroya followed a similar path. After returning from Germany, where he survived in a castle prison, he became heavily involved in the creation of a socialist (noncommunist) party. In 1953, following a first trip to Israel, he decided to relocate to a country that seemed to fulfil his dream of an actual workers' state.[108]

The legacy of Jewish socialists and communists was cloaked in postwar oblivion. The Left challenged the dominant state dogma of being non-Greek by emphasizing its patriotic contribution to the national resistance movement. In this context, the interwar years were brushed aside, along with all references that questioned the Greekness of the movement. The Greek Left rebranded itself as purely Greek, leaving little, if any, room for memorializing the Jewish comrades of the past, who were quickly forgotten.[109] A similar process defined the memory politics of the Jewish community of Salonica. The reconstruction of a cohesive narrative, which under the specter of the Holocaust sidelined the internal divisions of the past, dovetailed with the internalization of institutional anti-communism. The retrospective marginalization of the Federation and Jewish communism served the strategic aim of presenting the members of the community as law-abiding citizens and true Greeks.[110] This logic proved resilient over time. Even in the recent rediscovery of multiethnic and Jewish Salonica, the dominant narrative pays little attention to the class divisions within the community, favoring cosmopolitan stories of wealth and success, while passing references to Benaroya's era are often followed by silence regarding the interwar communist activities of his disciples.[111]

The sole exception to this trend was the effort of a younger generation of leftist historians in the late 1970s, who were influenced by the works of George Haupt and Paul Dumont during the years of the military dictatorship a decade earlier. Their interest in the origins of the Greek socialist movement sparked curiosity about the Federation and particularly Benaroya, who was still alive in Holon.[112] Nonetheless, these endeavors remained confined to intellectual circles and did not lead to a broader reappreciation of Jewish radicalism in the broader public memory of the Left. In contrast, following the fall of the military dictatorship in 1974 and the subsequent political democratization, all competing parties of the communist Left constructed historical narratives and political genealogies of a resilient Greekness, prioritizing the formative experiences of the 1940s. Contemporary politics also contributed to the minimal interest in the Greek Jewish socialist tradition. The popularity of the Palestinian cause after 1967, and especially the Lebanon War of 1982, led to a systematic conflation between Jewishness and the policies of Israel. This, combined with sheer ignorance, leftist antisemitism cloaked in anti-imperialism, and minimal interest in the interwar period of the Left's history resulted in a cultural and political void regarding the Jewish contribution to the making of the Greek socialist and communist movement.[113]

The current state of historiography allows us to retrace how this marginalization became possible. Studies on the Ottoman years of the Federation have not been followed by a systematic interest in the years following Salonica's annexation to Greece, and even less so in the communist years of the movement. The flourishing studies on Jewish radicalism are predominantly focused on Eastern Europe and the history of the Bund, while the social history of the Balkan Sephardic communities has attracted attention only recently, mainly within the context of Ottoman socialism and, sporadically, labor history. In Greece, the emerging interest in Jewish history has challenged the long-standing nationalistic narrative that presented post-Ottoman Macedonia and Salonica as purely Greek. However, emphasis is often given to the Holocaust, with less attention to the interwar years and the social and political tensions within the community.[114] The history of the Jewish socialist and communist movement of Salonica does not easily fit in predefined intellectual paths and there is a resulting fragmentation of historiographical areas of interest. It is a history that challenges an insular understanding of Jewishness, as it was entrenched in emancipatory ideologies that connected the Jewish to the social question. At the same time, it escapes the boundaries of national histories of the Left, highlighting the intrinsic otherness of the movement and a vast world of transnational trajectories that in turn question the fundamental myth of the movement's Greekness and its evolution as a national project.

NOTES

1. On Salonica's diversity in the European imagination, see Mark Mazower, "Travellers and the Oriental City, c. 1840–1920," *Transactions of the Royal Historical Society* 12 (2002): 59–111.

2. The global turn informs the recent study of Frank Wolff, *Yiddish Revolutionaries in Migration: The Transnational History of the Jewish Labour Bund* (Leiden: Brill, 2020). However, the persistent conflation of Yiddish with Jewish radicalism is still evident in Alain Brossat and Sylvie Klingberg, *Revolutionary Yiddishland: A History of Jewish Radicalism* (London: Verso, 2016). For a persuasive plea to expand the historical study of Jewish communism in the twentieth century beyond Europe and the Americas, see Alma Rachel Heckman, "Jewish Radicals of Morocco: Case Study for a New Historiography," *Jewish Social Studies* 23, no. 3 (2018): 67–100.

3. Antonis Liakos, "Modern Greek Historiography (1974–2000): The Era of Transition from Dictatorship to Democracy," in *(Re)Writing History. Historiography in Southeast Europe After Socialism*, ed. Ulf Brunbauer (Münster: LIT Verlag, 2004), 351–378; Antonis Liakos, *O Ellenikos Eikostos Aionas* (Athens: Polis, 2019), 669–674; Efi Avdela, "E koinoteta ton istorikon kata ton 21o aiona," *Mnemon* 40 (2023): 1–6.

4. For an excellent but introverted history of Salonica's Jewish community, see Rena Molho, *Oi Evraioi tes Thessalonikes, 1856–1919: Mia idiaıtere koinoteta* (Athens: Themelio, 2001).

5. For a concise reflection on the current state of the field, see Sarah Abrevaya Stein, "The Field of In Between," *International Journal of Middle East Studies* 46, no. 3 (2014): 581–584. The best examples of this new wave include Michelle Campos, *Ottoman Brothers: Muslims, Christians, and Jews in Early 20th-Century Palestine* (Stanford: Stanford University Press, 2010); Devi Mays, *Forging Ties, Forging Passports: Migration and the Modern Sephardi Diaspora* (Stanford: Stanford University Press, 2020). For Salonica, see Devin Naar, *Jewish Salonica: Between the Ottoman Empire and Modern Greece* (Stanford: Stanford University Press, 2016).

6. On the place of class in history, the best account remains Geoff Eley and Keith Nield, *The Future of Class in History: What's Left of the Social?* (Ann Arbor: University of Michigan Press, 2007).

7. Georges Haupt, "Le début du mouvement socialiste en Turquie," *Le mouvement social* 45 (1963): 121–137; Paul Dumont, "Une organisation socialiste ottomane: La Fédération ouvrière de Salonique," *Études Balkaniques* 11 (1975): 76–88. Notable works upon which this chapter heavily relies include Mete Tunçay and Erik Jan Zürcher, eds., *Socialism and Nationalism in the Ottoman Empire and Modern Turkey, 1876–1923* (London: I. B. Tauris, 1994); Pelin Tığlay, "The Ideological Melting Pot: Salonican Socialists and 'Empire' During the Second Constitutional Period (1908–1912)," *Études Balkaniques* 58, no. 4 (2022): 609–639; H. Sükrü Ilicak, "Jewish Socialism in Ottoman Salonica," *Southeast European and Black Sea Studies* 2, no. 3 (2002): 115–146.

8. Axel B. Çorlu, "Anarchists and Anarchism in the Ottoman Empire, 1850–1917," in *History from Below—A Tribute in Memory of Donald Quataert*, ed. Selim Karahasanoglu (Istanbul: Istanbul Bilgi University Press, 2016), 553–583; Ilham Khuri-Makdisi, *The Eastern Mediterranean and the Making of Global Radicalism, 1860–1914* (Berkeley: University of California Press, 2013).

9. E. Tutku Vardağli, "Searching for Women's Agency in the Tobacco Workshops: Female Tobacco Workers of the Province of Selanik," in *A Social History of Late Ottoman Women: New Perspectives*, ed. Duygu Köksal and Anastasia Falierou (Leiden: Brill, 2013), 57–58; Maria Vassilikou, "Politics of the Jewish Community of Salonika in the Inter-War Years: Party Ideologies and Party Competition" (PhD diss., University College London, 1999), 106; Can Nacar, *Labor and Power in the Late Ottoman Empire: Tobacco Workers, Managers, and the State, 1872–1912* (London: Palgrave, 2019), 3–6, 47–168.

10. Richard Ayoun, "L'esprit de solidarité entre les travailleurs dans la Solidaridad Ovradera," *Revue Européenne des Études Hébraïques* 14 (2009), 31; Vassilikou, "Politics of the Jewish Community of Salonika," 106; Gila Hadar, "Jewish Tobacco Workers in Salonika: Gender and Family in the Context of Social and Ethnic Strife," in *Women in the Ottoman Balkans: Gender, Culture and History*, ed. Amila Buturović and Irvin Cemil Schick (London: I. B. Tauris, 2007), 131; Avraam Benarogias (Abraham Benaroya), *E prote stadiodromia tou ellenikou proletariatou* (Athens: Kommouna, 1986) 20.

11. On Salonica as a city of liberty, see Banu Turnaoğlu, "The New Ottoman Conception of War, State and Society in the Prelude to the First World War," in *European Revolutions and the Ottoman Balkans*, ed. Dimitris Stamatopoulos (London: I. B. Tauris, 2019), 223.

12. Yura Konstantinova, *The (In)visible Community: Bulgarians in Ottoman Salonica* (Istanbul: The Isis Press, 2021); Yura Konstantinova, "The Role of Bulgarians for the Spread of National, Anarchist and Socialist Ideas in Ottoman Salonica," *Études Balkaniques* 54, no. 3 (2018): 508–509, 513. On Bulgarian socialism, see Maria Todorova, *The Lost World of Socialists at Europe's Margins: Imagining Utopia, 1870s–1920s* (London: Bloomsbury, 2020).

13. Kostis Karpozilos, *Ellenikos kommounismos: Mia diethnike istoria (1912–1974)* (Athens: Antipodes, 2024), 62.

14. Aron Rodrigue, *French Jews, Turkish Jews: The Alliance Israélite Universelle and the Politics of Jewish Schooling in Turkey 1860–1925* (Bloomington: Indiana University Press, 1990).

15. Avram Benaroya, *Everiskiyat vipros y sotsialnata demokratsiya* (Plovdiv, 1908); Ayoun, "L'esprit de solidarité," 35–36; Tığlay, "The Ideological Melting Pot," 618; Abraham Benaroya, "A Note on 'The Socialist Federation of Saloniki,'" *Jewish Social Studies* 11 (1949): 70–71, 72; Benarogias, *E prote stadiodromia tou ellenikou proletariatou*, 24–30; Konstantinova, "The Role of Bulgarians," 520–523; Paul Dumont, "A Jewish, Socialist and Ottoman Organization: The Workers' Federation of Salonica," in *Socialism and Nationalism in the Ottoman Empire*, 64.

16. Konstantinova, "The Role of Bulgarians," 526, 529.

17. Vassilikou, "Politics of the Jewish Community of Salonika," 106–107; Dumont, "A Jewish, Socialist and Ottoman Organization," 64; Benarogias, *E prote stadiodromia tou ellenikou proletariatou*, 22.

18. Selim Yavuz Karakişla, "The 1908 Strike Wave in the Ottoman Empire," *Turkish Studies Association Bulletin* 16, no. 2 (1992): 153–177; Paris Papamichos Chronakis, *The Business of Transition: Jewish and Greek Merchants of Salonica from Ottoman to Greek Rule* (Stanford: Stanford University Press, 2024).

19. Benarogias, *E prote stadiodromia tou ellenikou proletariatou*.

20. Tığlay, "The Ideological Melting Pot," 618–619; Benaroya, "A Note on 'The Socialist Federation of Saloniki,'" 72; Benarogias, *E prote stadiodromia tou ellenikou proletariatou*, 43–44.

21. Dumont, "A Jewish, Socialist and Ottoman Organization," 59–61.

22. Benarogias, *E prote stadiodromia tou ellenikou proletariatou*, 50. Conforming to the Greek nationalist and European orientalist discourses of the early twentieth century, Benaroya referred to the Ottoman Empire as "Turkey."

23. Hadar, "Jewish Tobacco Workers in Salonika," 128; Benaroya, "A Note on 'The Socialist Federation of Saloniki,'" 70.

24. Nacar, *Labor and Power in the Late Ottoman Empire*, 137; Dumont, "A Jewish, Socialist and Ottoman Organization," 53.

25. Benaroya, "A Note on 'The Socialist Federation of Saloniki,'" 69.

26. Ilicak, "Jewish Socialism in Ottoman Salonica," 126–129; Benarogias, *E prote stadiodromia tou ellenikou proletariatou*, 79.

27. Ilicak, "Jewish Socialism in Ottoman Salonica," 126–127; Benarogias, *E prote stadiodromia tou ellenikou proletariatou*, 43–44; Nikos Potamianos, "Internationalism and the Emergence of Communist Politics in Greece, 1912–1924," *Journal of Balkan and Near Eastern Studies* 21, no. 5 (2019), 3; Julia Phillips Cohen, *Becoming Ottomans: Sephardi Jews and Imperial Citizenship in the Modern Era* (Oxford: Oxford University Press, 2016), 103–130.

28. Karpozilos, *Ellenikos kommounismos*, 72–73.

29. Dumont, "A Jewish, Socialist and Ottoman Organization," 53, 64; Vassilikou, "Politics of the Jewish Community of Salonika," 106–107.

30. Konstantinova, "The Role of Bulgarians," 525; Dumont, "A Jewish, Socialist and Ottoman Organization," 62; Tığlay, "The Ideological Melting Pot," 623–624; Burak Sayım, "A Communist Center in Thessaloniki at the Junction of Mediterranean and Post-Ottoman Spaces," *Mashriq & Mahjar* 9, no. 2 (2022), 33.

31. Tığlay, "The Ideological Melting Pot," 623.

32. Benarogias, *E prote stadiodromia tou ellenikou proletariatou*, 27, 53; Vardağli, "Searching for Women's Agency in the Tobacco Workshops," 60; Tığlay, "The Ideological Melting Pot," 613, 623; Dumont, "A Jewish, Socialist and Ottoman Organization," 63.

33. Benaroya, "A Note on 'The Socialist Federation of Saloniki,'" 71.

34. Dumont, "A Jewish, Socialist and Ottoman Organization," 62–64, 67; Tığlay, "The Ideological Melting Pot," 620–622, 624, 629–630; Benarogias, *E prote stadiodromia tou ellenikou proletariatou*, 27.

35. Dumont, "A Jewish, Socialist and Ottoman Organization," 65; Nacar, *Labor and Power in the Late Ottoman Empire*, 140.

36. Tığlay, "The Ideological Melting Pot," 614, 617–618; Benarogias, *E prote stadiodromia tou ellenikou proletariatou*, 10.

37. Dumont, "A Jewish, Socialist and Ottoman Organization," 52.

38. Cohen, *Becoming Ottomans*; Tığlay, "The Ideological Melting Pot," 609, 612.

39. Benarogias, *E prote stadiodromia tou ellenikou proletariatou*, 66–68; Tığlay, "The Ideological Melting Pot," 625, 631–632; Dumont, "A Jewish, Socialist and Ottoman Organization," 69–70.

40. Karpozilos, *Ellenikos kommounismos*, 79; Tığlay, "The Ideological Melting Pot," 621–622.

41. Tığlay, "The Ideological Melting Pot," 620, 628; Dumont, "A Jewish, Socialist and Ottoman Organization," 64–65.

42. Ilicak, "Jewish Socialism in Ottoman Salonica," 123; Can Nacar, "Labor Activism and the State in the Ottoman Tobacco Industry," *International Journal of Middle East Studies* 46, no. 3 (2014), 546; Benarogias, *E prote stadiodromia tou ellenikou proletariatou*, 30; Tığlay, "The Ideological Melting Pot," 617, 631; Dumont, "A Jewish, Socialist and Ottoman Organization," 58.

43. Benaroya, "A Note on 'The Socialist Federation of Saloniki,'" 71; Tığlay, "The Ideological Melting Pot," 620–621; Konstantinova, "The Role of Bulgarians," 524; Dumont, "A Jewish, Socialist and Ottoman Organization," 60–61.

44. Efi Avdela, "Class, Ethnicity, and Gender in Post-Ottoman Thessaloniki: The Great Tobacco Strike of 1914," in *Borderlines: Genders and Identities in War and Peace, 1870–1930*, ed. Billie Melman (London: Routledge, 1998), 426.

45. Nacar, *Labor and Power in the Late Ottoman Empire*, 130, 135–136; Ayoun, "L'esprit de solidarité," 30; Dumont, "A Jewish, Socialist and Ottoman Organization," 65–66, 70–71; Tığlay, "The Ideological Melting Pot," 620.

46. Dumont, "A Jewish, Socialist and Ottoman Organization," 54, 68; Benarogias, *E prote stadiodromia tou ellenikou proletariatou*, 69.

47. Benarogias, *E prote stadiodromia tou ellenikou proletariatou*, 66–68.

48. Malte Fuhrmann, *Port Cities of the Eastern Mediterranean: Urban Culture in the Late Ottoman Empire* (Cambridge: Cambridge University Press, 2020).

49. Karpozilos, *Ellenikos kommounismos*, 74–75.

50. Ayoun, "L'esprit de solidarité," 32; Dumont, "A Jewish, Socialist and Ottoman Organization," 55.

51. Dumont, "A Jewish, Socialist and Ottoman Organization," 56; Benarogias, *E prote stadiodromia tou ellenikou proletariatou*, 50; Hadar, "Jewish Tobacco Workers in Salonika," 137–138; Vassilikou, "Politics of the Jewish Community of Salonika," 106. Benaroya, "A Note on 'The Socialist Federation of Saloniki,'" 72; Antonis Liakos, *E Sosialistike Ergatike Omospondia Thessalonikes (Phederasion) kai e Sosialistike Neolaia: Ta katastatika tous* (Thessaloniki: Paratiritis, 1985).

52. Dumont, "A Jewish, Socialist and Ottoman Organization," 61–62, 67; Tığlay, "The Ideological Melting Pot," 622; Hadar, "Jewish Tobacco Workers in Salonika," 134; Karpozilos, *Ellenikos kommounismos*, 75.

53. Nacar, *Labor and Power in the Late Ottoman Empire*, 9–11, 154; Hadar, "Jewish Tobacco Workers in Salonika," 128, 133–134; Avdela, "Class, Ethnicity and Gender in Post-Ottoman Thessaloniki"; Ayoun, "L'esprit de solidarité," 35; Vardağli, "Searching for Women's Agency in the Tobacco Workshops," 58.

54. Avdela, "Class, Ethnicity and Gender in Post-Ottoman Thessaloniki," 424; Hadar, "Jewish Tobacco Workers in Salonika," 129.

55. Nacar, *Labor and Power in the Late Ottoman Empire*, 154; Avdela, "Class, Ethnicity and Gender in Post-Ottoman Thessaloniki," 426; Hadar, "Jewish Tobacco Workers in Salonika," 129, 131–133.

56. Avdela, "Class, Ethnicity and Gender in Post-Ottoman Thessaloniki," 424.

57. Benarogias, *E prote stadiodromia tou ellenikou proletariatou*, 77–78; Dumont, "A Jewish, Socialist and Ottoman Organization," 72 (extensive); Potamianos, "Internationalism and the Emergence of Communist Politics," 3.

58. Dumont, "A Jewish, Socialist and Ottoman Organization," 73.

59. Dumont, "A Jewish, Socialist and Ottoman Organization," 73.

60. Potamianos, "Internationalism and the Emergence of Communist Politics," 2–3, 6–8.

61. Dumont, "A Jewish, Socialist and Ottoman Organization," 73; Vassilikou, "Politics of the Jewish Community of Salonika," 107.

62. Leon Nar, *Oi Israelites vouleutes sto elleniko koinovoulio (1915–1936)* (Athens: Idryma tes Voules ton Ellenon, 2011), 32.

63. Horst Lademacher, ed., *Die Zimmerwalder Bewegung: Protokolle und Korrespondenz*, Bund II (Paris, 1967), 157–158.

64. Karpozilos, *Ellenikos kommounismos*, 90, 105–106.

65. Karpozilos, *Ellenikos kommounismos*, 95–96, 97.

66. Benarogias, *E prote stadiodromia tou ellenikou proletariatou*, 80–81; Karpozilos, *Ellenikos kommounismos*, 99.

67. *To proto synedrio tou SEKE: Praktika* (Athens: Synchrone Epoche, 1982); Benarogias, *E prote stadiodromia tou ellenikou proletariatou*, 114.

68. Benarogias, *E prote stadiodromia tou ellenikou proletariatou*, 118.

69. Benarogias, *E prote stadiodromia tou ellenikou proletariatou*, 82.

70. Karpozilos, *Ellenikos kommounismos*, 128–129.

71. Karpozilos, *Ellenikos kommounismos*, 124–128.

72. Papamichos Chronakis, *The Business of Transition*, 69–97.

73. Avdela, "Class, Ethnicity and Gender in Post-Ottoman Thessaloniki," 421.

74. Nacar, *Labor and Power in the Late Ottoman Empire*, 172.

75. Karpozilos, *Ellenikos kommounismos*, 90; Minna Rozen, "Salonika's Jewish Laborers from the Balkan Wars to the Metaxas Dictatorship (1912–1936): A Reevaluation of the Tobacco Crisis," *Analekta* 1 (2020), 23–24; Avdela, "Class, Ethnicity and Gender in Post-Ottoman Thessaloniki," 437.

76. Avdela, "Class, Ethnicity and Gender in Post-Ottoman Thessaloniki," 431–432. See also Paul Hanebrink, *A Specter Haunting Europe: The Myth of Judeo-Bolshevism* (Cambridge: Harvard University Press, 2020); Karpozilos, *Ellenikos kommounismos*, 133–134.

77. On the Greek Communist Party in the interwar period, see Nikos Marantzidis, *Under Stalin's Shadow: A Global History of Greek Communism* (Ithaca: Cornell University Press, 2023).

78. Karpozilos, *Ellenikos kommounismos.*

79. Dimitris Livanios, *The Macedonian Question: Britain and the Southern Balkans, 1939–1949* (Oxford: Oxford University Press, 2008), 3–41.

80. For instance, "Maniphesto," *Rizospastis*, April 29, 1933, 1. References to a colonizing process in Northern Greece were frequent. In March 1933, for instance, the newspaper wrote that "Greece is an imperialist state, which forcibly conquered entire regions inhabited by other ethnicities (Macedonia and Thrace), oppresses them, and subjects them to a colonial exploitation, which persecutes and exterminates national minorities (the Jews)." "Apophaseis tes IVes Olomeleias tes KE tou KKE," *Rizospastis*, March 6, 1932, 4.

81. "Ta zetemata tes evraikes meionotetas," *Rizospastis*, December 3, 1928, 2. The newspaper carried consecutive dispatches from Salonica "on issues of the Jewish minority."

82. "Oi Evraioi tes Thessalonikes," *Rizospastis*, June 3, 1925, 1; "Epauthe to *Avanti*," *Rizospastis*, December 4, 1926, 1. On the nationalizing policies of the Greek state and their impact on the Jewish and Macedonian minorities of Northern Greece, the reference works remain Bernard Pierron, *Juifs et chrétiens de la Grèce moderne* (Paris: L'Harmattan, 1986); Anastasia Karakasidou, *Fields of Wheat, Hills of Blood: Passages to Nationhood in Greek Macedonia, 1870–1990* (Chicago: University of Chicago Press, 1997). On minorities in national party politics and the centrality of minorities in communist politics, see George Th. Mavrogordatos, *Stillborn Republic: Social Coalitions and Party Strategies in Greece, 1922–1936* (Berkeley: University of California Press, 1983).

83. On Ventura's involvement in the youth section, see Chrestos Tzintzilones, *OKNE, 1922–1943: Leninistiko, machetiko scholeio ton neon* (Athens: Synchrone Epoche, 1989), 58; "To ethnikon symvoulion tou kommatos," *Rizospastis*, May 27, 1923, 2–3. Ventura was the editor of *Avanti* and of *L'Information*, a short-lived French-language publication that likely served as a news bulletin on Balkan communist affairs.

84. See, for instance, Ventura in parliament, *Ephemeris ton Syzeteseon tes Voules*, April 8, 1927. On his parliamentary activity and clashes with Zionist delegates, see Nar, *Oi Israelites vouleutes sto elleniko koinovoulio*, 84–98.

85. Mavrogordatos, *Stillborn Republic*, 262. For the communist ticket in Jewish community elections, see Vassilikou, "Politics of the Jewish Community of Salonika," 105; Photini Constantopoulou and Thanos Veremis, eds., *Documents on the History of the Greek Jews: Records from the Historical Archives of the Ministry of Foreign Affairs* (Athens: Kastaniotis, 1998), 239. For a report on the results, see "Oi edres tou Laikou Blok," *Rizospastis*, May 30, 1934, 4.

86. "E ge tes epangelias ton Evraion," *Rizospastis*, July 13, 1935, 3 (signed by a "group of Jewish workers").

87. An indicative report is "To martyrio mias vasanismenes meionotetas," *Rizospastis*, October 14, 1933, 1. Photos of young members of the clubs appeared in the journal of the communist youth. Veteran non-Jewish communists made passing references to the party's Jewish cultural clubs and other Jewish communist activities in their written memoirs and so did Holocaust survivors in their testimonies. See, for instance, Aura Partsalidou, *Anamneseis apo te zoe tes OKNE* (Athens: Synchrone Epoche, 2017); Joseph Israël, Interview 4971 by Raymond Reichenbach, Visual History Archive, USC Shoah Foundation, October 18, 1995, accessed August 01, 2024, https://vha.usc.edu/testimony/4971.

88. Kostis Karpozilos, *Red America: Greek Communists in the United States, 1920–1950* (New York: Berghahn, 2023)

89. Tzintzilones, *OKNE, 1922–1943*, 334. In "Sionismos kai evraikos fasismos," *Rizospastis*, March 20, 1928, 1, Zionists are described as "agents of British imperialism and stooges [of the ruling class]." "Oi erythroi en Thessalonike," *Makedonia*, November 13, 1926, 1 (citing *Avanti*).

90. Mazower, *Salonica, City of Ghosts: Christians, Muslims and Jews, 1430–1950* (New York: Knopf, 2005), 333–358, 375–391.

91. References in the communist press are systematic. On Jewish working-class neighborhoods, see Rena Molho, "Jewish Working-Class Neighborhoods Established in Salonica Following the 1890 and 1917 Fires," in *Salonica and Istanbul: Social, Political and Cultural Aspects of Jewish Life* (Istanbul: The Isis Press, 2010), 107–126.

92. Naar, *Jewish Salonica*, 78.

93. Paris Papamichos Chronakis, "A National Home in the Diaspora? Salonican Zionism and the Making of a Greco-Jewish City," *Journal of Levantine Studies* 8, no. 2 (2018): 59–84.

94. On Jewish tobacco workers, see Rozen, "Salonika's Jewish Laborers from the Balkan Wars to the Metaxas Dictatorship."

95. Passing references appear in Markos Vapheiades, *Apomnemoneumata*, vol. 1 (Athens: Difros, 1984); Agis Stinas, *Anamneseis* (Athens: Ypsilon, 2023). *Rizospastis* reported frequently on such clashes. See, indicatively, "E Thessalonike parousiazei apo chtes katastase polemikou stratopedou," *Rizospastis*, June 30, 1933, 1.

96. "Dichoniai israeliton: Makampe-Kommounistai," *Makedonia*, November 1, 1926, 4; "Ethriamveuse chthes e demokratia," *Makedonia*, November 8, 1926, 1.

97. Aristotle A. Kallis, "The Jewish Community of Salonica Under Siege: The Antisemitic Violence of the Summer of 1931," *Holocaust and Genocide Studies* 20, no. 1 (2006): 34–56. The pogrom was initiated after the fiercely antisemitic local Greek newspaper *Makedonia* falsely accused the Maccabi Sports Club of attending a conference in Sofia in favor of Macedonian independence from Greece.

98. On clashes with fascists, see "Oi phtochoi israelites apantoun stis prokleseis ton fasiston," *Rizospastis*, August 17, 1933, 6. Violent episodes were frequent in 1932 and 1933, while in 1934 the Communist Party organized various "anti-fascist conferences." See, for instance, "Ten Kyriake synelthe e panelladike antiphasistike kai antipolemike syndiaskepse tes neolaias," *Rizospastis*, June 7, 1934, 6. Four of the 103 delegates in the June 1934 conference were "young Israelites from Salonica."

99. Aristeides Andronikos, *Ti esti Bolsevikismos* (Athens: Koronaios, Denaxa & Co., 1925).

100. "Ta katapiestika metra enantion tes Israelitikes meionotetos," *Rizospastis*, April 11, 1927, 2.

101. "O antisemitikos agonas kai e Israelitike meionoteta," *Rizospastis*, August 9, 1929, 3; "Oi sionistai kai ai koutoponeriai tou Mallach," *Ephemeris ton Valkanion*, October 19, 1929, 1.

102. See, for instance, references to the displacement of the secretary of the Jewish youth section, "Echtopizoun tous agonistes ton meionoteton," *Rizospastis*, March 12, 1934, 3; police attacks, "Ai archai tes Thessalonikes apagoreusan ten semerinen synkentrosin tou Eniaiou Metopou," *Rizospastis*, August 5, 1928, 4; the imprisonment of Soulam, "Gyro apo to arthro tes *Avanti* epi tou Makedonikou," *Rizospastis*, July 31, 1933, 1; and the arrest of Leon Carasso, "Syllepsis kommounistou," *Makedonia*, May 11, 1931, 6. In 1932 and 1933 the editors of *Avanti* were condemned to seventeen years of imprisonment and exile; see "To *Avanti* 25 chronia stis protes grammes tou epanastatikou agona," *O Neos Rizospastis*, February 12, 1933, 1.

103. "Pantote!" *Makedonia*, December 19, 1932, 1.

104. Cazes remained in Moscow until 1938 or 1939. He then returned illegally to Greece and became involved in the chaotic realities of the communist movement under the Metaxas dictatorship. He was accused of being a police agent in late 1939, while he was already imprisoned. For more information, see his personal file in the Communist International Archive, Russian State Archive of Social and Political History (RGASPI), Fond 495, opis' 207, delo 95

105. Mazower, *Salonica, City of Ghosts*, 347–358; Kostas Foundanopoulos, *Ergasia kai ergatiko kinema ste Thessalonike, 1908–1936* (Athens: Nefeli, 2005), 280–310; Spyros Kouzinopoulos, ed., *O eroikos Maes tes Thessalonikes tou '36* (Athens: Synchrone Epoche, 1976).

106. Steven Bowman, *Jewish Resistance in Wartime Greece* (London: Vallentine Mitchell, 1996).

107. Katherine E. Fleming, *Greece: A Jewish History* (Princeton: Princeton University Press, 2007); Moyses Bourlas, *Ellenas, Evraios kai aristeros* (Thessaloniki: Nisides, 2000); Eleni Beze, "Ellenes Evraioi: Mnemes kai tautotetes meta ton B′ Pankosmio Polemo" (PhD diss., University of Thessaly, 2021).

108. For a biographical note, see Kostis Karpozilos, "Abraham Benaroya: Ein Sozialistisches Leben im Osmanischen Reich, in Griechenland und Israel," in *Die Arbeiter*innenbewegung als Emanzipationsraum: Jüdinnen und Juden in der Internationalen Linken*, eds. Riccardo Altieri, Bernd Hüttner, and Florian Weis, vol. 3 (Berlin: Rosa Luxemburg Stiftung, 2023), 25–29.

109. Manos Avgeridis, "Debating the Greek 1940s: Histories and Memories of a Conflicting Past Since the End of the Second World War," *Historein* 16, no. 1–2 (2017): 8–46; Demetres Eleutherakes, *To Olokautoma sten ellenike koultoura mnemes, 1945–1989* (Athens: Alexandria, 2023), 119–161.

110. Beze, "Ellenes Evraioi," 345–393.

111. See the permanent exhibition at the Jewish Museum of Thessaloniki. This is true of even the most sympathetic histories of Salonican Jewry. Mazower, *Salonica, City of Ghosts.*

112. Angelos Elephantis, "Introductory Notes," in *E prote stadiodromia tou ellenikou proletariatou*, by Avraam Benarogias (Athens: Kommouna, 1986), 9–16; Kostis Moskof, *Thessalonike, tome tes metapratikes poles* (Athens: Stohastis, 1978); Kostis Moskof, *Eisagogika sten istoria tou kinematos tes ergatikes taxes* (Athens: Kastaniotis, 1988); Liakos, *E Sosialistike Ergatike Omospondia Thessalonikes.* In the 1980s, Benaroya's own Greek-language texts were also collected and republished. Avraam Benarogia, *Elpides kai planes* (Athens: Stohastis, 1989).

113. There is no systematic study of Greek leftist anti-Zionism. For a broader discussion of post-1967 Greek antisemitism, see Tobias Blümel, "Antisemitism as Political Theology in Greece and Its Impact on Greek Jewry, 1967–1979," *Southeast European and Black Sea Studies* 17, no. 2 (2017): 181–202.

114. The singular exception remains Vassilikou, "Politics of the Jewish Community of Salonika."

PART IV

Unorthodox Radicalisms

Radical Jewish politics generally took the form of competing parties on the Left. Some were explicitly Jewish in orientation, such as the Bund and different versions of labor Zionism, and some, such as the wide range of socialist and communist organizations across the Middle East and North Africa, lacked a specifically Jewish orientation but nevertheless attracted many Jewish members and, in some cases, were even founded or led by Jews. And yet, in addition to these parties, what might be described as unorthodox formations of radical Jewish politics also emerged, sometimes in what would seem to be the most unlikely of contexts. In this section, we include two such formations: anarchism and Revisionist Zionism. Despite their own profound differences from one another, these movements fiercely opposed the parties that constituted the radical Jewish orthodoxy of their day. Nevertheless, they were also products of the same atmosphere of radicalism that gave rise to their Bundist, Zionist, socialist, and communist rivals and, in a variety of ways, they were influenced by their opponents, sometimes profoundly. They were part of a radical Jewish political spectrum that illustrates the interrelated histories of the far right and the far left.

Although Jewish anarchists, like their non-Jewish counterparts, staunchly opposed the nation-state and traditional religious hierarchies, not all of them abandoned cultural modes of Jewish identity or even, in some cases, aspects of Jewish religious tradition, including core texts, rituals, and movements that they creatively subverted, reimagined, and plumbed for inspiration. In chapter 15, Anna Torres explores what she calls the "religious genealogies of [Jewish] anarchism," examining figures such as Emma Goldman, the most famous and influential Jewish anarchist, who argued that the Hasidic movement possessed important anarchistic elements, and Rabbi Yankev-Meir Zalkind, an Orthodox rabbi who developed an anarchist philosophy from Talmudic texts.

At the opposite end of the spectrum, Revisionist Zionism, despite its right-wing character, was also, in part, an unorthodox outgrowth of the hothouse atmosphere of radical Jewish politics that existed in the first decades of the twentieth century.

In chapter 16, Arie Dubnov relates the often obscured tale of Revisionist Zionist admiration for Italian fascism and how some of Ze'ev Jabotinsky's disciples elaborated their own "Hebraic Mediterranean" ideology while living in Mussolini's Italy. Significantly, Dubnov argues, these borrowings from Italian fascism complemented, rather than contradicted, the Revisionist Zionist commitment to anti-colonial militancy. In chapter 17, Avery Weinman explores another understudied aspect of the same movement, revealing the crucial role played by Mizrahi Jews in the Irgun and Lehi—two Revisionist Zionist paramilitary organizations. Weinman offers an important corrective to the typical narrative of Revisionist Zionist history, emphasizing the particular roles Mizrahi members played in the movement due to their facility with Arabic and ability to "pass" as non-Jewish Arabs. Moreover, Weinman asserts, despite their ideological differences, Revisionist Zionism and radical movements in the Middle East and North Africa shared key similarities.

CHAPTER 15

Jewish Anarchism

Anna Elena Torres

Anarchism denounces institutions of statehood, capitalism, coercive authority, and all social hierarchies such as sexism, racism, and class. Anarchists refuse to defer this vision until after a revolution or regime change, but demand that it be practiced in the present. As a self-identified credo, anarchism emerged in Europe during the nineteenth century in conversation with broader labor movements.[1] Many European anarchists, however, claimed to trace genealogies of anarchistic social practices from ancient histories and throughout the non-Western world.[2] While some anarchist ideals converge with those of other movements—such as libertarian communist critiques of nationalism and capitalism—anarchists insist that state hierarchy is inherently violent and ethically unjustifiable, a stance borne out by their own persecution under Vladimir Lenin.[3] The various schools of anarchism all share a commitment to mutual aid, direct action, and cultivating comradeship in the present. As Jesse Cohn notes, "[Anarchist] ethics refuses to locate the desired good in some utopian elsewhere or elsewhen, in the afterlife or after the revolution, a deferral which authorizes the dualism of 'ends' versus 'means' . . . but insists that means contain their own ends, that a genuinely transformative movement 'prefigures' the society it seeks to bring about in its practices here and now."[4] Anarchism has been a long-suppressed, little-studied, but persistent thread running through two centuries of Jewish radical politics, art, literature, and ethics and was profoundly shaped by Jewish experiences of statelessness.

What Was "Jewish" About Jewish Anarchism?

European universalist definitions of anarchism left little space for ethnic particularism or religiosity. The English poet Percy Bysshe Shelley, for example, aspired in "Prometheus Unbound" (1810) toward a vision of Romantic anarchy unmarked by identity: "Sceptreless, free, uncircumscribed, but man / Equal, unclassed, tribeless and nationless."[5] What role could there be for Jewishness within such a "tribeless and nationless" politics? Why would so many Jews embrace a movement so seemingly close to complete assimilation? I argue that Ashkenazim articulated their own form of *diasporic anarchism* or stateless anti-statism, infusing the revolutionary working-class movements with anti-nationalist aspirations, often beside a passionate attachment to Jewish culture, texts, and traditions.

Jewish anarchism emerged as a transnational movement in the late nineteenth and early twentieth centuries, when many European Jews were radicalized through their experiences of migration and statelessness. Its adherents were primarily Ashkenazim, whose status was distinct from the spectrum of legal citizenship statuses available to Jews under the Ottoman Empire, for example.[6] Another factor that helped to shape the development of Jewish anarchism in Europe was the antisemitism of other anarchists. Mikhail Bakunin (1814–1876), a prominent Russian anarchist, invoked a range of paranoid antisemitic canards from parasitism to vampirism in his work: "This whole Jewish world, comprising a single exploiting sect, a kind of blood sucking people, a kind of organic destructive collective parasite, going beyond not only the frontiers of states, but of political opinion, this world is now, at least for the most part, at the disposal of Marx on the one hand and Rothschild on the other."[7] Bakunin linked Jews and capital indelibly, claiming that "where there is centralisation of the state, there must necessarily be a central bank, and where such a bank exists, the parasitic Jewish nation, speculating with the Labour of the people, will be found." Rather than celebrating the revolutionary potential of transnationalism, Bakunin excoriated Jews for "going beyond the frontiers of states."[8]

Against the backdrop of European antisemitism, Yiddish anarchists articulated anarchism in their own vernacular, drawing from their experiences of diasporic existence. Against the anti-Jewish typologies of Bakunin and the French anarchist Pierre-Joseph Proudhon (1809–1865), Jewish anarchists mobilized their own histories of diaspora and textual interpretation. The editor and poet Yosef Luden, for example, took Jews' status as "the most international people of the world" as an ethically generative position, recasting Bakunin's term of slander into something positive. In *Kurtse geshikhte fun anarkhistishe gedank* (Brief History of Anarchist Thought), Luden draws a genealogy of Jewish anarchism, from the biblical Gideon's refusal to become king; to the Essenes, an all-male egalitarian movement whose members have been identified by some as the authors of the Dead Sea Scrolls; to the Viennese Jewish philosopher Martin Buber.[9]

Jewish anarchists took a variety of positions toward religion, which sometimes put them at odds with their fellow Jews, as when militantly atheist anarchists famously hosted riotous Yom Kippur balls in the streets outside High Holiday services in London, New York, Havana, and other cities between 1888 and 1905.[10] Writing in English, Emma Goldman expressed a view that was common among many Jewish anarchists: "Religion! How it dominates man's mind, how it humiliates and degrades his soul. God is everything, man is nothing, says religion. But out of that nothing God has created a kingdom so despotic, so tyrannical, so cruel. . . . Anarchism rouses man to rebellion against this black monster."[11] Yet, in a 1907 Yiddish-language interview with the Zionist journalist Reuben Brainin, Goldman constructed a genealogy of anarchism *within* Judaism, itself, citing Jesus of Nazareth, Hasidic mutual aid societies, and the radical Jewish thinker Moses Hess as links in a single chain, while claiming that nationalism, including Zionism, was "antithetical to the Jewish spirit": "You want to come up with a new, Jewish state. No, I think that the task of the Jews and their assignment in the world is to demolish and make a furnace of the states. The state is an obsolete and rusted institution that stands while collapsing. We see with our own eyes that the so-called 'promised' land will bring us closer to our end, while you, Zionist, fantasize about a Jewish state in Asia. . . . No, we will not permit that!"[12] This remarkable passage represents Goldman's attempt to claim the essential Jewishness of anarchism, arguing that statehood is profoundly un-Jewish, by contrast. Moreover, while historiographic attention has focused on strains of anticlericalism and atheism in early twentieth-century anarchism, there is new scholarly interest in religious Jewish anarchists, such as the rabbis Yankev-Meir Zalkind and Aaron Shmuel Tamaret, as well as the broader phenomenon of Hasidic theological anti-militarism.[13]

Rabbi Yankev-Meir Zalkind's capacious politics thoroughly confound any binary of religious conservatism versus leftist atheism. His writings anticipate the rise of the "spiritual Left" and critiques of political secularism in the late twentieth century. Zalkind derived a political philosophy of anarchism from his study of Talmudic ethics, retaining the particularity of Jewish identity and cultural autonomy within a vision of life liberated from capitalism, militarism, statism, and institutional oppression. Rather than retrofitting secular radicalism, Zalkind articulated an anti-statist position *through* the language and logics of Jewish scripture while fiercely opposing anarchist strains of atheism, universalism, and antisemitism, as well as the pressures of assimilation.[14] Between 1922 and 1932, Zalkind published his translations of the first four tractates of the Talmud, which are related to labor, agriculture, redistribution of wealth, and other practices of daily life.[15] Although anarchism has been characterized by the authoritarian Left as a utopian project, deferring realization of "the Idea" into the future, Zalkind's gaze was trained on tradition. Utopian Jewish writing is arguably a more strongly developed Zionist tradition, from Edmund Eysler's *Ein Zukunftsbild* (1885) to Theodore Herzl's *Altneuland* (1902). In contrast to those speculative statist tendencies, Zalkind labored throughout his life to establish a defiantly Jewish anarchist lineage through philology, scripture, and religious study.

One can analyze the historical relation between anarchism and Zionism through the levels of movement strategies, philosophical debates, and individuals' attachments and identities. The majority of the anarchist labor movement considered their anti-statist political aspirations to be incompatible with Zionism. European anarchist groups, such as Chernoe Znamia (Black Banner, Białystok 1903–1906), with large numbers of Jewish adherents, responded to pogrom violence with militancy and expropriation, rather than advocating for a Jewish state. Others who experienced anti-Jewish terror negotiated between their political universalism and need for community safety. Mina Grauer's essay "Anarcho-Nationalism: Anarchist Attitudes towards Jewish Nationalism and Zionism" examines their understanding of peoplehood.[16]

A philosophical tradition also aimed to wed the two approaches. Samuel Hayim Brody describes Martin Buber's theopolitics as "bordering on anarchism," and Hayyim Rothman describes varied streams of "anarcho-Judaism" which sought to synthesize anti-statism with religious and national attachments to Zion.[17] Oral histories and newspaper sources further reveal the life trajectories of some Jewish anarchists who eventually embraced Zionism. Some of Paul Avrich's interviews with Jewish anarchists in *Anarchist Voices* describe an arc of multiple or partial affiliations between anarchism and Zionism over a lifetime. Bessie Zoglin, an interviewee who wrote for *Fraye arbeter shtime* (Free Voice of Labor), reflects: "As for my years in the anarchist movement, I have no regrets . . . It was the chance of a lifetime. I've been a pretty good student of human nature. Anarchism is a philosophy, an ideal. We want to see life organized on the principle of social justice, as in the kibbutz, for example. True anarchism will never materialize as long as ignorance exists in this world. So I think it is a long, long way to Tipperary. But who knows what the future will bring?"[18]

The Yiddish Anarchist Press

Anarchists outnumbered Marxists in North America during the 1880s, and they continued to comprise a significant percentage of the Left until World War II.[19] North American anarchist communities developed in the late 1880s, largely radicalized by the Chicago Haymarket Tragedy. By 1902, anarchist movements' global adherents were estimated at one million. The historian Kenyon Zimmer has identified 208 anarchist newspapers published in North America between 1880 and 1940; his research shows a peak circulation of 120,000 papers in 1910, with a far larger projected readership, as papers were shared and read aloud on the factory floor. Yiddish anarchism emerged within this multilingual movement, and anarchists in the United States were more likely to speak Yiddish, Italian, Russian, or Spanish than English.[20] The Yiddish anarchist press flourished in New York and London, with dozens of newspapers published between the 1880s and World War I. Yiddish anarchists were among the largest and most prolific of the immigrant groups: They published more than twenty newspapers, twelve of which were founded in the first two decades of the twentieth century, and these generally grew out of radical social groups and mutual aid societies. Learning Yiddish thus became a part of radical acculturation: In England, *Arbeter fraynt* (Workers Friend) was edited by Rudolf Rocker, a non-Jew who learned Yiddish, Spanish, and other languages to better organize in London's East End. In New York, *Fraye Arbeter Shtime* was edited by the Russian-born poet Dovid Edelshtat, who learned Yiddish for the same reasons (the son of a Cantonist, he had been raised in a Russian-speaking family).

The Yiddish anarchist press gained a transnational presence. In Buenos Aires alone, nearly forty Yiddish anarchist books, newspapers, and pamphlets were published until the Argentine government shut them down in the mid-1970s. Just after the Russian Revolution, about two dozen anarchist newspapers were published, critiquing Bolshevik statist control of art. Before their offices were firebombed in 1918, Abba and Wolf Gordin, the editors of *Anarkhiia* in Moscow, published a manifesto calling for "the complete liberation of people from property, children from schools, society from the state, nations from empire, and women from men."[21] The Gordin brothers' manifesto articulated an awareness of the collusion between racism, colonialism, and gender oppression, anticipating aspects of contemporary intersectional feminist analysis. In the city of Białystok, Poland, the Anarchist Black Banner movement grew alongside the Bund and the Polish Socialist Party, chronicled by one of its organizers, Eliezer Hirschauge.[22]

In Mandatory Palestine and during the early years of Israeli statehood, the domestic Yiddish press was regulated and taxed as a "foreign" import by a young government seeking to establish Hebrew-language hegemony. Among the ranks of Yiddish-speaking Israeli anarchists could be found some surprising figures like Paula Ben-Gurion (née Munweis), a Minsk-born, fluent Yiddish speaker and the wife of Israel's first prime minister David Ben-Gurion. In a recently discovered recording from 1968, the prime minister spoke candidly about his wife: "She was a remarkable woman . . . she was an anarchist. At that time, all the progressive youth were anarchists. And her hero was an anarchist woman, [Emma] Goldman."[23] Among the Israeli anarchist papers was *Problemen/Problemot*, a bilingual Yiddish/Hebrew journal with a literary emphasis, which was printed until 1997. Its title, a Hebraization of the Yiddish, indicates its origins before the fuller adoption of Modern Hebrew. Its first editor was the prolific Abba Gordin, followed by the poet and novelist Yosef Luden, whose younger brother, Yitzhak Luden, edited the Bundist *Lebnsfragn* (Life-Questions). Upon passing away in 2002, Yosef Luden (b. 1907) was described in his obituary as "the last of the Orthodox Anarchists."

In New York City, the anarchist newspaper *Fraye arbeter shtime* shone as a literary journal. Its editor Saul Yanovsky launched the careers of many poets, including Dovid Edelshtat, Mani Leyb, Anna Margolin, Fradl Shtok, and Yankev Glatshteyn. Another prominent editor was Joseph Cohen, who wrote an encyclopedic Yiddish-language history of anarchism and founded the short-lived Sunrise Co-operative Farming Community in Michigan in 1933. Although this experiment in utopian country living was doomed by members' incompetence as farmers, it had many illustrious visitors in its heyday, including Albert Einstein. *Fraye arbeter shtime* was published for eighty-seven years—from 1890 (seven years before the launch of Abe Cahan's socialist *Forverts*) until 1977—making it the longest-running anarchist newspaper in the world. (In comparison, no other anarchist Yiddish paper in the United States lasted more than five years.) While some Jewish anarchists denounced publishing in Yiddish as cowardly, other non-Jewish anarchists hailed the newspaper as an example of cultural resistance.

In celebration of its anniversary in 1971, *Fraye arbeter shtime* ran an article titled "The Dean of All the Anarchist Journals in the World" by Federica Montseny, the novelist and anarchist minister of health in revolutionary Spain. In it, Montseny identified the exile of Spanish anti-fascists with the Yiddish diaspora: "the most admirable, the most extraordinary thing about [*Fraye arbeter shtime*] is that this paper has always been inspired, sustained, distributed within a community in exile.

For these Jewish comrades in America have always constituted an ethnic group as distinct as that which we, Spanish exiles, scattered all over the world, have formed. . . . There is no racism in this preservation of an ethnic community."[24]

Anarchist literature of the 1880s and 1890s was often elegiac, memorializing lost comrades, deportations, prison sentences, liminal triumphs. Such elegies and genealogical poems strove to reposition historical figures within a grander frame. There were prolific Yiddish literary responses to three court cases against immigrant anarchists in particular: the Haymarket Tragedy in Chicago (1886); the Italian American workers Nicola Sacco and Bartolomeo Vanzetti in Boston (1920); and the Russian poet-assassin Sholem Shwartzbard in Paris (1927). Each trial was a public spectacle: The execution of the Haymarket defendants instigated the first mass wave of anarchist organizing in the United States; Sacco and Vanzetti's deaths after seven years' incarceration galvanized the labor movement; and Shwartzbard's acquittal solidified his heroic status in Jewish communities in the United States, Europe, and South Africa.[25] Poets such as Dovid Edelshtat folded these historical events into religious temporalities, Judaizing the memory and vocabulary of labor "martyrs."

The explicitly anarchist *Svetshop* (Sweatshop, or Proletarian) poetry of the 1890s continued to inform modernist poets well into the 1920s and 1930s. Some reinvented the aesthetic forms of Proletarian verse to contextualize new labor struggles in a longer genealogy of struggle, drawing from Svetshop poetry as an archive of verse. Rather than a supercessionist model, where experimental forms replace Romanticism and poets' attention moves from the masses to the psychology of individuals, later poets continually returned to Svetshop poetry as a resource. In a Yiddish-language essay of 1986, Yosef Luden claimed a "deep bond between anarchism and literature," asserting that "Anarchism has never been an established policy, but a movement in process."[26] In these models, anarchism has a natural affinity with literature, as both are imaginative exercises.

Beyond artistic sympathy for experimental form, anarchists were particularly willing to fight at the front lines of free speech, notably during the 1919 Supreme Court case *Abrams v. United States*.[27] English-language modernist and avant-garde journals were also deeply informed by Jewish anarchism. Influenced by her friendship with Goldman, Margaret Anderson's *Little Review* published Pound, Hemingway, and—scandalously—Joyce; the journal was considered for its first three years to be "largely an anarchist publication."[28] Goldman and her circle supported the editors of the *Little Review* when its copies were seized by the U.S. Post Office in 1923 on charges of obscenity for publishing Joyce's *Ulysses*. Both materially and creatively, then, anarchists were key to the emergence and circulation of new literary movements.

Mutual Aid and Direct Action

While mutual aid practices can and often do exist without the vocabulary of anarchism, mutual aid is central to anarchist thought. A theory of mutual aid within the Ashkenazi radical Left in the late nineteenth and early twentieth centuries in some ways anticipated twenty-first-century discourses of care and reproductive labor. As Gustav Landauer, the influential German Jewish anarchist, wrote: "The state is a social relationship; a certain way of people relating to one another. It can be destroyed by creating new social relationships; i.e., by people relating to one another differently."[29] Landauer's comrade Erich Mühsam described him: "Landauer never saw anarchism as a politically or organizationally limited doctrine, but as an expression of ordered freedom in thought and action. . . . His revolutionary activity was never limited to the fight against state laws and social systems. It concerned all dimensions of life."[30] Judith Butler has followed Landauer and Russian-born Jewish anarchist Mollie Steimer's definitions, emphasizing that anarchism is "an ethos of sociability."[31] For Yiddish anarchists, sociality was cultivated in the form of balls, picnics, fundraisers held on steamboats sailing up and down the Hudson River, free medical programs, Ferrer Modern Schools, and mutual aid societies.

Since comradeship is both the primary aim and means of anarchism, cultivating it was of great importance. The contemporary anarchist legal scholar Dean Spade defines mutual aid as "work that directly addresses the conditions the movement seeks to address, such as by providing housing, food, health care, or transportation in a way that draws attention to the politics creating need and vulnerability." Spade notes that this "politicized survival work . . . intentionally departs from charity frameworks."[32] Women's cultural practices of care, nourishment, and community organization undergirded the development of an anarchist theory of mutual aid. As Saidiya Hartman writes: "Collaboration, reciprocity, and shared creation defined the practice of mutual aid. . . . Mutual aid did not traffic in the belief that the self existed distinct and apart from others or revere the ideas of individuality and sovereignty, as much as it did singularity and freedom."[33] Indeed, a key part of Emma Goldman's public persona was her labor of care for comrades: Goldman's memoir describes the pleasure she took in nourishing her comrades with traditional Eastern European Jewish cuisine. Friends attempted to convince her to open a restaurant, but she refused to run it as a kosher kitchen. We have the address of her ice cream shop in Worcester, Massachusetts (86 Winter Street) and her blintz recipe, in which she used the Yiddish word *bleter* (leaf or page) for crepes: "They are the principal thing; they must be as fine as tissue paper."[34]

Jewish anarchists also sought to reclaim public space for celebration, like projecting movies onto the side of the *Forverts* building on East Broadway on the Lower East Side of Manhattan. Goldman is often misquoted as writing in her memoir "if I can't dance, it's not my revolution," though Goldman did indeed dance, as Isidore Wisotzky wrote in his unpublished memoirs, describing a fundraising ball for the magazine *Mother Earth*: "Emma Goldman, elegantly dressed, and beaming like a proud and happy mother on the wedding day of her youngest daughter, circulated among the crowd and greeted everyone with her warm words and soft smile. The crowd grew gayer, happier, livelier. We danced all kinds of dances—from a *Cossacki* to a *Sher* and a *Freylechs*. Everybody asked Emma to join in. Modestly, she thanked everyone for their invitation. But she could not refuse to dance the *Sher* with us."[35] By enumerating these traditional Eastern European Jewish dances, Wisotzky illustrated how profoundly culturally Jewish these celebratory anarchist social spaces were.

The term *mutual aid* was popularized in the 1880s, then elaborated as a theory in the book titled *Mutual Aid: A Factor of Evolution*, published by the Russian anarchist Piotr Kropotkin (1842–1921). *Mutual Aid* argues against Social Darwinism, mustering the ethnographic, historical, and zoological data Kropotkin gathered from his expeditions funded by the Imperial Russian Geographical Society. Though he was not Jewish, Kropotkin's work was widely translated and circulated in Yiddish, inspiring other anarchist researchers such as Joseph Cohen and Y. A. Merison. Unlike his fellow "classical anarchists" Mikhail Bakunin and Pierre-Joseph Proudhon, Kropotkin was not antisemitic. The London anarchist paper *Arbeter fraynd* (Workers Friend), edited by Zalkind, ran serialized Yiddish translations of *Mutual Aid* in the early 1920s. Kropotkin enjoyed close comradeship with Jewish anarchists, including the poet Anna Margolin, who brought "the Jewish question" to his attention.[36] She maintained correspondence with the Kropotkin family even after leaving Europe.[37] In 1901, Emma Goldman helped arrange a tour of the United States for Kropotkin.[38]

Kropotkin claimed mutual aid was a universal law of nature, not an emotion or mere affective bond:

> It is not love to my neighbour—whom I often do not know at all—which induces me to seize a pail of water and to rush towards his house when I see it on fire; it is a far wider, even though more vague feeling or instinct of human solidarity and sociability . . . an instinct that has been slowly developed among animals and men in the course of an extremely long evolution, and which has taught animals and men alike the force they can borrow from the practice of mutual aid and support, and the joys they can find in social life.[39]

Kropotkin identified mutual aid within both animal and human societies, notably describing the "alliance of mothers" found in Whitechapel, an impoverished Jewish neighborhood in London's East End:

> This habit [of mutual aid] is general. It is mentioned by all those who have lived among the poor. In a thousand small ways the mothers support each other and bestow their care upon children that are not their own. Some training—good or bad, let them decide it for themselves—is required in a lady of the richer classes to render her able to pass by a shivering and hungry child in the street without noticing it. But the mothers of the poorer classes have not that training. They cannot stand the sight of a hungry child; they *must* feed it, and so they do.[40]

While Kropotkin emphasized mutual aid as the scientific basis of anarchism, he was also fascinated by grassroots and traditional practices within current society. In short, his ethnographic research and construction of an anarchist genealogy was key, not only to legitimate anarchism as a scientific discipline, but to prove its underlying presence within current society, always about to burst forth. Kropotkin sought to prove that mutual aid is present within and undergirding the world already—a force to build from, not an alien impulse. In insisting upon the immanence of anarchism, Kropotkin anticipated the abolitionism of Ruth Wilson Gilmore, who states: "First: abolition requires that we change one thing, which is everything. Contemporary prison abolitionists have made this argument for more than two decades. Abolition is not absence, it is presence. What the world will become already exists in fragments and pieces, experiments and possibilities. So those who feel in their gut deep anxiety that abolition means knock it all down, scorch the earth and start something new, let that go. Abolition is building the future from the present, in all of the ways we can."[41]

Contemporaneously with Kropotkin's ethnographic articles, Dr. Katherina Yevzerov-Merison published her own studies of global matriarchal societies in the Yiddish anarchist paper *Fraye gezelshaft* (Free Society), later collected in the book *Di froy in der gezelshaft* (Woman in Society, 1902). An anarchist, gynecologist, journalist, and anti-racist suffragist, Yevzerov-Merison inhabited multiple radical worlds not often thought to intersect. Her journalism analyzed racial segregation as a gender issue, advocated for reproductive rights, and supported women's suffrage while critiquing state power. Born in Vitebsk (now in Belarus), she was raised in a traditional Jewish home, mastered Hebrew by age ten, studied Aramaic and Hasidic thought, and then encountered nihilism through her own reading. She earned a medical degree at New York University in 1893 or 1895. It has been claimed that Isaac Bashevis Singer's character Yentl is based upon her early life. Yevzerov-Merison's articles appeared in an array of leftist newspapers, including *Fraye Arbeter Shtime*, *Tsukunft*, *Der Tog*, *Forverts*, and *Zherminal* under the pseudonyms Rosa Ziserman and, grandly, Ezra Sofer, a reference to the biblical scribe and priest who returned from Babylonian exile and reintroduced the Torah in Jerusalem.

Yevzerov-Merison frequently covered children's health, child factory labor, and women's rights in her essays. She provided a combination of history lessons, reflections on personal experience (such as being barred from applying to Columbia University's medical school in 1890), and analysis of the intersections of abolition, militarism, and class in the struggle for women's rights. Yevzerov-Merison also befriended Emma Goldman and, with her husband, Y. A. Merison (himself a physician) became an honored member of anarchist and socialist circles.[42] Only a year after she immigrated to the United States in 1888, Yezerov-Merison's satirical "confessional prayers" became standard features of Kol Nidre Balls, the infamous street carnivals held between 1889–1893 in front of synagogues in New York City on the holiday Yom Kippur to spite pious worshippers.

Like Kropotkin, Yevzerov-Merison turned to anthropology to cultivate political visions of life before and beyond the state. Written decades before the emergence of feminist anthropology, Yevzerov-Merison's book *Di froy in der gezelshaft* (Woman in Society) spans several genres, from polemic to history lesson to anthropological gender and racial analysis. While Kropotkin's *Mutual Aid* aimed to demonstrate that current political systems were far from inevitable, Yevzerov-Merison's genealogies of women's history sought to disprove the claim of women's biological and cultural inferiority. In its pages, Yevzerov-Merison constructs a figure of liberated womanhood persisting across centuries and territories. Her treatment of ancient Greece does not glory in the early days of democracy, but critiques Plato and portrays women's struggle for freedom within a patriarchal system.

Yevzerov-Merison critiques Plato's valorization of the state above the autonomy of the individual and attributes Plato's belief in the equality of male and female souls (though not bodies) to his unnamed female contemporaries. Anticipating David Graeber's *Fragments of an Anarchist Anthropology* (2004), Yevzerov-Merison's genealogy decenters ancient Greece and Rome as the primary influences of democracy, instead highlighting the contributions of those who lived at the margins of the ancient world and taking to task its most central philosophers. Yevzerov-Merison stood simultaneously among the ranks of anarchists and suffragists, advocating both anti-statism and expansion of citizenship. Her work provokes the question: What did it mean to advocate for women's suffrage as an anarchist? Yevzerov-Merison's final page calls to the reader: "One must take notice that women are capable of producing and contributing to all branches of human endeavor, if they merely have the inclination and strong will. One must expose the false idea lying at the root of women's enslavement, and say to women themselves: Think independently, rely on yourself alone, be free!"[43]

Drawing on both Jewish religious customs and theories of care, mutual aid societies embodied Jewish anarchist praxis. Michael Cohen, another editor of *Fraye arbeter shtime*, kept the ledger books of anarchist mutual aid groups. These document the contingency and precarity of women's lives, particularly when facing abandonment. In some cases, loans were made; in others, doctors were sent to care for clients. No mention is made of clients' politics. Those administering mutual aid societies, however, had to determine the most efficient use of funds, and so their anarchist instincts contended with discourses of need, worthiness, and perhaps respectability. Anarchist mutual aid societies were also organized to help survivors of the Nazi genocide and anarchist fundraising flyers featured photos of emaciated Jews after the liberation of the camps.

Yiddish anarchists' idealized forms of comradeship mimicked the reproductive and emotional labor performed by women. Actions that were idealized as mutual aid were in practice often the labor of nurturance already performed by women within the movement. Their labor was linked to the beginning of sexology and the reproductive rights movement.[44] This reproductive labor included Emma Goldman's own practice of nursing and midwifery, which included helping the young Jewish anarchist Hilda Adel arrange an abortion. Goldman's partner Ben Reitman was a gynecologist serving sex workers in Chicago, and the Jewish anarchist and labor organizer Chaim Weinberg noted the strong presence of Jewish female sex workers at anarchist meetings in Pittsburgh.[45] In an unpublished memoir, Isidore

Wisotzky, an anarchist who was also active the Industrial Workers of the World, detailed the dangerous logistics of circulating birth control information:

> [I] was given my first difficult assignment: to publish a Yiddish pamphlet (it was also printed in English) on *Birth Control*. This was against the law. Bill Sanger, the husband of Margaret Sanger, was sentenced to jail for passing out this type of literature. Emma Goldman and Dr. Reitman also went to jail for the same crime. Anthony Comstock, the keeper of American morals at that time, saw to it. One of our friends, a doctor, made a good, simplified translation in Yiddish. . . . Every baby carriage on the East Side, Harlem, Bronx, Brownsville, Williamsburg, got a birth control pamphlet. . . . It was a successful job. No arrests.[46]

Wisotzky and other anarchists' health care agitation may be considered both mutual aid and direct action. Voltairine de Cleyre—a Catholic anarchist and poet who learned Yiddish—defined direct action in 1912 thus:

> Every person who ever had a plan to do anything, and went and did it, or who laid his plan before others, and won their co-operation to do it with him, without going to external authorities to please do the thing for them, was a direct actionist. All co-operative experiments are essentially direct action. Every person who ever in his life had a difference with anyone to settle, and went straight to the other persons involved to settle it, either by a peaceable plan or otherwise, was a direct actionist. Examples of such action are strikes and boycotts; many persons will recall the action of the [Jewish] housewives of New York who boycotted the butchers, and lowered the price of meat.[47]

Direct action may be violent or nonviolent, and Jewish anarchists had differing stances on the question of assassination—strikingly more ambivalent than other leftists—colored by the imperial Russian government's retaliations against whole Jewish communities. The assassination of Tsar Alexander II in 1881 was followed by pogroms, justified by antisemites since one of the women involved in the conspiracy had a Jewish background. The assassination of U.S. president William McKinley in 1901 received ambivalent coverage in the Yiddish anarchist press.[48] The killing of Ukrainian pogromchik Symon Petliura by the poet-assassin Sholem Shwartsbard, however, was widely celebrated by many Jewish anarchists.[49] Shwartsbard went on the worldwide lecture circuit, but disappointed some audiences who had expected a charismatic hero and instead experienced his modest presence.[50]

In Palestine during the 1910s–1920s, argues James Horrox, anarchist strains informed the communal ideals of the kibbutz movement.[51] In the later twentieth century, the discourse of anarchist direct action reemerged in Israeli activism, notably by the group Anarchists Against the Wall. Jewish philosopher Judith Butler—who identified as a "provisional anarchist"—has linked anarchism and anti-Zionism:

> [Anarchists Against the Wall protests are] a case in which direct action against a military force and a segregationist politics is a very powerful event. . . . There

> is an important "queer anarchist" component to these demonstrations, and it has to do with episodic, direct action, drawing on older traditions from ACT UP, for instance. But it also has to do with exposing and stopping the violence of an ostensibly legal authority. I think this last is important to point out, since when the legal regime is itself a violent regime, and legal violence consumes all recourse to due process or legal intervention, then anarchism becomes the way of contesting and opposing the violent operation of the state.[52]

Butler's statement frames the ongoing, weekly protests of Anarchists Against the Wall within a longer genealogy of queer activism, notably ACT UP, which fought for HIV/AIDS care and policies. In her view, anarchist protest remains a spectacular, "episodic" and "disorganizing" force.

Conclusion: Who Are the Jewish Anarchists?

Jewish anarchism has seen a recent resurgence both in response to the rise in antisemitism and white nationalism in the United States and Russia and as a political tradition in opposition to Zionism. Contemporary Jewish anarchist groups have organized for refugee rights and freedom of movement, in solidarity with Gaza, queer liberation, veganism, and other anti-authoritarian ideals. Emma Goldman's emphasis on beauty and pleasure within a revolutionary politic continue to resonate with feminist women of color such as Audre Lorde, photographed grinning in a shirt printed with Goldman's portrait. In Russia, Jewish anarchists have recently turned for inspiration to earlier movements.[53] In Glasgow, a queer vegan cafe called *Di Rozeve Pave* (The Pink Peacock) successfully raised money to open as a Yiddish-speaking anarchist center.[54] And during the COVID-19 pandemic, an anarchist vocabulary of care aid became widespread, as neighborhoods organized mutual aid societies to deliver food to the elderly and physically vulnerable; some community groups are new, and others draw from long-standing activist networks that emerged in response to Hurricanes Maria, Katrina, and Sandy.[55]

Today, a number of Jewish cultural and activist groups draw explicitly from the archives of anarchist resistance. The zine *Don't Just Do Nothing: 20 Things You Can Do to Counter Fascism* was collectively written after the reelection of Trump. Alongside mutual aid suggestions on childcare, distributing food, and N95 masks, the contributors embrace ritual:

> Take time to mourn your losses and grieve your dead—as inseparable from fighting and organizing for the living; as part and parcel of mending the world and ourselves. Set up temporary and ongoing public altars. Paint murals to honor lost friends and comrades. Lean on the deep wisdom of grief rituals that have sustained life for millennia, such as saying Kaddish for the dead or doing shiva after a loss. Make rituals part of your resistance, queering and self-organizing them in collectivity with others. Take those rituals out into your community—by a river, on a street corner, at a DIY space or radical bookfair, during a forest defense or as a direct action.[56]

Their approach extends the heterogeneity of traditional Jewish anarchism, emphasizing mutual aid and direct action as an ethics and practice or *minhag*.

NOTES

1. On Marx's expulsion of anarchists from the London International in 1864 and its aftermath, see Robert Graham, *We Do Not Fear Anarchy, We Invoke It! The First International and the Origins of the Anarchist Movement* (Chico: AK Press: 2013), 2–3.

2. As Robert Graham notes, "If during an era of social upheaval in China around 300 C.E., a Daoist like Bao Jungyan expressed views substantially similar to those expressed 1,500 years later by European anarchists during another era of social upheaval, and the latter's views are generally accepted as 'anarchist,' then there is no reason why Bao Jingyan cannot be described as an anarchist too. Bao Jungyan's motto was 'Neither Lord Nor Subject,' which is remarkably similar to the nineteenth-century anarchist battle cry, 'Neither Lord Nor Master.'" Graham, *We Do Not Fear Anarchy*, 2–3.

3. See Paul Avrich, *Kronstadt 1921* (Princeton: Princeton University Press, 1991); Nina Gourianova, *The Aesthetics of Anarchy: Art and Ideology in the Early Russian Avant-Garde* (Oakland: University of California Press, 2012).

4. Jesse Cohn, "What is Anarchist Literary Theory?" *Anarchist Studies* 15, no. 2 (Autumn–Winter 2007), 115. Landauer quoted in Eugene D Lunn, *Prophet of Community: The Romantic Socialism of Gustav Landauer* (Berkeley: University of California Press, 1973), 227; Daniel Colson, *Petit Lexique Philosophique de l'Anarchisme*, trans. Jesse Cohn (Paris: Librairie générale française, 2001), 119; Graeber, David, "The New Anarchists," *New Left Review* 13 (2002), 62.

5. Percy Bysshe Shelley, *Prometheus Unbound: A Lyrical Drama in Four Acts* (London: J.M. Dent, 1898), 99.

6. See Sarah Abrevaya Stein, *Extraterritorial Dreams: European Citizenship, Sephardi Jews and the Ottoman Twentieth Century* (Chicago: University of Chicago Press, 2016).

7. Bakunin wrote these lines in a letter to the Bologna section of the International in December 1871. On this historical context and for a slightly different translation, see Hal Draper, *Karl Marx's Theory of Revolution*, Vol. IV, Critique of Other Socialisms (New York: Monthly Review Press, 1990), 296. For this version of the quote, see Chaia Heller, "Questioning Öcalan's Jewish Question," *Harbinger: A Journal of Social Ecology*, no. 2, https://harbinger-journal.com/issue-2/questioning-ocalans-jewish-question/.

8. Heller, "Questioning Öcalan."

9. *Brief History of Anarchist Thought* begins with the Essenes as a model of Jewish egalitarianism and ends with Martin Buber, whom Luden claimed as an important part of Jewish anarchist genealogy. Yosef Luden, *A kurtse geshikhte fun anarkhistishe gedank* (Tel Aviv: Problemen, 1984).

10. See Rebecca Margolis, "A Tempest in Three Teapots: Yom Kippur Balls in London, New York, and Montreal," *The Canadian Jewish Studies Reader*, ed. Richard Menkis (Markham: Red Deer Press, 2004), 52.

11. Emma Goldman, *Anarchism and Other Essays*, second revised edition (New York: Mother Earth Publishing Association, 1911), https://theanarchistlibrary.org/library/emma-goldman-anarchism-and-other-essays#toc3.

12. Ruben Brainin, "Fun shabes biz shabes," 1935, courtesy of the Emma Goldman Papers Project, University of California, Berkeley. Author's translation.

13. See also Hayyim Rothman, "Rediscovering Radical Rabbi Abraham Bick at the Site of the Former *Institut far Yidisher Bildung*," *In geveb*, January 12, 2020, https://ingeveb.org/blog/rediscovering-radical-rabbi-abraham-bick-at-the-site-of-the-former-institut-far-yidisher-bildung; Lilian Türk and Jesse Cohn, "Yiddish Radicalism, Jewish Religion: Controversies in the *Fraye Arbeter Shtime*, 1937–1945," in *Essays in Anarchism and Religion: Volume II*, ed. Alexandre Christoyannopoulos and Matthew S. Adams (Stockholm: Stockholm University Press, 2018), 20–57.

14. Anna Elena Torres, "The Anarchist Sage/*Der Goen Anarkhist*: Rabbi Yankev-Meir Zalkind and Religious Genealogies of Anarchism," *In geveb*, February 27, 2019, https://ingeveb.org/articles/the-anarchist-sage-der-goen-anarkhist.

15. Accounts suggest that Zalkind completed translating the entire Talmud and much of the Zohar, but he does not seem to have finished publishing his translations.

16. Mina Grauer, "Anarcho-Nationalism: Anarchist Attitudes towards Jewish Nationalism and Zionism," *Modern Judaism* 14, no. 2 (1994), 1–19.

17. See Samuel Hayyim Brody, "This Pathless Hour: Messianism, Anarchism, Zionism, and Martin Buber's Theopolitics Revisited," (PhD. diss., University of Chicago, 2013) and Hayyim Rothman, *No Masters but God: Portraits of Anarcho-Judaism* (Manchester: Manchester University Press, 2021).

18. Paul Avrich, *Anarchist Voices: An Oral History of Anarchism in America* (Princeton University Press, 1995), 183–186; see also articles in *Fraye arbeter shtime* from 1948.

19. Kenyon Zimmer, *Immigrants Against the State: Yiddish and Italian Anarchism in America* (Urbana, IL: University of Illinois Press, 2015), 1.

20. Andrew Cornell, *Unruly Equality: U.S. Anarchism in the Twentieth Century* (Oakland: 2016), 22.

21. The manifesto was published in 1917, with a collective called the Union of the Oppressed Five. Michael G. Smith, *Rockets and Revolution: A Cultural History of Early Spaceflight* (Lincoln: University of Nebraska Press, 2014), 129.

22. See Eliesor Hirschauge, *Ṭroym in farẏirḳlekhung zikhroynes-fartseykhenungen un bamerḳungen vegn der anarkhisṭisher baẏegung in Poyln* (Tel Aviv: Dina Hirshauge, 1964). See also I. S. Grossman Roshchin, "History of the Anarchist 'Black Banner' Movement in Bialystok," *Biloye (The Past)*, no. 27/28 (1924): 172–182.

23. Alon Hadar, "Ben-Gurion: 'Since Paula Died, I've Been Alone, I'm Half a Man,'" *YNET News*, July 25, 2016, https://www.ynetnews.com/articles/0,7340,L-4833044,00.html.

24. Federica Montseny, "Di eltste anarkhistishe tseytshrift in der velt," trans. Anna Elena Torres, *Fraye arbeter shtime*, February 1, 1971, 5.

25. See Kelly Johnson, *Sholem Shvartsbard: Biography of a Jewish Assassin* (PhD diss., Harvard University, 2012). See also the writings of Bernard Lazare, the first Dreyfusard and a Jewish anarchist.

26. Yosef Luden, "Anarkhizm un literatur," in *Shturem-glokn: Eseyen* (Tel Aviv: Problemen, 1986), 229–232.

27. See Richard Polenberg, *Fighting Faiths: The Abrams Case, the Supreme Court, and Free Speech* (Ithaca: Cornell University Press, 1987).

28. Modernist Journals Project, "Modernism Began in the Magazines," https://modjourn.org/journal/little-review/.

29. Gustav Landauer, *Revolution and Other Writings: A Political Reader*, ed. and trans. Gabriel Kuhn (San Francisco: PM Press, 2010), 214.

30. Landauer, *Revolution and Other Writings*, 25.

31. Judith Butler, "Palestine, State Politics, and the Anarchist Impasse," The Anarchist Turn conference at the at the New School, May 5–6, 2011, https://www.youtube.com/watch?v=tosUmZbwJ1M

32. "Dean Spade: Mutual Aide for Survival and Mobilization," accessed July 8, 2025, https://www.hendersonville.com/event/dean-spade-mutual-aide-for-survival-and-mobilization/?instance_id=551887. See also: Dean Spade, *Mutual Aid: Building Solidarity During This Crisis (and the Next)* (Verso Books, 2020).

33. Saidiya Hartman, "The Anarchy of Colored Girls Assembled in a Riotous Manner," *The South Atlantic Quarterly* 117, no. 3 (July 2018), 471.

34. Emma Goldman, *Living My Life* (New York: Alfred A. Knopf, 1931), chapter 30.

35. Isidore Wisotzky, "Such a Life," 270, Box 1, Folder 5, Joseph A. Labadie Collection, University of Michigan Library, Ann Arbor, MI

36. Reuben Iceland, *From Our Springtime: Literary Memoirs and Portraits of Yiddish New York* (Judaic Traditions in Literature, Music, and Art), trans. Gerald Marcus (Syracuse: Syracuse University Press), 143.

37. Margolin's archive includes letters from Kropotkin's family after his death.

38. Goldman, *Anarchism*.

39. Piotr Kropotkin, *Mutual Aid: A Factor of Evolution*, (New York: McClure Phillips, 1902), 5. Orig. pub. 1902; essays written and published serially 1890–1896.

40. Kropotkin, *Mutual Aid*, 137.

41. Ruth Wilson Gilmore interviewed by Léopold Lambert, "Making Abolition Geography in California's Central Valley with Ruth Wilson Gilmore," *The Funambulist* 21 (January–February 2019), https://thefunambulist.net/magazine/21-space-activism/interview-making-abolition-geography-california-central-valley-ruth-wilson-gilmore.

42. Her husband Y. A. Merison translated the work of Malatesta, Darwin, and Kropotkin into Yiddish—with her assistance. When he passed away, a huge parade was held in his honor, winding through the Lower East Side to East Broadway near the *Forverts* building.

43. Katerina Yevzerov-Merison, *Di froy in der gezelshaft* (New York: Grupe zsherminal, 1907), 82. Translation by Anna Elena Torres.

44. See Terence Kissack, *Free Comrades: Anarchism and Homosexuality in the United States, 1895–1917* (Oakland, CA: AK Press, 2008).

45. See Chaim Weinberg, *Forty Years in the Struggle: The Memoirs of a Jewish Anarchist*, trans. Naomi Cohen, annotated by Robert P. Helms (Sacramento: Litwin Books, 2009).

46. Wisotzky, "Such a Life."

47. Voltairine de Cleyre, *Selected Works of Voltairine de Cleyre* (Czechia: DigiCat, 2022) 221.

48. See Ayelet Brinn, "Translation, Politics, Pragmatism, and the American Yiddish Anarchist Press," in *With Freedom in Our Ears: Histories of Jewish Anarchism*, ed. Anna Elena Torres and Kenyon Zimmer (Champaign: University of Illinois Press, 2023), 110–130.

49. See Anna Elena Torres, *Horizons Blossom, Borders Vanish: Anarchism and Yiddish Literature* (New Haven: Yale University Press, 2023), 183–194.

50. For a more in-depth discussion of the discrepancy between Shwartsbard's rhetoric and presence as an orator, see Torres, *Horizons Blossom*.

51. James Horrox, *A Living Revolution: Anarchism in the Kibbutz Movement* (Edinburgh: AK Press, 2009).

52. Jamie Heckert, "On Anarchism: An Interview with Judith Butler," *Anarchism & Sexuality: Ethics, Relationships and Power*, ed. Jamie Heckert and Richard Cleminson (New York and London: Routledge) 93–100.

53. See work by Ania Aizman, including "From Representation to Sabotage: New Practices of Russian Antiwar Groups," *The Russian Review* 83, no. 1 (January 2024), and interviews with contemporary Russian anarchist groups (e.g., "BOAK: The anarchist partisans sabotaging Russian railways," https://thelead.uk/boak-anarchist-partisans-sabotaging-russian-railways).

54. Pink Peacock, "About," https://pinkpeacock.gay/about/.

55. See, for example, Mutual Aid Disaster Relief (MADR), "Collective Care Is Our Best Weapon Against Pandemic and Endemic Disasters," accessed June 18, 2025. https://mutualaiddisasterrelief.org/collective-care/?fbclid=IwAR2yTkuTVSG5faQjMXJiReAq5Cda7eHj8ETHCy6A7bmwDjQbE6xdyA5J2Tw.

56. It's Going Down, "Don't Just Do Nothing: 20 Things You Can Do to Counter Fascism," November 21, 2024, https://itsgoingdown.org/dont-just-do-nothing-20-things-you-can-do-to-counter-fascism/.

CHAPTER 16

Politics of the Comparative Gaze

THE THREE LANGUAGES OF RIGHT-WING ZIONIST RADICALISM

Arie M. Dubnov

And I said: Malchut *[Kingdom], how much you loathed that word!*
Not as splendor, but as hot coal to a burnt scar came this word!
Far sweater to your hearts was the word: surrender!
—*Uri Zvi Greenberg, "Shir asher za'akti" [A poem I bellowed]*

"The word intellect stinks in the normal Americo-English nostril," wrote Ezra Pound in his vile pro-fascist tract *Jefferson and/or Mussolini* (1936). "The academic ass exists in a vacuum with a congeries of dead fixed ideas, or with a congeries of fixed ideas which may be 'good' and not quite dead," Pound argued, his habit of discussing abstract ideas allied to his desire for eloquence. It was a curious twist to find a modernist poet loathing "intellect." Yet this foreign-sounding term, Pound insisted, had nothing to do with knowledge or a desire to learn. Worse, it concealed the fact that real intelligence does not exist before it evolves into action. It was one of the symptoms of diseased liberal societies that were incapable of eliminating unemployment yet continued destroying traditional social bonds. Infamously, it was Italian fascism, with its cult of the state and the Great Leader, that was seen by him as offering a bold alternative, hailed as the ultimate "anti-snob movement."[1] Mussolini's anti-elitism and anti-intellectualism, his obsession with *Romanità*, the desire to juxtapose Ancient Rome with the modern Italian state, appealed to Pound. He welcomed Il Duce's call to make use of the full power of the modern state, including his celebration of symbolic and actual violence, and, ultimately, his rabid racist policies. All were justified as serving a vital therapeutic function, a vigorous protest against liberalism, a fending off of a rotten bourgeois order.[2]

When examined from a post-Holocaust perspective, it would be difficult to think of Jews as anything but victims of this kind of sinister sermon. And yet, at the time Pound was making his political pronouncements, right-wing Jewish radicals in Mandatory Palestine as well as Europe were gravitating in similar ideological directions. Like Pound, they were also constantly shifting between the social and aesthetic realms, and like the expatriate American poet their writings also reveal the essential inconsistency of fascist anti-intellectualism: the need for silver-tongued poetics and sophisticated prose to articulate their disgust of bourgeois refinement. Whether it is because we are fond of writing the histories of underdogs and struggles for lost causes, or because of the difficulty of imagining twentieth-century Jews, the ultimate victims of fascism, to be active participants in interwar right-wing discourse, our understanding of Jewish variants of right-wing radicalism remains lacking and insufficient. This chapter will offer a sketch of a specific kind of right-wing radicalization: that of "maximalist" revisionist Zionists from the late 1920s to the late 1940s, the somewhat forgotten apostles of revolt. My account differs on purpose from traditional historiographical interpretations of the origins of the Israeli Right, which tend to focus exclusively on Vladimir (Ze'ev) Jabotinsky, the founding father of revisionist Zionism and the leader of its youth movement, *Betar*, or Menachem Begin, the leader of the militant *Irgun* who later became the first right-wing prime minister of Israel.[3] Instead, the next pages will be looking at a lesser-known, somewhat eclectic group of Jabotinsky's disciples-turned-contenders, who operated in pre-statehood Palestine as well as the fascist Italy of the 1930s. Though they were rarely the ones to occupy leadership positions in the revisionist movement, these radical activists produced a steady stream of publications expressing sweeping, contentious political notions that ultimately helped push the entire movement in an increasingly radical direction. What made them radical, I will argue, was not the way they took Jabotinsky's right-wing ideas to their extreme, but the way they quickly transcended and departed from this opening position in three major directions, developing a theory of a revolutionary avant-garde, a vision of a Hebraic Mediterraneanism, and a doctrine of anti-colonial terror. Never forming independent organizations or a viable mass movement that competed with the revisionist party, the importance of these right-wing intellectual warriors lies elsewhere: in their ability to provide the vocabulary, pathos, imagery, and poetics of struggle. These ultimately fueled the paramilitary groups *Irgun* and *Lehi* that chose the path of open confrontation and violent struggle against both Palestinian Arabs and the British mandatory forces during the last stages of the mandatory period in Palestine. Most strikingly, as I will argue, the willingness of these radicals to borrow fascist notions did not contradict their commitment to an anti-colonial struggle.

To explain this seemingly paradoxical position, I will be using the intellectual historian's toolbox. In particular, I suggest that the processes of ideological radicalization we identify among the members of this group would be better understood by reconstructing the political language developed by these maximalists. More specifically, I would like to highlight the diverse, continually evolving and not necessarily consistent maximalist rhetoric that evolved as a product of the incorporation of diverse ideas, including Leninist theories of revolution, Italian fascist conceptions of the state, and even Irish notions of anti-colonial insurgency. In other words, I suggest that the multilayered maximalist imagination was a result of a "remix"—an eclectic borrowing of ideas, sensibilities, political vocabulary, and programs that were put forward elsewhere, in different European contexts, and were creatively meshed together with Jewish messianic idioms and adapted to meet Mandatory Palestine's unique political situation. Maximalist revisionist language, in this sense, was at once a local fruit and a result of borrowing of foreign idioms and an outward-looking, comparative gaze. Understanding its development requires us to track the global itineraries of radical ideas during the interwar period, and to explain the way in which Jews activated processes of borrowing and adaptation and developed an "analogical lexicon": a series of comparisons that allowed them to see themselves as similar to contemporaneous non-Jewish radicals elsewhere and provided justification for this borrowing.

We shall proceed in three steps, corresponding to the three main types of ideological borrowings. The first section focuses on the self-described radical avant-garde group known as *Brit Habiryonim* as it transitioned during the 1920s from admiration of Leninist revolutionary methods to praise of Italian fascism. Moving from Palestine to Italy, the next section looks at lesser-known Betar movement activists who provided crucial personal and ideological bridges connecting Palestine's radicals with the fascist regime during the mid-1930s. The third section, focusing on the 1940s, shows how in the context of growing anti-British sentiment, Palestine's radicals began seeing themselves in comparison to the Irish republicans.

The Birth of "Revolutionary Zionism" (or Lenin on My Mind)

Before its ideology had crystallized and its party institutions were installed, revisionist Zionism was first and foremost an ethos and an artistic sensibility emerging in the wake of the First World War. Famously, Vladimir Jabotinsky took much pride in the fact that he (alongside Joseph Trumpeldor and the eccentric British lieutenant-colonel John Henry Patterson) played such a central role in creating a Jewish Legion that fought alongside the British during the war.[4] Less known was the fact that he, like numerous other veterans, also suffered from that dizzying, confusing disconnect between wartime dreams of grandeur and meager postwar realities once the war ended. This disconnect bred feelings of frustration and uncertainty. At other times, it fed into a machismo aesthetic and *Sittlichkeit* (vision of an ethical order) and a deep contempt toward the postwar order. It is a sentiment we find in abundance among postwar European avant-garde thinkers. In Italy in particular, proto-fascists found inspiration in the words and deeds of Gabriele D'Annunzio, the controversial nationalist poet who formed a short-lived Italian Regency in Fiume (in present-day Croatia), a self-fashioned new man of action who combined the virtues of daring warrior with the sophistication of refined poet. D'Annunzio, as historian Robert Wohl put it, "sang vaguely but seductively of a new race of young Italian heroes who would supplant the old and corrupt ruling class."[5] Such songs seduced Jabotinsky as well, who admired Italian culture since the time he spent in Rome as a student. In 1919 Jabotinsky described D'Annunzio to the readers of the Hebrew daily *Ha'aretz* as "the poet of spiritual aristocracy in our generation . . . standing above a cliff and longing for something sublime, which he himself could not yet grasp." Shortly thereafter, while imprisoned by the British, Jabotinsky translated his poems into Hebrew.[6] To a large degree, the Jabotinsky of the early 1920s modeled himself after the eccentric Italian poet-warrior. The commemoration of the great deeds of the Jewish Legion played a central role in this respect. Above all, for Jabotinsky the legion provided the world with the ultimate proof that when needed, Jews could pick up the sword and fight. That sense of pride and splendor was projected onto Betar, the new youth movement established in 1923. The Betarist code of *hadar* (glory, impeccability) was very close to the iconic images of Lieutenant Jabotinsky dressed in British army uniform, an Odessa Jew performing the English stiff upper lip.

It is noteworthy that these sentiments of grandeur did not lend themselves to an anti-colonial, anti-British revolt. In the political circumstances that were established in Palestine in the early 1920s, as British military rule was replaced by a mandatory regime under the auspices of the League of Nations, a continuing reliance on a British imperial partnership was imperative. This political premise provided the foundation for many of Jabotinsky's political writings from the 1920s. Even Jabotinsky's most famous essay on the Arab question, "On the Iron Wall" ("O Zheleznoi Stene," 1923) testified to it, stating boldly that Zionism is a movement of colonization that could "continue and develop only under the protection of a force independent of the local population—an iron wall which the native population cannot break through."[7] The question whether the iron wall would be based on Jewish or British bayonets—that is, of whether it would require a Jewish militia that would be established under the auspices of the British, or that British colonial police and army forces would be solely in charge of—remained open, and purposely so. It was clear that for Jabotinsky the iron wall required British permission and active support. This reliance on imperial support is often muted in accounts produced by Jabotinsky's heirs, who appropriated him retroactively as the father of the 1940s revolt against the British. In the early years of the mandate, this was not only a distant horizon, but a course of action that was dismissed as needless, dire, and potentially disastrous. First frictions with the British mandatory government notwithstanding, especially in light of Jabotinsky's calls for a more assertive and aggressive approach to Jewish self-defense, the last thing Jabotinsky was contemplating was an anti-colonial insurgency. Not coincidentally, during the same year the iron wall essay was published, Jabotinsky authored another article criticizing young mavericks from within his own camp who began using the anti-British slogan "Perfidious Albion" to reprimand British policies.[8] His political analysis was premised on the belief that a deeper bond between Britain and the new-old Jewish nation, modeled on this camaraderie-in-arms, was to guarantee the Zionists' success in colonizing the land.

Jabotinsky's slow evolutionary vision of politics resting on a vertical alliance with the British was challenged from within his own circles by the members of *Brit*

Habiryonim (The Zealots' Alliance)—a trio composed of the essayist and activist Abba Ahimeir (1897–1962), the modernist poet Uri Zvi Greenberg (1896–1981), and the journalist and translator Yehoshua (Joshua) Heschel Yevin (1891–1970). In particular, it contrasted the way in which the trio understood and came to admire the Leninist revolutionary methods that quickly, though counterintuitively, led them to admire Italian fascism.

Abba Ahimeir was the first Zionist to describe himself openly and proudly as a fascist, but his journey to fascism occurred via the October Revolution. Born in Bobruisk (Mogilev Region in today's eastern Belarus) as Abba Shaul ben Isaac Gaissinovitch, Ahimeir started his writing career as a foreign affairs correspondent for *Izvestia*, the Bobruisk Soviet's journal. A revolutionary zeal colors much of these early articles, which were signed with the pen name Johan Geschalski (John of Giscala, aka Yohanan Ish-Halav), after one of the leaders of the Jewish revolt against Rome in 70 C.E.[9] Forging a new persona, he began calling himself Ahimeir shortly prior to his immigration to Palestine (1924), in memory of his younger brother Meir, an officer in the Red Army and a committed Bolshevik who was killed in a battle against Polish forces in April 1919. More than its message of equality and social justice, he admired Bolshevik Communism, to use the words of a prominent historian, "as an example of what single-mindedness, ruthless expediency and revolutionary determinism could achieve."[10]

Turning Zionist did not mark an ideological conversion for him. Even after becoming an active member of the socialist *Ahdut Ha'avoda* (Labor Unity) party, Ahimeir continued expressing his admiration of the Bolshevik leader explicitly, declaring that "[o]ur teacher is not Herzl or Jabotinsky, but Lenin. We reject the doctrines and philosophies of Lenin and his followers, but they were correct in their practical path. This is the path of violence, blood, and personal sacrifice."[11]

Early signs of Ahimeir's transition from Bolshevism to fascism can be found in "A Few Ideas About Fascism," an article he wrote for *Ha'Toren* (The Mast), a Hebrew monthly published in New York.[12] Written in August 1923, a few months before Ahimeir immigrated to Palestine and three months before Jabotinsky's "On the Iron Wall" was published, Ahimeir's article drew a clear line connecting the two authoritarian ideologies. According to Ahimeir, both fascists and Bolshevik revolutionaries should be admired for their heroism, their readiness for self-sacrifice, their embrace of violence, and their unique psychological disposition.

> From the psychological point of view, there is no difference between fascism and Bolshevism. There is a great distance between these two movements when it comes to their aspirations, but their living spirit is basically the same. There is an ideological distance, but not a psychological one. Both movements try to install their opinions within society, and both stand out in their impatience toward other opinions; both hinder mutual understanding within their societies. These are the slaves of *Losung* [solutions] of our times. Results do not interest them: The man of action thinks only of the day; the man of thought is preoccupied with the future and the past. For the psychologists, the carriers of

> fascism and Bolshevism, as well as the masses supporting these two movements, belong to the same psychological type. And in the eyes of the historians of the future to come as well, there will be no big gap separating these two movements.[13]

Ahimeir's 1923 article provides a vivid illustration of Ze'ev Sternhell's famous thesis regarding the origins and essence of fascism. According to Sternhell, fascism was first and foremost a form of a radical cultural revolt stemming from the ideological Left, originating in attempts to offer nonmaterialist revisions of Marxism while sharing Marxism's vehement rejection of bourgeois, rationalistic and procedural forms of politics. Soon enough, Sternhell suggested, fascists embraced a myth of violence, thereby transcending traditional ideological divisions and ending up in that liminal space of "ni droite, ni gauche" (neither Left nor Right). Crucially, this curious mix could be maintained only by visions of permanent struggle, a myth of violence, and constant revolution.[14] Fascism, as Ahimeir defined it, fits Sternhell's theoretical model exceptionally well. Ahimeir saw Italian fascism as a revolutionary movement that took the élan and intrepid energy of the Bolsheviks, yet without the false communist belief in internationalism and class struggle. Not surprisingly, like Pound, who despised intellectual abstractions, Ahimeir was also taken with the way both Bolsheviks and fascists were privileging action over contemplation, or what he called *Losung*—the German word for solution, which carried the meaning of a sophisticated theory and a mobilizing slogan. It was not so much a revolution derived from philosophical principles as a revolt of a spirit unbound.

Ahimeir's soon-to-become partners, Uri Zvi Greenberg and Joshua Yevin, followed a similar trajectory. Born in Eastern Galicia and Ukraine respectively, both immigrated to Palestine at the same time as Ahimeir (1923–1924), and like him, both were initially affiliated with the two Zionist socialist parties, *Hapoel Hatzair* and *Ahdut Ha'avoda-Poale Zion*. Greenberg published his first poems in *Davar*, the Labor Party's daily newspaper, and Yevin earned his living as a translator and teacher, working for the cultural committee of the *Histadrut*.[15] A verbose virtuoso, Greenberg played a more significant role than his two compatriots Ahimeir and Yevin in shaping the political language and imagination of the Right. Like Ahimeir, Greenberg also admired Lenin, whom he eulogized in 1924 in *Kuntras*, the Labor Party's journal prior to *Davar*, as the benefactor of "a bleeding Torah" (*torah medamemet*), a creator of "a dictatorship that a miracle accompanies, as well as glory."[16] It did not take long for him to lose hope that the labor Zionist ideologues and leaders would forge a local revolutionary avant-garde. His Hebrew poetry from those years—lush, excessive, expressionist—was already infused with messianic and irredentist language. In "Yerushalayim shel Matah" (Earthly Jerusalem, 1924), written with what became his trademark prophetic tone, he envisioned a pregnant Jerusalem, carrying in its womb a future kingdom (*malchut*) that would stretch from El-Arish to Damascus.[17]

Although Greenberg had his moment of ideological conversion around the same time as Ahimeir and Yevin, and despite the fact the three shared a similar temperament, his background—a Galitsianer with a strong Hassidic pedigree—set him somewhat apart. Unlike his Russian-Jewish peers who were intimate friends of key labor Zionists (Ahimeir and Berl Kaznnelson, the key labor Zionist pundit, shared the same hometown and were friends before immigrating to Palestine), Greenberg never enjoyed an "insider" status within labor Zionist institutions, nor did he have any sentimental attitude toward the Russian-speaking, Tolstoyian *Halutzim* (pioneers) that captured the imagination of the socialist Zionists at the time. He also had a far more fraught relationship with Europe and European culture. Two horrendous near-death experiences that occurred before his immigration and scarred Greenberg deeply played a significant role: first was the sight of carnage he witnessed as a soldier in the battlefields of WWI, and soon afterwards, in November 1918, Greenberg barely survived the Armistice Day pogrom in Lwów (Lemberg), during which Polish soldiers celebrating their victory almost slaughtered him and his family. Dubbed *malkhes fun tseylem* (the Kingdom of the Cross) in his early Yiddish poems, Europe was never mentioned by name and regarded as a place of great terror. Violence was not abstract or remote for him. It colored his expressionist poetry, depicting a godless world and the horrors of the tormenting, tortured human flesh.[18] Further, it was in his poetry, not his newspaper columns, that the term *Malchut Yisrael* (Kingdom of Israel) makes its first appearance.[19] The question of whether Greenberg introduced the term to envisage a modern sovereign nation-state or a larger kingdom or empire (the Hebrew root M.L.Ch means "King") remains open. What was clear was his open rejection of the mandatory regime, which was not described as a nucleolus of a future state but as a form of servitude. In the 1940s, the phrase would become a battle cry regularly used by anti-British insurgents.

All three men started drifting away from labor Zionist circles after spring 1926 and officially joined Jabotinsky's movement in February 1928. The revisionist movement provided them with the political home they were looking for, and the new association allowed them to fashion themselves as scion-followers of Jabotinsky, constantly quoting his blazing rhetoric of "In blood and fire Judah fell, in blood and fire Judah will rise!" Nevertheless, at no stage did they become blind admirers of Jabotinsky. Ahimeir, for example, was highly skeptical of Jabotinsky's reliance on British protection and described him in a private letter as a quixotic figure, a prisoner of his own naïve hallucinations.[20] Their rhetoric became more violent in the wake of the 1929 riots.[21] Having no access to concealed weapons, they remained preachers of the clenched fist. They adopted the name Brit Habiryonim in October 1931, effectively making themselves a political faction within the revisionist camp. The name, chosen by Greenberg, was indicative of their self-fashioning and self-understanding: "Biryonim" was the name given by the authors of the Babylonian Talmud to Second Temple era zealots, Jewish extremists who notoriously assassinated Romans as well as Jews who collaborated with the Romans or were considered their sympathizers.[22] Perhaps the trio chose this name because they conceived of themselves as an elite group of professional revolutionaries, modern heirs of the Second Temple's zealots. Relying on Second Temple imagery was a savvy move that provided a Jewish cover to what was, to no small extent, a Leninist conception of a revolution. They were calling the youth to find the courage needed to fight a far stronger foreign empire and, no less importantly, to dismiss with scorn the authority of the rabbis. What the Zionist movement needed, Ahimeir argued in 1932, was not more Zionist congresses that would deliberate endlessly but one decisive "Zimmerwald conference"—a reference to the 1915 communist conference in which Lenin distanced his faction from the reformist socialists and began building a committed, revolutionary party instead.

As far as Jabotinsky was concerned, the three men proved to be an asset and a liability at the same time. Though on the face of it they lacked real political power, the trio manifested shrewdness and remarkable sophistication in exploring and utilizing new media channels that helped them spread and amplify their message.[23] Notably, a series of articles Ahimeir published in *Doar Hayom* under the title "From the Diary of a Fascist" attracted much attention. In between, the trio played a significant extra-Palestinian role in radicalizing Polish and Baltic members of the Betar youth movement, who were intoxicated by the fiery self-described maximalists from Palestine who distinguished themselves from the all too obedient and impotent "Salon Revisionists."[24] Jabotinsky, realizing that he must ride the tiger or else be eaten by it, was afraid to dismount. His February 1932 article "On Adventurism," which warned against the excessive ideas of the new revisionist phalanx, revealed the tension between the leader and his rebel children, as well as his limitations in restraining them. Sugarcoating what was in fact a disruptive, disobedient attempt to challenge Jabotinsky, the three explicitly called him to declare himself a dictator or simply Il Duce in 1932, thereby abandoning his outdated law-abiding beliefs in parliamentary politics and considerable Anglophile biases.

Startlingly, it was after the Arlosoroff assassination (June 1933) and its ensuing trial that the triumvirate dwindled in influence, which saved Jabotinsky's young movement from being hijacked from within.[25] Though acquitted of murder, Ahimeir was convicted of heading an illegal organization and sentenced to two years in prison; the newspaper *Doar Hayom* was also shut down and ceased publication.[26] Greenberg's fiery poetry gained its second political life during the 1940s, after Jabotinsky's death, mainly thanks to Avraham ("Yair") Stern and the members of the paramilitary group Lehi. In the context of an open, violent rebellion against the British authorities, Greenberg came to be revered as prophetic, inspirational, and exciting and was practically crowned the poet laureate of the underground group. It was in this context that his poetic vocabulary acquired new meaning. Once it was contrasted with the specter of a future Lilliputian partitioned "state"—and not only with the preservation of colonial subjugation—a term like *Malchut Israel* was no longer an expressionist abstraction devoid of concrete political meaning. On the contrary, it resurfaced in the insurgents' writings and shaped their horizon of expectations. Still, in between these two phases, another discursive development became noticeable: the emergence of a vision of a Hebraic *mare nostrum*, modeled after the Italian fascist fantasy of the Mediterranean basin.

The Dream of a Hebraic *Mare Nostrum*

The Italian ingredients of revisionist Zionism, discernible as they may be, remain understudied. Jabotinsky's writings, for example, which reveal little admiration for Russian Bolshevism, are rich in sympathetic allusions to the Italian *Risorgimento*, which he considered the paradigmatic nineteenth-century Romantic nationalism. The Italy of Mazzini and Garibaldi he admired was referred to by him as his spiritual homeland, and "Altalena," the pen name he started using when he arrived in Rome to study law at Sapienza University (1898–1901), made this Italophilia part of Jabotinsky's public and intellectual persona.[27] But was Mussolini's Italy the same? Jabotinsky's references to fascist Italy as more efficient, clean, and orderly in comparison to its predecessor state were abundant during the early 1930s, especially in light of a global economic meltdown. It led many Zionists to flirt with the Italian dictator while maintaining a critical distance from the authoritarian cult of power and youth and without completely subscribing to the new ideology. Numerous non-revisionist Zionist activists, including Itamar Ben-Avi, Nahum Sokolow, Victor Jacobson, and the leader Chaim Weizmann himself met with the Duce (including after the rise of the Nazis to power in Germany in 1933 and the Italian invasion of Abyssinia [Ethiopia] in 1935, but not after the passing of the *leggi razziali*, the Italian racial laws, in 1938). In this respect, Jabotinsky was not unique in seeking, somewhat cautiously, stronger ties with Rome. These ambiguous contacts did not appear in a vacuum. They corresponded with Mussolini's Middle Eastern foreign policy that sought to counterbalance French and British hegemony by forging ties with local forces who were equally unhappy with the mandates system. After all, Italian colonial Libya notwithstanding (which Italy acquired in 1911, before mandates), it was clear that the distribution of post-Ottoman territories during the 1920s solidified British hegemony. This process was not only incompatible with Italy's own irredentist desires but made the fascist talk of a *mare nostrum* (Latin for "our sea")—the dream of making the Mediterranean basin into the beating heart of a new empire—into a laughingstock.[28]

It was in the context of the fascist *mare nostrum* policy that Mussolini gave his blessing to the opening of a naval training academy for Betar members in Civitavecchia, a port city northwest of Rome. Careful and suspicious, Jabotinsky accepted the generous offer but refused on principle to accept money from the Italian government. *Sarah I*, the training vessel used in the new naval academy, was purchased with funds donated by Yfim Kirshner, a Jewish fur merchant from Paris. In a letter dispatched to the cadets, Jabotinsky urged them to be respectful but remain politically neutral: "If you are to be asked about your political and social beliefs, answer: 'I am a Zionist, my heart craves from a Hebrew State in our country, and I oppose the war between the classes. That is all I believe.'"[29] Many of the cadets ignored the leader's advice. Ideological radicalization, like the work of consolidating stronger ties with the fascist regime, was accomplished at the rank-and-file level by a group of second-tier and somewhat forgotten intellectuals and activists such as Zvi Kolitz (1912–2002), Isacco ("Yitzhak") Sciaky (1896–1979), Leone Carpi (1887–

1964), and Yirmiyahu ("Irma") Halpern (1901–1962). They were the ones who provided the crucial personal and ideological bridges connecting Palestine's radicals with the Italian fascists. Unlike the members of Brit Habiryonim, the political idioms they incorporated and developed did not rely on Leninist theories of revolution but were taken from an arsenal of Italian political imageries. Crudely, this loose assembly could be subdivided into two branches: While the more cerebral members of the group translated terms and ideas taken directly from the writings of Benito Mussolini and Giovanni Gentile (Mussolini's court philosopher and the person to coin the term *totalitarianism*) into Hebrew, the more adventurous and artistically inclined members of the group, mesmerized by the Mediterraneo-centric notion of *mare nostrum*, sought to develop a Hebraic variant of the same ideals.[30]

Zvi Kolitz, who published the first (and to this day, only) Hebrew biography of Mussolini, belongs to the first branch of thinkers who were fascinated by the new fascist conceptions of the corporate post-liberal and anti-liberal state. Born to an Orthodox Lithuanian family, he moved to Italy in the 1930s to study political science at the University of Florence and to attend the Betar Naval Academy in Civitavecchia. During these formative Italian years, he realized the importance of a strong political leadership, arguing that fascism was the most significant ideology in Europe and the Italian state was his concrete realization. Published in Tel Aviv in 1936, the biography he authored dissociated fascism from antisemitism, presenting the former as free of any Jew-hatred. Similar to Ahimeir's, Kolitz's depiction of Mussolini emphasized the "exceptional will-power [of] a man who knows what he wants and wants the favor and the future of Italy to the best of his belief. . . . An idea without a leader is like a corpse without a soul. . . . [Subsequently] strong ideas depend on strong personalities." [31] In its appendix, the book provided translated excerpts of some of Mussolini's speeches and essays, including his famous doctrine of fascism (*La dottrina del fascismo*; ghostwritten by Gentile) of 1932, appearing in Hebrew for the first time. Later, he joined the Irgun (aka the *Etzel*, the revisionist's underground paramilitary organization) and was arrested by the British. He reinvented himself after the Second World War as a film producer and fiction author. As far as we know, he never acknowledged his fascist past in later years.

Isacco Sciaky was the main theoretician and ideologue of revisionism in Italy. A Sephardi Jew born in Salonica (Thessaloniki), Sciaky was the *enfant terrible* of Italian Zionism, known for his fiery temperament and radical ideas. He was an enthusiastic follower of Giovanni Gentile's neo-Hegelian philosophy since his days as a student of philosophy at La Sapienza University. In November 1922, soon after the fascist March on Rome, Sciaky wrote to Gentile to express his hope that the fascist cultural regeneration "will be better able to meet our eastern populations (*nostre popolazioni orientali*) at the time of the awakening of those countries," and that stronger contacts between Italians and Jews would provide the common framework of civilization in the East, spreading light and boasting pride in the "two immortal nations (*di due popoli immortali*)."[32] Siacky did not fear to challenge the socialist Zionist teachings of Enzo Sereni and mainstream Italian Zionists who preached agricultural life and sought to model Italy's Zionism after the Yishuv's labor movement.[33] Instead, he formulated an authoritarian political theory of the "corporative state" that would replace the liberal and antisocial vision of a competitive economy with a planned economy that replaced the egoistic interests of individual citizens, trade unions, and social classes with the unitary interest of the State, which would synthesize and harmonize all the productive forces of the nation.[34] Jabotinsky remained unimpressed.[35] The highly abstract style of Sciaky's writings, infused with neo-Hegelian language defining the "true state" as an entity living "within the consciousness, or better the true state is the consciousness of citizens," might further suggest why much of this high talk fell on deaf ears.[36] Sciaky viewed the passing of the racial laws in Italy as a betrayal, prompting his 1939 immigration to Palestine, where he began a second career as a professor of law and economics in Tel Aviv. The densely metaphysical tone did not disappear from the Hebrew textbook on the history of Western philosophy he authored in later years for his Israeli students.[37]

Leone Carpi, the *naziv* (commander) of Civitavecchia's Naval Academy, was less philosophically inclined than Sciaky. Older than most of his Betar comrades, he was also the only Italian Jew by birth, scion to one of Italy's most distinguished Jewish families. He took much pride in his family's patriotic pedigree: His grandfather—also called Leone—was a friend of Mazzini's, a supporter of the short-lived Roman Republic (1849) and the first Jew to be elected to the Italian Parliament, by the city of Ferrara. Serving as an officer in the Italian army during WWI, he was decorated for his courage under fire, after which he obtained a law degree and began drifting toward Zionism. It did not take long for him to be revolted by what he saw: a pale, tiny movement, which he described as "completely bogged down, monopolized by a few people, and focused narrowly on economic problems and financial needs."[38] Revisionism, seen by him as a brave revolt against this oligarchical group, reminded him of the Romantic nationalism of 1848. He saw fascism as an organic continuation of the Risorgimento.

The founding editor of the revisionist newspaper *L'Idea Sionistica* (The Zionist Idea, 1930–1938), Carpi made himself the ideal bridge figure between the revisionist Zionist movement and Italy's fascist regime. The translation of Jabotinsky's history of the Jewish Legion into Italian first appeared in the newspaper, alongside many other translations of revisionist Zionist texts. Carpi's own articles and editorials depicted the revisionist leader as a superhuman figure combining the qualities of the revolutionary theorist Mazzini and the diplomat Cavour, or as the "Jewish Garibaldi."[39] Advocating a spiritual affinity between Italians and revisionists, he emphasized that "in Jabotinsky's words, we often find references, reminiscences, and associations inspired [by] the Italian artistic and political atmosphere of that time."[40] Yet, if Carpi made himself instrumental in the establishment of the Naval Academy, it was to a large degree thanks to his ability to add a considerable dose of realpolitik to this enthusiastic idealism. It was critical when communicating with fascist representatives. When he approached Mussolini during the early 1930s, he argued that the establishment of a Jewish National Homeland would be in the interest of Italy's Mediterranean aspirations. When he contacted Admiral Paolo Camillo Thaon, the commander of the Royal Italian Navy, Carpi stressed the reciprocal advantages both fascism and revisionism would draw from the training facility. The academy, he brazenly added, was much more than a training facility, "because we want our youth to learn and later promote fascist culture and Italian language, to facilitate the penetration of the fascist civilization into the Near East."[41]

Jabotinsky feared that a golem was emerging: Would the efficient apparatchik who helped him spread the revisionist word in Italy gain too much power and ultimately challenge him? He had good reasons for concern. During the fifth World Revisionist Conference in Vienna (1932), Carpi sided with Ahimeir and the Palestinian maximalists, who demanded a stronger leadership and gave the fascist salute before he delivered his speech on "the affinities between fascism and Revisionism." Jabotinsky, he believed, had to make himself a Jewish Duce: "Gentlemen, we have a leader who has what it takes to be a dictator. . . . It is necessary to let him choose the right moment and the right way to act for the protection of the movement, for the salvation of Herzl's original idea, and the redemption of the Jewish State."[42]

Undoubtedly, if there was a person who personified the zeal for the Mediterranean, more than anyone else it was the free-spirited and dashing captain Yirmiyahu ("Yirma") Halperin. Halperin had acquired a reputation as one of the legendary leaders of Betar, the revisionist proto-militarist youth movement, long before landing at Civitavecchia. Born in Smolensk but growing up in Palestine, he was the commander of Betar's 41st Battalion in Tel Aviv and founded Betar's school of instructors before being invited by Jabotinsky to Poland in 1928, where he established a national school for Betar leaders and oversaw the activities of Betar camps in Austria and Latvia. Like Carpi, Halperin took pride in his family lineage, as the son of Michael Halpern, member of the anti-Tsarist underground *Narodnaya Volya* who became a legendary pioneer in Palestine, supported the Young Turks after 1908, and inspired the founders of *Hashomer*, Palestine's first Jewish defense organization.[43] "Yirma" proved unruly from the very beginning of his involvement, accusing Betar's leadership of deficient enthusiasm and petite-bourgeoisie thinking. Stories about Yirmiyahu Halperin's fearlessness during the 1920 Nebi Musa riots and the 1929 riots—tales that contained a nucleus of truth to which much melodrama and hyperbole were added—further helped to build a myth around the man. Though he had no formal military training nor real battle experience, he was idolized, and he pushed his cadets to replace the reigning defensive ethos with a more stern, offensive attitude.

Halperin was captivated by the sea from an early age. He served as a sailor on *Hechalutz*, the first ship acquired by the Yishuv in 1919, established the Jewish Maritime League in 1933, and began publishing pamphlets in Russian and Hebrew, describing the future benefits the Jews of Palestine would gain from sailing, trade, and economic development in the Mediterranean. He arrived at Civitavecchia accompanied by his close ally Arieh Bayevski (born Gleb Alexeyevich Boklebecki), an eccentric ex-officer in the Russian Imperial Navy who fled Russia during the Civil War and ended up living in Palestine. Bayevski was among the founders of the Zebulon Naval Association in Tel Aviv, an organization seeking to promote marine training and development, and in Civitavecchia he served as Halperin's deputy.

For both men, Betar's Italian initiative was the necessary vehicle to accomplish their dream of *kibush ha-yam* (conquest of the sea), a slogan that surfaced in Halperin's publications from the early 1930s. The suggestion that aquaculture should also be part of Palestine's economic development did not originate with the revisionist movement. Yet early attempts to promote such initiatives, including the creation of a special "water committee," as it was called at the time, either died out quickly or lacked the necessary funding. Halperin brought much of the needed energy to help promote such initiatives, but he also charged the project with a new political meaning. For the catchphrase *kibush ha-yam* was first and foremost a tool in intra-Zionist ideological struggles. It allowed the revisionists to counterbalance the labor Zionists' emphasis on *kibush ha-adama* (conquest of the land) through agriculture. Halperin explicitly accused the labor Zionists of suppressing any initiative or attempt to invest in Hebrew seafaring, instead focusing myopically on fostering the kibbutz movement, which he argued was not viable economically. Next, the conquest of the sea went hand in hand with an open challenge to British hegemony in the region and what the hawkish revisionist described as a British as well as Zionist policy of appeasing the Arab population. "Those who saw the struggle for the rebirth of an independent Hebrew state as a provocation to British rule and the status of the Arabs . . . and were careful to avoid taking steps that might be interpreted as 'provocation,'" Halperin wrote, were also the ones who "deterred from aspiring to revive Hebrew seamanship and to cultivate the merchant fleet, the Hebrew Navy and a Hebrew fishing fleet."[44]

Third, and probably most significant, was the term *yamaut 'ivrit* (Hebrew seafaring). This term, popularized by the journalist Itamar Ben-Avi (né Ben-Zion Ben Yehuda), rested on an original claim of nativity according to which a significant number of the ancient Israelite tribes were, in fact, seafaring tribes. Based on a somewhat whimsical interpretation of biblical stories, it looked at the ancient Israelites, like the Phoenicians, as an ancient nation that lived by the sea and from the sea.[45] Zebulon, the tribe that occupied a territory bordering the Mediterranean and whose symbol was a ship, gave its name to the association dedicated to promoting naval training "and deepening of marine consciousness" that was practically hijacked by these new hawkish Betarists. [46] This discursive innovation armed the revisionist ideology with a powerful primordial claim, making the modern return to the sea a project of reconnecting with an autochthonic, pre-Rabbinical mode of living. It competed with Ben-Gurion's efforts to read socialist Zionists back into the ancient Jewish prophets, which he insisted on describing as the heralds of calls for social justice and equality in modern times. It collided most sharply with Chaim Weizmann's favorable allegory, which compared the institutions of higher learning that the Jews established in Palestine, in Jerusalem and in particular in Rehovot, to Yavneh, the famous Yeshiva established by Rabbi Yohanan ben Zakkai after the destruction of the Second Temple by the Roman Legions.

Turning to the sea, in other words, was also about creating a new political language anchored in a historical phantasm. Revisionist Mediterraneanism underscored a romantic desire to reconnect with a fantastic Hebraic, pre-exilic past. Similarly, the irredentist potential of these fables was evident. The less domesticated versions of the Hebraic Mediterranean discourse went as far as suggesting that ancient Hebrew-speaking tribes ruled the Mediterranean basin, that the Carthaginians originated in the Land of Canaan, and that there was good reason to suggest that Hannibal spoke Hebrew. The parable mirrored the Italian fascist *mare nostrum* vision, which presented Mussolini's expansionist politics as part of a transhistorical, monumental project of reconnecting with the Roman past. At the same time, the Hebraic fleet was not about to join the neo-Roman empire. The new *Judaea Navalis* was to be the substitute and the answer to *Judaea Capta* (Judea Conquered), the humiliating term inscribed on the coins issued by the Roman emperor to celebrate the destruction of the Second Temple.

A vast gap separated Halperin's boastful statements and his modest results. In October 1935, *Sarah I*, with twenty Jewish cadets in military uniform, embarked on its first long voyage to Spain and Algeria. The journey was interrupted when, on the way to Seville, the ship almost sank after water penetrated it. When the ship docked in Algiers, the appearance of Jews in uniform created a riot, leading the local Italian consulate to intervene and warn against further provocations. At first, the summer 1937 cruise seemed to be a success. The nonsocialist Hebrew press in Palestine followed Halperin and his men as they visited Genoa, Livorno, and Cyprus, before arriving in Haifa and organizing a mini military parade in Tel Aviv. From there they continued to Rhodes, Salonica, and Malta, and even stopped in Tunisia, where they were welcomed warmly by the local Jewish community. On the island of Corsica, a fierce storm hit the ship, and it got stranded and had to be evacuated. Halperin was the last to abandon ship, which was later dragged by an Italian hauler. The rescue operation cost a fortune and the vessel was decommissioned. Soon after that, with the passing of Italy's racial laws and the closing of the academy, the entire Hebrew Mediterranean scheme evaporated. With characteristic pathos and melodrama, Halperin insisted in later years that the Civitavecchia was the place where the future Israeli navy was born. In practice, even his proposal to convert the vessel into a "floating exhibition" that would display the achievements of the Yishuv failed.

A Jewish *Sinn Féin*: Constructing a Culture of Anticolonial Martyrdom

It was on June 29, 1938, at the same time the revisionists had begun to dismantle their Italian project, that the British hanged a twenty-five-year-old member of the paramilitary Irgun (Etzel) named Shlomo Ben-Yosef. Born as Shlomo Tabachnik in Lutsk (Łuck), Poland, Ben-Yosef immigrated to Palestine in 1937. He was sentenced to death for carrying ammunition and discharging firearms after a failed attempted shooting and throwing a hand grenade at an Arab bus near Safed. Though his attempted ambush flopped miserably, once he was put on trial before the Haifa Military Court, the Irgun press wing seized the opportunity to turn the trial and execution into a media propaganda event. Ben-Yosef insisted on wearing his Betar uniform on his death row walkthrough (a request that was denied), sang the Betar hymn and the Hatikvah, and called out "Long live Jabotinsky!" before the rope tightened around his neck.

Most historians agree that the execution inaugurated a new and far more violent phase in the history of the revisionist movement. The new strand of Jewish militants who joined the Irgun and later on the *Lehi* (acronym for *Lohamei Herut Yisrael*; lit. fighters for the freedom of Israel, established August 1940) saw themselves as anonymous soldiers in a war of national liberation against a foreign and hostile colonial rule. The 1938 hanging, which was merely the first in a list of executions that would continue into the late 1940s, played a vital role in the new political mythology that emerged during the war and its immediate aftermath, weaving a legend around "the martyrs of the gallows."[47] In the hands of underground newspapers and pamphlet writers, the trials and executions were converted into heroic stories of courage in the face of the oppressor, surpassing even the bravery of the soldier dying in battle. The hangings triggered retaliation and revenge attacks and were used as a recruitment tool for new fighters. The cycle of violence followed a vicious new logic, identified in later years by Carl Schmitt, the German ex-Nazi legal and political theorist: "The modern partisan expects neither justice nor mercy from his enemy. He has turned away from the conventional enmity of the contained war and given himself up to another—the real—enmity that rises through terror and counter-terror, up to annihilation."[48] Undoubtedly, in this new toxic environment, executions proved to be one of the most counterproductive tools of counterinsurgency.

The new climate necessitated a new action model. Ireland, and its famous 1916 armed insurrection against British rule known as the Easter Rising, provided a new source of inspiration. In fact, the shift in attitude among the revisionists toward Ireland is one of the most reliable barometers to measure the movement's radicalization. In 1916, while working as a correspondent for the Russian newspaper *Russkiye Vedomosti* (which was closed down by the Bolsheviks after the Russian Revolution), Jabotinsky expressed empathy for the Irish cause but not sympathy with the methods of struggle employed by the rebels. It was pointless to declare a war of liberation, he argued, which only lead to the senseless sacrifice of many.[49] This cautious expression of solidarity with the Irish comes as a small surprise given the vertical alliances Jabotinsky sought to strengthen between the Zionist movement and Great Britain through schemes like the Jewish Legion. By 1939, however, he had changed his mind, stressing the affinity between the two movements and befriending Robert Briscoe, the famous Jewish-Irish politician and perhaps the only Jew in the Irish Republican Army (IRA), who was charmed by the leader of

Betar. The purpose of his visit to Ireland, Jabotinsky told Briscoe, was "to learn all he could of the methods we had used in training our young men and boys for the Revolution against England."[50] The similarity between Betar and *Fianna Éireann*, the Irish nationalist youth movement, did not escape both men, and Briscoe, who boastfully recalled in his memoir how he appointed himself "to a full professorship with the Chair of Subversive Activity against England," described to Jabotinsky how the boys were secretly trained during times of peace, what the British military weaknesses were, and what the most effective ways of orchestrating a revolt against them were.[51] The signs of change were also apparent during the winter of 1940, when *HaMashkif*, the revisionist party's Hebrew daily newspaper, published a series of three articles portraying Éamon de Valera and the 1916 Easter Rising in a highly positive light.[52]

In these same months, a small Irgun delegation that included Eri Jabotinsky (Jabotinsky's son) and Hillel Kook (aka Peter Bergson) toured the United States. Using letters of introduction from Jabotinsky and Briscoe, they met with Irish Americans in New York who might support their campaign to permit the formation of a Jewish army in Palestine.[53] Paul O'Dwyer (1907–1998), a prominent Irish-born lawyer, political activist, and younger brother of New York City's Mayor William O'Dwyer, was certainly convinced. He supported the American League for a Free Palestine, the Irgun's fundraising arm in the United States, and was probably involved in drafting the public statement that made the Zionist-Irish analogy explicit, declaring: "It is not the first time that oppressed and subjugated people of a foreign land have appealed to America for help. . . . Free Czechoslovakia and Free Ireland are living examples of our response."[54] In a later interview O'Dwyer returned to these stormy years and explained: "While you're engaged in a war of revolution, you don't question the ideology . . . of your compatriots . . . when it's all over and the victory is won, you can make your decision whether you bring back the kin of David and make them kings of Israel or you want a workers' republic. . . . But while there's a common enemy and while you don't have your freedom you can't enjoy the luxury of an internal fight."[55]

Above all, the Irish cause provided an opportunity to endorse the more hawkish stance of Ahimeir and his maximalist peers, which came with a radical reinterpretation of Zionism itself. A permanent avant-gardist never afraid to take a different stance than Jabotinsky, Ahimeir published articles expressing support for Sinn Féin as early as 1927. In a typical manner, Ahimeir went as far as suggesting that the very term *Sinn Féin*, literally meaning "We Ourselves," was a direct equivalent of Hillel the Elder's famous Hebrew proverb, "*Im ein ani li, mi li*?" ("If I am not for myself, then who will be for me?").[56] Ahimeir's original interpretation, to be sure, was not meant to tie the Irish Republican passion with the ancient Jewish religious figure alone, but with the Jewish national movement. For Hillel's famous dictum was used as the motto for Leon Pinsker's famous proto-Zionist manifesto, "Autoemancipation!" (1882). He returned to the subject in 1930, expressing his pro-Irish sympathies in a series of articles written in response to the Passfield White Paper, which sought to restrict Jewish settlement.[57] His comrade, Joshua Yevin, went even further: "Akko [Acre] could be a second Cork, if only the Jewish People knew what all other nations know: how to eradicate internal treason!"[58]

Unsurprisingly, such positive references became more frequent after Jabotinsky's unexpected death (August 4, 1940), especially within the circles of the Lehi. Avraham Stern (1907–1942), the founder of the underground group, came to the Irish analogy at a very late stage in his short but dramatic life. He evinced an early interest in classics as a student at the Hebrew University, and thanks to a scholarship he won to study at the University of Florence, he came to know the Italian fascist regime intimately. While in Italy contemplating how to write his planned dissertation on eros in ancient Greek literature, Stern also penned some of his poems, which were inspired by Russian modernism, Polish nationalist poets, and Uri Zvi Greenberg's expressionist poetry.[59] Back in Palestine, he chose "Yair" as his nom de guerre. The name, which was a tribute to Eliezer Ben Yair, the commander of the Jewish zealots at Masada, was taken from the same Second Temple repository of cultural associations Greenberg borrowed from. Similarly, the term *Malchut* (Kingdom), which made its first appearances with Greenberg's poetry, resurfaced in Stern's poems, only now it gained a more concrete political shape: *Malchut* was to mark Jewish national sovereignty and full independence to be achieved through armed struggle and guerilla warfare. It was clear, however, that neither fascist Italy nor the Second Temple era could provide a clear plan of action for such an anticolonial rebellion. In 1941, not long before the British police killed him, Stern began translating into Hebrew Patrick Sarsfield O'Hegarty's book, *The Victory of Sinn Féin: How It Won It and How It Used It*, which told the story of the 1916 Easter Rising. The opening chapter was published in *Ba-mahteret* (The Underground), Lehi's newspaper.[60] The main lesson to be drawn from the chapter was that although the Easter Rising failed to accomplish its declared mission, the Irish struggle gained new martyrs whose memory perpetuated the rebellion. Becoming a Jewish martyr himself, Stern had no opportunity to further develop the Irish analogy. Symbolically, the underground name chosen by the commander who replaced him, Yitzhak Shamir (born Yitzhak Yezernitsky) was "Michael," after Irish Republican revolutionary leader Michael Collins. The assassination of the secretary of state for the colonies Lord Moyne, planned by Shamir and executed by his men, was a copycat murder inspired by the IRA.[61]

The Irish analogy found its way into the circles of the Irgun as well, especially after Menachem Begin assumed its leadership in December 1943. The authors of the Irgun's announcement about an open "rebellion against British rule," printed on banners that were posted on billboards and house walls on the night of February 1–2, 1944, used the Proclamation of the Provisional Government of the Republic of Ireland (i.e., the announcement of the Easter Rising) from April 1916 as their template.[62] Crucially, under Begin, who wanted a paramilitary organization free of political shackles, the formal ties with the revisionist party, which were diluted even beforehand, were finally cut. This also meant that the new recruits who joined the underground were not necessarily drawn from Betar, and they did not necessarily have to subscribe to the precise ideological stance advocated by Jabotinsky, the former "Supreme Commander" of the Irgun. In that respect, the Irgun fighters, despite their intense political commitment, were not partisans in the German, Schmittian sense nor in the Leninist sense, for they were dissociated from a specific *Partei* [political party] and were not necessarily *Parteigänger* [party adherents]. Reserving the term for the irregular troops who fought the Axis powers in Europe, Palestine's Jewish insurgents rarely applied it to their actions. No less significant was the fact that both the Irgun and the Lehi took much pride in their ability to recruit and integrate into their fighting force a growing number of non-Ashkenazi youth, including from the margins of society.[63] Tellingly, of the dozen Lehi and Irgun insurgents executed by the British, six were non-Ashkenazi, six were native born, and three had gained military experience before joining the underground during their service in the British army during WWII. This demographic makeup was a marker of difference distinguishing the *Haganah* and the *Palmach*, the paramilitary groups affiliated with the labor Zionist parties, from the Lehi and the Irgun, but it also illustrates the shift from the two previous decades, during which extremist ideas were promoted by Ashkenazi men born and raised outside Palestine.

At this stage of "party-free" and "gloves-off" struggle, intricate ideological sophistry was less relevant to Menachem Begin than folktales of Irish resistance, endurance, and martyrdom. These ideas were encapsulated in the affidavit Avshalom Haviv, an Irgun fighter captured by the British during the Acre Prison break, presented before the British judges during his trial:

> I assume you know the bloody history of your own tyrannical rule in Ireland. You probably remember that there too you overran a small country and a civilized nation by force of arms and by treacherous perfidy under the foul pretext of protecting religion and maintaining law and order. . . . And when the sons of Ireland rose against you, when the Irish underground waged a war of liberation, you tried to drown the rebellion against tyranny in streams of blood. You erected gallows, you murdered innocent people in the streets, you deported patriots into a God-forsaken wilderness, you tortured the people and looted their homes and you believed, in your stupidity, that by doing so you would break the spirit of resistance of the Irish people. That spirit which is a God-given gift to every man created in His image. You failed. The Irish rebellion went from strength to strength. The blood of the fighters and the blood of the tortured united the whole nation around the flag of liberation until you were forced to retreat, leaving behind a bloody trail and memories that will never be forgotten. Ireland rose to freedom and you were left with eternal shame.[64]

While *Olei Hagardom* (literally, "those who rose to the gallows") was the collective name most frequently used during the 1940s to describe the Jewish insurgents executed by the British, Menachem Begin began referring to them as *Harugei Malchut*.[65] The term, taken from elegies read during Yom Kippur and Tishah B'Av services, traditionally referred to the ten Jewish sages who were killed by the Romans in the second century C.E. Begin's renaming thus not only drew once more a direct line connecting the British control in Mandatory Palestine with ancient Roman subjugation but also Judaized the language of revolt.

To be sure, a similar sacralization of politics was characteristic of Irish Republicanism too, drawing upon fables and historical memories of Catholic martyrs and past rebels who were recast as heralds of the modern IRA. Similar "cultures of martyrdom," to use a contemporary phrase, continued to be constructed elsewhere, whether they were reliant on an indigenous storage house of cultural memories or products of imitation and importation.[66] However, in the context of Jewish anti-British radicalism, the Judaizing of the language of anticolonial revolt was not problem-free. Ultimately, it exposed the inherent tension between two incompatible conceptions and political visions. The one was a conception of *yehudiyut* (Jewishness), which tied the modern violent struggle to a lachrymose narrative of continuous Jewish suffering and brave spiritual standing in the face of oppression. The other was the proto-Canaanite vision of *'ivriyut* (Hebraism), which read the anticolonial conflict as a daring attempt to reconnect with the pre-Rabbinic, primordial and indigenous "Semitic" past. These proto-Canaanite ideas were already visible, as the previous section has shown, in the writings and actions of the fervent advocates of Hebraic Mediterraneanism.[67] It was not by coincidence that the poetry and teachings of Yonatan Ratosh (born Uriel Halprin, 1909–1981), the founder of the Committee for the Formation of the Jewish Youth (1943) and the mainspring behind the neo-Hebraic idea, were highly popular among the underground fighters. Eventually, Ratosh and other followers of the Canaanite idea had alienated themselves from their revisionist right-wing colleagues and set out on a separate path.[68]

These internal points of friction were almost unnoticeable during the years leading up to the 1948 War. The analogical imagination, the tendency to read one's unique political predicament in juxtaposition with other historical precedents, can explain, in part, why the Israelis dubbed it a War of Independence (*milhemet ha'atzmaut*) or a War of Liberation (*milhemet hashihrur*). There was nothing evident in the path the 1948–1949 conflict took to explain this framing: The Jewish forces were, by and large, not fighting the British mandatory forces, who left the country out of their own will, but their Palestinian Arab neighbors. After 1948, the exclusion of the veterans of these underground fighting groups from the national pantheon by the labor Zionist hegemony created deep-seated bitterness and helped to create an image of a united "fighting family." More than anything, the family metaphor, like the commemorations that returned time and again to the gallows myth, functioned as a veil. Beneath it one could hardly notice the difference between a Jewish conceptualization of the armed struggle and a "Canaanite" reading of the revolt, seeing it as on par with other decolonization struggles. As far as the story of Zionist radicalism is concerned, however, these different interpretations determined the different post-independence routes of these radicals and, ultimately, the fragmentation of the pre-1948 radical movement. This dynamic, however, requires a separate study and cannot be discussed here.

Epilogue

Radicalization is dependent on political languages and semiotics of violence. Systems of oppression need languages too, to be sure. The "prose of counter-insurgency," to use a term coined by Indian historian Ranajit Guha, is a system of narration that affirms the imperialist's view of himself as "firm but benign, authoritarian but understanding." Ultimately it is a form of colonialist knowledge and a system of justifications.[69] One does not need to study Hegelian dialectics to notice the extent to which the colonial prose of counter-insurgency mirrors the images introduced by the expressive poetics of the defiant rebel. For the historian reconstructing the language of rebellion, this language becomes intoxicating. The liberal historian's challenge is to neither accept the antiseptic logic used in systems of subjugation nor allow the spell of a poetics of blood and fire to take over. The scorn for pragmatism or willingness to compromise was an essential feature of this radicalization, which could not avoid turning violent. Between this violent politics of defiance and nonviolent civil resistance lies an abyss. It is not a question of degree but of quality, of essence.

Political languages and poetic imagination of the kind described in this chapter were a means to an end. They were applied to generate a cognitive map and a script for political action. The three languages of radicalism examined in this chapter—the Leninist-revolutionary language, the maritime Italo-fascist language, and the Irish-inspired language of rebellion—were, I have argued, the products of the politics of a comparative gaze, manufactured thanks to constant comparison, borrowing, and appropriation. Of the three languages, the turn to the sea was perhaps the least violent but the most radical. This somewhat naive naval fancy, I suggested, had more to do with a conscious effort of intellectuals to forge a new political language and historical imagination than with the actual, technical practice of recreating a new seafaring Jewish subject. There is no doubt a profound irony in the way in which a neo-Roman fascist fancy inspired the neo-Zealot Jewish radicals to restore Jewish pride and reverse *Judaea Capta*. Here, however, lies their radicalism in the literal sense: This was not simply an eccentric rebelliousness but an attempt to go to *radix* (Latin for root), to unearth the stems and roots of Jewish existence and reconnect with an imagined, pre-Rabbinical and monumental Hebraic past.

This imaginative process, to be sure, was not unique to revisionist Zionism nor was it confined to Palestine alone; rather, it was shared by numerous contemporaneous nationalist movements. It was, in essence, the Jewish hyper-nationalist equivalent of the Wagnerian Teutonic mythologies that allowed German nationalists to imagine themselves as reconnecting with a pure, pre-Christian age.[70] Uncoincidentally, it paralleled the phenomenon of "Phoenicianism" we find among Maronite intellectuals in the Lebanon of the 1920s, who cultivated dubious myths of origin reconnecting them with the monumental maritime culture that roamed the seas since the second millennium B.C., prior to the Arab conquest of the region.[71]

And similarly, it bears resemblance to the invocations of an ancient Celtic past that were put in service of racist mythologies of pan-European, pre-Christian and non-Roman origin.[72] We are still missing a synthetic study that compares these nationalist appeals to a lost golden age and identifies their relations to each other. The common denominator of these phantasms was their reliance on modern archeology and philology, and their naturalization of political communities that were prescribed a primordial monumental past. In the Middle Eastern arena, French and British archeology in the Ottoman Empire and Ernst Renan's musing about Semitism and Phoenicianism played a major role in providing the foundations for these intellectual fashions. All too often, these mythical conceptions of the past supplemented a deep suspicion if not contempt toward the liberal, bourgeois and "artificial" order, a bold attempt to surpass a narrow Christian-classical canon and an eagerness to fuel new empire-building imaginativeness. Contrary to an ideology of Jewish exceptionalism and separateness of a people dwelling alone (and, perhaps, the noticeable anxieties of incorporation one finds among Jewish studies scholars who resist this paradigm), studying Jewish radicals suggests their integration into broader intellectual and political fashions of the day and their active participation in them.

The three languages of radicalization surveyed here were not, by any means, the sole sources of inspiration for these Jewish radicals. Multiple references to authoritarian Poland and the autocratic methods of Kemalist Turkey, for example, lived side by side with ideological imports from Russia, France, and Ireland. What matters is the logic of continuous eclectic borrowing and remix. This logic was summarized by Ahimeir, who declared in 1920: "if our national disease does not have a national remedy, we will take it from the treasures of our neighbors."[73] Nor would it be accurate to suggest that at each phase of this evolution a new language replaced the former. Rather, like scales of onion, they formed new layers on top of previous layers, forming a composite.

Ultimately, the only place where these radicals revealed astonishing flexibility was in their categories of thought. Men who prided themselves on their rigid stubbornness and iron consistency were, in fact, constantly evolving and changing their language, adapting it to changing conditions like a chameleon. Even the semiotics of violence, apparently, cannot escape the logic of mimicry.

Acknowledgments

This paper grew out of the workshop "Radical Jewish Politics" at the University of California, Santa Cruz, May 24–25, 2017, and an abbreviated version of this chapter was published in *Palestine/Israel Review* 2, no. 2 (2025), published by Penn State University Press. I would like to thank the workshop organizers for encouraging me to put my thoughts into writing and for their invaluable feedback on earlier versions of this chapter. Some of the descriptions of figures discussed in the second section benefited much from research done by Matteo Quadrifoglio in his "Statism and Italophilia: Risorgimento and the Italian State in the Zionist-

Revisionist Imagination, 1922–1940" (unpublished master's thesis, University of Haifa, 2018). I would like to thank Mr. Quadrifoglio for his assistance in tracking down and translating the Italian sources, and Professor Amir Goldstein for his comments and advice. Additional archival research conducted for this chapter was supported by the Institute for Middle East Studies at the George Washington University.

NOTES

Epigraph: Uri Zvi GreenberSg, "Shir asher za'akti" [A poem I bellowed], can be found in *Reḥovot ha-nahar* [The streets of the river] (Tel Aviv: Shocken, 1951), 74. The English translation is mine.

1. Pound, Ezra. *Jefferson and/or Mussolini: L'idea Statale; Fascism as I Have Seen It* (New York: Liveright, 1936), 18, 26, 58.

2. The literature surveying Pound's fascism is vast. For a good introduction to the subject, see Catherine E. Paul, *Fascist Directive: Ezra Pound and Italian Cultural Nationalism* (Clemson: Clemson University Press, 2016).

3. The term *revisionist Zionism* was used by Jabotinsky as the political alternative to both labor (socialist) Zionist ideology and the Jewish Agency's leadership, which worked in close coordination with the British mandatory authorities. It led to the formation of a separate Union of Zionist Revisionists (*Berit ha-Tzohar*) headed by Jabotinsky in 1925. The youth movement Betar (acronym of *Berit Yosef Trumpeldor*, the Joseph Trumpeldor Alliance), was founded 1923 in Riga. Within a short time, Betar opened branches throughout Eastern Europe and Palestine, half of which were based in Poland. Menachem Begin became the head of Betar in Poland in 1938. The Irgun (shorthand for *Irgun T'zvai Le'umi*, National Military Organization) was an underground paramilitary group that was established in 1931 in protest of what its founders considered to be a restrained and defensive approach of the Jewish Agency and the mainstream *Yishuv* leadership. It accepted Jabotinsky's authority and carried out armed reprisals against the Palestinian Arabs and, after 1939, the British mandatory forces as well. Begin arrived in Palestine during the Second World War with the Free Polish Army (*Armia Andersa*) a couple of years after Jabotinsky's death and took the leadership of the Irgun. He disbanded the Irgun in 1948 and formed the *Herut* party and later (1973) the *Likud* party. He served as prime minister between 1977 and 1982.

4. Jewish Legion was the popular shorthand given to three battalions (numbered 38th, 39th, and 40th) of the Royal Fusiliers, an infantry regiment of the British Army during World War I. The 38th Battalion (also known as the Judean Regiment or the "First to Judah") was the first one to be established (spring 1917) and had a distinctive Jewish character, with uniforms featuring a menorah and Star of David. The two other battalions attracted Jewish volunteers from Palestine, Australia, the United States, and other European countries.

5. Robert Wohl, *The Generation of 1914* (Cambridge: Harvard University Press, 1979), 164.

6. Vladimir (Ze'ev) Jabotinsky, "D'Annunzio, Fiume and Zara [in Hebrew]," *Hadshot Ha'aretz*, November 25, 1919, 2. The translations were included in Jabotinsky, *Shirim* [Poems] (Jerusalem: Eri Jabotinsky, 1947). A letter from September 1915 that Jabotinsky sent to the Russian author Maxim Gorky, asking him to introduce him to D'Annunzio, discloses an even earlier fascination. See Jabotinsky to Maxim Gorky, September 8, 1915, aleph 1-5/2, Jabotinsky Institute Archives (hereafter JIA), Tel Aviv.

7. The essay was originally published in Russian in November 1923 in the Berlin-based periodical *Rassvyet* (*Рассвет*). The English translation (excerpted) is included in Itamar Rabinovich and Jehuda Reinharz, eds., *Israel in the Middle East: Documents and Readings on Society, Politics, and Foreign Relations, pre-1948 to the Present* (Hanover: University Press of New England, 2007), 41–43. The full version is available online at http://en.jabotinsky.org/media/9747/the-iron-wall.pdf.

8. Vladimir Jabotinsky, "Laḥaṣ," [Pressure], in *Ha-derekh el ha-revizyonizm ha-tsiyoni: Kovets maamarim be-"Razsvyet" la-shanim 1923–1924* [The road to Zionist revisionism], ed.

Joseph Nedava (Tel-Aviv: Mekhon Z'abotinski be-Yisrael, 1984), 64–75. For further details, see Arie M. Dubnov, "On Vertical Alliances, 'Perfidious Albion' and the Security Paradigm," *European Judaism* 52, no. 1 (2019): 67–110.

9. Avraham Heller, "Ha-historiosof," in *Abba Ahimer: Ha-ish shehita et ha-zerem* [Abba Ahimeir: The man who turned the tide], ed. Joseph Nedava (Tel Aviv: The Association for the Dissemination of National Consciousness, 1987), 187. For a fuller, authoritative intellectual biography, see Peter Bergamin, *The Making of the Israeli Far-Right: Abba Ahimeir and Zionist Ideology* (London: I. B. Tauris, 2020).

10. Colin Shindler, *The Triumph of Military Zionism: Nationalism and the Origins of the Israeli Right* (London: I.B. Tauris, 2010), 156.

11. Quoted in Colin Shindler, *The Rise of the Israeli Right: From Odessa to Hebron* (New York: Cambridge University Press, 2015), 90.

12. Established in 1913, *Ha'Toren* was the organ of the Hebraist society *Achieber*, which promoted Hebrew in the United States. After being funded initially by the Zionist Organization of America (ZOA), from 1921 it became an independent magazine, edited by the critic and translator Reuben Brainin. In contrast to Hebrew newspapers in Palestine, which were organs of specific political parties, *Ha'Toren* was known for its political and religious diversity. This may explain Ahimeir's decision to publish his ideas outside Palestine. The periodical ceased publication shortly thereafter, in 1925.

13. Abba Ahimeir, "Ra'ayonot bodedim al ha-fashism" [A few ideas about fascism]. *Ha'Toren* 4–5 (1923), 154 (my translation).

14. Zeev Sternhell, Mario Sznajder, and Maia Ashéri, *The Birth of Fascist Ideology: From Cultural Rebellion to Political Revolution*, trans. David Maisel (Princeton: Princeton University Press, 1996).

15. *Hapoel Hatzair* (The Young Worker) was a socialist Zionist party, formed in 1905 by A. D. Gordon and Yosef Sprinzak. Its non-Marxist practice and ideology (its founders rejected Marx's class struggle) put much emphasis on Hebraism, productivity, and agricultural work. It never enjoyed a mass following and was supported predominantly by members of nonurban collectives (*kibbutzim* and *moshavim*). *Ahdut Ha'avoda* (Labor Unity) was established in 1919 and led by Yitzhak Ben Zvi (Israel's second president) and Berl Katznelson, who also served as the general editor of the daily *Davar*. Both parties merged in 1930 into *Mapai* (Party of the Workers of the Land of Israel), led by David Ben-Gurion.

16. Uri Zvi (Greenberg), "El ever Moskva" [Toward Moscow], *Kuntras* 8, no. 15 (January 25, 1924), 3.

17. Uri Zvi Greenberg, "Yerushalayim shel matah," in *Eimah gedolah ve-yareah*, 57. The poem was originally published in *Hapoel Hatzair*, April 18, 1924.

18. The title of Greenberg's first Hebrew book is also noteworthy—*gedolah veyareah* (Great Terror and Moon; 1925)—which captures a similar sentiment of horror. For further details, see Dan Miron, *Akdamut le-atzag* [Prolegomenon to U. Z. Greenberg] (Jerusalem: Mosad Bialik, 2003). Notably, Yevin also put his traumatic experiences from WWI, during which he served in the Russian army as a military surgeon, in writing. See Y. H. (Yehoshua Heschel) Yevin, *Be-mazal ma'adim* [Mars zodiac] (Tel Aviv: Ahdut, 1928).

19. The first appearance of the term can be found in his 1924 poem "Yerushalayim shel matah" (translated as "Jerusalem" by Charles A. Cowen in 1939).

20. Abba Ahimeir, letter to Berl Katznelson, June 30, 1925, as quoted in Anita Shapira, *Berl: Biyografyah* [Berl Katznelson: Biography], (Tel-Aviv: Am Oved, 1980)389–390.

21. A series of weeklong demonstrations and violent clashes between Jews and Arabs in Palestine that resulted in 133 Jews and 116 Arabs killed and almost twice as many injured on both sides. For further details, see Hillel Cohen, *Year Zero of the Arab-Israeli Conflict 1929*, trans. Haim Watzman (Waltham, MA: Brandeis University Press, 2015).

22. For example, Tractate Gittin 56a speaks of Abba Sikkara as the leader of the zealots (*biryonei*) of Jerusalem.

23. These included *Sadan* (a short-lived literary journal founded, edited, and to a large extent also written by, Greenberg, 1924–1927), *Doar Hayom* (a daily founded by Itamar Ben-Avi and

edited for a brief but significant period, 1928–1931, by Jabotinsky), and *Hazit Ha'am* (lit. The Nation's Frontier, 1931–1934).

24. Daniel K. Heller, *Jabotinsky's Children: Polish Jews and the Rise of Right-Wing Zionism* (Princeton: Princeton University Press, 2017), chapter 3.

25. Chaim (Victor) Arlosoroff was the head of the Political Department of the Jewish Agency and one of the leaders of *Mapai* (see note 16). He was assassinated in June 1933 in Tel Aviv. The main suspicion fell on the revisionist movement, leading to the arrest of Ahimeir, who campaigned against Arlosoroff, alongside two other revisionist Zionist activists. Ahimeir, suspected of incitement to murder, was detained for a year. After a lengthy trial and appeal, the two main suspects were acquitted. Although it was decided not to prosecute Ahimeir for murder-related charges, he was prosecuted for his role as leader of Brit Habiryonim and sentenced to one and a half years in prison. The toxic affair underscored a deepening schism between the revisionist and the labor Zionists in Palestine.

26. Ahimeir's prison diaries, in which he further developed his ideas, were brought to print recently by his children: Abba Ahimeir, *Ayalah bein ha-homot: Yoman ha-mishpat ve-ha-soher 1934–1935* [A Doe inside the Walls: Trial and Prison Diary, 1934-1935], ed. Zeeva Ahimeir-Zabidov (Tel-Aviv: Jabotinsky Archive, 2023).

27. See, in particular, Vladimir Jabotinsky, "Garibaldi," in *Feullitons*, F1912/501/FR, JIA. For discussion, see Svetlana Natkovich, *Ben 'anene zohar: Yetsirato shel Vladimir (Zeev) Z'abotinski ba-heksher ha-hevrati* [Among radiant clouds: The literature of Vladimir (Ze'ev) Jabotinsky in its social context] (Jerusalem: Magnes Press, 2015).

28. For additional information, see Nir Arielli, *Fascist Italy and the Middle East, 1933–40* (New York: Palgrave Macmillan, 2010) as well as Daniel Carpi, "Weizmann's Political Activity in Italy in 1923–1934" [Hebrew], *Zionism—Studies in the History of the Zionist Movement and of the Jewish Community in Palestine* B (1971): 169–208.

29. Vladmir Jabotinsky, letter to students of Betar Naval School in Civitavecchia, November 20, 1934, letter 2414, aleph 1-2/24/3, JIA.

30. Gentile served as Mussolini's minister of education (1922–1924), was involved in drafting the 1925 "Manifesto of the Fascist Intellectuals," and was the author of the infamous 1932 Doctrine of Fascism that Mussolini attributed to himself. See A. James Gregor, *Giovanni Gentile: Philosopher of Fascism* (New Brunswick: Transaction Publishers, 2001). For the history of the term *totalitarianism* and its Italian fascist roots, see Abbott Gleason, *Totalitarianism: The Inner History of the Cold War* (New York: Oxford University Press, 1995); M. E. Moss, *Mussolini's Fascist Philosopher: Giovanni Gentile Reconsidered* (New York: P. Lang, 2004).

31. Zvi Kolitz, *Mussolini: Ishiyuto ve-torato* [Mussolini: His personality and teachings] (Tel Aviv: Tevel, 1936), 5–82. For additional information, see Dan Tamir, *Hebrew Fascism in Palestine, 1922–1942* (New York: Palgrave Macmillan, 2018).

32. Isacco Sciaky to Giovanni Gentile, November 8, 1922, in fascicule "Sciaky," Archivio della Fondazione Giovanni Gentile, Rome.

33. On Sereni and the socialist Italian Zionists, see Shira Klein, *Italy's Jews from Emancipation to Fascism* (Cambridge: Cambridge University Press, 2018), chapter 6.

34. Many of these ideas were summarized by Sciaky in the presentations he prepared for a conference he helped organize in Tel Aviv in January 1935, under the title "The Fascist Corporatism." The original handwritten notes for Sciaky's speech (in French) are available at the Jabotinsky Institute; see "Le Corporativisme Fasciste," pe307—3/1, JIA.

35. See Vladimir Jabotinsky and Isacco Sciaky, *Stato E Libertà: Il Carteggio Jabotinsky-Sciaky: 1924–1939* [State and liberty: The Jabotinsky-Sciaky exchange, 1924–1939], ed. Vincenzo Pinto (Soveria Mannelli, Catanzaro, Italy: Rubbettino, 2002).

36. Isacco Sciaky, "Recensione di 'La libertà nello Stato Moderno' di Harold J. Laski," in *La Nuova Italia*, III.2 (February 20, 1932): 64–65.

37. Isacco Sciaky, *He-hagut ha-filosofit be-hishtalshelulatah ha-historit* [Philosophic thought in its historical development], 2 vols (Jerusalem: Mishpat u-medinah, 1953). On Sciaky, see also Vincenzo Pinto, "Between Imago and Res: The Revisionist-Zionist Movement's Relationship with Fascist Italy, 1922–1938," *Israel Affairs* 10, no. 3 (2004): 90–109.

38. Leone Carpi, "Il Revisionismo in Italia," *L'Idea Sionistica* 2, no. 10/11 (November–December 1932): 10–14.

39. Leone Carpi, "Il Sionismo Nazionale di Zeev Jabotinsky," in Jabotinsky, *Verso lo Stato; Scritti E Discorsi Di Politica Sionistica*, ed. Leone Carpi (Milano: L'idea sionistica, 1960), xiv.

40. Leone Carpi, "Il Revisionismo in Italia," *L'Idea Sionistica* 2, no. 10/11 (February–March 1932): 10–12.

41. Leone Carpi to Thaon di Revel, October 28, 1934, A73/35, Central Zionist Archives, Scuola Marittima di Civitavecchia, Italy.

42. Leone Carpi, "Discorso, Vienna 1935" (handwritten notes), pe 189/4, JIA.

43. See Yermiyahu ("Yirma") Halperin, *Avi, Mikhael Halperin* [My father, Michael Halperin] (Tel-Aviv: Hadar, 1964). Halperin also emphasized the fact that he was the nephew (on his maternal side) of Hermann Kallenbach, the Lithuanian-born doctor who was Gandhi's closest friend and right-hand man during his time in South Africa.

44. Yermiyahu Halperin, *Tehi'yat ha-yamaut ha-'ivrit* [The revival of Hebrew seamanship] (Tel Aviv: Hadar, 1961), 10–11.

45. Itamar Ben-Avi, *Ha-Yama!* [Into the sea] (Tel Aviv: Zebulon, 1936).

46. Ben-Avi, *Ha-Yama!*, 1.

47. Amir Goldstein, "The Roots of the Gallows Myth in the Revisionist Movement During the 1930s," *The Journal of Imperial and Commonwealth History* 48, no. 1 (2019): 127–148,quote found on 131.

48. Carl Schmitt, *Theory of the Partisan: Intermediate Commentary on the Concept of the Political*, trans. G. L. Ulmen (New York: Telos Press, 2007), 7. The lecture, which was written against the backlash of decolonization struggles, was originally delivered by Schmitt in 1963.

49. Vladimir Jabotinsky, "Ирландия (От Нашего Корреспондента)" [Ireland (from our correspondent)], *Russkiye Vedomosti*, May 15 1916, resh-samech (רס)/910/1916—tav (ת), JIA; Jabotinsky, "Дублин" [Dublin], *Russkiye Vedomosti*, July, 24, 1916, resh-samech (רס)/918/1916—tav (ת), JIA; "О Новой Ирландии" [Russian: About New Ireland] *Russkiye Vedomosti*, August 19, 1916, resh-samech (רס)/920/1916—tav (ת), JIA. See also Joseph Heller, "Jabotinsky's Use of National Myths in Political Struggles," *Studies in Contemporary Jewry* 12 (1996), 190.

50. Robert Briscoe, *For the Life of Me* (Boston: Little, Brown, 1958), 264.

51. Robert Briscoe, *For the Life of Me* (Boston: Little, Brown, 1958), 264.

52. Abba Ahimeir, "Devalira—manhiga u-meshahrera shel Ayer" [De Valera—Éire's leader and liberator]. *HaMashkif*, February 2, 1940 (part I), February 23, 1940 (part II), February 3, 1940 (part III).

53. Monty Noam Penkower, "Vladimir (Ze'ev) Jabotinsky, Hillel Kook-Peter Bergson, and the Campaign for a Jewish Army," *Modern Judaism* 31, no. 3 (2011): 332–374. Penkower also mentioned a petition, organized by a fighting Irishman from Brooklyn named Andrew Somers, which demanded the His Majesty's Government permit the formation of the Jewish army.

54. Paul O'Dwyer, *Counsel for the Defense: The Autobiography of Paul O'Dwyer* (New York: Simon & Schuster, 1979), 152.

55. Paul O'Dwyer, "Paul O'Dwyer: Oral History Memoir (July 1980)," William E. Wiener Oral History Library of the American Jewish Committee, New York Public Library, 172 pp., on 55–56.

56. Abba Ahimeir, "Im Ein Ani Li, Mi Li?" [If I am not for myself, then who will be for me?] *Ha'aretz*, November 15, 1927, 2.

57. Abba Ahimeir, "Shin Fein" [Sinn Féin], *Doar Hayom*, October 28, 1930, 2.

58. Quoted in Yosef Heller, *Lehi: Ideologiyah u-folitikah 1940–1949* [Lehi: Ideology and politics 1940–1949] (Jerusalem: Shazar Center, 1989), 63.

59. Abraham Stern, *Mikhtavim le-Roni* [Letters to Rony], trans. David Stern, ed. Aharon Amir (Tel-Aviv: Ya'ir 'a. sh. Avraham Shṭern, 2000). Stern was among the early cohorts at the Hebrew University and earned his MA in January 1934. During his studies he joined a circle of revisionist students and joined the underground. His principal mentor in Jerusalem

was Moshe (Max) Schwabe, a German-born philologist specializing in classical epigraphy. Stern wrote his private correspondence primarily in Russian.

60. P. S. O'Hegarty, "Ha-hitkomemut bi-shnat 1916" [The 1916 Uprising], excerpt from *The Victory of Sinn Féin: How It Won It and How It Used It*, trans. Avraham Stern, *Ba-mahteret*, no. 5 (1941): 53–56.

61. For additional information, see Shulamit Eliash, *The Harp and the Shield of David: Ireland, Zionism and the State of Israel* (London: Routledge, 2007); Shlomo Shpiro, "The Intellectual Foundations of Jewish National Terrorism: Avraham Stern and the Lehi," *Terrorism and Political Violence* 25, no. 4 (2013): 606–620; Bruce Hoffman, *Anonymous Soldiers: The Struggle for Israel, 1917–1947* (New York: Vintage, 2016); Aidan Beatty, "Zionism and Irish Nationalism: Ideology and Identity on the Borders of Europe," *The Journal of Imperial and Commonwealth History* 45, no. 2 (2017): 1–24. To be sure, the Zionist-Irish analogy did not escape British attention. See Rory Miller, "'An Oriental Ireland': Thinking About Palestine in Terms of the Irish Question During the Mandatory Era," in *Britain, Palestine, and Empire: The Mandate Years*, ed. Rory Miller (Farnham: Ashgate, 2010), 157–176.

62. As reported by Yohanan (Jan) Bader (1901–1994), who was close to Menachem Begin and joined the Etzel a short time after moving from Poland to Palestine in 1943. See Yohanan Bader, *Darki le-Tsiyon, 1901–1948: Oṭobiyografyah* [My way to Zion, 1901–1948: An autobiography] (Jerusalem, Tel Aviv: Mekhon Z'aboṭinsḳi; Ha-Sifriyah ha-Tsiyonit, 1999), 361–362.

63. Sephardi and Mizrahi Jews constituted 42 percent of the Irgun and 35 percent of the Lehi. See Abigail Jacobson and Moshe Naor, *Oriental Neighbors: Middle Eastern Jews and Arabs in Mandatory Palestine* (Waltham: Brandeis University Press, 2016), 174.

64. "Statement by Absalom [*sic*] Habib," *The Answer*, August 1, 1947, kaf (כ) 16-6/15, JIA. Reprinted alongside additional letters in Avshalom Haviv, *Arba'Ah tse'adim la-mavet: Avshalom Haviv u-mikhtavav mi-tsinok ha-gardom* [Four S\steps to the gallows: Avshalom Haviv's death row letters], ed. Aryeh Eshel (Tel Aviv: Misrad ha-bitahon, 1997). The statement was most likely written not by Haviv but by his supreme commander, Menachem Begin.

65. Amir Goldstein, *Gevurah ve-hadarah: 'Olei ha-gardom ve-ha-zikaron ha-yisreeli* [Heroism and exclusion: The 'Gallows Martyrs' and Israeli Collective Memory] (Jerusalem: Yad Yitzhak Ben-Zvi, 2011), 132–143.

66. Mia Bloom, "Constructing Cultures of Martyrdom Across Religions, Time, and Space," in *Constructions of Terrorism: An Interdisciplinary Approach to Research and Policy*, ed. Michael Stohl, Richard Burchill, and Scott Englund (Oakland: University of California Press, 2017), 181–192.

67. I prefer using the term *proto-Canaanite* here to avoid anachronism, since the term *Canaanites*, introduced by poet Avraham Shlonsky as a derogatory term, was coined only during the 1950s.

68. Yehoshua Porath, *Shelah ve-'et be yado: Sipur hayav shel Uri'el Shelah* [Yonatan Raṭosh] [Weapon and pen in his hand: The life of Uriel Shelah] (Tel Aviv: Maḥberot le-sifrut, 1989); Elliott Rabin, "'Hebrew' Culture: The Shared Foundations of Ratosh's Ideology and Poetry," *Modern Judaism* 19, no. 2 (1999): 119–132.

69. Ranajit Guha, "Prose of Counter-Insurgency," in *Selected Subaltern Studies*, ed. Ranajit Guha and Gayatri Chakravorty Spivak (New York: Oxford University Press, 1988), 45–84, quote on 70.

70. A good introduction to the topic, old but not outdated, remains George L. Mosse, *The Crisis of German Ideology: Intellectual Origins of the Third Reich* (New York: Grosset & Dunlap, 1964). The picture is further complicated and nuanced in Suzanne L. Marchand, *German Orientalism in the Age of Empire: Religion, Race, and Scholarship* (Cambridge: Cambridge University Press, 2009).

71. Asher Kaufman, *Reviving Phoenicia: The Search for Identity in Lebanon* (London: I. B. Tauris, 2004); Sarah Griswold, "Allies in Eastern Trenches: Archaeological Salvage Operations in the French Mandate for Syria and Lebanon," *Journal of Levantine Studies* 8, no. 1 (2018): 121–144.

72. Michael Dietler, "'Our Ancestors the Gauls': Archaeology, Ethnic Nationalism, and the Manipulation of Celtic Identity in Modern Europe," *American Anthropologist* 96, no. 3 (1994): 584–605.

73. In the original Hebrew: "אם אין למחלה הלאומית מרקחת לאומית, ניקח אותה מאוצר שכנינו." Abba Ahimeir, *'En ha-kore: Sofrim u-sefarim, 'itonaim ve-'itonim* [En-hakkore: Authors and books, journalists and newspapers (Tel Aviv: Ha-Va'ad le-hotsaat kitve Ahimeir, 2003), 163 (translation mine). The article originally appeared on October 8, 1920.

CHAPTER 17

Middle Eastern and North African Jews in the Irgun and Lehi in British Mandatory Palestine

Avery Weinman

On November 6, 1944, Eliyahu Beit-Tzuri and Eliyahu Hakim—two young members of the radical paramilitary organization *Lohamei Herut Israel* (Freedom Fighters for Israel)—rode rented bicycles to the lavish Cairo mansion of the British minister-resident of the Middle East, Lord Moyne Sir Walter Edward Guinness, and assassinated him as he returned home for his regular afternoon nap. Slumped over in the back seat of his car, bleeding from several bullet wounds from Eliyahu Hakim's handgun, Lord Moyne commented in shock, "Oh, we've been shot!" before passing out, never to regain consciousness.[1] At the time of his death, Lord Moyne was the highest-ranking British imperial official in the Middle East. His assassination and the subsequent murder trial of his assassins—which culminated in Beit-Tzuri's and Hakim's execution by hanging on March 22, 1945—captivated the world. This episode, sometimes mythologized as the tale of "the two Eliyahus" is well-known in historiography and in the popular consciousness of Zionist radicalism during the British Mandate, in no small part because of its melodrama and its memorable details such as the assassins' shared first name. However, what is less well-known is that both Eliyahu Beit-Tzuri and Eliyahu Hakim were of Middle Eastern, and specifically Sephardi, backgrounds. On his mother's side, Beit-Tzuri descended from a multigenerational Sephardi family from the Old City of Jerusalem.[2] Hakim came from a Sephardi Damascene-Shami family and grew up in Beirut before moving to Haifa at age seven.[3] Indeed, it was their backgrounds that made the two Eliyahus exemplar clandestine operatives and the ideal candidates to assassinate Lord Moyne in the first place. The fact that they were both born in the Middle East and were both raised in Palestine meant that they were familiar with local slang, dress, customs, and traditions. Their backgrounds gave them the firsthand knowledge that enabled them to blend-in—undetected—when carrying out high-stakes operations, such as the assassination of Lord Moyne.

Eliyahu Beit-Tzuri and Eliyahu Hakim were not the only two radicals who fit this profile, and the drama of the two Eliyahus embodies a larger history. During the British Mandate over Palestine from 1918 to 1948, hundreds of Jews of Middle Eastern and North African (MENA) background participated in the two most radical Jewish paramilitary organizations operating in Palestine: the *Irgun Zvai Leumi* (National Military Organization), known as the *Irgun*, and *Lohamei Herut Israel*, known by its acronym, *Lehi*. These two organizations grew out of the crucible of the interwar period and the mandates system and were radical in both their ideological turn to anti-imperial armed struggle and in the ways that they used violence and active retaliation to try to achieve their goals. MENA Jews constituted a significant proportion of the Irgun and Lehi as key leaders, as members of the rank and file, and as supporters and collaborators who were less explicitly involved in the organizations' operations. They played integral roles in the organizations' daily activities—which included propaganda, intelligence, and recruitment—and in their extreme actions such as terror bombings, prison breaks, and assassinations. Since MENA Jews were essential to the Irgun and Lehi, two organizations that are, in turn, essential to the history of Jewish radicalism in the interwar period in general and to Zionist radicalism in particular, it follows that these MENA members of the Lehi and Irgun are an essential part of the history of Jewish radicalism.

And yet, there is a gap in historical scholarship on MENA Jews in the Irgun and Lehi. One reason for this is that the Irgun and Lehi are both associated with revisionist Zionism, which historians and the public—especially in Israel—have historically dismissed and excluded from academic scholarship, official state institutions, and popular collective memory. Revisionist Zionists were, and in some ways still are, the archrivals of the labor Zionists, whose adherents were the most powerful force within Zionist institutions before the establishment of the State of Israel in 1948, and who maintained hegemonic control over Israeli academia, government, and culture through the mid-1970s. The marginalization of revisionist Zionists in the history of Zionism and the State of Israel mirrors attempts to delegitimize and exclude revisionist Zionists from positions of political power in the Israeli government.[4] Another reason is these radicals' MENA backgrounds. While Jewish studies as a whole has made and continues to make strides in writing the histories of MENA Jews, historians of Zionism in general and of revisionist Zionism in particular have overwhelmingly neglected them. The historiography of revisionist Zionism remains mostly a collection of political and intellectual histories that focus on a narrow set of famous Ashkenazi leaders such as Vladimir "Ze'ev" Jabotinsky and Menachem Begin.[5] These histories of revisionist Zionism rarely, if ever, analyze the presence and significance of MENA Jews in the Irgun and Lehi, despite their prevalence in and importance to these organizations and despite a wealth of historical and archival material. This neglect of MENA members of the Irgun and Lehi exists in scholarship written by professional historians as well as in nonprofessional histories that were written by affiliates or former members of the Irgun and Lehi. MENA Jews in the Irgun and Lehi, then, are at the center of two overlapping circles of historiographical marginalization.

In this chapter, I analyze the largely unstudied Jewish radicalism of MENA members of the Irgun and Lehi in British Mandatory Palestine. First, I ask what makes the Irgun and Lehi "radical" to begin with. I scrutinize revisionist Zionism, overview the Irgun and Lehi, and situate the two organizations in a larger global and regional interwar context. Then, I provide a social history and prosopography of MENA Jews in the Irgun and Lehi. Throughout this chapter, I return to a regular cast of notable characters—for instance, the two Eliyahus—but it is critical to note that there are hundreds of other MENA members of the Irgun and Lehi who I do not write about at length, but who also embody the patterns I will discuss in this chapter. Additionally, I highlight the importance of social relations and structures in British Mandatory Palestine, particularly with connection to space, identity, class, youth, and gender. Ultimately, with this chapter I aim to complicate the idea of Jewish radicalism by highlighting one of its neglected forms.

Revisionist Zionism, the Irgun and Lehi, and Interwar Radicalism

Before discussing MENA Jews in the Irgun and Lehi, it is first necessary to understand revisionist Zionism, the Irgun and Lehi, and what made these two organizations "radical." Revisionist Zionism is one of many different types of Zionism, which is itself an agglomeration of many different ideas, tactics, and goals. Typically, historians attribute the beginning of revisionist Zionism to the resignation of influential Zionist thinker and leader Vladimir "Ze'ev" Jabotinsky from the World Zionist Congress in 1923, and his subsequent founding of the political party *HaTzionim HaRevizionistim* (The Revisionist Zionists, also known by the acronym *Hatzohar*) in 1925.[6] At different times and for different leaders, revisionist Zionist ideas have included bourgeoise capitalism, territorial maximalism, liberalism, democracy, Romantic vitalism, ethnonationalism, fascism, militarism, imperial federalism, anti-imperialism, and religious messianism. This is to say that there is not, nor has there ever been, a single static revisionist Zionism.[7] Instead, revisionist Zionism is—like all ostensible ideologies—a constellation of complex, contradictory, and often irreconcilable beliefs, all of which changed over time. These contradictions existed at the movement level and at the level of individual personalities. For example, at the movement level, the leaders of the Irgun put tremendous stock in the pageantry of military rank and hierarchy, whereas the leaders of Lehi eschewed formality in favor of a deep underground based on total secrecy. Contradictions were equally as acute at the individual level. Jabotinsky was a pragmatist and ardent Anglophile up to his death in 1940 and never wavered from his conviction that collaboration with the British Empire was the best way to achieve an autonomous Jewish polity. On the other hand, enigmatic and charismatic Lehi founder Avraham "Yair" Stern offered a mystical vision of Jewish revolution and redemption, and opposed the British Empire so strongly that he pushed the Lehi to ally itself with Nazi Germany and Mussolini's Italy.[8] Before this, Stern had been a part of the group of young Palestine-based dissidents who challenged Jabotinsky's authority among revisionist Zionist organizations in a dramatic face-to-face showdown at the Third Betar World Conference in 1938 in the wake of the British Empire's execution of Shlomo Ben-Yosef, a famous Zionist figure who was a member of the revisionist Zionist youth group *Betar* (an acronym for *Brit Yosef Trumpeldor*, meaning "the Alliance of Josef Trumpeldor") and who died at Tel Hai in 1920.[9] Another leader, Nathan Yellin-Friedman (later Hebraized to Nathan Yellin-Mor)—who, along with Israel Scheib (later Hebraized to Israel Eldad) and Yitzhak Yezernitsky (later Hebraized to Yitzhak Shamir) formed one third of the triumvirate that resuscitated Lehi in 1943, after Stern's death at the hands of British police in 1942—preserved Stern's basic idea of revolution but harnessed his unbridled vision into a program of Soviet-oriented anti-imperialism. For Yellin-Friedman, other anti-imperial national liberation movements in the Arab world and globally were natural allies, not enemies.[10] As these examples show, there was no one true, fixed version of revisionist Zionism, but rather a collection of multiple revisionist Zionist ideas that evolved from the same shared intellectual and political heritage.

Despite the inherent problems with trying to write about a coherent revisionist Zionism, there were two main organizations associated with revisionist Zionist ideas. One was the Irgun Zvai Leumi, which was also known simply as the Irgun or by its acronym in Hebrew, *Etzel*. The other was Lohamei Herut Israel, which was also known by its acronym in Hebrew, Lehi, or by its pejorative nickname, "the Stern Gang," after its founder Avraham "Yair" Stern. The Irgun was established in 1931, when several influential officers in the older and larger Zionist paramilitary organization the *Haganah* (Defense) quit over the Haganah's policy of *havlagah* (restraint) in the face of mounting tensions and violent confrontations with other nationalist movements in Palestine and with the British Empire. The leaders of the Irgun believed in active armed struggle instead of restraint, and they fused the idea of sovereignty and self-determination for Jews in Palestine, which they called *Eretz Israel* (in Hebrew, "The Land of Israel"), to the spiritual and emotional liberation of the Jewish people. Lehi also began as a splinter movement. In 1940, amid the factional splits and plays for power that occurred in the wake of Jabotinsky's death, Stern established Lehi as a more extreme revolutionary alternative to the Irgun. Like the Irgun, Lehi espoused armed struggle and connected physical and spiritual liberation, but Lehi was more violent in its actions, more messianic and utopian in its ideology, less concerned with military rank, and uniquely uncompromising on its principal goal of ending British imperial rule. While financial hardships, political persecution, and a revolving door of different leaders with different capabilities and personalities meant that the Irgun and Lehi operated in fits and starts, both were active in the interwar period and during World War II. They were particularly active between the so-called Revolt—the Irgun's declaration of active armed struggle against British imperial rule in February 1944, of which Lehi was also a part—and the establishment of the State of Israel in 1948.[11] Both organizations were always much smaller than the labor Zionist paramilitary organization the Haganah. At its peak in the mid-1940s, the Irgun numbered a few hundred to a thousand active, full-fledged and officially registered members. Lehi never numbered more than a few dozen active members. Lehi's leaders intentionally structured the organization around a secretive cadre of dedicated revolutionaries, which meant that its small size was a built-in asset, not a drawback.[12]

The Irgun and Lehi were radical in both the content of their ideas and the form of their actions. Radicalism, in a basic sense, means fundamentally different than preceding norms. By this measure, the Irgun and Lehi were radical in a number of key ways, including an ideological shift from collaboration with empire to anti-imperial armed struggle; intergenerational divides, particularly over the proper relationship to empire and the use of violence; strong emphasis on youth movements and organizing youth; flirtation with illiberal politics, including fascism and communism; and the use of new methods of violence and politics, such as terror bombings and radio propaganda broadcasts.

It is critical to note that the radicalism of the Irgun and Lehi is not exceptional. Rather, it resembles that of other radical organizations in the interwar period. The Irgun and Lehi were similar to other radical interwar organizations globally; more specifically, they were similar to other radical organizations in the Middle East, including Palestinian nationalist organizations. These similarities are visible, for example, in the shift in power to a younger generation of more radical leaders, which occurred in the Irgun and Lehi and in Palestinian nationalist organizations at roughly the same time, in the late 1930s and early 1940s. Up-and-coming figures who ascended the hierarchies of their respective organizations at this time—such as Avraham "Yair" Stern, Izz ad-Din al-Qassam, Menachem Begin, and Hajj Mohammed Amin al-Husseini—were all part of a wave of new political leaders who rejected older elites' collaboration with empire and pushed for anti-imperial armed struggle.[13] While these leaders' respective movements and goals often directly opposed each another—including in periods of violent confrontation such as the 1936–1939 Great Revolt/General Strike—they developed in a common context and shared key features. This accentuates a larger truth about radical organizations in the interwar period. While the particular messages, symbols, and objectives of these groups differed, at their cores they were structurally similar. The differences between them in terms of slogans, iconography, anthems, and uniform colors were superfluous in comparison to more important similarities in ideological positions, power hierarchies, and tactics, all of which diverged from prewar norms in like ways.

Middle Eastern and North African Radicals in the Irgun and Lehi

Defining the Irgun and Lehi members at the center of this chapter is an essential but difficult task. I use a geographically based adjective—Middle Eastern and North African (MENA), capaciously imagined—because it captures the wide range of locales from which these Irgun and Lehi members came, as well as the diversity of their religious, linguistic, class, and cultural backgrounds.[14] None of the popular terms that scholars often use—whether they be regional, like Mashriqi, Levantine, or Maghrebi; historical, like Oriental, *bnei ha'aretz* (sons of the land), *edot hamizrach* (communities of the East), or *mista'arvim* (those who live among the Arabs, from the Arabic *musta'arabi*); or ethno-cultural, like Sephardi, Mizrahi, or Arab Jew—neatly suit the group that is the focus of this chapter. While not a perfect term, particularly in the limits of its geographic reach, MENA sufficiently conveys features that differentiate this particular group of Irgun and Lehi members. It describes a group whose experiences with empire, colonization, and racialization differed from the Ashkenazim—immigrants and Palestinian-born—who constituted the majority of the Irgun's and Lehi's membership. And, frankly, it describes a group of historical subjects for whom there is still a lack of historical scholarship, particularly with regard to Zionism and revisionist Zionist organizations in British Mandatory Palestine.

With this terminological caveat in mind, it is possible to establish the basic characteristics of MENA Jews in the Irgun and Lehi. The memoirs, nonprofessional histories, edited primary source volumes, and encyclopedias published by former members of the Irgun and Lehi or their heritage foundations are indispensable in this regard.[15] Geographically, MENA Jews in the Irgun and Lehi came from places of origin that stretch the limits of the notion of Middle Eastern and North African. Using the locations of modern-day states, their places of origin included Bulgaria, Greece, and Turkey in the Balkans and Anatolia; Afghanistan and Iran in Southwest Asia; Yemen; Iraq (including Kurdistan), Syria, Lebanon, Palestine/Eretz Israel, and Egypt in the Mashriq/Levant; and Tunisia, Libya, and Morocco in the Maghreb. Overall, there were far more members from the Balkans and the Middle East than there were from North Africa. More specifically, most members were Sephardim from around the Eastern Mediterranean or were of Yemenite background. While some members were born outside of Palestine and immigrated as children or teenagers, the vast majority of members were born in Palestine itself. The length of time that the families of Palestinian-born members had lived in the land varied. Some belonged to established wealthy families of local notables with multigenerational roots in major cities such as Jerusalem or Hebron. Others belonged to first-generation working-class families. Their knowledge of Arabic varied depending on their different backgrounds. Sephardim were likely to have grown up with Ladino as their first language but may have acquired Arabic later. Their degree of fluency in Arabic and their familiarity with local dialect would have varied on an individual basis. Conversely, others grew up with Arabic as their first language and were native speakers. These distinctions, among others, are important for understanding that there was no single archetypal profile for MENA members of the Irgun and Lehi, but rather a variety of types. Differences in their identities shaped how and why they came to the Irgun and Lehi, as well as the roles that they played in these organizations.

In terms of age, MENA members of the Irgun and Lehi skewed young. Most were born between the very end of the 1910s and the very beginning of the 1930s, making the average age range for members the late teens through the mid-to-late twenties at the height of the Irgun's and Lehi's activities in the mid-1940s. As such, these particular radicals in the Irgun and Lehi fit into a larger pattern of youth radicalism in the interwar period. Youth led radical organizations and made up the rank-and-file of these organizations throughout the Middle East and around the world in the interwar period, not just in the Irgun and Lehi.

Statistically, MENA Jews were a significant percentage of the Irgun and Lehi, although they were always the minority when compared to the percentage of Ashkenazim. In a survey of the composition of the Irgun and Lehi, Israeli sociologist Shlomo Resnik concluded that "Sephardi and Oriental Jews" made up as much as 26.7 percent of the Irgun and 25.5 percent of Lehi.[16] This jumped to 42 percent of the Irgun and 35 percent of Lehi when Resnik narrowed his sample to Palestinian-born members.[17] Resnik's figures corroborate Menachem Begin's estimate that between 25 and 35 percent of the Irgun's total membership was of "Sephardi" descent.[18] That number rose to between 40 and 50 percent in the Irgun's intelligence division *Yechidat Mahatz* ("Shock Unit," also called *Mahatz* for short), which made a concerted effort to recruit members who could pass as Palestinian Arabs because they were the most likely to successfully execute intelligence operations without arousing suspicion.[19] However, these figures do not account for the larger sphere of collaborators and supporters who were involved in the Irgun or Lehi, nor is it clear how Resnik or Begin qualified who counted as "Sephardi" or "Oriental" Jews.

A significant number of these proportions of MENA Jews in the Irgun and Lehi were women. In his history of women in the Irgun, Yehuda Lapidot—a former member of the Irgun, and one of its most prolific nonprofessional historians—listed more than 890 women who were involved with the Irgun in some capacity during the entirety of its operations from 1931 to 1948.[20] This number does not distinguish what percentage of these women were of MENA background, nor does it include the number of MENA women who were involved in Lehi. However, a survey of 840 biographies that are collected in the two-volume encyclopedia of Lehi members confirms that women played a considerable role in Lehi operations as well.[21]

MENA Jews were integral at all levels of the Irgun and Lehi, including in key leadership positions. They held some of the most important, highest-ranking positions in each of the Irgun's three main divisions: *Hel Tamulah HaMahapahnit* (Revolutionary Propaganda Force; acronym *HaTam*), *Hel HaKrav* (Assault Force; acronym, *Hok*), and its intelligence division Mahatz.[22] For example, Shlomo Levi (later Hebraized to Shlomo Lev-Ami)—born in 1919 in Hartuv to a family of Bulgarian Sephardim who migrated to Ottoman Palestine with the wave of Sephardi members of Hovevei Zion in 1895–1896, and who later moved to Petah Tikvah in 1930 after the 1929 riots—served as the Irgun's chief commanding officer, general chief of staff, active commander, and as a member of the Irgun High Command alongside Menachem Begin, Arieh Ben-Eliezer, Ya'akov Meridor, and Eliyahu Lankin.[23] Moshe Nehmad—born in 1912 in Iran to a family who migrated to Palestine through Iraq, Syria, and Lebanon—served as the Irgun's commander in

Haifa and the Northern District.[24] Ya'akov Sika Aharoni—born in 1921 as one of ten siblings to a father from Isfahan in modern-day Iran and a Sephardi mother whose family had lived in Jerusalem for generations—was one of the foremost members of the Mahatz division.[25] Levi, Nehmad, and Aharoni—along with other MENA commanders in the Irgun—planned, organized, and executed the operations without which the Irgun would have ceased to function. Lehi did not have a formal hierarchy like the Irgun, but MENA Jews played similarly important leadership roles in its assault, intelligence, and propaganda activities. For example, Geulah Cohen—born in December 1925 in Keren HaTemanim in Tel Aviv as one of ten siblings to father who was a prominent politician in the Yemenite Association and a mother who was half Maghrebi-Moroccan and half Turkish-Sephardi with old roots in the Old City of Jerusalem—was an active militant, a Lehi Youth Section leader, and one of the lead broadcasters for Lehi's radio propaganda program, *Kol HaMakhteret HaIvrit* (Voice of the Hebrew Underground).[26] Another MENA Lehi member, Yitzhak Hasson—who was born in the Neve Tzedek neighborhood of Tel Aviv into a Ladino-speaking Sephardi family and had an ethnic Turkish father—served as head of Lehi operations in Jerusalem.[27] Hasson and Cohen were, in fact, directly connected through one of Lehi's prison breaks. Hasson led the successful operation to free Geulah Cohen from the Bethlehem Women's Prison in 1947 after British police arrested her for her involvement with Lehi the year prior. He carried out this mission with the help of one of Lehi's Palestinian Muslim allies, Yosef Abu Gosh.[28] All five of the MENA Irgun and Lehi members mentioned here—Levi, Nehmad, Aharoni, Cohen, and Hasson—later wrote histories of the Irgun or Lehi or memoirs of their own experiences in these organizations. But they were not the only MENA Jews who held key leadership positions in either the Irgun or Lehi.[29] Yosef "Uzi" Levi—Shlomo Levi's older brother—served as the Irgun's regional commander in Tel Aviv.[30] Yisrael "Giddy" Levi—born in Jerusalem to a Sephardi family—became the Irgun's chief of operations in his twenties.[31] In this role, Levi designed and executed many of the Irgun's most notorious and most consequential operations, including the assault on British intelligence offices in the Russian Compound in Jerusalem on March 23, 1944; the bombing of the King David Hotel on July 22, 1946; and the Acre Prison break on May 4, 1947. Levi was also one of the Irgun's most creative inventors. He devised the "milk-can" bombs that subsequently became a staple of the Irgun's operations, a time-delay device for explosives, railway track mines for the Irgun's sabotage missions, and the below-ground ventilation machine that enabled the Irgun to produce propaganda at its own secret printing-press location on the border of Jaffa and Tel Aviv.[32]

Many more MENA radicals in the Irgun and Lehi who did not hold key leadership positions or who did not later write histories or memoirs nonetheless sustained the organizations as rank-and-file members. Their roles as secretaries, couriers, propagandists, radio technicians, nurses, spies, and low-ranking soldiers and militants may have been of lesser individual responsibility, but they were no less consequential to the Irgun's and Lehi's ability to function. Take, for example, Rachel Meiri (born Rachel Yemeni), who was a member of the Irgun and who went underground using the codename "Ruhama" after the declaration of armed revolt against the British Empire in 1944.[33] She was born in Petah Tikvah to a Yemenite family, joined the revisionist Zionist youth group Betar at age fourteen, graduated to the Irgun at age sixteen, and quickly rose through the Irgun's ranks. Meiri successfully completed a training course to become a commander of her own Irgun combat unit and participated in some of the Irgun's more dramatic operations, including a diamond robbery on January 30, 1945. But it was her role as the main liaison between members of the Irgun's High Command and as Menachem Begin's personal scribe that best demonstrates the essential role she played in the organization. She was the one who transcribed Begin's chicken-scratch handwritten notes into legible typed sheets that then became the posters and fliers for the Irgun's print propaganda, as well as the articles for the Irgun's newspaper, *Herut* (Freedom).[34] Meiri is just one example of a lower-ranking Irgun member who played an essential role in the organization's operations, and she even belonged to the exclusive circle of members who went underground and abandoned their real identities between 1944 to 1948. The majority of MENA members of the Irgun and Lehi maintained their regular lives as they participated in their operations in smaller ways. Among them were a plethora of others who are not discussed in this chapter, including Shlomo Alkalai, Yehudah Bakar, Yehudit Cohen-Maguri, David de-Boton, Yocheved Tobiana, Malka Yefet, and dozens of other active members whose biographies appear in published works on the Irgun and Lehi, not to mention additional untold numbers of unregistered members, collaborators, and supporters.[35]

These smaller ways were, in fact, the relatively mundane daily activities that made up most of what MENA Jews did in the Irgun and Lehi. These daily activities can be broken down into three categories: propaganda, intelligence, and recruitment. Each of these three categories demonstrate how social structures in British Mandatory Palestine affected MENA members of the Irgun and Lehi, particularly in dimensions of space, identity, class, and youth.

Propaganda was arguably the most common of the Irgun's and Lehi's daily activities and demonstrates the importance of space.[36] Both the Irgun and Lehi produced two main forms of propaganda: print and radio. One way that the Irgun and Lehi published their print propaganda was in their multiple journals and newspapers, including the Irgun's *Herut* and Lehi's *HaHazit* (The Front), *HaMa'as* (The Deed), *Hazit HaNoar* (The Youth Front), and *Hazit HaHayal* (The Soldier's Front).[37] Another way that the Irgun and Lehi spread their print propaganda was in leaflets, bulletins, fliers, and posters that members of the Irgun and Lehi plastered on the walls of busy neighborhoods in major cities including Jerusalem, Tel Aviv, and Haifa.[38] Members of the Irgun's and Lehi's propaganda divisions were responsible for every stage in the design, production, organization, and dissemination of print propaganda. They collected the propaganda materials from the organizations' clandestine production sites; distributed the allocated amount of materials to the proper cells of the propaganda divisions; cooked the sticky glue that members used to plaster print materials to the walls of public spaces; and did the actual plastering itself, often in the dead of night when they were the least likely to attract unwanted attention from nosy neighbors or be arrested by British police.[39] While seemingly innocuous, these activities were quite dangerous. After February 1944, British police adopted a policy of shooting live rounds at those whom they caught plastering propaganda on the walls of public spaces, wounding and sometimes even killing several members of the Irgun and Lehi.[40] Radio broadcasts—the Irgun's *Kol Zion HaLohemet* (The Voice of Fighting Zion) and Lehi's *Kol HaMakhteret HaIvrit*—required fewer members to produce, but were essential pieces of the Irgun's and Lehi's propaganda activities and reached a significant number of listeners.

Space, including both physical locations and how those locations embodied complex social relations, was essential to print and radio broadcast propaganda. More specifically, the working-class neighborhoods of large cities—which had historically mixed demographics—served as the principal locations of propaganda production and distribution. In their pathbreaking 2016 book *Oriental Neighbors: Middle Eastern Jews and Arabs in Mandatory Palestine*, one of a small number of studies whose main focus is MENA Jews in British Mandatory Palestine, historians Abigail Jacobson and Moshe Naor termed these areas "frontier neighborhoods."[41] According to Jacobson and Naor, these frontier neighborhoods were sites of vibrant—and sometimes violent—cohabitation between Jews and their non-Jewish neighbors, with whom they lived in close proximity, cultivated a common cultural identity, spoke Arabic, and dealt with similar economic conditions. Examples of frontier neighborhoods include Nachlaot, Mahane Yehudah, and the Bukharan Quarter in Jerusalem, and Keren HaTemanim, Neve Tzedek, Neve Shalom, Mahane Yosef, Manshiya, and the Hatikvah Quarter in Tel Aviv.[42] The Irgun and Lehi based their propaganda operations in these frontier neighborhoods because they were close to densely trafficked urban spaces and because they were where a significant number of the rank-and-file members of their propaganda divisions and their supporters lived. For example, the Irgun's secret in-house printing press—for which Yisrael "Giddy" Levi invented his below-ground ventilation system—was located under a carpentry shop in a frontier neighborhood between Tel Aviv and Jaffa.[43] Before the Irgun set up this printing press, it produced its print propaganda at a small shop run by a Sephardi businessman and his sons on the Tel Aviv-Jaffa border for several years.[44] Menachem Begin wrote about this man and his role producing the Irgun's print propaganda in his memoir, *The Revolt*, but did not provide his name or any of his biographical information, making him among the many anonymous supporters who should also be included in a more comprehensive evaluation of MENA Jews in the Irgun and Lehi. Even more frequently than opening their businesses to the Irgun and Lehi, MENA residents of frontier neighborhoods offered the homes where they lived with their families as bases for propaganda production and distribution. This was the case for Miriam (née Rabbi) and Shlomo Alon (born Shoshan Yaziri), a young married couple, both of whom were born in Afghanistan in the early 1920s and were active members of Lehi.[45] The Alons turned their Jerusalem apartment into a hub of propaganda operations where Lehi members came to cook wall-plastering glue, obtain posters and fliers, and convene before setting out to post propaganda materials on the walls of the city.[46] The Alons did this with their infant children in the house. Radio was also a domestic endeavor. Throughout the 1940s, the Irgun and Lehi broadcast their radio programs out of amateur recording studios that they set up in the houses or apartments of the organizations' members and supporters. Most often, these homes belonged to MENA Jews in frontier neighborhoods in Tel Aviv. This was the case with Regina and Yosef Sheetrit, another married couple of Greek Sephardi background who were both members of the Irgun.[47] They converted the apartment at 28 Rehov HaShuk in Tel Aviv that they shared with Regina's parents—complete with a spacious roof that made it the perfect location for a high-powered antenna—into a broadcast studio for the Irgun's radio program, *Kol Zion HaLohemet*. Sometimes, Regina's mother provided the Irgun broadcast technicians and program hosts with home-cooked meals, while the whole family stood guard and watched for British police activity or suspicious neighbors.[48]

Intelligence activities also reflected the importance of space, but even more so they reflected the importance of identity. More specifically, the Irgun's and Lehi's intelligence activities illustrated how some MENA members' identities were similar to those of their non-Jewish Arab neighbors and how their intimate knowledge of local norms were assets because they allowed them to conduct operations undetected. Intelligence activities included collecting information about important individuals, rival political movements, and the British imperial administrative and policing apparatus for the purposes of planning future operations, evading arrest, and general knowledge-gathering. For example, intelligence operatives surveilled key military camps and tracked the routes of vehicles that belonged to high-ranking British officials or Palestinian nationalist leaders in order to construct a dependable record of daily patterns, routines, and habits.[49] The Irgun and especially Lehi put the utmost emphasis on secrecy. Intelligence operatives usually did not know the real identities of the other members in their intelligence division cells, nor did they often know the context for their activities. They used codenames and submitted their reports to higher-ranking members of the intelligence divisions without knowing their ultimate purpose.[50] The point of this secrecy was to make it harder for the British police to rout the Irgun or Lehi at the organizational level when they captured individual operatives. The greater the degree of anonymity and the less that operatives knew about what they were doing, the harder it was for British police to piece together networks of Irgun and Lehi members, identify the organizations' leaders, or prevent the organizations' planned activities. With this emphasis on secrecy and evading detection, it is not surprising that a significant percentage of the Irgun's and Lehi's intelligence operatives were of MENA background and had characteristics that made it easier for them to pass in mixed Arab spaces. In his memoir, Menachem Begin estimated that "Sephardim and members of the Eastern Communities" made up between 40 and 50 percent of the Irgun's intelligence division, Mahatz.[51] Aharoni's description of Mahatz, of which he himself was a part, suggests that the percentage of MENA intelligence operatives could potentially be higher.[52] Many of these MENA intelligence operatives were born and raised in frontier neighborhoods. As Jacobson and Naor argue in *Oriental Neighbors*, it was precisely the fact that the Jewish residents of these frontier neighborhoods shared a basic common identity with their non-Jewish neighbors, knew Arabic, and had intimate knowledge of local slang, dress, interpersonal relationships, and customs that made them ideal intelligence operatives.[53] Using these attributes, they could blend into mixed spaces and pass as non-Jewish Arabs with ease, collecting information and executing operations without arousing suspicion from neighborhood residents or from British police. For example, before they assassinated Lord Moyne, Eliyahu Beit-Tzuri and Eliyahu Hakim put their ability to pass to good use as Lehi intelligence operatives. When Beit-Tzuri and Hakim helped plan one of Lehi's many failed attempts to assassinate High Commissioner of Palestine Sir Harold MacMichael, Beit-Tzuri used his fluency in Arabic and real-life job as a surveyor in Jenin to dupe roving British police and to avoid detection while he scouted the route of MacMichael's motorcade during one operation in 1944. In the same operation, Hakim disguised himself as a young Arab laborer working with Beit-Tzuri and pretended to idly thumb through surveyor's maps while the pair actually searched for the best spots to bury mines in the road.[54] In this case, Beit-Tzuri's and Hakim's backgrounds and their understanding of local identity played an essential role in their efficacy as intelligence operatives.

However, at the same time as MENA Jews' familiarity with long-standing local characteristics and norms made them assets for intelligence operations, identity itself was changing. During the British Mandate, new discourses and new ways of categorizing populations created new exclusive boundaries within communities where boundaries had not previously existed in Palestine in prior generations, at least not to the same extent. These new identities often marked the fault lines for intergroup tensions. Foremost among these new identities was nationality. In a global period of ethnonationalism and during heightened violence between Zionists and Palestinian nationalists, nationality divided communities in Palestine in unprecedented ways and made conflict ever harder to solve. While prior generations were able to relate to a common local identity or even to a broad civic Ottoman identity, during the British Mandate the nationalization of Jewish and Arab identities broke communities into different distinct groups.

Another type of identity that became more consequential in Palestine during the British Mandate was race. In British Mandatory Palestine, MENA Jews, especially Yemenites, were increasingly racialized as Black.[55] This racialization paralleled a larger pattern in the Mandates period.[56] European imperial powers and international diplomatic and legal systems used racism to delegitimize colonized peoples' claims to national equality and to forfend their self-determination. These powers, understanding that colonized peoples' national self-determination would require the termination of the mandates system and the end of direct European imperial rule, accentuated racial hierarchy as one method of maintaining their control and protecting their imperial interests.[57] At the smaller scale of MENA Jews in British Mandate Palestine, race functioned similarly as a method of political delegitimization. British officials and the leaders of Zionist institutions who opposed the Irgun and Lehi—and who were often affiliated with labor Zionist organizations, the historic rivals of revisionist Zionist organizations—insinuated that there was a causal link between the large number of MENA Jews in the Irgun and Lehi and their radicalism and violent activities.[58] This was the case, for instance, in the pejorative nickname given to the Irgun's Mahatz intelligence division—"The Black Squad"—and in attempts to disparage the Irgun as an organization made up only of "black Yemenites."[59] MENA members of the Irgun and Lehi also internalized this racialization at the individual level, as was the case when Ya'akov Sika Aharoni gave himself the nickname "King of the Blacks" during the 1936–1939 Great Revolt/General Strike.[60] Aharoni's self-appointed royal title was part prideful boast about his centrality to Mahatz's operations, part gesture at the greater context of racializing MENA Jews. He co-opted the descriptor "Black" for his own subversive interpretation, but nonetheless recognized that race—and more specifically a hierarchical racial spectrum in which "Black" carried a negative political and social connotation—was a salient marker of identity and difference in British Mandatory Palestine.

The last of the Irgun's and Lehi's three main types of daily activities, recruitment, demonstrated the interconnected importance of class and youth. Established veteran members of the Irgun and Lehi were the primary force behind recruiting new members. They intentionally recruited from within a certain demographic profile, namely frontier neighborhood youth from impoverished working-class families. Economic conditions in Palestine in the mid-1940s were dire after the three difficult years of the 1936–1939 Great Revolt/General Strike and because of World War II.[61] Many MENA youth, especially those of working-class backgrounds from frontier neighborhoods, had to drop out of school in their early teens to find work and help support their families. For added perspective, in the mid-1940s only 23.4 percent of Sephardi boys, 30.3 percent of Sephardi girls, 17.2 percent of non-Sephardi MENA boys, and 13.1 percent of non-Sephardi MENA girls who lived in cities finished the standard eight years of elementary education.[62] Dropping out of school to support one's family was a consistent trend among MENA members of the Irgun and Lehi. It was the case, for instance, for Mordechai Alkahai, a member of the Irgun who was born in Petah Tikvah in 1923 to a Turkish Sephardi family.[63] Alkahai left school at age ten to help his parents run the family inn, where they were known to have welcomed weary travelers and guests in Ladino.[64] Ya'akov Sika Aharoni, Moshe Barzani, Shlomo Levi, and dozens of others also left school and got jobs in order to support their families.[65] One reason that the Irgun and Lehi recruited new members from this particular demographic group was that the local knowledge that these youth had from growing up in frontier neighborhoods made them valuable assets. Another, more abstract, reason was that this demographic group symbolized acute political and social anxieties. Large numbers of MENA youth on the streets and out of school posed a problem of community reputation for Zionists in general and for Sephardi elites with long-standing roots in Palestine in particular. During the British Mandate, Sephardi elites grappled with the so-called Sephardi Question. As Sephardi elites lost their role as intercommunal mediators that they had cultivated in the Ottoman Empire, they struggled to solidify the Sephardi community's place in Palestine in the era of Zionism and exclusive nationalism. Facing intense political and social scrutiny, Sephardi elites identified youth as one potential answer to the challenges that they faced.[66] The confluence of these worries converged in the figure of David Sitton. Sitton is perhaps best known as a prominent Sephardi Jerusalemite politician and as a journalist for Avraham Elmaleh's Sephardi-oriented newspaper *Hed HaMizrach* (Echo of the East) and for the bourgeois newspaper *HaBoker* (The Morning), but he was also a member of Lehi. Sitton recollected his time in Lehi in his 1978 memoir *Ba-or u-va-seter: Dapim me-yemeno shel atsir* (In the Light of Day and in Secret: Pages from the Diary of a Prisoner), in which he also recounted being arrested by the British police and his time at the Latrun detention camp.[67] In the memoir, Sitton acknowledges that he and others in Lehi prioritized recruiting MENA youth from impoverished frontier neighborhoods because of their symbolic value. The general reasoning was that this group of purposeless youth listlessly roaming the city streets could be indoctrinated and shaped in Lehi's vision of national strength and honor, in the process restoring the pride of the community and the nation.[68]

The main method by which the Irgun and Lehi recruited and indoctrinated new members was through youth movements. The Irgun and Lehi were not unique in this regard. Youth movements and emphasis on youth as the vital wellspring and future vanguard of the nation was a standard feature of radical interwar organizations in the Middle East and globally. Indeed, the differences between youth movements that were connected to the Irgun and Lehi—including Betar, *Degel Zion* (Flag of Zion), *HaTa'im HaLe'umi'im* (The National Cells), and *Maccabi HaTzair* (The Young Maccabi)—and *al-Qumsan al-Hadidiyya* (The Steel Shirts) in Syria, *al-Futuwwa* (Nobility) in Iraq, and the Young Egypt Green Shirts were largely superfluous.[69] At their cores, each of these youth groups used militarism, arms drills, uniforms, anthems, and flags to instill the idea that the future of the nation lay in the hands of youth in similar ways.[70] Each youth group that was connected to the Irgun or Lehi had a slightly different focus. Betar, for example, served as the most direct link to the Irgun and to revisionist Zionist political parties. HaTa'im HaLe'umi'im—of which Eliyahu Beit-Tzuri and Yitzhak Hasson were alumni—was also linked to the Irgun, although unlike Betar it had fewer links to revisionist Zionist organizations in Europe and was more squarely rooted in Palestine. Degel Zion, alternatively, explicitly served MENA and Sephardi youth.[71]

While these daily propaganda, intelligence, and recruitment activities constituted the majority of the Irgun's and Lehi's operations, there were also extreme actions, particularly from 1936 to 1939 during the Great Revolt/General Strike, and from 1944 to 1948 after the declaration of armed revolt against the British Empire and up to establishment of the State of Israel. The most common forms of these extreme actions were terror bombings, both for the purpose of causing high-casualty events and to destroy symbols of imperial rule; raids of military arms depots; sabotage of strategically valuable sites; and bank robberies, assassinations, and prison breaks. Examples of notable extreme Irgun and Lehi actions, some of which have already been mentioned in this chapter, include the assassination of Lord Moyne on November 6, 1944; the "Night of the Trains" attacks on November 1, 1945; the bombing of the King David Hotel on July 22, 1946; and the Acre Prison break on May 4, 1947. As Eliyahu Beit-Tzuri's and Eliyahu Hakim's roles in the assassination of Lord Moyne and Yisrael "Giddy" Levi's role as the mastermind behind the King David Hotel bombing and the Acre Prison break make clear, MENA radicals were as integral to these extreme actions as they were to daily activities.

In addition to the basic fact of the indispensability of MENA members to extreme Irgun and Lehi actions, these operations further accentuate the importance of social structures, namely space, identity, and gender. The roles that space and identity played in extreme actions were similar to the roles they played in daily activities. Just as Irgun and Lehi members and supporters turned their homes into distribution hubs for print propaganda or ad hoc radio broadcast studios, they also turned their homes and community spaces into safe houses, weapons caches, and pre-operation meeting locations. For example, Eliyahu Hakim turned the vacant Haifa apartment that belonged to his older brother Joseph into a safe house for Lehi leader Yitzhak Yezernitsky after Yezernitsky escaped from Mazra Prison in 1943.[72] In another example, Moshe Lehi Nahum—the Yemenite *mukhtar* (in Arabic, "chosen one"; the title of local village chiefs in the Ottoman Empire) of the Tel Aviv frontier neighborhood Keren HaTemanim—allowed the Irgun and Lehi to use his home as a storehouse for guns and explosives.[73] In yet another example, the Irgun operatives who carried out the King David Hotel bombing met up at the neighborhood Talmud Torah school in Jerusalem—one of many schools in a larger religious school system that often served MENA Jews—before setting out on the mission.[74] Similarly, the local knowledge that allowed Irgun and Lehi operatives to pass undetected in intelligence-gathering and surveillance operations also allowed them to avoid suspicion when carrying out terror bombings, sabotage, or assassinations. As for many others, this was the case for Ya'akov Sika Aharoni, the self-styled "King of the Blacks." It was precisely his knowledge of Arabic, access to customary Arab dress, and self-described "swarthy face and black hair" that let Aharoni perpetrate a number of high-casualty terror bombings without being captured, including two attacks on popular Arab vegetable markets in Haifa in July 1938, in which Aharoni and his brother, also an Irgun operative, killed a combined total of at least seventy bystanders.[75]

Gender played a more complex role in the Irgun's and Lehi's extreme actions. First, plainly put, MENA women constituted a significant number of active militants. Irgun and Lehi operatives including Geulah Cohen, Rachel Ohevet-Ami (born Rachel Habshush), and Malka Yefet trained as military commanders, learned how to assemble and use guns and explosives, and carried out robberies and terror attacks.[76] The Irgun and Lehi also weaponized ideas about gender—more specifically, the assumption of feminine docility—in their extreme actions. This was the case, for example, when Malka Yefet—born in 1925 to a Yemenite family in the

Neve Tzedek neighborhood of Tel Aviv—and the six other women who participated in the Irgun's January 12, 1946, Hadera "Money Train" robbery helped smuggle more than 35,000 Palestinian silver lirot away from the crime scene in nylon stockings that they tied around their bodies to make themselves look pregnant.[77] In another example, a Lehi operative with the codename "Yael" used a baby carriage to conceal a bomb that she had intended to use to kill General Sir Evelyn Barker, at the time the highest-ranking military officer in British Mandatory Palestine.[78] In both examples, women in the Irgun and Lehi utilized hollow gendered presumptions about their innocence and passivity.

These extreme actions—and the violence, deep trauma, and stress that they left in their wake—raise the point of how families felt about the Irgun and Lehi. After all, members of the Irgun and Lehi were, at the end of the day, sons, daughters, cousins, brothers, sisters, fathers, mothers, friends, and lovers whose involvement in radicalism induced complex and ambivalent reactions in their loved ones. On one end of the spectrum, there were a number of families who fully supported and actively participated in the Irgun and Lehi. This was the case for Ya'akov Sika Aharoni, whose entire twelve-person family was either directly or indirectly involved with the Irgun or Lehi.[79] It was also the case for Moshe Barzani, a Lehi member who was born to a Kurdish Jewish family in Baghdad in June 1926. His brothers Benyamin, Yehezkel, and Shaul were also in Lehi.[80] Indeed, it was common for groups of siblings or cousins of similar ages to join the Irgun and Lehi together. Familial ties proved to be one of the most consistently effective tools of recruitment. On the other end of the spectrum, some families reacted to their loved ones' involvement in the Irgun or Lehi with horror and outright condemnation, often stemming from a mix of political ideology and personal worry. This was the case for Eliyahu Hakim's family. Hakim's wealthy, locally prominent, and well-respected family responded to his involvement with the Irgun and later with Lehi with shock and denunciation. Sometime during the first few months of 1944, a few weeks after Hakim joined Lehi and disappeared into the underground, his father Simon offered him a large sum of money to quit Lehi and leave Palestine for Paris.[81] Simon and the other members of Hakim's family both disagreed with Lehi's radical tactics and feared for Eliyahu's life. Obviously, Eliyahu declined his father's offer, devastating the family. However, more often than either of these polar reactions, families supported the individual out of love and responsibility, but did not fully support their radicalism or the organizations that they were in. This was the case for Geulah Cohen and her mother, Miriam. Miriam knew about her daughter's involvement in Lehi, and while she did not wholeheartedly support Lehi's operations and her daughter's involvement in them, she did indirectly support Lehi by helping Geulah with her activities and by trying to protect her from social persecution or arrest by British police. One particularly memorable anecdote about Miriam's support for her radical daughter comes from Cohen's memoir. In it, she recounts her mother pushing her out of the kitchen in a fit of exasperation as Geulah tried, and failed, to cook wall-plastering glue for her propaganda missions using the family's kitchen utensils and pantry stock. Hoping to spare the family's pots, wooden spoons, and cooking starch from further abuse and waste, Miriam stepped in and finished the glue herself.[82]

Miriam's relationship with her daughter, and the support for Lehi that stemmed from it, raises the question of how a more capacious conceptualization of radicalism changes the definition of who is a radical. One aspect of radicalism that changes in a more expanded framework is gender. Like Miriam, many of the covert supporters of the Irgun and Lehi were the mothers of active members. Shoshana Levi—the mother of Yoav Levi, a member of the Irgun's Mahatz division who was of Yemenite background—used the family home to hide her son and his fellow spies from British police.[83] Simcha Avhar—the mother of Amnon Avhar, a Lehi member who was born to a Yemenite family in the frontier neighborhood of Mahane Yosef in Tel Aviv in 1930—opened the family home as a safe house for members of Lehi.[84] Hannah Nehmad—the mother of Moshe Nehmad, the Irgun's commander of Haifa and the Northern District—similarly opened the family home in the Bukharan Quarter of Jerusalem as a safe house for members of the Irgun.[85] These examples affirm that a conceptualization of radicalism that is expanded to include supporters makes possible a more diverse understanding of who a radical is, especially in terms of gender.

Another aspect of the history of the Irgun and Lehi in which MENA radicals played an important role was the British imperial legal and prison systems. When the Irgun and Lehi escalated their operations against the British Empire after February 1944, the British intensified their efforts to arrest and punish Irgun and Lehi members. In this period of heightened policing, which lasted from 1944 to 1948, the British arrested hundreds of Irgun and Lehi members and detained them—often in violation of habeas corpus—at a number of different prisons. British prisons where the imperial administration detained Irgun and Lehi radicals included the Jerusalem Central Prison at the Russian Compound, a detention camp at Latrun, the Acre Prison and—most infamously—a network of concentration camps in Eritrea, Sudan, and Kenya. There was also a prison specifically for women, the Bethlehem Women's Prison, which housed more than 350 women who were affiliated with the Irgun and Lehi at its peak after February 1944.[86] A significant number of these imprisoned Irgun and Lehi radicals were of MENA background. Among many others were the previously mentioned Geulah Cohen, Ya'akov Sika Aharoni, Yosef "Uzi" Levi, and Moshe Nehmad. An additional prisoner of note was Eliezer Kashani, an Irgun member who was born in 1923 to a large Persian and veteran Sephardi family in Petah Tikvah and who was among the *Olei HaGardom* (those who ascended the gallows).[87] The Olei HaGardom were the twelve members of the Irgun and Lehi that the British Empire arrested and executed by hanging for their involvement in militant or terror operations between 1938 and 1948. They later became mythologized as martyr figures in Zionist and Israeli consciousness, and embody Irgun and Lehi radicals' experience in and reaction to the British imperial legal apparatus and court system in Palestine.[88] Six of the twelve Olei HaGardom were of MENA background: Eliyahu Beit-Tzuri, executed on March 22, 1945, for the assassination of Lord Moyne; Eliyahu Hakim, also executed on March 22, 1945, for the assassination of Lord Moyne; Mordechai Alkahai, an Irgun member who was born to a Turkish Sephardi family in 1943 and who was executed on April 16, 1917; Eliezer Kashani, an Irgun member who was also executed on April 16, 1917; Moshe Barzani, a Lehi member who was born to a Kurdish Jewish family in Baghdad in June 1926, and who committed suicide on April 21, 1947, the day before his scheduled execution; and Meir Nakar, an Irgun member who was born to a religious Iraqi family in Jerusalem in 1926 and who was executed on July 29, 1947.[89] At their trials, the Olei HaGardom gave highly political testimonies that were scathing indictments of British imperial rule and law, and which reflected the broader currents of interwar Middle East radicalism and anti-imperialism. The speech that Eliyahu Beit-Tzuri gave while he was on trial for the assassination of Lord Moyne in Cairo is a particularly strong example of this. In his testimony, Beit-Tzuri compared the British Empire's respected international reputation and the brutal reality of its rule in Palestine to the famous story of Dr. Jekyll and Mr. Hyde, bemoaning the ongoing presence of British police and administrators and calling for an end to what he described as the rule of an illegitimate foreign power characterized by "all the ugliness of imperialism and colonialism."[90] The trial testimonies of other MENA Olei HaGardom reflect similar themes, as do the other forms of recollection and witnessing given by other MENA radicals in the Irgun and Lehi who went through the British imperial legal and prison systems.

Conclusion

The Middle Eastern and North African Jews who joined the Irgun and Lehi in British Mandatory Palestine are an understudied case of Jewish radicalism. Their history sits at the center of two overlapping marginalizations: the political marginalization of revisionist Zionism, and the ethno-cultural marginalization of MENA Jews. In this chapter, I addressed the historiographical lacuna created by these dual marginalizations by putting the Irgun, Lehi, and revisionist Zionism in a larger global and regional context of interwar radicalism, and by writing a social history of MENA members of the Irgun and Lehi. In these two organizations, MENA Jews were key leaders, members of the rank and file, and quiet supporters. They played essential roles in the Irgun's and Lehi's daily propaganda, intelligence, and recruitment activities, as well as in extreme actions such as terror bombings, prison breaks, and assassinations. The social structures of British Mandatory Palestine—especially space, gender, identity, class, and youth—all affected the roles that MENA Jews played in the Irgun and Lehi. Ultimately, despite a lack of existing historical work, this chapter affirms that the history of MENA Jews in the Irgun and Lehi is important and enriches the overall understanding of Jewish radicalism.

NOTES

1. For a vivid description of Lord Moyne's death, see Gerold Frank, *The Deed* (New York: Simon & Schuster, 1963), 22–25.

2. For Beit-Tzuri's biography, see Nechamia Ben-Tor, David Blau, Ruth Kotlitzky, and Menachem Klein, eds., *Lehi anashim: Sipur hayehem shel 840 lohamim ve-lohamot*, 2 vols. (Tel Aviv: Yair Publishing, 2002), 1:149; Frank, *The Deed*, 39–60, 70–120; "Olei HaGardom, Eliyahu Beit-Tzuri and Eliyahu Hakim," K16-2, Jabotinsky Institute Archives (hereafter JIA), Tel Aviv.

3. For Hakim's biography, see Ben-Tor et al., *Lehi anashim*, 1:339; Frank, *The Deed*, 36–44, 171–183; "Olei HaGardom, Eliyahu Beit-Tzuri and Eliyahu Hakim," JIA.

4. For more on the exclusion of revisionist Zionism from scholarship, state commemoration, and collective memory, see Tuvia Friling, "A Blatant Oversight? The Right-Wing in Israeli Holocaust Historiography," *Israel Studies* 14, no. 1 (Spring 2009): 123–169; Amir Goldstein, "*Olei HaGardom*: Between Official and Popular Memory," *Journal of Israeli History* 34, no. 2 (2015): 159–180.

5. One exciting recent history that breaks the pattern of political and intellectual histories is Daniel Kupfert Heller's *Jabotinsky's Children: Polish Jews and the Rise of Right-Wing Zionism* (Princeton: Princeton University Press, 2017). Heller's book is a social history of the revisionist Zionist youth group *Betar* in interwar Poland.

6. Jabotinsky was a ubiquitous presence in Zionist politics at the beginning of the twentieth century and remains one of the most compelling Zionist thinkers. In his lifetime, Jabotinsky was an authoritative and revered leader among revisionist Zionist organizations, though a younger generation of revisionist Zionist leaders challenged his power toward the end of his life. A multitude of historians have written about Jabotinsky's life, political career, literary work, and philosophy. For more on the origins of revisionist Zionism and *Hatzohar*, see Ya'akov Shavit, *Jabotinsky and the Revisionist Movement, 1925–1948* (New York: Frank Cass & Co., 1988), 28–58.

7. For recent scholarship, much of it from the last decade, that complicates the picture of revisionist Zionism, see Peter Bergamin, *The Making of the Israeli Far Right: Abba Ahimeir and Zionist Ideology* (London: I. B. Tauris, 2020); Arie Dubnov, "Shuvo shel HaZev HaGadol," *HaZman HaZeh* (November 2020), https://hazmanhazeh.org.il/jabotinsky/.; Amir Goldstein, "The Roots of the Gallows Myth in the Revisionist Movement During the 1930s," *The Journal of Imperial and Commonwealth History* 48, no. 1 (2020): 127–148; Kupfert Heller, *Jabotinsky's Children*; Joseph Heller, "The Zionist Right and National Liberation: From Jabotinsky to Avraham Stern," *Israel Affairs* 1, no. 3 (1995): 85–109; Eran Kaplan, *The Jewish Radical Right: Revisionist Zionism and Its Ideological Legacy* (Madison: University of Wisconsin Press, 2004); Avi Shilon, "Tugat ha-fashistan," *HaZman HaZeh* (January 2021), https://hazmanhazeh.org.il/ahimeir/.

8. For more on Stern's relationship to Nazi Germany, see Heller, "The Zionist Right and National Liberation," 97–101.

9. Amir Goldstein, "The Roots of the Gallows Myth."

10. This picture is further complicated by the general problems with intellectual history. The position of ideological leaders and elites within political movements do not necessarily represent the positions of average rank-and-file members. Additionally, revisionist Zionists, like all good politicians, were savvy strategists who knew how to tailor their messages in ways that would best connect to different intended audiences. Additionally, revisionist Zionists were human beings whose individual backgrounds, subjective beliefs, interpersonal squabbles, and idiosyncratic dispositions shaped their politics.

11. Menachem Begin game the name "the Revolt" to this period in the title of his memoir. It is not, however, a universally recognized proper name for the Irgun's and Lehi's anti-British operations between 1944 and 1948.

12. For further reading on the Irgun and Lehi, including more in-depth analyses of their positions, leaders, and memberships, see J. Bowyer Bell, *Terror Out of Zion: Irgun Zvai Leumi,*

Lehi, and the Palestine Underground, 1929–1949 (New York: Avon Books, 1977); Joseph Heller, *The Stern Gang: Ideology, Politics, Terror, 1940–1949*, reprint ed. (London: Routledge, 2004); Shavit, *Jabotinsky and the Revisionist Movement*.

13. Stern and Begin belonged to the younger generation of leaders in revisionist Zionist movements that challenged Jabotinsky's authority and political strategy after the British executed Shlomo Ben-Yosef on June 29, 1938. For more on this generational split, see Dubnov, "Shuvo shel HaZev HaGadol" and Goldstein, "The Roots of the Gallows Myth." Al-Qassam and al-Husseini similarly challenged the power hierarchy of Palestinian politics in the 1930s and 1940s. Historians have written about them both at length. For texts that deal with how Al-Qassam and al-Husseini fit into the change in the Palestinian political hierarchy, see Rashid Khalidi, "The Palestinians and 1948: The Underlying Causes of Failure," in *The War for Palestine: Rewriting the History of 1948*, ed. Eugene L. Rogan and Avi Shlaim, 2nd ed. (New York: Cambridge University Press, 2007), 12–36; Mark Sanagan, "Teacher, Preacher, Soldier, Martyr: Rethinking 'Izz al-Dīn al-Qassām," *Die Welt Des Islams* 53, no. 3/4 (2013): 315–352.

14. The two main challenges in deciding how to describe the group at the center of this chapter were terminological and methodological. Regarding terminology, scholars of Middle Eastern and North African (MENA) Jewish history have labored over and debated which terms are the most contextually accurate or politically effective for years. I do not resolve this chronic conundrum in this chapter. There were also methodological challenges in defining this group of MENA radicals. Hebraization—changing one's family name to Hebrew—was common in British Mandatory Palestine, which makes it difficult to guess geographic or ethnic origin from family name alone. Marriage between Jews of different backgrounds and the mixed families that came from these marriages add another layer of complication. An even more consequential methodological challenge comes from the fact that the Irgun and Lehi were both, to varying degrees and at different times, underground organizations that were secretive by design and necessity. They destroyed paper trails and demanded the use of codenames between operatives, erasing critical threads of archival material and historical reconstruction. Yet another methodological challenge comes from the distinction between active members of the Irgun and Lehi, who are in the organizations' histories and membership encyclopedias, and the larger sphere of collaborators and supporters, who were not collected in these works but who nonetheless played integral roles in the Irgun's and Lehi's operations.

15. See Ya'akov Banai, ed., *Mekorot le-toldot tnuat Lohamei Herut Yisrael* (Tel Aviv: Yair Publishing, 2006); Ben-Tor et al., *Lehi anashim*; Frank, *The Deed*; Yehuda Lapidot, *Lida shel makhteret* (Tel Aviv, Israel: The Alliance of Irgun Soldiers, 2001); Lapidot, *Hayom Sara Ha-Ketana: Siporei shel lohamot ha-Etzel* (Tel Aviv: Jabotinsky Institute and Irgun Museum Association, 2003); Lapidot, *Nashim ba-Etzel* (Givat Shaul, West Bank: Herzog College; Daat: Limudei Yahdut Ve-Ruah, 2015); Lapidot, *Olei ha-gardom* (Givat Shaul, West Bank: Herzog College; Daat: Limudei Yahdut Ve-Ruah). For memoirs, see Ya'akov Sika Aharoni, *Be-ikvot ha-Mufti 'im David Raziel* (Ramat Gan, Israel, 2000); Menachem Begin, *The Revolt: The Dramatic Inside Story of the Irgun* (Los Angeles: Nash Publishing, 1972); Geulah Cohen, *Woman of Violence: Memoirs of a Young Terrorist, 1943–1948*, trans. Hillel Halkin (New York: Holt, 1966); Yitzhak Hasson, *Ha-zaken ve-ani* (Tel Aviv, Israel: Breirot Publishers, 1993); David Sitton, *Ba-or u-ve-seter: Dapim me-yemene shel atsir* (Jerusalem: Ba-Ma'arakhah, 1978). See also the websites for the Etzel Museum (https://etzelmembers.org.il/) and of the Association for Commemorating the Legacy of the Freedom Fighters of Israel (Lehi) (https://lehi.org.il/he/%d7%91%d7%99%d7%aa-%d7%97%d7%93%d7%a9/), as well as the archives of the Jabotinsky Institute (https://en.jabotinsky.org/archive/search-archive/).

16. Shlomi Resnik, "Ha mordim: Nituah sozyologi shel Lohamei Etzel ba-shanim 1944–1948," in *Ha-mordim: Ma'avak ha-Etzel ba-Britim 1944–1948: Diyun mehudash*, ed. Ya'akov Markowizki (Jerusalem, 2008), 189.

17. Resnik, "Ha-mordim," 189.

18. Begin, *The Revolt*, 79.

19. Begin, *The Revolt*, 79.

20. See the index to Lapidot, *Hayom Sara Ha-Ketana*, for his list of women in the Irgun.

21. Ben-Tor et al., *Lehi anashim.*

22. For the organizational structure of the Irgun, see Begin, *The Revolt*, 76, as well as Yehuda Lapidot's histories of the Irgun.

23. Begin, *The Revolt*, 62; Aharoni, *Be-ikvot ha-Mufti 'im David Raziel*, 206–207.

24. Begin, *The Revolt*, 78.

25. Aharoni provides his family background in the introduction to his memoir. For more on Aharoni, see also Abigail Jacobson and Moshe Naor, *Oriental Neighbors: Middle Eastern Jews and Arabs in Mandatory Palestine* (Waltham: Brandeis University Press, 2016), 156–157.

26. Ben-Tor et al., *Lehi anashim*, 1:480. See also Cohen, *Woman of Violence.*

27. Hasson, *Ha-zaken ve-ani*, 28.

28. Hasson, *Ha-zaken ve-ani*, 154–162. See also Cohen, *Woman of Violence*, 246–260. Hasson is the Lehi commander that Cohen refers to by the codename "Lot."

29. Levi's articles and books include "Ha-saison ha-gadol," *HaUmah* 122 (1995): 174–183; *Be-me'abek u-be-mered: Haganah, Etzel, ve-Lehi, 1918–1948* (Tel Aviv, Israel: Ministry of Defense Publishing, 1977); and *Mefakedet ha-Etzel ba-shanot ha-mered* (Jerusalem, 2004). For mention of Nehmad's writings, see his obituary in *Ba-Ma'arakha*, October 11, 1963. Aharoni's memoir is *Be-ikvot ha-Mufti 'im David Raziel.* Cohen's memoir is *Woman of Violence.* Hasson's memoir is *Ha-zaken ve-ani.*

30. Begin, *The Revolt*, 78; Yehuda Lapidot, "Yosef 'Uzi' Levi," Etzel Heritage Site, Accessed April 15, 2022.

31. Begin, *The Revolt*, 67.

32. Begin, *The Revolt*, 71–72, 86.

33. Lapidot, *Hayom Sara Ha-Ketana*, 161–164.

34. Lapidot, *Hayom Sara Ha-Ketana*, 161–164.

35. For the biographies of the members listed here—and for the biographies of hundreds of others—see Lapidot's histories of the Irgun, the encyclopedic entries on Lehi members on the website of the Association for Commemorating the Legacy of the Freedom Fighters of Israel (Lehi), and the index at the back of Aharoni's memoir.

36. Estimations for patterns among members of the Irgun and Lehi come from an analysis of the hundreds of biographies that are collected in Lapidot's histories of the Irgun, the encyclopedias of Lehi members, and memoirs. Along with participation in propaganda activities, the other most common pattern was participation in revisionist Zionist–affiliated youth movements.

37. For *Herut* and other Irgun publications, see "Irgun Tzvai Leumi Collection," K4, JIA. For the listed Lehi publications, see "Lehi Collection," K5, 2/7-12, JIA.

38. Many of these leaflets, bulletins, fliers, and posters are available online through the archives of the Jabotinsky Institute. See "Irgun Tzvai Leumi Collection," K4, JIA and "Lehi Collection," K5, JIA.

39. Ruth Kolitzky, "Mahleket noar ve-tironut: Ha-ma'agar ha-anushi le-shorot Lehi," in *Mekorot le-toldot tnuat Lohamei Herut Yisrael*, ed. Ya'akov Banai (Tel Aviv: Yair Publishing, 2006), 387–388.

40. This was the case for Asher Tratner, a member of the Irgun who died of sepsis from a bullet wound he sustained after a British policeman shot him while he was posting propaganda materials around Haifa. See Begin, *The Revolt*, 92.

41. For Jacobson's and Naor's concept of "frontier neighborhoods," see *Oriental Neighbors*, "Introduction," 9, and chapter 4, "Mixing and Unmixing in the Oriental Ghettoes," 121–149. See also Moshe Naor, "The Sephardi and Oriental Jews of Haifa and Arab-Jewish Relations in Mandate Palestine," *Middle Eastern Studies* 55, no. 6 (2019): 1020–1036.

42. This list of neighborhoods comes from Jacobson and Naor's *Oriental Neighbors*, as well as from an analysis of the biographies that appear in Ben-Tor et al., *Lehi Anashim* and in other secondary source materials.

43. Begin, *The Revolt*, 87.

44. Begin, *The Revolt*, 86.

45. Ben-Tor et al., *Lehi anashim*, 1:85–86.

46. Ben-Tor et al., *Lehi anashim*, 1:85–86.

47. Lapidot, *Hayom Sara Ha-Ketana*, 170. Lapidot does not clarify what he means by Greek or go into greater depth about a particular city or community of origin in this biography of Rachel Sheetrit.

48. Lapidot, *Hayom Sara Ha-Ketana*, 170.

49. Kolitzky, "Mahleket noar ve-tironut," 387.

50. Kolitzky, "Mahleket noar ve-tironut," 387.

51. Begin, *The Revolt*, 79.

52. The majority of Mahatz operatives that Aharoni identifies at the end of his memoir were of MENA origin. Further, at the beginning of the book Aharoni makes a point of explaining that Mahatz purposely recruited MENA Jews for its membership.

53. See the chapter 5 of *Oriental Neighbors*, "Crossing the Lines: The Security Border Between Jews and Arabs," 150–195.

54. Frank, *The Deed*, 161–163.

55. For analysis of the racialization of Yemenite Jews as Black, see Jacobson and Naor, *Oriental Neighbors*, 166–171.

56. For an analysis of the characteristics of the Mandates period, see James L. Gelvin, "Was There a Mandates Period? Some Concluding Thoughts," in *The Routledge Handbook of the History of Middle East Mandates*, ed. Cyrus Schayegh and Andrew Arsan (London: Routledge, 2015), 420–432.

57. See Michael Provence, *The Last Ottoman Generation and the Making of the Modern Middle East* (Cambridge: Cambridge University Press, 2017), 74, 81.

58. See Jacobson and Naor, *Oriental Neighbors*, 168, 179, 181; Begin, *The Revolt*, 76–79.

59. Begin, *The Revolt*, 76, 78.

60. Aharoni, *Be-ikvot ha-Mufti 'im David Raziel*, 52. Aharoni used the Hebrew *shachor*, meaning both literally the color black and the concept of darkness. Other members of the Irgun and Lehi had the term *Cushi* as their codename, which carries a similar racial connotation but derives from biblical textual and historical precedent and not from modern racism and colorism. See, for example, Yoav "Cushi" Levi from the Irgun's Mahatz division (Aharoni, *Be-ikvot ha-Mufti 'im David Raziel*, 185–186) and Ya'akov "Cushi Habakkuk" Bezalel (Ben-Tor et al., *Lehi anashim*, 1:93).

61. In his memoir, Aharoni emphasizes how the 1936–1939 Great Revolt/General Strike and the economic crises it caused affected his family. See Aharoni, *Be-ikvot ha-Mufti 'im David Raziel*, 10.

62. Jacobson and Naor, *Oriental Neighbors*, 142–143. Jacobson and Naor pulled these statistics from the estimates of a December 7, 1946, issue of *Hed HaMizrach*, a newspaper whose target audience was Sephardim in Palestine.

63. For Alkahai's biography, see Lapidot, *Olei ha-gardom*, 18–19.

64. Aharoni, *Be-ikvot ha-Mufti 'im David Raziel*, 177.

65. See Ben-Tor et al., *Lehi anashim*, for a list of more than 840 biographies of Lehi members, many of whom fit this pattern.

66. For more on the "Sephardi Question," see Jacobson and Naor, *Oriental Neighbors*, 5–6, 151.

67. David Sitton, *Ba-or u-va-seter: Dapim me-yemene shel atsir* (Jerusalem: Ba-Ma'arakhah, 1978).

68. Sitton, *Ba-or u-va-seter*, 211–212.

69. I identified which youth movements were closely related to the Irgun and Lehi from the historical literature and encyclopedias published by former members of the Irgun or Lehi and their heritage foundations. See also Jacobson and Naor, *Oriental Neighbors*, 145; Moshe Naor, *Iyunim* 34 (2020): 200–233. For more on the other youth movements listed here, see James P. Jankowski, "The Egyptian Blue Shirts and the Egyptian Wafd, 1935–1938," *Middle Eastern Studies* 6, no. 1 (1970): 77–95; Provence, *The Last Ottoman Generation*, 240–241; Keith Watenpaugh, "Steel Shirts, White Badges and the Last Qabadāy: Fascism, Urban Violence and Civic Identity in Aleppo Under French Rule," in *France, Syrie et Liban 1918–1946: Les ambig-*

uïtés et les dynamiques de la relation mandataire, ed. Nadine Méouchy, 325–347 (Damas: Presses de l'Ifpo, 2002).

70. Another similarity across these youth movements is that their leaders intentionally modeled them on European fascist youth movements. Indeed, a shared fascination with fascism, and illiberal politics more generally, is yet another common characteristic among radical interwar movements in the Middle East, including the Irgun and Lehi.

71. For analysis of the distinctions between and competition among youth movements, see Jacobson and Naor, *Oriental Neighbors*, 73–78, 145, 162. See also Moshe Naor, "Degel Tzion ve-hitargenut ha-noar ha-sephardi ve-ha-mizrahi be-tekufat ha-mandat."

72. Frank, *The Deed*, 124.

73. Jacobson and Naor, *Oriental Neighbors*, 123.

74. Sharon Geva, "Malka Yefet Fine," *Proyekt ma'alim erekh: Makhazirot nashim le-historiah*, September 24, 2016, accessed April 16, 2022.

75. Aharoni, *Be-ikvot ha-Mufti 'im David Raziel*, 52; Jacobson and Naor, *Oriental Neighbors*, 156–157.

76. For Rachel Ohevet-Ami, see Lapidot, *Hayom Sara Ha-Ketana*, 28–32. For Malka Yefet, see Lapidot, *Hayom Sara Ha-Ketana*, 257; Geva, "Malka Yefet-Fine."

77. Lapidot, *Hayom Sara Ha-Ketana*, 109.

78. Cohen, *Woman of Violence*, 18.

79. Aharoni, *Be-ikvot ha-Mufti 'im David Raziel*, 6, 11.

80. Ben-Tor et al., *Lehi anashim*, 1:215–218.

81. Frank, *The Deed*, 179–180.

82. Cohen, *Woman of Violence*, 43.

83. Aharoni, *Be-ikvot ha-Mufti 'im David Raziel*, 185–186.

84. Ben-Tor et al., *Lehi anashim*, 1:37.

85. "Moshe Nehmad zichron livracha me-rishonei ha-machteret," *Ba-Ma'arakhah*, October 11, 1968.

86. Lapidot, *Hayom Sara Ha-Ketana*, 201.

87. For more on Yosef Levi, see Begin, *The Revolt*, 78; Lapidot, "Yosef 'Uzi' Levi." For more on Eliezer Kashani, see Lapidot, *Olei ha-gardom*, 19–20; Na'ama Volcani, "Olei ha-gardom," in *Mekorot le-toldot tnuat lohamei herut Yisrael*, 48.

88. For the Olei HaGardom and public consciousness, see Amir Goldstein, "Olei HaGardom: Between Official and Popular Memory," *Journal of Israeli History* 34, no. 2 (2015): 159–180.

89. For basic bibliographic information on each of the Olei ha-gardom, see Lapidot, *Olei ha-gardom*; Volcani, "Olei HaGardom," in *Mekorot le-toldot tnuat lohamei herut Yisrael*, 44–57; and the Irgun and Lehi heritage websites. Additional, more specific details appear in Ben-Tor et al., *Lehi Anashim*, and in various memoirs and nonprofessional histories.

90. "Olei Hagardom, Eliyahu Beit Tzuri and Eliyahu Hakim—Trial in Cairo," Beit-Tzuri Testimony Transcript, K16-2/3, JIA.

Acknowledgments

This book emerged out of a workshop hosted by the Center for Jewish Studies at the University of California, Santa Cruz, in 2017. The workshop, titled "Radical Jewish Politics," included many of the contributors to this volume and more. We would like to thank the original workshop participants for their thoughtfulness in generating a comparative discussion of radical Jewish politics, including Bettina Aptheker, Orit Bashkin, Joel Beinin, Arie Dubnov, Peter Kenez, Lior Sternfeld, and Bob Weinberg. We are grateful as well to the contributors to this volume who did not participate in the original workshop and have enriched the current work greatly. Thank you to Irena Polic, Evin Knight, and Jessica Guild for their work in making that workshop possible.

There are many who have encouraged this project over time in some capacity, including David Epstein, David Myers, Devin Naar, and Sarah Abrevaya Stein. We extend our thanks to the staff at Rutgers University Press, and particularly Carah Naseem for believing in this project and shepherding it to completion.

Finally, we dedicate this volume to the memory of Maya Karin Peterson (1980–2021), a brilliant historian of Russia and Central Asia and a dear friend and colleague in the history department at UC Santa Cruz.

Acknowledgments

Notes on Contributors

ORIT BASHKIN is a historian who studies the intellectual, social, and cultural history of the modern Middle East. She teaches modern Middle Eastern history in the Department of Near Eastern Languages and Civilizations at the University of Chicago. Her publications deal with Iraqi history, the history of Iraqi Jews, the Arab cultural revival movement (the Nahda) in the late nineteenth century, and the connections between modern Arab history and Arabic literature. Her books are: co-edited with Joshua Levinson (eds.), *Jews and Journeys: Travel and the Performance of Jewish Identity*; co-edited with Margrit Pernau, Helge Jordheim, Christian Bailey, et al., *Civilizing Emotions: Concepts in Nineteenth-Century Asia and Europe*; *Impossible Exodus: Iraqi Jews in Israel*; *New Babylonians: A History of Jews in Modern Iraq*; and *The Other Iraq: Pluralism and Culture in Hashemite Iraq*.

MICHAEL CASPER is the coauthor, with Nathaniel Deutsch, of *A Fortress in Brooklyn: Race, Real Estate, and the Making of Hasidic Williamsburg*. He received a PhD in history from the University of California, Los Angeles, and has held postdoctoral fellowships at Yale University, the University of Pennsylvania, and Fordham University–New York Public Library.

PARIS PAPAMICHOS CHRONAKIS is lecturer in modern Greek history at Royal Holloway University of London, where he teaches and researches on the history and memory of the modern Mediterranean. His work explores questions of transition from empire to nation-state, bringing together the entangled histories of Jews, Muslims, and Christians from the late Ottoman Empire to the Holocaust. In recent years, his research and publications have expanded to Balkan War refugees, Salonica in World War I, Greek interwar Zionism and anti-Zionism, the Holocaust's impact on Sephardi Jewry, and digital Holocaust studies. He was a member of the scientific committee that developed the Database of Greek-Jewish Holocaust Survivors' Testimonies and is currently spearheading a digital history project on the social networks of Greek Jewish Holocaust deportees and escapees. His most recent book is *The Business of Transition: Jewish and Greek Merchants of Salonica from Ottoman to Greek Rule.*

Nathaniel Deutsch is distinguished professor of history and Baumgarten Endowed Chair in Jewish studies at the University of California, Santa Cruz. He is the author of a number of award-winning books, including *The Maiden of Ludmir: A Jewish Holy Woman and Her World*, *Inventing America's Worst Family: Eugenics, Islam, and the Fall and Rise of the Tribe of Ishmael*, and *The Jewish Dark Continent: Life and Death in the Russian Pale of Settlement*, for which he received a Guggenheim Fellowship. His coauthored (with Michael Casper) book *A Fortress in Brooklyn: Race, Real Estate, and the Making of Hasidic Brooklyn* won a National Jewish Book Award.

Arie M. Dubnov is an associate professor of history and the Max Ticktin Chair of Israel studies at the George Washington University. His publications include *Isaiah Berlin: The Journey of a Jewish Liberal*, and two edited volumes, *Zionism—A View from the Outside* (in Hebrew), and *Partitions: A Transnational History of Twentieth-Century Territorial Separatism* (coedited with Laura Robson).

Rami Ginat is a professor of Middle Eastern politics in the Department of Political Studies (which he chaired until recently) at Bar-Ilan University. He has published extensively on Middle Eastern affairs with special reference to Egyptian politics and ideology. Among his recent books are *A History of Egyptian Communism: Jews and their Compatriots in Quest of Revolution* and *Egypt and the Struggle for Power in Sudan: From World War II to Nasserism.*

Alma Rachel Heckman is associate professor of history and Neufeld-Levin Endowed Chair in Holocaust studies at the University of California, Santa Cruz. Her first book is *The Sultan's Communists: Moroccan Jews and the Politics of Belonging*. She has published numerous chapters and articles regarding questions of Moroccan Jewish politics and communism in Morocco, as well as on the Alliance Israélite Universelle. She is currently at work on a book about Jewish and Muslim anti-fascism in interwar Morocco.

Kostis Karpozilos is a historian who served as the director of the Greek Contemporary Social History Archives (ASKI) from 2016 to 2023. He authored several works, including *Stavros Kallergis: Sketching the Socialist Polity* (in Greek), *Red America: Greek Immigrants and the Quest for a New World, 1900–1950*, and (with Dimitris Christopoulos) *10 + 1 Questions & Answers on the Macedonian Question.* His latest book is *Greek Communism: A Transnational History (1912–1974)* (in Greek). Karpozilos currently teaches at Panteion University and has held postdoctoral fellowships at Columbia University, Princeton, and Oxford.

Peter Kenez is professor emeritus of history at the University of California, Santa Cruz. He was born in Hungary and came to the United States after the Revolution of 1956. He is the author of numerous books and articles, including *The Coming of the Holocaust: From Antisemitism to Genocide* and *A History of the Soviet Union from the Beginning to Its Legacy*, now in its third edition.

Pierre-Jean Le Foll-Luciani is a historian working on the social history of Algerian communism and of Algerian Jews. He studied at the École normale supérieure of Lyon and was previously a research associate at the University of Rennes 2 (France). He is the author of *Le Camp des oliviers. Parcours d'un communiste algérien* and *Les juifs algériens dans la lutte anticoloniale. Trajectoires dissidentes.*

Richard Mendelsohn taught for many years in the history department of the University of Cape Town, where he served as chairman of the department and as deputy dean in the university's faculty of humanities. He has published extensively on the history of Jewry in South Africa, including *Sammy Marks: "The Uncrowned King of the Transvaal," The Jews in South Africa: An Illustrated History* (with Milton Shain), *Memories, Realities and Dreams: Aspects of the South African Jewish Experience* (co-edited with Milton Shain), and, most recently, *The Jews of Parow: The History of a South African Community.*

Dario Miccoli is assistant professor of modern Hebrew and Jewish studies at the Department of Asian and North African Studies, Ca' Foscari University of Venice. His research and publications deal with the history and memory of the Jews of the modern Middle East and North Africa, notably Egypt, and Israeli literature and society. He is the author of *A Sephardi Sea: Jewish Memories Across the Modern Mediterranean* and *Histories of the Jews of Egypt: An Imagined Bourgeoisie, 1880s–1950s.*

Tony Michels is the George L. Mosse professor of American Jewish history at the University of Wisconsin-Madison. He is the author of *A Fire in Their Hearts: Yiddish Socialists in New York*, which won the Salo Baron Book Prize for best first book in Jewish studies, and the editor of *Jewish Radicals: A Documentary History* and (with Mitchell Hart) *The Cambridge History of Judaism. Volume Eight: The Modern World, 1815–2000.* He is currently completing "Soviet America: Communism, Anti-Communism, and Jews."

Kamilia Rahmouni is an associate professor at the School of World Studies at Virginia Commonwealth University. Her interdisciplinary research interests include sociolinguistics, the use of AI in education, second language acquisition and teaching, discourse analysis, and curriculum design and development.

Michael Rom is the visiting assistant professor of modern Jewish history and culture at Hebrew Union College, Los Angeles. He received a PhD in history at Yale University, and has held postdoctoral fellowships at Harvard University, the University of British Columbia, and the University of Cape Town. His research has appeared in *Jewish Social Studies*, the *Jewish Quarterly Review*, and the *Luso-Brazilian Review.*

MILTON SHAIN is emeritus professor of historical studies at the University of Cape Town. He has written, coauthored, and co-edited over a dozen books on South African Jewish history, South African politics, and the history of antisemitism, including *The Roots of Antisemitism in South Africa*, *A Perfect Storm: Antisemitism in South Africa, 1930–1948*, and *Holocaust Scholarship: Personal Trajectories and Professional Interpretations*, co-edited with Christopher Browning, Susannah Heschel, and Michael Marrus. His latest book, *Fascists, Fabricators and Fantasists: Antisemitism in South Africa from 1948 to the Present*, is the final volume in his trilogy on the history of antisemitism in South Africa. In 2014 he was elected a fellow of the Royal Society of South Africa.

LIOR B. STERNFELD is associate professor of history and Jewish studies at Penn State University. His work focuses on the modern Middle East with an emphasis on Iran and Jewish histories of the region. He is the author of *Between Iran and Zion: Jewish Histories of Twentieth-Century Iran* and coauthor of *Jews of Iran: A Photographic Chronicle* (with Hassan Sarbakhsian and Parvaneh Vahidmanesh).

ANNA ELENA TORRES is an assistant professor in the departments of Comparative Literature and Race, Diaspora, and Indigeneity at the University of Chicago. Torres is the author of *Horizons Blossom, Borders Vanish: Anarchism and Yiddish Literature* and co-editor of *With Freedom in Our Ears: Histories of Jewish Anarchism* (with Kenyon Zimmer). Torres's publications include work in *Prooftexts*, *Jewish Quarterly Review*, *Nashim*, *Make/shift: A Journal of Feminisms in Motion*, *In geveb*, and *ArtsEverywhere*. Torres's creative practice has included work as a poet and translator, community arts organizer, muralist, and conceptual artist exhibited at the Venice Biennale's Yiddishland Pavilion and the POLIN Museum, Warsaw.

ROBERT WEINBERG is Isaac H. Clothier professor of history and international relations at Swarthmore College. Over the years he has published on the Jewish question in late imperial Russia and the early Soviet Union. His publications include books and articles about the Revolution of 1905 in Odessa, anti-Jewish pogroms, the ritual murder trial of Menahem Mendel Beilis, the history of Birobidzhan (the Jewish Autonomous Region), and antisemitic policies on the part of the tsarist and communist regimes.

AVERY WEINMAN is a PhD student in the Department of History at the University of California, Los Angeles. She completed her BA in history and Jewish studies at the University of California, Santa Cruz, where she served as the editor-in-chief of *Leviathan Jewish Journal*.

Index

Note: page numbers in italics refer to figures. Those followed by n refer to notes, with note number.